n

THE SUPPLEMENT TO
THE TENTH MENTAL
MEASUREMENTS YEARBOOK

D1264963

EARLIER PUBLICATIONS IN THIS SERIES

INSTITUTE DIRECTOR
BARBARA S. PLAKE

EDITORIAL ASSISTANT
ARLIE M. PROKOP

PRODUCTION
ROSEMARY G. SIECK

ADMINISTRATIVE AND SECRETARIAL
DEBRA S. RUTHSATZ
NANCY SCHWAB

RESEARCH ASSISTANTS

JANET ALLISON   MARK SHRIVER
CAROL BERIGAN   RICHARD SONNENBERG
MICHAEL BONNER   RICHARD TAFFE
HAEOK KIM   LORI WENNSTEDT
MARIA POTENZA

THE SUPPLEMENT TO THE TENTH MENTAL MEASUREMENTS YEARBOOK

JACK J. KRAMER and JANE CLOSE CONOLEY

Editors

LINDA L. MURPHY

Managing Editor

The Buros Institute of Mental Measurements
The University of Nebraska-Lincoln
Lincoln, Nebraska

1990
Distributed by The University of Nebraska Press

Copyright 1990 and published by the Buros Institute of Mental Measurements of The University of Nebraska-Lincoln, 135 Bancroft Hall, Lincoln, Nebraska 68588–0348. All rights reserved. No part of this publication may be reproduced in any form nor may any of the contents be used in an information storage, retrieval, or transmission system without the prior written permission of the publisher.

LC 39-3422
ISBN 910674–32–9

Manufactured in the United States of America.

The paper used in this publication meets the minimum requirements of American National Standard for Information Sciences — Permanence of Paper for Printed Library Materials, ANSI Z39.48–1984.

Note to Users

The staff of the Buros Institute of Mental Measurements has made every effort to ensure the accuracy of the test information included in this work. However, the Buros Institute of Mental Measurements and the Editors of *The Supplement to the Tenth Mental Measurements Yearbook* do not assume, and hereby expressly and absolutely disclaim, any liability to any party for any loss or damage caused by errors or omissions or statements of any kind in *The Supplement to the Tenth Measurements Yearbook*. This disclaimer also includes judgments or statements of any kind made by test reviewers, who were extended the professional freedom appropriate to their task; their judgments and opinions are their own, uninfluenced in any way by the Buros Institute or the Editors.

All material included in *The Supplement to the Tenth Mental Measurements Yearbook* is intended solely for the use of our readers. None of this material, including reviewer statements, may be used in advertising or for any other commercial purpose.

TABLE OF CONTENTS

INTRODUCTION

The Supplement to the Tenth Mental Measurements Yearbook (10MMY-S) is the second Supplement to be published by the Buros Institute. This volume is designed as a bridge between the publication of the Tenth Mental Measurements Yearbook in 1989 and the forthcoming publication of the Eleventh Mental Measurements Yearbook (projected in 1991). This yearly publication schedule has been implemented to allow test users rapid access to reviews of commercially available tests in psychology and education.

Feedback from readers suggests the Supplement is a useful addition to the libraries of test specialists and consumers who require timely information to expedite their decision making. The frequent appearances of Buros Institute reference works is in keeping with the Buros Institute's mission to improve testing practices by educating test consumers.

THE SUPPLEMENT TO THE TENTH MENTAL MEASUREMENTS YEARBOOK

The 10MMY-S contains reviews of tests that are new or significantly revised since the publication of the Tenth MMY in 1989. We have included reviews of tests that were available before our production deadline of April 1, 1990. Reviews of additional new or revised tests since 1989 will appear in the Eleventh MMY. Reviews, descriptions, and references associated with older tests can be located in other Buros publications such as previous MMYs and Tests in Print III.

The contents of the 10MMY-S include: (a) a bibliography of 98 commercially available tests, new or revised, published as separates for use with English-speaking subjects; (b) 183 critical test reviews by well-qualified professional people who were selected by the editors on the basis of their expertise in measurement and, often, the content of the test being reviewed; (c) bibliographies of references for specific tests related to the construction, validity, or use of the tests in various settings; (d) a test title index with appropriate cross-references; (e) a classified subject index; (f) a publishers directory and index, including addresses and test listings by publisher; (g) a name index including the names of all authors of tests, reviews, or references; (h) an index of acronyms for easy reference when a test acronym, not the full title, is known; and (i) a score index to refer readers to tests featuring particular kinds of scores that are of interest to them.

The volume is organized like an encyclopedia, with tests being ordered alphabetically by title. If the title of a test is known, the reader can locate the test immediately without having to consult the Index of Titles.

The page headings reflect the encyclopedic organization. The page heading of the left-hand page cites the number and title of the first test listed on that page, and the page heading of the right-hand page cites the number and title of the last test listed on that page. All numbers presented in the various indexes are test numbers, not page numbers. Page numbers are important only for the Table of Contents and are indicated at the bottom of each page.

INDEXES

As mentioned earlier, The 10MMY-S includes six indexes invaluable as aids to effective use: (a) Index of Titles, (b) Index of Acronyms, (c) Classified Subject Index, (d) Publishers Directory and Index, (e) Index of Names, and (f) Score Index. Additional comment on these indexes will be presented below.

Index of Titles. Because the organization of the 10MMY-S is encyclopedic in nature, with the tests ordered alphabetically by title throughout the two volumes, the test title index does not have to be consulted to find a test for which the title is known. However, the title index has some features that make it useful beyond its function as a complete title listing. First it includes cross-reference information useful for tests with superseded or alternative titles or tests commonly (and sometime inaccurately) known by multiple titles. Second, it identifies tests that are new or revised. It is important to keep in mind that the numbers in this index, like those for all *MMY* indexes, are test numbers and not page numbers.

Index of Acronyms. Some tests seem to be better known by their acronyms than by their full titles. The Index of Acronyms can help in these instances; it refers the reader to the full title of the test and to the relevant descriptive information and reviews.

Classified Subject Index. The Classified Subject Index classifies all tests listed in the *10MMY-S* into 14 major categories: Achievement, Behavior Assessment, Developmental, Education, English, Intelligence and Scholastic Aptitude, Mathematics, Miscellaneous, Neuropsychological, Personality, Reading, Social Studies, Speech and Hearing, and Vocations. Each test entry includes test title, population for which the test is intended, and test number. The Classified Subject Index is of great help to readers who seek a listing of tests in given subject areas. The Classified Subject Index represents a starting point for readers who know their area of interest but do not know how to further focus that interest in order to identify the best test(s) for their particular purposes.

Publishers Directory and Index. The Publishers Directory and Index includes the names and addresses of the publishers of all tests included in the *10MMY-S* plus a listing of test numbers for each individual publisher. This index can be particularly useful in obtaining addresses for specimen sets or catalogs after the test reviews have been read and evaluated. It can also be useful when a reader knows the publisher of a certain test but is uncertain about the test title, or when a reader is interested in the range of tests published by a given publisher.

Index of Names. The Index of Names provides a comprehensive list of names, indicating authorship of a test, test review, or reference.

Score Index. The Score Index is an index to all scores generated by the tests in the *10MMY-S*. Test titles are sometimes misleading or ambiguous, and test content may be difficult to define with precision. But test scores represent operational definitions of the variables the test author is trying to measure, and as such they often define test purpose and content more adequately than other descriptive information. A search for a particular test is most often a search for a test that measures some specific variables. Test scores and their associated labels can often be the best definitions of the variables of interest. It is, in fact, a detailed subject index based on the most critical operational features of any test—the scores and their associated labels.

HOW TO USE THIS SUPPLEMENT

A reference work like *The Supplement to the Tenth Mental Measurements Yearbook* can be of far greater benefit to a reader if a little time is taken to become familiar with what it has to offer and how one might most effectively use it to obtain the information wanted. The first step in this process is to read the Introduction to the *10MMY-S* in its entirety. The second step is to become familiar with the six indexes and particularly with the instructions preceding each index listing. The third step is to make actual use of the book by looking up needed information. This third step is simple if one keeps in mind the following possibilities:

1. If you know the title of the test, use the alphabetical page headings to go directly to the test entry.

2. If you do not know, cannot find, or are unsure of the title of a test, consult the Index of Titles for possible variants of the title or consult the appropriate subject area of the Classified Subject Index for other possible leads or for similar or related tests in the same area. (Other uses for both of these indexes were described earlier.)

3. If you know the author of a test but not the title or publisher, consult the Index of Names and look up the author's titles until you find the test you want.

4. If you know the test publisher but not the title or author, consult the Publishers Directory and Index and look up the publisher's titles until you find the test you want.

5. If you are looking for a test that yields a particular kind of score, but have no knowledge of which test that might be, look up the score in the Score Index and locate the test or tests that include the score variable of interest.

6. Once you have found the test or tests you are looking for, read the descriptive entries for these tests carefully so that you can take advantage of the information provided. A description of the information provided in these test entries will be presented later in this section.

7. Read the test reviews carefully and analytically, as described earlier in this Introduction. The information and evaluation contained in these reviews are meant to assist test consumers in making well-informed decisions about the choice and applications of tests.

8. Once you have read the descriptive information and test reviews, you may want to order a specimen set for a particular test so that you can examine it firsthand. The Publishers Directory and Index has the address information needed to obtain specimen sets or catalogs.

Making Effective Use of the Test Entries. The test entries include extensive information. For each test, descriptive information is presented in the following order:

a) TITLES. Test titles are printed in boldface type. Secondary or series titles are set off from main titles by a colon.

b) PURPOSE. For each test we have included a brief, clear statement describing the purpose of the test. Often these statements are quotations from the test manual.

c) POPULATION. This is a description of the groups for which the test is intended. The grade, chronological age, semester range, or employment category is usually given. "Grades 1.5–2.5, 2–3, 4–13, 13–17" means that there are four test booklets: a booklet for the middle of first grade through the middle of the second grade, a booklet for the beginning of the second grade through the end of third grade, a booklet for grades 4 through 12 inclusive, and a booklet for undergraduate and graduate students in colleges and universities.

d) PUBLICATION DATE. The inclusive range of publication dates for the various forms, accessories, and editions of a test is reported.

e) ACRONYM. When a test is often referred to by an acronym, the acronym is given in the test entry immediately following the publication date.

f) SCORES. The number of part scores is presented along with their titles or descriptions of what they are intended to represent or measure.

g) ADMINISTRATION. Individual or group administration is indicated. A test is considered a group test unless it may be administered *only* individually.

h) FORMS, PARTS, AND LEVELS. All available forms, parts, and levels are listed.

i) MANUAL. Notation is made if no manual is available. All other manual information is included under Price Data.

j) RESTRICTED DISTRIBUTION. This is noted only for tests that are put on a special market by the publisher. Educational and psychological restrictions are not noted (unless a special training course is required for use).

k) PRICE DATA. Price information is reported for test packages (usually 20 to 35 tests), answer sheets, all other accessories, and specimen sets. The statement "$17.50 per 35 tests" means that all accessories are included unless otherwise indicated by the reporting of separate prices for accessories. The statement also means 35 tests of one level, one edition, or one part unless stated otherwise. Because test prices can change very quickly, the year that the listed test prices were obtained is also given. Foreign currency is assigned the appropriate symbol. When prices are given in foreign dollars, a qualifying symbol is added (e.g., A$16.50 refers to 16 dollars and 50 cents in Australian currency). Along with cost, the publication date and number of pages on which print occurs is reported for manuals and technical reports (e.g., '85, 102 pages). All types of machine-scorable answer sheets available for use

with a specific test are also reported in the descriptive entry. Scoring and reporting services provided by publishers are reported along with information on costs. In a few cases, special computerized scoring and interpretation services are given in separate entries immediately following the test.

l) FOREIGN LANGUAGE AND OTHER SPECIAL EDITIONS. This section concerns foreign language editions published by the same publisher who sells the English edition. It also indicates special editions (e.g., Braille, large type) available from the same or a different publisher.

m) TIME. The number of minutes of actual working time allowed examinees and the approximate length of time needed for administering a test are reported whenever obtainable. The latter figure is always enclosed in parentheses. Thus, "50(60) minutes" indicates that the examinees are allowed 50 minutes of working time and that a total of 60 minutes is needed to administer the test. A time of "40–50 minutes" indicates an untimed test that takes approximately 45 minutes to administer, or—in a few instances—a test so timed that working time and administration time are very difficult to disentangle. When the time necessary to administer a test is not reported or suggested in the test materials but has been obtained through correspondence with the test publisher or author, the time is enclosed in brackets.

n) COMMENTS. Some entries contain special notations, such as: "for research use only"; "revision of the ABC Test"; "tests administered monthly at centers throughout the United States"; "subtests available as separates"; and "verbal creativity." A statement such as "verbal creativity" is intended to further describe what the test claims to measure. Some of the test entries include factual statements that imply criticism of the test, such as "1980 test identical with test copyrighted 1970."

o) AUTHOR. For most tests, all authors are reported. In the case of tests that appear in a new form each year, only authors of the most recent forms are listed. Names are reported exactly as printed on test booklets. Names of editors generally are not reported.

p) PUBLISHER. The name of the publisher or distributor is reported for each test. Foreign publishers are identified by listing the country in brackets immediately following the name of the publisher. The Publishers Directory and Index must be consulted for a publisher's address.

q) FOREIGN ADAPTATIONS. Revisions and adaptations of tests for foreign use are listed in a separate paragraph following the original edition.

r) SUBLISTINGS. Levels, editions, subtests, or parts of a test available in separate booklets are sometimes presented as sublistings with titles set in small capitals. Sub-sublistings are indented and titles are set in italic type.

s) CROSS REFERENCES. For tests that have been listed previously in a Buros Institute publication, a test entry includes—if relevant—a final paragraph containing a cross reference to the reviews, excerpts, and references for that test in those volumes. In the cross references, "T3:467" refers to test 467 in *Tests in Print III*, "8:1023" refers to test 1023 in *The Eighth Mental Measurements Yearbook*, "T2:144" refers to test 144 in *Tests in Print II*, "7:637" refers to test 637 in *The Seventh Mental Measurements Yearbook*, "P:262" refers to test 262 in *Personality Tests and Reviews I*, "2:1427" refers to test 1427 in *The 1940 Yearbook*, and "1:1110" refers to test 1110 in *The 1938 Yearbook*. In the case of batteries and programs, the paragraph also includes cross references—from the battery to the separately listed subtests and vice versa—to entries in this volume and to entries and reviews in earlier *Yearbooks*. Test numbers not preceded by a colon refer to tests in this *Yearbook*; for example, "see 45" refers to test 45 in this *Yearbook*.

If a reader finds something in a test description that is not understood, the descriptive material presented above can be referred to again and can often help to clarify the matter.

ACKNOWLEDGEMENTS

The publication of the *Supplement to the 10th Mental Measurements Yearbook* could not have been accomplished without the contributions of many individuals. The editors acknowledge gratefully the talent, expertise, and dedication of all those who have assisted in the publication process. Foremost among this group is Linda Murphy, Managing Editor. Her constant effort, knowledge, editorial skill, and cheerful attitude made our job as editors easier than we could have imagined. Nor would the publication of this volume be possible without the efforts of Arlie Prokop, Editorial Assistant, and Rosemary Sieck, Word Processing Specialist. As always, their efforts go far beyond that required as part of normal job responsibilities. We are also grateful to Debra Ruthsatz, Administrative/Marketing Coordinator, and Nancy Schwab, Secretary/Receptionist. We are pleased to acknowledge the continuous assistance available from the Director of the Buros Institute, Dr. Barbara Plake. Her enthusiasm for our work, visionary leadership, and skill in building a cohesive team effort are important to us all. The sense of accomplishment and pride we feel with the publication of the *10MMY-S* is shared by our entire staff and our heartfelt thank you is extended to the individuals mentioned above.

Our gratitude is also extended to the many reviewers who have prepared test reviews for the Buros Institute. Their willingness to take time from busy professional schedules to share their expertise in the form of thoughtful test reviews is appreciated. The *Mental Measurements Yearbook* would not exist were it not for their efforts.

Many graduate students have contributed to the publication of this volume. Their efforts have included reviewing test catalogs, fact checking reviews, looking for test references, and innumerable other tasks. We thank Janet Allison, Carol Berigan, Mike Bonner, Haeok Kim, Maria Potenza, Mark Shriver, Richard Sonnenberg, Richard Taffe, and Lori Wennstedt for their assistance.

Appreciation is also extended to our National and Departmental Advisory Committees for their willingness to assist in the operation of the Buros Institute. During the period in which this volume was prepared the National Advisory Committee has included Luella Buros, Stephen Elliott, William Mehrens, Lawrence Rudner, Douglas Whitney, and Frank Womer. The Buros Institute is part of the Department of Educational Psychology of the University of Nebraska-Lincoln and we have benefited from the many departmental colleagues who have contributed to our Departmental Advisory Committee including Robert Brown, Roger Bruning, Collie Conoley, Terry Gutkin, Gregory Schraw, Gargi Sodowsky, and Steven Wise. We are also grateful for the contribution of the University of Nebraska Press, which provides expert consultation and serves as distributor of the *MMY* series.

We thank Dave Spanel and his colleagues at the UNL Computing Resource Center for valuable assistance in preparing the indexes and organizing our information for printing.

Our Institute is fortunate to have as a constant benefactor Mrs. Luella Buros. Mrs. Buros supports our work in many, many ways. We are grateful for her interest in the continuation of Oscar Buros' work and honored by our close friendship with her.

SUMMARY

The *MMY* series is a valuable resource for people interested in studying or using testing. Once the process of using the series is understood, a reader can gain rapid access to a wealth of information. Our hope is that with the publication of the *10MMY-S*, test authors and publishers will consider carefully the comments made by the reviewers and continue to refine and perfect their assessment products.

Tests and Reviews

[1]

Adult Basic Learning Examination, Second Edition.

Purpose: "Designed to measure the educational achievement of adults who may or may not have completed twelve years of schooling . . . also useful in evaluating efforts to raise the educational level of these adults."

Population: Adults with less than 12 years of formal schooling.

Publication Dates: 1986–87.

Acronym: ABLE.

Administration: Group.

Levels, 3: 1, 2, 3 and screening test (SelectABLE).

Forms, 2: E, F (equivalent forms).

Price Data, 1988: $23 per examination kit containing test booklets and directions for administration for 1 form of each of the 3 levels, hand-scorable answer sheet, Ready Score™ Answer Sheet and group record for Level 2, and SelectABLE Ready Score™ Answer Sheet; $15 per handbook of instructional techniques and materials ('86, 67 pages); $15 per norms booklet (specify level); $5 per Reading Supplement; ABLE Computer Scoring™ software program also available for local computer scoring.

Authors: Bjorn Karlsen and Eric F. Gardner.

Publisher: The Psychological Corporation.

a) SELECTABLE.

Purpose: A screening test to determine which level of ABLE is most suitable for use with a particular individual.

Price Data: $26 per 25 Ready Score™ Answer Sheets; $23 per 50 hand-scorable test sheets; $13 per scoring key; $5 per SelectABLE Handbook ('86, 15 pages).

Time: (15) minutes.

b) LEVEL 1.

Population: Adults with 1–4 years of formal education.

Scores, 5: Vocabulary, Reading Comprehension, Spelling, Number Operations, Problem Solving.

Price Data: $33 per 25 hand-scorable test booklets and directions for administering including group record (specify Form E or F); $28 per scoring key (specify Form E or F); $8 per directions for administering ('86, 38 pages).

Time: (130–165) minutes.

c) LEVEL 2.

Population: Adults with 5–8 years of formal education.

Scores: Same as *b* plus Language.

Price Data: $33 per 25 hand-scorable or reusable test booklets (specify Form E or F); $28 per scoring key (specify Form E or F); $27 per 25 Ready Score™ Answer Sheets (specify Form E or F); $23 per 50 hand-scorable answer sheets and 2 group records; $8 per directions for administering Levels 2 and 3.

Time: (175–215) minutes.

d) LEVEL 3.

Population: Adults with 9–12 years of formal schooling who may or may not have completed 12 years of schooling.

Scores: Same as *c*.

Price Data: Same as *c*.

Time: Same as *c*.
Cross References: See also T3:121 (6 references), 8:2 (4 references), and T2:3 (3 references); for a review by A. N. Hieronymus of the earlier edition and excerpted reviews by Edward B. Fry and James W. Hall of Levels 1 and 2 of the earlier edition, see 7:3.

Review of the Adult Basic Learning Examination, Second Edition by ANNE R. FITZPA-TRICK, Manager of Applied Research, CTB/McGraw-Hill, Monterey, CA:

This second edition of the Adult Basic Learning Examination (ABLE) has many qualities not present in the first edition. Language mechanics and usage are assessed in the second and third levels of the new edition. The objectives assessed by all subtests are described in detail. The norms groups consist of comprehensive samples of distinct reference groups. Finally, a Handbook of Instructional Techniques and Materials and a Reading Supplement will help teachers of adults plan effective instruction. All tests, manuals, and ancillary materials are well written and easy to use, and the test items appear suitably adult-oriented in content.

SELECTABLE. This multiple-choice locator test has 30 items that measure verbal concepts and 15 items that measure numerical concepts. Once an examinee's total score has been calculated, a table of cut-scores is used to decide what level of ABLE to administer. No evidence of how accurately examinees are placed using these cut-scores is provided. Also not explained is why an examinee's total score is calculated rather than separate verbal and numerical scores, so that an examinee's verbal and quantitative skill levels could be differentiated.

ABLE TEST CONTENT. At Level 1, the Vocabulary and Spelling subtests are entirely dictated so that reading skills are not taxed. The items in the Problem Solving subtest are read aloud by the examiner, although they are also printed in the test booklets.

The term "auditory comprehension" best describes what is measured by the Level 1 Vocabulary subtest, because examinees must listen to a sentence and then choose from three alternatives the word that best completes the sentence. The Vocabulary subtests at Levels 2 and 3 are not dictated.

The Reading Comprehension subtest at Level 1 requires examinees to read signs, short passages presented in a modified cloze format, and short passages followed by questions. At Levels 2 and 3 the reading material consists of passages of an educational nature and letters, forms, instructions, and notices of the kind that adults may confront in everyday life. At all levels there are items designed to assess inference skills, although these items are not particularly challenging. In Form E of Level 2, for example, only 4 of the 24 inference items had p-values less than .50 for the ABE/GED and prison norms groups combined. The Reading subtest is among the easiest at each level.

In contrast, the mathematics subtests appear relatively difficult. For example, the average adult in each ABE/GED norms group answered only about half of the Problem Solving items correctly. Among the most difficult items at Levels 2 and 3 were those that involved ratios, percents, travel rates, and geometric formulae.

The Spelling and Language subtests at Levels 2 and 3 require examinees to identify the correct or incorrect versions of words or phrases. They appear to be suitable in content and difficulty.

ABLE NORMS. Adult reference-group norms expressed in terms of percentile ranks, stanines, and normal curve equivalents accompany each level of ABLE. At Levels 1 and 2, the norming program involved two reference groups, adults in ABE/GED programs and adults in prison education programs. At Level 3, the norming program also involved adults in vocational/technical high school programs.

Grade equivalents (GEs) and scale scores are also given. These scores were developed when the Stanford Achievement Test (SAT) series was normed with public and nonpublic school students in 1981 and 1982. ABLE was linked to these score scales through a 1984 equating study. A discussion of the meaning of the GEs provided in each ABLE norms booklet aptly notes limits that should be applied when interpreting adults' performance in terms of a GE score scale that was developed using students' performance.

The adults comprising the reference groups for each test level are described in terms of their sex, age, race, and geographic location. Each adult was assigned to an ABLE level in light of the last grade completed by the adult in school. Because this variable of last grade completed was central in the process of defining the reference groups for each level of ABLE, data should have been provided to describe the last grades completed by the members of each reference group. Such data would allow users of ABLE to better determine the similarity between each reference group and the adults they are testing.

ABLE RELIABILITY AND VALIDITY. The internal consistency estimates of reliability (KR-21s) that were reported seem reasonable, generally ranging between the low .80s and low .90s. Given that one stated use of ABLE is to evaluate educational programs for adults, test-retest reliabilities and/or alternate forms reliabilities also should have been reported.

The evidence of validity that is reported consists of intercorrelations among the ABLE subtests and correlations between ABLE and the Stanford Achievement Test series. Although these correlational findings are quite respectable, it is important to note the version of ABLE used in the correlational studies was one of the experimental forms from which the items for the published version of ABLE were selected. Therefore, the correlational evidence must be interpreted with caution, because it does not directly pertain to the published ABLE forms.

It is stated that the content of the items in ABLE were reviewed for possible ethnic and/or sex bias, although the characteristics of the reviewers are not specified. A more serious omission is that no data analyses were conducted to assess ethnic or sex bias in responses to these items.

SUMMARY COMMENTS. ABLE and the Test of Adult Basic Education (TABE; 94) are the two preeminent batteries available to assess adults' educational achievement. Both batteries are professionally developed and of high quality. To choose between them, users should evaluate each measure in terms of how well its content matches their curricular and/or assessment objectives. For adults who wish to earn a high school equivalency certificate, the TABE may be preferable because estimates of their scores on the Tests of General Educational Development (GED) can be derived from TABE scale scores using a conversion table that is provided.

Review of the Adult Basic Learning Examination, Second Edition by ROBERT T. WILLIAMS, *Professor, School of Occupational and Educational Studies, Colorado State University, Fort Collins, CO:*

The second edition of this battery is a high-quality, professional publication. The test booklets, directions for administering and scoring the tests, norms booklets, supplemental materials, and handbook of instructional techniques and materials are all well developed and organized, readable, attractive, and useful. SelectABLE is a useful addition to the three-level ABLE of the previous edition.

SelectABLE is a 45-item, untimed (estimated time needed is 15 minutes) screening test for placing examinees at the appropriate ABLE level. Item development, analysis, and selection are clearly and completely described. Procedures for administering, scoring, and interpreting SelectABLE are clear and meaningful. Tables are simple and easy to read. SelectABLE is a useful screening device, especially when limited educational information about the examinees is available.

There are no time limits for any subtest at any level; there are suggested time guidelines. Therefore, the ABLE is a power test that allows examinees to demonstrate their abilities without time constraints. For Level 1, examinees mark in the test booklet; for Levels 2 and 3, answer sheets are used. Following is a discussion of the subtests of ABLE, Levels 1, 2, and 3.

VOCABULARY. The examinee is to recognize the meaning of words encountered in everyday situations (16 words), in the natural and physical sciences (8 words), and in the social sciences (8 words). The examinee chooses the word or group of words that best completes each sentence. For Level 1, the sentence and the options are read to the examinee. The examinee marks the answer booklet. For Levels 2 and 3, the examples are read to the examinee, then the examinee reads and answers the 32 items.

This task is appropriate in adult content; it should be noted that nouns dominate the words. Having few items to represent a wide range of grade equivalent scores causes difficulties, as discussed below.

READING COMPREHENSION. At Level 1 (40 items) the examinee gets information from simple signs (9 items), completes sentences within short reading passages using the cloze technique (18 items), and reads and comprehends advertisements and short reading passages (13 items). In each item, the examinee selects the word or phrase that best completes the sentence. Levels 2 and 3 (48 items) evaluate functional reading, printed material that is typically encountered in everyday life (24 items), and educational reading, material found in informational pieces and content area textbooks (24 items). Both literal (24 items) and inferential (24 items) comprehension are evaluated. After reading the information, the examinee is to select from four alternatives the response that best completes a statement or answers a question.

This subtest has items of adult content in an appropriate format. The cloze technique recognizes the metacognitive and metalinguistic aspects of reading comprehension.

SPELLING. At Level 1, 30 items are dictated to the examinee, who writes the word in the test booklet. At Level 2, for 30 items of four words each, the examinee is to select the misspelled word. At Level 3 (30 items), 6 items have four phrases each (each phrase has an underlined word) and the examinee is to select the misspelled word; 24 items have four words each and the examinee is to select the misspelled word. This reviewer questions the construct validity of this subtest at Levels 2 and 3. The ability to identify a misspelled word is not a measure of spelling ability; such a skill is proofreading and should be identified as such. Level 1 measures spelling ability; Levels 2 and 3 do not.

LANGUAGE. At Levels 2 and 3 only (30 items at each level), the examinee selects the correct punctuation (11 items) and capitalization (7 items) for complete sentences. For 12 items the examinee selects the word or group of words that provide the grammatical completion of a sentence.

These items are appropriate to assess the mechanics of written language. There is no assessment of the examinee's production of written or oral expressive language. Users will want to recognize the limits of this language assessment.

NUMBER OPERATIONS. At Level 1 (20 items), concepts of number items (5 items) are dictated to the examinee, and computation items (15 items) are completed by the examin-

ee. All responses are written in the test booklet. At Levels 2 (36 items, 7 concepts of number and 29 computation) and 3 (40 items, 7 concepts of number and 33 computation), the examinee selects the correct solution to a problem from five alternatives, one of which is sometimes "NG" or not given.

At Level 1, some of the first five items seem difficult; the examinee is required to "write thirty-two thousand, forty-five in numerals" and to write 1,257 in words. Other items at this level and items in the other levels seem appropriate.

PROBLEM SOLVING. At Level 1, the 20 items and the four alternative answers, one of which is often "NG" or not given, are read to the examinee, who responds in the answer booklet. At Level 2 (30 items) and Level 3 (40 items), problems are solved by the examinee and answers are selected from five alternatives, one of which is sometimes "NG" or not given.

The items seem appropriate in difficulty and adult in content.

The authors present users with detailed guidance in understanding the types of scores generated by ABLE. There is a clear, usable discussion of content-referenced scores and norm-referenced scores. Tables of scores are well labeled, clear, and easy to read. There are enlightening, useful tables of the objectives and p-values (percentage of the combined group sample answering the item correctly) given for each subtest at each level.

Test-item tryout and standardization was completed using 3,471 adults involved in 132 adult basic education and high school equivalency programs in school, community, and prison settings, and vocational-technical school settings for Level 3, in 41 states. Demographic data of the participating adults suggest that characteristics of sex and race are not proportionally represented by the sample. Age and geographic region are more balanced. The user is encouraged to be aware of the demographics of the research sample and to consider the characteristics of their examinees when selecting a norm table. The authors recommend the development of local norms.

Norms for ABLE are not discussed adequately. The final forms of the ABLE were "equated to the experimental forms" described by the authors. The authors state, "Percentile rank and stanine norms for each level of ABLE, based on the performance of the adult groups taking each level, were developed for the final test forms as an outcome of the equating process." No further discussion of the norms is offered. Users are directed to the publisher for a more detailed description of this equating process. All normative data, reliability, and validity information seem to be based upon the 3,471 subjects drawn from adults involved in 132 community, school, and prison adult basic education and high school equivalency programs or joint vocational-technical high school programs in 41 states. These sample sizes are: at Level 1, ABE/GED $N = 291$; Prison Group $N = 565$; at Level 2, ABE/GED $N = 436$; Prison Group $N = 472$; and at Level 3, ABE/GED $N = 474$; Prison Group $N = 515$; Vocational-Technical Group $N = 718$.

Reliability was determined using Kuder-Richardson Formula 21. For Level 1, Forms E and F, all subtests are reliable ($> .80$) for the ABE/GED population; for the prison population, Vocabulary, Number Operations, and Problem Solving have questionable reliability ($< .80$), although Reading and Spelling are reliable; for the combined group, all subtests are reliable except Form E, Number Operations and Problem Solving, and Form F, Problem Solving. For Level 2, Forms E and F, all subtests of both forms are reliable for all groups except for Vocabulary (both forms) for the prison group (.79). For Level 3, Forms E and F, all subtests are reliable for all groups except for Vocabulary (Form E) for the ABE/GED group (.78). Note that these reliabilities approach an acceptable reliability of .80.

All subtests for all levels, except for Spelling, Level 1, have a range of PK (pre-kindergarten) to PHS (post-high school). Few items in a subtest and such a wide range of scores cause wide differences in grade level equivalents from a change of a few raw score points. For example, in the Vocabulary subtest, a range of raw score points from 11 to 20 yields a difference in grade equivalence scores of 2.3 at Level 1, 2.9 at Level 2, and 4.2 at Level 3. In the Problem Solving subtest, the raw score range from 11 to 20 yields a difference in grade equivalence scores of 6.9 at Level 1, 3.2 at Level 2, and 3.1 at Level 3.

Not all subtests or all levels are as significantly influenced as these examples. The user is encouraged to examine each subtest at each level for each sample to determine the impact on their examinees' performances. Further, all subtests have a standard error of measurement of at least 2 raw score points. Users will want to be aware of these facts when interpreting scores.

There is a discussion of the validity of each level of ABLE. Objectives measured by each level are stated and related to specific items, allowing users to evaluate content validity easily. This reviewer's opinion is that the content validity is good, except for Spelling in Levels 2 and 3, as noted above. Intercorrelations among the subtests of experimental forms are as follows: for Level 1, $\leq .68$; for Level 2, $\leq .71$; and for Level 3, $\leq .71$. This suggests each subtest is measuring separate elements of skill or knowledge. ABLE was equated to the Stanford Achievement Test series. The correlations were: for Level 1, .69 or less; for Level 2, .68 to .81; and for Level 3, about .80. One wonders why the Stanford Achievement Test might not be used instead of ABLE Level 3. Perhaps the adult content of ABLE Level 3 argues for its use with the population for whom ABLE is intended.

ABLE is a useful, efficient assessment of the educational level of adults with limited education. This edition follows in the tradition established by the earlier edition. SelectABLE, a screening device for placement in the correct level of ABLE, is a useful addition. The lack of specific information about the norm development is disappointing. The problem of having a few test items represent a wide range of grade level equivalents persists. SelectABLE and ABLE are useful tools for their intended purposes. Consumers are encouraged to use them with the test limitations in mind.

[2]

Adult Growth Examination.
Purpose: "For use in the assessment of individual adult aging."
Population: Ages 19–71.
Publication Dates: 1981–86.
Acronym: AGE.
Scores, 4: Near Vision, Hearing Loss, Systolic Blood Pressure, Body Age.
Administration: Individual.
Price Data, 1987: $14 per test manual ('86, 70 pages including score sheet).
Time: (10–15) minutes.
Comments: Other test materials (e.g., portable electronic blood pressure monitor, portable

audiometric monitor, portable visual near point indicator) must be provided locally.

Author: Robert F. Morgan.
Publisher: Robert F. Morgan.

Review of the Adult Growth Examination by CAMERON J. CAMP, Associate Professor of Psychology, and CAROLYN TRIAY, Department of Psychology, University of New Orleans, New Orleans, LA:

The Adult Growth Examination (AGE) requires 10–15 minutes to administer and is designed for the assessment of individual adult aging. The author states, "A test of individual bodily aging may be used for information, enjoyment, self awareness, research, and social change." Specifically, the test is designed to measure the "body age" of adults from age 19–71 by measuring an individual's near point of vision (NPV), hearing loss (HL), and systolic blood pressure (SBP). (A portable electronic blood pressure monitor, portable audiometer monitor, and portable visual near point indicator must be provided locally.) The individual's body age in years is then computed by comparing raw scores of these three measures to normative body-age scores provided in conversion tables (separate tables are given for men and women). In normative samples, birth age is within 10 years of body age in two out of every three persons tested, body age was more than 10 years older than birth age in one out of six persons, and body age was more than 10 years younger than birth age in one out of six persons tested. The AGE is described as "the most valid (and only) indicator of relative bodily aging in standardized test form available." The author states the test can ultimately be used to predict life expectancy, and "In theory, AGE should be a better survival predictor for an individual than insurance company actuarial tables."

RELIABILITY. Test-retest reliabilities for the overall AGE and the three subtests were computed for 50 male volunteer Nova Scotians. Reported reliability for the AGE was .88, with subtest reliabilities of .93 (NPV), .92 (HL), and .75 (SBP).

TEST STANDARDIZATION. Subtests were standardized by Morgan and his colleagues in Hawaii, New York, and Nova Scotia from 1966 to 1972.

NORMATIVE DATA. Normative data for men and women are described as being derived from

studies conducted primarily in the 1960s. The latest referenced data set is from 1972, though the author claims these data remain valid for normative purposes.

VALIDITY. Validity for AGE scores was determined by computing correlations between these scores and chronological age for 107 Nova Scotians (56 females and 51 males). AGE total scores correlated with chronological age ($r = .8$ using product-moment coefficients) for both genders. Correlations between subtest scores and chronological age ranged from .57 to .69 for raw scores, and from .67 to .78 for body-age scores.

From this same sample, correlations between subtest scores and AGE total scores ranged from .64 to .84 for raw scores, and from .74 to .85 for body-age scores. In addition, subtest intercorrelations ranged from .43 to .47 for raw scores, and from .52 to .63 for body-age scores. The standard error of the AGE scores estimated in years of chronological age was 9.3 years for AGE total score, and ranged from 8.1 years to 14.3 years for the subtests.

The AGE can be critiqued on two levels. The first level involves the general manner in which subtest scores are gathered and interpreted. An obvious problem is the possibility of variation introduced by different examiners using different brands of testing equipment. In addition, there will be varying levels of expertise in administration and scoring of the subtests if, as the author states, the AGE will be administered by "any intelligent adult" after "sufficient supervised practice."

The norms for creating body age out of subtest raw scores are dated. In addition, they might not be appropriate for some purposes. As the author notes, local norms may need to be developed. In addition, the norms and body-age conversion data reach only to age 71. Given the rapid increase in the "old-old" segment of our population, the AGE will be of limited utility for the study of aging. Finally, data for body-age declines across decades are presented in some detail for a variety of measures separately for men (in Table 1 of the test manual) and women (in Table 2). However, the data in the two tables are identical in every feature, representing either redundancy or missing data for one of the genders.

A second level of criticism involves problems for specific subtest measures. These will be described below.

MEASUREMENT OF BLOOD PRESSURE. The AGE instructions do not take into account several factors that can affect accuracy of SBP readings. The arm used to measure blood pressure should not be restricted by clothing and should be slightly flexed at the elbow, with the brachial artery approximately at heart level and forearm flat on a table. Nothing should be held in either arm, and legs should not be crossed (Schein, 1987). The inflatable bag encased in the cuff should be about 20% wider than the diameter of the arm and long enough to encircle the arm; thin and obese persons will require different cuff sizes. Irregular rhythms also produce variations in systolic pressure that can reduce reliability of measurements (Bates & Hoekelman, 1974). The test author's admonition that examiners acquire "highly practiced familiarity with test materials" does not seem to go far enough in dealing with these potential confounds.

MEASUREMENT OF HEARING LOSS. The abbreviated hearing loss measure used in the AGE differs from standard methods of measurement (Newby, 1979). For example, the AGE tests the right ear first, whereas it is advisable to test the better ear first. This allows the examiner to plan on masking the better ear if the difference in sensitivity between the ears is so great that the better ear will participate in the test of the poorer ear. Testing begins at 50db, which might be uncomfortably loud for some examinees, rather than beginning at a lower reading and then increasing the dbs. In addition, the AGE uses only a descending method of obtaining threshold, rather than a series of ascending and descending sweeps.

MEASUREMENT OF VISION. Although each ear is tested in the hearing loss subtest, eyes are not tested individually in the NPV subtest.

SUMMARY. The AGE is designed to measure body age by assessing measures of near point vision, systolic blood pressure, and hearing loss in individuals aged 19–71. These raw scores are then converted into body-age scores using tables based on normative data for individuals of different ages, thus allowing individuals to determine if their abilities are at, above, or below levels that might be expected for someone of their age. Supposedly, the AGE score

could also be used to detect the influence of life style changes or interventions, as well as to make predictions regarding individual longevity.

The lack of standardized testing equipment and training could severely compromise the reliability and validity of the AGE. The very simplicity of the instructions assures that the sophistication necessary to measure complex physical phenomena may not be achieved by testers. Normative data may be inappropriate or outdated. The writing style of the test manual at times is quite colloquial (e.g., Comfort "left England for sunny California"; "correlational analysis of age-sensitive factors remains in high gear"; etc.). Reviews of the test presented in appendices often include newspaper articles written by reporters rather than reviews in professional journals. Finally, by ignoring factors such as individual personality and coping variables, social support systems, and so on, the AGE becomes severely limited in its ability to measure constructs such as survivability or functional age.

In short, the AGE highlights the need to develop reliable and valid measures of body age and related constructs, as well as how very far the testing community still has to evolve before such goals are achieved.

REVIEWER'S REFERENCES

Bates, B., & Hoekelman, R. A. (1974). *A guide to physical examination* (pp. 138-141). Philadelphia: Lippincott.
Newby, H. A. (1979). *Audiology* (4th ed., pp. 117-124). Englewood Cliffs, NJ: Prentice-Hall.
Schein, J. (1987). Monitoring your blood pressure at home. *Consumers' Research Magazine, 70* (Part 3), 31-34.

Review of the Adult Growth Examination by JACLYN B. SPITZER, Chief, Audiology and Speech Pathology, Veterans Administration Medical Center, West Haven, CT, and Associate Clinical Professor, Department of Surgery (Otolaryngology), Yale University School of Medicine, New Haven, CT, and GAIL M. SULLIVAN, Chief, Geriatric Medicine, and Associate Chief of Staff for Education, Veterans Administration Medical Center, Newington, CT, and Assistant Professor of Medicine, University of Connecticut, Farmington, CT:

The manual begins with the statement, "You do not have to be a psychologist or a physician to give the Adult Growth Examination (AGE)." The author apparently intended to provide guidelines for screening several different aspects of physiology. Unfortunately, the guidelines provided contain numerous inaccuracies that could result in serious failures to detect health problems. The flaws relate to both the methods described and the validation of the test.

For example, the methodologic guidelines given for hearing examination conform to no published screening methods for the geriatric patient or any other target clinical population. The technique described should not be applied, as the intensity levels suggested far exceed any definition of hearing impairment in professional usage and also bear no semblance to levels shown to correlate to hearing handicap (e.g., see Weinstein, 1986). Furthermore, if a person or group was interested in providing hearing screening with minimal audiologic training, there are alternative methods that can be provided with greater accuracy than the one described. Specifically, the AudioScope by Welsh-Allen can be used routinely by nursing or health care professionals where an audiologist or otologist is not available. Similar methodologic criticisms can be made of vision and blood pressure screening as outlined in the AGE manual.

The validation, both face and construct, of this test is absent. As a clinician, it makes no sense at all that these "scores" (Systolic BP ≤ 160, Near Vision, and Hearing) have much to do with biological aging, chronological aging, or *survival*. Patients can survive very well with congenital hearing and visual deficits and with systolic hypertension. No sensible geriatrician would accept the unsubstantiated assertion, by the author, that these scores have any relationship to the immensely complex, and poorly understood, process of physiologic aging.

No acceptable validation data are provided. Dr. Morgan quotes 1884 and 1932 (not very recent!) data as proof that presbyopic patients die at younger ages (p. 21). These data clearly were not stratified by what we now know are major risk factors for decreased survival (e.g., heart disease, lung disease, renal failure, functional class). No validation for the "scoring" of the test (p. 9) is given at all. The statement that a systolic blood pressure of 160 mm Hg (p. 10) is "definite hypertension" is grossly inaccurate. We do not know, although there are clinical trials to study this underway (e.g., SHEP study; Black, Brand, Greenlick, et al., 1987), the import of elevations of systolic blood pressure in different age groups and sexes. In fact, most studies show no significance whatsoever for an elevated systolic blood pressure in adult females, unless it is extremely high.

The statement that this test has been "field" tested with "apparent success" (p. 28) is not adequate validation data. Indeed, there is currently no accepted "gold standard" for "biological" age, aside from chronological age; the author certainly does not attempt to put forth his own description of a gold standard (p. 32).

At various points, the author appears to suggest the score can be used to predict chronological age (p. 35), predict survival (pp. 21, 35), or perhaps spur an individual to "reverse" his aging process (p. 10), for unclear reasons and/or benefit.

In summary, the reviewers seriously question both the intent and the execution of the manual for this examination. We believe it can have serious negative consequences in failing to identify health problems that may require treatment and rehabilitation. It is irresponsible to suggest individuals should focus on the test results and even perhaps try to improve them. Great harm may result from focusing on these probably irrelevant parameters to the exclusion of well-documented risk factors for determination of function and health: diastolic blood pressure, functional class, cholesterol level, smoking, and weight, to name just a few.

REVIEWER'S REFERENCES

Weinstein, B. (1986). Validity of a screening protocol for identifying elderly people with hearing problems. *Asha, 28*, 41-45.

Black, B. M., Brand, R. J., Greenlick, M., et al. (1987). Compliance to treatment for hypertension in elderly patients: The SHEP Pilot Study. *Journal of Gerontology, 42* (5), 552-557.

[3]

The Affective Perception Inventory/College Level.

Purpose: Focuses on the academic dimension of self-perceptions, measuring the self as a person, a student, against the school settings and exploring the feelings about the self relative to specific subject areas.

Population: Postsecondary school students.

Publication Dates: 1975–89.

Acronym: API.

Scores: 10 scales: Self Concept, Student Self, English Perceptions, Mathematics, Science, Social Studies, Business, Arts, Humanities, Campus Perceptions.

Administration: Group.

Price Data, 1988: $.30 per single scale; $4 per booklet of 10 scales; $8 per College Level manual ('85, 83 pages); $15 per composite test manual (information on all levels, '89, 22 pages).
Time: (45–60) minutes.
Comments: Ratings by self and others; fourth of 4 levels; highest level and most recent addition to the Affective Perception Inventory (9:59).
Authors: Anthony T. Soares and Louise M. Soares.
Publisher: SOARES Associates.
Cross References: For reviews by Rosa A. Hagin and Gerald R. Smith of the first three levels, see 9:59.

Review of The Affective Perception Inventory/College Level by JOHN R. HESTER, Associate Professor of Psychology, Francis Marion College, Florence, SC:
The Affective Perception Inventory/College Level (API/CL) attempts to assess self-perception in relation to specific academic areas, and at the same time seeks to measure both a general and student self-concept. To accomplish these goals, the API/CL uses a multitrait/multimethod approach, whereby the instrument assesses each student with 10 scales (multitrait) completed by the student, a peer, and a teacher (multimethod). Such a multimethod approach seeks to measure and contrast differing perceptions of each student. The College Level is similar to previously developed levels of the API (Primary Grades 1–3, Intermediate 4–8, Advanced 9–12), requiring on each item a forced choice from among four descriptors along a continuum between a pair of dichotomous phrases (i.e., "enjoys math—does not enjoy math"). Student, peer, and teacher ratings on each of the 10 scales are all completed using the same items. The College Level scales are similar to previous API scales, with the exception of Humanities substituted for Physical Education and the addition of a Business Scale. The authors cite research as the primary purpose of the instrument, but also present the API/CL as an applied tool to measure the perceptions of individual students. The manual cautions users against using measured self-perceptions to categorize individuals.

Information concerning the authors' clustering model of self-concept, as well as technical data for earlier levels of the test and the College Level, are all included in the same manual. Unfortunately, at times the manual is unclear as to which level of the test it is referring, and as a result the manual has the appearance of having been pieced together over the years. The outcome is a manual that is at times confusing and very difficult to use. Users are cautioned that norms and technical information for the Business Scale are currently available only in a supplement to the test manual.

Administration instructions in both the scale booklet and the manual are rather straightforward and clear. Simple scoring directions are provided, with numeric values attached to ratings, and an algebraic sum computed for each of the 10 scales. A table is provided for converting raw scores on each scale to a stanine. As always, stanines represent a band of scores, with more specific information lost. The manual states that both a total score and subscale scores (for seven scales) can be computed, but no norms are provided for these scores. The purported advantage of having three ratings for an individual is diminished by the fact that no guidelines are included to assist in interpreting the significance of any discrepancy among scores.

An inadequate description is provided as to how items were developed for the API/CL. The norms for the test are based upon 450 college students who are broken down by sex, but no information is provided as to race, year in school, major, grades, or how the subjects were chosen. The normative sample consists of one group of 100 students from an urban, private university and 350 from a rural, public university. No other data concerning the two academic institutions are provided. It is unlikely that using students from only two universities provides a representative sample.

Reliability in terms of internal consistency (method of computation undefined) for the API/CL is .91 for self-ratings, .83 for peers, and .69 for teachers. No internal consistency data are provided for the 10 individual scales. Test-retest reliability coefficients, based on an 8-week interval, vary from a low of .69 on Campus Perceptions to a high of .94 for Mathematics. Reliability coefficients for Arts (.77), English (.76), Humanities (.73), Social Studies (.72), and Campus Perceptions (.69) are, at best, adequate. No *SEM*s are provided to aid in interpreting individual scores. Reliability studies reported in the manual have no information as to the number of subjects included or other demographic information.

Convergent validity was assessed through comparisons among the three raters (self, peers, and teachers). Moderate correlations were obtained, but no information was provided as to the number of raters in each group or how they were chosen; nor were there correlations among raters for individual scales. The manual did not report any validity studies comparing the API/CL to external criteria. Note should be made that Byrne and Shavelson (1986) in using the Advanced Level of the API found significant correlations of .56 to .86 between portions of the API (Student, Self, English, Mathematics) and portions of the Self Description Questionnaire III and the Self-Concept of Ability Scale. Intercorrelations of nine API/CL scales as presented in the API manual were moderate; however, no factor analysis was provided.

In summary, the authors of the API/CL conceived of a cluster of academic self-concepts that are to some degree dependent on experiences in different academic situations. Unfortunately, minimal information is provided as to item selection, and guidelines to interpret scores are generally lacking. The normative group seems limited and only generally described. While the test appears to have adequate reliability, inadequate information is provided about reliability studies to draw firm conclusions. External criterion validity studies are notably lacking. Normative, reliability, and validity data presented in the manual are generally confusing and incomplete. It should be noted that more extensive data for the other levels of the test are presented in the manual. In short, the API/CL cannot be recommended for applied/clinical uses. Rather, the test is best considered a research tool.

REVIEWER'S REFERENCE

Byrne, B., & Shavelson, R. (1986). On the structure of adolescent self-concept. *Journal of Educational Psychology, 78,* 474-481.

Review of The Affective Perception Inventory/College Level by MICHAEL J. SUBKOVIAK, Professor and Chair of Educational Psychology, University of Wisconsin-Madison, Madison, WI:

The College Level of The Affective Perception Inventory (API) is an extension of forms of this instrument designed for use in primary and secondary schools. The inventory consists of 10 scales composed of items measuring self-concept relative to specific subject areas (English, Mathematics, etc.) or other aspects of student life. Items employ a semantic differential format in which dichotomous traits (e.g., strong vs. weak) are positioned on either side of four ordered categories scored -2, -1, +1, +2. A raw score is calculated for each scale by summing these values across items; the raw score is then converted to a stanine, indicating the strength of an individual's self-concept in a given subject area as compared to a norm group. In addition, self-ratings can be compared for congruence to peer or instructor ratings derived from equivalent forms completed by others.

The authors recommend that the API be used primarily for research purposes, which is a responsible position to adopt in light of limited information provided in the manual regarding its technical characteristics. One would hope that the API would not be used for admission, course placement, or other purposes for which it has not been validated. In its current stage of development, the API/College Level cannot and should not be recommended for general use.

RELIABILITY. Test-retest correlations, with an 8-week interval between testings, are reported for each scale of the API. The Self Concept (.88), Student Self (.85), Mathematics (.94), and Science (.90) scales have acceptable test-retest reliabilities. However, the reliabilities of the other scales range between .69 and .76 and are substandard for a commercial instrument.

Internal consistency estimates are also reported for self-ratings (.91), peer ratings (.83), and instructor ratings (.69). Although the manual does not explain how these coefficients were derived, apparently they are Rulon (1939) split-half reliabilities for composite scores obtained by summing ratings across all items and subscales. The results suggest that self-ratings are consistent, whereas those for instructors are substandard.

VALIDITY. The information provided in the manual pertaining to validity is also sparse. A matrix of intercorrelations among self, peer, and instructor ratings is reported—apparently for ratings on the Self Concept subscale, but the manual is not clear on this point. In any event, self-peer ratings correlated .59 and self-instructor ratings correlated .49, which suggests that self ratings are at least moderately correlated with the perceptions of others. Peer-instructor ratings correlated a relatively low .36.

A second matrix provides information about intercorrelations among all subscales for self ratings. About half of these intercorrelations are relatively low (.20–.38), while the other half are moderate to high (.40–.71). These mixed results suggest that some, but not all, subscales of the API are independent of each other. The need for factor analysis of API subscales to identify independent dimensions of self-concept has been noted by others. Such analysis might suggest combining highly correlated subscales like Science and Mathematics (.71), which appear to be measuring much the same trait, thereby reducing the number of subscales to be administered.

A table of "construct validity" coefficients for the various subscales is also reported in the manual, but the table is not explained or discussed. Apparently these coefficients are based on judgments of experts regarding the appropriateness of items on a particular subscale of the API. However, it is difficult to evaluate the results, given the dearth of information provided about the analysis.

NORMS. The tables for converting raw scores to stanine equivalents are based on administration of the API to 450 students at two universities. The representativeness of this reference group ought to be questioned by potential users of the API. The self-perceptions of this restricted group may differ in certain respects from those of college students in other settings.

The manual provides cryptic information about the norm group of 450 students. About 75% are from a public/rural university and 25% are from a private/urban university. About 48% are female and 52% are male. Separate norm tables are *not* provided for various subgroups, although there are obvious differences in perceptions, for instance, between females and males on the Mathematics and Science subscales.

The Affective Perception Inventory/College Level is at best an "experimental model" about which little is known. Information on the reliability is mixed—some subscales are reliable and others are not. Evidence of validity is extremely limited—Self Concept ratings are moderately correlated with peer and instructor ratings. Norm groups are restricted to two

universities. The manual is cryptic in many respects. As such, the API cannot be recommended for general use, and its use for research purposes should be carefully considered.

REVIEWER'S REFERENCE

Rulon, P. J. (1939). A simplified procedure for determining the reliability for a test by split halves. *Harvard Educational Review, 9,* 99-103.

[4]
The Alcadd Test, Revised Edition.

Purpose: "Designed to: a) provide an objective measurement of alcoholic addiction that could identify individuals whose behavior and personality structure indicated that they were alcoholic addicts or had serious alcoholic problems; b) identify specific areas of maladjustment in alcoholics to facilitate therapeutic and rehabilitation activities; and c) obtain better insight into the psychodynamics of alcoholic addiction."
Population: Adults.
Publication Dates: 1949–88.
Scores, 6: Regularity of Drinking, Preference for Drinking over Other Activities, Lack of Controlled Drinking, Rationalization of Drinking, Excessive Emotionality, Total.
Administration: Individual or group.
Editions, 2: Paper-and-pencil, microcomputer.
Price Data, 1989: $35 per complete kit including 25 AutoScore test booklets ('88, 4 pages) and manual ('88, 24 pages); $22.50 per 25 AutoScore test booklets; $12.70 per manual; $185 per microcomputer edition (IBM) including diskette (tests up to 25) and user's guide.
Time: (5–15) minutes.
Comments: Self-administered.
Authors: Morse P. Manson, Lisa A. Melchior, and G. J. Huba.
Publisher: Western Psychological Services.
Cross References: See T3:152 (3 references), T2:1098 (1 reference), and P:7 (3 references); for a review by Dugal Campbell, see 6:60 (6 references); for reviews by Charles H. Honzik and Albert L. Hunsicker, see 4:30.

TEST REFERENCES

1. Elkins, R. L. (1980). Covert sensitization treatment of alcoholism: Contributions of successful conditioning to subsequent abstinence maintenance. *Addictive Behaviors, 5,* 67-89.

Review of The Alcadd Test, Revised Edition by WILLIAM L. CURLETTE, *Professor of Educational Foundations, Georgia State University, Atlanta, GA:*

According to the revised edition of The Alcadd Test manual (1988), the purposes of The Alcadd Test are threefold: namely, to "provide an objective measurement of alcoholic addiction," to "identify specific areas of maladjustment," and to "obtain better insight into the psychodynamics of alcoholic addiction." These objectives are accomplished by having respondents answer yes or no to 65 items resulting in scores on the following five subscales: Regularity of Drinking (12 items), Preference for Drinking Over Other Activities (11 items), Lack of Controlled Drinking (20 items), Rationalization of Drinking (20 items), and Excessive Emotionality (20 items). The test and the manual are produced with an attractive format.

The original Alcadd manual (1965, 1978) provided by Western Psychological Services consisted of only two pages and one-paragraph descriptions of validity, reliability, and administration. Thus, the revised manual with 19 pages of text and 4 additional pages for test form and profile form samples represents a substantial revision.

Previous reviewers of the test (Campbell, 6:60; Hunsicker, 4:30) have commented on the lack of a theoretical support for the dimensions used in the test. The revised manual reports a factor analysis of the five Alcadd subscales; hence, providing through empirical research some basis for the total score. Ultimately, however, the meaningfulness and usefulness of the subscales come from the studies employing the Alcadd. The revised manual reports a number of studies.

As the previous reviews of the Alcadd and the test manual indicate, scores on the test could be influenced by the response set of social desirability. This occurs because the responses to the items are obvious if a person desires to fake a nonalcoholic response. Furthermore, there is no social desirability subscale to measure faking on the test. The manual suggests the MMPI validity scales or the Social Desirability Scale by Crowne and Marlowe (1960) may be used in conjunction with the Alcadd if there is concern about faking. The discussion of this issue in the test manual is brought to a close by stating that the use of the Alcadd in voluntary treatment settings should not be a problem.

Based on information in the previous manual, scoring has improved with the new revision. Previously, scoring was done by hand using a template (or sheet next to the person's responses). Now scoring is done on a form having carbon paper underneath the sheet on which the examinee takes the test. The carbon paper eliminates one step in the hand-scoring process. Also included in the test booklet are profile sheets that convert raw scores to centiles and T-scores, and the probability of being an alcoholic. In addition, the manual states that a microcomputer disk (IBM $5^1/_4$ in. or $3^1/_2$ in.) is available to administer, score, and print a report (two pages long) for The Alcadd Test.

Two key aspects for using any test are the amount of time required to administer the test and its reading level. On both accounts the Alcadd appears very good. The test manual reports that it requires between 5 and 15 minutes to take the 65 items in the test. Although there are many readability formulas and approaches, there are several ways to obtain a quick estimate of the grade level for reading. The Flesch-Kincaid, as calculated by the RightWriter computer program for the first 99 words and the last 101 words of the Alcadd, was 3.0. Using the SMOG index on the same selections, the reading was at the 4.7 grade level. Thus, reading level appears low enough to be used with most populations. The manual also suggests it is appropriate to read the items to examinees.

Two bothersome technical aspects are overlapping items between subscales and 40-year-old norms. A technical aspect of the test, which may be a limitation for the use of the test in research, is the assignment of some items to more than one subscale (although many tests do this). In fact, there are 23 items that are scored on more than one subscale. Even though it may reduce test-taking time, the effect of overlapping items between subscales is to induce spurious correlation between subscales. This means the correlation between subscales sharing items may be artificially inflated unless statistical adjustments are made. Whether due to overlapping items or not, the intercorrelation (.81) between two subscales (Rationalization of Drinking and Excessive Emotionality) seems high, if only from the perspective that subscales on a test battery are typically created to measure distinct attributes and, thus, would not be expected to correlate highly.

The norms shown in a sample 1988 score report in the test manual are based on a 1949 sample. Subsequent research on norms by Dunlop is reported in the manual; however, the results do not appear to provide direct support for the 1949 norms. More recent norms are needed for score interpretation.

There is a lack of information in the test manual on topics considered necessary (primary standards) in the *Standards for Educational and Psychological Testing* (AERA, APA, & NCME, 1985). Missing from the manual are standard errors of measurement, reliabilities for the subscales, and cultural fairness research information.

A unique aspect of the test is translating an examinee's total test score into the probability of being an alcoholic. Interestingly, for both males and females in any preassigned risk group, a total raw score of exactly 22 or higher yields a .99 probability of being in the alcoholic group. This observation might be helpful as a benchmark for quickly interpreting test scores.

On a PsychALERT and PsychINFO computer literature search run during Fall 1989, two citations (not listed in the test manual) (Ramsay, 1979; Zeh, 1985) were found. Ramsay (1979) administered the Alcadd, the MMPI, and the 16PF to patients suffering from alcoholism. Zeh (1985) compared scores on the Michigan Alcoholism Screening Test, the MacAndrew Alcoholism Scale, and the Alcadd in a sample of 80 incarcerated male adolescent felons. An Educational Resources Information Center (ERIC) literature search on Alcadd using SilverPlatter V1.5 for 1/83 to 6/89 did not provide any citations.

In conclusion, the concerns of previous reviewers regarding the lack of control of social desirability and the potential to fake scores on the Alcadd still limit the use of the Alcadd. Disregarding this concern, the Alcadd does approach all three of its objectives. Additional work is needed, however, to bring the Alcadd manual into closer agreement with basic test standards.

REVIEWER'S REFERENCES

Crowne, D. P., & Marlowe, D. A. (1960). A new scale of social desirability independent of psychopathology. *Journal of Consulting Psychology, 24*, 349-354.

Ramsay, S. A. (1979). Statistical information on three personality measures used with alcoholics. National Institute for Personnel Research, Johannesburg, South Africa (Afrikaans Abstract).

American Educational Research Association, American Psychological Association, & National Council on Measurement in Education. (1985). *Standards for educational and psychological testing.* Washington, DC: American Psychological Association, Inc.

Zeh, R. S. (1985). Alcoholism and incarcerated adolescent males: Knowledge and testing (Doctoral Dissertation, The University of Akron, 1985). *Dissertation Abstracts International, 45,* 3593A. (ISSN: 04194209)

Review of The Alcadd Test, Revised Edition by PAUL RETZLAFF, *Assistant Professor of Psychology, University of Northern Colorado, Greeley, CO:*

This 65-item (60 items scored) inventory of obvious yes/no alcohol-related behaviors purports to "identify" alcoholics. Its scoring results in a total score and five subscales: Regularity of Drinking, Preference for Drinking over Other Activities, Lack of Controlled Drinking, Rationalization of Drinking, and Excessive Emotionality. It was originally developed in 1949 and remains substantially unchanged in its 1988 revision.

It is brief and easy to administer, score, and determine sophisticated hit rate statistics. The new Autoscore multipart test forms and scoring sheets are particularly noteworthy. Finally, the adoption of positive and negative predictive power statistics is found in few other tests.

There are a number of problems with the test, however. First, all items, norms, and hit rates are from the original 1949 development. The test was developed via empirical group separation at an item level. The problem with this is that empirical group separation results in poorer operating characteristics than domain theory test construction. Further, in the last 40 years it is very likely that different items would be better and that "alcoholics" as a group may have changed. This is particularly true in light of the relatively low N employed in the original study—282 split four ways, male-female and alcoholic-nonalcoholic. The reliability and validity statistics are also disturbing. Although the test as a whole has an internal consistency of .92 and .96, there are no reliabilities for the five subscales reported in the manual. There is also a problem with the independence of the five subscales. They were subjectively derived and as such have no empirical basis. Further, the manual attempts to put a positive face on their very high intercorrelations by saying this proves high internal consistency. Finally, although the test as a whole has been examined for validity indices, there are no validity estimates reported for any of the five subscales.

The most positive aspects of the test are the hit rate statistics integrated into the scoring process. The test publisher is applauded for adopting the operating characteristics of positive and negative predictive powers. The reliance on the 1949 norms, however, greatly reduces the validity of these data.

In summary, The Alcadd Test is substantively unchanged from 1949 and as such is limited by its construction, norms, and other developments. A better test is probably the Alcohol Use Inventory (AUI) (Horn, Wanberg, & Foster, 1987). Its subscales were empirically derived, have high reliabilities, and add additional dimensions. The most recent revision of the AUI has added scales, items, and norms. Although longer than the Alcadd, it is a far superior test.

REVIEWER'S REFERENCE

Horn, J. L., Wanberg, K. W., & Foster, F. M. (1986). Alcohol Use Inventory. Minneapolis, MN: National Computer Systems.

[5]
American High School Mathematics Examination.

Purpose: "To identify, through friendly competition, students with an interest and a talent for mathematical problem solving."
Population: High school students competing for individual and school awards.
Publication Dates: 1950–88.
Acronym: AHSME.
Scores: Total score only.
Administration: Group.
Price Data, 1989: $15 per school registration fee; $.60 per exam (specify English or Spanish); $4 per 10 solutions pamphlets; $.50 per specimen set of prior year exams (specify year and English or Spanish); price data available from publisher for additional study aids and supplementary materials.
Foreign Language and Special Editions: Spanish, braille, and large-print editions available.
Time: 90(100) minutes.
Comments: Test administered annually in February or March at participating secondary schools.
Authors: Sponsored jointly by the Mathematical Association of America, Society of Actuaries, Mu Alpha Theta, National Council of Teachers of Mathematics, Casualty Actuarial Society, American Statistical Association, and American Mathematical Association of Two-Year Colleges.
Publisher: Mathematical Association of America; American Mathematical Society.
Cross References: For a review by Thomas P. Hogan, see 8:252 (1 reference); see also T2:598 (3 references).

Review of the American High School Mathematics Examination by CAMILLA PERSSON BEN-

BOW, *Professor of Psychology, Iowa State University, Ames, IA:*

The Mathematical Association of America's (MAA) Committee on the American Mathematics Competitions writes and administers each year a sequence of four challenging mathematics examinations: The American Junior High School Mathematics Examination (AJHSME; 7), the American High School Mathematics Examination (AHSME), the American Invitational Mathematics Examination (AIME; 6), and the USA Mathematical Olympiad (USAMO). All tests, except the first, serve as screening devices for the U.S. International Mathematical Olympiad (IMO) team. Students who achieve a predetermined cutoff score on the AHSME (i.e., 100) are invited to take the AIME, a 3-hour, 15-question, short-answer test, administered 3 weeks after the AHSME. The top 50 to 75 students on the AIME are invited to take the USAMO, a 3½-hour, five-question, "essay" examination. The eight top scorers on the USAMO are honored in Washington, DC, and the top 20 to 25 students are invited to a training session for the IMO. The top students emerging from the training session are then selected to participate in the IMO as representatives of the United States.

The AHSME is the very first test students take as part of this long screening process for the IMO. It serves as a filter. A secondary objective of the AHSME, however, is to identify, through friendly competition, students with an interest and a talent for mathematical problem solving. Approximately 380,000 students in the U.S. and Canada each year take the AHSME in February or early March. Unofficially participating are several thousand students in schools in other countries.

The AHSME comprises 30 multiple-choice questions to be solved in 90 minutes. (Arrangements can be made for visually handicapped students and for Spanish-speaking students.) The items on the test are based on noncalculus mathematics and are of varying difficulties. The problems are rather clever and ingenious. They appear to tap problem-solving or mathematical reasoning ability rather than emphasize the application of learned facts and knowledge. To do well on the examination, however, students must have mastered all of precalculus mathematics. For such talented students, the

AHSME should be challenging and stimulating.

Given that the test has been administered for 40 years and that the American Mathematics Competitions, of which the AHSME is a part, are sponsored by such distinguished associations as the Mathematical Association of America, the American Statistical Association, and the National Council of Teachers of Mathematics, I was surprised to find no reliability or validity data. Presumably a new test is devised each year. Nonetheless, pilot testing of the examination must have taken place. Internal reliability estimates could be computed from such data. Moreover, retest data or testing students with examinations from several years, as well as results from past testings, could have provided reliability and validity data. Including results of an item analysis along with the answers would have been most useful. In addition, we are not informed how the items that comprise the test are selected or written. What are the criteria? What is the purpose of the items? Given the important screening function the AHSME serves and its expressed use to identify talented mathematical problem solvers, the lack of technical information is difficult to overlook.

Nonetheless, the AHSME should be an educationally stimulating experience for our nation's mathematically talented students. The Committee on the American Mathematics Competitions should be commended for providing this opportunity.

Review of the American High School Mathematics Examination by RANDY W. KAMPHAUS, *Associate Professor of Educational Psychology, The University of Georgia, Athens, GA:*

According to the publishers, the American High School Mathematics Examination (AHSME) exists for the following purpose: "The purpose of the AHSME is to identify, through friendly competition, students with an interest and a talent for mathematical problem solving." The examination consists of 30 multiple-choice items and takes 90 minutes to administer.

The AHSME student test booklet has a number of design flaws. One is first struck by the amount of superfluous information included in the test booklet. It includes various insignias of the organizations that sponsor the examination, a great deal of information about the program in general, and information on how to order copies of publications associated with the testing program. The test book is also a rather nonstandard small size. Consequently, students work on a page of mathematics problems that is considerably smaller than they typically encounter. The typeface used in the examination booklet is very small and "busy." The organization of the multiple-choice distractors varies from item to item. As such, the student has to expend cognitive resources to search actively for a place to mark an answer to individual items. In some cases the distractors are aligned horizontally, in others vertically, and in yet others are in two different horizontal lines. As is mentioned on the front of the test booklet, the figures are not necessarily drawn to scale. Not only are the figures not drawn to scale, but in some cases they are not completely clear. There is also no space available in the test booklet for students to use in working through their answers. While they are allowed to use scratch paper, it still seems the items are too closely spaced. All in all, the AHSME test booklet is extremely poorly designed for use by high-school-age pupils.

The psychometric properties of the AHSME are unknown. They were not included with the information sent with the test. There is no information or evidence that the 30 items included are placed in appropriate difficulty order. There is no distractor analysis indicating relative quality of the individual items. There is no evidence regarding reliability or validity. The criterion for a passing score has no obvious evidence of empirical support.

Many publishers have long ago eliminated corrections for guessing because of their controversial nature and lack of proven effectiveness. Yet, the AHSME continues to use a correction for guessing. The scoring rules are given as follows: "You will receive 5 points for each correct answer, 0 points for each incorrect answer, and 2 points for each problem left *unanswered.*"

The 2 points for an unanswered question is essentially a correction for guessing because if a child guesses incorrectly he/she would receive 0 points for the item, whereas if the child does not guess he/she would receive 2 points. Unless the AHSME has some empirical data to support the use of a correction for guessing, which I doubt is readily available, it should be eliminated.

In summary, the AHSME is in many ways an unknown entity. Its psychometric properties are either not available or not published. Hence, crucial psychometric information cannot be evaluated to determine the quality of the exam. The AHSME does not seem even minimally adequate, as it has an exceedingly poorly designed response booklet. Unless psychometric information is forthcoming on the AHSME, it is difficult to have any faith in the quality of this instrument in order to meet its stated purpose—to select mathematically precocious youth.

[6]
American Invitational Mathematics Examination.

Purpose: "Provides challenge and recognition to high school students in the United States and Canada who have exceptional mathematical ability."
Population: American and Canadian high school students.
Publication Dates: 1983–88.
Acronym: AIME.
Scores: Total score only.
Administration: Group.
Manual: No manual.
Price Data, 1989: $1 per practice examination set including past exam (specify year desired, 1983–present) and solution pamphlet; other price data available from publisher.
Time: 180 minutes.
Comments: Administered annually, 3 weeks after the American High School Mathematics Examination (5), to students attaining a predetermined cutoff score on the AHSME.
Authors: Sponsored jointly by the Mathematical Association of America, Society of Actuaries, Mu Alpha Theta, National Council of Teachers of Mathematics, Casualty Actuarial Society, American Statistical Association, and American Mathematical Association of Two-Year Colleges.
Publisher: Mathematical Association of America; American Mathematical Society.

Review of the American Invitational Mathematics Examination by ROBERT W. LISSITZ, Professor of Education and Psychology and Chairperson, Department of Measurement, Statistics, and Evaluation, University of Maryland, College Park, MD:

This test is one in a series having to do with national and international competitions in mathematics. The Mathematical Association of

America Committee on Mathematics Competitions writes and administers four mathematics examinations: The American Junior High School Mathematics Examination (7), the American High School Mathematics Examination (5), the American Invitational Mathematics Examination, and the U.S.A. Mathematical Olympiad. In addition to test construction and administration, they also claim to oversee U.S. participation in the International Mathematical Olympiad.

The American Invitational Mathematics Examination (AIME) is described as a 3-hour, 15-question, short-answer examination and that is consistent with the sample examination made available to the reviewer. The test is taken by students who passed a predetermined cutoff on the American High School Mathematics Examination. No description of this cutoff or the process used to determine it is provided, other than to say that the AIME is a "challenge" to students with "exceptional mathematical ability." The results of the testing are to recognize highly able students from the United States and Canada and to select those with ability to participate in further competitions. Again, how this is done is not specified in the material provided.

One of the difficulties with writing this review is the almost total lack of information. The one-page (two sides) information sheet supplements an 11-page pamphlet (10 pages are a presentation of how to answer the sample test questions and one page is a listing of the organizations and persons involved in organizing the effort) and a sample test form, both from 1986. There are no norms, reliability, validity, item analysis, table of specifications, or almost any other information that is supposed to be a part of any serious testing effort. Despite the lack of appropriate information, this is a serious testing effort in the sense that it is important to the children involved and very important to the prestige of the United States and Canada. It is strongly recommended that a manual be prepared for this test that would summarize in one place the most important testing information.

The instructions to the test do indicate that scoring is simply the number correct, with no partial credit or correction for guessing. It would be interesting to know if there are formal rules for setting the cutoff for this test, what the distribution of scores is, and the reliability of the 15 items. It would also be interesting to see if the test serves to select those students who would do best at the next level of competition (i.e., validity evidence). At least one other mathematics talent search effort in the United States uses the mathematics score of the Scholastic Aptitude Test, and it would be interesting to see how the two efforts differ in selecting students. The test booklet is pleasing to look at, although the answers are to be placed on a computer card and it was unavailable for examination. Procedures for verifying the uniqueness and accuracy of the answer key are also unspecified.

In summary, this effort is a very important one and may be done well. The evidence provided does not support a feeling of confidence, nor does it necessarily raise any alarms. Attention to the design of the test and to gathering evidence about the test is an important next step for the relevant mathematics committees.

Review of the American Invitational Mathematics Examination by CLAUDIA R. WRIGHT, Assistant Professor of Educational Psychology, California State University, Long Beach, CA:

The American Invitational Mathematics Examination (AIME) has been prepared by the Mathematical Association of America (MAA) Committee on the American Mathematics Competitions (CAMC) and is used to select those students who demonstrate exceptional ability in mathematics for competition in the U.S.A. Mathematical Olympiad (USAMO) invitational examination (which is the precursor of the International Mathematical Olympiad).

The AIME is administered annually 3 weeks after the American High School Mathematics Examination (AHSME) to those high school students in the United States and Canada who attain a predetermined cutoff score on the AHSME and who accept the invitation to participate in this competition. Requiring 3 hours for administration, the AIME consists of 15 short-answer items that can be solved using precalculus mathematics. The test is normally administered by the staff at the school attended by the examinees. A total score is obtained based upon the number of correct responses achieved by the student. Depending upon the test item, more than one solution may be possible (e.g., algebraic vs. geometric, computational vs. conceptual, elementary vs. advanced). No partial credit is awarded and there is no penalty for wrong answers. The use of scratch paper, a ruler, a compass, and erasers is encouraged; however, no calculators or slide rules are allowed during testing.

A test packet that includes the test booklet, a computer card for recording answers, and the AIME Solutions Pamphlet is provided for students and teachers. The Solutions Pamphlet has been designed to provide clear explanations and illustrations of correct answers and, in some instances, expanded explanations are offered detailing alternative methods that may be employed to arrive at appropriate solutions. Additional practice materials are available upon request for a modest fee.

No reports of normative or descriptive data were cited and no detailed psychometric information pertaining to the reliability and validity of the AIME was provided or referenced in any of the test materials made available by the sponsors of the examination. In a search of the literature, no validity-related investigations or behavioral (e.g., student attitude) studies were found that employed AIME scores as a variable.

It is likely that those students who are tested represent a homogeneous scoring group in mathematics. Consequently, validity estimates associated with the AIME may be quite low. However, to establish psychometric properties of the test, including factorial or construct validity as well as concurrent and predictive validities, a more heterogeneous group could be sampled. To further this type of investigation, any number of variables could be employed from scores provided by standardized achievement tests in mathematics, performance scores from other competitive mathematics examinations, and/or indicators of academic success. In addition, the establishment of the reliability of the instrument, based upon a more heterogeneous group of students, would be relatively straightforward. Any number of approaches would be appropriate, including internal-consistency estimates and parallel forms (assuming that the new tests that are prepared each year can be shown to be nearly equivalent—once again, this task would be relatively easy to accomplish as, at this writing, there are approximately eight or nine versions of the test, with new versions added each year).

Overall, the AIME appears to have been a thoughtfully and expertly constructed test designed to challenge our most precocious mathematicians and logicians. It would seem that a carefully directed study targeting the psychometric properties of this series of tests could provide the empirical evidence necessary to support the selection process for which the test was developed and to confirm what appears to be a conceptually strong instrument. In addition, a thorough psychometric treatment of the test could provide those investigators in the areas of critical thinking and mathematics as well as those interested in related curriculum development with much needed insights and tools for improving instruction in these areas.

[7]
American Junior High School Mathematics Examination.

Purpose: "To increase interest in mathematics and to develop problem solving ability through a friendly competition."
Population: American and Canadian students in Grade 8 or below.
Publication Dates: 1985–88.
Acronym: AJHSME.
Scores: Total score only.
Administration: Group.
Price Data, 1988: $10 per school registration fee; $10 per 25 exam booklets.
Special Edition: Braille and large-print editions available.
Time: 40 minutes.
Comments: Test administered annually in December at participating schools.
Authors: Sponsored jointly by the Mathematical Association of America, Society of Actuaries, Mu Alpha Theta, National Council of Teachers of Mathematics, Casualty Actuarial Society, American Statistical Association, and American Mathematical Association of Two-Year Colleges.
Publisher: Mathematical Association of America; American Mathematical Society.

Review of the American Junior High School Mathematics Examination by JOHN M. ENGER, Professor of Education, Arkansas State University, State University, AR:

Undoubtedly spurred by the success of the American High School Mathematics Examination (AHSME; 5), seven mathematical societies in 1985 introduced the American Junior High School Mathematics Examination

(AJHSME). These sponsors are: the Mathematical Association of America, the Society of Actuaries, Mu Alpha Theta, the National Council of Teachers of Mathematics, the Casualty Actuarial Society, the American Statistical Association, and the American Association of Two-Year Colleges. The purpose of the AJHSME is to increase interest in mathematics and to develop problem-solving ability through a friendly competition.

This test consists of 25 multiple-choice items that cover a wide range of topics taught in junior high school (Grades 7 and 8) mathematics. Because it is a competitive exam that will identify the clearly superior junior high school math students, most of the items are quite difficult. A content analysis of the AJHSME suggests that most of the items deal with number concepts. There are some items on area, ratio/proportion, graphing, and spatial concepts.

The test and solutions manual from one administration provides the student and teacher with a description of the format and type of problems to be expected on the next administration. Most junior high school mathematics teachers who administer the AJHSME will receive only this information about the test.

The schools receive a series of certificates with the AJHSME. A gold certificate is awarded to the student recording the highest test score, a silver certificate for second, and a bronze-colored certificate for third. A white certificate, which can be copied, is included for other students participating in the examination. Exceptional mathematics achievement, as measured by the test, can be recognized and rewarded with these certificates.

Because the AJHSME will be quite difficult for the majority of junior high school students, the mathematics teacher should forewarn students prior to taking the exam. The AJHSME is markedly more difficult than current nationally standardized achievement test batteries. Standardized achievement test batteries are not intended to discriminate as well as the AJHSME at higher levels of achievement. Junior high school personnel might encourage students to take the AJHSME to demonstrate particularly high levels of mathematics achievement as a motivational strategy.

The AJHSME is administered in December. No calculators are permitted in taking the exam. There is no correction for guessing in scoring the exam; thus, the student should attempt to answer every item. Security in administration of the examination is stressed by having the principal verify the seal of the examination packet was not broken prior to one-half hour before the administration of the examination.

As noted in an earlier *MMY* review (8:252) of the high school mathematics examination (the AHSME), a limitation of the junior high school mathematics examination (the AJHSME) is the lack of a technical manual. The seven mathematical societies sponsoring these examinations may have assured the content validity of the items. Yet, little technical information (e.g., reliability and validity) is afforded the user. The test authors should consult the *Standards for Educational and Psychological Testing* (AERA, APA, & NCME, 1985) and provide test consumers with crucial psychometric information.

The AJHSME is one way of identifying and promoting exceptional mathematics achievement. Rewarding exceptional mathematics achievement on the basis of scores on the AJHSME appears appropriate in light of the commitment of the mathematics organizations sponsoring this testing program. Further technical information would support this speculation with data.

REVIEWER'S REFERENCE

American Educational Research Association, American Psychological Association, & National Council on Measurement in Education. (1985). *Standards for educational and psychological testing*. Washington, DC: American Psychological Association, Inc.

Review of the American Junior High School Mathematics Examination by DARRELL SABERS, Professor of Educational Psychology, University of Arizona, Tucson, AZ:

This is an unusual test to be reviewed in the *MMY* series. There is no manual for interpretation and no information on development, test or item bias studies, reliability, validity, scaling, norming, or equating. The materials reviewed for this review consist of the 1985 exam booklet and the solutions pamphlet. Each year a new exam booklet and a new solutions pamphlet are developed, permitting complete disclosure of all of the items used the previous year.

The exam booklet includes simple directions informing the student there is no penalty for guessing and that the answers can often be

obtained by eliminating options and estimating. Calculators are not permitted. The 40-minute time limit for 25 five-option items permits hand calculation for some of the problems for a fast student, but many students may find that estimation and elimination need to be used to finish the test in the allotted time.

Anyone questioning whether computation must be included in an instrument to assess mathematical reasoning is encouraged to examine this test. All of the problems can be answered without routine computation, although some computation may be useful in finding the answer. Graph paper and rulers are permitted, although I did not find it necessary to use more than a small piece of scratch paper in order to answer all 25 items in less than 25 minutes. Taking the test was a very enjoyable experience, and it is likely the exam does indeed serve its purpose "to increase student interest in mathematics."

There are no "tricky" items in the exam. The items are fair and very well written. They appear to be good measures of mathematical reasoning, although there are no item statistics provided to support this belief. Content validity typically should be evaluated by considering relevance and representation. Every item in this exam appears to be relevant. Because there is no implication that high scorers have learned the mathematics intended for their grades, there is no need for the test to be representative of the complete seventh- and eighth-grade curriculum. Also, given the nature of the program in which this exam is used, there is no implication that the low scorers have failed to learn necessary prerequisites for further instruction. Thus, it is difficult to suggest cautions about misuses of the test. However, if there were any attempt to use the number (or percentage) correct scores for purposes of comparing performances across years, all the problems associated with volunteer samples and all the concerns about representative sampling of curriculum content, meaning of scores for low-scoring examinees, and others that plague the SAT and ACT would immediately become issues.

The solutions pamphlet contains the correct choice and at least one solution for each item. Several items have more than one solution included. There is no implication that any of these solutions is better than any other one the student could have used. One of the praiseworthy features of the solutions pamphlet is that for most problems so little computation is done in the solutions presented.

As an overall evaluation, it should be stated the exam really delivers what the program intends and suggests. The exam appears to be a fair and good measure of mathematical reasoning. As long as it is used for the purpose intended, there is no need for the additional supporting material that definitely would be required if selection or placement decisions were to be influenced by students' scores on the exam.

[8]
Basic English Skills Test.

Purpose: Designed to test listening comprehension, speaking, reading, and writing skills at a basic level when information on the attainment of basic functional language skills is needed.
Population: Limited-English-speaking adults.
Publication Dates: 1982–88.
Acronym: B.E.S.T.
Scores, 9: Oral Interview Section (Listening Comprehension, Communication, Fluency, Pronunciation, Reading/Writing, Total) and Literacy Skill Section (Reading Comprehension, Writing, Total).
Subtests, 2: Oral Interview Section, Literacy Skills Section.
Administration: Individual in part.
Parts: 4 forms (Forms B and C only in current circulation).
Price Data, 1989: $100 per complete test kit; $9 per picture cue book ('88, 15 pages); $10 per 5 interviewer's booklets ('88, 13 pages); $20 per 100 interview scoring sheets ('88, 2 pages); $40 per literacy skills testing package including 20 literacy skills test booklets ('88, 20 pages) and 20 literacy skills scoring sheets ('88, 2 pages); $15 per manual ('88, 79 pages).
Time: [75] minutes.
Comments: Orally administered in part; subtests available as separates; other test materials (e.g., 3 $1 bills, 2 dimes, etc.) must be supplied by examiner.
Authors: Center for Applied Linguistics (test), Dorry Kenyon (revised manual), and Charles W. Stansfield (revised manual) with assistance from Dora Johnson, Allene Grognet, and Dan Dreyfus.
Publisher: Center for Applied Linguistics.

Review of the Basic English Skills Test by ALAN GARFINKEL, Associate Professor of Spanish and Foreign Language Education, Purdue University, West Lafayette, IN:

The Basic English Skills Test is advertised as a standardized, criterion-referenced, elementary-level test for determining placement, prog-

ress, diagnosis, screening decisions, and program evaluation. It is a well-constructed test that provides qualitative and quantitative evidence of its validity. Further, despite the fact that the test does not achieve all of its declared purposes equally well, it is a superb instrument, especially for assessment of progress and for overall evaluation in basic programs.

Face validity is clearly self-evident. The test was developed and published by The Center for Applied Linguistics (CAL) under a U.S. government contract. This center is widely known across the nation as the operator of two ERIC Clearinghouses and as perhaps the single most important source of information on second- and foreign-language teaching and learning. The instrument was field tested in several of the nation's best known centers for bilingual education.

Content validity is similarly well established. The test is intended to function in classes where survival skills have been emphasized and its content is clearly aimed at this kind of instruction. It is, however, partly a content issue that makes the test less valuable as a placement test. Its focus on survival skills has been provided at the expense of knowledge about English (linguistic competence). The Basic English Skills Test could still be used for placement when placement is not a matter of selecting one of several levels. In those cases, the Test of English Proficiency Level (TEPL; 91; Rathmell, 1985) would be a better choice because its content includes some (but admittedly fewer) emphases on survival skills along with a focus on more knowledge about language, and because the TEPL uses a scale of results labeled in letters rather than numbers to avoid confusion with chronologically labeled levels.

The Basic English Skills Test manual provides extensive information on quantitative efforts to establish validity. It cites the *Standards for Educational and Psychological Testing* (AERA, APA, & NCME, 1985) and indicates both the oral interview and the literacy skills portions have reliability quotients (.911 and .966, respectively) that exceed the .90 standard. Means and standard deviations are provided for each of seven student-performance levels. Interscorer reliability is only slightly lower. Subsequent efforts to establish interscorer reliability should include a larger N than 29 and more than two scorers.

An exceptionally well-written manual with clear instructions for testing without contaminating results completes the Basic English Skills Test package. This reviewer recommends the test very highly for assessment of progress or program evaluation in elementary survival-skills-oriented English as a Second Language classes.

REVIEWER'S REFERENCES

American Educational Research Association, American Psychological Association, & National Council on Measurement in Education. (1985). *Standards for educational and psychological testing*. Washington, DC: American Psychological Association, Inc.

Rathmell, G. (1985). Test of English Proficiency Level. Hayward, CA: The Alemany Press.

Review of the Basic English Skills Test by PATSY ARNETT JAYNES, *Second Language Program Evaluation Specialist, Jefferson County Public Schools, Golden, CO:*

The purpose of the Basic English Skills Test (BEST) is to assess the English as a Second Language (ESL) skills of adults using a nonacademic format. The authors describe the BEST as a standardized, criterion-referenced test of basic functional skills in English at an elementary level.

The battery consists of two sections: the Oral Interview Section and the Literacy Skills Section. These two sections can be used in tandem or separately. The Oral Interview Section (15 minutes) is an individually administered interview that simulates basic, real-life language tasks. The three subtests of this section consist of Listening Comprehension, Communication, and Fluency. Other items included in the Oral Interview Section are a rater-judgment of the student's pronunciation and a screening device for the Literacy Skills Section.

The Literacy Skills Section (1 hour) can be individually or group administered. The student is expected to complete a variety of reading and writing tasks in a consumable student book. The reading items are increasingly more difficult as the student goes through the exercises and include multiple-choice cloze passages. The writing tasks are in short paragraph format asking for three to four sentences on a given informal topic. Verbal and written answers are given a numerical score. These scores are added for a total score.

The training and testing procedures are presented in the Test Manual in a step-by-step, clearly understood manner. The authors emphasize very strongly that test examiners must have guided training prior to administering the BEST. Practice and interrater agreement are essential for compliance to the standardization component, especially in the Oral Interview Section. The instructions are brief, explicit, and complete. The scoring directions are clear, and extra samples for examiner training are included in Appendix C for additional practice prior to giving the exam. There is a Student Performance Level Document (Appendix B) in the Test Manual that describes survival English in 10 different levels of proficiency. The emphasis given to having a complete understanding of test administration is important, as the examiner must make scoring decisions quickly during the actual test procedure. There is no time to stop and reference the manual for guidance. Examiner preparation is also required to assemble the $3.84 before testing occurs. The exercises using these bills and coins reflects the authors' desire to have a language assessment that is pragmatic, with natural content that is suitable to the target population.

The BEST content has been structured to include items similar to real-life adult language situations. The topics of survival English situations for adults have been selected to include (*a*) basic grammar and (*b*) language functions of seeking, giving, and clarification of information within a U.S. cultural context. This attention to survival skills suggests the BEST has high content validity. This measure may also address what Cohen (1980) points to as a problem of validity in language assessment: interference with communicative competence. His definition of a language proficiency test requires that the measure of a student's knowledge in a language be applied functionally. Thus, strong support can be given to the BEST's construct validity as well.

Perhaps the BEST's solid predictive validity is of most value. The normative group of 987 for the Oral Interview Section and 632 for the Literacy Skills Section was drawn from adult speakers of Vietnamese, Hmong, Lao, Cambodian/Khmer, Chinese, Spanish, and Polish. Items were selected for level of difficulty and discrimination with an r-biserial coefficient item analysis, and the performance of the normative group was used to establish seven Student Performance Levels (SPL) using a modified contour analysis on all subsections of the test.

These seven student levels were correlated to the most frequent performance levels of the preexisting Mainstream English Language Training Project (M.E.L.T.) funded by the Office of Refugee Resettlement that included geographically as well as linguistically diverse populations. Even though affective factors such as personality, cognitive style, and motivation cannot be taken into account, this instrument matched student ability to existing instructional program levels. The BEST does very well at predicting appropriate levels of instruction for adult English class placement and instruction. The test is able to identify different levels for lower level placement which other instruments are unable to do (Eakin & Ilyin, 1987).

The authors report their test has high internal reliability. By section, the Oral Interview has a reliability factor of .911 for Form B and the Literacy Skills Section has a reliability factor of .966. This provides stable classification of language performance to the language-learning continuum. For those instructors who followed the authors' directions, the interrater reliability for Form B ranged from .842 to .999.

The BEST can provide achievement information as well as predictive information. For program screening, student placement, student evaluation, and exit criteria data, this assessment will meet the needs of adult ESL programs. Student progress can be documented, diagnostic information on the student's ability to respond in linguistic form and appropriate situational context is available, and most importantly, accurate student placement in levels of instruction is assured. The BEST also provides pre/post data that are so necessary for program funding survival. It is an appropriate screening instrument for English-medium vocational training programs. The one drawback to using the BEST is having to juggle multiple books and scoring sheets. Having a consumable booklet for an adult learner seems unnecessary.

In summary, the BEST responds to a real need in the field of adult ESL education. It is technically strong, normed to an appropriate group, and addresses the typology of situations students will encounter.

REVIEWER'S REFERENCES

Cohen, A. D. (1980). *Testing language ability in the classroom.* Massachusetts: Newbury House.
Eakin, E., & Ilyin, D. (1987). Basic English Skills Test. In J. Alderson, K. J. Krahnke, & C. W. Stansfield (Eds.), *Reviews of English Language Proficiency Tests* (pp. 9-10). Washington, DC: Teachers of English to Speakers of Other Languages.

[9]
Battelle Developmental Inventory Screening Test.

Purpose: For general screening, preliminary assessment, and/or initial identification of possible developmental strengths and weaknesses.
Population: Birth to age 8.
Publication Date: 1984.
Acronym: BDI Screening Test.
Scores, 10: Personal-Social, Adaptive, Motor (Gross Motor, Fine Motor, Total), Communication (Receptive, Expressive, Total), Cognitive, Total.
Administration: Individual.
Price Data, 1988: $70 per screening test including 30 test booklets, test item book (108 pages), and examiner's manual (52 pages); $15 per 30 screening test booklets.
Time: (10–30) minutes.
Comments: Short form of the Battelle Developmental Inventory (10:25); other test materials must be supplied by examiner.
Authors: Initial development by Jean Newborg, John R. Stock, and Linda Wnek; pilot norming study by John Guidubaldi; completion and standardization by John Svinicki.
Publisher: DLM Teaching Resources.

Review of the Battelle Developmental Inventory Screening Test by DAVID W. BARNETT, Professor of School Psychology and Counseling, University of Cincinnati, Cincinnati, OH:

The Battelle Developmental Inventory Screening Test (BDI Screening Test) is described as a short form of the Battelle Developmental Inventory (BDI; 10:25). The authors suggest that applications of the BDI Screening Test include general screening of preschool and kindergarten children, monitoring of individual student progress, assessing the "preliminary" status of at-risk children, and identifying strengths and weaknesses of children to determine the need for comprehensive assessments. The instrument is intended to be administered by program staff members and assessment specialists within a 10-to-30-minute time span.

The BDI Screening Test comprises 96 items selected from the more extensive BDI. There are two items for every age level in each domain, except for the Communication and Cognitive Domains for the 12-to-17- and 18-to-23-month age groups. The Screening Test is not recommended for children less than 6 months of age. Another feature is the availability of administrative adaptations for handicapped children. Many materials need to be supplied by the examiner. The domains and subdomains are as follows:

Personal-Social Domain (20 items): Adult interaction, expression of feelings/affect, self-concept, peer interaction, coping, and social role.

Adaptive Domain (20 items): Attention, eating, dressing, personal responsibility, and toileting.

Motor Domain (20 items representing fine and gross motor skills): Muscle control, body coordination, locomotion, fine muscle, and perceptual motor.

Communication Domain (18 items representing receptive and expressive skills): Receptive communication and expressive communication.

Cognitive Domain (18 items): Perceptual discrimination, memory, reasoning and academic skills, and conceptual development.

A significant feature of the BDI Screening Test is that three assessment methods may be used: administration of items to children, observations in natural settings, and interviews with caregivers. Examiner judgment is used to determine which procedures should be used to acquire test information. Even though the authors state, "Regardless of the procedure used, examiners can be confident that scoring and interpretation will be equally sound because the criteria are so clearly stated" (p. 7), a considerable amount of research indicates that agreement between observations and ratings may be modest, and that rater differences (i.e., parents, teachers) are often significant. Furthermore, the authors suggest that under ideal circumstances, observations should occur over "a few weeks' time" (p. 10)—a sound practice but also an important qualification for a "brief" screening instrument. In fact, many places in the manual describe procedures applicable to the BDI rather than the screening instrument.

The normative information for the BDI Screening Test is based on the development of the parent BDI. The authors used stratified random sampling to select children by geographic region, race, and sex. Children of poverty may be underrepresented. A total of 42 test administrators represented by a broad array of backgrounds and training levels (including elementary school teachers, paraprofessionals, specialists in early childhood education, psychologists, nursery school and day-care center staff) administered the BDI at sites in 24 states. Data collection was carried out in 1982–83. The sample is collapsed into 6-month age levels for infants and 1-year age levels for toddlers and older children. Although the total norming sample contained 800 children, the actual decisions are based on subsamples that vary from 49 to 108 children. The overall sample included approximately 16% minority children. However, depending on the specific age level and sex, the subsample may be quite small (i.e., $n = 1$ for a minority male in the age range 12 to 17 months).

The validity information for the BDI Screening Test is limited to correlations between items on the Screening Test and the parent BDI ($n = 164$). As may be expected, the correlations are quite high.

In the manual, reliability information for the parent BDI is stressed rather than for the Screening Test. Test-retest and interrater reliabilities for the BDI (*not* the Screening Test) are generally quite high. The retest interval is not reported in the manual, nor is the method used to calculate interrater reliability.

Scoring criteria are based on three categories. Two points are credited based on the child meeting the specified criteria; 1 point for the child's *attempts* at the task; and 0 points for the circumstances when a child will not or cannot attempt the item, the performance is judged as "extremely poor," or for tasks that the child has no opportunity to perform. Basal and ceiling rules are used to guide decisions concerning the beginning (first item is at the child's estimated developmental age) and ending of testing (when 0 points are scored for both items at an age level). The five domain raw scores are summed to yield a total score.

In order to assist with screening decisions, cutoff scores are provided both in standard deviations and probabilities (from a z table based on properties of the normal curve). Levels are provided that vary presumably with state criteria (or selection ratios) from -1 standard deviation (probability of .16) to -2.33 standard deviations (probability of .01). However, "if the raw score is higher than all five cutoff scores," the "*largest*" cutoff score is entered (i.e., -1 standard deviation) and the column is marked as passed. This practice may lead to misinterpretations.

The authors recommend a cutoff score of -1 standard deviation, which is described as a borderline performance. For children falling at or below this level, a complete administration of the more extensive BDI is recommended. Although many major assessment sources argue against the use of age-equivalent scores and cautions are described in the manual, tables are provided for determining scores and are prominently featured on the child's summary. Another problem is that the manual refers to screening decisions as *placement decisions* (emphasis added, p. 13), and point out the use of the Screening Test for eligibility and placement purposes on page 18 of the manual.

The potential concerns for the wide-scale use of the BDI Screening Test are many. Beyond basic concerns with reliability and validity, there is an inadequate ceiling and floor for domain scores. Also, item gradients are inadequate. These factors seriously affect the reliable use of cutoff scores and profile interpretations.

The following examples illustrate some of the concerns. For many age levels and domains, one or two raw score points separate a performance of -1 standard deviation from -2.33 standard deviations. In fact, for 46% of the age levels, the range of raw scores used to "discriminate" a severely discrepant performance (- 2.33 standard deviations) from a "borderline score" (-1 standard deviation) was either 0, 1, or 2 points. As another example, for the Receptive Score at age level 18 to 23 months, a raw score of 5 is described as being from -1 to -2.33 standard deviations below the mean. Children receiving nearly perfect scores at the upper age levels (e.g., 39/40 for the Motor Domain) have performances described as -1 standard deviation. To sum, in many cases the number of items separating extreme from marginal (or average) performances is small or even nonexistent. This factor is likely to lead to unreliable *decisions* (as distinct from test reliability) and unreliable profiles. A problem described by Boyd (1989) for the parent BDI is particularly potent for the Screening Test Total Score for children whose birthdays are at the borderlines of the age intervals. The difference of a day can alter significantly the way a child's performance is interpreted.

In summary, the BDI Screening Test cannot be recommended for use in consideration of stated purposes of the measure. The interpreta-tion chapter is two paragraphs long. Reliability and validity information is based on the parent BDI. The differentiation of reliable and meaningful profiles is untenable, given its reported technical characteristics. Furthermore, the error rates associated with screening decisions may be considerable. Alternatively, those interested in early childhood screening will need to consider a wide range of factors including educational experiences provided to children, parent needs, parent-child and other interactions, and curricular-based methods of assessment.

REVIEWER'S REFERENCE

Boyd, R. D. (1989). What a difference a day makes: Age-related discontinuities and the Battelle Developmental Inventory. *Journal of Early Intervention, 13,* 114-119.

Review of the Battelle Developmental Inventory Screening Test by JOAN ERSHLER, Postdoctoral Student, School Psychology Program, and STEPHEN N. ELLIOTT, Professor of Educational Psychology, University of Wisconsin-Madison, Madison, WI:

INTRODUCTION. The Battelle Developmental Inventory Screening Test is a relatively new norm-referenced and criterion-referenced measure of early development. A shortened (96-item) version of the 341-item Battelle Developmental Inventory (10:25; Newborg, Stock, Wnek, Guidubaldi, & Svinicki, 1984), it is an individually-administered instrument using a combination of direct observation and interview assessment methods to evaluate developmental skills in children from birth to 8 years. Intended as a general screening measure for preschool and kindergarten children, the BDI Screening Test has as its purpose the identification and placement of infants and young children "at risk" for developmental delay, as well as the identification of specific areas for educational remediation. It may also be used to identify normally developing children's areas of strengths and weaknesses and to evaluate the effectiveness of intervention programs. The 96 items on the test represent five areas, or domains, of functioning with 18 to 20 items on each: Personal-Social, Adaptive, Motor, Communication, and Cognitive. Examiner-gathered materials are administered in a 10- to 30-minute period of time.

PRACTICAL FEATURES OF THE TEST. The examiner presents each item in one of three ways, depending on which is most appropriate for the particular testing situation: directly administering an item to the child, observing the child performing an item, or interviewing a parent or teacher. The decision of whom to interview is left to the best judgment of the tester. Some items are more suited for administration according to one of the three methods; in fact, most of the items measuring the Personal-Social domain are best obtained through interview. Nonetheless, instructions for giving the items in alternative ways are included. Although instructions for interviewing are given, the examiner is encouraged to adjust the questioning to obtain enough information. Thus, the actual administration of this test may vary for individual children, making comparability of scores questionable. In addition, the items are to be administered in order. This aspect of this test has been criticized because it prevents the flexibility considered necessary when working with very young children (Boyd, Welge, Sexton, & Miller, 1989; McLean, McCormick, Bruder, & Burdg, 1987). However, administering the items in the specified order is necessary for applying the basal and ceiling rules that permit normative comparisons to be made on this test.

Several other points regarding the features of the BDI Screening Test are noteworthy. For those items requiring specific materials, descriptions of the materials are given, and it is the examiner's responsibility to provide them, again raising the question of the standardized nature of the test. There is one form of the BDI Screening Test, and the authors recommend becoming thoroughly familiar with the items and administration formats through conducting at least one practice administration with a normally developing child before administering the test. It has been suggested, however, that for the complete BDI, one administration is insufficient preparation for accurate administration (McLean et al., 1987). Finally, the authors report testing time to be one-half hour or less, but there is no available research addressing the accuracy of this assessment time.

Children's responses to the items are scored according to a 3-point system that allows one to "capture" skills in the process of being acquired, an advantage when measuring progress over time. Computing raw scores for each domain and a total raw score is described straightforwardly. However, difficulties and inaccuracies in scoring have been reported by

those investigating the characteristics of the complete BDI. In their study of administration of the BDI, Bailey, Vandiviere, Dellinger, and Munn (1987) found that only 14.5% of their sample of experienced test administrators had no scoring errors.

Raw scores are not converted to standard scores, but are instead compared to cutoff raw scores corresponding to different standard deviations and probabilities for false positives (based on a standardized distribution of z-scores). The derivation of each of the cutoff scores is not explained, and there is no information provided regarding the mean scores achieved by each age group in the normative sample, or standard score equivalents. In the absence of standard scores, one cannot assume the scores from each test are comparable (Anastasi, 1988), and with a test that purports to determine placement, the process of deriving cutoff scores needs to be made explicit. Age-equivalent scores are also provided in table form, but again, no explanation as to their derivation is given.

CHARACTERISTICS OF THE MANUAL. The BDI Screening Test Manual provides clear and complete descriptions of the subtests and the areas within each subtest that are tapped. An example of a protocol and scoring instructions are also provided, as is a listing of the items both on the complete BDI and on the Screening Test. This enables one to see the scope of the screening test in relation to the complete BDI.

Administration and scoring instructions are presented in the Manual, but not clearly enough to ensure standardization and objectivity. For example, a score of 1 point is earned for some items according to a criterion of "attempts but is often unsuccessful." This descriptive criterion does not represent objective, consistent scoring. Although many items do contain objective criteria for scoring in the test book itself, this standard is not consistently applied across all items. A good deal of clinical judgment in interviewing is necessary for acquiring information, which may provide a rich pool of information but does not lend itself to consistent, objective scoring criteria. To the authors' credit, the Manual does provide extensive examples of interviews in the Appendix.

The BDI Screening Test Manual also makes note of specific administration instructions for use with children having a variety of handicapping conditions that are further described in conjunction with specific items in the test book. Adaptations are provided for children with speech and hearing, vision, motor, and emotional difficulties. With regard to the complete BDI, however, only half of these adaptations have been found to be appropriate (Bailey et al., 1987).

Although there is little research reported in the Manual, psychometric properties of the BDI Screening Test are addressed in an organized manner. The standardization process, including date of standardization and characteristics of the normative sample, is adequately described. There is no information regarding the reliability of the Screening Test, however; readers are referred to a table for information regarding the complete BDI's test-retest and interrater reliability. Unfortunately, there is no information provided concerning the methods for obtaining reliability, characteristics of the sample (size, age), or interval of time elapsed, in the case of test-retest reliability. Thus, it is not possible to evaluate completely the reliability of the BDI Screening Test from the information presented in the Manual.

Validity information is limited, as well, with the criterion for selecting the Screening Test items described without the provision of supporting data, and only one study comparing the Screening Test with the complete BDI is reported in the manual. It is thus also difficult to evaluate the validity of the BDI Screening Test based on the information given. Finally, interpretive guidelines are described, but an explanation of their derivation is missing.

In summary, the Manual is strongest in its description of domains, interviewing techniques, and the standardization process. It is somewhat helpful in its provision of guidelines for administering the test to handicapped children. It is inadequate in providing scoring criteria, the rationale for interpreting raw scores, and a description of reliability and validity.

Psychometric characteristics of the test.
NORMS. The normative sample for the BDI Screening Test was part of the complete BDI's norming sample of 800 children. The number of children identified as the normative sample for the Screening Test is not mentioned, however; nor are the number of children and descriptive data regarding their BDI Screening Test scores included for each age group.

Normative data for the complete BDI was collected over a 4-month period from 1982 to 1983 (Newborg et al., 1984). Using a stratified random sampling procedure, children were selected on the basis of sex, age, geographic location, and race. The proportions of children in each of these categories were equivalent to U.S. Bureau of the Census data.

Several problems exist with the sample chosen for the complete BDI. First, of the total 800 children in the standardization sample, 301 comprised the 0- to 35-month range. Of these, approximately 50 children were selected for each of the infant age groups (0 to 5 months, 6 to 11 months, 12 to 17 months, and 18 to 23 months), and 99 were selected for the 24- to 35-month range. The number of children comprising this age component of the sample has been considered inadequate (Boyd et al., 1989), especially when one compares these figures to the Bayley Scales of Infant Development (1,262 children from 0 to 30 months, with 90 children representing 1- or 2-month intervals within the 30-month range).

A second problem deriving from the relatively broad sampling across ages during infancy is the likelihood of obtaining very different scores for the identical performance of children whose chronological age falls close to either side of the cutoff points between age groups (Boyd, 1989). These potential differences in scores could result in the under- or overestimation of developmental levels, important to note when considering the placement, educational remediation, and program evaluation decisions for which the authors are recommending the BDI be used.

There was also no effort made, across the entire sample, to obtain a representative number of children according to parental socioeconomic status, occupation, or income level. The authors do address this issue, stating they controlled for this potential bias through selection of test sites that included a wide range of socioeconomic levels. No data about socioeconomic status is provided, however, and one is left with the impression that little is known about the socioeconomic levels represented in the normative sample.

Another difficulty lies in the nature of the minority population represented. Although the total proportion of minority children is comparable to the overall proportion in the United

States, the authors make no mention of including Asian or Native American children. Minorities included in the normative sample were Black and Hispanic. There is no mention of handicapped children being included in the normative sample, an important omission considering the authors promote this test as a means of assessing children with a variety of handicapping conditions. One final point worth reiterating is the fact that no information is provided about the exact nature—size and characteristics—of the normative sample for the Screening Test. Only normative information about the complete BDI is provided.

RELIABILITY. There is no published reliability information for the BDI Screening Test. The limited information available related to reliability refers to the complete BDI.

Test-retest reliability of the complete BDI, using an "item-by-item" procedure, has been reported in two studies. The first, reported in the BDI Screening Test Manual and further described by McLinden (1989), reported total test-retest reliability on a sample of 183 children, tested with a 4-week interval, to be .88, with coefficients ranging from .81 to .97. The "item-by-item" procedure is not described, however; nor are the means and standard deviations for the two testings provided. The second study, using the same procedure with a sample of five children and a 6-week interval, reported a coefficient of .80 (Boyd et al., 1989). Again, the method of determining reliability is not described, and there are no data presented concerning means and standard deviations. This lack of procedural and data specificity contributes to the tentativeness of concluding adequate test-retest reliability for the complete BDI.

Internal consistency of the complete BDI using Cronbach's Alpha procedure has been evaluated with a sample of 40 children from birth to 30 months with a variety of handicapping conditions (McLean et al., 1987). The coefficients for all five domains were found to be very high, ranging from .89 to .96.

The majority of the reliability research with the complete BDI has been concerned with interrater reliability. As reported in the BDI Screening Test Manual, for the complete BDI (no method described, no means and standard deviations presented, no sample size provided), this was very high, with a total interrater reliability of .97, ranging from .95 to .99 across domains. Mott (1989) further elaborated this finding, reporting that the sample comprised the same 148 children from the norming sample used to determine test-retest reliability, as well as a group of handicapped children. However, no additional information is presented regarding the number of children in differing age groups in the normative sample or the characteristics of the handicapped children. Additional evidence for test-retest reliability is reported by Boyd et al. (1989), who found in a sample of seven children (few sample characteristics provided) a reliability coefficient of .97. Similarly, McLean et al. (1987) reported an overall interrater reliability of .93 in their sample of 20 children (no sample characteristics provided). Again, the lack of method specification, descriptive statistics, and information about the samples used in these studies causes us to question the evidence for interrater reliability.

VALIDITY. Validation studies concerning the complete BDI have been conducted, investigating its content, construct, and criterion validity. In addition, the issue of the content validity of the BDI Screening Test has been addressed.

As with the complete BDI, each item on the BDI Screening Test was assigned to an age category, based on the age level in the normative sample at which approximately 75% of the children earned full credit. One can assume that the 96 items comprising the Screening Test qualified for inclusion, but there are no data concerning the proportion of children in each age level in the norming sample achieving full credit for the items placed in each age category. In addition, the 75% criterion has been considered a conservative criterion compared, for example, to the 50% criterion for the Bayley, and most likely contributes to the significantly lower total age-equivalent scores that have been found on the BDI when compared to those earned on the Bayley (Boyd et al., 1989). However, McLean et al. (1987) did not find the two tests to yield significantly different composite scores.

Other information is lacking regarding content validity of the BDI Screening Test. Items included in the complete BDI, however, were selected by experts from 4,000 items found in a variety of developmental tests. Although the sequence and placement of skills generally have been deemed appropriate, there has been some criticism concerning the equivalency of increasing item difficulty between age levels. For example, McLinden (1989) identified a math item requiring addition and subtraction and noted the absence of any items assessing prerequisite number skills. Bracken (1987) also noted the problem of gaps in the sequence of skills that are assessed on the BDI.

Although there will necessarily be a steep gradient of skills assessed on a screening measure designed to sample behavior across a wide age range, a slightly different problem is evident on the BDI Screening Test. The items selected to tap each domain do not systematically represent their respective subdomains. That is, the subdomains that are measured vary from level to level, so that for different age groups, the subskills being assessed differ. Thus, the degree to which items are representative of their respective domains and the functional equivalence of items across age levels within each domain are questionable.

Although evidence of the construct validity of the BDI Screening Test is lacking, several investigators have evaluated the complete BDI. As mentioned above, McLean et al. (1987) found high internal consistency between the BDI total score and the five domains, ranging from a low of .89 for Cognition to a high of .96 for Motor. There is no information, however, regarding the internal consistency of items within domains. Newborg et al. (1984) presented similar evidence for internal consistency among the BDI domains in the BDI Manual. Although the specific domain scores are omitted and the correlation between the total score and the Cognitive domain score is missing, intercorrelations for the other domains are given, equal to .98 (for Personal-Social) and .99 (for Adaptive, Communication, and Motor). Again, no data are mentioned concerning the intercorrelation of items within domains. Finally, Boyd et al. (1989) found a wide range of intercorrelations among the BDI component scores, with coefficients ranging from a low of .52 (between the Motor and Communication domains) to a high of .97 (between the Adaptive domain and the Total Age Equivalent score). The majority of coefficients were in the .70s and .80s, suggesting good internal consistency between the domain and total scores. Again, the specific domain scores are not

included, the sample size of 30 was relatively small, and there is no information regarding item consistency within each domain.

Factor analysis has revealed an age-related factor structure for the complete BDI, with only the performance of children between 2 and 5 years of age explained by five factors consistent with the five domains (Newman & Guidubaldi, cited in Newborg et al., 1984). This lends partial support to the construct validity of the complete BDI, but it should be noted that this research was based on pilot data, and its applicability to the final version of the BDI is unknown.

Two final aspects of construct validity evidence are again provided by Newborg et al. (1984). In developing the BDI, the authors found that with increasing age, scores reflected increasingly mature performance. McLinden (1989) has questioned the meaningfulness of this finding, however, given the wide age groupings on the BDI. In addition, Newborg et al. (1984) found no significant differences in scores between boys and girls and between White and minority groups in the normative sample.

Probably the most investigated aspect of validity regarding the BDI has been criterion-related validity. Again, most of the evidence has come from studies evaluating the complete BDI, rather than the BDI Screening Test.

Several investigations of the concurrent validity of the complete BDI have yielded mixed findings. In their investigation of the relationships among the BDI, the Bayley Scales of Infant Development, and the Vineland Adaptive Behavior Scale, McLean et al. (1987) found, in their sample of 40 children from birth to 30 months with a variety of handicapping conditions, high correlations between the BDI and the Bayley total scores ($r = .88$ and .90), as well as high correlations between their respective domains, ranging from .74 to .92. Correlations between the BDI and the Vineland were also high, with coefficients for the BDI total scores and Vineland subdomain scores ranging from .86 to .92, and coefficients for the BDI domain scores and Vineland subdomain scores ranging from .73 to .95. Information concerning the concurrent validity of the BDI and the Bayley also has come from the research of Boyd et al. (1989), comparing the scores of his sample of handicapped children ranging in age from birth to 36 months on these two measures. Unlike the findings of McLean et al. (1987), the mean total age-equivalent score of the BDI was significantly lower than the Bayley. Further analysis revealed the discrepancy to be due to the significantly different motor domain scores. In an attempt to remediate the problem of small sample size, Sexton, McLean, Boyd, Thompson, and McCormick (1988) pooled the McLean and Boyd samples and subjected them to canonical correlational analysis. Their findings revealed correlation coefficients for the BDI domain scores and Bayley total scores ranging from .65 to .95, and they included means and standard deviations for the scores presented.

Strong relationships were found by Newborg et al. (1984) when they compared the complete BDI to the Vineland Social Maturity Scale, Developmental Activities Screening Inventory, Stanford-Binet Intelligence Scale, Wechsler Intelligence Scale for Children—Revised, and Peabody Picture Vocabulary Test. McLinden (1989) has pointed out, however, that the number of children used in these comparison groups was very small (from 13 to 37 subjects), and several of the criterion measures themselves have outdated norms.

One final investigation of the BDI's concurrent validity looked at the relationship between the Communication domain and several measures of expressive and receptive language. In this study of 20 speech- and language-disordered children, ages 35 to 60 months, Mott (1987) compared performance on the BDI Communication domain with performance on the Peabody Picture Vocabulary Test—Revised, Preschool Language Scale—Revised, and Arizona Articulation Proficiency Scale—Revised. Results showed that the BDI domain of Communication was most highly related, although moderately, to the Peabody Picture Vocabulary Test—Revised. The BDI total Communication domain score also was most strongly related to the Preschool Language Scale—Revised ($r = .81$), but its Expressive Communication subdomain and Cognitive domain were comparably correlated ($r = .75$, $r = .79$, respectively), indicating the overlap between the content measured by these two areas of the BDI. With regard to the Arizona Articulation Proficiency Scale—Revised, only the BDI Expressive Communication subdo-

main correlated moderately ($r = .68$). Thus, there is moderate evidence for the criterion validity of the Expressive Communication subdomain of the BDI, but the Receptive Communication domain does not appear to be measuring the same content as other measures of receptive language.

The only investigation concerning the criterion validity of the BDI Screening Test itself examined its predictive validity. A sample of 164 children was administered the BDI Screening Test prior to their inclusion in the normative sample for the complete BDI. High correlations between the components of the Screening Test and the components of the complete BDI were found, with coefficients ranging from .92 to .98. Correlations between the BDI Screening Test total score and the BDI components were similarly high, with coefficients ranging from .96 to .98, whereas the correlation between the total scores of the two measures was .99. Although it is unfortunate that characteristics of the sample (e.g., number of children per age group) and the scores on which the correlations are based were not given, it is not surprising that the BDI Screening Test appears to be measuring the same skills as the complete BDI.

Three final points regarding the evidence for validity of the BDI Screening Test warrant mention. First, only one study has reported validity findings using the Screening Test itself, and that has provided incomplete data. Second, the evidence for the concurrent validity of the complete BDI must be considered in light of the caveat argued by Boyd (1989), that group studies hide the inherent problem with the BDI's cutoff scores (explained above), contributing to either over- or underestimation of developmental scores and lending doubt as to their validity. Third, there is a noticeable absence in the literature of evaluation studies that have employed the BDI or the BDI Screening Test. Thus, while gross age-related differences in scores have been found, evidence for changes in scores over time as a result of intervention is still lacking.

SUMMARY OF OVERALL TEST QUALITY AND CONCLUSIONS. It is difficult to evaluate the Battelle Developmental Inventory Screening Test comprehensively at this time because of the lack of research concerning its psychometric properties, both in the Manual and in the literature. It appears that this test is reliable across examiners and successive testing times, but the omission of complete data regarding these types of reliabilities diminishes the strength with which this conclusion can be made. It also appears the BDI Screening Test is highly related to the complete BDI, and based on the BDI's content validity, seems to have a valid group of items. However, criticisms noting the inconsistent representation of subdomains across age levels, as well as an unequal succession of items in terms of their difficulty levels across age categories, also lessen the strength with which one may conclude the test has good content validity. The final bit of information relating directly to the Screening Test concerns its standardization process, and one would be well advised to use caution when applying the cutoff scores. There is much that is unknown (or at least unwritten) about the normative sample, including the age groups evaluated, their mean scores, the variability of their scores, and their socioeconomic status.

Additional information concerning the psychometric properties of the Battelle Screening Test must be inferred from the complete BDI, a less than satisfactory occurrence. Evidence from the standardization of the BDI has revealed a limited sample size, especially in the youngest age ranges, and wide age groupings that can result in over- or underestimation of developmental levels. Moreover, minority populations are underrepresented, and handicapped children are not included in the normative sample. All of these factors make one uneasy about using this test to make normative comparisons.

Although reports of test-retest and interrater reliability reveal high consistency, the data provided are inadequate and the sample sizes are small. Internal consistency between the domains and the total BDI scores does seem adequate, but the research is limited in scope and there is no research concerning the internal consistency within domains.

The complete BDI has been shown to be related to a variety of other measures of early development and expressive language. However, using group means may misrepresent the scores derived on the BDI, the validation studies that have been conducted have been based on small sample sizes, and several of the measures used as criteria have outdated norms.

Thus, sound conclusions concerning the validity of the BDI cannot clearly be made at this time.

Given the paucity of research, the unclear findings, and original deficiencies of the normative process, what recommendations can be made regarding use of the BDI Screening Test? The test does include relevant items for assessing young children, and the use of multiple assessment methods lends itself to flexible assessment that could provide a wealth of information. The use of a developmental milestone approach also lends itself easily to remedial planning and intervention. For these reasons, the BDI Screening Test could be a useful *adjunct* in one's assessment repertoire. The Screening Test provides a relatively quick assessment of areas of weakness, and it indicates areas to assess more fully for possible educational programming. These advantages would increase one's clinical judgment about individual children. At this point, however, it would be imprudent to use the Screening Test cutoff scores alone for placement decisions, in spite of the enthusiasm noted in the literature (e.g., McLean et al., 1987).

The BDI Screening Test, like its parent measure, has the potential of being a valuable addition to the assessment options available to practitioners and researchers working with young children. However, additional research needs to be done concerning the psychometric properties of the Screening Test, for it should be judged on its own merits, not on the qualities of the BDI. Moreover, a useful addition to the literature would be longitudinal evaluation research using the Screening Test as a measure of change. The addition of this research to the existing literature would enable potential consumers of the BDI Screening Test to make informed decisions about its utility.

REVIEWER'S REFERENCES

Newborg, J., Stock, J., Wnek, L., Guidubaldi, J., & Svinicki, J. (1984). Battelle Developmental Inventory. Allen, TX: DLM Teaching Resources.
Bailey, D. B., Vandiviere, P., Dellinger, J., & Munn, D. (1987). The Battelle Developmental Inventory: Teacher perceptions and implementation data. *Journal of Psychoeducational Assessment, 3*, 217-226.
McLean, M., McCormick, K., Bruder, M. B., & Burdg, N. B. (1987). An investigation of the validity and reliability of the Battelle Developmental Inventory with a population of children younger than 30 months with identified handicapping conditions. *Journal of the Division for Early Childhood, 11*, 238-246.
Mott, S. E. (1987). Concurrent validity of the Battelle Developmental Inventory for speech and language disordered children. *Psychology in the Schools, 24*, 215-220.

Anastasi, A. (1988). *Psychological testing* (6th ed.). New York: Macmillan.

Sexton, D., McLean, M., Boyd, R. D., Thompson, B., & McCormick, K. (1988). Criterion-related validity of a new standardized developmental measure for use with infants who are handicapped. *Measurement and Evaluation in Counseling and Development, 21,* 16-24.

Boyd, R. D. (1989). What a difference a day makes: Age-mostly related discontinuities and the Battelle Developmental Inventory. *Journal of Early Intervention, 13,* 114-119.

Boyd, R. D., Welge, P., Sexton, D., & Miller, J. H. (1989). Concurrent validity of the Battelle Developmental Inventory: Relationship with the Bayley Scales in young children with known or suspected disabilities. *Journal of Early Intervention, 13,* 14-23.

McLinden, S. E. (1989). An evaluation of the Battelle Developmental Inventory for determining special education eligibility. *Journal of Psychoeducational Assessment, 7,* 66-73.

[10]
Bennett Mechanical Comprehension Test.

Purpose: "Measure(s) the ability to perceive and understand the relationship of physical forces and mechanical elements in practical situations."
Population: Industrial employees and high school and adult applicants for mechanical positions or engineering schools.
Publication Dates: 1940–80.
Acronym: BMCT.
Scores: Total score only.
Administration: Group.
Forms, 2: S, T (equivalent forms).
Price Data, 1987: $30 per examination kit; $55 per 25 test booklets (Form S or T); $27 per 50 IBM answer sheets; $11 per hand-scoring key (Form S or T); $12 per manual ('69, 14 pages); $52 per cassette or reel-to-reel recording of test questions (Form S or T); scoring service offered by publisher.
Time: 30(35) minutes.
Comments: Tape recordings of test questions read aloud are available for use with examinees who have limited reading abilities.
Author: George K. Bennett.
Publisher: The Psychological Corporation.
Cross References: See T3:282 (7 references); see also T2:2239 (9 references); for reviews by Harold P. Bechtoldt and A. Oscar H. Roberts, and an excerpted review by Ronald K. Hambleton, see 7:1049 (22 references); see also 6:1094 (15 references) and 5:889 (46 references); for a review by N. W. Morton of earlier forms, see 4:766 (28 references); for reviews by Charles M. Harsh, Lloyd G. Humphreys, and George A. Satter, see 3:683 (19 references).

Review of the Bennett Mechanical Comprehension Test by HILDA WING, Personnel Psychologist, Federal Aviation Administration, Washington, DC:

The Bennett Mechanical Comprehension Test (Bennett) is a venerable measure of mechanical ability, an ability important for success in a wide variety of technical skilled and professional occupations. I have a number of concerns about the Bennett, concerns that some test users might share and the publisher might be encouraged to correct. However, I believe the Bennett to be a reasonably well-developed and well-documented instrument whose use should be considered whenever the assessment of mechanical ability in youth and adults is required.

My most critical remarks concern the appearance of the test. It just looks old. The test copy I reviewed listed "copyright renewed" no later than 1969, and figures in test item diagrams reflect their pre-Civil Rights Act origins. Of the 68 test items in Form S, 5 had male figures and 3 had female figures. All of the figures were Caucasians. The males were all active: workmen, soldier, hiker. The female figures were decidedly more passive: One young woman was on a hammock (!), another was demonstrating a trapeze, and two girls were on swings. Tests should not have items that inadvertently offend examinees, as offensive items could bias test scores. The current work force is much more female and much more minority than when these test items were developed.

The Test Manual, also copyrighted in 1969, is mostly helpful. In describing the history of the forms of the Bennett, the Manual includes the item budget, a list of the number of items in each of 18 content categories covered by the test. It would be useful to have more detailed information, such as, for example, the average and spread of item difficulties within each category. Such information would be very helpful to the test user in developing a content validity justification for use of the Bennett.

The 1969 Manual presents much useful data. First, there are correlations with other tests, including the Differential Aptitude Test (DAT) of Mechanical Reasoning, Forms L and M, as a parallel version of the Bennett. The Psychological Corporation publishes both these tests. In addition, Mechanical Comprehension as measured by the Bennett is not very independent of verbal and numerical ability, although it is more strongly related to spatial ability and tool knowledge.

Additional statistics are included whose utility depends somewhat on the test user's tolerance for the psychometric attitudes shared over 20 years ago. The Bennett's normative data in this 1969 Manual are elderly and limited to male samples. The discussion of sex differences struck me as patronizing. Because the Bennett was developed for occupations that are traditionally male and are only now opening up to women, it is perhaps unfair to fault a 1969 Manual with sexism. However, using the Bennett effectively with women now will require, at the least, better norms, a deficit partially met by the 1980 Manual Supplement, discussed below.

The critical employment statistics of the Bennett, albeit based on all male samples, are given in the 1969 Manual and are mostly acceptable. On the one hand, corrected reliabilities are in the high .80s; validities for a variety of criteria range from .10 to .64, with median validities in the mid-30s. It is not clear whether these validity coefficients were corrected for attenuation. On the other hand, the studies of form equivalence and short-term practice effects did not strike me as sufficiently rigorous.

The 1980 Manual Supplement would be required for anyone seriously considering the use of the Bennett for employment in today's environment. It includes additional normative and validity data collected in business organizations between 1969 and 1977. First, there are nine new norms groups and more recent data for three of the 1969 norms groups, with some separate norms for race and gender groups. Both applicant and employee groups are included. One norms group combines white females with minority males, the logic of which is not clear. Second, there are 14 additional validity studies, with two-digit *Dictionary of Occupational Titles* codes. (I cannot help but wonder why, with an instrument of the age and quality of the Bennett, there are not many more cited validation studies.) Third, the 1980 Supplement includes a discussion of critical issues in validity studies, such as the relevance of the test and the quality of the criteria. Fourth, there is also a table providing raw score equivalents of the DAT Mechanical Reasoning (Form T) and the Bennett. For a sample of 175 employees, the correlation between these two tests is over .80.

In summary, if you need a test of mechanical aptitude for occupational guidance or selection,

the Bennett is worth your consideration. Its positive attributes include an adequate description of its character and contents, acceptable normative data and validity, and a history of useful service. On the negative side is the datedness of the test contents and statistics for new members of applicant pools for traditionally male jobs: women and minorities. I would surmise that most of the older statistics would generalize adequately to new situations, but I would recommend that individual users decide for themselves how serious this datedness is for any prospective use. A more positive recommendation I will make is based on information in both the 1969 Manual and the 1980 Supplement that supports the parallel forms equivalence between the Bennett and the DAT Mechanical Reasoning. I would judge that improvements in appearance and norms for the more recently revised DAT might permit the expansion of the generalizability of the reliability and validity statistics for the older Bennett. Perhaps in subsequent editions, the Psychological Corporation will do this for prospective test users.

[11]

Career Assessment Inventory, Second Edition (Vocational Version).

Purpose: "A vocational interest assessment tool for individuals planning to enter occupations requiring a four-year college degree or less."
Population: Grade 10 through adult.
Publication Dates: 1973–84.
Scores, 125: 2 Administrative Indices (Total Responses, Response Patterning), 4 Nonoccupational (Fine Arts-Mechanical, Occupational Extroversion-Introversion, Educational Orientation, Variability of Interests), 6 General Themes (Realistic, Investigative, Artistic, Social, Enterprising, Conventional), 22 Basic Interest Area Scales (Mechanical/Fixing, Electronics, Carpentry, Manual/Skilled Trades, Agriculture, Nature/Outdoors, Animal Service, Science, Numbers, Writing, Performing/Entertaining, Arts/Crafts, Social Service, Teaching, Child Care, Medical Service, Religious Activities, Business, Sales, Office Practices, Clerical/Clerking, Food Service), 91 Occupational Scales (Aircraft Mechanic, Auto Mechanic, Bus Driver, Camera Repair Technician, Carpenter, Conservation Officer, Dental Laboratory Technician, Drafter, Electrician, Emergency Medical Technician, Farmer/Rancher, Firefighter, Forest Ranger, Hardware Store Manager, Janitor/Janitress, Machinist, Mail Carrier, Musical Instrument Repair, Navy Enlisted, Orthodontist/Prosthetist, Painter, Park Ranger,

Pipefitter/Plumber, Police Officer, Printer, Radio/ TV Repair, Security Guard, Sheet Metal Worker, Telephone Repair, Tool/Die Maker, Truck Driver, Veterinary Technician, Chiropractor, Computer Programmer, Dental Hygienist, Electronic Technician, Math-Science Teacher, Medical Laboratory Technician, Radiological Technician, Respiratory Therapeutic Technician, Surveyor, Advertising Artist/Writer, Advertising Executive, Author/Writer, Counselor-Chemical Dependency, Interior Designer, Legal Assistant, Librarian, Musician, Newspaper Reporter, Photographer, Piano Technician, Athletic Trainer, Child Care Assistant, Cosmetologist, Elementary School Teacher, Licensed Practical Nurse, Nurse Aide, Occupational Therapist Assistant, Operating Room Technician, Physical Therapist Assistant, Registered Nurse, Barber/Hairstylist, Buyer/Merchandiser, Card/Gift Shop Manager, Caterer, Florist, Food Service Manager, Hotel/Motel Manager, Insurance Agent, Manufacturing Representative, Personnel Manager, Private Investigator, Purchasing Agent, Real Estate Agent, Reservation Agent, Restaurant Manager, Travel Agent, Accountant, Bank Teller, Bookkeeper, Cafeteria Worker, Court Reporter, Data Entry Operator, Dental Assistant, Executive Housekeeper, Medical Assistant, Pharmacy Technician, Secretary, Teacher Aide, Waiter/ Waitress).

Administration: Group.
Price Data, 1988: $4.15 or less per Profile Report; $8.25 or less per Narrative Report; $14 per manual ('84, 152 pages).
Foreign Language Editions: Spanish and French editions available.
Time: (30–45) minutes.
Author: Charles B. Johansson.
Publisher: National Computer Systems, Inc.
Cross References: See T3:367 (1 reference); for additional information and reviews of an earlier edition by Jack L. Bodden and Paul R. Lohnes, see 8:993.

Review of the Career Assessment Inventory, Second Edition (Vocational Version) by JERARD F. KEHOE, District Manager, Selection and Testing, American Telephone & Telegraph Co., Morristown, NJ:

The Career Assessment Inventory (CAI) is a comprehensive occupational interest assessment system designed specifically for persons seeking occupations not largely dependent on 4 years of college education. In many ways the CAI is closely related to the Strong-Campbell Interest Inventory (SCII; 10:43, 9:1195, and 8:993), as described in the earlier reviews. And even though the 1982 version includes a few significant changes from the 1976 version, the link

with the SCII remains. This 1982 version has eliminated the Infrequent Response administrative index and added four new nonoccupational style scales to the set of Administrative Indices: Fine Arts-Mechanical, Occupational Extroversion-Introversion, Educational Orientation, and Variability of Interests. Also, the 1982 version has increased the number of Occupational Scales to 91, and perhaps most significantly, has introduced 32 combined-gender Occupational Scales. The 1982 CAI continues to include Holland's six types of general themes and 22 basic interest areas.

The reliability and validity data presented are extensive and supportive of CAI applications. Of particular interest is the result that the concurrent validities of the 32 combined-gender Occupational Scales decreased only slightly due to the exclusion of items not valid for both males and females. This slight loss of "gender-related uniqueness" is an acceptable price to pay for the increase in generality and reduction in complication of these Occupational Scales.

The purpose of the Fine Arts-Mechanical Scale is to represent a meaningful overall orientation to work without explicit gender labels. The Fine Arts-Mechanical Scale capitalizes on the typical result that fine arts, creative, and culturally oriented interests are associated with a feminine orientation and mechanical and trades-type interests are associated with a masculine orientation. The remaining three new administrative indices derive from earlier research with the Strong inventories. The Extroversion-Introversion Scale is well understood and is likely to be useful based on its relationship to occupational groups. The Educational Orientation Scale and the Variability of Interests Scale together seem to form what might be described as a CAI relevancy scale. The CAI has been developed primarily as a tool for persons generally not oriented to education and generally not focused on a particular occupational category. As a result, I would expect these scales to have relatively low value in aiding the interpretation of CAI profiles. More likely, they would provide an indication that some other type of assessment might be more appropriate.

The manual continues to be an excellent example of a comprehensive, yet focused and easy-to-use, document. Although it is now up to 142 pages, it continues to succinctly report a large volume of supporting evidence. Previous reviews suggested more descriptive information about the normative samples for the general themes and basic interests and more information about the predictive validity of interests both for the CAI in particular and as represented in the literature. Unfortunately, there are no improvements in these areas, in spite of the fact that requests for additional descriptive information about normative samples should be easy to accommodate and that at least some literature review of predictive validity for interests would be well worth the modest effort required. Previous reviewers were divided about the merits of more Occupational Scales. In my view, the additional Occupational Scales make the CAI better, not worse. The disadvantage of somewhat more crowded (if not more complex) profiles is more than offset by the benefits of the wider range of occupations. The CAI is more likely to have value to a wider range of potential users. The profiles are presented clearly enough that the relatively uninformative information on the Occupational Scales does not interfere with the more distinctive information. In fact, for most profiles that have an orderliness about the grouping of interests and occupations, the additional occupations may actually increase the meaningfulness to users of the relationship between interests and specific occupational choices.

SUMMARY. The CAI continues to be an excellent inventory that deserves widespread application. The combined-gender Occupational Scales reflect and facilitate significant progress toward freer access by males and females to desired occupations.

Review of the Career Assessment Inventory, Second Edition (Vocational Version) by NICHOLAS A. VACC, Professor and Chairperson, Department of Counselor Education, University of North Carolina, Greensboro, NC:

The Career Assessment Inventory, Vocational Version (CAI-VV), is designed to be used by counselors and other educators who work with non-college-bound students or adults seeking immediate career entry, or with individuals interested in work requiring some postsecondary education. In essence, the CAI-VV is intended for use with individuals seeking careers that do not require a baccalaureate degree. Another version (i.e., the Career Assess-

ment Inventory, Enhanced Version [10:49]) exists, for which the intended audience is individuals seeking professional careers. Readers should not confuse the two versions; although the titles are deceptively similar, the purpose and intended audiences of the two versions are dissimilar.

The rationale for the CAI-VV's development was a need for what has been described as a "blue collar version" of the Strong-Campbell Interest Inventory (SCII), because a large percentage or a majority (estimated at 80%, p. 3) of the work force is characteristically employed in technical, vocational, or other nonprofessional types of employment. (The SCII is now called the Strong Interest Inventory.) As reported by the author, the inventory has been designed to (a) be applicable for careers requiring no postsecondary training or those requiring training from, in general, a vocational-technical level through 4 years of postsecondary college; (b) be applicable for lower reading levels; (c) be reflective of the three levels of analysis, types (Theme Scales), and traits (Basic Interest Areas Scales), as well as specific career levels (Occupational Scales); and (d) provide a reporting format that is easy to understand, applicable for employment selection, and useful in career exploration.

The CAI-VV is a comprehensive instrument that comprises only one form for both males and females. More specifically, the 305 items included in the CAI-VV, as reported by the author, contain 151 items (i.e., 50%) that are "activity items," 43 items (i.e., 14%) that are related to school subjects, and 111 items (i.e., 36%) that are associated with job titles. The manual reports that wording of the items was designed to reduce biasing, be responsive to low reading levels (i.e., sixth-grade level, p. 10), and be relevant to individuals interested in vocational-technical jobs. Test-takers respond to items using one of five alternatives as follows: *Like Very Much, Like Somewhat, Indifferent, Dislike Somewhat,* and *Dislike Very Much.* The inventory takes approximately 30 minutes to complete by an adult. It appears to require somewhat longer for adolescents or individuals with reading problems.

The organizational format of the CAI-VV is essentially the same as previous versions and is very similar to that of the Strong Interest Inventory. No apparent changes appear to have been made in the 1984 version compared to the 1982 version; the inventory has remained the same. The content of the manual and the test was appreciably changed between the 1976 and 1982 versions. Changes between the 1976 and 1978 versions existed basically in the Occupational Scales. The 1978 version contained 68 gender-common occupations, and 21 separate male and female occupations, whereas the 1982 and 1984 versions contained 91 gender-common occupations. The Occupational Scales were designed to help individuals understand how their preferences fit with those of employed persons in a variety of occupations that are relevant to individuals who are interested in nonprofessional occupations. The specific occupational groups included were derived from surveys of high school counselors in 1975 and community college counselors sometime after 1978 (p. 66).

The organizational format of the CAI-VV and the scoring profiles for both the test taker (Narrative Scoring Report) and counselor (Counselor's Summary) are attractive and appealing. The main subsection includes General Theme Scales (Holland's six types), Basic Interest Area Scales (developed using the organization of Holland's typologies), and the Occupational Scales. The manual provides technical information, interpretative guidelines, and two case studies. Also included are illustrative score reports and informative interpretative information. The manual would be enhanced if the interpretative information was separated from the inventory's development procedures and data. Otherwise, the manual is very functional for acquiring knowledge concerning the interpretation of scores.

The major focus of the technical presentation is scale construction; lacking is adequate information supporting the predictive validity of the instrument. Although the instrument has been in existence about a decade, the manual is void of reported studies that examined the CAI-VV. It would be helpful if greater focus was directed toward reporting evidence that the CAI-VV has been successful in helping clients find highly satisfying occupations (prediction). Many of the relevant data in the manual need updating; some of the empirical information presented reflects work done in the mid-seventies. It is also unfortunate the manual does not document the reading levels for both the inventory and

the narrative-scoring report using a standardized readability index, because the sensitivity to level of reading was such an important component in the construction and merchandising of the inventory. Lastly, the author reports the instrument can be used for employment selection, but no evidence is presented to support this claim. Because the technical information has not changed appreciably, the reader is directed to earlier reviews for additional comments.

In summary, the CAI-VV has merit, particularly because it addresses a population for which comprehensive instruments are needed, and the items and manual are presented in gender-neutral terms. However, it is difficult to judge adequately some of the psychometric aspects of the inventory due to insufficient information. The noticeable small number of cases used in the development of some of the Occupational Scales is of concern. Also of questionable value is the construction of Theme Scales by choosing the items "rationally" or by inspection, rather than empirically demonstrating that the Themes adequately reflect the hexagonal model of Holland.

I would use the CAI-VV selectively with its intended population. Its cost and the time needed for appropriate interpretation preclude using it with large groups. It also should be noted that although the instrument is targeted for individuals with lower reading levels, the narrative scoring report will require an individual who has greater command of reading and a good ability to conceptualize.

[12]
Child Behavior Checklist.
Purpose: To assess the competencies and problems of children and adolescents through the use of ratings and reports by different informants.
Population: Ages 2–18.
Publication Dates: 1980–88.
Price Data, 1989: $25 per 100 Child Behavior Checklists (specify Ages 2–3 or Ages 4–16); $25 per 100 CBCL profiles (specify level); $5 per CBCL scoring template (specify level); $25 per 100 Teacher Report Forms; $25 per 100 TRF profiles; $5 per TRF template; $25 per 100 Youth Self-Report Forms; $25 per 100 YSR profiles; $25 per 100 Direct Observation Forms; $18 per CBCL manual ('83, 243 pages); $18 per TRF manual ('86, 205 pages); $18 per YSR manual ('87, 222 pages); computer programs available for computer scoring and profiling.

Comments: Behavior checklists; forms available as separates.
Authors: Thomas M. Achenbach and Craig Edelbrock.
Publisher: Thomas M. Achenbach, Ph.D.

a) CHILD BEHAVIOR CHECKLIST.
Purpose: "To record in a standardized format the behavioral problems and competencies of children . . . as reported by their parents or others who know the child well."
Comments: Ratings by parents.
1) *Ages 2–3.*
Population: Ages 2–3.
Publication Dates: 1986–88.
Acronym: CBCL/2–3.
Scores: 6 scales: Social Withdrawal, Depressed, Sleep Problems, Somatic Problems, Aggressive, Destructive.
Time: (15) minutes.
2) *Ages 4–16.*
Population: Ages 4–16.
Publication Dates: 1980–83.
Acronym: CBCL/4–16.
Parts: 6 profiles: Boys Aged 4–5, 6–11, 12–16, Girls Aged 4–5, 6–11, 12–16.
Scores: 13 to 14 scores depending on profile used: Boys Aged 4–5 Profile: Behavior Problems (Internalizing, Externalizing, Social Withdrawal, Depressed, Immature, Somatic Complaints, Sex Problems, Schizoid, Aggressive, Delinquent), Social Competence (Activities, Social, School); Boys Aged 6–11 Profile: Behavior Problems (Internalizing, Externalizing, Schizoid or Anxious, Depressed, Uncommunicative, Obsessive-Compulsive, Somatic Complaints, Social Withdrawal, Hyperactive, Aggressive, Delinquent), Social Competence scores same as above; Boys Aged 12–16 Profile: Behavior Problems (Internalizing, Externalizing, Somatic Complaints, Schizoid, Uncommunicative, Immature, Obsessive-Compulsive, Hostile Withdrawal, Delinquent, Aggressive, Hyperactive), Social Competence scores same as above; Girls Aged 4–5 Profile: Behavior Problems (Internalizing, Externalizing, Somatic Complaints, Depressed, Schizoid or Anxious, Social Withdrawal, Obese, Aggressive, Sex Problems, Hyperactive), Social Competence scores same as above; Girls Aged 6–11 Profile: Behavior Problems (Internalizing, Externalizing, Depressed, Social Withdrawal, Somatic Complaints, Schizoid-Obsessive, Hyperactive, Sex Problems, Delinquent, Aggressive, Cruel), Social Competence scores same as above; Girls Aged 12–16 Profile: Behavior Problems (Internalizing, Externalizing, Anxious Obsessive, Somatic Complaints, Schizoid, Depressed Withdrawal, Immature Hyperactive, Delinquent,

Aggressive, Cruel), Social Competence scores same as above.
Time: (15) minutes.

b) TEACHER'S REPORT FORM.
Purpose: "To obtain teachers' reports of their pupils' problems and adaptive functioning in a standardized format."
Population: Ages 6–16.
Publication Dates: 1982–86.
Acronym: TRF.
Forms: 4 profiles: Boys Aged 6–11, 12–16; Girls Aged 6–11, 12–16.
Scores: 16 to 17 scores depending on profile used: Boys Aged 6–11 Profile: Behavior Problems (Internalizing, Externalizing, Anxious, Social Withdrawal, Unpopular, Self-Destructive, Obsessive-Compulsive, Inattentive, Nervous-Overactive, Aggressive), Adaptive Functioning (School Performance, Working Hard, Behaving Appropriately, Learning, Happy, Sum of Items); Boys Aged 12–16 Profile: Behavior Problems (Internalizing, Externalizing, Social Withdrawal, Anxious, Unpopular, Obsessive-Compulsive, Immature, Self-Destructive, Inattentive, Aggressive), Adaptive Functioning scores same as above; Girls Aged 6–11 Profile: Behavior Problems (Internalizing, Externalizing, Anxious, Social Withdrawal, Depressed, Unpopular, Self-Destructive, Inattentive, Nervous-Overactive, Aggressive), Adaptive Functioning scores same as above; Girls Aged 12–16 Profile: Behavior Problems (Internalizing, Externalizing, Anxious, Social Withdrawal, Depressed, Immature, Self-Destructive, Inattentive, Unpopular, Delinquent, Aggressive), Adaptive Functioning scores same as above.
Time: (15) minutes.
Comments: Ratings by teachers.

c) YOUTH SELF-REPORT.
Purpose: "To obtain 11- to 18-year-olds' reports of their own competencies and problems in a standardized format."
Population: Ages 11–18.
Publication Dates: 1983–87.
Acronym: YSR.
Forms: 2 profiles: Boys Aged 11–18, Girls Aged 11–18.
Scores: 10 to 11 scores depending on profile used: Boys Aged 11–18 Profile: Problem Scales (Internalizing, Externalizing, Depressed, Unpopular, Somatic Complaints, Self-Destructive/Identity Problems, Thought Disorder, Delinquent, Aggressive), Competence Scales (Activities, Social); Girls Aged 11–18 Profile: Problem Scales (Somatic Complaints, Depressed, Unpopular, Thought Disorder, Aggressive, Delinquent), Competence Scale scores same as above.
Time: (15) minutes.

Comments: Ratings by self.

d) DIRECT OBSERVATION FORM.

Purpose: "To obtain direct observational data in situations such as school classrooms, lunchrooms, recess, and group activities."

Population: Ages 4–16.

Publication Date: 1981.

Acronym: DOF.

Scores, 10: Behavior Problems, Internalizing, Externalizing, Withdrawn-Inattentive, Nervous-Obsessive, Depressed, Hyperactive, Attention-Demanding, Aggressive, On-Task Behavior.

Time: (10) minutes for each observation period.

Comments: Ratings by trained observer.

Cross References: For additional information and reviews by B. J. Freeman and Mary Lou Kelley, see 9:213 (5 references).

[The following reviews pertain to the Teacher's Report Form and Youth Self-Report. The CBCL/4–16 and Direct Observation Form were reviewed in an earlier *MMY*. The CBCL/2–3 will be reviewed at a future time.—Ed.]

TEST REFERENCES

1. Larson, C. P., & Lapointe, Y. (1986). The health status of mild to moderate intellectually handicapped adolescents. *Journal of Mental Deficiency Research, 30*, 121-128.

2. Aram, D. M., Ekelman, B. L., & Nation, J. E. (1984). Preschoolers with language disorders: 10 years later. *Journal of Speech and Hearing Research, 27*, 232-244.

3. Bond, C. R., & McMahon, R. J. (1984). Relationships between marital distress and child behavior problems, maternal personal adjustment, maternal personality, and maternal parenting behavior. *Journal of Abnormal Psychology, 93*, 348-351.

4. Dishion, T. J., Loeber, R., Stouthamer-Loeber, M., & Patterson, G. R. (1984). Skill deficits and male adolescent delinquency. *Journal of Abnormal Child Psychology, 12*, 37-54.

5. Emery, R. E., & O'Leary, K. D. (1984). Marital discord and child behavior problems in a nonclinic sample. *Journal of Abnormal Child Psychology, 12*, 411-420.

6. Feinstein, C., Blouin, A. G., Egan, J., & Conners, C. K. (1984). Depressive symptomatology in a child psychiatric outpatient population: Correlations with diagnosis. *Comprehensive Psychiatry, 25*, 379-391.

7. Ferrari, M. (1984). Chronic illness: Psychosocial effects on siblings—I. Chronically ill boys. *The Journal of Child Psychology and Psychiatry and Allied Disciplines, 25*, 459-476.

8. Garbarino, J., Sebes, J., & Schellenbach, C. (1984). Families at risk for destructive parent-child relations in adolescence. *Child Development, 55*, 174-183.

9. Garrison, W., Earls, F., & Kindlor, D. (1984). Temperament characteristics in the third year of life and behavioral adjustment at school entry. *Journal of Clinical Child Psychology, 13*, 298-303.

10. Gordon, M., Post, E. M., Crouthamel, C., & Richman, R. A. (1984). Do children with constitutional delay really have more learning problems? *Journal of Learning Disabilities, 17*, 291-293.

11. Kazdin, A. E., & Heidish, I. E. (1984). Convergence of clinically derived diagnoses and parent checklists among inpatient children. *Journal of Abnormal Child Psychology, 12*, 421-436.

12. Kazdin, A. E., Matson, J. L., & Esveldt-Dawson, K. (1984). The relationship of role-play assessment of children's social skills to multiple measures of social competence. *Behaviour Research and Therapy, 22*, 129-139.

13. Kendall, P. C., & Fischler, G. L. (1984). Behavioral and adjustment correlates of problem solving: Validational analyses of interpersonal cognitive problem-solving measures. *Child Development, 55*, 879-892.

14. Loeber, R., & Dishion, T. J. (1984). Boys who fight at home and school: Family conditions influencing cross-setting consistency. *Journal of Consulting and Clinical Psychology, 52*, 759-768.

15. Rosenberg, L. A., Harris, J. C., & Singer, H. S. (1984). Relationship of the Child Behavior Checklist to an independent measure of psychopathology. *Psychological Reports, 54*, 427-430.

16. Seagull, E. A. W., & Weinshank, A. B. (1984). Childhood depression in a selected group of low-achieving seventh-graders. *Journal of Clinical Child Psychology, 13*, 134-140.

17. Stiffman, A. R., Feldman, R. A., & Evans, D. A. (1984). Children's activities and their behavior: Are activities worth manipulating? *Child Psychiatry and Human Development, 14*, 187-199.

18. Telzrow, C. F. (1984). Practical applications of the K-ABC in the identification of handicapped preschoolers. *The Journal of Special Education, 18*, 311-324.

19. Walker, E., Bettes, B., & Ceci, S. (1984). Teachers' assumptions regarding the severity, causes, and outcomes of behavioral problems in preschoolers: Implications for referral. *Journal of Consulting and Clinical Psychology, 52*, 899-902.

20. Webster-Stratton, C. (1984). Predictors of treatment outcome in parent training for conduct disordered children. *Behavior Therapy, 16*, 223-243.

21. Webster-Stratton, C. (1984). Randomized trial of two parent-training programs for families with conduct disordered children. *Journal of Consulting and Clinical Psychology, 52*, 666-678.

22. Cantrell, V. L., & Prinz, R. J. (1985). Multiple perspectives of rejected, neglected, and accepted children: Relation between sociometric and behavioral characteristics. *Journal of Consulting and Clinical Psychology, 53*, 884-889.

23. Cohen, N. J., Gotlieb, H., Kershner, J., & Wehrspann, W. (1985). Concurrent validity of the internalizing and externalizing profile patterns of the Achenbach Child Behavior Checklist. *Journal of Consulting and Clinical Psychology, 53*, 724-728.

24. Cooley, E. J., & Ayres, R. (1985). Convergent and discriminant validity of the mental processing scales of the Kaufman Assessment Battery for Children. *Psychology in the Schools, 22*, 373-377.

25. Costello, E. J., Edelbrock, C. S., & Costello, A. J. (1985). Validity of the NIMH Diagnostic Interview Schedule for Children: A comparison between psychiatric and pediatric referrals. *Journal of Abnormal Child Psychology, 13*, 579-595.

26. Dulcan, M. K., & Piercy, P. A. (1985). A model for teaching and evaluating brief psychotherapy with children and their families. *Professional Psychology: Research and Practice, 16*, 689-700.

27. French, D. C., & Waas, G. A. (1985). Behavior problems of peer-neglected and peer-rejected elementary-age children: Parent and teacher perspectives. *Child Development, 56*, 246-252.

28. French, D. C., & Waas, G. A. (1985). Teachers' ability to identify peer-rejected children: A comparison of sociometrics and teacher ratings. *Journal of School Psychology, 23*, 347-353.

29. Hasselt, V. B. V., Hersen, M., & Kazdin, A. E. (1985). Assessment of social skills in visually-handicapped adolescents. *Behaviour Research and Therapy, 23*, 53-63.

30. Heath, G. A., Hardesty, V. A., Goldfine, P. E., & Walker, A. M. (1985). Diagnosis and childhood firesetting. *Journal of Clinical Psychology, 41*, 571-575.

31. Janos, P. M., Fung, H. C., & Robinson, N. M. (1985). Self-concept, self-esteem, and peer relations among gifted children who feel "different." *Gifted Child Quarterly, 29*, 78-82.

32. Kolko, D. J., Kazdin, A. E., & Meyer, E. C. (1985). Aggression and psychopathology in childhood firesetters: Parent and child reports. *Journal of Consulting and Clinical Psychology, 53*, 377-385.

33. Last, J. M., & Bruhn, A. R. (1985). Distinguishing child diagnostic types with early memories. *Journal of Personality Assessment, 49*, 187-192.

34. McConaughy, S. H., & Ritter, D. R. (1985). Social competence and behavioral problems of learning disabled boys aged 6-11. *Journal of Learning Disabilities, 18*, 547-553.

35. Resnick, G. (1985). Enhancing parental competencies for high risk mothers: An evaluation of prevention effects. *Child Abuse & Neglect, 9*, 479-489.

36. Stolberg, A. L., & Garrison, K. M. (1985). Evaluating a primary prevention program for children of divorce. *American Journal of Community Psychology, 13*, 111-124.

37. Webster-Stratton, C. (1985). Comparison of abusive and nonabusive families with conduct-disordered children. *American Journal of Orthopsychiatry, 55*, 59-69.

38. Webster-Stratton, C. (1985). The effects of father involvement in parent training for conduct problem children. *The Journal of Child Psychology and Psychiatry and Allied Disciplines, 26*, 801-810.

39. Wolfe, D. A., Jaffe, P., Wilson, S. K., & Zak, L. (1985). Children of battered women: The relation of child behavior to family violence and maternal stress. *Journal of Consulting and Clinical Psychology, 53*, 657-665.

40. Wood, B. (1985). Proximity and hierarchy: Orthogonal dimensions of family interconnectedness. *Family Process, 24*, 487-507.

41. Campbell, S. B., Breaux, A. M., Ewing, L. J., & Szumowski, E. K. (1986). Correlates and predictors of hyperactivity and aggression: A longitudinal study of parent-referred problem preschoolers. *Journal of Abnormal Child Psychology, 14*, 217-234.

42. Campbell, S. B., Ewing, L. J., Breaux, A. M., & Szumowski, E. K. (1986). Parent-referred problem three-year-olds: Follow-up at school entry. *Journal of Child Psychology and Psychiatry and Allied Disciplines, 27*, 473-488.

43. Davis, J. M., Elfenbein, J., Schum, R., & Bentler, R. A. (1986). Effects of mild and moderate hearing impairments on language, educational, and psychosocial behavior of children. *Journal of Speech and Hearing Disorders, 51*, 53-62.

44. Dodge, K. A. (1986). A social information processing model of social competence in children. *The Minnesota Symposia on Child Psychology, 18*, 77-125.

45. Elander, G., Nilsson, A., & Lindberg, T. (1986). Behavior in four-year-olds who have experienced hospitalization and day care. *American Journal of Orthopsychiatry, 56*, 612-616.

46. Friedlander, S., Weiss, D. S., & Traylor, J. (1986). Assessing the influence of maternal depression on the validity of the Child Behavior Checklist. *Journal of Abnormal Child Psychology, 14*, 123-133.

47. Fuhrman, M. J., & Kendall, P. C. (1986). Cognitive tempo and behavioral adjustment in children. *Cognitive Therapy and Research, 10*, 45-50.

48. Guidubaldi, J., Cleminshaw, H. K., Perry, J. D., Nastasi, B. K., & Lightel, J. (1986). The role of selected family environment factors in children's post-divorce adjustment. *Family Relations, 35*, 141-151.

49. Hoge, R. D., & McKay, V. (1986). Criterion-related validity data for the Child Behavior Checklist—Teacher's Report Form. *Journal of School Psychology, 24*, 387-393.

50. Jacob, T., & Leonard, K. (1986). Psychosocial functioning in children of alcoholic fathers, depressed fathers and control fathers. *Journal of Studies on Alcohol, 47*, 373-380.

51. Jaffe, P., Wolfe, D., Wilson, S. K., & Zak, L. (1986). Family violence and child adjustment: A comparative analysis of girls' and boys' behavioral symptoms. *American Journal of Psychiatry, 143*, 74-77.

52. Jaffe, P., Wolfe, D., Wilson, S., & Zak, L. (1986). Similarities in behavioral and social maladjustment among child victims and witnesses to family violence. *American Journal of Orthopsychiatry, 56*, 142-146.

53. Kazdin, A. E., & Kolko, D. J. (1986). Parent psychopathology and family functioning among childhood firesetters. *Journal of Abnormal Child Psychology, 14*, 315-329.

54. Kazdin, A. E., Colbus, D., & Rodgers, A. (1986). Assessment of depression and diagnosis of depressive disorder among psychiatrically disturbed children. *Journal of Abnormal Child Psychology, 14*, 499-515.

55. Kazdin, A. E., Rodgers, A., & Colbus, D. (1986). The Hopelessness Scale for Children: Psychometric characteristics and concurrent validity. *Journal of Consulting and Clinical Psychology, 54*, 241-245.

56. Kendall, P. C. (1986). Comments on Rubin and Krasnor: Solutions and problems in research on problem solving. *The Minnesota Symposia on Child Psychology, 18*, 69-76.

57. Li, A. K. F. (1986). Low peer interaction in kindergarten children: An ecological perspective. *Journal of Clinical Child Psychology, 15*, 26-29.

58. McConaughy, S. H. (1986). Social competence and behavioral problems of learning disabled boys aged 12-16. *Journal of Learning Disabilities, 119*, 101-106.

59. McConaughy, S. H., & Ritter, D. R. (1986). Social competence and behavioral problems of learning disabled boys aged 6-11. *Journal of Learning Disabilities, 19*, 39-45.

60. McIntyre, A., & Keesler, T. Y. (1986). Psychological disorders among foster children. *Journal of Clinical Child Psychology, 15*, 297-303.

61. Nussbaum, N. L., & Bigler, E. D. (1986). Neuropsychological and behavioral profiles of empirically derived subgroups of learning disabled children. *Clinical Neuropsychology, 8*, 82-89.

62. Nussbaum, N. L., Bigler, E. D., & Koch, W. (1986). Neuropsychologically derived subgroups of learning disabled children: Personality/behavioral dimensions. *Journal of Learning Disabilities, 19*, 57-67.

63. Pianta, R. C., Egeland, B., & Hyatt, A. (1986). Maternal relationship history as an indicator of developmental risk. *American Journal of Orthopsychiatry, 56*, 385-398.

64. Rosenberg, L. A., & Joshi, P. (1986). Effect of marital discord on parental reports on the Child Behavior Checklist. *Psychological Reports, 59*, 1255-1259.

65. Shiller, V. M. (1986). Joint versus maternal custody for families with latency age boys: Parent characteristics and child adjustment. *American Journal of Orthopsychiatry, 56*, 486-489.

66. Shoemaker, O. S., Erickson, M. T., & Finch, A. J., Jr. (1986). Depression and anger in third- and fourth-grade boys: A multimethod assessment approach. *Journal of Clinical Child Psychology, 15*, 290-296.

67. Stiffman, A. R., Jung, K. G., & Feldman, R. A. (1986). A multivariate risk model for childhood behavior problems. *American Journal of Orthopsychiatry, 56*, 204-211.

68. Stouthamer-Loeber, M., & Loeber, R. (1986). Boys who lie. *Journal of Abnormal Child Psychology, 14*, 551-564.

69. Tharinger, D. J., Laurent, J., & Best, L. R. (1986). Classification of children referred for emotional and behavioral problems: A comparison of PL 94-142 SED criteria, DSM III, and the CBCL system. *Journal of School Psychology, 24*, 111-121.

70. Van Hasselt, V. B., Kazdin, A. E., & Hersen, M. (1986). Assessment of problem behavior in visually handicapped adolescents. *Journal of Clinical Child Psychology, 15*, 134-141.

71. Weisz, J. R. (1986). Contingency and control beliefs as predictors of psychotherapy outcomes among children and adolescents. *Journal of Consulting and Clinical Psychology, 54*, 789-795.

72. Wolfe, D. A., Zak, L., Wilson, S., & Jaffe, P. (1986). Child witnesses to violence between parents: Critical issues in behavioral and social adjustment. *Journal of Abnormal Child Psychology, 14*, 95-104.

73. Yu, P., Harris, G. E., Solovitz, B. L., & Franklin, J. L. (1986). A social problem-solving intervention for children at high risk for later psychopathology. *Journal of Clinical Child Psychology, 15*, 30-40.

74. Bathurst, K., & Gottfried, A. W. (1987). Untestable subjects in child development research: Developmental implications. *Child Development, 58*, 1135-1144.

75. Bierman, K. L., & McCauley, E. (1987). Children's descriptions of their peer interactions: Useful information for clinical child assessment. *Journal of Clinical Child Psychology, 16*, 9-18.

76. Burke, A. E., Solotar, L. C., Silverman, W. K., & Israel, A. C. (1987). Assessing children's and adults' expectations for child self-control. *Journal of Clinical Child Psychology, 16*, 37-42.

77. Johnston, J. R., Gonzalez, R., & Campbell, L. E. G. (1987). Ongoing postdivorce conflict and child disturbance. *Journal of Abnormal Child Psychology, 15*, 493-509.

78. Kashani, J. H., Shekim, W. O., Burk, J. P., & Beck, N. C. (1987). Abuse as a predictor of psychopathology in children and adolescents. *Journal of Clinical Child Psychology, 16*, 43-50.

79. Kazdin, A. E., Esveldt-Dawson, K., French, N. H., & Unis, A. S. (1987). Problem-solving skills training and relationship therapy in the treatment of antisocial child behavior. *Journal of Consulting and Clinical Psychology, 55*, 76-85.

80. Kazdin, A. E., Rodgers, A., Colbus, D., & Siegel, T. (1987). Children's Hostility Inventory: Measurement of aggression and hostility in psychiatric inpatient children. *Journal of Clinical Child Psychology, 16*, 320-328.

81. Lobato, D., Barbour, L., Hall, L. J., & Miller, C. T. (1987). Psychosocial characteristics of preschool siblings of handicapped and nonhandicapped children. *Journal of Abnormal Child Psychology, 15*, 329-338.

82. McCauley, E., Kay, T., Ito, J., & Treder, R. (1987). The Turner syndrome: Cognitive deficits, affective discrimination, and behavior problems. *Child Development, 58*, 464-473.

83. Mooney, K. C., Thompson, R., & Nelson, J. M. (1987). Risk factors and the Child Behavior Checklist in a child mental health center setting. *Journal of Abnormal Child Psychology, 15*, 67-73.

84. O'Brien Towle, P., & Schwarz, J. C. (1987). The Child Behavior Checklist as applied to archival data: Factor structure and external correlates. *Journal of Clinical Child Psychology, 16*, 69-79.

85. Reich, W., & Earls, F. (1987). Rules for making psychiatric diagnoses in children on the basis of multiple sources of information: Preliminary strategies. *Journal of Abnormal Child Psychology, 15*, 601-616.

86. Reid, J. B., Kavanagh, K., & Baldwin, D. V. (1987). Abusive parents' perceptions of child problem behaviors: An example of parental bias. *Journal of Abnormal Child Psychology, 15*, 457-466.

87. Rey, J. M., Plapp, J. M., Stewart, G., Richards, I., & Bashir, M. (1987). Reliability of the psychosocial axes of DSM-III in an adolescent population. *The British Journal of Psychiatry, 150*, 228-234.

88. Shaw, D. S., & Emery, R. E. (1987). Parental conflict and other correlates of the adjustment of school-age children whose parents have separated. *Journal of Abnormal Child Psychology, 15*, 269-281.

89. Sollee, N. D., & Kindlon, D. J. (1987). Lateralized brain injury and behavior problems in children. *Journal of Abnormal Child Psychology, 15*, 479-490.

90. Stark, K. D., Reynolds, W. M., & Kaslow, N. J. (1987). A comparison of the relative efficacy of self-control therapy and a behavioral problem-solving therapy for depression in children. *Journal of Abnormal Child Psychology, 15*, 91-113.

91. Susman, E. J., Inoff-Germain, G., Nottelmann, E. D., Loriaux, D. L., Cutler, G. B., Jr., & Chrousos, G. P. (1987). Hormones, emotional dispositions, and aggressive attributes in young adolescents. *Child Development, 58*, 1114-1134.

92. Wertlieb, D., Weigel, C., & Feldstein, M. (1987). Stress, social support, and behavior symptoms in middle childhood. *Journal of Clinical Child Psychology, 16*, 204-211.

93. Wolfe, V. V., Finch, A. J., Jr., Saylor, C. F., Blount, R. L., Pallmeyer, T. P., & Carek, D. J. (1987). Negative affectivity in children: A multitrait-multimethod investigation. *Journal of Consulting and Clinical Psychology, 55*, 245-250.

94. Asarnow, J. R. (1988). Peer status and social competence in child psychiatric inpatients: A comparison of children with depressive, externalizing, and concurrent depressive and externalizing disorders. *Journal of Abnormal Child Psychology, 16*, 151-162.

95. Barkley, R. A., Fischer, M., Newby, R. F., & Breen, M. J. (1988). Development of a multimethod clinical protocol for assessing stimulant drug response in children with attention deficit disorder. *Journal of Clinical Child Psychology, 17*, 14-24.

96. Bodiford, C. A., Eisenstadt, T. H., Johnson, J. H., & Bradlyn, A. S. (1988). Comparison of learned helpless cognitions and behavior in children with high and low scores on the Children's Depression Inventory. *Journal of Clinical Child Psychology, 17*, 152-158.

97. Edelbrock, C., & Costello, A. J. (1988). Convergence between statistically derived behavior problem syndromes and child psychiatric diagnoses. *Journal of Abnormal Child Psychology, 16*, 219-231.

98. Lewin, L., Hops, H., Aubuschon, A., & Budinger, T. (1988). Predictors of maternal satisfaction regarding clinic-referred children: Methodological considerations. *Journal of Clinical Child Psychology, 17*, 159-163.

99. Massman, P. J., Nussbaum, N. L., & Bigler, E. D. (1988). The mediating effect of age on the relationship between Child Behavior Checklist hyperactivity scores and neuropsychological test performance. *Journal of Abnormal Child Psychology, 16*, 89-95.

100. McConaughy, S. H., Achenbach, T. M., & Gent, C. L. (1988). Multiaxial empirically based assessment: Parent, teacher, observational, cognitive, and personality correlates of child behavior profile types for 6- to 11-year-old boys. *Journal of Abnormal Child Psychology, 16*, 485-509.

101. Romano, B. A., & Nelson, R. O. (1988). Discriminant and concurrent validity measures of children's depression. *Journal of Clinical Child Psychology, 17*, 255-259.

102. Smets, A. C., & Hartup, W. W. (1988). Systems and symptoms: Family cohesion/adaptability and childhood behavior problems. *Journal of Abnormal Child Psychology, 16*, 233-246.

103. Wallander, J. L., Hubert, N. C., & Varni, J. W. (1988). Child and maternal temperament characteristics, goodness of fit, and adjustment in physically handicapped children. *Journal of Clinical Child Psychology, 17*, 336-344.

104. Webster-Stratton, C., & Hammond, M. (1988). Maternal depression and its relationship to life stress, perceptions of child behavior problems, parenting behaviors, and child conduct problems. *Journal of Abnormal Child Psychology, 16*, 299-315.

105. Achenbach, T. M., Conners, C. K., Quay, H. C., Verhulst, F. C., & Howell, C. T. (1989). Replication of empirically derived syndromes as a basis for taxonomy of child/adolescent psychopathology. *Journal of Abnormal Child Psychology, 17*, 299-323.

106. Connolly, J. (1989). Social self-efficacy in adolescence: Relations with self-concept, social adjustment, and mental health. *Canadian Journal of Behavioural Science, 21*, 258-269.

107. Doering, R. W., Zucker, K. J., Bradley, S. J., & MacIntyre, R. B. (1989). Effects of neutral toys on sex-typed play in children with gender identity disorder. *Journal of Abnormal Child Psychology, 17*, 563-574.

108. Gallucci, N. T. (1989). Personality assessment with children of superior intelligence: Divergence versus psychopathology. *Journal of Personality Assessment, 53*, 749-760.

109. Kazdin, A. E. (1989). Identifying depression in children: A comparison of alternative selection criteria. *Journal of Abnormal Child Psychology, 17*, 437-454.

110. Konstantareas, M. M., & Homatidis, S. (1989). Parental perception of learning-disabled children's adjustment problems and related stress. *Journal of Abnormal Child Psychology, 17*, 177-186.

111. Lambert, M. C., Weisz, J. R., & Thesiger, C. (1989). Principal components analyses of behavior problems in Jamaican clinic-referred children: Teacher reports for ages 6-17. *Journal of Abnormal Child Psychology, 17*, 553-562.

112. McArdle, J., & Mattison, R. E. (1989). Child behavior profile types in a general population sample of boys 6 to 11 years old. *Journal of Abnormal Child Psychology, 17*, 597-607.

113. Trieber, F. A., Mabe, P. A., III, Riley, W., Carr, T., Levy, M., Thompson, W., & Strong, W. B. (1989). Assessment of children's Type A behavior: Relationship with negative behavioral characteristics and children and teacher demographic characteristics. *Journal of Personality Assessment, 53*, 770-782.

114. Weigel, C., Wertlieb, D., & Feldstein, M. (1989). Perceptions of control, competence, and contingency as influences on the stress-behavior symptom relation in school-age children. *Journal of Personality and Social Psychology, 56,* 456-464.

115. Fletcher, J. M., Ewing-Cobbs, L., Miner, M. E., Levin, H. S., & Eisenberg, H. M. (1990). Behavioral changes after closed head injury in children. *Journal of Consulting and Clinical Psychology, 58,* 93-98.

Review of the Child Behavior Checklist by SANDRA L. CHRISTENSON, Assistant Professor of Educational Psychology, University of Minnesota, Minneapolis, MN:

The purpose of the Child Behavior Checklist (CBCL) is to obtain parents' reports of their children's problems and competencies. Items were selected for inclusion on this checklist because of a significant relationship between the item and referral for social-emotional problems. The development of the Teacher's Report Form (TRF) and Youth Self-Report (YSR) of the Child Behavior Checklist creates a comprehensive assessment approach for describing the social-emotional development of children and youth. These two new self-report checklists are the focus of this review.

The TRF was designed to provide standardized descriptions of behavior rather than diagnostic inferences. Similarly, the YSR was designed to provide standardized self-report data on adolescents' competencies and problems rated by teachers on the TRF and parents on the CBCL. A comparison of parent, teacher, and student perceptions of items significantly related to referral for social-emotional problems in children and youth is facilitated by similarity in items across the three checklists.

Assessing social-emotional development for students or describing problems in social-emotional development in a standardized way is a difficult and complex task. The use of the TRF and YSR by well-trained professionals (e.g., master's level) is highly recommended for several reasons. Specific strengths include:

1. The manuals are well written, informative, and very "user friendly." Information presented in each manual follows a consistent format. Essential information about users' qualifications, checklist purposes, scoring and administration procedures, reliability and validity data, and interpretation of data are clearly provided. The authors are to be commended for the instructive value of the manual. Definitions of technical terms, such as *criterion-related validity,* are given, and many explicit illustrations are provided in varied ways, such as graphic portrayal of assessment results, case studies, and descriptions of interpretations of the TRF profile score or YSR profile scores for specific cases. The manuals, which are organized similarly, are so well written that either could serve as a prototype for development of other instruments.

2. The comprehensiveness of the CBCL, TRF, and YSR is a major strength. The use of these checklists allows professionals to gather standardized information in the area of social-emotional assessment from multiple sources. The congruence of items across parents, teachers, and students allows for an ecological perspective and greater understanding of student behavior. Although the purpose of these checklists is to provide standardized descriptions of behavior, the authors' assessment approach and interpretation of data are directed at achieving an assessment-to-intervention link for students. The authors provide information on how the empirically derived scales relate to commonly used clinical diagnoses, but are very explicit that the names of the scales were selected to summarize item content of each scale, not to be used as diagnostic categories or equivalents of particular diagnoses. Rather, the authors provide examples about how the differing perceptions of parent, teacher, and student must be considered, in relation to *all* other assessment information available on the student, to plan an intervention program. In addition, the gathering of qualitative information is encouraged on both the TRF and YSR. Thus, major strengths of these instruments (CBCL, TRF, and YSR) are that (*a*) examiners are provided with a means to gather multiple sources of data in the assessment of children and adolescents, and (*b*) examiners are instructed in the benefits of a multiaxial approach. No one type of informant is likely to provide the same information as other informants because the student's functioning may be different under different conditions. It is precisely this comprehensive and ecological interpretation of student behavior that makes the CBCL, TRF, and YSR so valuable to clinicians.

3. The TRF and YSR are reliable and valid checklists. The authors have provided strong, sound evidence for an explanation of three forms of reliability data (test-retest reliability, stability of ratings, and interrater agreement) and three forms of validity data (content,

construct, and criterion related). Of particular importance is the evidence provided for criterion-related validity of the TRF and YSR. Using referral for professional help with behavioral and social/emotional problems as a criterion, the authors found significant differences in TRF and YSR ratings between demographically similar referred and nonreferred pupils. In addition, explicit information is provided about the empirical derivation of the behavior-problem scales and item scores for both the TRF and YSR.

The development of norms based on empirical evidence for both checklists is a major strength. Norms are available separately for age groups of 6–11 years and 12–18 years by sex. The authors examined effects of race and SES but found that differences were too small to warrant separate norms. In sum, the norming procedures are impeccable.

4. The authors should be commended for their strong commitment that assessment practices (and interpretation) should be firmly grounded in research. The instrument typologies are based on empirical evidence. For example, the authors eliminated a typology of teacher-profile patterns on the TRF, despite the fact there was an analogous empirically derived parent typology found on the CBCL. The authors are engaged in an ongoing research program using CBCL, TRF, and YSR data, and advise users of the checklists to be aware that interpretation of scores could be subject to change. Users of the CBCL, TRF, and YSR are responsible for staying informed and need to be certain they are using the most recent manuals.

In addition to these four strengths of the checklists, specific features make the use of the checklists strongly recommended. Examples of these features include:

1. Specific directions for use of the checklists in unusual situations, such as appropriate use of norms when comparing a student who crosses from one age range to the next between ratings.

2. Specific directions for hand scoring, the provision of templates to assist scoring, and availability of computer scoring.

3. Clear description of multiple applications of the TRF and YSR, such as research, reevaluation of students after intervention implementation, and comprehensive evaluation of students for special services.

4. The last chapter in each manual addresses commonly asked questions and reviews salient points for accurate administration, scoring, and interpretation of TRF and YSR ratings.

In summary, the TRF and YSR, as part of the multiaxial assessment approach of the CBCL, are well-designed and well-researched instruments to provide standardized descriptions of students' problems and competencies in the social-emotional area. Use of these instruments by mental health professionals is highly recommended because of the conceptual and empirical basis for the checklists.

Review of the Child Behavior Checklist by STEPHEN N. ELLIOTT, Professor of Educational Psychology, and R. T. BUSSE, Graduate Student, Department of Educational Psychology, University of Wisconsin-Madison, Madison, WI:

The following review is divided into two parts. The first section critiques the Teacher Report Form and the second, the Youth Self-Report of the Child Behavior Checklist (CBCL).

The Teacher's Report Form or TRF is a teacher version of the Child Behavior Checklist "designed to provide standardized *descriptions* of behavior, rather than diagnostic inferences" (p. iii). The TRF is an empirically derived rating scale that covers a wide range of potential problem behaviors and a small number of academic and prosocial competencies. It is used by many psychologists and educators to screen and to classify children in need of special services. Achenbach and Edelbrock's record of scholarly research and sensitivity to psychometric and practical issues with the CBCL has done much to establish the TRF as one of the most frequently used problem-behavior rating scales with children ages 6 to 16 years.

CONTENT AND USE. The TRF has a separate user's technical manual, one rating form, and four (girls 6–11, girls 12–16, boys 6–11, and boys 12–16 years) Child Behavior Profile sheets for scoring and interpretation. The TRF includes 118 items, 5 comprising the Adaptive Functioning Scale and 118 the Behavior Problems Scale.

The Adaptive Functioning Scale items (e.g., How hard is he/she working? How happy is he/she?), the first items confronted on the rating form, are rated on a 7-point scale whereby a teacher compares the target child to "typical pupils of the same age." This scale seems poorly named and, consequently, may be misleading to many consumers familiar with adaptive behavior scales for assessing potentially retarded children. More importantly, it is of limited practical use. Furthermore, the development of the Adaptive Behavior Profile sheet for reporting results from individual items on this brief scale is likely to lead to overinterpretation of the ratings in this area.

The Behavior Problems Scale is the centerpiece of the TRF and, unlike the Adaptive Functioning Scale, is quite comprehensive and is conceptually consistent with several other problem-oriented behavior rating scales. Items are assumed to characterize objectively an overt behavior or state of functioning and are rated on a 3-point scale (0 = *Not True*, 1 = *Somewhat or Sometimes True*, and 2 = *Very True or Often True*). For the most part, the items are objective and clearly interpretable; however, several cause puzzlement, such as Item 5 ("Behaves like opposite sex") or Item 51 ("Feels dizzy"). The first example is highly subjective and the latter item is more reliably handled through self-report. Several items are designed to allow the rater to personalize the content. For example, Item 84 reads "Strange behavior (describe): _____" and Item 73 reads "Behaves irresponsibly (describe): _____." Such personalized items can be a plus, but often are a minus; the plus is that a rater can do a more accurate job of communicating about the behavior of a given child. The minus involves the scoring and interpretation of these items within a normative subscale structure. This structure includes eight to nine scoreable subscales (e.g., Anxious, Social Withdrawal, Unpopular, Self Destructive, Aggressive) and a large (19 to 30 items depending on the sex and age of the student) catch-all subscale appropriately titled "Other Problems." The Other Problems items are scored but do not contribute to a specific subscale; they are for descriptive use. A Profile sheet with percentile and *T*-score scales is used when the TRF is hand scored and provides a graphic portrayal of a teacher's ratings. The use of the now familiar broad-band Internalizing and Externalizing characterizations of problem behavior is a featured interpretive schema for the ratings.

Completion of this rating scale is rather easy and can be done by most teachers in 20 to 25 minutes. Scoring, on the other hand, is more complicated; hand scoring is tedious work and can take up to 25 minutes if one double-checks his/her work of transferring ratings from the rating form to the Profile sheet and the subsequent addition and graphing of subscale rating totals. A computer-scoring option is available, but is not described in the manual. Separate information on the computer program is available. A final and somewhat minor point about scoring: An error was observed in the raw score ranges for girls 6–11 that are equivalent to a *T*-score of 71 (see page 151 of the Manual). The raw score range should be 67 to 71 rather than 70 to 71. [More recently printed manuals have corrected this error.-Ed. note]

STANDARDIZATION SAMPLES AND NORMS. Two separately collected samples of students, a nonreferred and a referred group, were used to standardize and norm the TRF. Specifically, a sample of 1,100 students in Grades 1 through 10 from schools in three large cities (Omaha, Nashville, and Pittsburgh) was used to norm both the Adaptive Functioning Scale and the Behavior Problems Scale. This sample had equal numbers of girls and boys and was characterized racially as 77% White and 23% Black. This sample's racial mix slightly overrepresents both Whites and Blacks, and obviously underrepresents Hispanics, Asians, and Native Americans. Sex and race information about the teachers ($N = 665$) who completed all the ratings was not provided.

Before the Behavior Problems Scale was normed, a sample of 1,700 students referred for school and mental health services were rated and their scores analyzed to determine the factor structure of the scale. An equal number of girls and boys characterized as 76% White, 24% Black, and 2% mixed and other comprised this referred sample. Thus, the interpretive structure for the core of the TRF is based on referred children, but the norms were derived from a smaller sample of nonreferred children, somewhat unrepresentative of the U.S. population. This approach to determining a factor structure is reasonable, although infrequently done without confirming the structure for the second known group.

RELIABILITY AND VALIDITY. The authors of the TRF have demonstrated a sound knowledge of psychometric issues and techniques in constructing this rating scale. With regard to the scale's reliability, they report test-retest reliabilities for a 2-week period (mean $r = .89$), test stability for periods of 2 months ($r = .74$) and 4 months ($r = .68$), and interrater (teacher with teacher aides) reliabilities or agreements (median $r = .57$). No coefficient alphas or internal consistency data are presented as evidence for reliability. These latter traditional forms of scale reliability are assumed to be high and technically are unnecessary, given the factor analytic data presented in the manual. The reliabilities reported for the TRF are very respectable and compare well to other teacher rating scales such as the Revised Behavior Problem Checklist (Quay & Peterson, 1983) or the Social Skills Rating System (Gresham & Elliott, 1990).

The validity of the TRF, the authors argue, is based on its substantive content and the congruence of its constructs with many of the problem behaviors cited in the child psychopathology literature. Thus, the primary validity data for the TRF focus on the Behavior Problems Scale and are the result of factor analytic work and a concurrent validity study with the Conners Revised Teacher Rating Scale. The validity coefficient resulting from Pearson correlations between total problems scores on the TRF and the Conners scale was high ($r = .85$). In addition, good convergent validity was documented for TRF subscales concerning Aggressive, Nervous-Overactive, and Inattentive behaviors and those subscales respectively labelled Conduct Disorder, Hyperactivity, and Inattentive-Passive on the Conners.

The authors of the TRF spent significant effort to examine its criterion-related validity. Using multiple regression methods, the authors found for all ages and both sexes that referral status consistently accounted for the largest percent of the variance in ratings on the TRF. This is a desirable result, considering the purpose of the TRF.

In addition to this multiple regression approach to criterion-related validity, the authors conducted discriminant analysis to test the classification accuracy of the TRF for known referred and nonreferred samples. Overall, using just TRF scores, they misclassified approximately 28% of the sample with false-positives and false-negatives being observed almost equally. This level of classification accuracy is considered adequate, given that only one measure was used and the stated purpose of the TRF is for description, not classification!

CONCLUSIONS. The TRF is a useful contribution to the assessment arsenal of psychologists interested in gaining a broad picture of the behavioral functioning of a school-aged child. It is consistent with the presently popular empirical/descriptive approach to childhood psychopathology and generally has good to very good reliability and validity data to support its use as a method for describing children's behavior. The instrument was standardized on a sample of adequate size; however, it was unrepresentative of the U.S. population with regard to racial status and regional representation. The TRF's Adaptive Functioning Scale is weak conceptually and psychometrically, and consequently detracts from an otherwise rather attractive instrument. The Behavior Problems Scale is comprehensive, although we believe that eliminating the Other Problems items would be desirable and would not significantly affect the end product. Hand scoring is time consuming and tedious; computer scoring seems desirable, but little information is provided about it in the otherwise readable, informative TRF manual. (Other manuals are available for computer scoring.)

On balance, the TRF offers one a reasonable instrument for documenting the problem behaviors of school-age children. It has been developed from the mold of the CBCL, which has become one of the most frequently used descriptive tools of child psychopathology researchers. It is not as user friendly as some of its competition (e.g., Walker Problem Behavior Identification Checklist [9:1345]), but its psychometric qualities and research base are superior to much of its competition (e.g., Behavior Rating Profile [10:27], Devereux Elementary School Behavior Rating Scale II [9:330]). The TRF Manual is well written, which suggests its authors are knowledgeable developers and users of rating scales. This scale should be considered for use by those looking for more teacher input into the assessment and decision-making process for children referred for severe behavior difficulties.

The Youth Self-Report (YSR) is a relatively brief (120 items) multidimensional scale designed to measure adolescents' ratings of their personal competencies and problems. The scale requires reading abilities at the fifth-grade level and provides a potentially useful measure for cross-informant comparisons when employed concurrently with parent and teacher reports, such as the Child Behavior Checklist and the Teacher's Report Form. The Competence Scales are designed to assess adolescents' involvement in activities, their social relationships, and their academic performance. The Problem Scales yield scores for total behavior problems, broad-band problems (Internalizing and Externalizing), and several narrow-band syndromes (e.g., Unpopular, Depressed, Aggressive). Scoring is done by hand or by a computer program available from the author. The separate YSR scoring profiles for boys and girls allow for ready comparison between a respondent's ratings and those of the normative group. The manual is thoughtfully laid out, with ample information regarding scale usage and psychometrics. A section answering commonly asked questions concerning the YSR is a particularly useful feature.

STANDARDIZATION. The YSR was standardized in 1985–86 with 344 boys and 342 girls aged 11–18 from eight communities in Worcester, Massachusetts. Adolescents included in the norms had not received mental health services within 12 months prior to their ratings. Random cluster sampling in 34 residential census tracts stratified by income yielded similar proportions and mean Hollingshead ratings of upper, middle, and lower socioeconomic status families. Racial distribution was 81% White, 17% Black, and 3% mixed/other. Unfortunately, age distribution and handicap/nonhandicap status are not presented.

SCALE CONSTRUCTION. The YSR is an extension of the Achenbach Child Behavior Checklist (CBCL). Most of the items from the CBCL were retained or altered slightly, appearing in a parallel first-person format. The response format for problem behaviors is identical to the Likert-type rating used in the CBCL (0 = *Not True*, 1 = *Somewhat or Sometimes True*, 3 = *Very True or Often True*). Sixteen problem behaviors deemed inappropriate for adolescents were replaced by socially desirable items. The Competence Scales also parallel the CBCL, with the exception of a separate academic competence scale that is not used in the YSR.

Separate problem-behavior syndromes were empirically derived from statistical analyses of YSRs completed by adolescents referred for mental health services. Data were obtained between 1981–86 for 486 boys and 441 girls from 25 mental health services located predominantly in the eastern United States. Orthogonal varimax rotations were performed, with loadings $\geq .30$ as the criterion for retention on eight principal components and resulted in seven narrow-band syndromes for boys and six narrow-band syndromes for girls. Items that did not meet the criterion level are listed under Other Behaviors. In contrast to the Aggressive syndrome on the CBCL, the Depressed syndrome on the YSR accounted for the largest proportion of variance for both sexes. The remaining syndromes are similar across the measures, with the exception of the Self-Destructive/Identity Problems factor for boys.

Unfortunately, several problems exist with the referral group. As with the normative sample, no age distribution is reported. A further problem is that socioeconomic status (SES) is "unknown" for a rather large percentage of the sample (38%). Thus, the representativeness of SES is questionable. Finally, information concerning the selection and the presenting problems of the referred sample is lacking. Although the author states the purpose of employing referred adolescents was to "detect the syndromes that characterize individuals having severe enough problems to warrant referrals," the level of severity within the sample remains unknown and, as such, the validity of the derived syndromes is suspect.

A final note regarding scale construction concerns the inclusion of the 16 socially desirable items. These items do not effectively discriminate between referred and nonreferred youths and, as such, are not scored on the YSR profile. They do provide mitigation for the problem items and may help ensure against indiscriminate responding.

RELIABILITY AND VALIDITY. Given that the YSR is an empirically derived scale, internal consistency is not required to establish reliability. Therefore, reliability for the YSR is appropriately presented as test-retest stability. The authors used Pearson correlations and *t* tests to calculate rank order *and* mean differences in the determination of the reliability of the scale.

Overall scale test-retest reliability for a 1-week interval is satisfactory (median $r = .81$), with adequate broad-band and total behavior reliabilities (range $r = .83-.87$), and small mean differences. Reliabilities for age differences indicate lower stability for 11- to 14-year-olds (median $r = .77$) than 15- to 18-year-olds (median $r = .89$). The small sample size (22 boys, 28 girls), however, limits strong conclusions regarding stability. Further, the range of narrow-band and Competence Scale reliabilities (.39-.83) for the total sample is somewhat large for the small retest interval. Eight-month stability of YSR ratings with a "general population sample" of 48 boys and 54 girls yielded very small mean differences and satisfactory broad-band and total behavior reliabilities (range $r = .64-.67$), although overall scale stability was somewhat low (median $r = .51$). Unfortunately, the 8-month reliabilities were calculated on a restricted sample of 12- to 14-year-olds. Given the age differences reported above, reliability data for older adolescents should have been included to provide an indication of the stability of the scale for different age groups.

Although content validity is not a principal requirement for the validation of an empirical scale, content validity is offered and appears adequate. By employing referral status as the validity criterion, the authors have demonstrated satisfactory concurrent validity, as evidenced by lower competence and higher problem scores for referred adolescents. The YSR also appears to possess adequate discriminant validity for the Problem Scales, but not for the Competence Scales. The Competence Scales have limited, if any, clinical utility. To their credit, the authors acknowledge the shortcomings of the Competence Scales.

The overall validation of the YSR was managed appropriately and is well documented. However, a possible problem exists with the cross-validation study. Cross-validation with a sample other than the derivation group is a necessary component of the validation of any empirical scale. Although cross-validation was performed, it is unclear whether a new sample was employed. If, as it appears, the same sample or subsamples of the derivation group were used in cross-validation, there is a high probability that the results are inflated.

Validity for the use of the YSR as a means to obtain cross-informant data is clearly presented by correlations with the CBCL and its counterpart in the school setting, the TRF. Correlations between these measures also provide an index of construct validity. Mean correlations are acceptable between the YSR and CBCL ($r = .41$ for boys, .45 for girls). Similar correlations are reported for the YSR and TRF. Interestingly, nonreferred adolescents and referred girls reported significantly more problems than parents or teachers, whereas the YSR problem scores of referred boys exceed only teacher ratings. These differences underscore the need for measures such as the YSR to ascertain cross-information regarding the functioning of youths.

More direct evidence for the concurrent and construct validity of the YSR is not provided in the YSR Manual, due to the reported paucity of relevant child and adolescent self-report measures. Recent research, however, has provided some evidence that the YSR Problem Scales correlate negatively ($r = -.33$) with prosocial behaviors and that the Competence Scales correlate positively ($r = .23$) with the prosocial behaviors as measured by the Social Skills Rating System (Gresham & Elliott, 1990).

SUMMARY. The YSR is a useful self-report measure of the problems and competencies of adolescents. The instrument is *not* to be used for diagnosis or classification, but rather to provide an adjunct to decision making and for guiding clinical interviews. Clinicians and researchers will find the measure particularly useful for cross-informant comparisons. To date, the YSR has been employed in only a handful of published studies. Continued research is needed to further substantiate the reliability and validity of the scale.

REVIEWER'S REFERENCES

Quay, H. C., & Peterson, D. (1983). Revised Behavior Problem Checklist. Coral Gables, FL: University of Miami.
Gresham, F. M., & Elliott, S. N. (1990). Social Skills Rating System. Circle Pine, MN: American Guidance Service.

[13]

Children's Depression Inventory.

Purpose: A self-rating assessment of children's depression.
Population: Ages 8–17.
Publication Dates: 1977–82.
Acronym: CDI.
Scores: Total score only.

Administration: Individual and small groups.

Price Data: Available from publisher for test, instructions for administration, scoring template, reference list, and manuscripts.

Foreign Language Editions: Translations available in Arabic, Bulgarian, Italian, Hungarian, Hebrew, Spanish, German, French, and Portuguese.

Time: [10–15] minutes.

Comments: For research use only.

Author: Maria Kovacs.

Publisher: Western Psychiatric Institute and Clinic.

TEST REFERENCES

1. Borden, K. A., Brown, R. T., Jenkins, P., & Clingerman, S. R. (1987). Achievement attributions and depressive symptoms in attention deficit-disordered and normal children. *Journal of School Psychology, 25,* 399-404.

2. Feshbach, N. D., & Feshbach, S. (1987). Affective processes and academic achievement. *Child Development, 58,* 1335-1347.

3. Finch, A. J., Saylor, C. F., Edwards, G. L., & McIntosh, J. A. (1987). Children's Depression Inventory: Reliability over repeated administrations. *Journal of Clinical Child Psychology, 16,* 339-341.

4. Jouriles, E. N., Barling, J., & O'Leary, K. D. (1987). Predicting child behavior problems in maritally violent families. *Journal of Abnormal Child Psychology, 15,* 165-173.

5. Stark, K. D., Reynolds, W. M., & Kaslow, N. J. (1987). A comparison of the relative efficacy of self-control therapy and a behavioral problem-solving therapy for depression in children. *Journal of Abnormal Child Psychology, 15,* 91-113.

6. Trieber, F. A., & Mabe, P. A., III. (1987). Child and parent perceptions of children's psychopathology in psychiatric outpatient children. *Journal of Abnormal Child Psychology, 15,* 115-124.

7. Vincenzi, H. (1987). Depression and reading ability in sixth-grade children. *Journal of School Psychology, 25,* 155-160.

8. Wolfe, V. V., Finch, A. J., Jr., Saylor, C. F., Blount, R. L., Pallmeyer, T. P., & Carek, D. J. (1987). Negative affectivity in children: A multitrait-multimethod investigation. *Journal of Consulting and Clinical Psychology, 55,* 245-250.

9. Worchel, F., Nolan, B., & Willson, V. (1987). New perspectives on child and adolescent depression. *Journal of School Psychology, 25,* 411-414.

10. Altmann, E. O., & Gotlib, I. H. (1988). The social behavior of depressed children: An observational study. *Journal of Abnormal Child Psychology, 16,* 29-44.

11. Benfield, C. Y., Palmer, D. J., Pfefferbaum, B., & Stowe, M. L. (1988). A comparison of depressed and nondepressed disturbed children on measures of attributional style, hopelessness, life stress, and temperament. *Journal of Abnormal Child Psychology, 16,* 397-410.

12. Bodiford, C. A., Eisenstadt, T. H., Johnson, J. H., & Bradlyn, A. S. (1988). Comparison of learned helpless cognitions and behavior in children with high and low scores on the Children's Depression Inventory. *Journal of Clinical Child Psychology, 17,* 152-158.

13. Kaslow, N. J., Rehm, L. P., Pollack, S. L., & Siegel, A. W. (1988). Attributional style and self-control behavior in depressed and nondepressed children and their parents. *Journal of Abnormal Child Psychology, 16,* 163-175.

14. Robins, C. J. (1988). Attributions and depression: Why is the literature so inconsistent? *Journal of Personality and Social Psychology, 54,* 880-889.

15. Romano, B. A., & Nelson, R. O. (1988). Discriminant and concurrent validity measures of children's depression. *Journal of Clinical Child Psychology, 17,* 255-259.

16. Rowlison, R. T., & Felner, R. D. (1988). Major life events, hassles, and adaptation in adolescence: Confounding in the conceptualization and measurement of life stress and adjustment revisited. *Journal of Personality and Social Psychology, 55,* 432-444.

17. Slotkin, J., Forehand, R., Fauber, R., McCombs, A., & Long, N. (1988). Parent-completed and adolescent-completed CDIS: Relationship to adolescent social and cognitive functioning. *Journal of Abnormal Child Psychology, 16,* 207-217.

18. Spirito, A., Williams, C. A., Stark, L. J., & Hart, K. J. (1988). The Hopelessness Scale for Children: Psychometric properties with normal and emotionally disturbed adolescents. *Journal of Abnormal Child Psychology, 16,* 445-458.

19. Strauss, C. C., Last, C. G., Hersen, M., & Kazdin, A. E. (1988). Association between anxiety and depression in children and adolescents with anxiety disorders. *Journal of Abnormal Child Psychology, 16,* 57-68.

20. Strauss, C. C., Lease, C. A., Last, C. G., & Francis, G. (1988). Overanxious disorder: An examination of developmental differences. *Journal of Abnormal Child Psychology, 16,* 433-443.

21. Allen, D. M., & Tarnowski, K. J. (1989). Depressive characteristics of physically abused children. *Journal of Abnormal Child Psychology, 17,* 1-11.

22. Belter, R. W., Lipovsky, J. A., & Finch, A. J., Jr. (1989). Rorschach Egocentricity Index and self-concept in children and adolescents. *Journal of Personality Assessment, 53,* 783-789.

23. Cole, D. A. (1989). Validation of the Reasons for Living Inventory in general and delinquent adolescent samples. *Journal of Abnormal Child Psychology, 17,* 13-27.

24. Kazdin, A. E. (1989). Identifying depression in children: A comparison of alternative selection criteria. *Journal of Abnormal Child Psychology, 17,* 437-454.

25. Lipovsky, J. A., Finch, A. J., Jr., & Belter, R. W. (1989). Assessment of depression in adolescents: Objective and projective measures. *Journal of Personality Assessment, 53,* 449-458.

26. Meyer, N. E., Dyck, D. G., & Petrinack, R. J. (1989). Cognitive appraisal and attributional correlates of depressive symptoms in children. *Journal of Abnormal Child Psychology, 17,* 325-336.

27. Nieminen, G. S., & Matson, J. L. (1989). Depressive problems in conduct-disordered adolescents. *Journal of School Psychology, 27,* 175-188.

28. Curry, J. F., & Craighead, W. E. (1990). Attributional style in clinically depressed and conduct disordered adolescents. *Journal of Consulting and Clinical Psychology, 58,* 109-115.

29. Kovacs, M., Iyengar, S., Goldston, D., Obrosky, D. S., Stewart, J., & Marsh, J. (1990). Psychological functioning among mothers of children with insulin-dependent diabetes mellitus: A longitudinal study. *Journal of Consulting and Clinical Psychology, 58,* 189-195.

30. Ollendick, T. H., & Yule, W. (1990). Depression in British and American children and its relation to anxiety and fear. *Journal of Consulting and Clinical Psychology, 58,* 126-129.

31. Worchel, F., Little, V., & Alcala, J. (1990). Self-perceptions of depressed children on tasks of cognitive abilities. *Journal of School Psychology, 28,* 97-104.

Review of the Children's Depression Inventory by MICHAEL G. KAVAN, Director of Behavioral Sciences and Assistant Professor of Family Practice, Creighton University School of Medicine, Omaha, NE:

The Children's Depression Inventory (CDI) is a 27-item self-report instrument aimed at measuring depression in children and adolescents between the ages of 8 and 17. According to the author, the CDI was modeled after the Beck Depression Inventory (an adult scale) due to support in the literature that overlap exists among the salient manifestations of depressive disorders in children, adolescents, and adults.

This viewpoint has been echoed by the recently revised *Diagnostic and Statistical Manual of Mental Disorders—Third Edition* (DSM-III-R) (APA, 1987). The DSM-III-R indicates the essential features of depression in children and adolescents are similar to those in adults with some recognition of age-specific effects. With this in mind, CDI items cover fully or partially all nine of the DSM-III-R symptom categories for diagnosing major depressive syndrome in children.

ADMINISTRATION AND SCORING. The CDI was designed for individual administration in clinical research settings, but may also be administered in a group format to "normal" individuals. The respondent is handed a copy of the scale and asked to read along silently, marking the appropriate response as the administrator reads the items aloud. Older children and adolescents may continue on their own after a few items, because reading level for the CDI is estimated at the first-grade level (although Berndt, Schwartz, & Kaiser [1983] estimate reading level to be at the third-grade level). Each item contains a three-choice response format (i.e., 0, 1, or 2) reflecting increasing severity of disturbance. Respondents are requested to select the statement from each group that "describes you best for the past two weeks." Scoring simply involves the addition of numerical values assigned to each selected item response. Total scores may therefore range from 0 to 54. Although the CDI is not meant to be a diagnostic instrument, the author does provide cutoff scores for determining depression.

Unfortunately, a cutoff score of 11 has a sensitivity of 67% (i.e., about 33% of the clinically depressed cases will be missed) and a specificity of 60% (i.e., 40% of children taking the CDI will be identified mistakenly as having a depressive disorder). A cutoff score of 13 has a sensitivity of 51% and a specificity of 75%. Predictive values (i.e., the number of true positives *divided* by the number of true positives and false positives multiplied by 100) for the cutoff scores of 11 and 13 are 62% and 67%, respectively.

RELIABILITY. The unpublished manuscript that accompanies the CDI provides information on several reliability studies. Internal consistency (coefficient alpha) has been found to be .86 with a diagnostically heterogeneous, psychiatrically referred sample of children ($n = 75$), .71

with a pediatric-medical outpatient group ($n = 61$), and .87 with a large sample of Toronto public school children ($n = 860$). Item-total score correlations for these three samples range from .08 to .62. One-month test-retest data on 29 recently diagnosed children with diabetes were .43 (when two outlying subjects were dropped in subsequent analysis, reliability improved to .82). Nine-week test-retest data on a subsample of 90 school children were .84. Because the CDI is supposed to measure a state as opposed to a trait, however, the author recommends a 2-week test-retest interval may be most appropriate. No data are provided in the accompanying manuscript to indicate level of stability of the CDI over this time period. Saylor, Finch, Spirito, and Bennett (1984) found 1-week test-retest reliability to be .87 in 28 emotionally disturbed children and .38 in 69 normal fifth- and sixth-grade children.

VALIDITY. Concurrent validity of the CDI was determined against two self-rating instruments that assess constructs related to depression. CDI scores were found to correlate positively with scores from the Revised Children's Manifest Anxiety Scale and to correlate negatively with scores from the Coopersmith Self-Esteem Inventory. Evidence of criterion-related validity and construct validity of the CDI was provided by Carlson and Cantwell (1979) and Cantwell and Carlson (1981), who examined the relationship between CDI scores and independent psychiatric diagnoses in 102 children aged 7 to 17 years who were undergoing inpatient or outpatient psychiatric treatment. Results indicated that patients with higher self-rated depression as measured by the CDI received higher global severity ratings of depression on the basis of a semistructured interview administered without knowledge of patients' CDI results. The high-scoring patients were also more likely to receive a formal diagnosis of major depressive disorder. Factor analysis completed on data collected from the Toronto public school system yielded one principal factor, whereas studies with clinic-referred children yielded as many as seven separate factors.

NORMS. Limited normative data are available on several groups. Information is presented in a disjointed manner in the accompanying manuscript. Means, modes, standard deviations, ranges, and standard errors are made available on recently diagnosed juvenile diabetics ($n = 61$), child psychiatric outpatients ($n = 75$), and Toronto public school children ($n = 860$). In addition, means, standard deviations, and standard errors are provided for various small psychiatric diagnostic samples (range of $n = 10$–40). Means are not provided for specific age groups or for minority populations. In light of the age-specific features associated with depression (highlighted in DSM-III-R) and recent research suggesting age-related (Helsel & Matson, 1984) and race-related (Politano, Nelson, Evans, Sorenson, & Zeman, 1986) differences on the CDI, these would seem most important for proper interpretation. As a result, the clinician is left with little information on how to appropriately interpret CDI score results.

SUMMARY. The CDI is a self-report instrument designed to assess depressive symptomatology in school-aged children and adolescents. Its easy and efficient administration and scoring are very beneficial to clinicians. Although further studies need to be completed on the test-retest reliability of the CDI, internal consistency and validity appear adequate for a research instrument. As a result, the CDI shows promise as an instrument to measure childhood depression. However, limited normative data are provided by the author, and thus, the CDI should be interpreted cautiously.

Until more research is collected on the CDI, its use, as its author suggests, should be limited to that of "clinical research settings." Unfortunately, due to the absence of a solid self-report instrument to assess childhood and adolescent depression, many clinicians may be pressed to use this scale for purposes beyond those recommended by the author.

REVIEWER'S REFERENCES

Carlson, G. A., & Cantwell, D. P. (1979). A survey of depressive symptoms in a child and adolescent psychiatric population. *Journal of the American Academy of Child Psychiatry, 18,* 587-599.

Cantwell, D. P., & Carlson, G. A. (1981, October). *Factor analysis of a self-rating depressive inventory for children: Factor structure and nosological utility.* Paper presented at the annual meeting of the American Academy of Child Psychiatry, Dallas, TX.

Berndt, D. J., Schwartz, S., & Kaiser, C. F. (1983). Readability of self-report depression inventories. *Journal of Consulting and Clinical Psychology, 51,* 627-628.

Helsel, W. J., & Matson, J. L. (1984). The assessment of depression in children: The internal structure of the Child Depression Inventory (CDI). *Behaviour Research and Therapy, 22,* 289-298.

Saylor, C. F., Finch, A. J., Spirito, A., & Bennett, B. (1984). The Children's Depression Inventory: A systematic evaluation of psychometric properties. *Journal of Consulting and Clinical Psychology, 52,* 955-967.

Politano, P. M., Nelson, W. M., Evans, H. E., Sorenson, S. B., & Zeman, D. J. (1986). Factor analytic evaluation of differences between black and Caucasian emotionally disturbed children on the Children's Depression Inventory. *Journal of Psychopathology and Behavioral Assessment, 8,* 1-7.

American Psychiatric Association. (1987). *Diagnostic and statistical manual of mental disorders* (3rd ed. rev.). Washington, DC: Author.

Review of the Children's Depression Inventory by HOWARD M. KNOFF, Associate Professor of School Psychology and Director of the School Psychology Program, University of South Florida, Tampa, FL:

In formulating this review, the following documents were read and considered: (*a*) the Children's Depression Inventory (CDI) protocol along with its two-page photocopied "Instructions for the Administration of the Children's Depression Inventory" dated March 1978; (*b*) an unpublished manuscript (April 1983) by Maria Kovacs, the CDI's author, entitled "The Children's Depression Inventory: A Self-Rated Depression Scale for School-Aged Youngsters"; (*c*) an article describing the CDI's construction and some psychometrically-related research (Kovacs, 1985); and (*d*) a three-page list of references of research with the CDI copywritten 1982 but dated October 1987. The review of these documents is notable, given the fact that the CDI is available only from the author and that a user might not have access to these materials so as to understand how to best use (if at all) this inventory.

As noted correctly by the author, the CDI should be used only as a research tool. However, given the scale construction and psychometric concerns discussed below, it is recommended that research with the CDI be used only for further scale refinement or to demonstrate its own reliability and validity across multiple samples, both clinically-involved and normal. Any other use of the CDI at this time, for example as a functional dependent or independent variable, would be premature and unsupportable.

Currently the CDI is a 27-item self-report scale that is purported to be suitable for school-aged children and adolescents aged 8 to 17. Based on the adult Beck Depression Inventory (Beck, 1967), the CDI has been developed in four phases from 1975 to 1979, the most significant of which used data from 39 consecutively admitted 8- to 13-year-old patients from a child guidance center, 20 age-matched "normal" controls, and 127 children from the Toronto public schools aged 10 to 13. While the use of such small and geographically-confined samples for a scale's initial development might be acceptable, the CDI has never been nationally normed using appropriate stratification processes, its use with and generalizability to multiple (research) samples has been unsystematic, and its evaluation has consisted of various reliability and validity studies that have been equivocable in their results.

Yet, the CDI's author recommends this inventory for research, and in her unpublished April 1983 manuscript states that "it is best used as a severity measure in appropriately selected samples . . . [because] . . . the investigator who does not have the resources to conduct clinical interviews does need a tool for subject selection" (p. 19). The author then continues by suggesting a CDI cutoff score, to identify children with depressive disorders in research studies, that, by her own admission, misses "about 49% of the clinically depressed cases . . . [yet] . . . will include the lowest number of false positives" (p. 21). Given the CDI's construction and lack of systematic and consistent psychometric data, the author's recommendations regarding the use of the CDI in research and her suggestion of a clinical cutoff score appear premature and ill-advised. In fact, many recommendations for the scale have gone beyond the evaluation data thus far collected. Indeed, even in such a basic area as test administration, a conclusion that CDI group administration procedures appear acceptable because a number of studies using this approach "reported no difficulties" is based more on anecdotal reports than actual research data.

Expanding on administration, the CDI's items are written at the first-grade level, and children respond to each item by identifying which of three choices best describes their feelings and ideas over the past 2 weeks. Fifty percent of the items start with the choice reflecting a "more depressed" status or correlate, and the rest start with the "less depressed" choice. Although the directions and protocol are clear and easy to read, separate booklets for younger (elementary school) versus older (high school) respondents are suggested. The former booklet might provide fewer items per page and more space between item choices, whereas the

latter might be printed to appear more "grown up." Relative to actual administration, examiner directions are clear, and appropriate recommendations for individualization for children with reading or attentional problems are made. Overall, the CDI's administration procedures appear clear-cut and efficient. Perhaps the instruction sheet provided for the test will soon be integrated into a comprehensive manual including both administration and technical data.

Relative to reliability, a number of studies using different normal and clinical samples have reported inconsistent results. For example, reported studies suggest that the CDI's internal consistency is acceptable for separate samples of clinically-referred, psychiatrically distressed youngsters and normal children, but that less consistency was noted for a pediatric-medical outpatient group. Similar inconsistent results occurred with the same samples when item-total score correlations were evaluated. These inconsistencies were of such a magnitude the author concluded that the CDI "does not have the same 'reality' to different respondent groups" (Kovacs, 1983, p. 12). Although test-retest reliability ranged from .43 over a 4-week period for diagnosed juvenile diabetics to .84 over a 9-week period with 90 children from the Toronto "standardization" sample, overall a number of serious reliability questions exist that must be addressed by future research. Among the most important questions are (*a*) to what degree does the CDI test-response pattern truly vary across research and/or clinical samples, and if it does vary, how can it be used with any consistency relative to interpretation and generalization; and (*b*) to what degree is the CDI a state-related versus trait-related instrument (i.e., what results should be expected when test-retest reliability is measured)?

Relative to validity, the CDI again seems to yield inconsistent results. Although concurrent validity with such scales as the Revised Children's Manifest Anxiety Scale and the Coopersmith Self-Esteem Inventory appear acceptable, construct, discriminant, and predictive validity data are problematic. For example, CDI factor analyses with the Toronto student sample yielded one principal factor, yet with a psychiatric-clinic referred sample, *seven* factors were found. Thus, again, the CDI appears to vary from sample to sample in its psychometric reactivity, making its research or clinical use difficult. CDI discriminant and predictive validity studies indicated the instrument (*a*) could not discriminate a normal from a heterogeneous child psychiatric sample; and (*b*) that it could discriminate certain outpatient children with major depressive disorders from children with adjustment disorders, with depression in remission, and with other pathologies but not depression even though *the actual score differences were not that substantive*. To summarize, the CDI has not been thoroughly validated, and more research in this area is critical. The author's caution not to use the CDI for patient selection, but as an adjunct to other diagnostic screening tools, is important and should be heeded.

Although the author is very forthright in describing the limitations and equivocable results of the CDI, it may be too early to conclude, as she does, that it "has clear promise as an assessment tool in treatment-outcome studies" (Kovacs, 1985, p. 998), depending on how one operationalizes "promise." For now, the CDI needs a great deal more research on its own psychometric properties. This is recommended *before* utilizing it as a dependent or independent variable in research investigating, for example, different characteristics of depressed children or the ability of certain interventions to decrease children's depression. The CDI *cannot* be used diagnostically at this time; thus, it is disconcerting to find a cutoff score to identify children with major depressive disorders even suggested—the fear being that someone not familiar with the CDI's current status might actually use the test and the cutoff in clinical practice. To summarize, there is clearly a need for a sound children's depression inventory in our field. Although the CDI has the potential to be one of those scales, a great deal more research on its own psychometric properties is needed at this time.

REVIEWER'S REFERENCES

Beck, A. T. (1967). *Depression: Clinical, experimental, and theoretical aspects*. New York: Harper & Row.

Kovacs, M. (1983). *The Children's Depression Inventory: A self-rated depression scale for school-aged youngsters*. Unpublished manuscript, University of Pittsburgh School of Medicine, Pittsburgh.

Kovacs, M. (1985). The Children's Depression Inventory (CDI). *Psychopharmacology Bulletin, 21*, 995-998.

[14]

Classroom Communication Screening Procedure for Early Adolescents: A Handbook for Assessment and Intervention.

Purpose: "To identify early adolescents who have not acquired some basic thinking strategies and communication skills considered to be essential for success in secondary school."
Population: Grades 5–10.
Publication Dates: 1986–87.
Acronym: CCSPEA.
Scores: Total score only.
Forms, 2: Short, long.
Administration: Individual or group.
Price Data, 1988: $35 for handbook ('87, 173 pages) including tests, information, scoring key, and answer sheets.
Time: Short form, (50–70) minutes; long form, (80–110) minutes.
Comments: Only to be administered to students who scored below the 40th percentile on the last annual reading test and/or teacher referral; "criterion-referenced."
Author: Charlann S. Simon.
Publisher: Communication Skill Builders.

Review of the Classroom Communication Screening Procedure for Early Adolescents: A Handbook for Assessment and Intervention by ESTHER E. DIAMOND, Educational and Psychological Consultant, Evanston, IL:

The Classroom Communication Screening Procedure for Early Adolescents (CCSPEA) draws on research from cognitive psychology, speech-language pathology, and education, indicating that communication deficits are the single most critical factor for students diagnosed as learning disabled or emotionally handicapped. A criterion-referenced, paper-and-pencil screening procedure for high-risk junior high students likely to drop out of school prematurely, it is designed to measure competence in comprehending directions, scanning for information in text, analyzing language, making inferences, interpreting math story problems, recognizing vocabulary, and engaging in written composition.

Both the long and short forms, which are suitable for classroom administration, have an accompanying observational checklist for observing the test-taking and interactive behaviors of students in Grades 6–9. The procedure can also be administered individually or in small groups. Approximately 75 percent accuracy in performance on CCSPEA tasks is claimed to be predictive of successful classroom performance in the middle and upper grades. The CCSPEA is administered only to students making the transition from elementary to secondary school who have scored below the 40th percentile on their last annual standardized reading test and/or have been referred by a teacher for underachievement in the classroom. The reading test requirement is based on research cited by the author indicating a strong relationship between reading performance and communication and thinking skills. The CCSPEA can be administered by teachers and a variety of specialists—speech-language pathologists, learning disability (LD) specialists, psychologists, and reading specialists. Ideally, it is administered at the "feeder" school.

RATIONALE. The author questions the clinic model of intervention and the practice of pinning diagnostic labels on marginal students such as those the CCSPEA is designed to identify. Ninety percent of language-learning special education students, according to the research literature cited, need to acquire school socialization skills and practical strategies to help them learn to learn. They are generally of normal intelligence, but they exhibit only marginal mastery of skills, strategies, and basic knowledge in subject areas. They generally do not qualify for special education. A teacher-student ratio between 1:12 and 1:18 is recommended in basic core subject classes—English, social studies, and science.

The CCSPEA can also be used with bilingual students who have been enrolled for 3 or more years in an elementary school transitional bilingual program or have been living in the United States for at least 3 years. Students from other than mainstream cultural backgrounds can also benefit from the CCSPEA. Because of their failure to use language and logic as well as middle-class children do, they are often perceived as lacking in ability rather than in training.

The rationale for the CCSPEA draws heavily from relevant research literature on communications skills, language proficiency, metalinguistic awareness, reading disabilities, and language and learning disabilities, which the author cites throughout the Handbook. CCSPEA tasks are designed to probe the underlying cognitive strategies and communication skills that research has shown to affect classroom performance in language proficiency, independent problem solving, language processing and analysis, and task persistence. No research studies on the CCSPEA itself are reported, although there is mention of preliminary reports from schools using the CCSPEA, including one instance in which the Screening Test of Adolescent Language (STAL), a one-to-one instrument, was administered to all students who failed the CCSPEA. An 85% overlap of the two measures was found.

CONTENT. The CCSPEA is divided into four sections:

1. This section taps content comprehension and metalinguistic skills. The administrator reads aloud a passage and the directions for each task, and the student must be able to understand numbers presented as words as well as in figures; write a clear phrase or sentence that includes all information requested; figure out a definition from the context; determine the noun or noun phrase to which a pronoun refers; and determine the total number of subpoints in a text that are related to the main topic.

2. This section contains 10 separate direction-following tasks involving listening to details within an oral direction, understanding multipart written directions, and other tasks requiring active listening and monitoring of task performance.

3. This section involves 10 different types of tasks, some with overlapping features—for example, unscrambling or rearranging words to make a sentence, solving riddles, adding a meaningful word to the end of an unfinished sentence, deciding if statements make sense, combining several short sentences into one, choosing an example that demonstrates a given fact, solving math story problems, finding the noun referent for a pronoun in a story, identifying terms in a story that have been substituted for a given term, and using all of a given set of words to make up a descriptive sentence about a picture.

4. This section requires students to match synonyms or brief definitions with vocabulary words.

The CCSPEA is not a timed test, but approximately 80–90 minutes are generally needed for the long form and 50–60 minutes for the short form. The short form has been found useful with incoming and current seventh graders, whereas the long form is recommended for students above Grade 7. The item sequence is identical for the two forms.

A specific rationale is given for each task, and complete scoring instructions are provided. The CCSPEA administrator and a colleague from the feeder school make notations on the Observational Checklist during the session, rating as "good" or "inappropriate" such behaviors as on-task persistence, attention to directions, amount of time taken to settle down, daydreaming, and so on.

DETERMINING LOCAL PASSING SCORES. The CCSPEA is not a standardized test, and there are no norms. Two procedures are suggested for comparing achieving and nonachieving students and establishing local norms. The first, to be used where students are grouped by reading ability, is to administer the CCSPEA to approximately 30 students in average-ability classes at the grade level being screened, and to compute a mean percentage correct score for that grade level. The second procedure, to be used where grouping is heterogeneous, is to administer the CCSPEA to two classrooms at the grade level being screened, compute the percentage correct score, rank the students from highest to lowest, isolating the middle third of the students, and determine, in discussions with classroom teachers, grade-level classroom communication behavior. If all agree, compute a mean score for the middle-third group. It is suggested then that 15 points be subtracted from the mean percentage correct score for average students at the appropriate grade level for use with incoming students to that grade. No psychometric reason is cited, but the author claims the formula has been found to predict validly which students will have difficulty with curriculum content.

The authors do not suggest using the CCSPEA as a pre/post test, although at one school a preliminary version was used as part of a total assessment of an experimental curriculum in English, science, and social studies. A 6.5 percent increase in performance among seventh graders and a 9.4 percent increase among eighth graders between September and May was found.

FOLLOW-UP SCREENING. A procedure for follow-up screening is suggested for cases where students show borderline performance (just above or below the passing score) on the CCSPEA, and where students display exceptional difficulty, compared with classmates, in language processing and analysis, expressive language, and cognitive strategies, or where another teacher observes difficulties in a particular subject area. Some other follow-up screening suggestions are using supplementary measures—for example, STAL scores (Prather, Breecher, Stafford, & Wallace, 1980), any one of several suggested observational checklists, an adaptation of the Token Test and the Reporter Test included in the Handbook, and the Learning Style Inventory (Carbo, 1984).

SUMMARY. In summary, this revised edition of the CCSPEA is a practical handbook that offers the promise of being a useful screening instrument for identification of Grade 6–9 students who are marginal in their school skills and at risk for dropping out of school. However, users are well advised to use it only on an experimental basis—advice with which the author concurs—until there is clear-cut evidence of internal consistency, test-retest reliability, and construct and predictive validity to support the inferences drawn from performance on the instrument. Schools using the CCSPEA should be encouraged to engage in well-designed research studies toward that end, and also to examine more completely the relationship between the CCSPEA and related instruments, such as STAL and other measures that deal with speech and other communication disabilities.

In addition, although the Handbook offers a wealth of background historical, research, and philosophical information, the information is scattered too widely throughout the content, and much of it tends to be repetitious. It would be more helpful to the researcher to have all the background information that is not *directly* pertinent to CCSPEA rationale and development, such as "Notable Quotes: An Introduction to Philosophical Biases," placed in a separate section.

REVIEWER'S REFERENCES

Prather, E., Breecher, S., Stafford, M., & Wallace, E. (1980). Screening Test of Adolescent Language. Seattle, WA: University of Washington Press.

Carbo, M. (1984). Research in learning style and reading: Implications for instruction. *Theory Into Practice, 23*, 72-76.

Review of the Classroom Communication Screening Procedure for Early Adolescents: A Handbook for Assessment and Intervention by GARY J. STAINBACK, Senior Psychologist, Department of Pediatrics, East Carolina University, School of Medicine, Greenville, NC:

The Classroom Communication Screening Procedure for Early Adolescents: A Handbook for Assessment and Intervention (CCSPEA) is a criterion-referenced, paper-and-pencil screening procedure to help identify students in the sixth through ninth grades who possess communication difficulties. It was designed by a speech-language clinician who has strong interest and experience in learning-disabled adolescents, in addition to those with emotional handicapping and speech-language disorders. The CCSPEA is experimental, and can be either individually or group administered by a variety of educational personnel (teachers, speech-language pathologists, learning disability specialists, psychologists, and reading specialists). There are both short and long forms. Only a difference of six tasks separate the two forms. A recommended 50 minutes is allocated for the short form and 80 minutes for the long form. Scoring is done by hand and is reportedly (and apparently) uncomplicated.

The manual for the CCSPEA is inadequately organized. It is extremely difficult to find essential parts for administration or scoring instructions. There is extensive review of research supporting the need for the CCSPEA, why certain kinds of tasks are included, and discussion of speech pathologists' role; however, it would be better for the test user if such information was contained in a separate handbook.

The personal and professional feelings and thoughts of the author regarding the need for supportive services for early adolescents who may not respond adequately to established regular educational or special educational practices are very apparent from a reading of the CCSPEA. Ms. Simon (the author) makes a strong argument for providing a group intervention approach to help improve communication skills.

The CCSPEA is a screening measure for competence in comprehending directions, scanning for information in a textbook, analyzing language, making inferences, interpreting language in math story problems, recognizing vocabulary, engaging in written composition, and demonstrating task persistence. It is intended to be given to students who score below the 40th percentile on a recent standardized reading test, or by teacher referral for classroom underachievement. Ideally it can be given to students entering into the middle school or junior high from a "feeder school," so students who may require intervention can be identified early and planning done prior to their first day in the new school. The short form is intended for incoming seventh grade students (second semester sixth graders) and current seventh graders, whereas the long form is intended for students above the seventh grade. A cutoff of 70 percent accuracy level (conversion table available in the manual) is used to make a determination of whether or not a student should participate in a cognitive/communication development program.

The manual contains both the long and short forms of the CCSPEA, along with scoring directions, test directions, sample letters that can be sent to the teachers and parents, adaptions to some other test items, and some classroom activities. Test forms are reproducible from the manual. Directions are the same for the short and long forms, with an asterisk denoting short-form items. Care has been taken to develop the items to be equal to or below a fifth-grade ability level, so that communication skills are actually being measured; however, statistical data supporting this are lacking. The examiner is instructed to reread portions in the manual during the test administration. It is, however, difficult to find these portions quickly. Bold facing the type for the examiner's script and repeating those portions of the directions intended to be repeated will help reduce examiner confusion and aid in administration. Scoring is provided in the manual; however, it is not clear how misspellings should be scored except in vocabulary where the reader cannot recognize the letter.

Follow-up screening is recommended when a student shows a borderline level of performance on the CCSPEA, or if a student exhibits exceptional difficulty with language processing, language analysis, expressive language, and cognitive strategies. The author recommends specific recourse in some instances, to the exclusion of others. The recommendations are not explained or justified. Throughout the manual it is impossible to distinguish facts from opinions because necessary citations are not provided.

In summary, the CCSPEA is introduced as an experimental screening instrument to help identify early adolescents who may possess language disorders, and who might benefit from some group cognitive-communication intervention. The manual is poorly organized, and contains an excessive amount of material related to the personal and professional beliefs of the author regarding underachieving adolescents, in addition to the role of the speech-language pathologist in the school system. There are two forms available, short and long, separated only by a small number of items and about 30 minutes of allotted administration time. No statistical data exist to support whether the test items measure their purported skills, nor to indicate whether the screening procedure actually identifies children who have a mild language disability separate from some other handicapping condition. However, there appears to be excellent thought and planning given to initial item development. The test shows promise as an instrument worthy of further development, but is not developed sufficiently for application in the school system as a screening instrument or diagnostic tool.

[15]

Cognitive Behavior Rating Scales.

Purpose: "To allow a family member, or other reliable observer, to rate the presence and severity of cognitive impairment, behavioral deficits, and observable neurological signs."
Population: Patients with possible neurological impairment.
Publication Date: 1987.
Acronym: CBRS.
Scores: 9 scales: Language Deficit, Apraxia, Disorientation, Agitation, Need for Routine, Depression, Higher Cognitive Deficits, Memory Disorder, Dementia.
Administration: Group.
Price Data, 1989: $32 per complete kit including manual, 25 reusable item booklets, and 50 rating booklets.
Time: (15–20) minutes.
Author: J. Michael Williams.
Publisher: Psychological Assessment Resources, Inc.

Review of the Cognitive Behavior Rating Scales by RON EDWARDS, Professor of Psychology and Director of School Psychology Training, University of Southern Mississippi, Hattiesburg, MS:

The Cognitive Behavior Rating Scales (CBRS) are designed to provide information regarding the cognitive functioning of brain-damaged individuals who are unable or unwilling to complete more formal tests of cognitive abilities. The items are rated by a family member or other reliable observer familiar with the everyday functioning of the client. Materials include a reusable Item Booklet containing 104 descriptive statements and 12 ability items (e.g., spelling, reading, drawing ability) and a separate Rating Booklet. The first 104 items are rated on a 5-point scale from *not at all* (1) to *very much* (5) like the person being rated. Items 105–116 rate the person's ability from *very low* (1) to *very high* (5). Completion of the CBRS is reported to take 15–20 minutes with raters generally needing assistance in completing only the first two or three items.

Identifying populations that can be expected to complete the CBRS reliably and validly may be a problem. No information is provided as to the age, race, ethnic, educational, or social class characteristics of the raters used in the development of the CBRS. The ability of informants to complete the CBRS may be influenced by such characteristics.

CBRS item ratings are entered in corresponding blocks in the Rating Booklet. The blocks are arranged so that column and/or row totals represent raw score totals or subtotals for each of the nine CBRS scales. The total raw scores for the nine CBRS scales are transformed to *T*-scores ($M = 100$, $SD = 15$) and percentiles using a table contained on the last page of the Rating Booklet. Because score distributions for the Apraxia and Disorientation scales were significantly skewed, only percentiles are provided for these scales. Higher raw scores on the CBRS represent more pathological ratings and yield lower *T*-scores and percentiles.

DEVELOPMENT OF THE CBRS. An initial pool of 170 nonredundant items was created based on interviews with families with a demented member, review of the literature on dementia-related illnesses, and popular guides describing behavioral aspects of cognitive impairment. The initial item pool was arranged into the nine CBRS scales and reviewed by 10 practicing neuropsychologists. Items that at least eight raters agreed belonged to a particular scale were placed in that scale. Items failing to meet this criterion were dropped, resulting in the final set of 116 items.

RELIABILITY AND VALIDITY. Reliability and validity data were obtained by analyzing CBRS ratings provided by either a child or spouse for three groups of subjects. A demented group consisted of 30 patients with a diagnosis of Alzheimer's disease but no other brain disease, psychiatric disorder, or cerebral vascular accident. A second group consisted of 30 normals matched on age and years of education. The third group consisted of 400 normal subjects with no history of brain disease or psychiatric disorder. Test-retest reliabilities (1-week interval) based on 31 of the normal subjects ranged from .61 to .94. Internal consistency reliability using the 400 normals yielded alpha coefficients ranging from .78 to .92. Although the reliability data would seem adequate, especially for a research instrument, the fact they are based solely on normal subjects limits their value. Reliability data for subjects similar to those for which the instrument is intended to be used are clearly needed.

Normative data were obtained for 688 individuals recruited by public newspaper advertisements and by "announcements to the membership of an Alzheimer's Disease and Related Disorders Association and the American Association of Retired People." All volunteers were screened for neurological and psychiatric disorders. The resulting data were used to construct the *T*-score and percentile tables for the CBRS.

Validity was assessed by comparing the scores of the 30 demented patients with those of the 30 matched normals. Based on paired *t*-test comparisons, the demented group received significantly higher ratings on all scales except Depression. A nonstepwise discriminant analysis resulted in 100% correct classification of the demented and normal subjects. These data suggest that the CBRS can discriminate between moderately impaired Alzheimer's patients and normals. Whether the CBRS can also discriminate mildly impaired patients or patients with other forms of brain damage is unknown.

A couple of puzzling aspects of the CBRS scoring system were noted. First, the initial 104 items are statements of pathology, with higher ratings reflecting greater pathology. On the other hand, higher ratings on the "ability" items (105–116) reflect positive characteristics. Although one would assume the normative data would control for this idiosyncracy, examination of data reported in the manual raises additional questions. For example, the Language Deficit (LD) scale consists of four pathology items (Cannot maintain a simple conversation, Has difficulty communicating thoughts, Substitutes an incorrect word that sounds similar to the correct word, and Has difficulty following instructions) and six ability items (Spelling, Writing, Reading, Ability to use language, Following directions or instructions, and Speaking). The LD mean for the normative group is 12.32 which, assuming the lowest ratings on the pathology items, means that they were rated as low or very low on all the ability items. Ratings of average ability would yield an LD scale score of 22. Anomalies of this sort raise questions as to the accuracy of the instructions for rating items 105–116.

Another curious situation occurs with Items 98 and 101. Item 98 states, "When asked to recall something, he or she is quick to say 'I don't know' rather than make up something," whereas Item 101 states, "Guesses or makes up an answer rather than saying 'I don't know.'" Ratings on these items would appear to cancel each other.

SUMMARY. The CBRS manual identifies the scale as a research instrument intended to document a family member's observations of cognitive impairments in the everyday functioning of brain-damaged individuals. The information yielded by the CBRS is intended to supplement other data available to the clinician and to suggest areas for further exploration. Based on available data, the CBRS would appear to be a useful instrument for obtaining such information for patients with Alzheimer's disease. Whether it will be as useful for patients with other forms of brain damage remains to be demonstrated. Advantages of the CBRS include its standardized format and normative data. The apparent ability of the CBRS to discriminate dementia from depression in the elderly, if substantiated by further research, would be another significant advantage. As a research instrument, the CBRS would seem to be an excellent alternative to informal interviews with family members.

Review of the Cognitive Behavior Rating Scales by DAVID J. MEALOR, Chair of Educational Services Department, College of Education, University of Central Florida, Orlando, FL:

The Cognitive Behavior Rating Scales (CBRS) is a 116-item instrument designed to rate the presence and severity of cognitive impairment, behavioral deficits, and observable neurological signs. The CBRS was published as a research edition to "interest other experimenters in the further development of the scales." Persons with cognitive impairment may be unable or unwilling to complete formal test batteries. The CBRS is designed to allow a family member or other reliable observer to rate an individual in nine specific areas (scales) designed to "elicit information about deficits as they are revealed in everyday behaviors." The nine scales are: Language Deficit (LD)—10 items; Apraxia (AP)—5 items; Disorientation (DO)—5 items; Agitation (AG)—6 items; Need for Routine (NR)—7 items; Depression (DEP)—24 items; Higher Cognitive Deficits (HCD)—12 items; Memory Disorders (MD)—21 items; and Dementia (DEM)—26 items.

The items were selected "from interviews with families who have a demented member, the scientific literature that describes dementia-related illnesses and their diagnoses . . . and the popular guides for families which describe behavioral aspects of cognitive impairment in everyday terms." An initial item pool of 170 items was reduced to the present number using an expert judge methodology. Ten practicing neuropsychologists were asked to group items, and items remained if at least eight of these experts agreed that an item belonged in a particular scale.

The CBRS consists of a reusable Item Booklet, Rating Booklet, and Manual. The Item Booklet is divided into three sections and the respondent rates the first 92 items on a scale of 1 (*not at all like this person*) to 5 (*very much like this person*). The second section has 12 items and assesses memory and intellectual stability. Completion of the second section is optional and the third section (12 items) employs a slightly different rating with 1 (*this person's ability is very low*) to 5 (*this person's ability is very high*). The method used to determine the rating descriptors is not mentioned. The actual ratings for the 116 items are recorded on the Rating Booklet. Respondents are instructed to read the instructions in the Item Booklet and record only one number in each box. Each item from the Item Booklet has a corresponding box in the Record Booklet. Scoring is entered in a horizontal direction and the total score for each scale is derived by summarizing in a vertical direction. It would be beneficial if the respec-

tive ratings were listed on the pages with the items. This would save the need to keep referring to the front page of the Item Booklet.

Total ratings for each of the scales are computed and transferred to the scoring grid on the back page of the Rating Booklet. It would be helpful if the boxes for total scale scores were provided. Transferring total scores to the scoring grid may result in errors. According to the author, most persons should be able to complete the CBRS in 15–20 minutes.

Although the intent of the CBRS appears to be very good, the technical aspects of the test present some major shortcomings. The CBRS manual is inadequate at best. The section dealing with reliability and validity simply does not provide enough information to determine if the CBRS is capable of doing what it purports to do. In addition, there is insufficient information provided about the subjects used in the reliability and validity study(ies). For example, comparisons were made utilizing three groups: "Demented" ($N = 30$), "Matched-Normal" ($N = 30$), and "Normal" ($N = 400$). The demented subjects came from a local chapter of the Alzheimer's Disease and Related Disorders Association. No other demographic information relating to any of the subjects is given. Any comparisons with others would be most difficult. The mean age of the "Normal" group is 2 standard deviations below that of the other two groups.

Test-retest reliability was conducted with the "Normal" subjects. Considering the intent of the CBRS, a test-retest study is needed with the "Demented" group. Concurrent validity studies centered on comparing the performance of the "Matched-Normals" with the ratings given the "Demented" group. It is inferred that "family members were able to judge reliably the disabilities of a demented family member," yet, no test-retest studies were conducted with this group.

The normative sample ($N = 688$) ranged in age from 30–89 years. Means and standard deviations for each of the nine scales by age group and total group for the normative sample are provided. However, a note appears at the bottom of the table informing the reader "ratings [were] not available for all subjects for all scales."

If the CBRS is to be used as a measure of cognitive decline, its use is not supported by the performance of the normative sample, where performance differed little between the 30–39-year age group and the 70–89-year age group. The data from all age groups were combined for purposes of normative comparisons. It is the use of the CBRS for comparative purposes that may present the most difficulty. The manual refers readers to the Appendix of percentile rankings and normalized T-scores for the CBRS scales. This same Appendix appears in the Rating Booklet. The basic tenets of measurement appear to be misunderstood. The means and standard deviations do not match the numbers presented in the Appendix, and measures of central tendency are ignored. The author notes that the Appendix contains normalized T-score transformations ($x = 100$, $SD = 15$); however, most T-scores have a mean of 50 and a standard deviation of 10. Regardless, the Appendix yields maximum scores to only 1 standard deviation above the mean. Higher scores are reported below a percentile ranking of 1 and are carried to 3 standard deviations below the mean. This Appendix forms the basis for the CBRS Rating Booklet.

In summary, any potential usefulness of the CBRS in its current form appears to be outweighed by the serious psychometric deficiencies with standardization, norming, and reliability. A great deal of technical work needs to be done before the test should be used for any clinical purpose. At best, the CBRS Item Booklet may serve as an initial survey for clinicians to gain insight about a person's present level of functioning in certain areas.

[16]
Computer Managed Screening Test.

Purpose: "Screens children for communicative disorders in articulation, receptive language, expressive language, voice and fluency."
Population: Ages 3–8.
Publication Date: 1985.
Scores, 3: Receptive Language, Articulation, Expressive Language; 2 ratings: Voice Test (pass/fail), Fluency Test (pass/fail).
Administration: Individual.
Price Data, 1989: $79.95 per complete kit including diskette, backup diskette, and manual (29 pages).
Time: (4) minutes.
Comments: Apple II microcomputer necessary for administration.
Author: James L. Fitch.
Publisher: Communication Skill Builders.

Review of the Computer Managed Screening Test by RONALD K. SOMMERS, Professor of Speech Pathology and Audiology, Kent State University, Kent, OH:

Screening tests seem particularly vulnerable to criticism. These tests invariably can be found wanting in one area or another, one common deficiency being that they skim the surface of factors evaluated and thus lose their sensitivity. The Computer Managed Screening Test has this deficiency, but it also has some potential for use for rapid screening and reporting if the user has an Apple computer available for use wherever screening is conducted. Apparently, this small program will not run on other microcomputers at this time.

Field testing was limited to 50 Head Start children 4–6 years of age. The examiners were laypersons who received 2.5 hours of training prior to testing these children. The Receptive Language portion subtest scores agreed with unspecified criterion measures of receptive language at 88%, the Expressive Language subtest 88%, and the Articulation subtest 68%. Thus, criterion-related validity is grossly understudied, and what was accomplished is meagerly described.

Basic test-construction information and a stated rationale for the selection of the subtests and items incorporated in the test are not provided. These deficiencies are reflected in the absence of information concerning any aspect of test validity, except that limited to the small tryout of the test that included the use of unidentified criterion measures of language and speech, as previously mentioned.

The construct validity, while not tested, may be promising. For example, the Receptive Language assessment uses colored blocks and verbal instructions on how they are to be manipulated, a strategy for testing comprehension similar to that of The Token Test for Children (9:1295), a test with a reasonably good reputation as a measure of children's language comprehension. The Expressive Language subtest is one of sentence imitation. At young age levels, imitative tests of this type seem to have more power to detect children's language impairments. However, after ages 4–5, there is some evidence that sentence imitation tests may not be adequate measures to reflect the overall quality of children's spoken language. The Articulation subtest is simple word imitation. Children with significant delays in articulation development will largely be identified on such a test, but some marginal cases will likely escape detection. Because rapid screening, data analysis, and reporting are major objectives of this computerized test, the word-imitation model may fit into this scheme. However, although a rapid assessment procedure, the practice of having a child count to 10 to judge whether a voice or fluency problem exists is a "bare-bones" determination. The author needs to provide some data to show how effective counting to 10 is in the detection of these two disorders. Some children may count to 10 without noticeable voice defects but have difficulty in connected speech, because simple counting fails to assess important aspects of vocal behavior.

Another vital consideration, test reliability, was not reported. Data showing interjudge reliability for examiners on the total test and its subtests were not reported. Determinations of test-retest reliability were also not included in the test manual.

This evaluator tried this screening test with a young child and found it very easy to use. The time required is essentially that stated by the author. The computer program is very simple to operate and user friendly. Student files are easily established and can be reentered easily. Three reports can be generated. The Individual Test Report shows the child's scores on each item of the five subtests. The Student List is a printed list of all students filed on a data disc, along with the date and whether or not a student has been tested. The Age Analysis Report is a breakdown of the Student List by 6-month age levels, listing each student's overall scores for the subtests. This appears helpful in comparisons of performances of children at different age levels. However, a user may accumulate data on children's performances (which may prove helpful as "local norms"), but test norms were needed to compare children's performances by age and other variables. This screening test was not standardized in any fashion.

The target population is children 3–8 years of age. However, the author feels, but does not justify with information, that the screening test is most useful with the middle range of this distribution. This vagary is typical of the greatest deficiency in the use of this instrument:

good scientific reporting of the accuracy of the screening test in the identification of children impaired in communication skills. Factors such as age, sex, ethnic background/race, and handicapping/nonhandicapping status were also needed to clarify the nature of the test scores and their interpretations.

Based upon a flurry of investigations reported in recent years of the validity of children's language tests, it seems likely that others will use and investigate this screening instrument. One would hope its author is a prominent member of this group.

[17]
The Creatrix Inventory.

Purpose: "To help people identify their levels of creativity as well as their orientations toward risk taking."
Population: Members of organizations.
Publication Dates: 1971–86.
Acronym: C&RT.
Scores, 2: Creativity, Risk Taking; plotted on matrix to determine 1 of 8 styles: Reproducer, Modifier, Challenger, Practicalizer, Innovator, Synthesizer, Dreamer, Planner.
Administration: Group.
Price Data, 1987: $5.95 per manual ('86, 26 pages) including inventory and scoring instructions plus administrator's guide (2 pages).
Time: Administration time not reported.
Comments: Catalog uses the test title Creativity and Risk-Taking.
Author: Richard E. Byrd.
Publisher: University Associates, Inc.

Review of The Creatrix Inventory by HARRISON G. GOUGH, Professor of Psychology, Emeritus, University of California, Berkeley, CA:

The Creatrix Inventory for "risk-taking" and "creativity" consists of two 28-item self-report scales. Each item is answered on a 9-step scale, going from 1 (*complete disagreement*) to 9 (*complete agreement*). Three illustrative items for risk-taking are "I feel free to be myself whatever the consequences," "Sometimes I cheat a little," and "I can accept my mistakes." For creativity, defined as the ability to generate unconventional ideas, three representative items are "Daydreaming is a useful activity," "I often see the humorous side when others do not," and "Complete ambiguity is more desirable than complete clarity."

The items within each scale appear to be reasonably homogeneous, but no intrascale reliability data are presented. The only statement in the manual concerning reliability reports a test-retest correlation of .72 for 25 persons readministered the test after a 1-week interval. Whether this coefficient refers to one scale, both scales, or some sort of index based on the 56 items is unspecified.

Also, nothing is said in the manual about the correlation between the two scales, even though the major interpretive model for the Inventory depicts them in a conjoint display. Eight regions on the bivariate surface are marked off and designated as discrete "orientations." Persons scoring very high on both scales are classified as Innovators, those scoring very low on both as Reproducers. Challengers are very high on risk-taking but low on creativity, and Dreamers are very high on creativity but low on risk-taking. In the center of the grid are found Practicalizers (average on creativity, above average on risk-taking), Synthesizers (average on risk-taking, above average on creativity), Planners (average on creativity, below average on risk-taking), and Modifiers (average on risk-taking, below average on creativity). No evidence is provided concerning the expected number of respondents to be found in each category.

The implications of each of the eight categories are elaborated in one-page digests suggesting how individuals in each class will think and approach problems, the positive contributions they might make to an organization, and the difficulties that can be anticipated. The sketches are plausible, but no data are furnished to substantiate the claims made for each way of functioning, or for the predicted assets and liabilities.

The manual closes with a one-page discussion of "norms," "effects of faking or extraordinary stress," and "validity." Under "norms," no means or standard deviations for any sample are given, although it is stated that women score higher than men on risk-taking, whereas on creativity no differences were detected.

Under "faking" it is asserted that attempts to fake good should seriously depress risk-taking scores, but only moderately depress those for creativity. Unfortunately, no data are given for samples tested under normal and fake-good instructions. Considering that the goal of the Inventory is to assess creative potential, the "fake creativity" set as explored in depth by

Harrington (1975) is more relevant than that for "fake good."

The short paragraph on validity offers no data whatsoever, and in fact carries the anomalous sentence, "Although the statistics necessary to support concurrent validity are not available, face validity is generally attested to by respondents." This assertion is an unacceptable substitute for the validity data that should have been provided.

Another serious deficiency in the manual is the absence of any attempt to relate risk-taking and creativity scores to widely used and well-known measures of these two phenomena. For instance, in the creativity domain, good examples are Welsh's (1975) scales for origence and intellectence, Barron's (1953, 1965) scales for independence of judgment and originality, and Cattell's (Cattell, Eber, & Tatsuoka, 1970) creativity equation for the 16PF. In the risk-taking domain, a good example is the scale of that name in the Jackson Personality Inventory (Jackson, 1976). Scores on the Creatrix Inventory should also be related to performance measures of creativity, such as those of Guilford (Wilson, Guilford, & Christensen, 1953), Harris (1960), and Torrance (1966), and linkage should also be established with the Innovator-Adaptor categories as defined by Kirton's (1976) measures.

To conclude, there may well be good potential in the scales of this Inventory, but at the present time there is little, if any, evidence of their value. Until such time as adequate evidence becomes available, the Inventory should be viewed only as a research device of undetermined worth.

REVIEWER'S REFERENCES

Barron, F. (1953). Some personality correlates of independence of judgment. *Journal of Personality, 21,* 287-297.

Wilson, R. C., Guilford, J. P., & Christensen, P. R. (1953). The measurement of individual differences in originality. *Psychological Bulletin, 50,* 362-370.

Harris, D. (1960). The development and validation of a test of creativity in engineering. *Journal of Applied Psychology, 44,* 254-257.

Barron, F. (1965). The psychology of creativity. *New directions in psychology* (Vol. 2, pp. 3-134). New York: Holt, Rinehart & Winston.

Torrance, E. P. (1966). Torrance Tests of Creative Thinking. Princeton, NJ: Personnel Press.

Cattell, R. B., Eber, H. W., & Tatsuoka, M. M. (1970). *Handbook for the Sixteen Personality Factor Questionnaire* (16PF). Champaign, IL: Institute of Personality and Ability Testing.

Harrington, D. M. (1975). Effects of explicit instructions to "be creative" on the psychological meaning of divergent thinking test scores. *Journal of Personality, 43,* 434-454.

Welsh, G. S. (1975). *Creativity and intelligence: A personality approach*. Chapel Hill, NC: University of North Carolina Institute for Research in Social Science.

Jackson, D. N. (1976). *Jackson Personality Inventory manual*. Goshen, NY: Research Psychologists Press.

Kirton, M. J. (1976). Adaptors and innovators: A description and measure. *Journal of Applied Psychology, 61*, 622-629.

Review of The Creatrix Inventory by JOHN F. WAKEFIELD, Associate Professor of Education, University of North Alabama, Florence, AL:

The Creatrix Inventory (C&RT) is a 56-item instrument designed to measure creativity and risk-taking orientations on a grid-like matrix. Each variable is measured by degree of agreement or disagreement with 28 statements. Degrees range from 1 (*complete disagreement*) to 9 (*complete agreement*), and the instrument is self-scored. Total scores for creativity and risk-taking are then plotted by the respondent on the two axes of the matrix. The matrix itself is divided into eight areas to indicate different types of individuals. The four central personality types (Modifier, Practicalizer, Synthesizer, and Planner) are purportedly more socialized than the other four, which lie at corners of the grid. Individuals are encouraged to interpret their combined orientation in light of descriptions of all eight types supplied in the C&RT booklet.

The strength of the C&RT lies in the logic of the rationale. If one accepts the author's definition of creativity as "the ability to produce unconventional ideas," it follows that people who live "in a phantasmagoric world of wildly imaginative ideas" are highly creative. This definition also permits the Inventory author to distinguish risk-taking from creativity and describe four extreme types based on this distinction. The Dreamer (creative but not a risk-taker) is described as an underachiever, whereas the Challenger (a risk-taker but not creative) is described as critical of others' ideas. The other two extreme types (Reproducer and Innovator) are self-explanatory and represent extremely low or high scores on both scales.

The weakness of the Inventory lies in the absence of statistical data to support the instrument. Means for the creativity and risk-taking scales can be estimated from the matrix, but standard deviations are not reported in the manual or the administrator's guide. Reliability is only reported through a test-retest coefficient (.72) for 25 subjects over 1 week. Statistical evidence of validity is not available, although the claim is made that respondents attest to face validity.

In the absence of more evidence of reliability and validity, the user should compare the C&RT with The Kirton Adaption-Innovation Inventory (KAI; Kirton, 1976). The KAI is also intended for use with organizational members, but it measures a personality dimension with an "Adaptive" type at one end and an "Innovative" type at the other. This continuum seems generally comparable to combined dimensions of the C&RT with Reproducer and Innovator at the extremes. The KAI measures a simpler construct than the C&RT, but the clear documentation of some of its psychometric characteristics would lead many potential users to prefer it over the C&RT.

Use of the KAI is made somewhat problematic, however, by the fact that at the time of this writing, it was no longer available from a publisher or distributor in the United States or Canada. This situation creates a possible dilemma for potential test users. Either they can request the KAI from its author at the Occupational Research Centre in Hatfield, England, or risk using the C&RT. The deciding factor in favor of the KAI is not that it is necessarily a better measure, but that it is a more thoroughly documented one.

At a minimum, efforts to document psychometric soundness should include descriptive statistics for both scales, scale reliabilities, and evidence of the validity of the matrix construct. Validation might begin with a factor analysis of scale items to demonstrate the distinction between creativity and risk taking, but to be convincing, it should also include correlations of the C&RT scales with other measures.

Overall, the C&RT presents a logical rationale for an inventory with inadequate research support. Currently, the Kirton Adaption-Innovation Inventory is a more thoroughly documented measure of a similar concept. The C&RT is more theoretically sophisticated and more easily accessible than the KAI, but the C&RT is not presented with adequate supportive information.

REVIEWER'S REFERENCE

Kirton, M. J. (1976). Adaptors and innovators: A description and measure. *Journal of Applied Psychology, 61*, 622-629.

[18]
Dallas Pre-School Screening Test.

Purpose: "Designed to screen the primary learning areas for children from three to six years of age."
Population: Ages 3–6.
Publication Date: 1972.
Scores, 6: Psychological, Auditory, Visual, Language, Motor, Articulation Development (optional).
Administration: Individual.
Price Data, 1987: $27.50 per 25 pupil record forms, stimuli book, and manual (42 pages).
Time: (15–20) minutes.
Authors: Robert R. Percival and Suzanne C. Poxon (stimuli book).
Publisher: Dallas Educational Services.

Review of the Dallas Pre-School Screening Test by JAMES E. YSSELDYKE, Professor of Educational Psychology, University of Minnesota, Minneapolis, MN:

The Dallas Pre-School Screening Test (DPST) was developed by a school psychologist and a speech therapist to eliminate excessive and unnecessary testing of small children, and to screen weaknesses and strengths in learning areas. The test falls very short of meeting even minimal criteria specified in *Standards for Educational and Psychological Testing* (AERA, APA, & NCME, 1985).

There are six subtests in the DPST: Psychological, Auditory, Visual, Motor, Language, and Articulation Development. These are not described adequately enough for the reader to decide what they are intended to assess. The author claims these are the major areas of learning for preschool children, but offers no evidence to support his conclusions. There is a list of references in the manual, but these are not cited in the text of the manual. Children who take this test are graded successful or unsuccessful in each of the areas relative to "expected normal development." Expected normal development is not defined.

The manual for the DPST is in need of a good editor. There are many spelling, grammatical, and typographical errors. Some of the sections are just incomprehensible. The test stimuli are clear, though crudely drawn.

The DPST was standardized on a random sample of approximately 3,000 children in a single community (Richardson, Texas). The authors describe the community as "above average in education, social and financial status." The authors do not specify the demographics of the standardization population,

though they do say that at least half the population tested was enrolled in private schools. They report that "approximately one hundred black children were evaluated."

Evidence for the technical adequacy of this scale is very poorly presented in the manual, and the evidence presented looks inadequate and inappropriate. The concepts of standardization and standardized scores are confused. Procedures for establishing reliability were incorrect and inadequate. Evidence for validity is based on correlations of performance of an unspecified sample on this test (or parts of it) and the Columbia Mental Maturity Scale (more than likely an old edition, because the scales were both published in 1972), the motor subtest of the Detroit Tests of Learning Aptitude (old edition), and the Draw-A-Man Test. There is little here to suggest the scale is reliable and valid.

The DPST is a very dated scale that falls far short of criteria necessary for a good test.

REVIEWER'S REFERENCE

American Educational Research Association, American Psychological Association, & National Council on Measurement in Education. (1985). *Standards for educational and psychological testing.* Washington, DC: American Psychological Association, Inc.

[19]

Dementia Rating Scale.

Purpose: Measures the cognitive status of individuals with known cortical impairment.
Population: Individuals suffering from brain dysfunction.
Publication Dates: 1973–88.
Acronym: DRS.
Scores, 6: Attention, Initiation/Perseveration, Construction, Conceptualization, Memory, Total.
Administration: Individual.
Price Data, 1990: $45 per complete kit including 25 scoring/recording forms, stimulus cards, and manual ('88, 28 pages); $24 per 25 scoring/recording forms; $15 per set of stimulus cards; $9 per manual.
Time: (15–45) minutes.
Author: Steven Mattis.
Publisher: Psychological Assessment Resources, Inc.

Review of the Dementia Rating Scale by R. A. BORNSTEIN, Associate Professor of Psychiatry, Neurosurgery and Neurology, The Ohio State University, Columbus, OH:

The Dementia Rating Scale (DRS) consists of 36 tasks distributed among five subscales. The test was designed to "provide a brief measure of cognitive status in individuals with known cortical impairment." The DRS was developed in the context of the examination of patients with progressive dementia. It was recognized that although most neuropsychological measures can discriminate normal from brain-impaired individuals, there are few measures that can discriminate reliably between different levels of dementia. Most available neuropsychological measures reach "floor effects" and are insensitive to progressive levels of dementia. The DRS was designed specifically to assess that lower level of cognitive function. Therefore, the DRS fills a needed and important niche in the assessment of higher cognitive function.

The DRS was designed to sample a broad range of functions based on clinical observations of the types of deficits observed in patients with dementing illnesses. There are five subscales measuring areas of specific ability including Attention, Initiation/Perseveration, Construction, Conceptualization, and Memory. The items are unevenly distributed among the five scales. The test also yields a summary score that enables users to examine a global level of performance in addition to specific abilities. In contrast to other scales, the broad range of measurement inherent in the DRS (total of 144 points) permits much better assessment and discrimination of different levels of impairment. The instructions for administration and scoring are clear and explicit. In addition, the DRS is structured with "skip patterns" so that satisfactory performance of certain tasks assumes normal performance of subordinate tasks. Therefore, considerable time saving can be achieved in some patients.

As would be expected, and by design, the DRS does not discriminate well at higher levels of performance. However, at the lower end of ability, the DRS is vastly superior to other measurement approaches in the discrimination of different levels of performance. This is based on the intentional structuring of the task to have a low floor effect which permits evaluation of even severely demented patients. This is an important feature in the longitudinal study of patients with progressive dementing disorders.

There have been relatively few studies of the reliability and validity of the DRS. However, those data that are available are very supportive. Split-half reliability and test/retest reliability

greater than .9 have been reported. Further, internal reliability (Cronbach's alpha) of .75 to .95 have been reported in control subjects and groups of mild and moderate dementia. Other validity data have demonstrated the correlation between DRS total scores and cerebral glucose metabolism in patients with Alzheimer's dementia. The demonstration of a relationship between degree of impairment and reduction in cortical glucose metabolism is strong evidence of the validity of the DRS. The one important potential use of the DRS relates to the differential diagnosis of dementia and depression. In this context, one study directly examining depressed and demented patients found that none of the depressed patients but 62% of the demented patients obtained scores below an identified cutoff score. This provides further construct validity support for the DRS.

The normative data base for the DRS is relatively weak. The largest control sample reported in the manual consists of 85 community living subjects between the ages of 65 and 81. Table 2 in the manual (p. 20) contains the actual frequency distributions of performance for the total DRS score as well as each of the subscales. Cutoff scores are proposed based on criteria of two standard deviations below the mean of the control subjects. The manual also presents means and standard deviations as well as normalized T-scores for a group of 30 dementia patients. Therefore, the manual provides the basis for comparison of an individual patient's performance with both a normal control group and a dementia group. Users of the DRS should be aware the percentiles and T-scores presented in Table 4 are in reference to a dementia population. Users who are interested in comparing the performance of an individual patient with a normal group can compute mean standard deviations and T-scores based on the frequency distribution presented in Table 2.

In summary, the DRS was developed to discriminate among individuals at the low end of the performance range. As such, the DRS is intended to represent an anchor point in the continuum of neuropsychological examination techniques. The DRS examines a broad range of functions and generates a wide range of scores. These clear strengths allow the DRS to accomplish its intended mission of discriminating between different levels of dementia. The DRS is the best measure of its kind and is strongly recommended for clinical and research evaluations designed to examine or differentiate among patients with various dementing disorders.

Review of the Dementia Rating Scale by JULIAN FABRY, Counseling Psychologist, Myers Rehabilitation Institute, Omaha, NE:

The Dementia Rating Scale (DRS) is a brief measure of cognitive status for individuals with known cortical impairment, particularly Senile Dementia, Alzheimer's Type. It was designed to measure the progression of behaviorial, neuropathological, and cognitive decline. The author has reported the DRS is sensitive to the differences at the lower end of functioning but it will not detect impaired cognitive ability in individuals who function within the average range of intellectual potential.

The assessment consists of 36 tasks subdivided into 5 subscales: (*a*) Attention (8 items), (*b*) Initiation/Perseveration (11 items), (*c*) Construction (6 items), (*d*) Conceptualization (6 items), and (*e*) Memory (5 items).

The tasks were derived from clinical procedures and what the author described as traditional assessment methods. They are presented in a fixed order with the most difficult item (within each subscale) presented first. If the person being examined passes the first item or two, credit is given for the remaining tasks (i.e., items). The examiner can then move to the next subscale, thereby shortening the total testing time. It would appear the DRS is easily administered and scored. It is portable and can be given in an office, in an examining room, or at bedside.

The Dementia Rating Scale consists of a technical manual, booklet of stimulus cards, and individual scoring form. The booklet containing the stimulus cards is used to complete several of the construction and memory tasks contained within the assessment. The manual contains four chapters: (*a*) Introduction, (*b*) Administration and Scoring, (*c*) Interpretation, and (*d*) Development and Validation of the procedure. The information contained in the manual is easily accessed and it is clearly written.

The DRS individual scoring form should assist the examiner in administering, scoring, and interpreting the assessment. Most of the instructions contained within the scoring form

make the administration easy to accomplish even without the use of the manual. Subscale raw scores are calculated by summing the task scores under each section. These scores can then be transferred to the front page of the form to a scoring grid. The grid provides for the raw score, cutoff scores, percentile, and *T* scores using the Senile Dementia, Alzheimer's Type normative sample.

Norms are presented in chapter 3 of the manual. Cutoff scores for each of the subscales as well as the total score were derived from 85 normal elderly subjects ranging in age from 65 to 81. The test performance of 30 Senile Dementia, Alzheimer's Type patients is also available.

As was previously indicated, specific test administrative instructions are contained in the manual and on the individual scoring form. The criteria for correct responses is available only in the manual. The author suggests practicing both the administration and scoring procedures prior to administration. The instructions to the patients can be repeated except for the attention tasks. Points are awarded for the correct response on the various tasks. The author maintains a liberal attitude toward scoring in general.

Test-retest correlations for a sample of Alzheimer patients range from .94 for the Conceptualization subscale to .61 for the Attention subscale. A coefficient of .97 was calculated for the total score.

On the basis of the total score, 62 percent of demented patients were correctly classified, whereas no depressed patients were found to have a score below the cutoff for cognitive impairment. The author reports a study that suggests the Initiation/Perseveration subscale, which is the longest subscale, differentiates controls from those with mild dementia. Apparently all scales differentiated mild from moderately demented subjects under study. Albert et al. (1986) reported significant negative correlations between fluid volume in the lateral ventricle of the brain and the Initiation subtest score, as well as the total score on the Dementia Rating Scale for senile Alzheimer's patients.

Some criticism can be made regarding the composition of each of the scales. For example, the Initiation/Perseveration subscale contains questions that deal with language, movement, and drawing. The scale seems heavily weighted

with naming objects and articulating consonants, compared to drawing designs and figures
and making alternative hand movements. Actual perseverations within the context of these
tasks is not accounted for in the scoring.
Individuals suffering from dysnomia, apraxia,
lack of visual synthesis, and/or memory deficits
could have problems responding to the items
within this particular scale, thereby giving the
impression of having difficulty initiating or
perseverating. For example, a person with
apraxia will not initiate, thereby earning a poor
score. In addition, someone with frontal lobe
deficits and possible memory deficits may
perseverate.

Other criticisms center on having only limited information regarding internal consistency
coefficients for the scale and the small number
of subjects used in many of the studies. The
Dementia Rating Scale does warrant further
research use with Alzheimer's patients, especially longitudinal research in order to continue in
its development, and to establish both its
validity as a diagnostic device and the reliabilities associated with its structure and its administration.

REVIEWER'S REFERENCE

Albert, M., Naeser, M., Duffy, F., & McNulty, G. (1986).
CT and EEG validators for Alzheimer's disease. In L. Poon
(Ed.), *Clinical memory assessment of older adults.* Washington, DC:
American Psychological Association.

[20]
Descriptive Tests of Language Skills.
Purpose: "To help college teachers assign entering
students to appropriate English courses, identify
students who may need special assistance in
particular aspects of reading and language use before
undertaking college-level work, tailor instruction in
reading and composition to individual student
needs, and plan instruction for classes or groups of
students."
Population: Beginning students in two- and four-
year institutions.
Publication Dates: 1978–88.
Acronym: DTLS.
Administration: Group.
Price Data, 1989: $.25 per student guide (16
pages); $.25 per score interpretation (4 pages);
$2.50 per user's guide (first copy free, 34 pages);
$7.50 per specimen set.
Comments: Revised edition; tests may be used
independently or in combination with other tests in
the series.
Author: The College Board.
Publisher: The College Board.

a) READING COMPREHENSION.
Scores, 4: Identifying Word and/or Phrase
Meaning Through Context, Understanding
Literal and Interpretive Meaning, Understanding
Writers' Assumptions/Opinions and Tone, Total.
Price Data: $3 per reusable test booklet
(minimum order of 25, '88, 12 pages); $.25 per
optional essay booklet (minimum order of 25, 7
pages); $.95 per self-scoring answer sheet
(minimum order of 25, 2 pages); $1 per
instructor's guide (first copy free, 43 pages); $.50
per scoring guide for writing sample (20 pages).
Time: 45(50) minutes; 50(55) minutes for
optional essay section.
b) CRITICAL REASONING.
Scores, 4: Interpreting Information, Using Information Appropriately, Evaluating Information,
Total.
Price Data: $.25 per essay booklet (minimum
order of 25, 4 pages); $1 per instructor's guide
(27 pages); $.50 per scoring guide for writing
sample (16 pages); other price data same as *a.*
Time: Same as *a.*
c) CONVENTIONS OF WRITTEN ENGLISH.
Scores, 4: Maintaining Consistency, Using
Standard Forms, Connecting Ideas Appropriately,
Total.
Price Data: $3 per reusable test booklet
(minimum order of 25, '88, 8 pages); $.25 per
essay booklet (minimum order of 25, '88, 8
pages); $1 per instructor's guide (41 pages); $.50
per scoring guide for writing sample (11 pages);
other price data same as *a.*
Time: 60(70) minutes for entire test; 35(40)
minutes for multiple-choice section; 25(30)
minutes for essay section.
d) SENTENCE STRUCTURE.
Scores, 4: Using Complete Sentences, Relating
Ideas in Sentences Logically, Making Meaning
Clear, Total.
Price Data: $3 per reusable test booklet ('88, 8
pages); $.95 per self-scoring answer sheet (2
pages); $1 per instructor's guide (39 pages).
Time: 30(35) minutes.
Cross References: See T3:685 (1 reference).

TEST REFERENCES

1. Boyle, G. J., Start, B., & Hall, E. J. (1989). Prediction of
academic achievement using the School Motivation Analysis
Test. *British Journal of Educational Psychology, 59,* 92-99.

*Review of the Descriptive Tests of Language
Skills by FRANCIS X. ARCHAMBAULT, JR.,
Professor of Educational Psychology and Depart-
ment Head, The University of Connecticut, Storrs,
CT:*

The Descriptive Tests of Language Skills
(DTLS) were developed in 1978 to help
college teachers and administrators assess the

needs of entering college students. The tests were updated in 1988 to reflect The College Board's Basic Academic Competencies, a set of skills that several hundred experts determined students needed to succeed in college. The six fundamental skills that comprise the Basic Academic Competencies are reading, writing, reasoning, speaking and listening, mathematics, and studying. The DTLS assesses the first three of these skill areas with four multiple-choice tests: (*a*) Reading Comprehension, (*b*) Critical Reasoning, (*c*) Sentence Structure, and (*d*) Conventions of Written English. Optional writing samples are also available, two for the Reading Comprehension test, two for the Critical Reasoning test, and two for either the Conventions of Written English test or the Sentence Structure test.

The multiple-choice tests are easy to administer and generally interesting to take. The essays also deal with interesting subject matter, but the Reading Comprehension and Critical Reasoning essays present activities that may be unfamiliar to some students. For the former, respondents must complete a prewriting exercise; for the latter, students must evaluate two statements or positions and compare them using certain specified criteria. Nonetheless, the competencies measured by the essays are important to success in college. Moreover, the well-written Student Guide gives examples of the questions, thereby eliminating, or at least reducing, a possible novelty effect.

A guide for interpreting test scores is also available for students. Because they can score their own exams, this is a useful aid. Also useful are the Instructors' Guides for each skill area and the Scoring Guides for each of the three types of essays. The Instructors' Guides provide good overviews of the Basic Academic Competencies measured by the test, as well as a good description of the tests themselves and the meaning of test scores. More importantly, they provide very good advice and strategies for remediating deficiencies uncovered by the tests. For example, the Reading Comprehension Guide provides an interview technique for determining a student's level of metacognitive awareness, a reading/study strategy and suggestions for helping students internalize it, and a set of sample lessons in areas such as identifying word meaning through context and understanding literal and interpretive meaning. The man-

uals are quick to point out that they are just guides for teachers to construct their own lessons and strategies, but they are very good. Likewise, although the Scoring Guides are not meant to be prescriptive, they provide sound advice and solid strategies for rating the essays. They also provide details on how one might have the essays scored through the Educational Testing Service, should that option be preferred.

It is clear that a great deal of work has gone into the development of the DTLS and that the tests are likely to be useful to a number of institutions. It is also clear from the User's Guide, which provides what little technical information is available on the tests, that much more work needs to be done. At this writing, only one of the two forms of the multiple-choice tests is available, but it is expected the alternate forms will be available soon. Some normative data, such as means, standard deviations, and scaled scores, are available, but these are based on relatively small samples. Moreover, there is no discussion of how the colleges participating in the standardization sample were selected, and no information on the ability levels of the students taking the tests. Perhaps because sound normative data are lacking, the authors suggest institutions develop their own norms, including cutoff scores for assigning students to different categories of instruction. Although some institutions may prefer this approach, it is hoped the authors will also provide normative data in the future, preferably separately for 2-year and 4-year institutions.

At present, only internal consistency measures of reliability are available for the multiple-choice tests. The coefficients of .88 for both Reading Comprehension and Conventions of Written English, .86 for Sentence Structure, and .78 for Critical Reasoning are within acceptable ranges, as are the standard errors of measurement. The same does not appear to be true, however, for the subscores, or cluster scores as they are called by the authors. As a result, caution must be exercised in interpreting these scores.

In addition to internal consistency estimates, the authors also plan to provide stability coefficients for the separate forms, as well as stability and equivalence measures across forms. These data will be useful in assessing the quality of the tests. It will also be informative to have data on the degree of overlap among the tests. It appears from the items that some redundancy may exist. Also desirable will be correlations between DTLS scores and measures such as the Scholastic Aptitude Test or the Academic Tests of the ACT Assessment because some of the information available from the DTLS may be available from these other measures. Some predictive validity data also should be provided.

In summary, the Descriptive Tests of Language Skills may be a valuable resource for institutions wishing to assess the needs of incoming students for planning, placement, and remediation purposes. Before these tests can be fully recommended, however, more technical information must be provided. Even without this information, some institutions may be interested in using these instruments with an eye toward determining how they perform at their location.

[21]
Draw A Person: A Quantitative Scoring System.

Purpose: "To meet the need for a modernized, recently normed, and objective scoring system to be applied to human figure drawings produced by children and adolescents."
Population: Ages 5–17.
Publication Date: 1988.
Acronym: DAP.
Scores, 4: Man, Woman, Self, Total.
Administration: Group or individual.
Price Data, 1989: $59 per complete kit including 25 student record/response forms, scoring chart, and manual ('88, 100 pages); $40 per scoring chart and manual; $19 per 25 student record/response forms.
Time: 15(25) minutes.
Author: Jack A. Naglieri.
Publisher: The Psychological Corporation.

Review of the Draw A Person: A Quantitative Scoring System by MERITH COSDEN, Assistant Professor of Education, University of California, Santa Barbara, CA:

The Draw A Person (DAP) is a revision of the popular Goodenough-Harris Drawing Test (Harris, 1963; 9:441), which was itself a revision of Goodenough's Draw-A-Man Test published in 1926. Harris adapted the original test by adding a drawing of a woman and a self-drawing to the drawing of a man, developing a more objective coding system, obtaining a nationally representative normative sample,

expanding the age range of the normative group, and replacing the ratio IQ used to evaluate performance with a deviation IQ. One prescient reviewer (Dunn, 1972) predicted the Harris revision would add 20 years to the life of the Goodenough procedure. Indeed, over 25 years have elapsed between the Harris revision and the current one.

The manual states the DAP was developed in response to criticisms of the Goodenough-Harris test. The following changes from the Goodenough-Harris system are reported: use of smaller (half-year and quarter-year) norm intervals, development of a more recent standardization sample, reduction in the ambiguity of the Goodenough-Harris scoring criteria, and development of norms for the self-drawing to permit calculation of a composite (man, woman, self) standard score. Although the value of updating the standardization sample and using smaller norm intervals is evident, the effects of the other changes on the utility of the test are less clear.

The changes to the scoring system are perhaps the most difficult to evaluate. The criteria used to score the DAP differ from those of the Goodenough-Harris, as do the total number of items for which one can gain credit. Although the manual describes the conceptualization of the DAP scoring system in some detail, its relationship to the Harris system is not addressed. This is surprising, as the DAP is promoted as a revision of the earlier test. It appears, however, the DAP scoring system was developed independently and without consideration of the Harris system. Nevertheless, the manual reports correlations between the two systems that range from .84 to .87. Further, the relationship between the two scoring systems and other measures of cognitive functioning appears similar. The advantage of one set of scoring criteria over another has not been demonstrated empirically.

Some internal problems with the DAP scoring system are apparent. Although the standardization sample was expanded to include children from ages 5 to 18, the system does not differentiate scores equally well for children at each age. Scores at quarter-year intervals could be developed only for children from ages 5 to 8-11, while half-year intervals could be obtained for 9- and 10-year-olds. For ages 11–18, mean scores on the DAP were too similar to provide separate age norms, so their scores are grouped together. The Goodenough-Harris system, on the other hand, yields progressively increasing raw scores for children at yearly intervals from age 5 to 15. Given the low age ceiling in the DAP scoring system, its utility as a measure of cognitive functioning for children over age 11 should be questioned.

The major weakness of this test, however, is the limited scope of its revision. The DAP follows the basic structure of the Goodenough-Harris test without substantively questioning its content or purpose. For example, the DAP adopts the Goodenough-Harris' use of three figures: drawings of the man, woman, and self. The DAP, in fact, reifies what was the experimental, auxiliary use of the self-drawing in the Goodenough-Harris test; in the DAP, all three figures are scored by the same criteria and summed to provide a composite score. What is missing in the manual is the rationale for the use of these particular three drawings. Why not rely on only one or two drawings? Is it essential that the drawings be of a man, woman, and self? We may assume the author of the test was interested in obtaining several samples of behavior in order to increase the reliability of the test results. However, one still needs to question the selection of these particular samples of behavior, and whether other samples (e.g., two drawings of a man; one of a man and one of a woman) would provide more accurate or reliable information. The lack of theoretical or empirical support for the structure of the test is troublesome.

The use of the three-figure composite score is supported only partly by the psychometric data presented in the manual. Internal consistency coefficients (coefficient alphas) for the individual drawings are lower (ranging from .56 to .78) than those for the composite score (.83 to .89). Interrater reliabilities are high for individual as well as composite scores (.86 to .95) and are comparable to those obtained for the Goodenough-Harris system.

Test-retest reliabilities are less impressive, however. The major study presented in the manual was conducted on a sample of 112 students over a 4-week period. Mean reliability coefficients were .74 for the composite score, .70 for the man, .65 for the woman, and .58 for the self-drawing. Examination of the reliability coefficients as a function of grade level, how-

ever, found some of the self-drawing coefficients strikingly low (.30 for sixth graders and .21 for seventh graders). Thus, one can question the inclusion of the self-drawing in the composite score on both psychometric and conceptual grounds. Given the self-drawing's intended experimental use on the Goodenough-Harris test, and the lack of a validated study to support its relationship to other measures of cognitive functioning, the nature of its contribution to a composite score warrants further study.

The validity of the DAP as a "nonverbal measure of ability" is a fundamental concern. The validity data presented in the manual are similar to those associated with the Harris scoring system: DAP scores increase as the child gets older, reflecting the effects of development on performance, and statistically significant correlations are obtained between the DAP and other measures of intellectual functioning. The manual reports that correlations between the DAP and the Matrix Analogies Test—Short Form (MAT-SF) and the Multilevel Academic Survey Test (MAST) range from .17 to .31. Although statistically significant, these correlations indicate the DAP accounts for only a small portion of the variance in the other cognitive tests. Similar correlations are obtained between the Goodenough-Harris system and the MAST and MAT-SF; this is not surprising, given the relatively high correlations between scores obtained from the DAP and Goodenough-Harris tests. These data suggest the two scoring systems are sampling similar cognitive skills, but that these skills vary in substantive ways from those sampled by other tests of cognitive functioning.

There is, in fact, a vast literature on the use of figure drawings for both emotional and intellectual assessment. The results of the studies on ability assessment have been inconclusive. Some have demonstrated statistically significant, if functionally low, relationships between figure drawings and other measures of ability, although others have found no relationship between children's drawings and other measures of cognitive performance. What is striking in the literature is the lack of attention given to defining the conditions under which one would select drawings to assess intellectual functioning over other available assessment devices. The DAP manual suggests the test may be particularly useful for some special populations. Included in this list are children with language impairments, individuals from minority cultures (particularly American Indians), and individuals with motor problems (including cerebral palsy) as the child is credited for the inclusion of body parts but not penalized for the precision of the drawings. The manual does not provide any data, however, to support these contentions. Normative data for individuals from the aforementioned special groups are not readily available. The manual provides normative data on two ethnic-minority groups, Blacks and Hispanics; the mean scores of these groups do not significantly differ from those of the rest of the sample. These data are suggestive, but the hypothesized role of the DAP as an ability assessment device for special populations remains unsubstantiated.

It is my feeling that despite the lack of "hard" data to support their use, figure drawings will continue to be a popular part of many assessment batteries. In addition to the ease with which they can be administered, drawings provide the clinician with a nonthreatening way to obtain information that is intuitively very rich. In fact, the implicit rationale for the use of the three figures in the DAP is that these drawings can serve double duty in a test battery; that is, they can be used for projective purposes as well as for ascertaining the child's cognitive abilities. The utility of the test for assessing ability, however, remains a question. The conditions under which figure drawings should be preferred over other tests of ability have neither been well defined nor empirically validated.

In sum, the major advantage of the DAP over the Goodenough-Harris system is that it uses a more recent normative sample. The advantage of one set of scoring criteria over the other has not yet been determined, and the high correlations between the two systems add to the ambiguity in choosing between them. Although the DAP appears to be as good an assessment tool as the Goodenough-Harris, it is unfortunate the revision stays so close to its predecessor. Dunn (1972) criticized the Goodenough-Harris manual for its limited discussion of the theoretical relevance of the Draw-A-Man test and its implications for future conceptualizations of intelligence. One finds similar flaws in the presentation of the DAP. Further theoretical and empirical analysis of the role of figure drawing in the assessment of ability is needed to make this test a more useful tool.

REVIEWER'S REFERENCES

Harris, D. (1963). *Children's drawings as measures of intellectual maturity.* New York: Harcourt, Brace & World.
Dunn, J. (1972). [Review of the Goodenough-Harris Drawing Test.] In O. K. Buros (Ed.), *The seventh mental measurements yearbook* (pp. 671-672). Highland Park, NJ: The Gryphon Press.

Review of the Draw A Person: A Quantitative Scoring System by W. GRANT WILLIS, Associate Professor of Psychology, University of Rhode Island, Kingston, RI:

The Draw A Person: A Quantitative Scoring System (DAP) is a carefully constructed and well-normed procedure that should prove useful in accomplishing its goal of providing a screening measure of nonverbal ability. The examinee is required to produce time-limited (i.e., 5 minutes) pencil drawings of three pictures (man, woman, and self) on separate pages of a response form. Instructions are provided for both individual and group administration. The DAP is intended for ages 5 through 17 years, but it does not provide enough discriminative power at the upper-age ranges to be of much utility for adolescents. The maximum age-equivalent score reported for the DAP is 11 years, which "results from a ceiling effect at the upper age levels of the normative sample" (p. 63); standard-score equivalents ($M = 100$, $SD = 15$) of raw scores are collapsed across the 11- through 17-year-old age range.

The quantitative scoring system is unambiguous and the record form is clearly organized along 14 criteria. High levels of interrater reliability ($rs = .86$ to $.95$), intrarater reliability ($rs = .89$ to $.97$), interrater agreement (91% to 94%), and intrarater agreement (94% to 96%) are reported in the test manual. The manual includes an excellent chapter on the scoring system, which provides explicit procedures, practice exercises, competency criteria, and (if needed) even remedial exercises.

The test manual is comprehensive and clearly organized. In addition to material on the scoring system, introductory (e.g., history, goals, appropriateness, user qualifications), test development and standardization, statistical properties, administration and scoring, and interpretation sections are included. The manual provides sufficient information for qualified users to evaluate the appropriateness and technical adequacy of the DAP.

The standardization sample is sufficiently large ($N = 2{,}622$) to ensure stability of the norms. Between 99 and 267 participants were included at each of 13 one-year age levels from 5 through 17 years stratified according to age, gender, racial, ethnic, and geographical proportions documented by 1980 U.S. Census data. Socioeconomic indicators of annual income and occupational type, documented on a district-wide basis, also closely matched 1980 U.S. Census data. Finally, community size was documented in the standardization sample as well. No gender differences were found for raw scores, and therefore norms were collapsed across gender. Age-related changes in raw scores showed the most rapid increase between 5 and 9 years, and then increased less rapidly. Thus, norms were established for quarter-year intervals for 5- through 8-year-olds, half-year intervals for 9- and 10-year-olds, and, as noted, one combined interval for the remaining 11- through 17-year-olds (for a total of 21 age intervals). Naglieri (p. 11) noted that "Because the raw score distributions are approximately symmetrical at all ages, they were not normalized," and argued that obtained standard scores closely matched those that would have resulted from a normalizing procedure. It is unfortunate no data were presented to support this claim, because the symmetry of a distribution of scores is unrelated to its kurtosis. This is an isolated weakness, however, in an otherwise exemplary test manual. Proper interpretation of standard scores, of course, rests on the assumption that those scores are based on a normal distribution; users of the DAP must trust this indeed is the case.

The internal consistency of DAP scores is good (median $r = .86$ for Total scores across the 13 one-year age groups in the standardization sample), and standard errors of measurement range from 5 to slightly over 6 standard score units. The stability of DAP scores was assessed for 112 individuals in one geographic region of the standardization sample. The mean test-retest coefficient for Total scores, computed over a 4-week interval for seven separate age levels (i.e., Grades 1 through 7) was .74. The lowest coefficient was reported at Grade 7 ($r = .60$) and the highest at Grade 4 ($r = .89$). Clearly, additional stability data should be collected, but DAP Total scores show promise of adequate stability for screening purposes, at least during childhood.

The construct and concurrent validity studies reported in the manual also show promise for the validity of the DAP Total score as a screening measure during childhood. Here, age-related increases in total raw scores were found in the standardization sample from ages 5 through 11, but not thereafter. DAP Total standard scores showed a fairly high correlation ($r = .87$) with the sum of the Man, Woman, and Self standard scores from the Goodenough-Harris for 100 9-year-olds, and, in other samples, low to moderate correlations with matrix analogies (r s $= .27$ and $.31$), reading ($r = .24$), and math ($r = .21$) tests. In addition to the analysis of gender differences, DAP total standard scores were compared to investigate potential Black/White and Hispanic/non-Hispanic differences. Results suggested that scores are unlikely to be influenced by these factors.

In summary, the recently published DAP is a carefully developed and well-described nonverbal screening test of general ability. Evidence for the reliability and validity of the standard scores is accruing, and although inadequate for individual diagnosis, is promising as a screening tool. The normative sample is stable and representative of 1980 U.S. Census data. The scoring system and test manual are clear. Results do not seem to be influenced by cultural (Hispanic/non-Hispanic) or racial (Black/White) factors. I would recommend its use through about age 11 for the purposes intended over other scoring systems, such as the Goodenough-Harris. As would be expected, use of the Total score is associated with substantially improved reliability relative to the Self, Man, or Woman drawings when scored separately. Thus, especially considering the minimal increase in administration time for the three drawings rather than only one, examiners should administer the DAP in its entirety. Finally, I would caution potential users that the DAP was neither intended nor validated as a personality measure, and it clearly should not be used for this purpose.

[22]

Early Mathematics Diagnostic Kit.

Purpose: "To provide the teacher with an effective means of diagnosing early difficulties in the learning of mathematics."

Population: Ages 4–8.

Publication Dates: 1977–87.
Acronym: EMDK.
Scores: 10 areas: Number, Shape, Representation, Length, Weight, Capacity, Memory, Money, Time, Foundation.
Administration: Individual.
Price Data, 1989: £63.25 per complete kit including 25 record booklets, book of test items, set of coloured cubes, set of 3 small boxes, and manual ('87, 32 pages); £6.35 per 10 record forms; £8.05 per manual.
Time: 30(35) minutes.
Comments: Item checklist.
Authors: David Lumb and Margaret Lumb.
Publisher: NFER-Nelson Publishing Co., Ltd. [England].

Review of the Early Mathematics Diagnostic Kit by JOHN M. ENGER, Professor of Education, Arkansas State University, State University, AR:

As evident from the price given in pounds, the Early Mathematics Diagnostic Kit (EMDK) is a British product. It was developed and field tested in England over a number of years. The administration of the EMDK to a young child, aged 4 to 8 years, is similar to the administration of an individualized IQ test. The intent, however, is to identify any deficiencies in mathematics in 10 different areas.

THE MANUAL. A 28-page instruction manual accompanies the EMDK. Background information about the test and administration procedures are included in the manual. It is imperative the user of the EMDK be well versed on the procedures covered in the manual prior to administering the instrument to a young child. These procedures are quite explicit and are explained very well. However, the American reader will sense a different culture base inherent throughout the manual in both the examples used (e.g., pence for coins) and the spellings of some words (e.g., colour, metre, programme).

In the manual, each of the 110 items of the EMDK is classified into 1 of 10 content areas. A table of specifications is not provided, so weights by content areas are not obvious to the reader. In constructing a table of specifications for the EMDK, the user will find a heavy representation on numbers (47 of 110 items, or 43 percent), yet there are fewer than 10 items in each of six content areas.

Information on reliability, validity, and normative data are scant in contrast to the recommendations of information for the publisher to provide given in the 1985 *Standards for Educational and Psychological Testing* (AERA, APA, & NCME). Validity is addressed in reporting the development of the instrument by groups of teachers in northeast England over a period of 7 years. Specific procedures and numbers of teachers involved in the development are not given.

A single reliability exercise was reported in which the EMDK was administered to 40 boys and 40 girls aged 7–8 who were judged by their teachers to have mastered the objectives covered by the EMDK. The items were administered by 20 individuals, and each child took a single administration of the instrument. The intent of this investigation was to examine the clarity of the items. This exercise resulted in the elimination of two of the original 112 items used in the instrument. Ten or more of the children failed these items. It is suggested in the manual that any normative data would be inappropriate because the instrument is intended only for those perceived to have deficiencies in mathematics.

THE INSTRUMENT. All of the 110 items or a subset of the items in the EMDK are presented by the examiner to a young child, aged 4 to 8. A convenient presentation is made through a loosely bound book, which lies flat, showing one item per page. A handy eight-page score sheet is kept by the examiner to record if the child's response to an item is correct or incorrect. If the child makes no response, the box is left blank.

Because the instrument is intended to be administered to young children and the children will be touching the pages of the test booklet, the pages should probably be plastic coated. In its present form, the pages are sturdy, but will soil with use. The cardboard boxes that accompany the instrument are loosely constructed and tend to come apart with use.

In administering the EMDK, the user will note little difference from administering an individual IQ test. Many of the items parallel the items and procedures found in commonly used intelligence tests, such as the WISC-R, the WPPSI, the WAIS-R, the Stanford-Binet, and the KABC. However, no reference is made to these or other tests.

Little information is given in the manual to guide the user in interpreting the child's performance. Learning difficulties are said to be identified by responses to the individual items. It is noted that a child's teacher would be in the best position to contrast achievement with expectations, based upon what had been covered in class.

USE OF EMDK RESULTS. In addition to the examination, the EMDK includes information on follow-up activities for the mathematics learning difficulties identified by the examination. More than half of the manual presents follow-up activities that correspond to the topics covered by various item groupings. Suggested follow-up activities are listed by referencing pages in 13 primarily British commercial textbooks.

In the suggested activities section, the items are grouped as 24 subtests containing from one to 26 items. Sixteen of the 24 subtests contain three or fewer items. A checklist of commonly taught mathematical topics is appended. Here, key concepts (called items) are grouped into eight content areas. Teachers are advised to record (*a*) when the student is introduced to the item, (*b*) when further involvement occurs with the item, and (*c*) when the item is consolidated (mastered).

OVERALL EVALUATION. By all appearances, the content and administration procedures of the EMDK model many of the commonly used individual IQ tests. In interpreting a child's performance on the EMDK, the user is advised to examine responses to individual items to determine deficiencies in mathematics achievement. The user could use subtests from IQ tests in much the same manner.

In the EMDK the test items are classified by topic and referenced to pages in various British commercial textbooks. To be applicable in American education, some items and the references should be changed.

For a young child suspected of having learning difficulties in mathematics, the EMDK would provide a systematic evaluation of performance on specific items. In writing an individualized education plan (IEP), commonly used in special education, the EMDK might be quite useful.

REVIEWER'S REFERENCE

American Educational Research Association, American Psychological Association, & National Council on Measurement in Education. (1985). *Standards for educational and psychological testing*. Washington, DC: American Psychological Association, Inc.

Review of the Early Mathematics Diagnostic Kit by G. MICHAEL POTEAT, Assistant Professor of Psychology, East Carolina University, Greenville, NC:

The Early Mathematics Diagnostic Kit (EMDK) was designed as part of a curriculum package. It was developed in England and is designed for use with children from 4 to 8 years of age who are experiencing learning difficulties in mathematics. The kit consists of a spiral-bound booklet of test items, a handbook (28 pages), test record booklets, a box of small cubes, and three small boxes of identical size and shape but of different weights. A pencil and sheet of paper for the child to make written responses are also required.

The EMDK has 110 items; all are contained in the test booklet. The spiral-bound booklet is placed between the child and the examiner and all of the items are presented by simply turning the page. The examiner's inquiry is printed on the page opposite the test item and the test materials and inquiries are oriented toward the child and examiner respectively. The instrument is designed to be administered not only by psychologists but by teachers and other school staff without training in assessment. Administration is relatively straightforward but is hampered by directions that are occasionally too abbreviated. The record booklet does not provide spaces for recording responses to all of the questions contained in the test booklet, nor is a system provided for grouping or summarizing performance in the variety of areas assessed. No guidelines are provided for where to start and stop administering items, and the handbook states only that the test may be administered in its entirety or as a collection of shorter subtests. The test-item hierarchy is ineffective in structuring the items in order of difficulty (e.g., Item 55 asks which of two fishes is smaller, whereas Item 50 requires the construction of sets of 2, 5, and 9 blocks).

The 110 items are inequitably divided into 10 areas of mathematics: Number (47 items), Shape (8 items), Representation (1 item), Length (11 items), Weight (2 items), Capacity (5 items), Memory (3 items), Money (11 items), Time (9 items), and Foundation (15 items). The content coverage of the instrument is consequently disparate. The Number area (the content areas are poorly defined by the authors) consists of items measuring everything from determining if there are equal numbers of knives and forks in a picture to naming two-digit numerals. All the mathematical operations (e.g., multiplication and addition) are also classified as in the Number area. The Foundation area includes several items reminiscent of the picture vocabulary on the Stanford-Binet. For the Memory area, a measure of "short-term" memory (Item 49) is obtained by asking the child what the two children shown in the Item 5 picture were doing. However, on Item 110 the same question is construed as a measure of "delayed recall." The 11 Money items are inappropriate for use in U.S. schools because they all involve British coins. The EMDK does contain some unusual items of potential value (e.g., weight discrimination). Still, no rationale for the selection and structure of the test content is given, although an appendix does contain a list of mathematical topics assigned to 8 of the 10 categories.

Almost no technical information is provided for the EMDK. The technical information consists of the report that the majority of a group of 80 seven- and eight-year-old boys and girls identified as not having problems in mathematics passed most of the items included on the instrument. No attempt to measure reliability and validity is mentioned. There is no evidence the information provided by the instrument is of any additional value other than that derived from the informal observations of teachers. No attempt is made to empirically link failure on any item or group of items to particular problems in mathematics, and only the most cursory attempt is made at the conjectural linking of test and classroom performance.

The EMDK cannot be considered to meet even the most minimal criteria for an educational test. No formal content analysis, or even a rationale, is provided. No data on reliability, validity, or normative performance are presented. The authors also state that attempts to norm reference the instrument are considered inappropriate. To be fair, the authors generally avoid the use of the word "test," referring to the materials as a "kit." Nonetheless, it is apparent the instrument is designed as a diagnostic, criterion-referenced measure. An essential requirement for any criterion-referenced measure is a well-defined domain of knowledge or skills to be assessed. Even this

most basic requirement has not been achieved. The classroom teacher might find some of the information provided by the EMDK useful, but this information could be collected less expensively using informal materials. Also, several other, better, instruments are available. These include the KeyMath Revised: A Diagnostic Inventory of Essential Mathematics and the Sequential Assessment of Mathematics Inventories. The EMDK can be recommended only as a supplemental instrument of limited value. It would probably be of most interest to researchers involved in the assessment and teaching of mathematics to young children.

[23]
Educational Leadership Practices Inventory.
Purpose: Reflects Ideal versus Actual attitudes for individual and group teaching style patterns.
Population: Teachers and administrators.
Publication Dates: 1955–79.
Acronym: ELPI.
Scores, 2: Ideal, Actual.
Administration: Group.
Price Data, 1988: $12.75 per specimen set including reusable test booklet, 25 self-scoring answer sheets, and manual ('67, 14 pages).
Time: (30–45) minutes.
Comments: Computer form available.
Authors: Charles W. Nelson and Jasper J. Valenti (inventory).
Publisher: Management Research Associates.

Review of the Educational Leadership Practices Inventory by ERNEST J. KOZMA, Professor of Education, Clemson University, Clemson, SC:
The Educational Leadership Practices Inventory is a self-scored survey consisting of 50 problem situations. Each problem has two practices offered as choices. The respondent must choose the ideal practice and the actual practice. The 50 problem situations are categorized into four styles of leadership. After categorizing the responses, teams of participants are formed to discuss the various categories and leadership styles. Group profiles can be determined and the scores in each area can be compared to a table of ideal scores for various known groups such as police department heads, auto manufacturing organizations, and route sales organizations.

The manual for administration, analysis, and interpretation contains the directions, explanations, and tables for interpretation. No statistical data concerning reliability or validity are included. The tables included in the manual do not have references or statistical explanations. One reference used to show that progress was made by the management of a company using the material was referenced to the years 1954, 1955, and 1956. The manual indicated a copyright date of 1967. The actual survey instrument indicates a revised form made in 1979. Accompanying material and references were all somewhat dated. Most of the sources cited, in the manual and the supportive material provided, were dated prior to 1974. Users of the survey should be cautious concerning the use of the tables and the ideal and actual scores. The material might be used by an effective discussion leader to introduce management development activities, particularly if some of the more recent materials and practices concerning leadership were added.

Review of the Educational Leadership Practices Inventory by DARRELL SABERS, Professor of Educational Psychology, University of Arizona, Tucson, AZ:

The Educational Leadership Practices Inventory (ELPI) is intended for in-service workshops and is not intended to be an instrument for providing assessments of individuals' leadership practices. Any evaluation of the survey based on criteria for tests and inventories will result in an extremely negative summation, especially when there is no evidence available to suggest the scores obtained from the survey are reliable or valid.

Most of the information presented to suggest the system of classifying styles is useful is dated (so dated that a footnote refers to a 1974 article as "recently published"). Some quantitative data supporting the obtained scores are from 1954 training results. These are most certainly not relevant to the 1979 revision. Other data are presented in two tables that might be used with in-service participants, but one cannot determine from reviewed materials where these data were obtained (or whether they are actual scores or examples of score differences). The information regarding reliability and validity is very limited, pertains to judgments made during development of the theory that guided the construction of this survey, and is based on data from a 1949 Ph.D. thesis.

While reading the material for the ELPI, I kept thinking the editors of the *Mental Measurements Yearbook* series must be using me for some experimental purpose. It is difficult to believe anyone would seriously propose the use (much less the purchase) of materials without better documentation. Based on these materials, one cannot judge the appropriateness of the in-service training provided by the authors (or others) who might use these materials. However, unless substantially better materials to support its use are made available to potential consumers, the ELPI cannot be recommended for any assessment purpose.

[24]
Emotional Behavioral Checklist.
Purpose: To assess an individual's overt emotional behavior.
Population: Children and adults.
Publication Date: 1986.
Acronym: EBC.
Scores, 8: Impulsivity-Frustration, Anxiety, Depression-Withdrawal, Socialization, Self-Concept, Aggression, Reality Disorientation, Total EBC.
Administration: Individual.
Manual: No manual.
Price Data, 1988: $10.50 per 25 checklists.
Time: Administration time not reported.
Authors: Jack G. Dial, Carolyn Mezger, Theresa Massey, and Lawrence T. McCarron.
Publisher: McCarron-Dial Systems.

Review of the Emotional Behavioral Checklist by WILLIAM A. STOCK, Professor of Exercise Science, Arizona State University, Tempe, AZ:

The Emotional Behavioral Checklist (EBC) is a 35-item behavior checklist that purports to measure seven factors, each with five items (Frustration-Impulsivity, Anxiety, Depression-Withdrawal, Self-Concept, Socialization, Aggression, and Reality Disorientation). Each of the 35 items can require three ratings. First, each behavior is rated as *definitely not observed* (0), *observed, but inconclusive* (1), or *definitely observed* (2). If an initial rating of 1 or 2 is given for an item, a second rating calls for a judgment as to whether treatment or intervention is or is not needed. Promotional materials claim the EBC may be used in school, rehabilitation, and/or clinical settings. However, technical and psychometric information accompanying the instrument fail to meet minimal standards, and, in this reviewer's opinion, potential users should be extremely cautious about adopting the instrument.

Absent from the documentation provided by the test publisher are (a) a rationale for the measure (including recommended uses and specific cautions against potential misuses); (b) a statement of qualifications required to administer and interpret the instrument; (c) a theoretical framework and definitions for the seven constructs; (d) specifications of observational domains for each construct; (e) descriptions of how behavior observations were selected; and (f) directions guiding judgments of the test user (who rates the client). Further, the evidence for reliability and validity claims seems to be primarily derived from data collected in settings where intervention programs of the test vendor were in operation.

Although recommended for school, clinical, and vocational settings, characteristics of the 567 adults (60% Caucasian, 26% Black, 11% Hispanic, 3% other) who comprise the normative sample do not support this recommendation. The sample is one of convenience and not from a well-specified population. About 40 percent of the sample were characterized as "diagnosed with neuropsychological disabilities (congenital or adventitious brain damage or dysfunction, mental retardation, CP, etc.) and were placed in various rehabilitation work settings." Forty-two further suffered either some or complete visual impairment. Of the 322 remaining individuals in the sample, 195 were visually impaired or blind, and 92 were *nondisabled*. An absence of systematic sampling from educational and clinical populations, and the opportunistic character of the sample with regard to vocational and rehabilitation populations, pose serious threats to inferences drawn from scores obtained from the scale.

Because primary evidence for reliability and validity of the EBC is also derived from this sample, an extremely cautious view on its adoption must be taken. Further, evidence provided for both the reliability and validity of the instrument suffers from several shortcomings. A single reliability estimate, reported for the total score of the EBC, of .83 is derived from a subsample ($N = 100$) of the 245 subjects with neuropsychological and visual impairments. The estimate is obtained by correlating scores obtained from two different raters at an interval of 7–14 days. As there are

identifiable subgroups within this subsample, a portion of the variance attributed to reliability of the instrument may, in fact, be attributed to subgroup mean differences on behaviors rated. The estimate of .83 should be regarded as generous. Further, with respect to reliability, there is an absence of attention to a number of test standards of primary importance. There are no standard errors of measurement reported. There are no separate reliability estimates for the seven purported observational domains comprising the instrument. There are no estimates for the subgroups comprising the sample, nor for populations where the instrument is claimed to be applicable (educational and clinical settings). Information regarding the qualifications, training, and selection of judges is absent. Internal consistency estimates are absent. In short, evidence for reliability is extremely restricted.

Evidence for the validity of the scale is not adequate. There is an absence of evidence for the validity of decisions made on the basis of the EBC in clinical or educational settings. Two of the primary pieces of validity evidence are correlations with two other instruments offered by this test vendor. As the EBC is a shorter version of one of these additional measures, characterizing the reported correlation of .91 as validity evidence stretches the concept of validity too far. Of the other validity evidence reported, a concurrent correlation of .70 between the EBC and placement level in a vocational program suggests the instrument may have applicability in that setting.

In sum, potential users are advised that this instrument falls short of professional standards for educational and psychological testing. Its adoption for clinical and educational settings is not recommended, and its adoption in vocational settings is questionable at present.

Review of the Emotional Behavioral Checklist by HOI K. SUEN, Associate Professor of Educational Psychology, Pennsylvania State University, State College, PA:

The Emotional Behavioral Checklist is a 35-item rating scale. For most items, ratings are to be assigned directly based on overt behaviors of the subject (e.g., "repetitive physical movements," "repeated expressions of worry"). For other items, however, ratings are assigned based on the rater's inference of a subject's covert attributes (e.g., "does not understand impact his/her behavior has on others," "limited self-awareness"). Based on these ratings, a norm-referenced score is derived. Subjects can then be classified as average, below average, or "deficit."

Whereas technical reliability and validity information is available for review, clearly stated explanations of purpose, theoretical background, or scoring scheme are not provided. Consequently, the intended appropriate use of the checklist is not clear. From various documents, the purpose of the checklist has been described as "to assess an individual's overt emotional behavior," "prediction of actual vocational functioning level," a measure of "emotional/behavioral functioning and adaptive behavior," and a substitute for the existing McCarron-Dial System measures of emotional functioning and adaptive behavior. It would be most helpful if the authors could provide clear statements specifying the purpose of the checklist, the intended use, and the situations under which the use of the checklist is appropriate.

SCORING SYSTEM. After ratings are assigned, the total raw score is converted into a standard score or a T-score based on a conversion table. Several problems are noted with the scoring procedure. First, the mean and standard deviation, which are needed to interpret standard scores meaningfully, are not provided. Second, the "T-score" does not appear to be based on the conventional T-score transformation. Specifically, conventional T-scores have a mean of 50 and a standard deviation of 10. This suggests that a score of 50 is average and scores less than 50 are below average. Based on the scoring instruction of the checklist, however, "T-scores" of above 70 are considered "average" and those at or below 70 (or standard scores below 85) are all considered "below average." If this is indeed a conventional T-score, this implies that 95% of the subjects will be considered "below average." Some clarification of this scoring system is needed. Finally, it is suggested in the scoring instructions that standard scores between 70 and 85 (i.e., "T-scores" between 60 and 70) indicate "below average" and standard scores below 70 (i.e., "T-scores" below 60) indicate "deficit" or "significant problem ratings." There is no explanation as to how these cutoff scores were chosen for this classification process. It might be helpful to a consumer if the authors

would present percentile scores in addition to the standard and T-scores.

NORMATIVE SAMPLES. The subjects for the normative samples consisted of 567 adults. Of these 567 subjects, 475 (or 84%) had been diagnosed as neuropsychologically disabled and/or visually impaired, with a mean IQ of 85. All subjects had functioned successfully in community employment situations. From this normative sample, it appears that the Emotional Behavioral Checklist might be intended to be used for subjects with various disabilities. If this is true, it would have been helpful to a consumer had the authors stated clearly as such. The ethnic and gender composition of the normative sample appears to be quite representative. It should be pointed out that 70% of the subjects were from the southwestern United States. Should this instrument be used in other regions of the United States, local norms need to be established. This accentuates the need to clarify the scoring and transformation process so that consumers may establish their own norms when needed.

RELIABILITY. A high estimate of test-retest reliability (.83) with a 7- to 14-day period between the first and the second administration is reported. A crossover method was used to estimate this test-retest reliability. Specifically, a subject was rated by one rater in the first administration and by a different rater in the retest. As a result, the estimate of interrater reliability is embedded in the test-retest reliability estimate. Given this design, the reliability estimate of .83 can be considered excellent. A drawback is the lack of information on the qualifications and training needed for a rater. Perhaps the authors should provide a description of the characteristics of the raters as well as any rater training procedures used in the reliability studies. This would assist the consumer in the choice of raters in order to sustain the high level of score reliability.

VALIDITY. Validity is not an absolute entity. Rather, it is relative to the intended use of an instrument. The scores on a given instrument may be valid for certain uses but not for others. Given that the intended use of this checklist is not clear, it is difficult to judge if sufficient evidence has been derived to indicate the validity of such usage.

As evidence of validity, the authors reported relatively high and statistically significant correlations between scores on the Emotional Behavioral Checklist and various measures of emotional functioning and adaptive behavior in the McCarron-Dial System. This provides good evidence of concurrent validity and indicates that scores on the checklist are a valid substitute for scores attained through the McCarron-Dial System. It also provides very limited evidence of construct validity in interpreting the scores on the checklist as measuring "emotional functioning and adaptive behavior."

It should be noted that the checklist is divided into seven sections with labels of Impulsivity-Frustration, Anxiety, Depression-Withdrawal, and so on. There is no statistical or other systematic evidence that scores from these sections form distinct subscores. For example, there is no evidence that a subject who scores high in the section labelled Impulsivity is different from one who scores high in the section labelled Anxiety. As such, the section scores should be considered convenient groupings of items, but not distinct subscales.

SUMMARY. The major limitation of the Emotional Behavioral Checklist is the lack of information on its intended use and the situations under which its use is appropriate. Without this information, many aspects of the quality of the instrument cannot be judged adequately. Based on the available information, scores on the instrument have an excellent level of reliability. However, the scoring procedure and interpretation need clarifications and justifications. Without a clear intended use, it is difficult to judge the validity of scores from the instrument. Local norms need to be established for uses of this instrument in areas outside of the southwestern region of the United States. In its present form, the Emotional Behavioral Checklist can best be considered experimental. Until the exact intended use of the checklist is clarified, the scoring scheme and rater training requirements clarified, and the classification criteria justified, the checklist is susceptible to misuse and abuse.

[25]
English Language Skills Assessment in a Reading Context.

Purpose: Assesses English language skills "measuring the understanding of meaning in a context, as well as grammatical ability."
Population: Beginning, intermediate, and advanced students of English as a Second Language from upper elementary to college and adult students.
Publication Dates: 1980–84.
Acronym: ELSA.
Administration: Group.
Levels, 3: Beginning, Intermediate, Advanced.
Price Data, 1987: $9.95 per 25 tests, 50 answer sheets, and answer key (specify test/level BC, BN, IC, IN, AN, or AL); $7.95 per 50 answer sheets and keys for use with all forms; $4.50 per technical manual ('81, 37 pages).
Time: (30) minutes per test.
Comments: "Criterion-referenced."
Authors: Cecelia Doherty and Donna Ilyin (technical manual) and others listed below.
Publisher: Newbury House Publishers, Inc.

a) BEGINNING LEVEL.
Scores: 2 tests: Conversation, Narrative.
Comments: Separate answer sheet/practice test for each test.
Authors: Donna Ilyin, Lynn Levy (Conversation test), and Lauri E. Fried Lee (Narrative test).

b) INTERMEDIATE LEVEL.
Comments: Details same as *a* above.

c) ADVANCED LEVEL.
Scores: 2 tests: Narrative, Letter.
Comments: Separate answer sheet/practice test for each test.
Authors: Cecelia Doherty, Donna Ilyin (Narrative test), and Philip Carleton (Letter test).

TEST REFERENCES

1. Spurling, S., & Ilyin, D. (1985). The impact of learner variables on language test performance. *TESOL Quarterly, 19,* 283-301.
2. Mori, C., & Yamada, J. (1988). Copying span as an index of written language ability. *Perceptual and Motor Skills, 66* (2), 375-382.

Review of the English Language Skills Assessment in a Reading Context by LYLE F. BACHMAN, Professor of Applied Linguistics, University of California at Los Angeles, Los Angeles, CA:

The English Language Skills Assessment in a Reading Context (ELSA) was developed for the purpose of placing adult students of English as a Second Language (ESL) into different language ability levels in ESL courses. Tests at three levels (beginning, intermediate, and advanced) are available and all utilize a four-choice, multiple-choice cloze test format. Passages are written to represent typical English conversational and narrative styles. The authors claim that the test is criterion-referenced and that it measures "understanding of meaning in a context" and "grammatical ability."

FEATURES. The ELSA has several desirable features. The test materials have been carefully edited, with reusable test booklets and separate hand-scorable answer sheets that provide clear instructions to test takers. There is a practice test to familiarize students with the multiple-choice cloze format. There are clear directions for the administration and scoring of the test, including scoring stencils. Each test can be administered to a group in about 30 minutes and scored in a few seconds per subject. The Technical Manual provides information on norms and tables for converting raw scores to placement levels based on the levels in the San Francisco Community College District. Discussions of the reliability and validity of the test are also included.

TEST CONSTRUCTION. The content of the ELSA is based on "the ESL structural syllabus curriculum taught in open enrollment adult centers" of the San Francisco Community College District. Two passages—one conversational and one narrative—were written specifically for the ELSA for each of the three levels. These passages were written in such a way that every seventh word was deleted, for a total of 33 deletions per passage. Each deletion is intended to elicit the specific grammatical and semantic features to be measured. These original passages were pretested as open-ended cloze tests with native speakers and students of the same levels of ability as those for which the test is intended. Errors made by students in this pretest were used as distractors for constructing 33-item four-choice multiple-choice cloze tests, which were then administered to a representative sample of ESL students. On the basis of classical item statistics, 25 items for each form were retained and the passages were revised a final time. These revised tests were then used for norming studies to establish cutoff points for placement levels.

VALIDITY. Although the Technical Manual discusses validity, the section headings do not provide accurate indications of the aspects of validity that are discussed, and evidence supporting the recommended interpretations and uses of the ELSA is scant. Under "face validity" (a concept that has long since been abandoned by the measurement profession), the authors make passing reference to what is essentially content validity, by stating that instructors reported that the ELSA "contained material that was taught at corresponding levels of instruction" (Technical Manual, p. 26). In the section entitled "content validity," the authors present evidence that pertains most directly to the predictive utility of the ELSA in placing students, and say virtually nothing about content validity. Evidence that pertains to the predictive utility (validity) of ELSA scores for placement is also presented in a separate section that describes the norming procedures. It would be most helpful if a summary of the curriculum on which the ELSA is based, along with the content specifications for the deletions that were made in the different forms, could be provided here. In this reviewer's opinion, content relevance is a strength of the ELSA, and it is disappointing to see that this is the aspect to which the authors have paid the least attention. The next section, entitled "empirical validity," should more accurately be called "concurrent validity," because it reports the results of studies designed to investigate the correlations among the ELSA and other measures of English language proficiency.

VALIDITY OF SCORE INTERPRETATIONS. Despite the authors' claim that the ELSA measures "understanding of meaning in a context" and "grammatical ability," they cite as a rationale for using the cloze, research that they interpret as supporting the interpretation of cloze test scores as indicators of "global proficiency," rather than of "specific skills or components in isolation" (p. 11). This research indicates that the cloze correlates highly with overall placement batteries, traditional tests of reading comprehension, speaking and listening, dictation, structure, and writing. In the section on "empirical validity," the authors cite studies of their own in which the ELSA correlates highly with a wide variety of language tests, including not only measures of grammatical structure and reading, but of listening. The fact that the cloze in general, and the ELSA in particular, is highly correlated with a wide variety of different types of language tests suggests indeterminacy in the definition of the construct measured by the ELSA, rather than support for the interpretation of scores as indicators of the specific language abilities it is claimed to assess. Furthermore, the authors ignore the considerable research in reading assessment, in which the nature of the constructs measured by the cloze has been controversial. More recent research in foreign language testing challenging the notion of "general language proficiency," which has led many language testers to abandon this as a viable construct in testing, is not discussed. Because of these problems, the construct validity of the proposed interpretations of ELSA scores has not been adequately demonstrated.

VALIDITY OF TEST USES. The research that the authors cite in support of the use of the ELSA in placement is problematic in that this research was not designed to adequately address the use of multiple forms across multiple ability levels. The authors would like to demonstrate that the ELSA has been equated vertically, or more accurately, scaled so that scores on the three level tests achieve comparability on a single developmental scale. However, the design of the studies they cite is inadequate for equating the three forms across even the levels for which they are intended. The vertical equating design that the authors used is essentially an equivalent-groups design, in which test takers from adjacent proficiency levels should be aggregated into a single group and then randomly assigned to two groups, each of which takes one of the two tests intended for the two levels. However, their implementation of this design was flawed in that they did not randomly assign the test takers to the forms to be taken, and they did not replicate the design for all pairs of proficiency levels. Thus, their results cannot be interpreted clearly as evidence that the three test levels form a multilevel ability scale. Although this does not necessarily vitiate the usefulness of the ELSA as a placement instrument, it certainly places in doubt the recommendation that it be used for achievement testing, especially for measuring gains in achievement.

RELIABILITY. Although the authors provide an extensive discussion of reliability, much of it is inappropriate in that it is based on classical internal consistency estimates, and does not report information relevant to the uses for which the test is intended. It is well-known that the internal consistency coefficients reported—Kuder-Richardson 20 and 21—overestimate reliability to the extent that test items are dependent upon each other. This is particularly problematic for a cloze test, in which the items are part of a whole text, and thus inescapably interrelated to each other. Thus, even though the reliability coefficients reported are lower-

bounds estimates, they are nevertheless likely to exaggerate the actual reliability. A more critical problem is the fact that even though the authors claim that the ELSA is criterion-referenced (CR), no CR dependability or agreement indices are provided. Test users are given no information about the consistency of ELSA scores as domain score estimates, nor about the consistency of placement decisions at the specific cutoff scores recommended for placement levels. Since the consistency of placement decisions will vary as a function of both the reliability of test scores and the cutoff score, a single reliability estimate and standard error of measurement for a given form provides inadequate information about how consistent placement decisions are across different levels. The authors do provide internal consistency reliability estimates for the different forms at different placement levels, but it would be most useful if they could take this a step further and provide the agreement indices and corresponding standard errors at each of the different cutoff scores they recommend for placement.

NORMS. Norms for placement were established with students in ESL classes in adult centers in the San Francisco Community College District and in intensive ESL programs at two universities in the San Francisco area. The samples used were all relatively small, ranging in size from over 100 per form per level for the beginning level forms to under 25 per form per level for the intermediate and advanced level forms. It is thus appropriate that the authors caution test users that the raw score to placement level conversion tables in the Technical Manual are a general guide only, and that programs should establish their own placement norms (p. 6). Although multilevel tests offer many advantages for test users, such tests also place upon test users the responsibility for assuring that each test taker is administered the appropriate level test. Neither the ELSA Technical Manual nor the instructions to test administrators offers adequate information about how to determine which level of ELSA is correct for a given student or group of students. The descriptions of ESL proficiency levels provided (p. 7) are too general to be of much use in this regard. Furthermore, if the test user knows the proficiency level of students in advance, there would appear to be little need to use the ELSA for placement. It would therefore be very useful if the authors could provide detailed procedures, including a locator test, for determining which level of the ELSA should be administered to a given group.

SUMMARY. The ELSA is a well-constructed ESL test, utilizing a procedure that offers efficient testing and at the same time requires test takers to process complete texts, as opposed to single items, of language. It is referenced to a specific content domain, and in this regard differs from many other ESL tests that are currently available for use. However, the evidence provided does not adequately support the intended interpretations of test scores as indicators of grammatical ability and the understanding of meaning in context. And although there is evidence that within the context of adult ESL classes in community colleges and university intensive programs the ELSA may provide useful information for placement purposes, the evidence does not support the use of the ELSA for the measurement of achievement or gains in achievement.

Review of the English Language Skills Assessment in a Reading Context by ALEX VOOGEL, Assistant Professor, TESOL/MATFL Program, Monterey Institute of International Studies, Monterey, CA:

The English Language Skills Assessment (ELSA) is a carefully designed test of reading and grammar in a multiple-choice, cloze format. It was developed in conjunction with a program for adult resident immigrants. For this reason, the ELSA appears most appropriate for use with adult education or beginning level university intensive language institutes. The test manual also indicates possible use with high school and upper elementary students. However, the beginning and intermediate test passages are written from an adult perspective, so the younger the population, the more questionable the ELSA's appropriateness.

The ELSA's test passages reflect the ESL curriculum of the San Francisco Community College District. In the sense that the ELSA contains structures and semantic content that relate to this curriculum as well as cutoff scores that refer to the performance of students proceeding through this curriculum, the ELSA is criterion-referenced. However, the test manual does not give specific information about skills, structures, or vocabulary domains cov-

ered by the test. Without this information, the score ranges in the manual cannot serve as criteria for mastery.

Interpretation of scores for placement is based on a table that converts raw scores into one of the levels of the San Francisco curriculum. No normative data are provided. Unless users follow a curriculum similar to San Francisco's, these score ranges cannot serve for placement. Local criteria or norms will have to be developed in these cases. The San Francisco ESL Master Plan, as well as information about establishing local levels, may be obtained by writing the ESL Resource Instructor at the San Francisco Community College District.

Some theory and research have suggested that the cloze format could provide a global picture of language proficiency (Oller, 1979). In addition to assessment of structure and vocabulary built into the ELSA, the authors hoped this test could serve as a more global measure of language proficiency. To explore this possibility, they ran correlations between the ELSA and several other tests. One finding is that the ELSA correlates well (.70s and .80s) with tests that emphasize structure and vocabulary (Michigan Test of English Language Proficiency, Structure Tests-English Language, Comprehensive English Language Test-Structure), but not so well (.56–.61) with listening comprehension tests (Comprehensive English Language Test-Listening, and the Listening Comprehension Picture Test, respectively). This finding is consistent with more recent research (Cohen, 1984) that disputes the global quality of cloze tests. Rather, student answers are seen as responses to contexts, structure, and vocabulary at a sentence or even more local level. In any case, the ELSA is at least appropriate for identifying degree of proficiency in sentence level reading skills.

In addition to the ELSA's use to sort students into different levels, the authors suggest that the ELSA may be used as a pretest and posttest to generate accountability data for federal funding. In this case stability over time is important, but no test-retest reliability data are reported. However, other aspects of reliability for which data are available look very favorable.

Internal consistency for each form of the ELSA is in the low .80s (KR-20). These are very respectable values, especially considering that a test form only contains 25 items. Equivalent form reliabilities for the beginning and intermediate levels are also in the .80s. Thus, alternate forms of the beginning and intermediate levels of the tests can be used with relative confidence. No statistics are given for the alternate advanced form (which is a more recent publication).

In addition to good reliability, the ELSA has several practical advantages. Administration of the ELSA does not require skilled personnel. Simple step-by-step instructions for the administrator are on the front of every test booklet. The front page of the test booklet also reports summary statistics for the test form, and the answer key has a conversion table for placing individual scores into levels in the San Francisco curriculum. The ELSA is time efficient. It takes 30 minutes and can be done in groups. Also, because of the multiple-choice format, scores can be generated quickly and reliably, either by hand or machine. Student answer sheets easily fit into a student's file. The test booklets are reusable and the cost of additional copies is nominal. These features make the ELSA very desirable from a practical standpoint. Finally, the technical manual is comprehensive and quite readable for the interested practitioner.

In summary, the ELSA appears to be a carefully designed test that has good reliability and practicality, especially where large numbers of adult students are tested. It can be used to identify placement and proficiency levels in sentence level reading skills, provided local norms are established or the program is similar to the one on which the ELSA is based.

REVIEWER'S REFERENCES

Oller, J. W. (1979). *Language tests at school.* London: Longman.
Cohen, A. D. (1984). On taking language tests: What the students report. *Language Testing,* 1, 70–81.

[26]
ETSA Tests.
Purpose: To measure "aspects of intelligence, specific abilities or aptitudes, and certain personality characteristics . . . to supplement the other factors upon which hiring, placing, training and promotion decisions are based."
Population: Employees and job applicants.
Publication Dates: 1959–85.
Scores: 8 tests: General Mental Ability Test, Office Arithmetic Test, General Clerical Ability Test, Stenographic Skills Test, Mechanical

Familiarity Test, Mechanical Knowledge Test, Sales Aptitude Test, Personal Adjustment Index.
Administration: Individual.
Price Data: Available from publisher.
Comments: Publisher recommends use of General Mental Ability Test (1A) and one or more others depending on nature of job.
Authors: Manual by Charles K. Stouffer and Susan Anne Stouffer; technical handbook by S. Trevor Hadley and George A. W. Stouffer.
Publisher: Educators'/Employers' Tests & Services Associates.
a) GENERAL MENTAL ABILITY TEST (1A).
Time: 45(50) minutes.
b) OFFICE ARITHMETIC TEST (2A).
Time: 60(65) minutes.
c) GENERAL CLERICAL ABILITY TEST (3A).
Time: 30(35) minutes.
d) STENOGRAPHIC SKILLS TEST (4A).
Subtests, 2: Typing Test, Shorthand Test.
Time: 45(50) minutes.
e) MECHANICAL FAMILIARITY TEST (5A).
Time: 60(65) minutes.
f) MECHANICAL KNOWLEDGE TEST (6A).
Time: 90(95) minutes.
g) SALES APTITUDE TEST (7A).
Time: 60(65) minutes.
h) PERSONAL ADJUSTMENT INDEX (8A).
Time: 45(50) minutes.
Cross References: For additional information, see 9:399 and T3:846; for reviews by Marvin D. Dunnette and Raymond A. Katzell of an earlier edition, see 6:1025.

Review of the ETSA Tests by ROLAND H. GOOD, III, Assistant Professor of Counseling and Educational Psychology, College of Education, University of Oregon, Eugene, OR:

PURPOSE. The stated purpose of the ETSA Tests is to "help provide . . . more satisfactory hiring, better employee placement, better selection of employees for special training, more effective measurement of training progress and more effective promoting with an objective data base." However, serious concerns regarding the reliability and validity of the tests as well as their normative samples, derived scores, and item selection severely limit the tests' ability to accomplish their stated purposes.

DESCRIPTION. Test 1A consists of 75 selection-type vocabulary, arithmetic reasoning, and visual analogies items. Test 2A has 50 items including computations, word problems, and graph and chart interpretations. Test 3A consists of 131 items measuring skills in alphabetizing, verifying, spelling, office vocabulary, and knowledge of postal rates and regulations. Test 4A consists of 120 items covering proofreading for spelling and grammar, alphabetical filing, and office procedures. Supplemental shorthand and typing tests also are available.

Test 5A requires selection of the corresponding picture for 50 tool or part names. Test 6A consists of 121 agree/disagree and matching items covering electrical, mechanical, drafting, and carpentry tools and terms. Test 7A includes 80 agree/disagree items representing sales lore/attitudes and 20 items matching a product to a slogan or sales pitch. Test 8A consists of 105 statements rated agree/disagree representing attitudes toward the community and employment.

The authors recommend administering test 1A to all examinees and test 8A when characteristic mode of life adjustment is a job consideration. Tests 2A through 7A assess job-specific skills and are to be used selectively.

ITEM SELECTION. Two concerns pertain to item selection. First, items for the specific tests were selected primarily from standard textbooks, handbooks, parts books, and other literature. It would be desirable instead to base item selection on an analysis of the knowledge, skills, and abilities necessary for successful job performance. Second, some items contain outdated material. For example, postcard postage of 13 cents is scored as correct.

SCORES. The primary score reported for the ETSA Tests is a performance classification that characterizes performance as either Poor, Questionable, Average, Good, or Excellent. The authors claim that "any further refinement of the derived scores obtained from ETSA Tests would not be helpful and might possibly be misleading" (p. 4). Two problems limit the utility of these performance categories. First, no information is provided on the criteria used to establish the performance categories; there is no explanation of just what made a questionable performance questionable. Second, there is a great deal of variability across tests in the proportion of examinees placed in each category. For example, based on the normative information provided, 12% of test 8A examinees and 32% of test 3A examinees obtained scores of Poor or Questionable.

RELIABILITY. The authors do not provide adequate information to judge whether the ETSA Tests have sufficient reliability to accomplish their purpose. The primary derived score for the ETSA Tests is the performance category—no reliability estimates are provided for performance categories. Performance categories will be less reliable than the raw scores because considerable variability is discarded in the conversion. In addition, subtest scores are reported for test 7A and 8A with *no* estimate of their reliability. No estimate of the standard error of measurement was provided for any scores.

Although reported raw score reliability estimates ranged from .77 to .94, insufficient information limits their value in evaluating the tests. On four tests, the sample used to estimate the reliability was not described at all; on none of the tests was the sample described adequately. Detailed descriptions are necessary to determine if the tests have sufficient reliability for the user's context and intended decisions. Furthermore, an unreliable test can appear highly reliable when using a sample of extreme scorers. Without a description of the samples used to estimate reliability, consumers must rely on hope that sample characteristics match their application.

NORMATIVE SAMPLE. Two problems severely limit the utility of the normative samples. First, an adequate description of the normative sample was not provided for any of the tests. Without the year(s) in which normative data were collected and a description of the sampling design and participation rates, the norms cannot be evaluated for appropriateness. Test 8A provides more information on the normative sample than the other tests, with serious limitations apparent. Although the occupational level of the normative sample was representative of the U.S., according to the 1958 Census, more recent comparative information was not reported. Furthermore, the sample was geographically restricted to the eastern United States and the distribution of the normative sample by age, educational level, racial/ethnic group, or community size was not reported.

Second, the normative samples often do not represent groups with whom users of the ETSA Tests would wish to compare examinees. Test 7A has the most appropriate normative sample: "2300 employed salesmen representing four aspects of the sales field" (p. 18). However, other norms were based, in part, on respondents from a college psychological clinic (4 tests), college applicants or students (4 tests), and high school students (2 tests).

VALIDITY. When tests are used to make performance predictions and employment decisions, the *Standards for Educational and Psychological Testing* (AERA, APA, & NCME, 1985) stress that "the principal obligation of employment testing is to produce reasonable evidence for the validity of such predictions and decisions" (p. 59). The most troubling limitation of the ETSA Tests is the lack of empirical support for the performance categories. For example, on test 8A an applicant scoring 65 or below is reported to be a poor risk for employment on a personal adjustment basis. However, no information is provided on the proportion of poor-risk applicants who are indeed unsatisfactory employees. Conversely, there is no indication that excellent-risk applicants have fewer personal adjustment problems. Predictive validity was not reported for any of the tests.

Although concurrent validity was reported for seven of the eight tests (raw scores only), a job performance criterion with job applicants or employees was employed for only two tests. Test raw scores were correlated with supervisor ratings of job performance for test 6A (.87) and 7A (.71 to .82). Instructor rating of student performance in college was the criterion for three tests, and college student test performance was the criterion for three tests.

Content validity was claimed for tests 2A, 3A, and 4A. However, that assertion was based solely on the item selection procedure: Items were obtained from standard textbooks. The extent to which test content corresponds to job requirements based on a job analysis was not reported.

Support for the construct validity of tests 4A and 5A was reported. Group means were significantly different for those with and without mechanical experience. However, the extent to which the tests are effective in differentiating individuals was not examined.

CONSUMER RESPONSIBILITY. Throughout the test manuals, the authors stress the desirability of the consumer developing local norms, conducting local reliability and validity studies, and developing local cutoff scores. In addition, the consumer is responsible for establishing the content validity of the ETSA Tests. If these tests are to be used for hiring, training, and

promotion decisions, *all* supporting data must be provided by the consumer.

SUMMARY. The manuals provide little data to support the use of these tests to assist with hiring, training, and promotion decisions. Thus, the consumer is responsible for all empirical support in defense of such uses. The concluding comment from the review of an earlier edition (6:1026) remains appropriate: Caveat emptor! Let the buyer beware!

REVIEWER'S REFERENCE

American Educational Research Association, American Psychological Association, & National Council for Measurement in Education. (1985). *Standards for educational and psychological testing.* Washington, DC: American Psychological Association, Inc.

Review of the ETSA Tests by HILDA WING, Personnel Psychologist, Federal Aviation Administration, Washington, DC:

The Educators'/Employers' Tests & Services Associates (ETSA) have published, in the Test and Personal Adjustment Index, a battery of eight measures: General Mental Ability, Office Arithmetic, General Clerical Ability, Stenographic Skills Test, Mechanical Familiarity Test, Mechanical Knowledge Test, Sales Aptitude Test, and Personal Adjustment Index. The copyright dates on these components of the test battery are 1984 and 1985. In addition to having copies of the tests, I also had access to the Administrator's Manual, copyrighted 1985, and the Technical Handbook of Norms and Testing Guidance, revised edition, copyrighted 1972.

The contents of these tests make the battery interesting and potentially useful, but evaluation is very difficult because the information available to me contained very few statistics providing critical details about the tests, such as item and test construction, reliability, validity, norms, and statistics. Any test user would be required to have or to develop such statistics to justify implementation of these measures. Although my general predilection is to require local norms whenever a test is used, I also believe test publishers should be required to provide an adequate psychometric and content foundation for this test selection process. The ETSA publishers have not met these requirements for this battery. Although I will describe the materials that were available to me, without the necessary psychometric and conceptual information I cannot recommend these tests.

The first six tests are power tests of cognitive abilities or skills. The remaining two are biodata instruments. All have fairly generous time limits; they are each scored Rights Only. There is no information about item characteristics and selection, or about test construction. Minimal information about reliability is provided, but the available statistics appear to be in acceptable ranges. The characteristics of the group(s) supplying the test data are mostly unknown. Validity statistics are few, as well as being inadequately described. There was an almost complete absence of information about normative groups.

The General Mental Ability Test includes different item types assembled in a spiral omnibus fashion, reminiscent of tests constructed decades ago, such as the Wonderlic (T3:2637). These types appear to include vocabulary, arithmetic reasoning, and figural/spatial analogies. More modern tests might cluster all items of a given type together, to minimize possible examinee confusion. The selection of item types was not documented here. For this, as for the other ETSA tests, several score categories are recommended (Poor, Questionable, Average, Good, Excellent) with little if any information concerning the origin of such scoring categories or their utility. Without appropriate justification, such scoring categories should not be used.

Each of the remaining seven measures are assembled to include several sections. The next three (Office Arithmetic, General Clerical Ability, Stenographic Skills) appear to tap clerical abilities and to include such traditional clerical item types as arithmetic, percentages, arithmetic reasoning, tables, graphs, alphabetizing, number and name matching, spelling, vocabulary, filing, and grammar. The sections on mailing, in the General Clerical Ability Test, and on general information, in the Stenographic Skills Test, should be checked for currency. The latter also provides for a test of shorthand and typing, with scoring rules to be provided by the test user.

Each of these clerical tests has generous time limits, although most clerical ability tests are quite speeded. No explanation is provided for this difference in speededness, and there are minimal validity data. It could be that power tests are appropriate for clerical abilities, perhaps more so than traditional speeded tests.

However, without a good explanation, including supporting data, I am dubious.

Mechanical Familiarity and Mechanical Knowledge both appear to be getting at some version of mechanical ability, with insufficient discussion of the benefits and drawbacks of either approach. The former test presents sets of pictures of tools and the examinee has to select the picture to go with a tool name. This approach might be useful for applicants with low levels of written English, but the representativeness of the selected tools is not documented. The latter test includes primarily statements with which the examinee agrees or disagrees, along with questions about diagrams exhibiting mechanical principles. Again, the content representativeness of the items requires more documentation. Verbal descriptions are provided concerning the procedures used to select and develop items used to assemble these tests of mechanical ability. Because part of the validity for each test appears to rest on a content strategy, item and test statistics combined with item budgets would have been useful. It would be interesting to know the correlations of these tests to each other and to similar tests, such as the Bennett Mechanical Comprehension Test (10). It is also important to have normative data and differential validity studies separately by gender and race.

The Sales Aptitude Test includes several categories: sales judgment, interest in selling, personality factors, matching occupations, level of aspiration, insight into human nature, and awareness of sales approach. Because sales occupations are purportedly poorly predicted by cognitive ability tests, the prospect of this biodata measure developed for prediction of successful salespeople is an exciting one. The information provided for this ETSA measure does not dampen such enthusiasm, but it does not enhance it greatly, either. While the content categories used may be right for sales jobs, insufficient data are presented in their support. Why these seven categories? Is each category unique or at least conceptually independent? Is there any theory behind this? A small table of validity data is provided for this test; the value of the median coefficient is .40. The table is a good start in providing adequate data for an instrument of potentially great utility, but highlights the insufficiency of the information.

The final ETSA measure, a biodata index of Personal Adjustability, is based on a theory of vocational adjustment that is not linked to the research literature by any citation. The format selection was not justified in an adequate manner. No criterion-related validity data are provided. Without more explicit reference to current research in personality theory and vocational adjustment, and with the minimal documentation provided here, it would not be wise to use this measure in employment selection.

To summarize: This is a potentially interesting test battery that requires extensive research and data collection before being used operationally. I would recommend the Sales Aptitude Test and the mechanical ability tests as the most worthy of the effort, although the impact of (the lack of) speededness on the assessment and validity of clerical abilities is an interesting question as well. The test user who selects one or more of these tests for operational purposes with only the available data does so at his/her own peril. The publisher has provided insufficient information.

[27]
Family Relations Test: Children's Version.

Purpose: "To assess the relative importance that different family members have for children" and to explore the child's emotional relations with his or her family.
Population: Ages 3–7, 7–15.
Publication Dates: 1957–85.
Administration: Individual.
Levels, 2: Form for Young Children, Form for Older Children.
Price Data, 1988: £70.15 for complete set including manual ('85, 59 pages), test figures and item cards, scoring and record sheets for older children, and record/score sheets for young children.
Time: 25(40) minutes.
Authors: Eva Bene (test and revised manual) and James Anthony (test).
Publisher: NFER-Nelson Publishing Co., Ltd. [England].
a) FORM FOR YOUNG CHILDREN.
Population: Ages 3–7.
Scores, 8: Outgoing Feelings (Positive Total, Negative Total), Incoming Feelings (Positive Total, Negative Total), Dependency Feelings, Sum of Positive, Sum of Negative, Total Involvement.
b) FORM FOR OLDER CHILDREN.

Population: Ages 7–15.
Scores, 12: Sum of Outgoing Positive, Sum of Outgoing Negative, Sum of Incoming Positive, Sum of Incoming Negative, Total Involvement, Sum of Positive Mild, Sum of Positive Strong, Sum of Negative Mild, Sum of Negative Strong, Maternal Overprotection, Paternal Overindulgence, Maternal Overindulgence.
Cross References: For information on the complete test, see 9:409 (3 references), T3:874 (33 references), 8:558 (18 references), and T2:1182 (4 references); for an excerpted review by B. Semeonoff of the Children's Version and the Adult Version, see 7:79 (7 references); see also P:81 (2 references); for reviews by John E. Bell, Dale B. Harris, and Arthur R. Jensen of the Children's Version, see 5:132 (1 reference).

Review of the Family Relations Test: Children's Version by CINDY I. CARLSON, Associate Professor of Educational Psychology, University of Texas at Austin, Austin, TX:

The Family Relations Test (FRT) for children is a clinical tool for examining the direction and intensity of a child's feelings toward family members, as well as his/her estimates of their reciprocal feelings. The measure is based upon psychoanalytic theory. Consideration of Piagetian cognitive development theory is employed in the construction of items for the younger and older child version, with items for older children reflecting greater complexity of emotions. The FRT is physically designed as a manipulation of objects (test figures) that are sufficiently stereotyped to permit the child to select figures that represent the members of his/her family. The test consists of the placement of items, each printed on a separate card, onto the figure(s) that the child associates with the item. Children have the option of selecting multiple family figures for items as well as selecting no family member for a particular item. The physical properties of the FRT are designed to maximize the collection of family relationship information from children less able or willing to express their thoughts and feelings about family members, such as younger, less verbal, or defensive children.

A comprehensive manual is available for the FRT. Directions for the administration and scoring of the test are clearly written. The primary shortcoming of the administration directions of the FRT is the limited guidance provided regarding the use of the younger or older form of the test. For children between the ages of 6 and 8, FRT users are directed to use their clinical judgment in determining the applicability of forms when it would appear that more specific guidelines could be identified (e.g., based on Piagetian cognitive measures, standard intelligence tests, or a series of pre-screening questions designed to identify the complexity of emotions understood by the child).

A considerable portion of the FRT manual is devoted to the clinical interpretation of test results. Numerous clinical examples are provided and discussion is organized around clinical syndromes (e.g., egocentric auto-aggressive, idealizing, paranoid). It would appear that use of the FRT is limited to the creation of hypotheses and clinical judgments, as neither the information regarding interpretation of scores nor the evaluation studies of the FRT are adequate to permit differential diagnosis based upon the test. A further shortcoming of the manual and interpretative information is that it does not conform to the widely used *Diagnostic and Statistical Manual—III*. Information contained in the FRT manual, therefore, may be limited in relevance to those clinicians who have been trained in and who practice within the psychodynamic framework.

Regarding the reliability of the FRT, the internal consistency of the measure was determined using a modification of the split-half procedure yielding corrected correlation coefficients ranging from .68 to .90. Although the FRT authors assert that the test-retest method of reliability is unsuitable for the test due to retest memory effects with short-term retest reliability or changes in home environment with longer retest intervals, this reviewer does not agree. Because the authors argue that children will be unable to remember their placement of items *within* the test administration, it seems unlikely they could remember placement *across* administrations. Short-term (1 week to 1 month) retest reliability evaluation appears both warranted and feasible with the FRT. Moreover, the occurrence of mediating home environmental changes could be measured and statistically controlled in retest analyses. It would appear that a critical concern regarding the FRT is the degree to which stable versus momentary subjective family relationship conditions are being measured.

The validity of the FRT, as a projective measure of "psychic reality," cannot be determined in the conventional manner, according to the authors (citing Cronbach & Meehl, 1955). The authors, however, have made an effort to examine the construct validity of the FRT from several points of view, including a comparison of the reciprocity of parent-child responses, the correspondence and reciprocity of sibling attitudes, the differentiation of theoretically relevant "pre-genital" and "genital" syndrome groups, and a comparison of child report with parent questionnaire responses. Although the FRT authors cite these data as supportive of construct validity of the measure, their primary reliance upon descriptive data without accompanying qualitative statistical analyses to confirm conclusions leaves this reviewer skeptical. In addition, current developmental research increasingly acknowledges the "nonshared reality" of members within a family, suggesting that efforts to establish construct validity by comparing within family member responses may be inappropriate. Rather, examining the relationship of FRT responses with other tests of the same construct would be more fruitful (see Grotevant & Carlson, 1989, for a review of relevant parent-child measures).

Adequate normative data are not available for the FRT. In the manual, descriptive data are provided that differentiate the ascribed parent items of nonclinical children and adolescents. This provides the clinician with an estimate of the differences between these developmental stages in children's parental perceptions. Similar data are provided regarding children's differing perceptions for brothers versus sisters and younger versus older siblings. Data are not provided that differentiate clinical from nonclinical child and adolescent perceptions of relevant family members. This would appear crucial for clinical use of the measure. Ideally cutoff scores, that have been empirically validated, would be available for users of the FRT. Finally, available descriptive data rely upon a single nonclinical sample (55 school-age children and 40 adolescents) and provide limited information regarding the characteristics of the sample. Without normative data, use of the FRT as a method of clinical diagnosis is inappropriate.

In summary, the strength of the FRT is its unique physical construction, which optimizes the collection of subjective family relationship information from children who are either developmentally or clinically less capable of completing objective self-report measures or reticent to share such information in a clinical interview. Given the few family relationship measures designed for children (see Grotevant & Carlson, 1989), the FRT provides an invaluable adjunct interview technique. Unfortunately, use of the FRT for clinical diagnostic or research purposes must await a more stringent test of the measure's psychometric properties. This reviewer does not agree with the FRT authors that such psychometric validation cannot be accomplished due to the "psychic reality" basis of the FRT. Rather, social scientists have increasingly recognized the importance of the subjective cognitive realities of individuals as determinants of their behavior, and have measured these in family and other close relationships (see Huston & Robbins, 1982). Rigorous psychometric standards are considered essential for family assessment measures, whether used in research or clinical practice (Carlson, 1989). Thus, the lack of adequate reliability, validity, and normative data on the FRT seriously limits its current utility in either clinical or research contexts except as an interview method.

REVIEWER'S REFERENCES

Huston, T. L., & Robins, E. (1982). Conceptual and methodological issues in studying close relationships. In L. H. Brown & J. S. Kidwell (Eds.), Methodology: The other side of caring (Special issue). *Journal of Marriage and the Family, 44* (4), 901-925.
Carlson, C. I. (1989). Criteria for family assessment in research and intervention contexts. *Journal of Family Psychology, 3* (2), 158-176.
Grotevant, H. D., & Carlson, C. I. (1989). *Family assessment: A guide to methods and measures.* New York: Guilford Press.

Review of the Family Relations Test: Children's Version by STEVEN I. PFEIFFER, Director, Institute of Clinical Training and Research, The Devereux Foundation, Devon, PA:

The Family Relations Test: Children's Version (FRT:C) is a semistandardized procedure that allows children to express their feelings and attitudes toward their families, as well as the children's perceptions of the families' reciprocal feelings toward them. The test consists of 21 cardboard schematic human figures representing a variety of family members of various ages and sizes, a set of red cardboard boxes with openings in the top, and a group of cards with printed statements reflecting a range of feelings and attitudes.

The FRT:C is presented in a play-like format and is individually administered. The child is asked to select a set of test figures to represent important family members, including the child, and a figure representing "Nobody." The child next reviews each of the statements—from 48 printed cards for younger children and 100 cards for older children—and sorts each card into the box behind the family figure for which each statement is most representative. Statements reflect feelings of like and dislike, love and hate, and attitudes such as overprotection and overindulgence. Administration time is 20–30 minutes, and scoring time is an additional 15 minutes. Scoring is straightforward—tallying statements for each particular family role. The manual provides some rather meager normative data and detailed clinical profiles for a few case vignettes to assist in interpreting a child's performance.

The test was originally published in 1957, with minor revisions in 1978 and 1985 that incorporated changes to five items and slight modifications in the administration procedure. The task is intrinsically appealing; it is easy to elicit the cooperation and interest of the child; and, as a relatively objective personality measure, the test has considerable heuristic value. In addition, the procedure is an ingenious device to assess the child's perceptions of emotional relationships within the family.

Although the test has strong face validity and inherent clinical appeal, the manual provides very little evidence to support the validity of the specific inferences made from the test profiles. The only validity studies compare test results with case history material for several small groups of clinical subjects, and equate profiles with predictions made from psychiatric diagnoses. Interpretation requires considerable clinical wisdom and extensive experience with the instrument, and is based on highly speculative and inferential psychological constructs founded in psychoanalytic thinking.

Reliability studies are somewhat more encouraging. However, the manual does not provide the user with enough information to judge whether the scores are sufficiently accurate for individual clinical decision making. As mentioned above, normative data are sketchy—

apparently local norms, with only a very small number of "normal families" included.

The test does not follow a standard administration procedure. For example, only the first and last two items are presented in a uniform sequence; all other items are simply presented in a "mixed order." In addition, it is left to the discretion of the examiner to determine whether items for the older children need to be read to the child. Perhaps the most telling procedural weakness is that the child is permitted to select from the 21 cardboard figures which family members to include or exclude. The family members the child selects may not necessarily coincide with his true family system—a not unlikely occurrence for younger children or for children whose parents are separated, divorced, or remarried, or with absent or deceased family members.

This test is innovative in design and of considerable heuristic value. However, until administration is restandardized, more extensive and carefully selected norms are obtained, and more rigorous examination of the technical adequacy of the scale is procured, the FRT:C should be used only as a clinical research instrument.

[28]
Group Achievement Identification Measure.

Purpose: "To determine the degree to which children exhibit the characteristics of underachievers so that preventative or curative efforts may be administered."
Population: Grades 5–12.
Publication Date: 1986.
Acronym: GAIM.
Scores, 6: Competition, Responsibility, Achievement Communication, Independence/Dependence, Respect/Dominance, Total.
Administration: Group.
Price Data, 1988: $10 per individual inventory including prepaid computer scoring by publisher; $80 per class set of 30 inventories including prepaid computer scoring by publisher; manual for administration and interpretation (12 pages) included with test orders.
Time: (30) minutes.
Comments: Self-report inventory.
Author: Sylvia B. Rimm.
Publisher: Educational Assessment Service, Inc.

Review of the Group Achievement Identification Measure by ROBERT K. GABLE, Professor of Educational Psychology, and Associate Director,

Bureau of Educational Research and Service, University of Connecticut, Storrs, CT:

The Group Achievement Identification Measure (GAIM) is a 90-item self-report measure that employs a 5-point Likert response format (*No, To a Small Extent, Average, More Than Average, Definitely*). No empirical evidence is presented to support the "equal interval" nature of this atypical Likert scale.

The 10-page Manual for Administration and Interpretation is extremely superficial and presents little comprehensive information regarding theoretical or empirical support for the measure. For example, the author states the "GAIM was created based on the psychological practice" of the author (p. 1) and refers readers to her nontheoretical book containing case studies of children's problems and strategies for assistance. No literature or appropriate judgmental data are presented to properly support the content validity of the measure.

Although the manual indicates the GAIM is appropriate for Grade 5–12 students, this reviewer doubts if lower grade students can reliably respond to a 90-item measure. Brief mention is made of percentiles, normal curve equivalents, and stanine scores; these scores are inadequately defined in a footnote (p. 3).

The most serious problems with the GAIM rest in the vague description of the process followed in its development and the empirical support offered for reliability and validity, which fall inexcusably short of the criteria set forth in the *Standards for Educational and Psychological Testing* (AERA, APA, & NCME, 1985). For example, reference is made to an item analysis that indicated "some items discriminated well for one sex and not the other" (p. 4), but no data are presented. Respectable Hoyt reliability coefficients were calculated for male (.92) and female (.90) scores on the 90 items, but no reliability data are presented for the five subscore areas assessed. Users are presented no empirical evidence that the subscore items are adequate samples of student characteristics from the intended domains of content, and thus cannot be confident that the subscores yield accurate assessments. Further, no stability reliabilities are reported.

A section on construct validity (p. 4) states the "construct validity of GAIM was based on items which Rimm used in developmental history interviews with parents of underachieving children." This evidence appears to address content validity and is not sufficient to support construct validity. The comment that "further theoretical background is provided" in the available book (p. 4) is insufficient, given the flyer for the book states that "the book is not theoretical." Construct validity evidence in the form of factor analysis of the items to support empirically the judgmentally designated item clusters is essential, but missing. No evidence is presented to indicate the factor structure of the student responses is constant across Grades 5–12.

A section is presented on criterion-related validity that states GAIM scores were compared with teacher ratings of student achievement (p. 4). A criterion-related validity correlation of .43 is reported for a sample of 215 students. No description of the sample (i.e., grade level) is presented and no data are presented for the subscales. The overall correlation of .43, while not interpreted in the context of theoretical expectations, appears more likely to address construct validity than criterion-related validity.

A section on norms states that the GAIM was normed on "over 950 school aged children" from various community types and geographic areas (p. 5). A more specific description of the norms is appropriate. The norms are apparently provided during the computer-scoring service, but no norm tables appear in the Manual for Administration and Interpretation. A final section in the manual offers well-written interpretive descriptions of the five subscales included in the 90 items. Unfortunately, the manual provides little judgmental (i.e., content validity) and no empirical (i.e., construct validity and alpha reliability) support for the item groupings employed to define the subscales.

Overall, in its current form the GAIM manual provides inadequate judgmental and empirical support for the validity and reliability of the proposed assessment of the "characteristics which distinguish achieving students from underachievers" (p. 1). Until these data are available in a manner consistent with the *Standards*, users cannot be confident that scores on the GAIM are meaningful or accurate.

REVIEWER'S REFERENCE

American Educational Research Association, American Psychological Association, & National Council on Measurement in Education. (1985). *Standards for educational and psychological testing*. Washington, DC: American Psychological Association, Inc.

Review of the Group Achievement Identification Measure by JEFFREY JENKINS, *Attorney, Keleher & McLeod, P.A., Albuquerque, NM:*

On its face, the Group Achievement Identification Measure (GAIM) seems to offer the user a thoughtful measure of student "underachievement." Closer examination, however, reveals shortcomings that leave the instrument with questionable usefulness.

The GAIM was based on a theory of underachievement derived from the clinical psychology practice of its author, Sylvia B. Rimm. This theory is summarized in general terms in the GAIM Manual for Administration and Interpretation as "the inability to deal with competition was key to causing children to underachieve." The user is referred to Dr. Rimm's book, *Underachievement Syndrome: Causes and Cures* for further theoretical background and suggestions on reversing underachievement. Because the theoretical debate over the concept of underachievement continues, such lack of more specific theoretical justification for the GAIM presents a significant stumbling block to confident recommendation of the instrument.

The measure is presented in a format clearly readable for students in Grades 5–12, and simply consists of a series of 90 statements with which students are to agree *definitely*, *more than average*, *average*, *to a small extent*, or *no*. The items, such as "The most important part of school for me is my social life" and "I believe I am smarter than my grades show me to be," comprise five dimensions and are scored by the publisher. The manual offers no guidance on how scoring is accomplished, nor is any indication given of which items fall into the various dimensions. Brief descriptions of the five dimensions are given. Total scores are reported as percentiles and NCEs (normal curve equivalents) with dimension scores reported as stanines.

Instructions for administration are straightforward, and teachers are free to explain words to students. No time limit is imposed, but the suggested usual time required is 30 minutes. Students mark in pencil on the instrument itself.

The manual offers very brief sections on reliability, validity, and norms, which are altogether inadequate for weighing the sufficiency of these characteristics. Hoyt reliability coefficients are reported as .92 for males and .90 for females, but no specific information is given on how these coefficients were computed, raising questions about the GAIM's actual reliability. A more common measure of reliability should have been reported with a simple explanation of its basis. In addition, although dimension scores are reported, no evidence of their reliability is offered.

Criterion-related validity was explored by correlating the GAIM scores of 215 students with teacher ratings of student achievement, resulting in a validity coefficient of .43. A value of this magnitude is generally adequate for this type of measure, and may support the instrument's purpose of differentiating between underachievers and achieving students.

In support of construct validity, the manual offers the following: "Construct validity of GAIM was based on items which Rimm used in developmental history interviews with parents of underachieving children." A one-sentence explanation of Dr. Rimm's theory is then offered. Given the theory-laden nature of this instrument, construct validity is of central importance. However, essentially no information is offered in support of the instrument's construct validity. Moreover, the five specific dimensions on which scores are obtained purport to reflect student strengths and weaknesses, yet no support for their presentation as separable constructs is offered. An article by Rimm (1985) suggests the dimensions are derived from a factor analytic study, but no specific information from such a study was given. These are flaws that should be remedied before any user gives serious consideration to the instrument.

Normative information is derived from "950 school aged children" including "rural, urban and suburban children as well as those representing different geographical areas of the country." Although more specific information about the norm group would be helpful, such as numbers of male and female students in each grade, the norm group is probably sufficient for the instrument's purpose.

The GAIM is an instrument presenting itself as a measure of underachievement, yet the publisher offers little specific information to support this claim. The instrument may have some usefulness for tentative assessments of students' underachievement, but insufficient evidence is available to warrant recommendation of even this. At this time, use of the GAIM should be limited to research settings.

REVIEWER'S REFERENCE

Rimm, S. (1985, November-December). Identifying underachievement: The characteristics approach. *G/C/T*, pp. 2-5.

[29]
Guidance Centre Classroom Achievement Tests.

Purpose: "To assist teachers in making informed decisions about the success of their instructional practices and the progress of their students."
Publication Dates: 1979–85.
Acronym: GC CATS.
Administration: Group.
Levels, 2: Elementary, Secondary.
Price Data, 1987: $1.75 per test; $55 per 35 of any 1 test; $1.75 per teacher's manual for any test.
Time: (45–60) minutes per test.
Comments: Curriculum-based achievement tests.
Author: Merlin Wahlstrom (Background, Scope, and Interpretation manual).
Publisher: Guidance Centre [Canada].
a) ELEMENTARY LEVEL.
Population: Grades 3–8.
Scores: 24 tests in 6 domains: Summative Mathematics, Scientific Processes, Scientific Literacy/Knowledge: Mathematics, Summative Reading, Reading, Language Arts: Writing.
Comments: Subtests available as separates.
b) SECONDARY LEVEL.
Population: Grades 9–12.
Scores: 22 tests in 9 domains: Reading, English/Writing, Chemistry, Consumer Education, Consumer Mathematics, Algebra, Number and Number Operations, Geometry and Measurement, Summative Mathematics.
Comments: Subtests available as separates.
[The publisher advised in June 1990 that this test is now out of print—Ed.]

Review of the Guidance Centre Classroom Achievement Tests by PAUL C. BURNETT, Lecturer in Psychology, Queensland University of Technology—Kelvin Grove Campus, Brisbane, Australia:

The Guidance Centre Classroom Achievement Tests (GC CATS) consist of 46 curriculum-based achievement tests designed and developed as classroom achievement tests based upon the instructional objectives for each curriculum domain. The tests are based on the instructional objectives from the Canadian Province of British Columbia's curriculum guide. The use of these tests in other provinces and countries is extremely limited, given the differences in curriculum content and the variation in the sequence of instruction that exist from classroom to classroom, province to province, and country to country. The eight-page manual, which addresses the background, scope, and interpretation of .the tests, partly addresses this issue by stating all items should be reviewed by teachers outside the Province of British Columbia (B.C.) to determine if instruction in their classrooms has covered the knowledge and skills required to answer each item. Consequently, the use of this test outside B.C. is questionable because of (a) the differences that exist in curriculum and instruction across educational environments, and (b) the laborious task of evaluating the suitability of each item for a particular classroom.

This review will now focus on the use of the GC CATS in B.C. The tests were developed using a curriculum-based criterion-referenced approach. There are 24 tests in three curriculum areas (Mathematics, Reading, and Language Arts: Writing) for elementary children (Grades 3–8) and 22 tests in six curriculum areas (Consumer Education, Mathematics, Reading, Chemistry, Algebra, and English: Writing) for secondary level students (Grades 9–12). The elementary tests are interpreted using either broad classifications such as (a) at or above grade expectations, (b) below grade expectations, and (c) inconclusive; a 5-point scale, A = Excellent, B = Very Good, C = Average, P = Pass, and F = Fail; means, standard deviations, percentile ranks, and stanines; or a combination of the above. The secondary level tests are interpreted using percentile ranks, stanines, means, and standard deviations, or grades of A, B, C, P, and F as above. Each of the 46 tests has its own manual that addresses test development, administration, scoring, and interpretation. The content of these manuals varies greatly and the criteria for interpreting the results are not always consistent. For example, an "A" on one test means an excellent performance in terms of some set criteria, but "A" on another test indicates the student is reading at an independent level. Some manuals report norm-referenced data and statistical characteristics such as means, standard deviation, reliability, and standard error of measurement, but most do not. The few

reliability coefficients reported are computed using different methods such as Hoyt's analysis of variance procedure for examining internal consistency and the Kuder-Richardson 20 formula. Each manual presents a different combination of information for interpreting the results of the test and for evaluating the psychometric properties of the instrument. No information pertaining to validity is presented. The inconsistent presentation of information is a major weakness of these tests.

One problem inherent in an externally developed evaluation of curriculum objectives is that many teachers view the tests as an assessment of their teaching effectiveness and consequently teach to the tests' content. Additionally, it is hoped each curriculum is tailored to the needs of the students in the class. Tailoring a curriculum to student needs requires flexibility, and teachers are not likely to be flexible if an externally developed curriculum evaluation is used to assess student achievement. An alternative exists with teachers assessing student performance in terms of curriculum objectives but with the understanding of the uniqueness of their class. The curriculum implemented in individual classrooms to adequately cater to student needs may vary from the general curriculum outlined by an educational authority.

In summary, the GC CATS is a curriculum-based criterion-referenced test developed using the Province of British Columbia's curriculum. It is not recommended for use outside B.C. because of curriculum differences and questionable suitability of items. The test manuals are inconsistent in the presentation of necessary information. The 46 manuals present little reliability data and there is no information about validity. A variety of methods for interpreting results are presented. Teachers in B.C. may find the tests useful because they are based on familiar curriculum goals and instructional objectives.

Review of the Guidance Centre Classroom Achievement Tests by ROLAND H. GOOD, III, Assistant Professor of Counseling and Educational Psychology, College of Education, University of Oregon, Eugene, OR:
The Guidance Centre Classroom Achievement Tests (GC CATS) consist of 46 tests covering Mathematics (24 tests), Reading (10

tests), Science (6 tests), English (4 tests), and Consumer Education (2 tests). Only 41 tests were available for review. The tests are intended for use in Grades 3 through 12, with 11 of the tests intended for the 7/8 grade level. Between 1 and 6 tests are available for other grade levels. Although the mathematics area and the 7/8 grade level are well represented, there is little consistency in the availability of tests for other academic areas across grade levels.

The purpose, description, instructions, norms, and interpretive guidelines are available in a separate Teacher's Manual for each test. All of the teacher's manuals contain information that is partially redundant with other manuals, and yet there also are substantial differences among the tests. Separate manuals allow test users to read and evaluate only that material directly relevant to the tests they are using. However, no overall teacher's manual or technical manual is available, which makes evaluation of the package of tests more difficult as, for example, when a school district would consider adopting the entire set of tests. This review focuses on those characteristics that typify the entire set of tests, although individual exceptions can usually be found. In the materials reviewed, the manual labeled Grade 4/5 Reading: Content Areas contained instead the manual for another test by mistake. Consequently, the Grade 4/5 Reading: Content Areas test is not included in this review.

Two types of tests are included in the GC CATS. The eight tests intended to provide only summative information regarding the mastery of curriculum objectives are to be used at only one grade level. The remaining tests are intended to provide summative information at one grade level and formative information at the next grade level. For example, a 3/4-level test covers the curriculum objectives for Grade 3. When administered at the end of Grade 3, the test provides summative information regarding student mastery of the curriculum. When administered at the beginning of Grade 4, the test is intended to provide formative information regarding pupil strengths and weaknesses to guide instruction.

Most of the tests are timed tests consisting of 40 multiple-choice items to be completed in 45 minutes. The six Reading tests, two Consumer Education tests, and two Summative Mathe-matics tests are not timed, however. The grade 11 and 12 summative tests are timed and require 100 to 120 minutes to administer. Production-type responses are required for three English tests where the students are required to write two letters, a newspaper article, and several short paragraphs, and to edit several short passages. Production-type responses also are required for the Grade 11 and 12 Algebra tests where the students are required to solve problems and graph functions. Scoring of production-type responses is subjective, although detailed scoring rules and criteria are provided. In addition, optional, open-ended questions with scoring criteria are provided for the six Reading tests.

SCORES. Letter grades (A, B, C, P[Pass], and F) indicating the level of student performance are available for all but two of the tests. For the most part, letter grades are based on experienced teacher judgment. The difficulty inherent in this approach is illustrated for the two Language Arts, Grade 7/8 tests that were the only tests to report the frequency of each letter grade. For one of the tests, 6% of the normative sample received an A or a B. In contrast, 47% received an A or a B for the other test. Relying on teacher judgment to establish letter-grade criteria may have resulted in similar disparities for other tests as well. A variety of other scores also are available, including percentiles (21 tests), quartiles (6 tests), stanines (14 tests), and percent correct (14 tests). For 11 of the tests, the only norm-referenced information provided is whether the score is above or below the mean. Although the interpretation of subtest performance is recommended for 27 tests, subtest percentile ranks are provided only for 3 tests. For the remaining 24 tests, whether the subtest raw score is above or below the mean is the only normative information provided.

NORMS. Norm-referenced information is provided for all but two of the tests, based on sample sizes ranging from 556 students to 30,000 students. All normative samples consist of students in British Columbia, Canada. The normative sample is described as either random or representative of British Columbia students for 14 of the tests. However, none of the tests describe the sample distribution by gender, race, socioeconomic status, geographic location within the province, or language spoken in the home. Test consumers would be wise to exercise caution in their interpretation of normative information when the tests are used with students in British Columbia. The norms are not appropriate for use in other locations.

RELIABILITY. No evidence of test reliability is reported for 16 of the tests. For those subtests without reliability information, the test consumer is completely responsible for demonstrating test reliability sufficient for intended uses. Reliability estimates sufficient for important individual educational decisions (.90 or above) are reported for 7 tests and reliability estimates sufficient for screening decisions (.80 to .89) are reported for 12 tests. Reliability estimates sufficient for group data and administrative decisions only (.71 to .79) are reported for 5 tests. Internal consistency estimates are the only type of reliability information provided, although the type of reliability was not indicated for 10 of the tests.

Estimates of interrater agreement are not provided for those tests requiring production-type responses. Less than satisfactory interrater agreement is reported for selected items and scales of the English 12: Writing test, but the standards by which satisfactory/unsatisfactory agreement were judged are not reported. The test consumer is left with some doubt regarding the extent to which the scoring criteria are clear enough for acceptable interrater consistency.

VALIDITY EVIDENCE. In general, excellent support is provided for the content validity of the tests with respect to the curriculum employed in the province of British Columbia as represented by the 1978 (24 tests), 1981 (4 tests), and 1982 (2 tests) curriculum guides. The close correspondence of the tests to the British Columbia Curriculum is a significant strength of the GC CATS, although it also limits the range of settings where the GC CATS would be appropriate. A table of specifications is provided for all of the tests, and 29 of the tables directly reference the objectives of the British Columbia Curriculum. In addition, teachers in British Columbia contributed substantially to the design and development of most, if not all, of the tests. The limited number of production-type responses limits both the types of objectives and the level of mastery that can be evaluated. For most items, the students must only select the correct answer from four alternatives.

No evidence is provided regarding the tests' criterion-related or construct validity. In particular, evidence that students performing well on the GC CATS were also judged by their classroom teachers to be mastering the curriculum objectives would provide valuable support for the GC CATS.

SUMMARY. Teachers in British Columbia using the B.C. Curriculum of 1978 who are seeking a classroom achievement test for one of the grade-academic area combinations supplied by the GC CATS will want to consider these tests carefully. Teachers in other settings using other curricula would be well advised to keep looking.

[30]
Happiness Measures.

Purpose: Assesses a respondent's perception of amount of happiness or unhappiness and estimate of time experienced as happy or unhappy.
Population: Ages 16 and over.
Publication Dates: 1980–87.
Acronym: HM.
Scores, 5: Scale, Happy Percentage Estimate, Unhappy Percentage Estimate, Neutral Percentage Estimate, Combination.
Administration: Group.
Manual: No manual.
Price Data: Available from publisher.
Time: (1–5) minutes.
Comments: Test booklet title is *Emotions Questionnaire*.
Author: Michael W. Fordyce.
Publisher: Cypress Lake Media.

Review of the Happiness Measures by WILLIAM A. STOCK, Professor of Exercise Science, Arizona State University, Tempe, AZ:

The Happiness Measures (HM) is most appropriately considered a social indicator instrument, historically linked to research in the domain of subjective well-being—a domain whose origins are primarily in general social survey research and social gerontology. Well-established constructs in this domain include mood, happiness, life satisfaction, and morale. The HM is a two-item instrument requiring a global assessment of degree of happiness, and of amount of time spent in happy, neutral, and unhappy states. The principal item, tapping degree or intensity of happiness, may be modified to assess any reasonable span of time. Although appropriate for a variety of research settings in which a global index of happiness is required, users are advised not to adopt it for clinical or diagnostic purposes.

In reviewing research on happiness, the test author (Fordyce, in press) competently places the HM in a network of theoretical constructs and empirical evidence. Further, he provides a variety of reliability and validity information on the instrument. Based on this reviewer's knowledge, Fordyce's claim that the HM displays equivalent or better reliability and validity than comparable subjective well-being measures is reasonable.

Generally, Fordyce obtained psychometric information using samples of community college students, a population younger than the general population. Use of representative samples from the general population would not, in my opinion, significantly alter the magnitude of estimates of reliability. However, these estimates would likely lead to lower mean scores than those reported by Fordyce, because samples from older populations historically have self-reported lower levels of happiness. Therefore, empirical support for the HM would be strengthened by expanding the normative base to include persons more representative of the general population. Also needed are estimates of standard errors of measurement (currently absent from the documentation). As significant gender, age, and ethnic differences have been consistently reported for subjective well-being measures, the empirical base of the HM should include reliability and validity information obtained within levels of these classifications.

Reported, short-term, test-retest reliabilities range from .98 to .62 as the retest period goes from 2 days to 4 months, and are consistent with results reported in psychometric summaries of the field (Okun & Stock, 1987a). Further, numerous concurrent validity estimates are reported both with other scales of subjective well-being (e.g., happiness, life satisfaction, positive mood), and with a variety of divergent constructs (e.g., anxiety, depression, negative affect). These estimates are consistent in magnitude and direction with those found in the field. Finally, experimental evidence from studies conducted by Fordyce indicates that HM scores change in a theoretically relevant manner after interventions designed to evaluate happiness.

This instrument is acceptable for use in research where happiness is the construct of interest and where the user is interested in assessment of a present-oriented time perspective (e.g., the last two weeks, the past few months, the past year). In addition, the user should be aware that subjective indices of well-being have stronger relationships with each other than with objective indicators of quality of life (Okun & Stock, 1987b). Therefore, a subjective index should not be used as a substitute in situations where objective quality of life is the construct of primary interest. Some appropriate uses of the HM would be as an outcome measure in program evaluations, in general and local social surveys, and in research assessing *mild* interventions designed to increase feelings of well-being. The measure should not be used as a diagnostic tool, nor should it be used to evaluate the impact of clinical interventions. Clinical interventions deal with stable negative traits (e.g., depression and neuroticism) that are manifestations of an independent construct, negative affectivity (Watson & Clark, 1984), and a different measurement tool is required. In clinical settings, the objective is to demonstrate effective long-term decreases in behaviors associated with negative affectivity, and here the user should select from among the well-established clinical scales.

REVIEWER'S REFERENCES

Watson, D., & Clark, L. A. (1984). Negative affectivity: The disposition to experience aversive emotional states. *Psychological Bulletin, 96,* 465-490.

Okun, M. A., & Stock, W. A. (1987a). The construct validity of subjective well-being measures: An assessment via quantitative research syntheses. *Journal of Community Psychology, 15,* 481-492.

Okun, M. A., & Stock, W. A. (1987b). Correlates and components of subjective well-being among the elderly. *Journal of Applied Gerontology, 6,* 95-112.

Fordyce, M. W. (in press). A review of research on the Happiness Measures: A sixty-second index of happiness of mental health. *Social Indicators Research.*

[31]
Human Resource Development Report.

Purpose: Assesses an individual's management style, "provides insights into the individual's personality, describes personal strengths, and identifies areas for potential growth and development."
Population: Managerial candidates.
Publication Dates: 1982–87.
Acronym: HRDR.
Scores: 5 dimensions: Leadership, Interaction with Others, Decision-Making Abilities, Initiative, Personal Adjustment.
Administration: Group.

Price Data, 1987: $27.95 per introductory kit including 16PF test booklet, answer sheet, prepaid processing form to receive Human Resource Development Report, and user's guide ('87, 47 pages); $17.50 per 25 16PF reusable test booklets; $6.25 per 25 16PF machine-scorable answer sheets; $12 per user's guide; $30 or less per Human Resource Development Report available from publisher scoring service.
Time: 45(60) minutes.
Comments: Based on the Sixteen Personality Factor Questionnaire; must be scored by publisher.
Author: IPAT staff.
Publisher: Institute for Personality and Ability Testing, Inc.

Review of the Human Resource Development Report by S. ALVIN LEUNG, Assistant Professor of Educational Psychology, University of Nebraska-Lincoln, Lincoln, NE:

The Human Resource Development Report (HRDR) is based on the Sixteen Personality Factor Questionnaire (16PF), a personality inventory. The scores from a number of 16PF (Form A) scales are used to generate an interpretive report concerning the potential effectiveness of an individual in a managerial position. The interpretive report is a narrative summary outlining the individual's personality, strengths, and areas for growth and development. The HRDR is designed to assist organizations in making personnel-related decisions.

The HRDR has five composite scales and each has several subscales. The five composite scales are: Leadership, Interacting with Others, Making Decisions, Initiative, and Personal Adjustment. These five dimensions of management are regarded as common characteristics of successful managers. Short-term (2 days to 2 weeks) test-retest reliabilities for the subscales are within a desirable range, between .58 and .94, with a mean of about .81. Long-term reliabilities (from 2.5 months to about 8 years) range between .08 and .89, with a mean of about .52. These reliability data were collected from a number of groups, including college students and working adults. However, information concerning internal consistency reliability is not available in the User's Guide.

The User's Guide provides only limited information concerning validity. It is suggested that because the 16PF was well documented as a valid instrument, users who are interested in validity information of the HRDR should refer to other sources. Although this may be true, the HRDR is actually extending the application of the 16PF to personnel selection and development. Past research data concerning the 16PF may not be relevant to the objectives and claims of the HRDR. The HRDR targets management personnel who are not trained in psychological testing and are unlikely to have knowledge about the 16PF. Consequently, it is reasonable to expect the User's Guide to give a more informed summary concerning the validity of the 16PF, as related to the composite scales and subscales being used in the HRDR.

A key to the utility of the HRDR is whether the interpretive statements are accurate and valid. The interpretive statements are derived from a statement library, and the selection of specific statements is determined by the elevation and configuration of the scales. The authors are rather vague on how statements were constructed. While empirical findings served as a general background, specific statements were linked to the scores based on expert opinions, not on findings of specific research studies. The User's Guide indicates the statement library was written by a team consisting of "a number of specialists" (p. 28) who had at least 4 years of experience in interpreting the 16PF profile. Information concerning the experts, such as training, educational background, and sex, were omitted. It is also not clear as to how many experts actually participated in writing the statements, and no information regarding reliability checks (e.g., inter-expert reliability) was provided. One gets the impression from this procedure that the statements were written based more on the experts' experience in interpreting the 16PF than on specific research findings. This is a very risky process. The interpretive statements should be based on specific research findings and if expert opinions are used, there has to be some form of reliability check. A review of the example statements in the User's Guide (pp. 11–12) suggests some statements are quite definitive (e.g., "He is not very trusting of the behaviors and motives of others") and extreme (e.g., "He may frequently seem inconsistent and prone to suddenly change his mind about things"). These statements can easily be abused by a user in making personnel-related decisions. If the statements are of questionable validity and accuracy, users who are not trained or experienced in psychological testing can be misled.

A so-called "stop-light model" is recommended for using the HRDR. The user initially generates a description of the ideal employee in a specified position. The user will then read the HRDR of a candidate, marking in red those interpretive statements that do not indicate a good match, marking in yellow those that are questionable, and green those that are indicative of a good match. The user is then encouraged to integrate and compare the marked statements with data from other sources, such as those from an interview. The stop-light model appears to be a useful method, particularly in its emphasis on integrating data from multiple sources.

The user is also encouraged to discuss and share the results of the HRDR with the respondent. Several useful guidelines and answers for commonly asked questions are provided in the User's Guide. Although interpretation of test scores is necessary, it is doubtful whether the user has the necessary skills, training, and information to perform such an interpretation, particularly when the HRDR includes so many extreme and definitive statements about an individual. The typical user is not likely to be equipped with basic knowledge about psychological measurement and the 16PF. Inaccurate interpretations could create confusion and problems for both the user and the test taker. This is perhaps an expected undesirable effect of having a nontrained person to interpret psychological test reports.

The 16PF may be a well-documented personality measurement, but the authors of the HRDR have to show how past and current research findings support the validity of the interpretive statements printed in the HRDR. The information reported in the User's Guide is not adequate. It is troubling to read the interpretive statements as they are rather extreme and definitive, and to think about the possibility they may be abused by users. Consequently, users of the HRDR have to be aware of its limited validity, and not use it as the only source of information when making personnel and hiring decisions.

Review of the Human Resource Development Report by MARY A. LEWIS, Director, Organizational and Employment Technology, PPG Industries, Inc., Pittsburgh, PA:

The Human Resource Development Report (HRDR) is a five- to six-page computer-based analysis of Cattell's Sixteen Personality Factor Questionnaire (16PF) designed to measure those personality dimensions that relate to management potential. The narrative portion of the report is organized around five areas: Leadership, Interaction with Others, Decision-Making Abilities, Initiative, and Personal Adjustment. The report is supported by a score summary sheet that reports and displays graphically the sten (standard ten) scores for the scales that correspond to each of the five areas.

The User's Guide for the HRDR refers the user to the 16PF Handbook (Cattell et al., 1970) for information on construction, reliability, and validity of the 16PF Scale, and contains a technical supplement describing both the development of the scales and the process by which the computer-generated report was developed.

SCALES IN THE HRDR. Four of the five topical scales in the HRDR (Interaction with Others, Decision-Making Abilities, Initiative, and Personal Adjustment) are second or third order factors of the primary 16PF scales that were developed and documented in other literature. The Leadership scale was developed specifically for this instrument and is a third order factor developed for the HRDR. This scale is based on Sweney's (1970) model of organizational power, and was developed through multiple correlations of 16PF scores with the Response to Power Measure (RPM; Sweney, 1977). The correlations of the scales with the RPM scores ranged from .42 to .51, although the specific correlations are not reported.

The documentation includes a description of the literature review that led to the selection of the scales used for the HRDR, and information about the validity and scale reliability. The average short-term reliability of the scales used in the HRDR is .81 for the basic scales and .87 for the composite scales. The long-term reliability average is .52 for the basic scales and .67 for the composite scales.

The validity of the scales is based on a content analysis of the management literature that identified 88 studies using 54 assessment instruments. No validity coefficients for the scales are reported; however, specific references are provided to studies that support the use of each of the subscales.

COMPUTER-GENERATED REPORT. The computer-generated report for the HRDR is built from a statement library that was built from summary reports prepared for managers who were candidates for hiring or promotion. A team of experts, each with at least 4 years of experience in interpreting the 16PF profiles, was involved in developing the statement library. The themes identified from the 88 studies mentioned above were linked to the statement library and to the logic that triggered the statements.

USE OF THE HRDR IN HUMAN RESOURCE DECISIONS. The HRDR User's Guide includes a detailed section on how to use the HRDR for personnel decision making, as a supplement to a selection interview, and as a developmental tool. It also includes instructions of feeding results back to the candidate. These sections are easy to follow and include detailed instructions on how to tie the report statements to the job, or to integrate the report into a selection interview.

STRENGTHS AND WEAKNESSES OF THE HRDR. Use of computer-generated interpretive statements to write reports such as the HRDR helps alleviate reliability problems associated with raters. The fact that the same answers will generate the same report on two different occasions assures consistency. The use of a team of experts to generate the statements and logic to generate the report should also help to improve the content validity of the report.

However, the long-term scale reliabilities of .52 raise questions about the use of instruments such as the 16PF for selection purposes. Although the User's Guide provides some detail on how to conduct a job analysis and tie the statements from the report to desirable job behaviors, the use of the report as a stand-alone decision maker would be difficult to justify, particularly if the dimensions being measured can change over time. Using it as a developmental tool, or as a tool to guide the development of a structured selection interview, seems more appropriate.

An additional concern with the use of instruments such as the 16PF in organizational settings is that nonprofessionals may have access to scale scores and may use them inappropriately. The User's Guide instructs the individual receiving the report to separate the attached scale scores from the report to prevent this, but the potential remains.

REVIEWER'S REFERENCES
Cattell, R. B., Eber, H. W., & Tatsuoka, M. M. (1970). *Handbook for the Sixteen Personality Factor Questionnaire (16PF)*. Champaign, IL: Institute for Personality and Ability Testing.
Sweney, A. B. (1970). Organizational power roles. *Professional Management Bulletin, 10*, 5-12.
Sweney, A. B. (1977). *Response to power measure handbook.* Wichita, KS: Test Systems, Inc.

[32]
Informal Reading Comprehension Placement Test.

Purpose: Assesses the instructional and independent comprehension levels of students from pre-readiness (Grade 1) through level eight plus (Grade 8).
Population: Grades 1–6 for typical learners and Grades 7–12 remedially.
Publication Date: 1983.
Scores, 3: Word Comprehension, Passage Comprehension, Total Comprehension.
Administration: Individual.
Price Data, 1989: $49.95 per complete kit including 1 diskette, 1 back-up diskette, management, and documentation (15 pages).
Time: (35–50) minutes for the battery; (15–20) minutes for Part 1; (20–30) minutes for Part 2.
Comments: Test administered in 2 parts; Apple II or TRS-80 microcomputer necessary for administration.
Authors: Ann Edson and Eunice Insel.
Publisher: Educational Activities, Inc.

Review of the Informal Reading Comprehension Placement Test by GLORIA A. GALVIN, Assistant Professor of Psychology, Ohio University, Athens, OH:

This test consists of two types of tasks: word analogies and a series of eight graded paragraphs. The paragraphs were developed using readability formulas to control for vocabulary and sentence length. Each paragraph is followed by four multiple-choice questions (each with three one-word answer choices) designed to test comprehension of each of the following: detail, main idea, inference, and vocabulary from the context. The major purpose of the test is to enable a student to be placed in curricular materials at the appropriate reading comprehension level. The authors' rationale for the test is "to use the findings to prescribe a developmental, corrective, or remedial reading program for the individual student."

The main advantage of this test over other commercial tests or typical teacher-made tests of this type is the computer format that lets the child take the test largely independent of a test administrator. However, this advantage is limited because there are points within the program where the student may be given the instruction, "Please call your teacher," so that an examiner must be available to advance or terminate the program appropriately. Further, there is a fundamental problem in having beginning or poor readers do a reading test independently when the instructions are printed on the screen and must be read and comprehended to be executed correctly. Children whose reading comprehension is at the lower reading levels may not be validly tested because they do not understand the printed program commands, and not because they cannot comprehend the lower level paragraphs. This limits the usefulness of the test with many young children and also with older children with reading problems.

A major problem with this test is the complete lack of reliability, validity, and normative information. Although the test is claimed to have been used with 3,000 children, no data are presented. Furthermore, how well this test places children into various curricular materials at various grade levels is not known. For the purpose of placing children accurately into reading materials, teachers would be better served by their own teacher-made materials that fit their specific curricula.

A second problem with this test is the authors' failure to fully utilize the computer technology. Although the variety of comprehension questions accompanying each paragraph is laudable, greater numbers of questions could have been incorporated to make the measurement more reliable. For example, questions could have been arranged so that a student answering 100% of the four basic questions would be given some higher level inferential questions, whereas the student falling below the criterion would be given additional easier questions. The process should lead to a fuller understanding of the student's level of comprehension. In addition, qualitative information on the student's test performance should be made available using computer technology, rather than limiting the output to a few summary scores. Given the rationale for the test by the authors as a way of helping plan for prescriptive and remedial help for the individual student,

information on the (a) number and types of errors made, (b) amount of rereading the student did (each paragraph can be recalled once per question), and (c) rate at which the student completed the test should also be made available. Such information would be available in many typical paper-and-pencil, examiner-administered tests.

In summary, this test offers some positive features, such as the variety of comprehension questions uniformly applied to each paragraph, minimum examiner time per student, and a test that ends smoothly without showing the student how many items were not presented. However, this test lacks the basic foundation for adequate measurement by ignoring the concepts of reliability and validity. Further, the test fails to utilize the computer format to provide analysis of student errors and actually is more limited in the information it provides and the flexibility with which it can be used than a well-constructed teacher-made test for a specific curriculum. Therefore, although time is saved in administration of this test, the information gleened is much less than it could have been. This test may be useful for a quick screening of reading placement level, but does not have much to offer the educator who has the goal of remediation for the individual student.

Review of the Informal Reading Comprehension Placement Test by CLAUDIA R. WRIGHT, Assistant Professor of Educational Psychology, California State University, Long Beach, CA:

The Informal Reading Comprehension Placement Test was developed by two educators with backgrounds as reading specialists in elementary and secondary school settings who also have worked as curriculum development consultants for public school districts located in New York. This test was designed to serve as a computer-facilitated screening and placement test providing a measure of reading comprehension levels for students in Grades 1 through 6 who may range in reading ability from prereadiness through eighth-grade levels and beyond. In addition, the test has been employed for remediation purposes with secondary and special education students.

The Informal Reading Placement Test is divided into two parts. The first section, identified as the Word Comprehension Test (Part 1), is made up of eight sets of eight word-meaning analogies for a total of 64 test items in a multiple-choice response format. Approximately 15 to 20 minutes is required for testing. Vocabulary levels for this part of the test have been validated, in part, by the employment of the EDL and Dolch Word lists as referents in the selection of words for each level. The second section, the Passage Comprehension Test (Part 2), is composed of eight reading passages which range in reading difficulty from prereadiness to eighth-grade-plus levels. Vocabulary and sentence length have been controlled for each level using Spache, Frye, and Dale Chall readability formulas. Each of the eight passages is followed by four multiple-choice test items that purportedly measure comprehension of detail, main idea, inference, and vocabulary. Completion time for Part 2 is 20 to 30 minutes. In addition to the two reading comprehension components, estimates of a respondent's total instructional level, independent reading level, and frustration level are also provided.

The entire test is administered and scored on the microcomputer. The test manual provides the teacher with clear instructions for the operation of the program through a sample testing session. The process is facilitated further by illustrations of the sequence for several test segments. The computer displays are personalized with the student's name, the content is easy to read and hierarchically organized, and the program is well suited for independent or teacher-assisted testing. In addition, explicit directions are provided for the interpretation of student performances. Teachers have access to five types of information for each student: (a) a word comprehension score that identifies the number of incorrect responses at each of the eight reading levels; (b) a passage comprehension score for each of the eight reading levels; (c) the total instructional level that is a composite indicator made up of a comparison of the word comprehension and passage comprehension levels to determine by how many levels the two scores differ; (d) a total independent level that identifies the level at which the student can read independently (operationally defined as that level at which the student correctly identifies words with 99% accuracy and passes the comprehension items at the 95% level); and (e) the total frustration level that signifies the lowest level of comprehension (less than 90% word accuracy and 50% or below in

correct responses to the comprehension items) and that is thought to indicate the extent to which the reading material is too difficult for the student. This reviewer assumes that conventional mastery-learning rationales have been employed for the selection of these particular percentages as cutoff scores, even though no rationales have been cited.

No reliability or validity information has been provided with the test materials. The authors acknowledge that the psychometric properties of the instrument are "undoubtably not the same as a typical standardized reading test"; however, they fail to report what information may have led them to this conclusion. Further, a relatively thorough search of the literature revealed that very little, if any, research has employed the Informal Reading Placement Test to support the validity of the instrument.

As noted in the test manual, the Informal Reading Placement Test has been used with over 3,000 students enrolled in Grades 1 through 6 as a tool for the classroom teacher to assess reading comprehension for placement and to provide information for remedial instruction. It would appear that with such a broadly based usage of the instrument, some data from standardized achievement tests could be made available for estimating construct and criterion-related validities.

The authors are encouraged to incorporate within the test manual any additional information that may be obtained from empirical studies to establish the reliability of the instrument, as well as the construct and criterion-related validities of the Informal Reading Placement Test. These data could serve to support the placement and remedial functions for which the test was developed. Even though a test has been designed to afford a "quick" assessment of behavior, the brevity of the assessment does not reduce the demand for an instrument with sound psychometric properties.

Overall, the Informal Reading Placement Test as a computer-assisted assessment device would appear to provide a promising approach for classroom applications. Caution, however, should be exercised in the use of this instrument if it is employed as the only criterion for placement or remediation purposes, particularly in light of the absence of reliability and validity data.

[33]
Informal Writing Inventory.

Purpose: To measure an individual's skills in written expression.
Population: Grades 3–12.
Publication Date: 1986.
Acronym: IWI.
Scores, 4: Formation Errors, Grammar Errors, Communication Errors, Total Errors.
Administration: Individual or group.
Price Data, 1988: $32.95 per complete set including 50 response forms, 20 student record folders, 14 picture prompts, and Administrator's Manual (36 pages).
Time: Administration time not reported.
Author: Gerard Giordano.
Publisher: Scholastic Testing Service, Inc.

Review of the Informal Writing Inventory by GABRIEL DELLA-PIANA, Professor of Educational Psychology, University of Utah, Salt Lake City, UT:

The Informal Writing Inventory (IWI) is designed as a "diagnostic procedure . . . for evaluating writing samples . . . analyzing [them] into categories that simplify a judgment about the presence, degree, and [to some extent] cause of writing disability. . . . [It also] specifies remedial exercises . . . for writers who commit errors that interfere with . . . formation [handwriting], grammar, and communication [comprehensibility]" (p. 1, Manual, bracketed words added). The instrument makes use of pictorial prompts to "motivate students to write." This review focuses on the procedures specified in the Administrator's Manual. Although the reviewer found much innovative about the IWI, it was found limited in its current stage of development.

The procedures for administration do not appear adequate for the uses intended. The test administrator is to "choose one from a set of 14 pictures" (p. 7, Manual) for the student to write about. However, no data are presented describing the differential effects of the writing prompts for the wide range of ages for which the test is designed. Furthermore, the instructions to the writer leave so much to the discretion of the test administrator that it is not clear what writing prompt will be presented. A portion of one key sentence is "ask the students to think about the picture you display and to create a record of their responses" (p. 7, Manual). One teacher following these instructions said to the students, "Look at the picture and write what the girl is thinking about." These instructions certainly focused attention differently than others would with the same general guide to administration. Additionally, the instructions indicate that there are "No limits . . . for . . . length of passage." However, they also suggest that "Typically, a minimum of twenty errors is required for an analysis" (p. 7). With such instructions, the "diagnosis" can certainly be quite different when conducted by different test administrators.

Scoring procedures could be improved with respect to the help given to the test user doing the scoring. The writing sample elicited is scored for three kinds of errors that are transformed into an "error index" and a "communication index." The error index is the percent of words analyzed that indicate any kind of error including Formation (handwriting), Grammar, or Communication (formation and grammar errors that interfere with comprehension and another category of communication error to be noted below). The communication index is the percent of total errors that are Communication errors. The scoring difficulty arises from the lack of detailed descriptions of the categories and the lack of sample analyses representing "disabled writers." On the latter point, there are three complete illustrative analyses none of which represent "disabled writers" (a writer who has *not* developed "functional writing skills"). For writers *with* functional writing skills, "at least 77% of [their] writing errors do not impede communication." Yet, of the three illustrative analyses, two of them have *no* communication errors (well above 77% that do not impede communication) and one has only three Communication errors out of a total of 31 errors (or about 90% of the errors being those that do not impede communication). As to the detail on description of scoring categories, Grammar errors are listed and well illustrated. However, Formation errors (handwriting) are not clearly described or illustrated. The only Communication error other than Formation errors that is illustrated or described is "joining of semantically irreconcilable concepts, e.g., 'He took a bite from the sleeping stone.'" Because the definition of disabled and nondisabled rests primarily on the extent of communication errors, these examples in the manual raise questions about the construct or domain definition of "disability."

Suggestions for correcting writing problems are outlined under 24 activities keyed to weaknesses in handwriting, spelling, grammar, and communication. These activities are of varying quality. What is most significant, however, is the lack of a clear guide to selection of an activity based on the diagnostic data. For example, once one eliminates instructional activities that are relevant to communication errors due to spelling, handwriting, or grammar, there are 14 of the 24 activities that are targeted to improve communication, and many of them indeed do appear to be helpful for this purpose. However, the diagnostic test does not identify kinds of communication errors in a way that would help in selecting among the activities. Also, there are six activities relevant to "spelling," three of which are independent of spelling error due to handwriting difficulties. But again there is no diagnosis of *kinds* of spelling difficulties (e.g., phonetically regular spellings, mispronunciations, regular spelling inappropriately generalized) and remediation relevant to the kind of spelling difficulty.

Perhaps what is most problematic about the IWI is that even though it is intended as an "informal" assessment instrument, its development does not appear to be guided by systematic procedures for performance assessment. There are no intercoder reliability data for the scoring system. The achievement domain is not defined clearly enough so that one can interpret a "communication index" or decide if the scoring operations appear to tap the domain or construct intended. The idea of using pictorial prompts is excellent because it can sidestep the difficulties in reading instructions that tell what to write about. But the IWI has too many problems in its current stage of development. What this reviewer would recommend to potential consumers of an informal writing inventory is that they read up on what is involved in writing skills assessment (e.g., Faigley et al., 1985; Ruth & Murphy, 1988; Quellmalz, 1986) and then survey available instruments.

REVIEWER'S REFERENCES

Faigley, L., Cherry, R. D., Jolliffe, D. A., & Skinner, A. M. (1985). *Assessing writers' knowledge and processes of composing.* Norwood, NJ: Ablex.

Quellmalz, E. (1986). Writing skills assessment. In R. A. Berk (Ed.), *Performance assessment: Methods and applications* (pp. 492-508). Baltimore: Johns Hopkins University Press.

Ruth, L., & Murphy, S. (1988). *Designing writing tasks for the assessment of writing.* Norwood, NJ: Ablex.

Review of the Informal Writing Inventory by DONALD L. RUBIN, *Associate Professor of Language Education, The University of Georgia, Athens, GA:*

In recent years, educational reformers have decried the once common medical pathology-oriented metaphor of teaching and learning. Rather than diagnosing and curing skill deficits, the new generation of metaphors instead urges educators to acknowledge the considerable prowess of even novice learners. The new models enjoin educators to nurture students as they move through predictable stages of development. The skill domain of written communication is at the forefront of this new order. Under slogans like "writing to learn" and "composing processes not written products," and in tandem with growing interest in teaching critical thinking, the teaching of writing is enjoying a strong revitalization as something a great deal more than just error-free scribing.

A writing assessment procedure that focuses exclusively on errors, therefore, is an anachronism, a throwback to deficit remediation models. Such is the case of the Informal Writing Inventory. The purpose of this instrument is to identify the writing problems of potentially disabled writers. The category of disabled writer to which the Inventory is aimed seems quite broad; the Administrator's Manual refers to students who experience difficulty forming letters, suffer from writer's block, and manifest inability to distinguish relevant from extraneous details. At least some of these disabling conditions are quite normal occurrences for most writers at least some of the time. They hardly serve to define some special population.

Moreover, the entire issue of error in writing is a good deal more complex than this Inventory acknowledges. The instrument analyzes elicited writing samples for relative frequencies of three kinds of errors: Formation errors (spelling and penmanship), Grammatical errors, and Communication errors. One issue not adequately addressed is the identification of error. For example, the society—if not the grammar handbooks—is rapidly moving toward acceptance of "they" as a generic third person *singular* pronoun (e.g., "If a person wants to write well they need to know what to say"). And although many people would regard starting a sentence with a conjunction as gravely egregious, the Administrator's Manual shows one such example (on page 8) but fails to mark it as a violation. As it happens, it is difficult to define the concept of error in writing. The phrase "gravely egregious" contains an element of redundancy. Is it therefore an error?

Beyond the issue of reliably defining the concept of error, categorizing types of errors can be problematic. Consider the sentence, "The manuscript went to the printed." It contains a formation error if one assumes that the final "d" should be "r." It contains a grammatical error if one assumes that a verb form cannot serve as object of a sentence (but compare, "The toils went to the vanquished"). It constitutes a communication error, the Administrator's manual rightly points out, only if one cannot make sense of it in context. Communicative errors are particularly important to interpreting results of the Informal Writing Inventory; the greater the proportion of communicative errors to total errors, the more disabled is the writer. Most teachers of basic writing are painfully aware, however, that in context—for example, in the context of a conversation with the writer—virtually all student sentences do make sense. The critical issue in judging writing quality is not so much one of sense as negotiating effort: How much effort ought the reader, relative to the writer, expend in order to reveal the sense of a text?

These concerns about the Inventory's emphasis on error, the fuzziness of the very concept of writing error, and lack of clear definition between categories of error all speak to the procedure's poor construct validity. They also bear on matters of reliability. The test publisher's materials provide no information about interrater reliability in identifying or categorizing error.

Test users will also be operating in the dark with regard to the reliability of elicitation procedures. The Inventory includes 14 stimulus pictures to be used in eliciting writing samples. The pictures depict incongruent events, intended to arouse mild anxiety in writers. According to the Administrator's Manual, this is an optimal way to elicit "meaningful writing samples." Optimal or not, the various pictures are likely not equivalent forms of the same test. (Elicitation instructions even permit the option of test-takers drawing their own stimulus pictures.) Students may produce different quantities of writing, or different modes of writing, in response to the different stimuli. Test users would also be interested in learning about test-retest reliabilities. To what extent does a student's error production represent a stable trait? Because motivation and attentiveness are important factors in error detection and correction, reliability across time is likely small. The Administrator's Manual does recommend that writing samples ought to include at least 20 errors. Too small a sample, according to the Manual, "decreases . . . one's confidence in the validity of the analysis of these errors." Using the number of errors as an index of sample length results in an odd enigma, however. An adequate language sample for a poor writer might be five sentences but a good writer might need to produce five pages. Still, the two writers' error proportions might end up looking quite similar.

The basic strength of the Informal Writing Inventory is that it attempts to measure writing ability directly. It samples holistic writing performance rather than isolated word writing and rather than indirect measures of error identification in supplied sentences. In using the Inventory with learning disabled populations, test administrators will be acknowledging that all students are capable of authentic composing. In addition, the Inventory quite properly recognizes that not all errors are created equal; those that disrupt communication engender greater concern than those that are mere violations of surface-level mechanics. Finally, as a diagnostic instrument the Inventory links various error profiles to one of 24 remedial writing exercises. These exercises range from simple procedures in which students label illustrations with descriptive words to more complex and diffuse activities, such as writing to request information from foreign consulates. The activities are sound instructional practices, though there is little reason to believe that any single exercise will remediate a pattern of error. In short, the Informal Writing Inventory is inadequate psychometrically, and it does reflect a paradigm of instruction generally regarded as outmoded, if not bankrupt. But at least it gets students writing, and that's not bad.

[34]
Jr.-Sr. High School Personality Questionnaire.

Purpose: Measures primary personality characteristics in adolescents.
Population: Ages 12–18.
Publication Dates: 1953–84.
Acronym: HSPQ.
Scores, 18: 14 primary factor scores (Warmth, Intelligence, Emotional Stability, Excitability, Dominance, Enthusiasm, Conformity, Boldness, Sensitivity, Withdrawal, Apprehension, Self-Sufficiency, Self-Discipline, Tension), 4 second-order factor scores (Extraversion, Anxiety, Tough Poise, Independence).
Administration: Group.
Forms, 4: A, B, C, D (authors recommend administration of 2 or more forms).
Price Data, 1987: $14.25 per 25 reusable test booklets (specify Form A, B, C, or D); $9.50 per scoring keys for all forms; $7.50 per 25 machine-scorable answer sheets; $7.50 per 50 hand-scoring answer sheets; $9.50 per 50 hand-scoring answer-profile sheets; $7.50 per 50 profile sheets; $7.50 per 50 second-order worksheets; $9.95 per manual ('84, 101 pages); $21.10 per introductory kit; computer scoring and interpretive services available from publisher at $16 or less per individual report depending upon quantity requested.
Time: (45–60) minutes per form.
Authors: Raymond B. Cattell, Mary D. Cattell, and Edgar Johns (manual and norms).
Publisher: Institute for Personality and Ability Testing, Inc.
Foreign Adaptation: British adaptation; ages 13–15; 1973; supplement by Peter Saville and Laura Finlayson; NFER-Nelson Publishing Co., Ltd. [England].
Cross References: See 9:559 (8 references), T3:1233 (22 references), 8:597 (68 references), and T2:1253 (37 references); for reviews by Robert Hogan and Douglas N. Jackson, see 7:97 (53 references); see also P:136 (29 references); for reviews by C. J. Adcock and Philip E. Vernon of an earlier edition, see 6:131 (17 references); see also 5:72 (4 references).

TEST REFERENCES

1. Bamber, J. H., Bill, J. M., Boyd, F. E., & Corbett, W. D. (1983). In two minds—Arts and science differences at sixth-form level. *British Journal of Educational Psychology, 53*, 222-233.
2. Castelli-Sawicki, D., Wallbrown, F. H., & Blixt, S. L. (1983). Developing a Motivational Distortion Scale for the High School Personality Questionnaire. *Measurement and Evaluation in Guidance, 16*, 43-51.
3. Gilbert, J. (1983). Deliberate metallic paint inhalation and cultural marginality: Paint sniffing among acculturating central California youth. *Addictive Behaviors, 8*, 79-82.
4. McGiboney, G. W., Carter, C., & Jones, W. (1984). Hand Test and the High School Personality Questionnaire: Structural analysis. *Perceptual and Motor Skills, 58*, 287-290.
5. Munson, R. F., & Blincoe, M. M. (1984). Evaluation of a residential treatment center for emotionally disturbed adolescents. *Adolescence, 19*, 253-261.
6. Munson, R. F., & LaPaille, K. (1984). Personality tests as a predictor of success in a residential treatment center. *Adolescence, 19*, 697-701.
7. Cattell, R. B., Rao, D. C., & Schuerger, J. M. (1985). Heritability in the personality control system: Ego strength (C), super ego strength (G) and the self sentiment (Q3); by the Mava Model, Q-data, and maximum likelihood analyses. *Social Behavior and Personality, 13*, 33-41.
8. Cattell, R. B., & Krug, S. E. (1986). The number of factors in the 16PF: A review of the evidence with special emphasis on methodological problems. *Educational and Psychological Measurement, 46*, 509-522.
9. Handford, H. A., Mayes, S. D., Bagnato, S. J., & Bixler, E. O. (1986). Relationships between variations in parents' attitudes and personality traits of hemophilic boys. *American Journal of Orthopsychiatry, 56*, 424-434.
10. Howard, R. C., Haynes, J. P., & Atkinson, D. (1986). Factors associated with juvenile detention truancy. *Adolescence, 21*, 357-364.
11. Richman, C. L., Brown, K. P., & Clark, M. (1987). Personality changes as a function of minimum competency test success or failure. *Contemporary Educational Psychology, 12*, 7-16.
12. Winkel, M., Novak, D. M., & Hopson, H. (1987). Personality factors, subject gender, and the effects of aggressive video games on aggression in adolescents. *Journal of Research in Personality, 21*, 211-223.

Review of the Jr.-Sr. High School Personality Questionnaire by RICHARD I. LANYON, Professor of Psychology, Arizona State University, Tempe, AZ:

The Jr.-Sr. High School Personality Questionnaire (HSPQ) is described as a self-report personality inventory for adolescents (ages 12–18) that measures 14 primary personality characteristics. It is one of the 16PF series of tests that share a common core of personality concepts. There are four forms (A, B, C, and D), and norms exist to use them in combination (A + B; C + D; A + B + C + D). Each form uses a common answer sheet and scoring key. Computerized scoring and interpretation services are available. The HSPQ was first published nearly 40 years ago (1953) as the *Junior Personality Quiz*. The current Manual states that although minor revisions have been made in the test, the last being in 1968, the test has remained essentially the same.

The test booklet provided to this reviewer was entitled Jr.-Sr. HSPQ, Form A, 1968–1969 Edition. This appears to be exactly the same test that was reviewed in detail by Robert Hogan and by Douglas Jackson in the *Seventh Mental Measurements Yearbook* (1972), and the reader is referred to those reviews. To summarize them, Hogan found the HSPQ to be convenient and easy to use. However, "the reliability of the scales is modest, and their validity is indeterminate." Jackson's conclusions were even more negative, citing "deceptive misuse of the concept of validity" in reporting test data, low equivalent-form correlations, low homogeneity of single scales, and the failure to report the specific procedures by which scales were constructed and items were selected. He found the HSPQ to be "perhaps characteristic of personality tests as they existed three decades ago."

The HSPQ Manual, updated in 1984, provides considerable additional validity and other data beyond what was available in 1972. However, it is noted that the *format* of the test was changed in the 1968/69 edition (to trichotomous from dichotomous items) and that some items were reworded. Thus, one cannot assume the pre-1968/69 HSPQ is the same as the current (1968/69) HSPQ. A cursory examination of the relevant references indicates that roughly half of them were published prior to the early 1970s, and thus may not be relevant to the current form of the test. This problem is not mentioned in the Manual. Another problem with the validity data is that the form of the HSPQ used is not indicated in any of the studies cited. Because the interform correlations are so low, it cannot be assumed that the forms are interchangeable. The median scale correlations of the combined Forms A and B with the combined Forms C and D is less than .60, based on the largest sample cited in the Manual.

Examination of the validity data leads to the conclusion that the promotional literature continues to oversell the test. For example, the *IPAT Catalog* states the computer interpretation "provides a complete report for . . . all personality characteristics of significance, as well as the individual's promise in areas of academic achievement, leadership, creativity, and vocational success." The accompanying brochure adds to this list tendencies for delinquency, chemical dependency proneness, longitudinal research, and rapid mental health screening.

The Manual cites only one longitudinal research study, in England and Wales. Regarding chemical dependency, the only published work cited is on glue sniffers, also in England. An examination of this and several unpublished studies shows some group differences, but no evidence of utility for individual assessment. The claim of utility for mental health screening relies mainly on group differences on Anxiety, which is a second-order factor to be computed as a weighted composite of seven regular scales. The brochure states that "since the HSPQ has been translated into German, French, Italian, Hebrew, Japanese, Spanish, and other languages, it is especially useful for cross-cultural studies." However, not a word about any of these translations is given in the Manual, let alone any recognition that the process of translating a personality inventory is a complex and tricky business that may not result in a test that is equivalent to the original-language version. Overall, the presentation of validity data falls far short of the 1985 *Standards for Educational and Psychological Testing* developed jointly by the American Psychological Association and other organizations.

There are many other problems and annoyances with the HSPQ. For example: (*a*) Although the norms are based on a large, geographically diverse sample, no information is given as to how the children were selected, so it is uncertain whether they are representative of teenagers in general. (*b*) One section of the Manual continues to refer to the scales by Cattell's neologisms (Sizia/Affectia, Harria/Presmia, etc.), a practice that is guaranteed to befuddle potential users. (*c*) The sample items on the front of the booklet are written as statements (they are the same sample items as on the 16PF booklet), but the items themselves are in question format. (*d*) The HSPQ uses the obsolete "sten" (standard ten) scale-score system, rather than a percentile or deviation score system. (*e*) Age corrections for the norms can be made only by applying an algebraic formula individually to each score, and this correction is not available for all forms of the test. (*f*) Despite the promotional literature, no substantive information is given to support computer interpretation of the HSPQ.

There is little else to say except that Jackson's conclusions still hold, nearly 20 years later. The HSPQ is not a viable test for contemporary use. Readers are steered toward the Personality Inventory for Children (10:281) for children up to the age of 16, and also to the Minnesota Multiphasic Personality Inventory (MMPI; 9:715) adolescent data. (The MMPI-2 for adolescents has been promised but is not yet available at the time of writing this review). Regarding the assessment of normal-range personality characteristics in adolescents, no alternative instrument comes readily to mind.

However, in view of the recent activity in developing inventories based on the five-factor system, it is hoped that an adolescent form of such an inventory will soon be forthcoming.

REVIEWER'S REFERENCES

Hogan, R. (1972). [Review of the Jr.-Sr. High School Personality Questionnaire]. In O. K. Buros (Ed.), *The seventh mental measurements yearbook* (pp. 207-208). Highland Park, NJ: The Gryphon Press.
Jackson, D. N. (1972). [Review of the Jr.-Sr. High School Personality Questionnaire]. In O. K. Buros (Ed.), *The seventh mental measurements yearbook* (pp. 208-211). Highland Park, NJ: The Gryphon Press.
American Educational Research Association, American Psychological Association, & National Council on Measurement in Education. (1985). *Standards for educational and psychological testing.* Washington, DC: American Psychological Association, Inc.

Review of the Jr.-Sr. High School Personality Questionnaire by STEVEN V. OWEN, Professor of Educational Psychology, University of Connecticut, Storrs, CT:

The Jr.-Sr. High School Personality Questionnaire is a multifactor battery whose aim is to measure a variety of personality characteristics of high-school-aged youngsters. Superficially, the HSPQ seems to assess 14 traits, but a careful reading will produce ambiguity about exactly what is being measured. Fourteen primary scores are produced. Although the authors claim each scale "measures a unique personality dimension" (Cattell, Cattell, & Johns, 1984, p. 1), one of the scores is termed *Intelligence*, a construct not usually considered to be a portion of personality. Further, the scale intercorrelations are so strong the claim of unique dimensions is misleading.

Modeled on Cattell's Sixteen Personality Factor Questionnaire (16PF; 9:1136), the HSPQ has evolved through four versions—the original, published in 1953 under a different title; and revisions in 1958, 1963, and 1968. The current test version is thus more than two decades old; item wording occasionally reflects an earlier vocabulary (e.g., "Are there times when you think, 'People are so unreasonable, they can't even be trusted to look after their own good'?"). The most recent manual (1984) is a consolidation of earlier references and later research, but the norms appear to be from students in 1968.

There are four versions (A, B, C, and D) of the HSPQ that appear to be equivalent forms, each requiring 45 to 60 minutes to complete. Equivalence estimates for each scale across the four versions are given in the manual, but the authors argue that one should not consider these versions equivalent forms. Rather, "they are better thought of as *extension* forms" (Cattell et al., 1984, p. 26) and the authors propose that every effort be made to administer two or more forms. No matter what the forms are called, the equivalence coefficients are low. In the worst cases, Factors E (Dominance) and J (Withdrawal) show average coefficients of .19 and .18, respectively. For Factor J, double forms (A + B versus C + D) give a coefficient of only .06. A quick scan of the table of equivalence coefficients suggests the "extension" scales share only about 50% of their variance.

Stability estimates are also given. Coefficients for brief intervals (misleadingly called "dependability coefficients" as though derived from generalizability analysis) average .79 for a single form. For longer intervals, the mean is .56. Internal consistency estimates are conspicuously absent. Reliability estimates would not be expected to be especially high, because the scales are so brief.

The standard error of measurement is mentioned briefly, and a very hopeful example is offered. An analyst interested in confidence intervals around obtained scores will have to calculate his or her own standard errors; the results may reduce optimism about the HSPQ. Here is an example using the scale with the best psychometric properties—Intelligence—measured on Form A, for a male with a raw score of 7. Using the long-interval reliability estimate, a 95% confidence interval gives a range of percentile ranks from 23 to 89, or an IQ range of 88 to 120.

Even test users with adequate measurement skills might be confused by the wide variation in reliability data, coupled with a notably upbeat narrative in the manual. In classical test theory, of course, there is no rule that various reliability estimates must be consistent; sources of error variance are different for each type of coefficient. For two decades, advances in generalizability theory and covariance modeling have offered ways to improve and consolidate reliability information. Some consolidation would have been useful here.

The intended users of the HSPQ—teachers, guidance counselors, and clinical psychologists—likely will be befuddled as they try to wade through the validity evidence presented for the test. Perhaps the authors assume users will believe promises that the test is psychometrically sound because the procedures sound impressive. The statement introducing factorial data is typical: "Factor analysis, another technique for establishing construct validity, is becoming the standard procedure for confirming the existence of a construct" (Cattell et al., p. 27). Even before the widespread use of covariance structural modeling, this statement would have exaggerated the confirmatory use of principal factor analysis.

When the scale scores from the four test versions are factor analyzed, inspection of the pattern matrices shows a sizable departure from simple structure, especially for males. Here, six of the scales show very weak evidence of factorial validity. Oblique rotations might be expected to produce correlated scale scores (15% of the scale intercorrelations for females are greater than .50), but they cannot explain such vague structure. Second-order factoring of the 14 scales gives pattern matrices that are even more opaque. As if to justify the covariation among factors, the authors give a table showing unique variance for each factor. Even these figures are unimpressive. The average unique variance for the factors is less than 40%.

Abundant validity evidence is presented. A frequent form is a known groups comparison, where, for example, the profiles of high- and low-achieving students are contrasted. The profile comparisons are somewhat inconsistent. The most authentic contrast would use a multivariate approach to take into account the scale covariances; none is seen. A few comparisons are based on visual inspection of the largest apparent scale differences, and others are based on significance tests for each scale. The repeated statistical tests offer a good object lesson in psychometric sleight of hand. Each test assumes the variance analyzed is error-free. When significances pop up, they are treated as genuine, with no mention of statistical power or experimentwise alpha. Under a different assumption—that the measures are fallible—the comparisons can be done using standard errors of measurement to construct confidence intervals. Using this method, the apparent display of significant differences (and thus validity evidence) evaporates.

Other validity arguments, too tedious to detail, can be summarized as a small question with no answer: What do we have here?

Despite the authors' persuasive remarks, putting the HSPQ scale scores to practical use is doubly difficult for the practitioner. First, the psychometric evidence is not at all convincing. Second, it is not clear how a counselor or teacher might use scores to diagnose or to guide students. Neither does it seem clear to the authors, who resort to a long table of standard scores from a different measure (the 16PF!) to suggest how the HSPQ can provide occupational advice.

Although earlier reviewers have given straightforward advice about improving the psychometric properties of the HSPQ, the comments have gone largely unheeded. The HSPQ now seems so distant from current psychometric practice that it might be regarded as a relic in the history of measurement.

REVIEWER'S REFERENCE

Cattell, R. B., Cattell, M. D., & Johns, E. (1984). *Manual and norms for the High School Personality Questionnaire.* Champaign, IL: Institute for Personality and Ability Testing.

[35]
Learning Preference Inventory.
Purpose: "To assist teachers in the task of identifying individual student learning preferences or styles."
Population: Elementary through adult students.
Publication Dates: 1978–80.
Acronym: LPI.
Scores: 6 preference scores: Sensing-Feeling, Sensing-Thinking, Intuitive-Thinking, Intuitive-Feeling, Introversion, Extraversion.
Administration: Group.
Price Data, 1988: $175 per complete kit including 35 inventories, 35 Student Diagnostic Behavior Checklist folders, 35 individual computer printouts, 1 class profile printout, 1 copy each of Learning Style Inventory and Teaching Style Inventory (for teacher self-assessment), Learning Styles and Strategies Manual, and user's manual ('80, 60 pages); $142 per complete kit without computer scoring; $3 per inventory with prepaid computer scoring; $2 per inventory without computer scoring.
Time: [30] minutes.
Comments: Identifies learning styles based on Jungian typology.
Authors: Harvey F. Silver and J. Robert Hanson.
Publisher: Hanson Silver Strong & Associates, Inc.

TEST REFERENCES

1. Cahill, R., & Madigan, M. J. (1984). The influence of curriculum format on learning preference and learning style. *The American Journal of Occupational Therapy, 38,* 683-686.

Review of the Learning Preference Inventory by BRUCE H. BISKIN, *Senior Psychometrician, American Institute of Certified Public Accountants, New York, NY:*

As described in its User's Manual, the Learning Preference Inventory (LPI) "is designed to assist teachers in the task of identifying individual student learning preferences or styles." The LPI is based on Jung's theory of psychological types and attempts to classify students in terms of their information-processing attitude (introversion [I] vs. extraversion [E]), perceptual function (sensing [S] vs. intuition [N]), and judgment function (thinking [T] vs. feeling [F]). Six scores are calculated—one for each attitude (I and E) and one for each possible combination of functions (ST, SF, NT, NF). Descriptions of "ideal" types representing the four function combinations, as well as the two attitudes, are included in the User's Manual.

Many readers may be familiar with the Myers-Briggs Type Indicator (MBTI; 10:206), which is also a Jungian-based measure of psychological types. The LPI differs from the MBTI in several important ways. First, the LPI is targeted at school-aged children, whereas the MBTI was developed for adults. Second, whereas the MBTI items were written to measure single dimensions (e.g., S-N), the LPI items yield scores for dimensional combinations (e.g., SF). Third, the MBTI items require that a choice be made among two or three statements, whereas the LPI requires that preferences be rank ordered.

The LPI comprises 36 item stems, each intended to assess different preferences for learning. Each item is followed by four choices that students rank order in terms of their preference for each.

Hand scoring the LPI is more complex than on many inventories, and some teachers may have trouble manually scoring the LPI accurately in the 2–3 minutes estimated in the User's Manual. Although the User's Manual suggests "older students can score their own inventories," answer sheets should be computer-scanned and scored whenever possible to ensure accuracy. The weighting scheme used in the scoring is not intuitive and, unfortunately, its rationale is not explained.

The LPI booklet I examined was printed in black and white on glossy paper. Because glossy paper is sometimes difficult to read, the publisher should consider printing the LPI on nonreflective paper.

The LPI comes with considerable documentation. My review materials included the *LPI User's Manual*, a *Teaching Styles & Strategies* manual, and two research monographs. These materials are geared to help the teacher understand Jung's typology, interpret results from the LPI, and provide examples of teaching exercises to use with students having different learning preferences. Teachers may find the pedagogical material useful in developing lesson plans.

Although the documentation may help teachers think about different ways to teach different types of students, it lacks the technical information needed to evaluate the LPI fairly. I was unable to find a statement about the minimum grade or age level for which the LPI is appropriate. The User's Manual does contain instructions for administering the LPI to "younger children" orally, but it provides no evidence to suggest that oral administration results in scores similar to the standard paper-pencil administration. The User's Manual reports no norms or reliability estimates.

The section in the User's Manual describing LPI profiles is confusing because it illustrates various profile configurations, but then does not suggest how the interpretations of these profiles differ.

Documentation to support the LPI's validity was limited to one research monograph describing a factor analysis of the LPI. The monograph was ambiguous about which of the two groups of students reported had its LPI responses factor analyzed. It was also unclear about which factoring method (principal factors or principal components) was used. The LPI's partially ipsative scoring, a result of the ranking procedure, places constraints on the factor structure that probably enhances the appearance of the results. Thus, this study's findings have limited value until they can be supported by further research.

As I noted earlier, I found much of the pedagogical material provided for review interesting. For those teachers who are comfortable with Jung's model, this material may be a useful source of ideas. However, the documentation includes no evidence of validity for differential effectiveness of teaching methods across student LPI types.

SUMMARY. The fundamental problem with the Learning Preference Inventory is the lack of technical information documented in materials available to users. Basic information is missing about its reliability, its validity in classifying student learning preferences, and its usefulness for increasing teaching effectiveness. The manuals and other information provided are aimed at the classroom teacher rather than the measurement specialist. It is laudable to provide "nuts and bolts" information in an administrator's manual and other documents. However, such information is not sufficient for users who wish to evaluate whether a measure suits their purposes. Because the authors include no information on norms, reliability, and validity in the documentation, the LPI's adequacy and usefulness as a measure of learning preference is questionable.

I would expect to see information regarding a measure's psychometric characteristics in its manual. A published measure without such information falls far short of the ideals set forth in the *Standards for Educational and Psychological Testing* (AERA, APA, & NCME, 1985). In the absence of information that would allow a user to evaluate its psychometric qualities, the Learning Preference Inventory should be considered a research measure at best. Any teacher using the LPI for diagnostic purposes should interpret student scores with extreme caution.

REVIEWER'S REFERENCE

American Educational Research Association, American Psychological Association, & National Council on Measurement in Education. (1985). *Standards for educational and psychological testing*. Washington, DC: American Psychological Association, Inc.

Review of the Learning Preference Inventory by JEFFREY JENKINS, *Attorney, Keleher & McLeod, P.A., Albuquerque, NM:*

The Learning Preference Inventory (LPI) is based on Carl Jung's Theory of Psychological Type; such a basis forms a well-known and studied theoretical foundation for assessing student preferences and learning styles. As a component of a larger kit that includes measures for assessing teachers' teaching and learning styles as well as student behaviors, the LPI is an integral part of a program developed to "create a classroom environment that will work for different teaching and learning styles."

The User's Manual outlines five phases for exploring learning styles: Phase 1, Teacher Self Assessment; Phase 2, Collecting Student Data; Phase 3, Scoring, Analyzing and Plotting Student Learning Styles; Phase 4, Using Student Data; and Phase 5, Sharing Student Data. In each phase are step-by-step instructions for analyzing and using learning styles in the classroom. Phases 4 and 5 comprise half of the manual and outline instructional techniques and classroom exercises for teachers. Thus, the User's Manual, unlike a typical test manual, actually serves as an instructional manual that outlines a method of assessing learning styles as well as procedures for applying learning styles in the classroom. This review is limited to consideration of the LPI apart from its companion measures.

The authors of the LPI adapt the Jungian theory of psychological type to theoretically define styles of learning. This adaptation is one of many that have appeared for the measurement of aspects of personality, with perhaps the most well-known of these being the Myers-Briggs Type Indicator (10:206). Whereas the Myers-Briggs provides a broad measure of personality constructs by assessing personal preferences suggested by the Jungian theory, the LPI simplifies these constructs and focuses on those preferences that are found to be most relevant to learning styles.

Briefly, the authors of the LPI characterize learning style in terms of two sets of "functions," Perception and Judgment. The Perception functions are methods of "finding out" about the world either through Sensing ("The sensor assumes that what he sees is what exists") or Intuition ("The intuiter . . . looks at what the potential significance or interpretations of what the situation might be"). Judgment involves the analysis of the perceived information either by Thinking ("based on external and verifiable information") or Feeling (based on "likes and dislikes"). The authors also identify the dimension of Introversion/Extraversion as typifying two "attitudes" that mediate "how the mind processes those data perceived and judged."

The LPI is a 144-item self-report measure that yields a student profile in terms of four learning styles: Sensing-Feeling, Sensing-Thinking, Intuitive-Thinking, and Intuitive-Feeling. Preference scores are computed in each of these areas and ordered according to a student's "dominant" learning style, "auxiliary" style, "supportive" style, or "least used" style. In addition, students' attitudes are designated as either Introversion or Extraversion. Although the 144 items are scored separately, they are presented as 36 statements with four choices each; students rank the choices according to preference. For example, statement number 1 is: "I'm good at: 1._____helping others, 2._____getting things done, 3._____organizing things, 4._____discovering things." The directions for responding are clear and the items are presented on three pages in an easy-to-read format.

Student responses can be hand scored, and detailed but uncomplicated instructions are given. Scoring results in numerical values of 0–125 for each of the four learning styles and a value of 0–80 for attitude. Values indicate the strength of a student's preference for each style and profiles can be summarized graphically.

Although the authors of the User's Manual state the LPI was developed "over a period of five years on a population of 3,000 students in inner city, urban, and suburban environments," no summary of technical characteristics of the Inventory is offered. Thus, although the instrument appears to measure clearly defined and theoretically supportable constructs, there is no evidence the instrument provides any valid or reliable information about learning styles. This is a fatal flaw that should cause any user alarm.

Although teachers may be tempted to try the LPI and its kit as an interesting exploration in learning styles, they are forewarned that use of the LPI as a measure of learning style may be a futile and unwarranted exercise. Although the program of which the LPI is a part may be useful for sensitizing teachers to the potential differences in learning styles that may exist, there is currently little reason to believe the instrument should be used as a diagnostic tool for teaching, learning, and curriculum planning, as claimed by the authors.

[36]
Learning Process Questionnaire.

Purpose: "To assess the extent to which a secondary school student endorses different approaches to learning and the more important motives and strategies comprising those approaches."
Population: Secondary students.
Publication Dates: 1985–87.

Acronym: LPQ.
Scores, 9: Surface Motive, Surface Strategy, Deep Motive, Deep Strategy, Achieving Motive, Achieving Strategy, Surface Approach, Deep Approach, Achieving Approach.
Administration: Individual or group.
Price Data, 1989: A$4.65 per 10 questionnaires; $2.50 per 10 answer sheets; $3 per score key; $29.95 per monograph entitled *Student Approaches to Learning and Studying* ('87, 151 pages); $12.70 per manual ('87, 36 pages).
Time: 20(40) minutes.
Comments: Tertiary counterpart of the Study Process Questionnaire (85).
Author: John Biggs.
Publisher: Australian Council for Educational Research Ltd. [Australia].
Cross References: For a review by Cathy W. Hall of the Study Process Questionnaire, see 85.

TEST REFERENCES

1. Ramsden, P., Martin, E., & Bowden, J. (1989). School environment and sixth form pupils' approaches to learning. *British Journal of Educational Psychology, 59,* 129-142.

Review of the Learning Process Questionnaire and the Study Process Questionnaire by ROBERT D. BROWN, Carl A. Happold Distinguished Professor of Educational Psychology, University of Nebraska-Lincoln, Lincoln, NE:

The Learning Process Questionnaire (LPQ) and the Study Process Questionnaire (SPQ) are highly related instruments designed to assess the motives, strategies, and approaches that students use to learn and to study. The LPQ is intended for high school students and the SPQ for college students. The instruments were designed by Australian John Biggs and much of the research performed on the instruments is based on Australian subjects.

The self-report questionnaires ask students questions that attempt to measure whether they approach learning and studying primarily from a Surface Motive (to meet minimal standards), a Deep Motive (an intrinsic interest in learning), or from an Achieving Motive (interest in competition and doing well). Corollary strategies are assessed to again determine whether strategies used are Surface (bare essentials learned through rote learning), Deep (attempts to grasp meaning and interrelationships), or Achieving (being well organized). Subscale scores are obtained for Motive and Strategy within each of the three basic approaches: Surface, Deep, and Achieving. The summation of the Motive and Strategy scores yield scale scores for each, referred to as the Approach scores. The sum of the Approach Scores for the Deep and Achieving scales is used as a Composite Approach Score. Thus, there are six subscale scores: Surface Motive and Surface Strategy, Deep Motive and Deep Strategy, and Achieving Motive and Achieving Strategy; three scale scores: Surface Approach, Deep Approach, and Achieving Approach; and one composite score.

The LPQ has 36 items (6 items per subscale) and the SPQ has 42 items (7 items per subscale). Each item asks the respondent to indicate whether the item is 1 = "never or only rarely true of me" or on up the 5-point scale to "is always or almost always true of me." Norms are available for secondary and tertiary students.

The instruments are derived from research on the learning and study process that has centered in Australia. The basic theory is cognitive and assumes that students vary in motives and strategies, study and learn differently, and should be taught differently. Students using surface strategies will learn unintegrated details, those using deep strategies will learn the meaning and interrelationships, and those using achieving strategies will study whatever is necessary to achieve high grades. Students may have a typically used strategy for all subjects, but may also vary their strategies from subject matter to subject matter depending on their interests.

The Research Monograph accompanying the test materials is replete with scale analysis data and reliability and validity information obtained in numerous studies involving the two instruments with correlations available between the scales and a variety of other student variables ranging from fathers' education to locus of control scores. The test author characterizes the test-retest reliability coefficients ranging from .49 to .72 for the subscales across two studies as "highly satisfactory," given that the responses could be affected by interventions, time of year of administration (e.g., just before final exams), and other variables that could affect responses. As might be expected, the scale scores have reported higher test-retest reliability (.60 to .78) and measures of internal consistency are typically in the .70s. These reliability estimates might be more accurately characterized as "good" or "satisfactory" and minimally sufficient for use in working with individual students.

Validity studies lend support to the construct validity of the instruments. Factor analysis supports the scale structure and though labelled differently, other researchers have also reported the distinctions between motivations and strategies, and between deep and surface approaches. Generally, the results support the instruments at the same time they provide disquieting information about what happens to students. Students with high LPQ scores on Deep Approach and Achieving Approach, for example, were more likely to have plans for future education and parents who had more education. Gender differences interacted with the various scale scores with boys, for example, scoring lower on Deep Approaches on the LPQ with increasing years in school. Studies of college students on the SPQ yielded similar results, but interactions were found between the kind of institution and score patterns.

More work needs to be done before these instruments can be highly recommended for use in counseling individual students, but these instruments and others like them can prove to be valuable tools for research on how college and high school students learn and study. The author provides general thoughts about counseling students with different profiles on the scales. As rough guidelines, these can be useful, but counselors must be alert to how the specific context of the test administration may have affected the student's responses. The implications of patterns of group scores for teaching may be more useful as instructors gain insights as to what will and will not work for students who use primarily deep strategies as opposed to those who use primarily surface strategies. The instruments could be invaluable for researchers investigating the impact of intervention programs, particularly the value of teaching metacognition skills and trying to strengthen the metalearning capabilities, on student learning.

Before deciding whether or not to use this particular set of instruments for counseling individual students, intervening with different instructional strategies, or conducting research on the cognitive process, the decision maker should at least examine other available tools such as the Approaches to Studying Inventory (Entwistle & Ramsden, 1983) and the Inventory of Learning Processes (Schmeck & Ribich, 1978). These instruments were designed by researchers pursuing similar lines of inquiry and their instruments and their respective subscales are similar to those of the LPQ and SPQ. Research results thus far are not sufficient to make conclusive comments about how much these instruments are measuring similar or identical constructs (Speth & Brown, 1988). Test users for any purpose will want to read carefully the specific items in these instruments to determine whether or not the phrasing is appropriate for American students.

These instruments, and others like them, could have a significant impact on future education even if they do no more than sensitize school and college instructors to individual differences among their students and alert them that how they teach and test affects what and how students learn.

REVIEWER'S REFERENCES

Schmeck, R. R., & Ribich, F. D. (1978). Construct validation of the Inventory of Learning Processes. *Applied Psychological Measurement, 2*, 551-562.

Entwistle, N. J., & Ramsden, P. (1983). *Understanding student learning.* London: Croom Helm.

Speth, C., & Brown, R. D. (1988). Study approaches, processes and strategies: Are three perspectives better than one? *British Journal of Educational Psychology, 58*, 247-257.

Review of the Learning Process Questionnaire by CATHY W. HALL, *Assistant Professor of Psychology, East Carolina University, Greenville, NC:*

The Learning Process Questionnaire (LPQ) is a 36-item, self-report questionnaire that measures the process factors of learning strategies and learning motives used by secondary students. The Study Process Questionnaire is an extended version of the LPQ for use with tertiary students. A student's approach to a given learning situation is seen as a function of both a motive and a strategy. A surface approach would entail meeting the basic requirements of a learning situation by the rote learning of information for the sole purpose of passing a test. The student demonstrating intrinsic motivation with a strong desire to gain additional information and knowledge would be employing a deep approach. The achieving approach is concerned with being regarded as competent in the subject area and the strategy employed would be organized and systematic study in order to obtain this goal. These three approaches are not necessarily exclusive, however. It is possible for a student to demonstrate a deep-achieving or surface-achieving approach.

Three primary learning approaches are measured (Surface, Deep, and Achieving) with each factor having two subscales consisting of motives and strategies for a total of nine scores. The range of scores is 6 to 30 for each of the motive and strategy subscales. Scoring of the LPQ may be done by hand, machine, or computer, or by sending the protocols to the Australian Council for Educational Research.

The purpose of the LPQ is to better assess students' approaches to learning and make appropriate instructional decisions as well as possible referrals. Profiles are obtained for the students and possible implications for learning are discussed. For example, a student demonstrating a surface-achieving profile is cognizant of the need to do well, but he/she may be approaching the learning situation by using rote memory and reproduction. This may lead to a lower achievement level than he/she wants and counseling could be warranted to help modify his/her strategies.

The LPQ was standardized on an Australian student population of 14-year-olds ($N = 1,366$) and Year 11 students ($N = 985$). A random sampling was achieved through the assistance of the Australian Council for Educational Research. Tables of norms are provided in the manual for males ($N = 1,117$) and females ($N = 1,234$) to be used in converting raw scores to decile scaled scores for Motives and Strategies (Surface, Deep, and Achieving) and Approaches (Surface, Deep, and Achieving). Significant effects for gender and year level supported the utilization of separate norms for the two age groups and genders (Biggs, 1987). Decile standard scores provide information on where a student falls (low, average, high) on the scales in comparison to the standardization group.

Reliability and validity data are presented in the manual. Test-retest reliability data yielded correlations ranging from .49 to .72 and demonstrated reasonable stability over a 4-month period. Internal consistency data also demonstrated satisfactory results with a range of .45 to .78. Construct validity was assessed by utilizing students' estimates of their performance, how satisfied they were with their performance, future educational goals, and correlations with a performance exam administered 15 months after the LPQ administration.

The manual does not provide information on minority representation, demographic variables, or socioeconomic status. However, a detailed account of these variables can be found in *Student Approaches to Learning and Studying* (Biggs, 1987). In addition to the above variables, Biggs' text offers detailed information concerning theoretical development, relevant research, and implications for the use of the LPQ.

Utilization of the LPQ outside Australia needs to be done with the understanding that the norms are limited. Future research with the LPQ in other countries needs to determine if the three factors (Surface, Deep, and Achieving) are identified in other populations. For example, in one study by Ramsden and Entwistle (1981), four factors emerged, three very similar to Biggs' and one additional factor they termed "disorganized and dilatory."

The LPQ provides a promising research tool for the assessment of learning approaches and for studying the development of metacognition. The author in no way suggests that the surface, deep, and achieving approaches are the only factors. Biggs (1987) suggests that certain strategies may indeed be taught. He also stresses the importance of future research in this area. The distinction between availability and production is made in regard to the teaching of strategies as well as personality factors such as internal versus external locus of control. It is strongly suggested that anyone choosing to utilize the LPQ also acquire the text, *Student Approaches to Learning and Studying* (Biggs, 1987).

REVIEWER'S REFERENCES

Ramsden, P., & Entwistle, N. (1981). Effects of academic departments on students' approaches to studying. *British Journal of Educational Psychology, 51,* 368-383.
Biggs, J. (1987). *Student approaches to learning and studying.* Melbourne: Australian Council for Educational Research Ltd.

[37]
Learning Style Inventory [Price Systems, Inc.].

Purpose: "Identifies those elements that are critical to an individual's learning style . . . [and] aids in prescribing the type of environment, instructional activities, social grouping(s), and motivating factors that maximize personal achievement."
Population: Grades 3–12.
Publication Dates: 1976–87.
Acronym: LSI.

Scores: 22 areas: Noise Level, Light, Temperature, Design, Motivation, Persistent, Responsible, Structure, Learning Alone/Peer Oriented, Authority Figures Present, Learn in Several Ways, Auditory, Visual, Tactile, Kinesthetic, Requires Intake, Evening/Morning, Late Morning, Afternoon, Needs Mobility, Parent Figure Motivated, Teacher Motivated, plus a Consistency score.
Administration: Group.
Price Data, 1987: $2.50 per 10 answer sheets for Grades 3 and 4 or for Grades 5 and above; $.40 per individual interpretative booklet; $9.50 per manual ('87, 109 pages); $3.25 per research report; $295 per computerized self-administered inventory program with 100 administrations ($60 per 100 additional administrations) (specify IBM or Apple); $395 per Scan and Score program; $.60 per answer forms to use with Scan and Score; $4 or less per individual profile available from publisher's scoring service; $7.50 or less per group and subscale summaries available from publisher only in addition to individual profiles.
Time: (20–30) minutes.
Comments: Apple, IBM, or IBM-compatible computer required for (optional) computerized administration; 3000 or 3051 NCS scanner required for (optional) Scan and Score system.
Authors: Rita Dunn, Kenneth Dunn, and Gary E. Price.
Publisher: Price Systems, Inc.

TEST REFERENCES

1. Carbo, M. (1984). Research in learning style and reading: Implications for instruction. *Theory Into Practice, 23* (1), 72-76.
2. Dunn, R. (1984). Learning style: State of the science. *Theory Into Practice, 23* (1), 10-19.
3. Dunn, R., Krimsky, J. S., Murray, J. B., & Quinn, P. J. (1985). Light up their lives: A review of research on the effects of lighting on children's achievement and behavior. *The Reading Teacher, 38,* 863-869.
4. Biberman, G., & Buchanan, J. (1986). Learning style and study skills differences across business and other academic majors. *Journal of Education for Business, 61,* 303-307.
5. Valle, J. D., Dunn, K., Dunn, R., Geisert, G., Sinatra, R., & Zenhausern, R. (1986). The effects of matching and mismatching students' mobility preferences on recognition and memory tasks. *Journal of Educational Research, 79,* 267-272.

Review of the Learning Style Inventory [Price Systems, Inc.] by JAN N. HUGHES, Associate Professor of Educational Psychology, Texas A&M University, College Station, TX:

Research and test development in the field of individual learning styles has been plagued by poor attention to issues of construct validity and theoretical development. The authors of the Learning Style Inventory (LSI) have not improved upon this state of affairs. Rather, their instrument exemplifies all of the problems characteristic of instruments designed to measure learning styles.

The authors' failure to provide a clear, theoretically based definition of learning styles contributes to their difficulty in establishing the content and construct validity of the LSI. The authors state the purpose of the LSI is to aid "in prescribing the type of environment, instructional activities, social grouping(s), and motivating factors that maximize personal achievement" (p. 5, manual). In the authors' published articles concerning the LSI (e.g., Griggs & Dunn, 1984), they clearly state the instrument is a diagnostic one, permitting educators to match instructional environments and activities to individual characteristics. This claim is not supported by the limited published data on the LSI.

The LSI has undergone several revisions since 1974, and it is impossible to know to which version information in the manual on reliability, item development, and construct validity pertains. In its current form, the inventory consists of 104 items that are grouped into 22 scales. Scores for each scale are reported as standard scores with a mean of 50 and a standard deviation of 10. The relationship between the subscales and the four types of preferences the instrument purportedly measures is not addressed, and the number of items on each scale is not provided. Given the small number of items on which at least some of the scale scores are based, it is likely the scales do not possess adequate reliability to make the type of diagnostic decisions for which the authors recommend the test's use. The authors do report reliability coefficients on the internal consistency for the scales, which range from .40 to .84. Most of these reliability coefficients are too low to justify making instructional decisions. Furthermore, the groups on which these coefficients were obtained are not adequately defined.

The types of student preferences the scale purports to measure include temperature (defined simply as "Many students 'can't think' when they feel hot, and others can't when they feel cold"); structure (student needs or does not need structure); and modality (e.g., auditory, kinesthetic, tactile, visual). The authors ignore an impressive amount of literature that lends no support to the educational usefulness of such factors on learning.

The authors do not provide evidence of the instrument's test-retest reliability, with the exception of one unpublished study that found one scale to be consistent across administrations. Given the instrument's widespread use in schools and the importance of demonstrating test-retest in any measure used to predict optimal learning environments, the lack of test-retest data is appalling.

The authors provide no information on the normative group on which the standard scores are derived, other than to state that the norms are based on "more than 500,000 students" (p. 11). In light of this paucity of information, the provided norms are meaningless.

The authors state the LSI was developed through "a content and factor analysis" (p. 6). Evidently, content validity refers to the authors' intuition as to which types of student preferences affect achievement. Results of factor analysis are reported for an earlier version of the LSI, for which the number of items is not given in the manual but is something less than 223 items. The principal components factor analysis resulted in 32 factors, each with an eigenvalue greater than 1.0, which collectively explained 62% of the variance. Because factor analysis is a device for simplifying correlations between related variables, the 32-factor solution does not accomplish what factor analysis is intended to do. Of greater significance is that the relationship between the factor structure and the authors' conceptualization of learning style is not addressed. Thus, the factor analysis represents a confused use of a sophisticated statistical tool, and the reported results obfuscate rather than clarify the constructs underlying the LSI. The authors do not apply acceptable rules for retaining factors, do not provide data on the number of items that load on each factor, and do not provide factor loadings of items.

A well-conducted factor analysis of the 104-item version of the LSI was reported by Ferrell (1983). Ferrell extracted four factors from the LSI, accounting for 23.5% of the variance. Sixty of the items loaded on one factor only. Twelve items had salient loadings on more than one factor, and 32 had no salient loadings. An inspection of the factor loadings provided no support for the authors' conceptualization of learning styles. Only the first factor was interpretable.

The manual is written to sell rather than to inform. The heavy use of statistical jargon and the exaggerated claims of the test's construct and predictive validity will impress the psychometrically naive reader. The unsophisticated reader will assume the 147 references provided attest to the instrument's scientific respectability. A closer inspection of these references reveals that a majority are unpublished dissertations, most of which were conducted under the supervision of one of the authors, Gary Price. The remaining references are nonempirical studies with titles such as "Breakthrough: How to Improve Early Reading Instruction" (Dunn, Carbo, & Burton, 1981). A search of PsychLIT (1974–1988) revealed two empirical studies on the LSI, both of which provided negative results (Pettigrew & Buell, 1986; Ferrell, 1983). Neither of these studies were referenced in the LSI manual.

The critical test of the validity of a prescriptive instrument is evidence the test predicts the conditions under which learning is optimized. The manual includes numerous recommendations for individualizing instruction based on students' scores on the 22 scales. Although it would be easy to design an experiment to test for such aptitude-treatment interactions, these investigations have not been undertaken.

In summary, the LSI has no redeeming values. Many of its limitations also apply to other measures of individual learning styles. Research to date has not supported the individual learning-styles paradigm. Whether this failure is attributable to inadequate measurement or to a faulty paradigm cannot yet be determined. If one is determined to use a measure of learning styles, he or she should consider Kolb's Learning-Style Inventory (Kolb, 1976; 10:173), for which some evidence of construct validity is available. Currently, no instrument provides a good substitute for a teacher's careful observations of student behavior and systematic collection of data to provide confirming or disconfirming evidence of hypotheses based on such observations.

REVIEWER'S REFERENCES

Kolb, D. A. (1976). *Learning-Style Inventory: Technical manual.* Boston, MA: McBer and Company.
Dunn, R., Carbo, M., & Burton, E. (1981). Breakthrough: How to improve early reading instruction. *Kappan, 62* (9), 675.
Ferrell, B. G. (1983). A factor analytic comparison of four learning styles instruments. *Journal of Educational Psychology, 75,* 33-39.
Griggs, S. A., & Dunn, R. (1984). Selected case studies of the learning style preferences of gifted students. *Gifted Child Quarterly, 28* (3), 115-119.
Pettigrew, F. E., & Buell, C. M. (1986). Relation of two perceptual styles to learning a novel motor skill. *Perceptual and Motor Skills, 63,* 1097-1098.

Review of the Learning Style Inventory [Price Systems, Inc.] by ALIDA S. WESTMAN, Professor of Psychology, Eastern Michigan University, Ypsilanti, MI:

The Learning Style Inventory (LSI) consists of 104 questions which take about 20 to 30 minutes to answer. The items are meant to explore some important aspects of the way in which a pupil prefers to learn (see the test entry above). The LSI explores some environmental, personality, social, and biological factors. The factors are well described and interpretation is easy. Application of the findings assumes that a pupil is adjusted enough to learn and that the pupil and teacher can implement the findings (for example, the time of day when learning is easiest).

ANSWER SHEET AND QUESTIONS. Some aspects of the LSI decrease ease of use and reliability. I will describe five of these. First, the instructions are in small print against the side of the identification box on the answer sheet and are easily overlooked. The vocabulary (e.g., "reliable") is too advanced for children. Second, some questions are repeated as a consistency check. However, the instructions not only point out that there are repetitions, they also tell the child to answer the questions the same way the second time as the first time. This means the child is urged to remember his or her answers. The child also may feel compelled to look back. Therefore, the consistency check is confounded by the instructions. Third, only three response alternatives are used with Grades 3 and 4, whereas a five-alternative Likert scale is used with older children. This incompatibility is not explained and in my experience is unnecessary. Fourth, some of the questions are simplistic and thereby may contribute to unreliability. For example, one question asks whether quiet is needed to study, but the material to be studied is not indicated and the answer may depend on what comes to the child's mind. The problem is noted in the Manual (pp. 34–35) but not resolved. Fifth, some questions are confusing. For example, Item 31 states, "I like to feel what I learn inside." Inside a classroom or the body? And is the subject matter bacteria, poisonous snakes, or shapes?

RESEARCH DESIGN AND STATISTICS. There are some attempts to establish a research base for the LSI, but many statistical problems are apparent. On occasion, the number of pupils studied was far too low to permit statistical analysis. For example, in one study the number of pupils in each condition was 3, 2, 4, 3, and 7, respectively (Manual, p. 41). In an analysis by grade, 11 boys and 11 girls represented the first grade (Research Report, p. 4). Much research is cited, which could be a strength, but usually only probability levels are indicated, whereas means, SDs, or F-values are not, and therefore interpretation of the research is difficult or impossible. For example, sometimes significant interactions are cited, but the results are described as main effects. Sex is said to interact with learning style in one case, such that both sexes do better in one condition than in another (Manual, p. 62, number 2). This is not interpretable without means. Sometimes the probability level indicates nonsignificant results, but subsequent interpretations are made as though the probability levels were significant (see Manual, pp. 51–52 and 79 for examples). With respect to the type of statistics used, 48 separate one-way analyses of variance were done for sex (Research Report, p. 12), even though much better statistical procedures are available. The corresponding table is mislabelled; it reads ANOVA *within* grades and should read *across* grades. It also is not clear which 500,000 people's scores were used to develop the standard scores (Manual, p. 11).

EXPENSIVE AND DIFFICULT TO USE. For many schools the test may cost $1 for each student if answer sheets need to be sent to the publisher for scoring. Group summaries cost extra. One group of principals found the LSI too expensive and demanding to use (NASSP, 1979, pp. 83–84). Sale of a template overlay for hand scoring would be very welcome.

VALIDITY. Content validity is based, in part, on a factor analysis. The factors seem logical.

RELIABILITY. The reliability coefficients cited are low to moderate. It would be worthwhile to investigate further why they are so low. A few reasons are mentioned above. Hoyt reliability for the English test showed a range of .35 to .85 for Grades 3 and 4 combined and a range of .40 to .84 for Grades 5 through 12 combined.

The French edition showed a range of .18 to .85 for Grades 6 through 12 combined. Test-retest reliability on an unspecified population with delay of unknown duration showed reliability coefficients between .43 and .69, except for one of .74 and one of .00 (Manual, p. 102, Table 4, which seems not to be mentioned in the text anywhere).

SUMMARY. The LSI provides some good indices on aspects of learning style. Application assumes that pupils are sufficiently adjusted to learn and that both they and their teachers can use the information gathered (e.g., whether to permit food intake during study). Many other learning-style indicators exist that also are helpful and many of these will be cheaper and less cumbersome to obtain than the LSI. To put the indices and learning styles into perspective, I recommend the books listed below.

REVIEWER'S REFERENCES

National Association of Secondary School Principals (NASSP). (1979). *Student learning styles.* Reston, VA: The Association.
National Association of Secondary School Principals (NASSP). (1982). *Student learning styles and brain behavior.* Reston, VA: The Association.
Wittrock, M. C. (Ed.). (1986). *Handbook of research on teaching* (3rd ed.). New York: Macmillan.

[38]
Learning Styles and Strategies.

Purpose: "Assists teachers and administrators in better understanding their own learning and teaching styles."
Population: Teachers.
Publication Date: 1980.
Scores, 4: Sensing/Feeling, Sensing/Thinking, Intuitive/Thinking, Intuitive/Feeling.
Administration: Group.
Price Data, 1988: $25 per manual (130 pages) including Learning Style Inventory and Teaching Style Inventory.
Time: Administration time not reported.
Comments: Self-administered, self-scored; tests available as separates.
Authors: Harvey F. Silver and J. Robert Hanson.
Publisher: Hanson Silver Strong & Associates, Inc.
a) LEARNING STYLE INVENTORY.
Purpose: "A self-diagnostic tool for adults to assess learning styles preferences."
Price Data: $2 per inventory including scoring key and information.
b) TEACHING STYLE INVENTORY.
Purpose: "A self-diagnostic tool to identify one's preferred teaching style."
Price Data: $2 per inventory including scoring key and information.

Review of Learning Styles and Strategies by
BERT A. GOLDMAN, *Professor of Education,*
University of North Carolina, Greensboro, NC:

The Teacher Self-Assessment (Learning Styles and Strategies) Manual includes information concerning two instruments: the Learning Style Inventory and the Teaching Style Inventory.

Authors Hanson and Silver based their instruments on Carl Gustav Jung's Theory of Psychological Types, about which they provide the reader a description and explanation. Their description and explanation of Jung's theory is detailed and informative.

Following the presentation of Jungian theory, the reader is led through a series of "warm-up" activities to introduce the process of self-analysis of one's learning style. These activities are followed by the Learning Style Inventory which, contrary to the authors' statement of being a "simple self-descriptive instrument," appears to this reviewer to be rather complex. It includes the four processes of (a) choosing self-descriptors through a weighting system, (b) preparing the self-analysis profile by rank ordering the styles, (c) computing the learning preference score for each of the learning styles, and (d) analyzing the learning preferences by plotting a learning profile. All of this is succeeded by a description of four possible profiles, any one of which might emerge. Next the reader is asked to read descriptions of each of the four basic learning styles and to rank order them according to how characteristic each one is of the reader. Following this task, the reader is asked to compare the ranking with the results obtained from the Learning Style Inventory by being led through a series of 17 self-diagnostic questions. This exercise is succeeded by a checklist of abilities for each of the learning styles. Those the reader would like to expand are to be checked and the strongest abilities identified by placing a plus sign next to them.

Any reader not exhausted at this point should not despair, for there is more to come. Now the authors provide the reader with a series of "warm-up" activities to prepare for the self-analysis of one's teaching style. These activities include three sets of myriad tasks and questions. Then the Teaching Style Inventory is proclaimed by the authors to be a simple self-descriptive instrument. First there are 10 sets of

four behaviors, each set to be ranked in order of preference. Next, the reader is asked to rank the four teaching styles according to how characteristic each is of the reader. This is followed by a request to complete the Teaching Style Profile. Now the reader is ready to compare the reader's personal analysis of teaching style preference with the style obtained from the Teaching Style Inventory. Next, the reader is led through a procedure for scoring teaching preferences and a few ways of interpreting the inventory are presented. Then several pages of detailed descriptions of the four teaching styles are presented so that the reader can rank them to further analyze the reader's teaching style. For the eager reader who has survived the preceding exercises, there are yet several pages of questions and checklists and checklists and questions to enable the teacher to indulge in further self-assessment of teaching.

Having read through the entire manual, which includes both the Learning Style Inventory and the Teaching Style Inventory, it appears to this reviewer that one cannot just respond to each of the instruments in order to evaluate one's learning and teaching styles. Instead it appears to this reviewer that one should engage in all of the exercises compiled in the manual in addition to addressing all items of both instruments in order to gain a comprehensive understanding of one's learning and teaching styles. A very cumbersome task, indeed!

The introduction to the manual indicates that its purpose "is to assist classroom teachers in diagnosing learning styles" and the Teaching Style Inventory indicates that its purpose is "to help you identify your own teaching profile based on your preferences for particular behaviors." Thus, the entire manual and the two instruments that it contains appear to be designed for teachers. However, the publisher's promotional materials tout the manual as a publication "for teachers and administrators." Nowhere does the manual indicate its use by administrators. However, it is conceivable that administrators may be interested in identifying their learning style but for administrators, there appears to be no application for teaching style.

C. G. Jung's treatment of psychological type is nicely described in the manual, as is its use as a basis for the development of the Teaching Style and Learning Style Inventories. This reviewer finds the initial chapter of the manual entitled "Dealing with Diversity" to be trite, trivial, and warranting deletion. Further, the illustrations included in the chapter as well as those throughout the publication are childishly insulting for any educator attempting to take the material seriously.

Not a single shred of evidence concerning the reliability and validity of either the Learning Style or the Teaching Style Inventories appears in the manual. Nor is there presented any evidence of validity supporting the Jungian personality theory upon which the two inventories are based.

Authors Hanson and Silver have identified two important educational processes that, if accurately assessed, could no doubt provide teachers with valuable information useful to their teaching decisions. Until the authors provide evidence their instruments are indeed reliable and valid, however, one should proceed with caution in their use.

Review of Learning Styles and Strategies by DAN WRIGHT, School Psychologist, Ralston Public Schools, Ralston, NE:

The Learning Styles and Strategies manual is one of a series of manuals developed by the authors to promote more effective teaching through processes of self-assessment and self-guided study. The entire series is based on the Jungian theory of personality types and its application to the teaching/learning process. Central to the part of the process embodied in this manual is the self-assessment by teachers of their own learning and teaching styles. Two brief inventories are employed in this task: the Learning Style Inventory and the Teaching Style Inventory. Each of these purports to analyze one's mode of functioning according to the feeling/thinking and sensing/intuiting dimensions of personality proposed by Jung. Results of the inventories are intended to give a measure of one's relative predisposition toward each of the four categories or styles yielded by the conjunction of these dimensions. The manual also provides some interpretive information dealing with the assets and liabilities that typify each style.

The inventories themselves are brief and simple, requiring test-takers to rate descriptions of behavioral or classroom characteristics according to preference. The Learning Style Inventory presents 20 sets of behavioral descriptors to be rated and should take less than half an hour to complete, including scoring. The Teaching Style Inventory presents 10 sets of classroom descriptions to be rated, and should take a bit longer to complete. Results are self-scored and self-interpreted according to guidelines presented in the manual.

Very little can be said about the adequacy of these two inventories for their intended purposes. The authors provide absolutely no information regarding test development. Although results from the inventories are ipsative, indicating only the strength of an individual's preferences relative to each other, items should have been developed through trials with various pools of subjects. However, there is no reference to any sort of subject group, nor any information supporting the reliability of results. According to a research monograph provided by the publisher at the reviewer's request (Research Monograph #4, undated), initial item development for an apparently similar inventory (the Learning Preference Inventory) was accomplished with a sample of 600 third through sixth grade students in New Jersey. If the methodology employed for the development of the teachers' inventories was similar, there is some cause for concern. Factor analytic treatment of item responses appears to have been somewhat unorthodox. Responses were compared *across* items after having been ranked *within* items; this would compromise the correlation matrix by restricting the variance for the group of responses presented with each item stem. The implications of this practice are unclear, but troubling.

Despite the basis of the inventories in recognized theory, there is no information presented regarding validity. According to the research monograph, the inventories were patterned, at least in part, on the Myers-Briggs Type Indicator (Briggs, K. C., Myers, I. B., & McCaulley, M. H., 1985; 10:206). Validity studies with the Myers-Briggs inventory would appear to be a necessary and early step in development, but no references to such appear in either the manual or the monograph. These inventories rest on face validity, period. Because of this, as well as the lack of information on reliability and item development, the inventories cannot literally be considered assessment instruments at all; at the present time, they must be considered as more similar to the self-assessment quizzes that frequently appear in popular magazines.

The unfortunate implication is that the process of guided study that follows the inventories is without foundation. Theory, educational practice, and test validity are all tightly linked in these inventories. As Wiggins (1989) observed of the Myers-Briggs Type Indicator, a construct-oriented test cannot be validated outside the bounds of the theory on which it is based. Thus, the soundness of the authors' observations and recommendations cannot be separated from the applicability of Jung's theories to education or from the validity of these inventories in particular. The authors may have much to say that is relevant to the improvement of teaching, but there is no reason to be confident their insights can be directed to individuals based on their learning or teaching styles. For example, teachers who complete the inventories are referred to descriptions of their type of learner or teacher, based on their dominant and auxiliary styles of functioning. The descriptions read rather like a horoscope, with many general statements that are either flattering or challenging. Most readers will likely identify with some of the characteristics in each of the descriptions, which is to be expected of an ipsative profile and which is acknowledged by the authors. Although one is directed by the inventories to a description of a dominant style, we must ask: If the descriptions were scrambled so they no longer matched inventory results, would anyone suspect? Without further information, we cannot suppose they would.

In summary, the inventories contained in the Learning Styles and Strategies manual must be considered of tentative utility at best. No great harm is likely to come of their use, but there is no reason to consider them adequate for their intended purpose. It is incumbent upon the authors to provide support for the technical adequacy of the inventories, because they provide the foundation for users' further self-study. This is a minimal and necessary (but not sufficient) step in demonstrating the overall value of their materials.

REVIEWER'S REFERENCES

Briggs, K. C., Myers, I. B., & McCaulley, M. H. (1985). Myers-Briggs Type Indicator. Palo Alto, CA: Consulting Psychologists Press, Inc.

Wiggins, J. S. (1989). [Review of the Myers-Briggs Type Indicator]. In J. C. Conoley & J. J. Kramer (Eds.), *The tenth mental measurements yearbook* (pp. 537-538). Lincoln, NE: Buros Institute of Mental Measurements.

Research Monograph #4. (undated). Moorestown, NJ: Hanson Silver Strong & Associates, Inc.

[39]
Leatherman Leadership Questionnaire.

Purpose: "To aid in selecting supervisors, providing specific feedback to participants on their leadership knowledge for career counseling, conducting accurate needs analysis, and screening for assessment centers or giving pre/post assessment feedback."

Population: Managers, supervisors, and prospective supervisors.

Publication Date: 1987.

Acronym: LLQ.

Scores, 28: Assigning Work, Career Counseling, Coaching Employees, One-on-One Oral Communication, Managing Change, Handling Employee Complaints, Dealing with Employee Conflicts, Counseling Employees, Helping an Employee Make Decisions, Delegating, Taking Disciplinary Action, Handling Emotional Situations, Setting Goals/Planning with Employees, Handling Employee Grievances, Conducting Employee Meetings, Giving Positive Feedback, Negotiating, Conducting Performance Appraisals, Establishing Performance Standards, Persuading/Influencing Employees, Making Presentations to Employees, Problem Solving with Employees, Conducting Selection Interviews, Team Building, Conducting Termination Interviews, Helping an Employee Manage Time, One-on-One Training, Total.

Subtests: May be administered in separate sessions.

Administration: Individual or group.

Price Data, 1989: $600 per complete set including 12 overhead transparencies, manual (336 pages), 10 sets of reusable test booklets, (may be reproduced for local use) NCS computer-scored answer sheets, and scoring service for 10 participants; $30 for each additional set of test booklets; $30 for each additional set of answer sheets including scoring service; $75 per additional manual; $1 each for "confidential service" (participant's scoring sheet sealed in an envelope).

Time: (300–325) minutes for battery; (150–165) minutes per part.

Comments: Complete test administered in 2 parts; machine-scored by publisher only (present norm of 5,000 participants); use of overhead projector for group instructions recommended; materials and scoring for legitimate research provided without charge.

Author: Richard W. Leatherman.

Publisher: International Training Consultants, Inc.

Review of the Leatherman Leadership Question-naire by WALTER KATKOVSKY, Professor of Psychology, Northern Illinois University, DeKalb, IL:

Carefully packaged in a carrying case, the Leatherman Leadership Questionnaire (LLQ) consists of 339 multiple-choice questions, divided into 27 supervisory tasks, that require 5 to 6 hours of testing time. A detailed administrative guide and overhead transparencies are included for group administration. Designed to be a "knowledge-based" based" measure of supervisory leadership, the criteria of "correct" responses and of the differential weights given items for scoring purposes were determined by the judgments of eight experts in management, supervision, and human resource development. Correct answers, item weights, and scoring procedures are not presented in the manual, and scoring and analysis require sending the completed answer sheet to a scoring service.

Two reports are returned. The first is directed to the organization and compares the scores on the 27 supervisory tasks of all subjects in that group with one another and with an "international population's average" (based on "everyone who has taken the LLQ") so that the group's strengths and weaknesses (needs) can be identified. The second report is on the individual, presenting and comparing his or her scores with other subjects in the organization and with the international averages, and designating the individual's strengths and needs.

A lengthy research report is included in the Administrator's Manual that contains commentary on competing measures and describes research conducted on the LLQ. The first phase of the research reports on the development of the instrument and its content validity. Beginning with the identification of distinctive supervisory tasks and effective ways of dealing with them culled from the literature, the instrument's content validity was established by agreement of six out of eight of the expert panel members on the importance of the tasks and the "correct" answers to items. Apparently, however, judgments concerning correct answers involved a suggestive bias in that the "correct" answers were presented to the judges with instructions to "agree" or "disagree" with them, rather than have the judges answer the actual test items independently.

An apparent problem in the construct validity of the LLQ concerns the differential weights assigned to items. The report notes that in addition to the experts, 229 subjects from seven organizations also "ranked" (actually rated) the tasks for their importance in a supervisory job, and that these ratings, together with the experts' ratings of the importance of tasks and behaviors, were "used in calculating the final score." Not only are the procedures for using the judgments of the different groups not explained clearly, but the report misinterprets the findings.

A statistically significant analysis of variance F of 2.4 is reported between groups' judgments, indicating differences in the importance they attached to the tasks for supervisory leadership. These findings, however, are erroneously cited in the report as a "correlation" that indicates the groups rated the tasks "similarly" (p. 77). The differences in judgments found concerning the importance of the tasks for supervision calls into question an underlying assumption of the LLQ, that distinctive areas of supervisory skill and knowledge can be identified that represent "an essential portion of the leadership part of a supervisor's job" (p. 45).

The second phase of research pertained to the internal reliability of the LLQ. Preliminary findings on the extent to which items correlated with task scores and with the total score resulted in the elimination of items and revision of the questionnaire. The internal consistency reported for the final version of the LLQ based on the Kuder-Richardson formula 20 is .9706 (KR-20 correlations of .91 and above also are reported for each of nine separate organizations). However, not presented are correlations between the 27 tasks and between the items within each task that are needed to establish the distinctiveness of the tasks or skill areas. The reporting format used by the author is difficult to decipher. Users would feel more confident in the internal reliability coefficients if all the necessary data were offered in the research report.

Given its reported high internal consistency, the LLQ appears to measure a homogeneous factor, rather than knowledge about 27 different supervisory tasks as intended. A factor analysis would help in determining the extent to which different factors are measured by the questionnaire. Also, data on the test-retest reliability of the LLQ are needed because no information on the stability of scores is given in the manual.

Concurrent criterion validity is the topic of the third phase of the research using assessment center findings as criteria. Three studies involving three separate assessment centers were conducted, in which Spearman *rho* correlations were obtained between rankings of subjects based on their assessment center evaluations of supervisory potential and rankings of their LLQ total scores. The findings indicated no relationship for the first study and significant relationships for the next two, with *rhos* of .01, .71, and .89 on samples of 23, 6, and 10, respectively. These inconsistent findings on small samples leave open to question the predictive validity of the LLQ for identifying and selecting leadership potential in accord with assessment centers. Without detailed information about the procedures of the different assessment centers, the meaning of the inconsistent findings remains obscure. Perhaps analyses of LLQ scores with ratings on separate assessment center dimensions would help determine the nature of possible relationships between these two measures. Also, as noted by the author of the test, additional validity studies are needed using a variety of criteria, such as job performance evaluations as a supervisor, promotions, and scores on other tests of supervisory abilities. In addition, if future analyses do, in fact, demonstrate that separate supervisory tasks or factors are measured by the LLQ, separate criterion validity research for each factor would be desirable.

Another weakness of the LLQ at present is the absence of norms in the manual and the failure to identify the subjects and groups included in the "international population's average" used in scoring analyses. The manual states "over 250 organizations have purchased the LLQ" (Introduction, p. 7). However, the research reported refers to only 10 organizations that participated in the reliability studies and three in the validity studies. To interpret scores meaningfully, norms are needed for different organizations and for subjects based on gender, education, race, and job level.

A question that must be addressed is, what does the LLQ measure? Inspection of items raises two issues. First, the assumption that a single "correct" answer exists for each item ignores the importance of situational variations and individual differences in subordinates. Second, many of the items appear to tap general intelligence rather than supervisory knowledge. If true, as may be determined readily by correlating LLQ scores with IQ, the value of the measure for the selection of supervisors may be no better than that of a general abilities measure that could be administered in one fifth the time required for the LLQ.

In conclusion, many questions exist concerning the LLQ and its potential value in evaluating supervisory leadership. And its claim of being a "lower cost alternative to assessment centers" for identifying effective supervisors is neither demonstrated nor justified. Additional research and clear presentations of findings are needed to further refine the measure and to determine its utility. The research report presently included in the Administrator's Manual would benefit considerably from careful editing to remove redundancies, shifts back and forth between topics, occasional errors, inconsistent use of the terms "ratings" and "rankings," and text references to materials not included in the appendices.

Review of the Leatherman Leadership Questionnaire by WILLIAM D. PORTERFIELD, *Academic Coordinator and Adjunct Assistant Professor of Educational Administration, Commission on Interprofessional Education and Practice, The Ohio State University, Columbus, OH:*

The Leatherman Leadership Questionnaire (LLQ) is part of a packet of training materials that includes the instrument, full reports of normative data, training and presentation materials, and suggestions for the use of the instrument. The packet is presented as a comprehensive assessment center for managers, supervisors, and individuals interested in testing their leadership knowledge. One complete set of the materials is priced at $600 (1989), with additional materials available at prices ranging from $30 for scoring services and additional questionnaires to $75 for additional administration guides. Although such prices may be reasonable market values for larger organizations and businesses, the costs will significantly reduce the possibilities of the LLQ being used for graduate research and furthering the validity of the instrument through the academy.

The theoretical base for the instrument is problematic in terms of a distinctive theoretical orientation. The author used a panel of eight human resource development specialists to validate the appropriateness of the questions and the subscales on the instrument. Thus, although providing some support for content validity, the theoretical base is diffuse and unclear. If application of the instrument in organizational settings is the primary use, such an instrument-development process may be acceptable. However, if the LLQ is intended as a research tool, a more clearly defined theoretical approach to leadership, human behavior, and perception should be developed and incorporated into the instrument.

The author makes a strong claim the instrument measures leadership knowledge versus perceptions of leadership knowledge. The questionnaire consists of 339 multiple-choice items, directed toward 27 subscales of leadership tasks. Within each of the questions are preferred responses that indicate the respondent's leadership knowledge. The instrument is designed to yield scores for each of the subscales that can be compared to normative data collected in eight different organizations ($N = 301$). Reliability and validity studies were conducted for the instrument and are extensively described in the packet of research materials. Data from test-retest reliability studies are missing and should be conducted with the instrument to increase the reliability data base. Additionally, continued item verification could strengthen the reliability of the instrument and its internal consistency. Validity studies were conducted using assessment center ratings for identified leaders, and comparing these ratings with scores on the LLQ. Validity studies might also be conducted by reviewing literature for each item and for each subscale.

Any new instruments in the leadership area must be designed in such a way that perspectives from various minority groups and both sexes are incorporated in the instrument. The author does not indicate if the panel of experts included minority individuals or a balance of men and women, or if any attention was given to these concerns in the actual design of the instrument. Additionally, the author notes there are little data on whether there are significant differences in test scores across racial and ethnic groups.

This lack of information is a serious weakness for the LLQ. Certainly, any instrument that is to be utilized in staff selection, needs assessment, career counseling, assessment centers, and evaluation should be thoroughly reviewed for sensitivity to various cultural and racial perspectives that may affect the theoretical basis and/or actual scores. This is a rich area for further research if the LLQ receives credibility for organizational development and planning.

The LLQ is a very lengthy instrument. It can be administered in 4 to 5 hours or in two separate sessions. This is a costly time commitment for respondents and for organizations choosing to employ the results of the LLQ for further planning and training purposes. The author makes the claim the LLQ yields comprehensive data on leadership knowledge. Such a claim suggests to businesses and trainers that time invested in administration may save time later. However, the practical barriers to an individual testing for a period of 4 hours may inhibit individual use of the LLQ and certainly would inhibit use of the LLQ by researchers. If possible, a consolidated version of the LLQ should be developed with a maximum administration time of $1^1/_2$ hours.

Scoring for the LLQ is completed electronically by the author for a price of $30. It seems much more practical, given current computer technology, to offer users a scoring package for test-site scoring. Additionally, it would be helpful for a hand-scoring key to be made available to users. On-site, reasonably priced scoring options might serve to broaden the use of the LLQ in nonbusiness settings.

Aside from the instrument, the packet of materials also contains an administrator's guide, research documentation, overhead transparencies, and a carrying case for materials, all quite nicely developed. The research documentation is more detailed than many instruments and provides potential users with the data necessary to make further judgments about the use of the LLQ in various settings.

In summary, the LLQ may be useful as a practical tool for assessing leadership knowledge in organizations. Attention should be given to explicating the theoretical base of the "knowledge" that is being tested. Further research needs to be conducted on the theoretical and practical validity of the instrument cross-culturally and with respect to gender differences. Due to the length of administration and the cost of the package, the instrument may not be the choice of researchers in the leadership arena at the academy. This is unfortunate, in that the LLQ needs more research and normative data in order for test results to be meaningful and generalizable. As a comprehensive assessment center, the LLQ may have some merits for organizations willing to commit themselves to the validity of the leadership knowledge incorporated in the instrument. However, businesses and trainers would be well advised to compare the LLQ to other instruments available in the areas of selection, needs assessment, career counseling, and evaluation.

[40]
Let's Talk Inventory for Children.
Purpose: "To identify children who have inadequate or delayed social-verbal communication skills; provides a uniform and standardized method of eliciting and probing selected speech acts, representing the ritualizing, informing, controlling, and feeling functions of verbal communication."
Population: Ages 4–8.
Publication Date: 1987.
Acronym: LTI-C. Scores, 2: Formulation, Association.
Administration: Individual.
Price Data, 1989: $69 per complete kit including 25 record forms, stimulus manual, and examiner's manual (82 pages); $15 per 25 record forms; $30 per stimulus manual; $25 per examiner's manual.
Time: 30(40) minutes.
Comments: Downward extension of Let's Talk Inventory for Adolescents (9:613).
Authors: Candice M. Bray and Elisabeth H. Wiig.
Publisher: The Psychological Corporation.

Review of the Let's Talk Inventory for Children by MERITH COSDEN, Assistant Professor of Education, University of California, Santa Barbara, CA:

The Let's Talk Inventory for Children (LTIC) provides a standardized method for assessing the verbal social-communication skills of children who have a background in standard American spoken English. It is not intended to identify the bases of verbal-communication problems or to be used as the sole criterion to determine placement in special programs. The LTIC is designed primarily for descriptive use. As such, it is structured to provide specific information on the ability of children to formulate or identify speech acts that perform different communicative functions.

The LTIC is based on a "parametric" taxonomy of social-verbal communication. Within this taxonomy, all interpersonal communications are defined by four controlling variables: participants, setting, topic, and task. Speech acts are categorized into five communicative functions: ritualizing, informing, controlling, feeling, and imagining. The first four of these are sampled in the Inventory. Omission of the fifth area is only weakly justified in the manual. Although at least four items using different situational communicative contexts were constructed to assess each speech act, no systematic method for analyzing the impact of the four control variables is provided.

There are three parts to the LTIC. The first, Speech Act Formulation-Peers, contains 24 items. Each item consists of a picture of a peer interaction and a short narrative describing the intent of the depicted communication. The examiner reads the narrative aloud and then instructs the child to verbalize the next communication that should occur between the characters. For example, in a trial story Mike and Debbie are shown playing together. Mike has a new toy; Debbie doesn't know the name of the toy and wants to ask him about it. The child taking the test is asked to formulate a verbal response to the question, "What did Debbie say to Mike?".

The second part of the Inventory, Speech Act Formulation-Adults, follows the same format. These 10 items are taken directly from the Peer Formulation section and rewritten to feature child/adult interactions in the same social contexts. Only two of the five speech functions, feeling and controlling, are sampled. The lack of complete crossover between audience (adult or child) and speech function is not well explained. The manual states that the Adult Formulation items are designed to indicate emerging formality features in the child's verbal repertoire; that is, to assess the child's skill in making distinctions between peer and adult communications.

The third part of the LTIC, Speech Act Associations, is optional and designed to assess receptive understanding of communicative intent in children who have difficulty formulating verbal responses. Items were selected from the informing, controlling, and feeling functions and were redesigned to reflect new task demands. The child is shown a stimulus page on which three interpersonal communicative contexts are pictured. Two of the pictures represent targeted speech acts and the third is a foil. The child is asked to point to the picture that best represents the intent of a speech act read by the examiner; then a second speech act is read and the child asked to make another selection from the same page. The authors' use of two targeted responses per stimulus page is a concern, however, as children who are sure of one answer can eliminate it when considering a response to the second item.

The LTIC is individually administered and does not require specialized training beyond familiarity with the test and general assessment procedures. The test easel is placed between the child and examiner so that the child can see the stimulus pictures while the examiner reads the accompanying narratives. There is no time limit for testing, but administration is estimated at 30 minutes. Demonstration items are provided at the beginning of the test and trial items are available for each section. Rules for determining when to discontinue testing are vague. Each narrative may be repeated once; repetition is not reflected in the child's score, although it may be noted in qualitative interpretation of the results.

All responses are transcribed on the Record Form. The manual suggests audiotaping Formulation responses for later transcription rather than noting them during the session. Preference for taping is based on a desire to increase accuracy in transcription without disrupting the flow of the test. It is this reviewer's experience, however, that one should not rely solely on taping, as machines may malfunction or children's voices may prove too soft to hear. The additional time required to transcribe taped data may also be too costly. Thus, examiner recording of verbal responses, with tape recording as a backup, is preferable to tape recording alone.

The manual presents both qualitative and quantitative systems for interpretation of test results. More emphasis is placed on the qualitative system. This system as described in the manual is highly subjective and relies on the clinical skills of the examiner. The manual provides several examples of this type of interpretation (e.g., if a child fails to understand the perspective of others across stories, a need to develop awareness of others' perspectives may be indicated). The manual suggests testing hypotheses generated in this manner through observation of the child in natural settings. Given the lack of knowledge on the empirical validity of the scale (discussed below), testing for the occurrence of problem behavior in natural settings should be mandatory.

Quantitative measures are obtained for each part of the LTIC. All Formulation items are scored for whether the intent of the speech act is "realized and expressed" in the response. An additional score is given to Formulation-Adult items to reflect the presence of formality structures; that is, the ability of the child to differentiate social communications between adults and peers. Association items are scored for correct identification of speech intent. Scoring is straightforward with adequate guidelines and examples provided. The utility of some of the scores, however, is unclear. No norms are provided for the scores of formal verbal structures obtained on Adult Formulation items or for scores on the Association items. Qualitative interpretation of scores reflecting formality is suggested, but not enough age-relevant information is provided to allow one to do this in an informed manner. Similarly, Association scores are discussed in regard to differentiating children who formulate poor responses but understand social communications from children who have problems in both areas. Unless the child provides a clear pattern of positive or negative scores on these subtests, however, interpretation of results based on the information provided in the manual will be difficult.

Normative data are provided only for the total intent score obtained by summing across all 34 (24 Child and 10 Adult) Formulation items. The normative data represent a small sample of children ($N = 214$), ages 4–8, and are presented for 1-year intervals. Although the manual states that the total score is the most reliable, the data supporting this statement are limited. Internal consistency coefficients (coefficient alphas) for the combined Child and Adult Formulation score range from .69 to .85 across age groups. Only one small study of interscorer reliability is reported, with high levels (94–96%) of agreement across categories. No studies substantiating reliability of responses or scores across test administrations are cited.

Using the total score as a representation of speech act formulation skill is questionable because speech acts are not equally sampled by the Inventory. The total score is more heavily weighted by controlling and feeling functions (13 items apiece) than by ritualizing or informing functions (4 items apiece). To the extent that students are differentially hampered by these communicative functions, the total test score will present a biased picture of skill level.

Although the instrument has a strong theoretical base, its validity as a measure of pragmatics is not apparent from the manual. The authors are very careful to frame the purpose of the test with caveats, noting that the Inventory is not designed to provide a diagnosis of language disorder, but rather to complement existing standardized tests and procedures. Nevertheless, the LTIC should contain items that tap into the needs of students known to have language and learning disorders. Recent literature reviews on pragmatic deficits in children are presented in the manual; however, test items were not selected to address these issues. Items were generated on the basis of their content validity for normal children; in fact, the small normative sample used to develop the scoring system consists solely of students with normal language skills. The only manner in which validity is addressed in the manual is by noting that test scores change as a function of age; that is, older children score higher on the test than do younger children, as would be predicted by developmental theories on social language development. Two types of studies are needed to determine the efficacy of this instrument even as an informal description of language skills. First, one needs to examine the validity of the test items for differentiating children known to have language deficits from those that do not. Second, given the novelty of this instrument's subject matter, there is a need to evaluate the effectiveness of this type of inventory for obtaining accurate information regarding children's skills in natural settings.

In sum, the LTIC presents an interesting model for systematically studying developing skills in the area of pragmatics. The importance of this area is well developed in the manual. The authors describe the LTIC as an informal assessment instrument to be used in association with other standardized tests. The advantages of using the Inventory over other types of informal observations, however, are unclear. It should be noted that the items in this Inventory correspond to an intervention program, *Let's Talk for Children*, also developed by the co-authors (Wiig & Bray, 1983). This Inventory opens a promising area for understanding more subtle social-communication problems in young children, but the utility of the test itself has not been established.

REVIEWER'S REFERENCE

Wiig, E., & Bray, C. (1983). *Let's talk for children*. Columbus, OH: Charles E. Merrill Publishing Co.

Review of the Let's Talk Inventory for Children by JANET NORRIS, Assistant Professor of Communication Disorders, Louisiana State University, Baton Rouge, LA:

The purpose of the Let's Talk Inventory for Children (LTIC) is to assess the ability to express and interpret speech acts representing the communication functions of ritualizing, informing, controlling, and feeling. Specifically, the ability to formulate or recognize speech acts that express the appropriate intent and degree of formality or politeness in both peer and adult/authority contexts is evaluated. The Speech Act Formulation items require the child to generate a speech act appropriate to a pictured situation presented with a lead-in narrative describing the situation. The Speech Act Association items probe the ability to associate spoken speech acts with pictured situational contexts, and are designed to be used in addition to or in place of the Formulation items when a child performs poorly on the latter.

The LTIC assesses a very limited aspect of language, measuring only one component of pragmatics and only four communication functions within this domain. However, the manual states that the test is not designed to be used as a single diagnostic tool, to determine educational placement, or to identify the bases for a delay. Rather, the primary purpose is to assist in the identification of children with inadequate or delayed social-verbal communication skills. To achieve this goal, the four communication functions assessed were selected because they are acquired early in development, are readily pictured and elicited by the task, reflect common experiences for young children (ages 4 to 8 are targeted), have been shown to be delayed in populations of children with language disorders or special needs, reflect increasing competence with increasing age, and correlate with items on the Let's Talk Inventory for Adolescents (Wiig, 1982; 9:613).

The test stimuli elicit natural communication to the degree that any contrived task is able to do so. The pictures and narratives used depict situations that are similar to the experiences of young middle-class children. They provide a meaningful situation and present characters with clear goals. The child is allowed to formulate a speech act using his/her own language rather than being limited to single word responses or imitations. The procedure has the advantage over spontaneous language assessment of assuring that a variety of speech acts are sampled. It is difficult to determine from naturally occurring interactions whether various language functions do not occur because of a lack of communicative competence or because the context failed to elicit the response.

However, the current task may present difficulties to young and/or language-disordered children. To formulate an appropriate speech act in response to the test stimuli, the child must be capable of understanding the situation from the perspective(s) of the characters depicted and be able to function in the role of another person. A language-disordered child may fail to formulate an appropriate response because of an inability to shift perspectives, while successfully performing similar communicative functions in real situations.

Minimal reliability data are reported. The manual does not report any stability of performance data, such as test-retest results. This is particularly problematic in that results from the adolescent version of the Inventory reported only moderate correlations for test-retest scores. Thus, the cautions that the Inventory not be used to provide a diagnosis of a language disorder or to determine educational placement must be taken seriously. Internal consistency coefficients for groupings of items by intent were relatively low. The author suggests that the Inventory is designed to assess a variety of speech acts that are not necessarily similar in function.

Only one preliminary study is reported concerning the interrater reliability for scoring the LTIC. This involved only five protocols and the scoring was conducted by trained professionals with backgrounds in test administration and linguistics. Although the percentage of interscorer agreements was high (94%–97%), this level of reliability cannot be assumed for practitioners who have not received training. The extensive rules and examples of possible responses provided in the manual would seem to enhance interscorer agreement and are a strength.

No measures of validity are reported. However, the manual provides an extensive literature review that describes various taxonomies used to categorize speech acts and establishes the rationale for the categories selected for inclusion in the Inventory. Literature is cited establishing the relative sequence and ages of acquisition of the functions assessed, ways in which the communicative functions are realized linguistically, and patterns of difficulty in using communicative functions exhibited by language-learning-disabled children. The author states that items were carefully designed to probe the functions targeted and to be developmentally appropriate, but no data are provided to support this claim. Thus, although the literature may indicate that children exhibit certain communicative functions at various stages of development, there is no evidence that these children are able to exhibit behaviors in response to the tasks required by the LTIC at these same ages.

Some support for validity is reported in a pilot study that showed increasing performance in speech act formulation on the test with increasing age, and moderate but significant correlations between groups of items that assessed similar functions expressed to peers versus adults.

The LTIC does not represent the universe of speech acts used by young children, but only four functions. More information is needed in order to determine if these four categories are sufficient to sample speech acts used by this population, or whether content validity is weakened by this restricted range. No studies establishing concurrent or construct validity are reported.

The Inventory does not purport to be a norm-referenced test. Results are evaluated based upon both quantitative and qualitative interpretations. Means and standard deviations are provided by age intervals of 1 year. These are based upon a small, nonrepresentative sample of 214 children who participated in field testing. In general, the sample consisted of normally developing, urban, middle-class, standard-English-speaking children from five eastern states. Language-disordered or special-needs children were not included by design. The author states that the score obtained on the LTIC can be compared to the means and standard deviations from the field-test group, with a substantial difference from the mean serving as a possible indication that the child's overall communication competence needs to be more completely examined. The examiner is further encouraged to make comparisons in relation to the standard error of measurement rather than the raw score.

Qualitative interpretations are recommended as well. The author suggests evaluating the speech acts obtained for patterns of inadequate responding, such as multiple examples of poor perspective taking across items, or a general inability to modify speech acts to reflect more polite forms in the adult context. These patterns can then be substantiated by interviews with individuals such as parents and teachers, as well as observations of the child in various settings. Confirmation of difficulties would suggest the need for specific intervention. An intervention program designed by the author, *Let's Talk for Children* (Wiig & Bray, 1983), provides a set of objectives and therapy materials for developing the functions assessed by the Inventory and thus provides continuity between assessment and intervention.

Use of the Inventory is time-consuming. Administration (30 minutes), transcription of the child's responses from audiotape, and scoring can take 2–3 hours. This represents a considerable amount of time that may not be clinically worthwhile in that only one limited aspect of pragmatic abilities is examined, there is no evidence that the results are reliable or valid, and no diagnostic claims beyond probable strengths and weaknesses can be made based upon results. There is considerable danger in attributing too much importance or emphasis on the types of behaviors assessed, particularly given the existence of the parallel intervention program. The speech acts included represent a restricted sample and not a comprehensive representation of the types of social-verbal communications produced by young children.

SUMMARY. Let's Talk Inventory for Children is an assessment instrument that has some appealing features. It provides an efficient method for eliciting four categories of early-developing, high-frequency speech acts. The Inventory is easy to administer and score (although time-consuming) and provides implications for intervention. However, the instrument is not well constructed, lacks evidence of both reliability and validity, and does not provide useful norms. The use of the LTIC for purposes of diagnostics is thus severely limited. Even more problematic is the test-teach paradigm that is encouraged by the authors of the Inventory. The focus upon discrete pragmatic language skills results in the perpetuation of the "splinter skill" approach to language assessment and remediation that has been largely ineffective in dealing with the language disorders of children in the past. If the Inventory is used, the examiner must be careful to interpret the results cautiously and to go beyond the narrow scope of the instrument when planning intervention.

REVIEWER'S REFERENCES

Wiig, E. (1982). *Let's talk inventory for adolescents.* Columbus, OH: Charles E. Merrill Publishing Co.

Wiig, E., & Bray, C. (1983). *Let's talk for children.* Columbus, OH: Charles E. Merrill Publishing Co.

[41]

Management and Graduate Item Bank.
Purpose: "For use in the selection, development or guidance of personnel at graduate level or in management positions."
Population: Graduate level and senior management applicants for the following areas: finance, computing, engineering, corporate planning, purchasing, personnel, and marketing.
Publication Dates: 1985–87.
Acronym: MGIB.
Scores, 2: Verbal Critical Reasoning, Numerical Critical Reasoning.
Administration: Group.
Price Data, 1986: £55 per administration set including manual ('87, 39 pages), supplementary norms manual ('87, 39 pages), test log, test booklets, answer sheets, administration instructions, and scoring stencils; £45 per 10 Verbal test booklets ('85, 16 pages); £65 per 10 Numerical test booklets ('85, 15 pages); £35 per 50 Verbal or Numerical answer sheets; £7 per Verbal or Numerical scoring stencil; £7 per Verbal (3 pages) or Numerical (3 pages) administration instructions; £22 per manual.
Time: 60(65) minutes.
Comments: Abbreviated adaptation of the Advanced Test Battery (9:57); subtests available as separates.
Authors: Saville & Holdsworth Ltd. and Linda Espey (supplementary norms manual).

Publisher: Saville & Holdsworth Ltd. [England].

Review of the Management and Graduate Item Bank by JAMES T. AUSTIN, Assistant Professor of Psychology, New York University, New York, NY, and H. JOHN BERNARDIN, University Professor of Research, Florida Atlantic University, Boca Raton, FL:

The tests of Verbal and Numerical Critical Reasoning from the Management and Graduate Item Bank are the first in a planned series of short tests with multiple parallel forms (hence the title Item Bank) for managerial selection and development in industry. Test takers are to be at the upper ranges of the respective ability distributions. The tests consist of short passages (Verbal) or statistical tables and figures (Numerical) with associated questions that call for critical evaluation by the examinee. Both entry-level college graduates and experienced managers are suggested as populations to which the tests apply. The authors acknowledge the tentative nature of inferences based on the scores at this stage in test and norm development.

The tests are short (1 hour total for both) to minimize practice effects and allow use throughout employees' careers. They were developed from the same firm's Advanced Test Battery (ATB; 9:57). The manual is available to anyone without restriction, but other materials are released only to those who meet the company's standards (based on British Psychological Society guidelines). Although internal and external selection is emphasized as a purpose for the tests in the Manual and User's Guide, no studies are cited or discussed that support this or other functions claimed for the tests. Moreover, the tests are based on the idea that critical reasoning is an important component in managerial and professional positions. One would therefore expect that construct validation or (at least) criterion-related validity evidence be presented (cf. Cook, 1988; Cronbach, 1988). Thus, the most critical flaw of the present tests and their supporting documentation is that no validity evidence is presented. This lack is especially distressing because the same firm has published other tests with no evidence of validity. Given the time lapse since the publication of the ATB, lack of time cannot serve as an excuse for this problem.

Reliability estimates (Cronbach's alpha) are presented in the Manual and User's Guide.

Normative data from relatively large overall samples, in the form of *T*-scores and percentiles, appear in a publication entitled *Normline Supplement No. 1*. These data, however, have problems of their own that we discuss below.

SPECIFIC EVALUATIONS. The tests have several strengths. One positive aspect is that the administration instructions are complete enough so that persons with relatively little training can give the test. Another is a discussion of equal employment opportunity in the context of British law (e.g., the Sex Discrimination Act and the Race Relations Act, 1975 and 1976, respectively). There is, however, no mention of the U.K. Commission on Racial Equality's Code (1984) and/or the Equal Employment Commission's Code (1985). There is a discussion of differential validity concepts with a question and answer section in the *Normline*. Third, the concept of a periodically updated norm supplement to which users can contribute data is a good one, provided that quality control is maintained. Finally, the authors seem to have a good grasp of basic psychometrics, as evidenced by their competent discussion of such concepts as standard scores, reliability and validity estimates, and user qualifications. A caveat to this final point is there is no discussion of range restriction, which is implied in the prescreening that many of the normative samples underwent. Taken as a whole, however, these strengths do not balance the test's critical flaws.

The reliability estimates (.74 and .82 for Verbal and Numerical respectively) are unimpressive, particularly given that the tests are recommended for important individual decisions. In addition, the samples for the final forms are too small (*n*s of 44), especially relative to the larger sample sizes for pilot forms. Oddly, the reliability estimates for both pilot forms (.77 for Verbal and .91 for Numerical) were higher than those of the final forms. Also, given that the test is supposed to discriminate at the high ends of the distribution, estimations of the standard error of measurement at different points along the test score distribution are advisable. There is no mention of any possible deficiencies in the reliability section of the manual other than a discussion of the advisability of considering the mean and variability of the sample when interpreting the standard error of measurement.

The lack of validity data is extremely troubling, although such information is promised in future editions of the *Normline*. Beyond a discussion of types of validity, no validity evidence for this test is presented, unless one considers a cursory discussion of a positive relationship between the two tests to be adequate (with no mention of the size of the relevant correlation; Manual, p. 23). Furthermore, evidence of construct validity is necessary, given that critical reasoning, a theoretical construct, is claimed as an important component of the managerial job.

The Watson-Glaser Critical Thinking Appraisal (9:1347), with forms for adults, appears to be the best alternative for assessing this construct at the present time. Although there are problems with the Watson-Glaser test, the authors of the tests under review here would do well to at least consider the conceptual work that went into the Watson-Glaser (i.e., the five-dimension structure) and to study the validation strategy used. An alternative assessment strategy might be to employ the techniques proposed and demonstrated by Borman, Rosse, and Abrahams (1980).

The norms presented consist of two sections: (*a*) Graduates (presumably recent undergraduates) and (*b*) Management. Sample sizes appear adequate at the overall level. There are some problems when the data are broken down into subsamples covering a wide range of occupations and firms. Overall sample sizes for the recent graduate group are 1,443 for Verbal and 1,439 for Numerical; the subsamples range in size from 72 (Mail Order Book Club) to 252 (Finance and Technical). The total sample for managers is 368 for both tests, with 277 managers who are graduates and 91 who are not. There is no discussion regarding the mean differences between the graduate and management samples. Even when managers who are graduates are compared to the graduate sample, there are mean differences in favor of the graduates (34.17 vs. 31.12 for Verbal; 23.63 vs. 20.56 for Numerical). These differences suggest the tests may assess aspects of schooling rather than job performance. This is a common complaint about general ability tests (cf. Frederiksen, 1986, although that critique was directed at "intelligence" tests). Some consideration and discussion should be given to the convenience sampling plan that apparently

governed the development of the norms. *Large numbers do not compensate for improper sampling.* Perhaps the ideal procedure would be to use a multistage procedure, in which firms would be randomly sampled from the U.K. population, followed by random sampling of managerial personnel within the firms. When state-of-the-art test development strategies are not used, mention of these shortcomings should be made in supporting manuals.

In summary, we cannot recommend the use of these tests for selection or development until more evidence is produced. The reported reliability estimates are low for individual decision-making purposes. More importantly, there is virtually no evidence for validity. Finally, the process of norm development has problems as well. The Manual has several strong sections, but references to many of the concepts and findings are lacking. A more complete manual would allow less experienced test users to fairly evaluate the tests.

REVIEWERS' REFERENCES

Mintzberg, H. (1973). *The nature of managerial work.* New York: Harper & Row.
Borman, W. C., Rosse, R. L., & Abrahams, N. M. (1980). An empirical construct validity approach to studying predictor-job performance links. *Journal of Applied Psychology, 65,* 662-671.
Stewart, R. (1982). A model for understanding managerial work. *Academy of Management Review, 7,* 7-13.
Frederiksen, N. (1986). Toward a broader conception of human intelligence. *American Psychologist, 41,* 445-452.
Cook, M. (1988). *Personnel selection and productivity.* Chichester: Wiley.
Cronbach, L. J. (1988). Five perspectives on the validity argument. In H. Wainer & H. Braun (Eds.), *Test validity* (pp. 3-17). Hillsdale, NJ: Erlbaum.

Review of the Management and Graduate Item Bank by R. W. FAUNCE, Consulting Psychologist, Minneapolis, MN:

The Management and Graduate Item Bank (MGIB) is described as the first stage in a series of new higher level cognitive tests being developed to rescue the Advanced Test Battery (9:57) from the ravages of practice effects and "potential" overexposure. The first two tests in this proposed series are the Verbal Critical Reasoning test (VMG1) and the Numerical Critical Reasoning test (NMG1). These new tests are reported to be similar in appearance to the Verbal and Numerical Critical Reasoning tests of the Advanced Test Battery (VA3 and NA4).

The test of verbal reasoning, VMG1, consists of 52 questions to be answered within 25 minutes. Answers are made by filling in boxes on a separate answer sheet. Scoring may be done manually or by machine. Thirteen paragraphs are presented and four statements are made about each paragraph. Respondents indicate whether each statement is true (follows logically), untrue (the opposite follows logically), or if neither the statement nor its opposite is true (or if more information is needed to make a determination).

The numerical reasoning test, NMG1, consists of 40 multiple-choice questions to be answered within 35 minutes. Half the items have 5 response options and half have 10 options. Questions are based on a number of statistical tables containing data on such things as production rates, inflation rates, and life expectancy.

Both tests are attractively packaged, printed on sturdy, high-gloss paper, have clear instructions, and are easy to handle. Answer sheets are also of high-quality construction. The hand-scoring plastic overlay keys make scoring simple and errors should be minimal. Scoring key instructions have one minor error. Scorers are directed to enter raw scores in a box at the top of the answer sheet; the box is actually at the bottom of the answer sheet.

The 41-page manual is also attractive and easy to read. More than a third of the manual (17 pages) is devoted to descriptions of the testing program, administration, and scoring. Another third (15 pages) presents boilerplate information on basic psychometric desiderata, which could apply to any test. Only nine pages refer to psychometric information specific to the MGIB. Eight pages present normative information and one page is devoted to reliability. No validity data are presented.

Users in the U.S. might be put off by language differences, such as instructions referring to the use of crayons, rubbers, and invigilators. Although language differences in instructions might have nuisance value, differences in item content could affect validity. It is hard to tell what impact questions involving petrol, pounds (instead of dollars), programmes, and tonnes would have on populations that do not speak "English."

The Management and Graduate Item Bank appears to be a direct competitor of another British developed test, Graduate and Managerial Assessment (10:129). Publishers of both tests appear to have pursued the same market-ing approach of publishing the basic test materials and then supplying supportive information as it becomes available. This approach has the advantage of getting the tests before the public with plenty of time to review them. It has the disadvantage of not supplying the potential user with sufficient psychometric data on which an informed decision to use or not to use must be based. It would be difficult to choose between the two tests, considering the available information. It appears unlikely that either test will have a substantial impact on the domestic U.S. market.

STANDARDIZATION AND NORMS. Little information is provided about standardization procedures. No information is given on item statistics. Norms, initially presented in 1986, were based on 252 "graduate applicants to a public utility." Presumably, these college graduates were applying for entry-level jobs because their average age was 21. Means, standard deviations, percentile ranks, and T scores are given. Similar information is also given for subgroups of the graduate applicant sample, based on the type of occupation to which they applied: Finance and Technical, Administration, or Commercial. Sample sizes in these subgroups were small, with Administration having only 46 applicants.

According to information found in the manual, applicants who did well on the verbal test also tended to do well on the numerical test. No supporting data are given. Males were described as doing better than females on the numerical test, but no sex difference was found on the verbal test. Again, supporting data are lacking. All norms are based on combined male-female scores and no evidence of predictive validity is provided. The publisher "plans to provide data on likely differences in test scores for different groups and, when appropriate, to issue differential norms."

A subsequent publication, in 1987 (*Normline Supplement No. 1*), provides additional norms, using the same format as the original norms. The new norms provide scores for 1,443 people in a Total Graduate Group and 368 members in a Total Management Group. Norms are also given for nine subgroups of the Graduate Group, with sample sizes ranging from 72 graduates applying for trainee positions at a mail-order book club to 252 graduate applicants for financial and technical positions in a public utility. Apparently, although not explicitly stated, this latter sample is the same sample included in the original norm group described in the manual. The sample sizes in the subgroups do not add up to the Total Graduate Group sample size for some unexplained reason.

The Total Management Group is divided into two subgroups: a Graduate Management Group and a Non-Graduate Group. Subgroup sample sizes do add up to the Total Management Group sample size. Mean scores for the Graduate Group were substantially higher than mean scores for the Non-Graduate Group, but large age differences between the two groups also existed. No studies of the influence of age have been reported thus far.

RELIABILITY AND VALIDITY. Information on reliability is sparse. Cronbach's alpha coefficients for 44 "young graduates in banking" were .74 for the verbal test and .82 for the numerical test. The reliability of the tests is critical to the success of the Management and Graduate Item Bank because a major purpose of the item bank is to permit the easy development of numerous alternate forms. Additional reliability information on larger and better described samples would be welcome and, of course, alternate form reliability needs to be established as the new tests are released.

Standard errors of measurement are provided for raw scores and T scores. Again, these measures are based on the 44 young graduates in banking and, presumably, on Cronbach's alpha coefficients. Standard errors typically were about 5 for the verbal test and about 4 for the numerical test.

The face validity of the two tests seems good, at least for Great Britain. No other validity information is presented, although it is promised.

SUMMARY. The Management and Graduate Item Bank is an attractively designed instrument that appears easy to administer and score. Its face validity is good for the British market. Its developers appear to be well aware of the criteria used to evaluate the adequacy of tests, and their descriptions of test desiderata are clearly presented in the manual. Up to this point, little evidence of reliability or validity has been offered. It remains to be seen if the developers can live up to their promising beginning. Until more information is forthcoming, the tests should be considered experimental.

[42]
Management Style Inventory [Training House, Inc.].

Purpose: "This exercise is designed to give you some insights into your management style and how it affects others."
Population: Industry.
Publication Dates: 1986–87.
Scores, 5: Team Builder, Soft, Hard, Middle of Road, Ineffective.
Administration: Group.
Price Data, 1988: $60 per 20 complete sets including test, answer sheet, and interpretation sheet.
Time: Administration time not reported.
Comments: Self-administered, self-scored.
Author: Training House, Inc.
Publisher: Training House, Inc.

Review of the Management Style Inventory [Training House, Inc.] by ERNEST J. KOZMA, Professor of Education, Clemson University, Clemson, SC:

The Management Style Inventory is a self-scoring inventory designed to help an individual make a self-assessment of his/her management style. The inventory contains 10 sets of statements. Each set includes five statements concerning a topic covered by the set. The individual using the inventory assigns a number to each of the statements. The highest number indicates the statement most representative of his/her view. The 10 topics covered are role perception, view of authority, setting goals and standards, view of work and workers, planning and scheduling work, giving feedback, team building, implementation, evaluation, and management philosophy.

An answer sheet is provided and the numerical ratings given each statement are recorded. A scoring sheet is attached and the answer is recorded and assigned a category. The totals for each category are compiled. The five categories are supposed to reflect five different management styles. After compiling the score in each of the five categories, the individual is referred to a four-page self-assessment folder that provides more detail concerning each of the categories or management styles.

The self-assessment folder begins with a very short review of various management styles that have been advocated since the first quarter of this century. The review contains no references or mention of some of the major management criticisms of the 1980s. A chart of factors affecting a person's management style with brief descriptive statements about each is included.

The styles are Hard style, Soft style, Middle of Road style, Ineffective style, and Team Builder. The entire folder includes only a few paragraphs of information about each of these.

No data or information are supplied as to the validity or reliability of the material. The claim is made that the material will provide some insights into personal management style and how it affects others. It is difficult to guarantee this result. As with most inventory-type instruments, individual differences in examinees greatly affect the value of the test-taking experience. The material overly simplifies the complex problems of management.

Review of the Management Style Inventory [Training House, Inc.] by CHARLES K. PARSONS, Professor of Management, Georgia Institute of Technology, Atlanta, GA:

The stated purpose of this inventory is to give the respondent some insights into his/her management style and its possible effects on other people. The inventory consists of 10 sets of five self-descriptive statements, on which the respondent is to rank order the five statements within each set on the degree to which each one is representative of him/her. The inventory is then self-scored and the respondent ends up with five scale scores representing his/her tendency to be a Team Builder, a Soft manager, a Hard manager, a Middle of the Road manager, or an Ineffective manager. Some explanation of these styles and when they might be effective is provided in an accompanying four-page folder.

This instrument is reported to be based on the "Managerial Grid" of Blake and Mouton (1964) and Blanchard and Hersey (1977). The resulting styles are virtually identical to those described by Blake and Mouton. The styles are the result of varying degrees of concern for people and production.

On the surface, this instrument appears to have some desirable features. First, each scale score ends up being the function of the responses to 10 items, thus improving chances of reliability. Second, the five statements within

each set appear to be somewhat equal in terms of social desirability. Each statement appears to represent a plausible statement by a manager. This characteristic could make the forced choice nature of the response format effective in eliminating social desirability effects.

The scoring routine is relatively easy, although I can imagine some respondents needing clarification. Because of the nature of the scoring, it is possible for a person to end up with five scores that are quite similar to each other (one for each of five styles) or five that are quite different (strongly suggesting one style is dominant). Neither the scoring instructions nor the four-page explanatory folder provides guidance on interpreting the differences in the scores. I recommend some guidance on what level of difference between scores suggests a dominant style. Also, I suggest providing guidance on interpreting a score profile for a person who scores about the same on all five scales.

One particular style and its description are problematic—that resulting from low concern for tasks and low concern for people and labeled "ineffective." For a respondent having this predominant style, the label could be devastating. Somewhat surprisingly, the explanation of the style goes on to describe situations in which this style might be effective. I recommend that a different label and description be associated with the low, low style.

Another shortcoming of this instrument is it provides only a report of how the manager sees him/herself, which might be quite different from how subordinates view this person. Although the sole use of a self-report instrument, like the Management Style Inventory, is an expedient way to get some information about one's management style, a more complete view can be obtained by getting parallel information from subordinates and co-workers. Several commercially available instruments provide this capability.

The theory upon which this instrument is based suggests that this sort of inventory is best used as a self-assessment tool prior to some form of management development intervention. It would be extremely useful if the author(s) included information regarding the intended use of the instrument. There is none provided presently.

A major disadvantage of this inventory is that it is not accompanied by a reference manual that includes standard psychometric characteristics of the instrument. There are no reports of reliability, validity, norms, and so on. The user is left only with the "face" validity of the items and the scales as the basis for use. I would strongly recommend the publisher of this inventory correct this glaring deficiency in the package.

REVIEWER'S REFERENCES

Blake, R. R., & Mouton, J. S. (1964). *The managerial grid.* Houston: Gulf Publishing Co.

Hersey, P., & Blanchard, K. H. (1977). *Management of organizational behavior: Utilizing human resources* (3rd ed.). Englewood Cliffs, NJ: Prentice-Hall.

[43]
Managerial Assessment of Proficiency MAP™.

Purpose: "Shows a participant's strengths and weaknesses in twelve areas of managerial competency and two dimensions of management style."

Population: Managers.

Publication Dates: 1985–86.

Acronym: MAP.

Scores, 17: Administrative Competencies (Time Management and Prioritizing, Setting Goals and Standards, Planning and Scheduling Work, Administrative Composite), Communication Competencies (Listening and Organizing, Giving Clear Information, Getting Unbiased Information, Communication Composite), Supervisory Competencies (Training/Coaching/Delegating, Appraising People and Performance, Disciplining and Counseling, Supervisory Composite), Cognitive Competencies (Identifying and Solving Problems, Making Decisions/Weighing Risk, Thinking Clearly and Analytically, Cognitive Composite), Proficiency Composite.

Administration: Group.

Price Data, 1988: $10,000 initial investment for purchase with licensing agreement (for high-volume users) including set of 4 videocassettes, 50 sets of participant materials including workbook (60 pages) and booklet entitled *Interpreting Your Scores* (24 pages), personal computer floppy disk for in-house scoring, scoring by publisher of first 25 participants, and 1¹/₂-day training and pilot cycle by senior instructor from publisher; $30 per person for additional participant materials; $30 per person for additional (optional) scoring by publisher; $200 per person (minimum of 12 persons) for contracting for in-house program including materials, scoring, and instructor/consultant time; $200–$250 per person for registration at public workshop held in Princeton, NJ by publishers.

Time: (360–420) minutes.

Comments: May be purchased with licensing agreement, contracted for in-house administration, or used by attending a public workshop provided by publisher; administered in part by videocassette.

Author: Scott B. Parry.

Publisher: Training House, Inc.

Review of the Managerial Assessment of Proficiency MAP™ by JERARD F. KEHOE, District Manager, Selection and Testing, American Telephone and Telegraph Co., Morristown, NJ:

The Managerial Assessment of Proficiency (MAP) is a video-based assessment exercise lasting 6¹/₂ hours designed to measure managers' competencies in 12 categories of performance and managers' style on two types of interaction, four types of communication, and four types of communication response. The developer suggests several applications: to diagnose individual and organizational training/development needs; to evaluate competency and style gains from training/development programs; and to make personnel selection decisions. Overall, a significant lack of evidence concerning reliability and validity makes the MAP a poor choice as a selection procedure. The lack of explanation about the origin of the 12 competencies and the development of the corresponding scoring rules limits the MAP's value as a diagnostic or evaluative tool to those training/development programs that adopt the MAP's companion training modules organized around the same competency categories and style dimensions.

ADMINISTRATION. The MAP can be administered in groups with a live "instructor" or individually with a PC-based guide. The MAP process has two basic components. One is a set of 12 videotaped exercises and the other is a set of 187 four-option items. In the videotaped exercises actors portray various combinations of managers playing out different, but sometimes related, scenarios. The scenarios consist of a staff meeting, an individual planning session, the preparation of a subordinate for a performance review, discussion of a problem situation, two examples of delegation, a job interview, a discussion of a problem employee, preparation of a memo, a performance review, counseling an employee with a performance problem, and reassignment meetings. The scenarios are uniformly well done with credible realism, plausible exchanges, and generally good acting. The 187 items are organized into 13 sets that are answered in turn after each scenario. One or more of the options in each item may be chosen, resulting in 748 scorable subitems. The items assess recall of facts, evaluations of depicted performance, beliefs and judgments about the specific situations depicted in the scenarios, and general beliefs and judgments about management principles related to the scenarios. Support materials include a participant's workbook, self-assessment procedures for the competencies and styles, development options and planning guides, a score interpretation workbook, and a personal interpretation worksheet with sample profiles and help materials describing the style dimensions. These participant-support materials are uniformly well organized and written at an informal level that is easy to use and avoids procedural confusion. However, they shed no light on the origin and development of the competency categories and style dimensions. With the exception of six style dimensions that are clearly derived from previous literature, the materials are virtually a closed system with no linkage to other research or theoretical domains in managerial assessment.

The following sections on scoring, reliability, and validity are based on two technical reports prepared by the developer in July 1985 and November 1986 describing results of field trials in 11 organizations.

SCORING. No information is presented to describe the theoretical or practical origins of the 187 items. Nor is any information presented describing what the scoring rules are or how they were developed. Some item revision took place during the field trials, based on participant input, resulting in changes in approximately 53 of the 187 items. Also, some unknown number of items were deleted because more than 90% of the participants answered in the same way. Because the same trials resulted in validity estimates as well as item revisions, this lack of information about item development and scoring rules creates uncertainty about the meaning of the validity results. The 12 competency scores, 10 style scores, and 5 composite scores are reported as percentile ranks based on normative data collected by the developer. In the 1986 report, normative data are reported for 1,400 participants from 52 organizations in 11 industry groups and one executive group.

The value of this normative data is limited because sample sizes are not provided, nor are any subgroup norms provided except by industry group. Also, the appropriateness of normative scoring is questionable due to the high sensitivity of MAP scores to training and other experience differences.

RELIABILITY. The developer claims two types of reliability evidence "verify the reliability of MAP." In fact, no reliability evidence is presented. Instead, the developer severely misconstrues the meanings of test-retest and split-half reliability, and presents evidence showing substantial score-level changes within one group of 13 participants from pre- to post-training and presents other evidence showing substantial score-level differences between two matched groups of 22 and 27 participants, one with and the other without related training. The irony of these data is that they indirectly imply the distinct possibility that the MAP has rather low reliability. In one case, intervening training changed the average percentile score on related competencies from 53 to 94. The average percentile score on competencies not directly addressed in training changed from 65 to 82. In the two-group study, the average percentile scores on the six training-relevant competencies for the trained and untrained groups were 49 and 30, respectively. For the six training-irrelevant competencies the difference was negligible, 45 and 47. These results have little utility because they are based on only 13 participants in the first case and 49 in the second. Nevertheless, they raise the distinct possibility that the MAP scores are highly sensitive to a variety of directly and indirectly relevant experiences, including the experience of taking the MAP itself. These types of influences are likely to negatively impact many types of reliability estimates. A further irony is the developer explicitly discounted the value of the appropriate split-half reliability estimation procedure that, in fact, would have provided the most appropriate estimate of reliability, given the available evidence.

VALIDITY. Most critical of all is the developer's claim that MAP scores predict managerial job performance. To evaluate its validity, the MAP was trialed in 11 organizations involving over 200 participants. Eight organizations complied by providing one or two managers' independent evaluations of the job performance of the participants. Within each organization, a validity estimate was computed as the correlation between ranked MAP scores and ranked performance evaluations. The number of participants within organizations varied from 18 to 32 with a total of 184 in the 1986 report. A number of inconsistencies plague the reports of these validity results, although the validities reported are remarkably high. In the 1985 report, seven validity coefficients for the overall composite competency score are reported ranging from .71 to .92. The 1986 report, which provides more detail about the same seven data sets plus one more, reports eight validities ranging from .71 to .90. For some reason, however, only three of the 1985 validity values are found in the 1986 report. No mention is made of any reason for the changes. Validities for the individual competency category scores are reported, although they were based entirely on one manager's rating of 12 participants on the 12 MAP competencies as his strategy for deriving an overall performance evaluation. Of course, using the predictor—the MAP—as the basis for producing the criterion artificially biases the validities. Nevertheless, the correlations between MAP competency scores and the corresponding manager-rated competency scores were reported and ranged from .39 to .83. No report was made of the correlations between different competency scores. Overall, the validity evidence is weak in spite of the high values reported. Sample sizes are small, differences in the two reports are not accounted for, the effects of item revision and scoring rule development in the same trials are not reported, individual competency validities are positively biased by the rating procedure, and MAP competency scores are likely to be sensitive to a variety of experiences.

SUMMARY. The ease, orderliness, and attractiveness of the MAP materials belie the significant lack of supporting evidence for the reliability and validity of MAP scores. Certainly, the available reliability and validity evidence fails to meet even the most minimal professional standards for assessment procedures and fails to meet the regulatory requirements for selection procedures. However, for managers and organizations who accept the MAP representation of manager competence and style, the entire MAP package of assessment and training modules may be an attractive tool for developmental

activities. Even developmental applications will be flawed, however, by the lack of appropriately reliable and valid outcome measures.

[44]
The Marriage and Family Attitude Survey.

Purpose: "A diagnostic and educational instrument for understanding relationship attitudes" in marriage and family life.
Population: Adolescents and adults.
Publication Date: No date.
Scores: 10 areas: Cohabitation and Premarital Sexual Relations, Marriage and Divorce, Childhood and Child Rearing, Division of Household Labor and Professional Employment, Marital and Extramarital Sexual Relations, Privacy Rights and Social Needs, Religious Needs, Communication Expectations, Parental Relationships, Professional Counseling Services.
Administration: Group.
Price Data, 1988: $15 per 25 test forms; $4.50 per examiner's manual (no date, 8 pages); $5 per specimen set.
Time: (4–10) minutes.
Authors: Donald V. Martin and Maggie Martin.
Publisher: Psychologists and Educators, Inc.

Review of The Marriage and Family Attitude Survey by MARK W. ROBERTS, Professor of Clinical Psychology, Idaho State University, Pocatello, ID:

The Marriage and Family Attitude Survey (MFAS) was designed to measure adolescent and adult expectations of various components of married life. Testing time is reported at 4 to 10 minutes. Respondents complete 5-point Likert scales for each of 58 items. For example, Item 1, "I believe it is wrong to engage in sexual intercourse before marriage," must be rated from "strongly agree" to "strongly disagree." Both item responses and total scale scores are suggested for use in counseling formats with individuals or couples or in educational formats with adolescents. By detecting deviations or conformity with either the available normative data or one's partner, the counseling or educational process is thought to be enhanced. The authors suggest that test items could also be used as a therapeutic exercise in seeking agreements for typical marital conflicts. Unfortunately, like the Marriage Role Expectation Inventory (9:655), the MFAS is severely limited by psychometric difficulties.

The standardization sample (*n* "exceeded" 5,000, 14 to 35 years of age, attending six different high schools, colleges, and universities) seems too heterogeneous to accomplish the stated objectives of the MFAS. As demonstrated by the authors in the manual, such variables as age, gender, ethnic background, parental marital status, and dating experience are significantly associated with some or all of the 58 MFAS items. Consequently, the assertion of normative data begs the question of "Normative for which subpopulation?" Subsequent to printing the MFAS manual, the authors (Martin & Martin, 1984) did publish norms for a more homogeneous sample (n = 5,237, 16 to 36 years, single, undergraduates). It is unclear if these are new subjects or a subset of the original sample.

Test items were generated following a review of the marriage and family literature and subsequently reviewed by a panel of clinical psychologists specializing in marital problems. The manual does not state the criteria used by the experts for item inclusion. A pilot study (n = 30 university students) was undertaken to determine readability and test duration and to perform item analyses for "offensive" or "unnaturally skewed" items. Each item was then compared to the five demographic and marital/dating variables cited above. Items yielding significant chi-square statistics with any two of these "criterion" variables were retained. All 58 items were retained. It is unclear if the pilot study sample data or the standardization sample data were used for the chi-square analyses.

Norms are provided in terms of the typical rating (strongly agree to strongly disagree) for each item by gender. Whether "typical" is a mean, median, or mode is not specified, nor are any data available on item variances. Recommended scoring consists of summing one point for each agreement with the categorical normative response across the 58 items. Total scores (0 to 58) are then categorized as "High Agreement" (48–58), "Normal" (39–47), "Low Agreement" (28–38), or "Conflicting" (27 or lower), using arbitrary 10-point cutoffs. Percent endorsement data for each category from strongly disagree to strongly agree are reported for 43 of the original 58 items by Martin and Martin (1984). These norms correspond closely to those in the manual, suggesting that the "typical" item rating in the manual is the modal endorsement and that the

1984 subjects were a subset of the original sample.

Additional psychometric problems with the MFAS are readily apparent. The manual does not report any reliability data. Martin and Martin (1984, p. 295), citing an earlier study (Martin, 1982), report "an internal reliability coefficient of .81 and a test rates and reliability coefficient of .79." This sentence does not include sufficient information for interpretation. Unfortunately, Martin (1982) was referenced incorrectly and is actually Martin, Gawinski, and Medler (1982), an article describing premarital counseling that does not include any information about MFAS reliability. Scale reliability is, therefore, uncertain. The standard error of the total scores is unknown. There are no internal consistency data or factor analyses to demonstrate the level of homogeneity within each of the 10 scales or to justify the summing of data across 10 scales to form total scores. Validity data consist of the chi-square analyses described above, rather than measurements of behavior responsive to the stated purpose of the MFAS. For example, total scores or couple agreement scores could be validated against independent measures of marital satisfaction. Couple agreement levels before and after counseling could be obtained. MFAS use versus non-use in high school formats could be contrasted on tests of student awareness of marital issues. In the absence of such studies, one must conclude that the MFAS total score is without criterion validation.

As currently researched, the MFAS represents an unproven instrument of questionable utility. It is not recommended. In a similar lament, Markman (9:655) recommended an unpublished instrument by Epstein and Eidelson called the Relationship Belief Instrument (RBI). The RBI, however, focuses on pathological expectations (e.g., Scale A, "Disagreement is Destructive"), rather than the comprehensive set of marital expectations attempted by the MFAS. Therefore, there does not yet appear to be a psychometrically adequate test of marital expectations.

REVIEWER'S REFERENCES

Martin, D., Gawinski, B., & Medler, B. (1982). Premarital counseling using group process. *Journal for Specialists in Group Work, 7*, 102-108.
Martin, D., & Martin, M. (1984). Selected attitudes toward marriage and family life among college students. *Family Relations, 33*, 293-300.

Review of The Marriage and Family Attitude Survey by DONALD U. ROBERTSON, Professor of Psychology, and VIRGINIA L. BROWN, Director, Institute for Research and Community Service, Indiana University of Pennsylvania, Indiana, PA:

The Marriage and Family Attitude Survey is a 58-item inventory that consists of statements grouped into 10 areas such as Religious Needs and Communication Expectations. Test takers indicate on a 5-point Likert scale how strongly they agree or disagree with each attitudinal statement. The initial item pool was generated by the test authors based on a review of the literature in the field of marriage and family therapy. This pool was then submitted to a panel of 10 licensed psychologists who also had supervisor status in the American Association for Marriage and Family Therapy. Items approved by seven of the panel members were included in the final test. The test manual does not indicate what the panel members were instructed to evaluate to determine whether an item was acceptable.

The ways the test can be used include facilitating discussion in classrooms from junior high through college and clarifying attitudes in the context of individual and couple counseling. An answer key is used to obtain scores on the test. The total test score is then assigned to high, normal, low, or conflicting ranges. Brief interpretive statements are provided for each of these ranges. There are no guidelines for interpretation of scores in the 10 areas.

The normative population consisted of over 5,000 people between the ages of 14 and 35, with slightly more females than males. No further information is provided in the manual. A far more serious problem is that the authors seem to have confused norms and answer keys. The answer key, labelled "Normative Distribution" in the only table contained in the manual, consists of a listing of the 58 items and the "typical" response for males, females, and combined males and females. The table is confusing and contradictory. For example, both males and females receive a point toward the total score if they disagree with the statement that it is wrong to engage in sexual intercourse before marriage. However, if one uses the combined key/norm, one obtains a point for either disagreeing or strongly agreeing! There is no information about how this table was constructed.

Even if we can accept the rather unusual scoring scheme, the only information that could possibly serve as norms are the ranges for total scores. There is no information about how the cutting scores were established or the basis of the interpretive statements.

The manual contains no information about reliability. In fact, the word "reliability" does not appear in the manual. The only evidence of validity is a brief statement that face validity was evaluated by administering the test to 30 undergraduates who were asked about the readability of the items. The only analysis of test data contained in the manual is a brief description of the results of cross-classifying six demographic variables with responses to the 58 items. The reader is told that 254 of the 348 tables produced values of chi-square that were significant at the .05 level or greater (sic).

The Marriage and Family Attitude Survey is a nice sample of 58 attitudes about marriage and families. The items could serve as a useful list of discussion topics. In its current form, however, it is not a test. There are no norms, no evidence of reliability, and no evidence of validity. The authors do not provide necessary technical information and its publication as a test is clearly inappropriate.

[45]

Mathematics 7.

Purpose: "Assess the mathematics attainment of children near the end of the school year in which they reach their seventh birthday."
Population: Ages 6-10 to 7-9.
Publication Date: 1987.
Scores: 1 individual total score, 4 item analysis categories: Understanding, Computational Skill, Application, Factual Recall.
Administration: Group.
Price Data, 1989: £6.25 per specimen set including Teacher's Guide (24 pages), test booklet, and group record sheet; £5.75 per Teacher's Guide; £10.30 per test booklets.
Time: (30–50) minutes.
Comments: Downward extension of Mathematics 8–12 Series; no norms for categories; orally administered.
Authors: Test Development Unit of the Foundation for Educational Research in England and Wales.
Publisher: NFER-Nelson Publishing Co., Ltd. [England].

Review of Mathematics 7 by CAMILLA PERSSON BENBOW, Associate Professor of Psychology, Department of Psychology, Iowa State University, Ames, IA:

Mathematics 7 was designed to assess the mathematics attainment of children near the end of the school year in which they reach their seventh birthday. This represents the final year of infant school for students in England. The items selected for the test were written to reflect guidelines issued by a number of local education authorities and to match the content of mathematics texts used by schools in England. Because the test was designed to be easy, it is argued that the test is suitable for identifying those children not making progress rather than for identifying advanced students. With this in mind, the fact that questions are read to students can be viewed as an advantage. Limitations in reading ability should not affect performance.

The test can be administered to small groups in either one or two sittings. Because the examiner does not proceed until every student has attempted the problem, it may take between 30 to 50 minutes to complete the 28 items. Some students may become frustrated by this procedure, however.

It is strongly recommended by the authors that the test be administered in the month of June. It is argued that data obtained during that month would be most useful to the junior schools receiving the pupils the following year. The disadvantage, as I see it, is that little time is left for the teacher in the infant school to provide remediation.

The items selected for the test represent four content areas: number, measures, shape, and pictorial representation. Four objectives are also tapped: understanding of basic concepts, computational skills, application of concepts and skills, and recall of basic facts. These two dimensions are crossed to produce a 4 x 4 grid. In this grid of 16 possible cells, items were designed to measure 10 cells or domains. Many of the items, however, are clustered in just one cell, the understanding of the basic concept of number. As a result, performance within certain domains is measured by only one question. To provide a specific diagnosis (except in the case of number), the number of items is clearly insufficient. I, therefore, question the utility of

this test for that purpose. Moreover, an alternate form of the test is lacking.

An appealing aspect of the test appeared to be its attempt at providing a diagnosis of wrong answers. Five types of errors were discussed. Although the potential user is instructed in how to approach such a diagnosis, there is little explicit information provided.

The accompanying manual or rather teacher's guide contains much information useful to an individual with little or no knowledge of psychometrics. Statistical terms, such as measurement scales, standardized scores, the normal curve, percentile ranks, errors of measurement, and confidence intervals are explained in depth. Much information is also provided as to how percentile ranks and confidence intervals can be computed and interpreted. The discussion assumes no knowledge on the part of the potential user and is clearly written. Finally, a strong emphasis was placed on controlling for the effects of age on performance. Scores were adjusted, with precision, according to age in months.

After such care was exhibited for providing clear explanations and instructions and for partialling out the effects of age, one became rather disappointed in the technical data available. The test was standardized on a sample of 3,965 students in various parts of Great Britain, who were administered the test in June 1986. The only reliability index reported, however, was the Kuder-Richardson 20, which was good (i.e., .90). Retest reliability estimates are most notably missing. In terms of test validity, the situation is perhaps even worse. The only evidence of test validity we are given are correlations between teacher's rankings of students and scores on Mathematics 7. The correlations ranged from .53 to .91 (median = .80) for the 16 classes studied. Even if one did not question the usefulness of these data, they are clearly insufficient to establish validity. Moreover, because the authors argue the test is especially suited for identifying students with deficient performance, one would have expected some sort of validation of this claim. But none was provided.

Finally, the test was explicitly made to be easy (mean difficulty index was 69%) so that low achievers could be identified. It is rather puzzling then that the authors did not choose to develop a criterion-referenced test. This would seem to coincide more closely with the stated purpose of the test.

In sum, this test was designed to assess children's performance in mathematics at the end of infant school in England. The authors claim that the test is especially useful for identifying students performing poorly. We are not provided, however, with sufficient evidence to know if the test is actually fulfilling this promise. On the other hand, the test may be useful in comparing the performance of groups on mathematics items designed to measure content covered by most widely used textbooks and items included in guidelines issued by local education authorities in Great Britain.

Review of Mathematics 7 by KEVIN MENE-FEE, Certified School Psychologist, Omaha Public Schools, Omaha, NE:

Mathematics 7 is a 28-item screening test, in booklet form, of mathematics skills in 7-year-old children. It is designed for oral administration to small groups or entire classes of children, with an estimated administration time of 30 to 50 minutes. The test covers a broad range of problems in number, money, measurement, and related concepts, and yields an overall standard score or percentile rank. Both the standardization sample and the content and language of items in this instrument restrict its usage to children in Great Britain.

The authors state the test's items were "written to reflect guidelines issued by a number of local education authorities and mathematics course books currently in use in schools" without specifying more precisely the exact authorities or course books consulted, or how this particular set of items was determined to be a balanced representation of the curricula in question. We are left, therefore, to presume that they do, in fact, fairly cover the typical mathematics content of "the final year of infant school." The authors' description of the development process, however (items were piloted to a stratified national sample in two consecutive trials, allowing ample opportunity for selection and modification of items based both on statistical findings and on input from participating schools), suggest a high probability of good content validity.

Standardization of the instrument, as reported in the manual, appears to have been very good, based on scores of nearly 4,000 students from 139 schools, proportionately stratified nationwide by region, type of school, class size, and rural versus urban counties throughout Great Britain. The authors base the test's claim to validity largely on its content (no predictive studies or comparisons to other instruments are reported), and on a concurrent validity study based on a sample of 11 schools involved in its standardization. In this study, teachers' rankings of their students' mathematics achievement were correlated with the students' ranked test scores, yielding a median Spearman's rank-order correlation of .80 between teachers' rankings and students' standard scores. The authors also report good internal consistency for the test, with a Kuder-Richardson 20 reliability of .90. No data regarding test-retest were reported.

As previously mentioned, Mathematics 7 yields a standard score for each age level (at monthly increments) from 6-6 to 7-11. The test was actually normed only on children ages 6-10 to 7-9; however, extrapolated scores are provided at each end of the age span. Children's scores change fairly dramatically with age in the norms tables, such that a raw score of 24 (for example) equates to a standard score of 100 for the oldest age level (7-11), but a standard score of 118 for the youngest (6-6). These substantial shifts in performance over a relatively narrow age span suggest the importance of adhering closely to the developers' recommendations for administering the test as near to the end of the school year (as was done with the standardization sample) as possible.

The test developers have also grouped the test items (with no supportive basis cited) into four item analysis categories (Understanding, Computational Skill, Application, and Factual Recall) based upon the hypothetical primary "processing" requirement of each item. The manual, however, provides no means of deriving or interpreting category scores, and the authors themselves appear to have completely ignored this feature of the test after having mentioned it, almost in passing, early in the manual. Users of the instrument are advised to likewise ignore these categorizations, as neither theoretical nor empirical support is provided for their validity, and, in fact, one of the categories is represented by only a single item on the test. It might have been more useful to provide a means of deriving category scores based upon a task analysis of item content (e.g., money vs.

measurement vs. computation, etc.), but given the brevity of the test, it is unlikely that reliable subscales for this instrument could be derived from any kind of breakdown of the total test.

A final significant issue limiting the utility of Mathematics 7 concerns its ability to discriminate achievement among the varying levels of math skill in the target population. As the authors point out, most of the subjects in the standardization sample enjoyed a relatively high rate of success on the test, producing a significant ceiling effect and lack of discriminative power at the upper levels of achievement (in fact, there were only two items on the entire test that were failed by more than 50% of the standardization sample). The test, therefore, is not a good instrument for comparing student performance across the full range of achievement, but is best used for detection of significantly underachieving students from amongst large groups. In other words, its true value is as a screening device for students in need of extra assistance in mathematics.

In summary, Mathematics 7 is limited to screening groups of children for underachievement in mathematics near the end of the school year in which they reach their seventh birthday. It is not a comprehensive test of an individual child's mathematics skills, and should not be used as the sole basis for making administrative decisions about a child's educational programming. It cannot be used for the identification of exceptionally high-achieving students. Only the total score should be utilized; item categories described by the manual should be disregarded. The test is applicable only to children who have been educated in the areas of Great Britain upon which it was standardized (which are listed in the manual). These limitations of Mathematics 7 are (to the authors' credit) discussed with clarity and candor in the test manual. Users who respect the authors' directions regarding use of the instrument are likely to find it to be valuable for its intended purposes.

[46]

MindMaker6™.

Purpose: To determine personality or personal style using hemispheric dominance theories for use in training, consulting, and counseling clients.
Population: Adults.
Publication Dates: 1985–87.

Scores, 6: Kins-Person, Loner, Loyalist, Achiever, Involver, Choice-Seeker.
Administration: Group.
Price Data: Price data for manual ('87, 22 pages), including test and scoring information, available from publisher.
Time: (30–40) minutes.
Authors: Kenneth L. Adams and Dudley Lynch.
Publisher: Brain Technologies Corporation.

Review of the MindMaker6™ by THOMAS A. WROBEL, Assistant Professor of Psychology, University of Michigan-Flint, Flint, MI:

The MindMaker6™ attempts to measure the values and belief systems of an individual, as presented in the authors' unique theory. They claim their theory is based on the developmental theories of Clare W. Graves, Abraham Maslow, Lawrence Kohlberg, Jean Piaget, Jane Loevinger, and Alvin Toffler, and reflects the notion that the building of values and beliefs occurs in stages. A detailed explanation of the theory may be found in Lynch (1984).

The test consists of a series of 20 items grouped under the headings of Self, Substance, Social, Work, Intimates, and Cosmic. Each item consists of a set of six statements, adjectives, or groups of statements. The test taker is asked to divide 9 points among one, two, or three of the statements for each item. The points are written on a color-coded answer sheet, and are added across the six possible systems (Kins-Person, Loner, Loyalist, Achiever, Involver, or Choice-Seeker). As there exists a possible total of 180 points, the sum of the system scores serves as a check on the addition of scores. The system scores are then combined to give a relative weighting for the individual on the continuua of Group versus Self and Past versus Future. In addition, the individual's score is presented in terms of the three historical eras defined by the MindMaker model, including the nomadic and survival-oriented era; the era of development of agriculture, industrialization, and commerce; and the post-modern era.

Interpretation of the MindMaker6™ Systems presented in the test includes the concept of reality, concept of human nature, personal inner reality, and assessment of situations for each system as well as the preferred organization type, preferred environments, possible strengths, and possible limitations of each. In addition, suggestions are made for motivating, communicating with, and changing each of the system types.

The test booklet is attractive and easy to follow. Administration and scoring should take approximately half an hour.

Unfortunately, according to the publisher, no manual exists for the MindMaker6™ other than the test booklet itself. Therefore, no information on the construction, norms, reliability, or validity of the test apparently exists. Further, there appears to be no information as to when, where, why, or to whom the test is to be given. Given that an individual obtains scores on each of the six systems, it seems necessary to present the difference between scores considered to be significant.

Overall, the MindMaker6™ appears to be a rather entertaining test with unknown psychometric properties. It should only be used with caution.

REVIEWER'S REFERENCE

Lynch, D. (1984). *Your high-performance business brain: An operator's manual.* New York: Simon & Schuster.

[47]

Mini Inventory of Right Brain Injury.
Purpose: To screen "for right hemisphere brain injury."
Population: Ages 18 and over.
Publication Date: 1989.
Acronym: MIRBI.
Scores, 16: Visual Scanning, Integrity of Gnosis, Integrity of Body Image, Visuoverbal Processing, Visuosymbolic Processing, Integrity of Praxis, Visual Processing Total, Affective Language, Higher Level Language Skills, Language Processing Total, Affect, Emotion and Affect Processing Total, General Behavior, General Behavior and Psychic Integrity Total, Total MIRBI Score, Right-Left Differentiation Subscale Score.
Administration: Individual.
Price Data, 1989: $59 per complete kit including examiner's manual (38 pages), 25 test booklets, and 25 report forms; $24 per 25 test booklets; $17 per 25 report forms; $21 per examiner's manual.
Time: (15–30) minutes.
Authors: Patricia A. Pimental and Nancy A. Kingsbury.
Publisher: PRO-ED, Inc.

Review of the Mini Inventory of Right Brain Injury by R. A. BORNSTEIN, Associate Professor of Psychiatry, Neurosurgery and Neurology, The Ohio State University, Columbus, OH:

The Mini Inventory of Right Brain Injury (MIRBI) consists of 27 items that purport to measure right-brain function. The rationale for the development of this test appears to be an alleged lack of appropriately standardized objective instruments for assessment of right-brain function, and the need to develop time-efficient assessment procedures. The latter rationale may well be true, but the former assertion is almost completely without merit. Numerous measures of a variety of right-hemisphere functions have been developed and are widely in use. The fact that some of these measures are time-consuming is not sufficient justification for development of a new test in the absence of demonstration that the proposed measure is as effective as those already available.

In addition to the questionable rationale, the theoretical basis and underlying assumptions for this test appear to be grossly flawed. The test manual on page 7 provides the classification scheme of syndromes that are assumed to reflect right-hemisphere function. It is noted on page 6 that available literature does not "provide an acceptable, comprehensive theoretical model of right brain injury." In spite of assertions presented in the manual, the classification of symptoms in Table 2 does not represent such a theoretical model. The items from the MIRBI are divided into 10 subsections, some of which have only one item and yield only 1 point. For example, Section 9 contains a single item in which the examiner rates the presence or absence of flat affect. Specific criteria for evaluation of this rather difficult concept are not provided. The items yield a total of 43 points that are used in a total point score to determine the severity of impairment. The content and structure of the MIRBI is apparently based on the principal author's understanding of disorders associated with right-hemisphere dysfunction. These disorders are listed in Table 1 on page 5 of the manual. It is clear from this table that the MIRBI is based on a flawed, incomplete, and unsophisticated understanding of brain-behavior relationships. Many of the deficits in Table 1 are equally associated with the left-hemisphere dysfunction, or typically require dysfunction in both hemispheres.

The flaws in test content become immediately apparent on review of the actual test items. In the second section on "Integrity of Gnosis," patients are asked to name a particular finger, as well as to name an object that is placed in their hand. These items are performed on the left hand, and one presumes the manual makes the assumption this is therefore a right-hemisphere task. However, because these tasks require a verbal response, there is some doubt about those assumptions. In contrast, comparable measures from the Halstead-Reitan Neuropsychological Test Battery (9:463) do not require a verbal response, and therefore make the presumption of right-hemisphere mediation somewhat more likely. The section on "Visuoverbal Processing" comprises approximately 25 percent of the MIRBI and is composed of unequivocally language-laden tasks. These tasks include reading and comprehension of a paragraph, writing to dictation and spontaneously, and writing alternating strings of letters. The section on "Higher Level Language Skills" consists of 16 points, or 37 percent, of the entire test. Again, the items in this section are expressly verbal and require such classic language-based tasks as proverb interpretation, a general comprehension of language, and verbal similarities. To assert that such tasks reflect right-hemisphere function ignores nearly 150 years of scientific investigation of the relationship between the left hemisphere and language function.

The item content, therefore, of the MIRBI is grossly flawed from a conceptual and theoretical point of view. The statistical development of the test is similarly flawed. In the selection of subjects, it is stated that patients in the unilateral lesion groups have confirmed cerebral lesions based on CT scans. It is not, however, stated whether there is any evidence of involvement of the other hemisphere. An initial pool of items was administered to 50 patients with right-brain injury to identify the most discriminating items. From this pool of 63 items, the final 27 items were selected and administered to 30 patients with right-brain injury, 13 patients with left-brain injury, and 30 controls. The manual alleges to evaluate the effects of age, education, sex, and duration of illness by computing Pearson correlations between these variables and the MIRBI total score within each group. Examining these relationships in the groups separately does not evaluate potential differences between the groups. This is particularly important in view of the goal of demonstrating that the MIRBI can discriminate between groups. In this context, it is a major problem that the duration of illness in the right-hemi-

sphere group was approximately 158 days, whereas the duration of illness in the left-hemisphere group was 689 days. It is well-known in neuropsychological evaluation that acute and chronic lesions have vastly different effects. Therefore, these data may simply be comparing the effects of acute versus chronic hemispheric lesions.

Comparison of the left- and right-lesions groups in Tables 6 and 7 (p. 21) also reveals the groups are not equivalent in terms of distribution of lesion location. Among those groups, 37 percent of the right- and 62 percent of the left-lesion groups have posterior lesions. As might be expected, the mean scores of the right- and left-lesion groups both differ from the controls, but do not differ from each other. Results of an analysis of covariance are presented that indicate a main effect for group, but no sex effect. No data on group by sex interaction are presented. Nevertheless, the manual reports a marginally significant difference between right- and left-lesion females. The manual then suggests the failure to detect differences between the left- and right-lesion groups may have been due to unequal sample size. The results of an unequal variances T-test are then presented without any evidence whatsoever that the groups, in fact, differ in regard to variance.

The manual presents a variety of reliability and validity data. Internal reliability using Cronbach's alpha was acceptable at .92. Interrater reliability was based on four protocols and yielded coefficients from .65 to .87, which is unacceptable. This lack of interrater agreement is likely a function of an insufficient number of protocols examined and the inadequate criteria for evaluation of responses. Information purporting to demonstrate the content, criterion, and construct validity of the MIRBI is included in the manual. The evidence presented represents little more than wishful thinking.

In summary, this is a poorly conceptualized and poorly validated measure that does not reflect current understandings of brain-behavior relationships. The test is based on a questionable rationale and a myriad of faulty assumptions. In brief, this is a bad test that has little chance of providing any meaningful data in the evaluation of patients with brain injuries. It is not recommended for use in any circumstance.

Review of the Mini Inventory of Right Brain Injury by JOHN E. OBRZUT, Professor of Educational Psychology, and CAROL A. BO-LIEK, Assistant Research Scientist, Speech and Hearing Sciences, University of Arizona, Tucson, AZ:

The Mini Inventory of Right Brain Injury (MIRBI) was developed as a standardized screening instrument for right-hemisphere injury, presumably because there is a dearth of assessment instruments and materials that specifically address suspected right-hemisphere dysfunction. Clinicians currently use subtests or portions of larger batteries in screening for right-hemisphere difficulties that were initially intended for cerebral assessment not specific to right-hemisphere functioning (Adamovich & Brooks, 1981). Furthermore, other examinations designed for right-hemisphere functioning lack test standardization and norming, and also experience inherent problems that occur when trying to combine subtests from a variety of other instruments (Adamovich & Brooks, 1981).

Pimental and Kingsbury (the MIRBI authors) state six general uses of the MIRBI: (*a*) identification of "deficits in visual, language, emotion, affect, general behavior, memory, orientation, and nonverbal processing"; (*b*) determination of the level of severity of right-brain injury ranging from "normal" to "profound"; (*c*) determination of specific areas of right-hemisphere dysfunction by linking various right-hemisphere syndromes with their specific underlying disorders of processing, based on Pimental's classification system of right-hemisphere syndromes (Pimental, 1987a, 1987b, 1987c); (*d*) determination of strengths and weaknesses for the purposes of differential diagnosis and development of individualized remedial strategies; (*e*) monitoring rehabilitative progress; and (*f*) research-related issues.

The MIRBI can be administered to English-speaking adults between the ages of 20 to 80 years. The inventory yields 10 subsections that cover four general domains, as follows: (*a*) Visual Processing, (*b*) Language Processing, (*c*) Emotion and Affective Processing, and (*d*) General Behavior and Psychic Integrity. The Visual Processing domain comprises six subsections including Visual Scanning, Integrity of Gnosis, Integrity of Body Image, Visuoverbal Processing, Visuosymbolic Processing, and In-tegrity of Praxis Associated with Visuomotor Skills. The Language Processing domain is characterized by two subsections including Affective Language and Higher Level Receptive and Expressive Language Skills. The Emotion and Affective Processing domain has Affect as its only subsection and the General Behavior and Psychic Integrity domain has General Behavior as its only subsection. The MIRBI also has a Right-Left Differentiation Subscale (RLDS), which contains 10 items that were statistically derived on the basis of their ability to differentiate right- from left-hemisphere injuries.

The MIRBI can be administered in approximately 15 to 30 minutes and requires the Examiner's Manual, the Test Booklet, and minimal additional materials (i.e., pencil, quarter, paper, etc.). There are no basal or ceiling levels because the administration rules require that all items be presented regardless of performance. Items are scored as correct (i.e., 3/3), partially correct (i.e., 2/3), or incorrect (0). The total MIRBI score is the sum of all correct responses: The higher the score, the better the performance.

A total of 63 items were initially developed based on Pimental's classification system and the deficit analysis paradigm (i.e., deficits can be identified by examining skill areas that are known to be diminished as a function of right-hemisphere involvement). All but two items were original. These initial 63 items were given to 50 right-hemisphere-injured patients (from 18 pilot sites), as documented by a neurological evaluation and a computer tomography (CT) scan. In addition, these patients were screened for medical problems, substance abuse, adequate vision and hearing acuity, mental retardation, and premorbid illiteracy, to name a few. The sample included 50% males and 50% females (mean age = 66.7 years). Using Cronbach's (1951) coefficient alpha technique, a .91 coefficient was obtained, indicating good internal consistency among items. Of the 63 original items, 27 items were retained in the final inventory, those that were failed by 54% to 98% of the right-brain-injured sample based on criteria recommended by Anastasi (1976).

The actual standardization sample consisted of 30 patients with a diagnosis of right-brain injury, 13 with left-brain injury, and 30 controls matched on the basis of age, education, and sex. Each brain-injured group was further divided into subgroups by site of lesion (right or left anterior, posterior, subcortical). The mean age for the standardization sample was between 59.06 to 63.9 years for the various groups. Using multiple Pearson product moment correlations, significant age effects were found for the normal and right-brain-injured groups. Using a two-way ANCOVA (age as a covariant) with total MIRBI points, the authors report that overall performances on the MIRBI were significantly different between the right-brain-injured and normal groups and left-brain-injured and normal groups. Only a borderline significant difference ($p = .0493$) was found between right- and left-brain-injured groups, even after an unequal variances t-test procedure was conducted.

The 27 MIRBI items were submitted to another ANCOVA comparing the least square mean values for each item. This analysis yielded 10 items that most strongly differentiated the right- from the left-hemisphere-injured groups. Optimal cutoff scores were determined for the purposes of differentiating among right-brain-injured, left-brain-injured, and normal groups resulting in a score of 10 (93.10% true positives and 78.57% true negatives). Severity levels were determined using univariate summary statistics, a frequency table, and a normal probability plot.

An alpha reliability coefficient of .9230 was reported as an index of internal consistency. Interrater reliability ranged from .65 to .87, but was performed on protocols of only four of the 73 participants for unacknowledged reasons. Standard error of measurement (SEm) was calculated for age groups by 10-year intervals and ranged from 0 to 5.5.

Content validity was established by selecting items that were representative of skill deficits often seen in right-hemisphere-impaired individuals. For example, making a string of cursive ms or ws, drawing a picture of a clock with a specific time, understanding a humorous sentence, and expressing emotional tone of voice during speaking activities. The authors state the items used in this screening device were selected for their representativeness of right-brain injury, according to their theoretical model and our current understanding of cerebral organization and function. Criterion-related validity was established using concurrent

measures, and performance on the MIRBI was compared to CT scans of the right- and left-brain-impaired groups. In addition, the MIRBI RLDS was apparently successful at differentiating between right- and left-brain-injured groups.

Construct validity was demonstrated by correctly classifying patients as right- or left-hemisphere-injured, as confirmed by CT scan. High item intercorrelations also indicated the MIRBI items are related to each other, presumably because they are measuring the same construct domain. In addition, the MIRBI total point score and the RLDS cutoff scores correctly differentiated right- from left-brain-injured patients, which would indicate that right-brain-injury phenomena are being measured (at least at a screening level). Initial diagnostic utility of the MIRBI also has been reported by the test authors.

Overall, Pimental and Kingsbury have accomplished the goal of developing a standardized instrument that screens for right-hemisphere injury and related dysfunction. The major strengths of the MIRBI are that it was normed on a group of right-hemisphere-injured patients and that it appears successfully to identify adults with such injury who are in need of further, more intensive evaluation. Additionally, the MIRBI demonstrates adequate internal consistency as well as initial criterion and construct validity.

Several limitations of the MIRBI are noted. There were no specific age ranges reported for any of the standardization groups. In addition, the MIRBI was not standardized on brain-injured or normal adults between the ages of 20–39 years and the 80–89 age group. The standardization sample was selected from hospital settings where patients were seen primarily for acute care. In order to use the MIRBI as a screening instrument in rehabilitative or long-term care settings, specific norms for these settings need to be developed. Most test sites were in the Midwest, and Blacks and Hispanics were underrepresented. Further, there are always difficulties in obtaining "pure" right-hemisphere-injured patients because often when there is an infarct in the right hemisphere there is also a concurrent lacunar infarct in the left hemisphere (the converse is true for left-hemisphere injuries). Thus, interpretations of "pure" cases should be made very cautiously when using the MIRBI. There was also no mention of determining handedness preferences, familial histories, or premorbid learning difficulties (with the exception of mental retardation) of patients in the standardization sample. A larger left-hemisphere-injured comparative population is also needed to further enhance the MIRBI's discriminative ability between right- and left-hemisphere-injured patients.

Most of the test items are straightforward with regard to administration and scoring; however, some subjective judgments must be made on general reading, writing comprehension, and expressive abilities. The authors have placed the scoring criteria for these items in the Test Booklet for easy reference. It would be helpful to have some examples from the standardization group on matters like poor spacing between words and letters (writing sample) and examples of scoring the spoken paragraph including typical mistakes. Also, the clinician should keep in mind that many of the items are given orally and require a verbal (primarily left-hemisphere) response from the patient.

It appeared the *SEm* was slightly larger for the right-hemisphere-injured group than for the left-hemisphere-injured group, with the lowest *SEm* reported for the normal group. This *SEm* difference would imply the targeted right-hemisphere-injured group was more variable in its performance on the MIRBI. This should be taken into consideration when assessing those patients who receive "borderline" scores and deciding upon a further evaluation. Whereas the MIRBI RLDS differentiated right- and left-brain-impaired groups and concurrent CT scans confirmed the classification, it is not evident whether the examiners were blind to the results of the CT scans prior to testing each patient. Diagnostic usefulness and clinical utility of the MIRBI will be obtained with the benefit of additional concurrent data from other more established neuropsychological instruments and achievement batteries. With these precautions, the practitioner will find this instrument a useful asset in clinical practice to determine further areas of needed assessment of right-brain injury.

REVIEWER'S REFERENCES

Cronbach, L. J. (1951). Coefficient Alpha and the internal structure of tests. *Psychometrika, 16*, 297-334.

Anastasi, A. (1976). *Psychological testing*. New York: Macmillan.

Adamovich, B. L., & Brooks, R. L. (1981). A diagnostic protocol to assess the communication deficits in patients with right hemisphere damage. In R. H. Brookshire (Ed.), *Clinical Aphasiology Conference Proceedings* (pp. 244-253). Minneapolis, MN: BRK.

Pimental, P. A. (1987a, October). *The MIRBI revisited: The first standardized right brain injury screening*. Paper presented at a meeting of the National Academy of Neuropsychology, Chicago.

Pimental, P. A. (1987b, October). *Deficit patterns and lesion site in right brain injured subjects*. Paper presented at a meeting of the National Academy of Neuropsychology, Chicago.

Pimental, P. A. (1987c). *The Mini Inventory of Right Brain Injury (MIRBI): Development and standardization of a new screening instrument for assessment of right hemisphere brain injury*. Unpublished dissertation, The Chicago School of Professional Psychology.

[48]
Missouri Kindergarten Inventory of Developmental Skills, Alternate Form.

Purpose: A screening battery providing a comprehensive assessment measure to use at or before kindergarten entrance.
Population: Ages 48–72 months.
Publication Dates: 1978–82.
Acronym: KIDS.
Scores: 6 areas: Number Concepts, Auditory Skills, Language Concepts, Paper and Pencil Skills, Visual Skills, Gross Motor Skills.
Administration: Individual.
Price Data, 1988: $.25 per answer sheet; $15 per specimen set including sample test materials, answer sheet, administration and scoring manual ('80, 78 pages), and instructional guide book ('81, 45 pages).
Time: (35) minutes.
Comments: Can be given anytime within the year preceding kindergarten as well as at kindergarten entrance.
Author: Missouri Department of Elementary and Secondary Education.
Publisher: Center for Educational Assessment, University of Missouri-Columbia.

Review of the Missouri Kindergarten Inventory of Developmental Skills, Alternate Form by MARY HENNING-STOUT, Assistant Professor of Counseling Psychology, Lewis and Clark College, Portland, OR:

The Missouri Kindergarten Inventory of Developmental Skills, Alternate Form (KIDS) is a broad-based screen of the developmental status of preschool children. The skills measured by this instrument were selected based on the learning objectives articulated in the Missouri Department of Elementary and Secondary Education report, *Focus on Early Childhood Education*.

The authors describe the inventory's coverage as including consideration of physical, cognitive, and behavioral development of children from 48 to 72 months of age. These areas are tapped via six subtests: Number Concepts, Auditory Skills, Paper/Pencil Skills, Language Concepts, Visual Skills, and Gross Motor Skills. The last subtest is the primary measure of physical development and behavior is gauged informally with observation during the assessment period (a period of approximately 35 minutes).

Cognitive development seems most directly screened with this instrument. The Guidebook accompanying the inventory provides suggestions for interventions by parents and teachers that are linked to the results of this screen.

ADMINISTRATION. The KIDS-Alternate Form is designed to be administered by the child's current or potential teacher. In the introductory pages of the administration manual, there are cautions about the importance of giving only standardized instructions to the child. In addition, special directions for recording scores and determining whether to give all items are presented. These instructions are not overly complex and with substantial practice could be mastered by classroom teachers. The test seems, however, to have characteristics of an instrument more appropriately administered by trained assessment specialists. The time required to become proficient in this test's standardized presentation and scoring may likely be prohibitive for most teachers unless special provisions are made.

The authors emphasize that behavioral observations should be collected throughout the administration. The back page of the response protocol provides prompts for recording the presence or absence of specific behaviors and environmental conditions. An additional questionnaire is included with the scale for completion by the parents. This questionnaire provides the parents' perspective on the child's developmental progress and personality.

It is suggested the scales be completed in the order they appear in the administration manual. The Gross Motor scale may be given to the child at any time for a change of pace. Generally, the items are immediately scorable as pass or fail. The authors suggest that, at the end of each subtest, the raw score for that subtest be recorded. These raw scores can later be transformed into percentiles, stanines, or Normal Curve Equivalents (NCE). NCE transformations provide normalized standard

scores by breaking the line beneath the normal curve into equal segments. The authors describe NCEs as indicating "how many tasks a child can perform in relation to the number of similar tasks that other children can perform" (Guidebook, p. 13). Although they indicate application of percentiles and stanines in determining the need a child has for supplementary learning opportunity, the authors give no indication of the utility of the NCE transformations.

When scoring is completed and a profile is developed, the results are surveyed to determine if any score falls below the 20th percentile or third stanine. According to the authors, if any of the six scores (there is no full-scale score) falls in this area, intervention should be implemented and reassessment should occur in 2–6 weeks to determine if additional assessment and long-term intervention might be necessary.

PSYCHOMETRIC PROPERTIES. This version of the KIDS includes a downward extension of the norms of earlier versions (1975, 1978) which were based on a sample of children aged 54–72 months. The sample for the KIDS-Alternate Form consisted of 4,709 children 48–72 months of age. These children were from school districts, preschools, and child care facilities throughout Missouri. Efforts to obtain a representative sample of Missouri children seems to have been largely successful.

The item development/selection information presented in the Guidebook is sparse. At least some items were selected by a panel of state experts. Additional item selection or development methods are not described.

Reliability and validity are also reported in the Guidebook. Internal consistency reliability was established. There are no other reports of reliability, however. Test-retest, split-half, or alternate forms data would strengthen the test user's understanding of the KIDS' psychometric characteristics. Content validity was described as emerging from the expert status of the individuals selecting the items for the inventory. The authors also demonstrate the instrument's construct validity; as children get older, their scores improve.

Four factors emerged with factor analysis of the inventory: visual-spatial relations, language development, recall of verbal material, and inferential-constructional skill. Of 29 subtasks, 24 loaded on at least one of these four factors. Most heavily represented was the visual-spatial relations factor where 11 tasks clustered. Items from the Gross Motor scale were not included in the factor analysis because of earlier evidence this was a noncognitive scale.

The results of the factor analysis are well substantiated by linking them with the test's discrete content and with the broader knowledge base of psychoeducational assessment. However, the relationship between the identified factors and the six scales into which the test is divided is left unarticulated. Careful comparison of the tasks making up the Number Concepts scale, for example, shows two tasks loading on the visual-spatial relations factor, one loading on the recall of verbal material factor, and two unaccounted for within the four-factor solution. The relationship between the Number Concepts scale and the findings of the factor analysis is unclear.

Because the KIDS is divided into six scales, and because there is no full-scale metric, the construct validity of these scales should be clearly established. More explicit linkage between factor analytic findings and scale construction seems necessary to clarify the statistical basis for the test's construct validity.

PRACTICAL UTILITY. This reviewer found it difficult to remember that the instrument under review was a screening measure. There are several ways in which the materials accompanying this test seem to overstretch its applicability. The authors suggest a direct link between the results of the inventory and intervention. They make good suggestions to parents about activities for preschoolers at home. The link between the data derived from the test and the interventions suggested is, however, unclear. If the activities are designed to teach the test, the link is evident. If, on the other hand, the activities are presented as ways to improve skills that are measured by the test and found lacking, the inferential leap from the inventory content to the specific intervention is great. The brief time and relatively few items devoted to assessment with this instrument provide an insufficient base for any intervention planning.

A step is missing. After the screen, there should be additional behavior-based assessment of what the child can and cannot do relative to her/his weak scale performance. With this additional data, remediation can be clearly focused, rather than inferentially derived with the potential for irrelevance or ineffectiveness.

SUMMARY. The Missouri KIDS provides a carefully conceived and constructed screening tool. However, the literature accompanying this instrument could encourage users to apply its results beyond what is psychometrically supported. This test is a screen for possible indications of cognitive and motor difficulties thought to be related to children's performance in early academic settings. The suggestions provided in the Guidebook are creative and would likely be helpful for any family readying their young child for school. However, by including these suggestions with the materials of this test, the authors imply a link between the test's results and the interventions they suggest.

The suggestions are good. The numbers derived from the test indicate children's standings relative to their peers and help parents and teachers know when to ask more questions about a child's particular academic needs. To prevent the overapplication of the numbers, perhaps it would be best to package the two sets of material separately. Both are helpful. This reviewer's concern is that the findings of this screen might be overapplied, sending children needlessly down the narrow path toward classification before sufficient exploration of their demonstrated abilities and resourcefulness in a classroom setting has occurred.

Review of the Missouri Kindergarten Inventory of Developmental Skills, Alternate Form by JAMES E. YSSELDYKE, *Professor of Educational Psychology, University of Minnesota, Minneapolis, MN:*

The Alternate Form of the Missouri Kindergarten Inventory of Developmental Skills (KIDS) is a 1982 revision of the scale originally developed in 1975–76. The Alternate Form is intended for use with children aged 48–72 months, a downward extension of the earlier scale. The KIDS is individually administered and takes about 35 minutes. The test includes a parent questionnaire designed to obtain relevant information about the child's development. Subtests are included for each of the six areas listed above; within each area are several subsections that sample a variety of activities ranging from easy to difficult.

The test manual and forms are clearly printed. The manual (Guidebook) for this scale includes learning objectives and activities for each subtest area, a section on communicating with parents, and an extensive section on additional related learning activities. There are many excellent suggestions for remediation. The manual could be described as long on intervention and short on assessment information.

The KIDS was standardized originally on a sample of 4,000 children representative of the kindergarten population of Missouri. The test was revised and restandardized in 1980. The current norms are for a sample of 4,709 children aged 48–72 months. The normative data were gathered from preschool measures administered to children in 1980 and were stratified on the basis of school district enrollment.

Data on reliability of this scale consist of internal consistency coefficients for five of the six subtests based on the performance of an unspecified sample of children. All coefficients exceed .78. The reliability of this scale is satisfactory for screening purposes. There are no data on test-retest reliability.

Three kinds of evidence for validity are presented in the manual. It is argued the scale has good content validity because the subtests and items were designed and selected by a task force of experts in early childhood education. The test is said to have good developmental or construct validity because the mean score increases as a function of age. A factor analysis was completed and was used to show the factors assessed in this scale are like those underlying other widely used measures of children's cognitive skills. There are no data on how performance on the KIDS compares to performance on other tests.

Use of the Missouri KIDS is limited by the fact that the scale was developed and normed in a single state. Those who use the scale outside of Missouri will be constrained to simple descriptions of their preschool and kindergarten children. Comparisons in the form of percentile ranks, stanines, and normal curve equivalents are relative to a population of children in Missouri. Data on technical adequacy of this scale are limited. The manual includes interesting and useful information on intervention, and limited information on the use of the scale.

[49]

The Multidimensional Self-Esteem Inventory.

Purpose: "Provides measures of the components of self-esteem."
Population: College students.
Publication Dates: 1983–88.
Acronym: MSEI.
Scores, 11: Competence, Lovability, Likability, Self-control, Personal Power, Moral Self-approval, Body Appearance, Body Functioning, Identity Integration, Defensive Self-enhancement, Global Self-esteem.
Administration: Individual or group. Price Data, 1989: $38 per complete kit (includes manual ['88, 22 pages], 25 reusable test booklets, 25 rating forms, and 25 profile forms); $12 per 25 reusable test booklets; $12 per 25 rating forms; $7 per 25 profile forms; $9 per manual.
Time: (15–20) minutes.
Comments: Originally called Self-Report Inventory.
Authors: Edward J. O'Brien and Seymour Epstein.
Publisher: Psychological Assessment Resources, Inc.

Review of The Multidimensional Self-Esteem Inventory by BARBARA J. KAPLAN, Associate Professor of Psychology, State University of New York College at Fredonia, Fredonia, NY:

The Multidimensional Self-Esteem Inventory (MSEI) is grounded in extensive writing, thinking, and research on a theory of the self-concept. Proponents of the model suggest the components of self-evaluation comprising self-esteem and self-concept are organized hierarchically in several levels from the general to the specific. Global self-esteem is the highest, most general self-evaluation in the model. Intermediate levels, as identified by eight component scales of the MSEI, are aspects of self-evaluations that generalize across situations in predicting behavior. Lower levels, which are not explicit parts of the MSEI, are specific to particular situations.

Two of the 11 MSEI scores are global measures of self-evaluation and self-concept, eight are intermediate-level scales, and the final scale is a validity check on the extent to which the test-taker is "defensively inflating his or her self-presentation." The MSEI requires a 10th grade reading level, and its authors suggest it is most appropriate for use with college students. The high reading level required may make it an inappropriate measure for populations with cognitive, educational, or psychological impairments.

There are 116 questions, each evaluated on a 5-point scale. The majority of scales contain 10 items. The validity scale contains 16 items. Items were selected only after they met fairly rigid standards. Among these were relative independence of the scales, internal consistency within the scales, range of response, balancing positive and negative presentation of items, and ensuring that items were free of gender bias.

Reliability studies of the MSEI show excellent internal consistency and test-retest reliability, with reliability coefficients ranging from a low of .78 to a high of .90. It is worth noting, however, that the original population on which the test was normed consisted primarily of college student volunteers.

The normative sample consisted of 785 college students, 487 women and 298 men, who were undergraduate volunteers. There are separate norms for males and females. The MSEI profile uses T scores with a mean of 50 and a standard deviation of 10. The test manual provides interpretive descriptions of high and low scorers on each scale.

As a research instrument the MSEI has a good deal to offer, not least of which is a coherent theory underlying its construction. It functions as well as other available self-esteem measures, and may be of interest to investigators who have reason to go beyond a global measure of self-esteem. As a clinical tool, MSEI scales may enhance treatment planning and goal setting.

Scores on the MSEI correlate with students' responses to success or failure on a major test, help-seeking behavior, and outcomes of depressed and/or alcohol-abusing inpatients. The range of populations studied using the MSEI suggests researchers are finding it a useful measure of self-esteem, but the available norms do not reflect these broader applications. The usual cautions about interpreting obtained scores must be heeded. Clinical applications of the test must await the development of a more diverse set of population norms.

Review of The Multidimensional Self-Esteem Inventory by JOSEPH G. PONTEROTTO, Associate Professor of Education, Division of Psy-

chological and Educational Services, Fordham University, New York, NY:

The Multidimensional Self-Esteem Inventory (MSEI) (formerly the Self-Report Inventory, O'Brien, 1980) is a 116-item, self-report instrument designed to measure components of self-esteem among college students in the United States. The underlying conceptual base of the MSEI posits that self-evaluation is an important component of personality. This self-evaluation consists of self-perceptions (self-concept) and evaluations associated with these perceptions (self-esteem). The MSEI is based on Epstein's (1980) self-esteem/self-concept model, which posits that self-esteem is organized in a three-stage hierarchical fashion. At the highest level of self-evaluation is global self-esteem, which represents the basic evaluation of self-worth. Influencing the global self-esteem are specific components of self-esteem linked to domains of life experience. These specific self-esteem domains represent the second level of self-esteem. The third and lowest level of self-esteem has minimal impact on global self-esteem, is situation-specific, and addresses self-evaluation in specific activities or tasks. The MSEI is designed to assess the two higher levels of self-esteem.

STRUCTURAL BASE OF THE MSEI. The MSEI operationalizes its multidimensional self-esteem/self-concept theory through the use of 11 scales divided into four categories: (*a*) Global Self-esteem; (*b*) eight components of self-esteem defined as Competence, Lovability, Likability, Personal Power, Self-control, Moral Self-approval, Body Appearance, and Body Functioning; (*c*) Identity Integration; and (*d*) Defensive Self-enhancement.

The rationale for the scales stems from the earlier conceptual and empirical work of the instrument developers (see Epstein, 1980; O'Brien, 1980; O'Brien & Epstein, 1985). Global Self-esteem is defined as a generalized summary of feelings of worthiness. The eight distinct components of self-esteem focus on broad domains representative of the types of experiences that effect self-esteem day-to-day. Identity Integration refers to the organization, processing, and the efficiency of integration of self-experiences into the overall self-concept. Finally, Defensive Self-enhancement examines one's tendency to be defensive and to overinflate his or her self-esteem to appear socially desirable. The MSEI assesses social desirability through the respondent's denial of common weaknesses and claiming of rare virtues.

ADMINISTRATION AND SCORING. The total MSEI package includes a 22-page Professional Manual, a four-page item booklet containing 116 items, a rating sheet, and a profile form. Section 1 of the item booklet presents 61 items written as self-descriptions. The respondents use a 5-point Likert scale (1 = *Completely false* to 5 = *Completely true*) to assess the veracity of the descriptions as they apply to them. In Section 2, respondents use a 5-point Likert scale (1 = *Almost never* to 5 = *Very often*) to report how often they experience thoughts and feelings reflected in 55 items.

The hand-scored rating sheet provides space for basic demographic information (i.e., name, date, age, and sex) and places items strategically so that the scorer simply adds numbered responses across rows to arrive at scale raw scores. Finally, the Profile Form provides a table of percentiles and *T* scores for both male and female norms onto which the raw scores can be easily plotted to develop a graphic profile.

The MSEI is appropriate for both individual and group administration with college students. A 10th-grade reading level is required to complete the instrument, and the average time of completion is 15–30 minutes. The MSEI reviewed here used rating form HS (hand scored). It took this reviewer 10–15 minutes to score and profile his own MSEI results. Although a computer-administered version of the MSEI was developed and validated (Fairchok & O'Brien, 1987), the availability of such, or of a computerized scoring version, was not mentioned in the manual.

Although paraprofessionals may administer and score the MSEI, the instrument should be interpreted only by professionals trained in personality assessment. To the extent that self-esteem can be perceived as an important component of personality, the instrument may be used as a personality measure; however, the MSEI *is not* a diagnostic instrument and *should not* be used to form any type of clinical diagnosis.

MSEI DEVELOPMENT AND ITEM ANALYSIS. The MSEI was developed, normed, and validated in a series of seven separate studies spanning a 7-year time period. Subjects in all studies were undergraduate college students from four different colleges and universities who volunteered to participate for course credit. Both qualitative and quantitative research methods were used in item selection. First, items were written to reflect the definitions of the 11 scales inherent in the theory. These items (approximately 30 per scale) were then evaluated by independent judges for congruence with the specific scale definitions. Second, the items remaining from this qualitative analysis were subjected to empirical item analysis. Criteria for the final selection of items included convergent and discriminant criteria, content representation, scale balancing in terms of positively and negatively worded items, a wide response range in an attempt to avoid ceiling and flooring effects, and sex balancing.

CONVERGENT CRITERIA. Using two subject samples from a large state university (*N* = 645 males and females), the authors (through item analysis) selected the 10 best items for each of the 11 scales. A point biserial correlation minimum of .50 served as the cutoff point. Ten of the 11 scales reached this minimum criteria, with correlations ranging from .52 for Likability to .69 for Body Functioning. The point biserial correlation for Defensive Self-enhancement was a low .35, necessitating that the developers add 6 items to bring the correlation up to the .50 cutoff point. Thus 10 scales include 10 items each, and the Defensive Self-enhancement scale consists of 16 items, bringing the grand total to 116.

DISCRIMINANT CRITERIA. There were two discriminant criteria for item selection: that items showed a higher correlation with their own scale than with any other MSEI scale, and that items demonstrated higher correlations with their own scale than with the Defensive Self-enhancement scale. This latter criteria served to minimize social desirability contamination.

In summary, the item analysis procedure was successful in selecting items that were homogeneous within scales and discriminant between scales. The practical considerations with regard to positively and negatively worded items, the avoidance of ceiling and flooring effects, and selecting items with nearly equal convergent and discriminant criteria results across sex were satisfactorily met.

Reliability and validity.

RELIABILITY. The MSEI's internal consistency was examined using a sample of approximately 298 male and 487 female students from a large state university and a private university. An analysis of sex differences revealed no significant differences and thus alpha coefficients are reported for the full sample. The resultant consistency measures were quite satisfactory, ranging from .78 for Defensive Self-enhancement to .90 for both Body Functioning and Global Self-esteem. Test-retest stability correlations over a 1-month span for approximately 58 male and 151 female students (again, no sex differences found) from two private colleges ranged from a low of .78 for Identity Integration to .89 for Body Functioning. The MSEI clearly demonstrates satisfactory internal consistency and short-term test-retest stability.

CONVERGENT AND DISCRIMINANT VALIDITY. MSEI scale scores were examined in relation to a host of other instruments designed to measure constructs that could be hypothesized to have either a positive or negative relationship to self-esteem. A number of validation studies generally supported a high level of convergent and discriminant validity of the MSEI construct relative to other measures of self-esteem (i.e., the Eagly [1967] and Rosenberg [1965] self-esteem scales), expectancy for success, depression, ego strength, perceived peer and parental acceptance, body perceptions, defensiveness, temperament, academic achievement, leadership, influence in intimate relationships, athletic involvement, and self-control behaviors. Collectively, the comparative correlations between relevant scale comparisons are in the expected direction (e.g., positive with other self-esteem measures; negative with depression measures) and support the validity of the MSEI for American college students.

FACTOR ANALYSIS. Using 1,086 students from a large state university and a private university, a confirmatory factor analysis constrained to extract 11 factors was conducted with the correlations among the 116 items used as input. With a factor loading restriction set at .40, strong factorial support was found for 7 of the 11 scales. Moderate factorial support was found for the Likability and Body Appearance scales. The Global Self-esteem and Identity Integration scales did not separate out as distinct factors. This is not surprising, however,

because both of these scales are conceptualized as generalized measures of self-adequacy, and therefore, their high intercorrelations with each other and with other MSEI scales would be expected. Thus, the factorial validity of the MSEI contruct is supported.

NORMS AND SEX DIFFERENCES. MSEI normative data are based on a sample of 298 men and 487 women from a large state university and a small private university (geographical region not specified). Students from the private university were predominantly from middle- and upper-class backgrounds, whereas the state university students were more varied in terms of social class and ethnic background. Analyses of variance indicated no MSEI differences due to university setting or to university setting X sex interaction. However, there were a number of significant differences for the main effect of sex. Men scored higher on Global Self-esteem, Competence, Personal Power, Body Appearance, and Body Functioning. Women scored higher on Lovability, Likability, Moral Self-approval, and Defensive Self-enhancement. In most cases the significant sex differences are small in magnitude; however, given the significant findings, the test developers appropriately report separate norms (reflected in the Profile Form and Professional Manual) by sex.

THE PROFESSIONAL MANUAL. The 22-page manual is well prepared and, generally speaking, easy to follow. Clear directions for administering, scoring, and interpreting the instrument are provided. Descriptive profiles of high and low scores on each of the 11 scales are meaningfully presented and assist the MSEI interpreter. The qualitative and quantitative development of the MSEI items is well presented, as are the studies on its psychometric evaluation. Clear tables in the manual help the interested reader. A strength of the manual, and the MSEI generally, is that the limitations of the instrument are adequately and candidly presented. The generalizability limits of the norming and validation samples are highlighted. The manual closes with a section on Supporting Research that summarizes 13 studies (from 1981 to the present) in which the MSEI was used. Generally, these studies provide additional support for the utility of the MSEI self-esteem construct as a mediating variable in the study of other personality traits. Noteworthy among these supporting studies is the initial utility of the scale with adult, nonstudent populations, and with some psychiatrically hospitalized patients.

SUMMARY. The MSEI is a content-valid measure of diverse components of self-esteem and self-concept. The construct and factorial validities of the MSEI have also been established, and are based on a series of well-designed studies spanning 7 years. The internal consistency reliability and short-to-moderate-term stability of the MSEI are high. The instrument is fairly easy to administer and score, and the manual is well organized, comprehensive, and generally easy to follow. This is an excellent self-esteem measure for use with the traditional college student population. At this time, the scale has not been validated or normed on nontraditional student populations (e.g., racial/ethnic minority groups, the returning adult student) or on any nonstudent populations.

REVIEWER'S REFERENCES

Rosenberg, M. (1965). *Society and the adolescent self-image.* Princeton, NJ: Princeton University Press.

Eagley, A. H. (1967). Involvement as a determinant of response to favorable and unfavorable information. *Journal of Personality and Social Psychology, 7,* 1-15.

Epstein, S. (1980). The self-concept: A review and the proposal of an integrated theory of personality. In E. Staub (Ed.), *Personality: Basic aspects and current research* (pp. 81-132). Englewood Cliffs, NJ: Prentice-Hall.

O'Brien, E. J. (1980). *The Self-Report Inventory: Development and validation of a multidimensional measure of the self-concept and sources of self-esteem.* Unpublished doctoral dissertation, University of Massachusetts, Amherst.

O'Brien, E. J., & Epstein, S. (1985). Unpublished research. Marywood College, Scranton, PA.

Fairchok, G. E., & O'Brien, E. J. (1987, October). *Computerization of paper-and-pencil psychological tests: Do custom and omnibus computerization procedures affect test validity?.* Paper presented at the Third Eastern Small College Computing Conference, Marist College, Poughkeepsie, NY.

[50]
Multiscore Depression Inventory.

Purpose: "To provide an objective measure of the severity of self-reported depression."
Population: Ages 13 through adult.
Publication Date: 1986.
Acronym: MDI.
Scores, 11: Low Energy Level, Cognitive Difficulty, Guilt, Low Self-Esteem, Social Introversion, Pessimism, Irritability, Sad Mood, Instrumental Helplessness, Learned Helplessness, Total.
Administration: Group.
Forms, 2: Short Form version available by administering first 47 items of questionnaire.
Price Data, 1987: $65 per kit including scoring keys, 100 hand-scored answer sheets, 2 prepaid

WPS Test Report answer sheets, 100 profile forms, and manual (111 pages); $12.50 per set of scoring keys; $13.50 per 100 hand-scored answer sheets; $9.25 or less per prepaid WPS Test Report answer sheet; $13.50 per 100 profile forms; $18.50 per manual; $185 per microcomputer diskette for administration, scoring, and interpretation (25 uses per diskette).
Time: (20–25) minutes; (10) minutes for Short Form.
Comments: Self-report format; IBM PC, XT, or AT or compatible computer required for optional computer administration or scoring.
Author: David J. Berndt.
Publisher: Western Psychological Services.

Review of the Multiscore Depression Inventory by DAVID N. DIXON, Professor and Department Chair, Department of Counseling Psychology and Guidance Services, Ball State University, Muncie, IN:

The Multiscore Depression Inventory (MDI) provides an overall measure of depression and 10 subscale scores. Not only is it a measure of severity of depression, but also it provides information related to sources of the depression.

The MDI is a well-constructed, objective measure of self-reported depression. The Inventory consists of 118 true-false items that typically can be completed in 20 to 25 minutes. For increased brevity a short form is available, requiring approximately half the administration time. The Inventory can be either hand or computer scored. A computer-generated interpretation is also available.

Development of the MDI followed the accepted methods of scale construction using a combination of rational and empirical approaches. The 10 subscales were identified initially from the literature on depressive symptoms and subsequently developed through empirical procedures such as item-total correlations, internal consistency and test-retest reliabilities, convergent-divergent validation, and cluster analysis. The Total Scale and subscales performed well in all of these tests, with the exception of the Learned Helplessness subscale. For example, average corrected item-total correlations with this subscale are no better than corrected item-total correlations with the Total Scale. This subscale is not included in the short form of the MDI. Validity data for the Learned Helplessness subscale are also not as impressive as are data for the other subscales.

Male and female norms for the MDI are available for adults, college students, and adolescents. Normative data for special populations are also reported for anorexic, bulimic, and weight-preoccupied patients; several high school students from differing SES levels; gifted adolescents; and family practice outpatients.

In addition to scores on the Total Scale and subscales, the individual profile is compared to criterion-group scores. Criterion groups include depressed, conduct disordered, mixed (depressed and conduct disordered), psychotic, suicidal, endogenomorphic, anorexic women, bulimic women, chronic pain sufferers, and theoretical groups of nondepressed and unselected prototypes. The individual profile is compared to these criterion groups for probability of belonging to each criterion group. Thus, a person's depressive symptomology is reported as resembling that of each criterion group at a particular level of probability. Users are cautioned not to make a diagnosis based on MDI scores alone but to use MDI scores as input into the diagnostic process.

The Manual for the MDI is quite complete. It provides a nice blend of conceptual and technical material. The case examples included in the manual illustrate how MDI results can be integrated into the diagnostic process. The emphasis throughout the manual is on the diagnostic process. As the Inventory gains wider acceptance and use, increased information integrating the MDI with treatment would be a welcome addition to the Manual. The section of the Manual on future research is particularly useful. The use of the MDI as a treatment outcome measure has promise for demonstrating differential effects for varied treatments.

It is difficult to compare the merits of the MDI to more established measures of depression. For example, the Beck Depression Inventory (BDI) has demonstrated its use both for diagnostic and research purposes. The MDI, because of its strong conceptual and psychometric development, has perhaps equivalent potential for significant contributions to practice and research. Like Aaron Beck and the BDI, the author of the MDI is not solely a test developer but has a research program focused on the diagnosis and treatment of depression. This, coupled with the existing level of development of the MDI, holds great promise for the future.

The MDI is built on a sound theoretical and empirical base. It has demonstrated acceptable levels of reliability and a solid, and developing, validity base. The subscale scores (with the previously noted exception of the Learned Helplessness subscale) seem to provide a method for understanding the overall depression score and for suggesting potential areas for intervention. Additional research is needed to support fully the utility of subscales in diagnosis and treatment, but initial data are supportive.

The MDI is recommended for clinical and research uses. Its development is exemplary and its potential is great.

Review of the Multiscore Depression Inventory by STEPHEN G. FLANAGAN, Clinical Associate Professor, Department of Psychology, The University of North Carolina at Chapel Hill, Chapel Hill, NC:

The Multiscore Depression Inventory (MDI) was developed as a measure of severity of depressive affect. It differs from other measures of depression in its standardization and use with nonclinical subjects, less intrusiveness of item content compared to other depression scales, and the availability of multiple subscales for interpretation, in addition to a full-scale depression score. The paper-and-pencil MDI includes forms that are intelligently designed for ease of scoring, profiling, and error checking. The computer report includes scoring and profile construction. The MDI is intended for use and interpretation by professionals with advanced training in psychological assessment. It can be administered to persons aged 13 and above with a sixth-grade reading level, and includes norms for adolescents, college students, and adults. This review is based on information provided in the MDI Manual.

The inventory consists of 118 true-false self-descriptive statements, nine scales of 12 items each, and a 10-item Guilt scale. Scale development started with rational derivation of 10 dimensions of depression, based upon clinical and research literature. An item pool was devised and a "character sketch" written for each concept. An initial pool of over 900 items was cut to 362, based on rated ambiguity and match to the character description from which each item was derived.

The remaining 362 items were administered to 200 college students who also completed a social desirability scale, and sequential criteria were used to select the final items: (*a*) rarely endorsed items were omitted; (*b*) corrected item-total correlations were computed and items removed if less than $r = .30$; (*c*) items were omitted if the corrected item-total correlation was lower than the item's correlation with another scale or the social desirability measure; (*d*) the final 118 items were selected on rational grounds considering the item's ranking in contribution to the scale independent of social desirability, and additional criteria of balancing true and false scored items, redundancy, and face validity.

Internal consistency (coefficient alpha) with five different samples ranged from .70 to .91 for subscales, and .96 to .97 for the full scale score. The MDI compared favorably on internal consistency to other measures of depression such as the Zung Scale and the Beck Depression Inventory. Test-retest reliabilities were likewise consistently significant and high for full scale and subscale scores immediately and over a 3-week interval (except Instrumental Helplessness, .38 in one study).

The Full Scale MDI has had high correlations with concurrent measures, including the Beck Depression Inventory ($r = .69$) and Depression Adjective Check List ($r = .77$) in a sample of 200 college students. The MDI correlated ($r = .66$) with the Hamilton Depression Rating Scale for an inpatient sample. The Manual reports the corrected item-total correlations with each subscale and with the full scale for each item, noting that all are highly significant (p < .001). A criterion measure was selected for each MDI subscale, and significant correlations are reported between each scale and its criterion. Correlations between subscale criterion measures and each of the other nine subscales are not reported. This makes the table of correlations less cluttered, but makes it difficult to evaluate the specificity of the correlation between criterion and subscale. A number of research studies are cited showing MDI validity for differentiating severity of depression in clinical samples. Results of factor and cluster analyses are supportive of construct validity.

Data are also presented in support of the Short Form, which consists of the first 47 items of the MDI (SMDI). There are nine subscale scores (Learned Helplessness was omitted) and a full scale score. Reliabilities are adequate, though generally lower than for the full MDI as expected with fewer items. Corrected item-total correlations are significant, as are correlations with criterion measures for each subscale. Significant correlations are reported between the Full Scale SMDI and the Beck Depression Inventory ($r = .68$) and the Depression Adjective Check List ($r = .76$) among 133 college students. Depressed medical patients scored significantly higher on the SMDI than nondepressed patients.

The optional computer report includes analyses for unusual patterns of item responses or statistical validity scales, including unusual patterns of true-false responses (Runs Test) and endorsement of rare items (Frequency Test). Also in the computer report is a histogram of normalized *T*-scores for the 10 subscales (9 for the SMDI) and Full Scale score, and an interpretive report with statements derived from subscale evaluations. The subject's profile is compared with prototypic profiles for several groups (e.g., depressed, suicidal, chronic pain sufferers) and the probability of group membership is calculated. The manual does not report on separate validation of inferences generated by the computer interpretation program.

The interpretive section of the manual provides guidelines for estimating validity, and discussion of how to detect response biases and faking. The hand-scored version of the inventory cannot include the computer "runs test," which requires extensive rapid calculations. It is unclear whether the frequency test could be adapted for use with hand scoring. The manual includes the caution that the MDI is not intended to be used to establish a diagnosis of depression, which would require careful assessment of symptomatic status and differential diagnosis in addition to any test battery employed. Guidelines are provided for estimating severity of depression, and a table provides corresponding ranges of MDI *T*-scores and Beck Depression Inventory scores corresponding to Nondepressed, Mild, Moderate, and Severe ranges of depression as defined by Beck. After providing interpretive sketches for each of the subscales, there is discussion of profile interpretation. The author appropriately cautions the user that greater elaboration of profile analysis awaits further research explicating empirical correlates of profile configurations.

In sum, the MDI is a reliable and easily administered objective measure of severity of depression that can be used in a wide range of settings with diverse populations. Scale development and validation meet high quality standards. The straightforward nature of the item content permits distortion of MDI responding, and professionals using the scale need to evaluate these risks to validity carefully. The computer report provides statistical indices of test-taking biases and validity not available with the hand-scored version. The MDI's characteristics make it highly suitable for research and clinical applications with a wide range of people, from college students and normal adults to severely depressed clients. Because the MDI is a relatively new instrument, additional research will be necessary to establish more firmly its usefulness with clinical populations. The Manual outlines recommendations for further research, including applications in family practice and medical settings, assessment of affective symptomatology in eating disorders such as anorexia and bulimia, and multiscore evaluation of response to treatment and changes in symptomatic status in depression.

[51]
Murphy-Durrell Reading Readiness Screen.

Purpose: "Provides information about a child's phonics abilities before entering a formal reading program."
Population: Grades K–1.
Publication Date: 1988.
Scores, 6: Lowercase Letter Names, Letter-Name Sounds in Spoken Words, Writing Letters from Dictation, Syntax Matching, Identifying Phonemes in Spoken Words, Total.
Administration: Individual or group.
Price Data, 1989: $29.95 per complete kit including 10 of each of 5 tests and manual (16 pages).
Time: (15–25) minutes per inventory.
Comments: "Developed from the Murphy-Durrell Prereading Phonics Inventory"; recommended that each of the 5 inventories be administered in separate sitting, over a period of 3 days.
Authors: Helen A. Murphy and Donald D. Durrell.
Publisher: Curriculum Associates, Inc.

Review of the Murphy-Durrell Reading Readiness Screen by DOUGLAS J. McRAE, Senior Evaluation Consultant, CTB, Ann Arbor, MI:

PURPOSE. The Murphy-Durrell Reading Readiness Screen is designed to identify grades K–1 students who will be successful in a formal reading program. The instrument is also designed to identify "at risk" students and note their reading readiness deficiencies. The instrument is based entirely on a child's phonics abilities.

DESCRIPTION. The Murphy-Durrell Reading Readiness Screen consists of five separately administered inventories: Lowercase Letter Names (26 items), Letter-Name Sounds in Spoken Words (22 items), Writing Letters from Dictation (26 items), Syntax Matching (10 items), and Identifying Phonemes in Spoken Words (25 items). Simple raw scores are computed for each inventory, and a level letter (A, B, C, or D) is assigned to each inventory using a table in the Teacher's Manual. A total score may also be computed and a level letter assigned, but the directions in the Teacher's Manual are unclear as to whether the total score level letter should be assigned based on the single numerical score or based on the pattern of level letters assigned to the five separate inventories. In any case, the manual is clear in indicating that students achieving level letters of A or B in all five inventories are ready for formal reading instruction.

Each inventory takes 15–25 minutes to administer, for a total administration time of 75–125 minutes. Either group or individual administration is acceptable.

RATIONALE. A brief statement of rationale, including broad references to research findings, is presented in the Teacher's Manual for each of the five inventories. The Teacher's Manual also provides possible reasons for low scores for each of the five inventories, along with suggestions for remediation. References to materials for remediation are given in the Teacher's Manual.

TECHNICAL INFORMATION. The Teacher's Manual provides no technical information to describe the development of the instrument, or to support the validity or reliability of the instrument. The Scoring Table in the Teacher's Manual indicates the assignment of level letters for each inventory is based on a frequency distribution of scores from 633 students, but gives no description for this reference group. The table is not entirely consistent with the instrument itself—for instance, it indicates a maximum score of 7 for Syntax Matching while the instrument itself has 10 items. No evidence for reliability is provided. Despite the express purpose of screening and placement, no evidence of predictive validity is provided.

EVALUATION. The Murphy-Durrell Reading Readiness Screen is a potentially useful instrument for reading teachers who believe that phonics abilities are necessary prerequisites for formal reading instruction. The instrument is based on research that supports this perspective. No evidence is presented that would suggest the instrument is psychometrically sound; the justification for the scoring rules appears to be particularly weak. The instrument's primary value may well be its lead into prereading instructional materials based on phonics. These materials are produced by the same publisher as the instrument itself.

Review of the Murphy-Durrell Reading Readiness Screen by STEPHANIE STEIN, Assistant Professor of Psychology, Central Washington University, Ellensburg, WA:

At first glance, the Murphy-Durrell Reading Readiness Screen's modest claim of providing "information about a child's phonics abilities before entering a formal reading program" is difficult to challenge or debate. After all, a series of inventories on letter names and sounds must provide *some* information about phonics skills. However, a closer look at the five inventories suggests that phonics skills are actually a fairly insubstantial part of the test and that more peripheral skills are being tested that may or may not be prerequisites to reading.

The inventories, which take 15 to 25 minutes each, all involve a combination of oral and printed stimulus items and require nonverbal responses from the child (either circling a letter/word or writing a letter). The first inventory is a fairly straightforward test of letter name identification which, although not a direct measure of phonics, is clearly related to reading readiness. The matching of the initial sound in a spoken word with a printed letter is assessed in the second inventory. In this inventory, the first sound does not always correspond to the first letter in the word. For example, the correct answer for "arm" is "r" and the correct answer for "Esther" is "s." The lack of correspondence between initial letter and initial sound could

understandably be confusing for many beginning readers.

The possibility for confusion increases, however, when the third inventory jumps back from a focus on letter sounds to letter names and asks the child to write the dictated letter in the space provided. No rationale is given as to why letter reversals are scored as correct responses in the initial administration but are scored as errors in follow-up assessments. The fourth inventory consists of short printed sentences that are read orally by the examiner. One word in the sentence is then repeated and the child is asked to circle that word on the worksheet. It is questionable what skill this inventory is actually testing, but phonics does not appear to be a substantial part of it. Children could respond to their knowledge of the actual printed word, memory of where they heard the word in the sentence, or the potentially misleading information provided in the picture that precedes the item.

Finally, the fifth inventory involves the visual presentation of a series of printed letters and the oral presentation of a brief sentence that contains two words that begin with the same letter. The two key words are repeated and the child is asked to circle the letter that is at the beginning of each word.

In all the inventories, the individual test item is preceded by a picture. The presence of the picture on each item is supposed to ensure the children do not lose their places because they are directed to put a finger on the particular picture before the item is presented. However, the picture also serves another purpose adding confusion and potential error to the test.

On three of the inventories, children are directed to circle the picture if they do not know the correct answer. The stated purpose of this practice is that "since the child is circling either a letter or the picture, the child doesn't experience failure." Although the intent is admirable, it is not clear the test-naive young child would not just choose to circle the picture because it is the most stimulating symbol in the row and because it appears to be an acceptable response to the examiner. Furthermore, it is unclear why suddenly in the fourth inventory, if children are unsure of the correct answer, they are simply directed to circle the answer they think is right rather than the picture. Why isn't this simple direction given throughout the test, for the sake of consistency if nothing else?

Another problem with the pictures in every item is that they do not always relate to the item in a consistent fashion. Sometimes the name of the picture represents the letter the child is supposed to select and other times it is very indirectly related to the item. The degree of relationship between the picture and the test item not only varies between inventories but also varies within an inventory. This inconsistent use of pictures represents a major distraction and downfall of the test materials.

If the manual stopped here, the Murphy-Durrell Reading Readiness Screen would simply be a mediocre classroom inventory of questionable usefulness and validity. However, the authors go one fatal step further and attempt to roughly quantify the child's test results into one of four categories. The categories of A, B, C, and D supposedly correspond to the norm group's scores in the top third, middle third, lowest third, and lowest fifth percentile, respectively. No explanation is given on why there is no overlap between the "lowest third" performance and the "lowest 5th percentile." The child's raw score on each inventory is assigned a letter depending on where it corresponds to the scores in the standardization categories, which are presented as a median score and a range of scores. The total letter score is obtained by adding up the raw scores from the five inventories, essentially ignoring the obtained raw total score, and then somehow averaging the letter scores from the five inventories (examples provided in the manual include AAABD = B and AABBC = B).

Although already clearly beyond the level of questionable measurement practice, the authors go even further and definitively state that a child with a score of A or B is ready for "formal reading instruction," implying that a child with a score of C or D is not ready. No definition is given of "formal reading instruction," and no information is provided about how this cutoff was determined. The manual does not provide any information about reliability, validity, or norms (other than $N = 633$).

Additional minor problems and weaknesses are present throughout the test and manual but are essentially inconsequential in comparison to the major, indefensible problems already discussed. The Murphy-Durrell Reading Readiness Screen is fraught with problems of distracting test items, lack of correspondence between stated purpose and actual inventories, imprecise scoring procedures, unsupported interpretation of test results, and complete lack of technical data in the areas of reliability, validity, and norms. Teachers would be better off to avoid this test and use either the readiness tests of major group achievement batteries or to design their own brief measure of phonics skills.

[52]
National Educational Development Tests.

Purpose: To provide students with information in their development of skills that are necessary to do well on college admissions tests and in college work itself.
Population: Grades 9–10.
Publication Dates: 1983–84.
Acronym: NEDT.
Scores, 6: English Usage, Mathematics Usage, National Sciences Reading, Social Studies Reading, Composite Score, Educational Ability.
Administration: Group.
Price Data: Available from publisher for combined test materials and standard scoring services, student materials consist of test booklets and answer sheets, Student Handbook, Certificates of Educational Development, and Student Information Bulletin; administrative materials consist of identification sheets, Supervisor's and Examiner's Manuals ('84, 14 pages), and Interpretive Manuals.
Time: 150(180) minutes.
Comments: Tests administered 2 times annually (October and February).
Authors: Science Research Associates, Inc.
Publisher: Science Research Associates, Inc.

Review of the National Educational Development Tests by PATTI L. HARRISON, Associate Professor of Behavioral Studies, College of Education, The University of Alabama, Tuscaloosa, AL:

The National Educational Development Tests (NEDT) assess ninth and tenth grade students' ability to apply what they have learned and to understand material that might be encountered in later education. Objectives for the tests include helping students, counselors, and administrators to understand students' strengths, weaknesses, and instructional and guidance needs. However, interpretive guidelines emphasize the use of test scores in making plans for college.

The four educational development tests, described in the Student Handbook as measures of intellectual skills, are English Usage, Mathematics Usage, Natural Science Reading, and Social Studies Reading. The term "intellectual" is misleading, as the tests are measures of academic skills, rather than general intelligence. The four tests are averaged to yield a composite. A fifth test, Educational Ability, contains five verbal and nonverbal subtests and is vaguely distinguished from the educational development tests as a measure of "developed abilities" associated with academic performance.

NEDT scores are comprehensively described in the manual, although several needed details are omitted from the interpretation section and are reported in the technical section only. For example, the interpretation section does not indicate that percentile bands and predicted test score ranges are based on a low 50% confidence level. The interpretation section also does not mention that predicted score ranges are based on data from tenth grade students only, and are inaccurate for ninth grade students.

Standard scores are non-normative and do not have the same meaning across tests, but guidelines for interpretation state incorrectly that standard scores may be used to compare performance on different tests. National, college-bound, and local percentile ranks are recommended as the best scores for interpreting performance. National percentile bands reflect measurement error and are used to compare performance on different tests. Expected percentile bands indicate predictions of performance on the educational development tests, given Educational Ability scores. Predicted ranges on the PSAT, SAT, and ACT are based on students' educational development scores.

Skill area data include percentages of items students answered correctly in specific categories. Strengths and weaknesses are identified by comparing percentages to average percentages of a norm group. Many skill areas are assessed with only a few items and data should be interpreted with caution.

Recommendations for using NEDT scores are directed toward making college plans, although materials appropriately state that other factors should also be considered. According to the manual, composite scores above the 85th percentile indicate students could succeed in most colleges; scores below the 75th percentile

indicate possible college success; and scores below the 25th percentile indicate questionable college success. Interpretive guidelines also suggest that scores on individual tests and skill areas may be used to identify and correct weaknesses. It should be noted, however, the manual reports no validity data for using scores to predict college success or remediate academic weaknesses.

A confusing array of studies were conducted for equating and norms development. Unfortunately, norms development was not based on a national standardization study for the NEDT; equating, interpolation, and convenient samples were used extensively. Several samples had small numbers of students, are not adequately described, or contained large numbers of church-related schools. The resulting normative data are questionable.

Studies with about 4,000 students equated the four test forms to each other and to an old test form and equated NEDT standard scores to Growth Scale Values. National percentile ranks for Growth Scale Values were obtained from the fall standardization of the Survey of Basic Skills. Spring percentile ranks were developed through interpolation.

Skill area data were obtained from a sample of an unspecified number of students, selected from the equating study to match standardization composite scores. Data from four samples of 100 students, also selected from the equating study, supplied internal consistency coefficients and correlations for developing national and expected percentile bands. Data for predicted PSAT, SAT, and ACT scores were obtained from a sample of 1,200 tenth grade students in five schools participating in the NEDT program. College-bound percentile ranks were based on all students participating in the 1983–84 NEDT program who indicated they definitely planned to go to college ($Ns = 21,178$ to 34,945).

Kuder-Richardson 20 and Spearman-Brown reliability estimates were obtained from fall and spring samples of ninth graders and fall and spring samples of tenth graders; 100 students in each of the four samples were selected from the equating study to match national standardization score distributions. KR-20 coefficients range from .75 to .91 for the educational development tests, .90 to .92 for the composite, and .79 to .85 for Educational Ability. Several questions can be raised about the reliability coefficients: Did time limits used for educational development tests result in overestimates? Did the different Natural Science and Social Studies passages and different item types of Educational Ability subtests result in underestimates? Were coefficients based on one form or were data pooled across all forms?

An alternate forms reliability study was conducted with about 2,700 students in 16 NEDT schools. Students were administered one complete form and a minitest of one of the other three forms. Correlations range from .37 to .75 for the five tests and .67 to .85 for the composite. Over 50% of the coefficients for the five tests fall below .60. Although the manual suggests that equating error in the minitests or fatigue may have resulted in low coefficients, many coefficients are alarmingly low and cast doubt on using forms interchangeably.

Limited validity data were obtained by correlating test scores with course grades from 11 schools. Correlations range from .02 to .81. Many of the correlations are based on very small samples and should be interpreted with caution. Correlations between the NEDT and PSAT, SAT, and ACT were determined for a sample of 1,200 tenth grade students and range from .60 to .80.

In conclusion, use of the NEDT is not recommended for several reasons. Normative and reliability data are questionable. The use of scores to predict college success or remediate academic weaknesses is not supported. A well-developed achievement/ability battery, such as the Stanford Achievement Test/Otis-Lennon School Ability Test (SAT/OLSAT; 9:1172/9:913), can better accomplish the NEDT objectives of determining students' academic skills and instructional and guidance needs.

Review of the National Educational Development Tests by HOWARD M. KNOFF, Associate Professor of School Psychology and Director of the School Psychology Program, University of South Florida, Tampa, FL:

The National Educational Development Tests (NEDT) consist of five tests designed "to test students' ability to understand the kinds of material they might encounter later in their education rather than to elicit recall of specific information." The first four tests assess students' educational development and correlate most highly with student grades in the specific curricular areas covered. These tests are: English Usage (50 items), Math Usage (40 items), Natural Sciences Reading (32 items), and Social Studies Reading (32 items). The fifth test assesses students' educational ability, those verbal, numerical, reasoning, and spatial abilities that students have developed over time and that correlate most highly with overall academic performance. This test is considered to be a power test in that it has been developed to provide all students with sufficient time to complete all items, and questions (55 items in all) in this test are grouped into verbal and nonverbal subtests.

Created for use with students in their early high school years (typically ninth and tenth grades), the NEDT was developed from a national standardization conducted in 1983–84 84 and a series of equating studies using representative samples of schools and students stratified by enrollment size, geographic region, and socioeconomic level. In all, the Fall 1983 standardization sample consisted of 96,185 ninth and tenth grade students from 208 schools in 55 districts. Significantly, this standardization process was preceded by an item development and test construction process in 1982 that involved (a) a curricular analysis of each test to ensure that individual items had appropriate content and difficulty; (b) an item selection analysis to eliminate items that were too easy or too difficult or that did not statistically conform to "best fit" lines; and (c) an item bias analysis to identify and eliminate any items that inherently differed across the black, white, and Hispanic groups that participated in the test revision, pretest process. Procedures and results of these three analyses and the standardization and equating process were well described in the NEDT Interpretive Manual. It appears that the NEDT's test construction was well organized, operationalized, and implemented, and that test bias was controlled to a large degree. While church-related schools seemed to be over-represented in the test revision sample (to an unknown degree as no data comparing public, private, and church schools were provided), the NEDT revision and standardization process appears to have yielded a test that accurately reflects its purported purpose.

As a result of the test revision process, four equivalent forms of the NEDT were developed. In the Natural Sciences and Social Studies Reading tests, these forms were balanced across a number of content dimensions (e.g., male versus female referents, urban versus suburban versus rural passage settings), as well as across passage readability and passage length. With average readability levels ranging from grade 8.5 (Form 33, Natural Sciences Reading) to 10.1 (Forms 32 and 34, Social Studies Reading) across the four forms, it is important to note that students whose reading skills fall below these tests' levels will be at a distinct disadvantage. While this may be desired given the NEDT's stated assessment goals (see above), the test's predictive validity will be questionable with students who can conceptually understand the material (e.g., if read orally to them), yet have reading decoding problems. Regardless, the four NEDT appear well equated from both statistical and content perspectives, and the Interpretive Manual again provides good documentation of this equating process.

From any of the four forms, the NEDT reports the following data: standard scores, national percentiles, college-bound percentiles, local (school-based) percentiles, national percentile bands, expected percentile bands, and predicted test scores. In addition, the NEDT Program Student Profile provides the number of correct items for specific skills in each test area (e.g., capitalization/punctuation, verb usage, pronoun usage), and if the student scored above, below, or equivalent to the national standardization group in those skill areas. The NEDT's standard scores range from 1 to 35 with a mean of 15 and a standard deviation of approximately 5 for students in the ninth and tenth grades combined. Although standard scores facilitate test interpretation and test-retest comparisons, the use of a more educationally familiar standard score format (e.g., a mean of 50 and standard deviation of 10; a mean of 100 and standard deviation of 15) would make interpretation even easier and allow functional comparisons across *other* tests of educational development.

The NEDT percentiles indicate an individual student's rank within a specific reference group. The national percentile ranks, for example, are based on data from the 1983 national

standardization and are best interpreted alongside the national percentile bands that utilize each test's error of measurement and indicate the range of scores wherein a student's true score rests. The local percentiles reflect a student's performance as compared to his or her same-school or same-community peers, while the college-bound percentiles were generated from students taking the NEDT in the Fall of 1983 and Spring of 1984 who indicated that they would definitely attend college. Finally, the expected percentile bands are generated from a student's performance on the NEDT's Educational Ability test, and they can be compared to a student's actual performance on the four Educational Development tests; while predicted test scores use NEDT standard scores to predict future student performance on the PSAT, SAT, and ACT college board tests. Overall, the derivation, interpretation, and implications of each type of percentile is clearly discussed in the NEDT Manual. The predicted test scores were based on data collected for the high school graduating class of 1983 (thus, their NEDT and PSAT data from 1980–1982 and their SAT and ACT data from 1982–1983). Correlations among the tests ranged from .631 to .764 for the NEDT and PSAT, from .477 to .610 for the NEDT and the SAT, and from .614 to .791 for the NEDT and the ACT.

Relative to reliability, the NEDT Manual reports both internal consistency data and alternative form data. The former form of reliability was obtained with the 1983–1984 standardization samples using the Kuder-Richardson Formula-20 (KR-20) and the Spearman-Brown Prophecy Formula (S-B). The KR-20 correlations ranged from .75 for Mathematics Usage (Grade 9 sample, First Semester) to .92 for the Composite Score (Grade 10 sample, First and Second Semesters), and the S-B correlations ranged from .85 for Mathematics Usage (Grade 9 sample, First Semester) to .93 for the English Usage test (Grade 10 sample, First and Second Semesters). Overall, these correlations indicate very acceptable internal reliability.

Alternative form reliability was assessed by administering a NEDT "minitest" consisting of 20% of the items of a complete test drawn from Forms 31, 33, and 34. Reliabilities here were acceptable, except that the Educational Ability test had the lowest correlations (.367 to .663). These correlations were considered lower than expected, but two hypotheses were forwarded to explain the results: the use of a minitest (as opposed to the full test) and fatigue due to the fact that the minitest was administered after the students had already completed a full NEDT. Regardless, additional research is needed to document the NEDT's alternative form reliability. Further, periodic updating of all of these reliability results is necessary as the test gets older and continues to depend on the 1983–1984 standardization.

Relative to validity, a series of concurrent validity studies were performed as part of the 1983 equating process by correlating students' NEDT scores and their year-end course grades. Approximately 2,000 students from 11 schools were utilized, and the data from each school were considered separately. While often statistically significant, the lower range of these correlations was quite low. For example, concurrent validity correlations were .253 and .34 for ninth and tenth graders, respectively, on English Usage; .14 and .244 in Mathematics Usage; .076 and .018 for Natural Sciences Reading; and .341 and .356 for Social Studies Reading. No other validity studies were noted in the NEDT Manual. Clearly, more validity research is needed, especially (a) concurrent validity studies involving other educational development/achievement tests, (b) predictive validity studies that confirm the utility of the predicted test scores, and (c) discriminant validity studies that demonstrate the NEDT's ability to discern successful from unsuccessful college-bound and college-matriculated students.

To summarize, the NEDT is designed to determine how well ninth and tenth grade students can apply what they have learned. The Interpretive Manual does an excellent job of describing all of the technical aspects of the test, from test construction to standardization to reliability/validity determination. The Manual is very well written, and it includes numerous examples that help to clarify critical interpretive elements and pragmatic uses of the test. Similarly, the other manuals reviewed (i.e., the Supervisor's and Examiner's Manual, the Student Information Bulletin, and the Student Handbook) were clear and easy to read. While additional research is needed in the areas of alternative form reliability and concurrent, predictive, and discriminant validity, the NEDT appears to be a well-developed test that successfully attains its primary goals and objectives: to help students—especially those with collegiate aspirations—to better understand their academic status and current educational potential.

[53]

New Jersey Test of Reasoning Skills—Form B.

Purpose: Assesses elementary reasoning and inquiry skills.

Population: Reading level grade 5 and over.

Publication Dates: 1983–85.

Scores: 22 skill areas: Converting Statements, Translating into Logical Form, Inclusion/Exclusion, Recognizing Improper Questions, Avoiding Jumping to Conclusions, Analogical Reasoning, Detecting Underlying Assumptions, Eliminating Alternatives, Inductive Reasoning, Reasoning with Relationships, Detecting Ambiguities, Discerning Causal Relationships, Identifying Good Reasons, Recognizing Symmetrical Relationships, Syllogistic Reasoning (Categorical), Distinguishing Differences of Kind and Degree, Recognizing Transitive Relationships, Recognizing Dubious Authority, Reasoning with 4-Possibilities Matrix, Contradicting Statements, Whole-Part and Part-Whole Reasoning, Syllogistic Reasoning (Conditional).

Administration: Group.

Manual: No manual.

Price Data, 1987: $2.40 per 12-month test booklet rental including scoring and analysis service for up to 4 answer sheets.

Time: (30–45) minutes.

Author: Virginia Shipman.

Publisher: Institute for the Advancement of Philosophy for Children.

TEST REFERENCES

1. Anderson, R. N., Greene, M. L., & Loewen, P. S. (1988). Relationship among teacher's and student's thinking skills, sense of efficacy, and student achievement. *The Alberta Journal of Educational Research, 34,* 148-165.

Review of the New Jersey Test of Reasoning Skills—Form B by ARTHUR S. ELLEN, Assistant Professor of Psychology, Pace University, New York, NY:

The New Jersey Test of Reasoning Skills—Form B (NJTRS) was designed to evaluate the Philosophy for Children program, an innovative curriculum that asks students to reflect on their thinking through carefully planned class discussion. The NJTRS is based upon a 22-

category taxonomy of children's elementary reasoning. Elementary reasoning is here defined as logic learned by children while they acquire language. It differs from higher level thinking, which occurs when students apply elementary skills to more advanced disciplines or solve problems using more than one elementary skill. True to this definition, the questions on the test tap basic logical operations by using an elementary-school reading level (Flesch reading grade level of 4.5 and a Fogg Index of 5.0).

The test consists of 50 multiple-choice questions, each in the form of a short dialogue with three possible answers. Directions are clearly given in the test booklet along with one practice item. The test, according to the publisher, should take about 45 minutes and a 1-hour time limit is suggested. An optical scan form goes back to the publisher, who will return for each class: (a) the Kuder-Richardson reliability index, (b) the mean and standard deviation, (c) the percent correct for each item, (d) a report for each of the pupils telling them the number correct in each of the 22 skill areas of the test, and (e) a chart of available test averages by grade from the publisher's data base.

The NJTRS appears to be used mainly with middle-school students, although it has been given experimentally to students from first grade to college (M. Lipman, personal communication, December 14, 1989). For students under fourth grade, the publisher suggests reading the test aloud. However, this may not work because many younger students will not remember or comprehend the questions and answers. As the test has been used to evaluate a year-long curriculum project, pre- and post-testing are possible with the same form if testing is completed during one school year.

Technical information is not provided in a manual, but instead the publisher furnishes four sources of information: (a) a portion of a 1982–83 curriculum evaluation report that used an earlier 55-item version of the test; (b) a 1983 three-page brochure from Montclair State College that briefly describes the test; (c) a sheet that reports correlations of the NJTRS with college-level measures of achievement; and (d) a sheet that contains grades 4 through 8 test means as of February 1986.

Although the current test has 50 items, the bulk of the technical information apparently

comes from a 55-item version used in the curriculum evaluation project. In 10 communities, that project sampled 2,346 fifth- through seventh-grade students in 74 experimental and 42 control classes. From this data the publishers derived item statistics, test reliability, and some of the rationale for the test's validity.

Item statistics included item difficulties and point-biserial correlations for item to total test score. Although not reported for each item, a good range of item difficulties with a preponderance of "moderately difficult items" was found. Seven items with low point-biserial correlations (.20 or less) were found, and perhaps these results helped to drop items from the 55-item version to make the final 50-item test.

Test reliability in the form of coefficient alpha, an index of internal consistency, was obtained from a random and representative sample of classrooms in the curriculum project. From grades 5 to 7, the coefficient alphas consistently increased from .84 to .94. These reasonably high indices agree with the reliability index of .83 found for a previous version of the test. Unfortunately, test stability was not examined by generating test-retest correlations.

One claim to validity is based upon the test's sensitivity to experimental intervention found in the year-long curriculum evaluation project. From the fall to spring of that school year, the matched-control classes, on the average, increased their test scores approximately 3 points. In contrast, experimental classes, on the average, increased their total test scores a little more than 6 points. These significant differences led the publishers to conclude that the NJTRS responds to changes caused by the Philosophy for Children program.

The publishers argue for at least four additional kinds of validity: content, construct, developmental, and concurrent. Content validity exists because the NJTRS is supposed to sample adequately the elementary reasoning skills taxonomy. Construct validity is based upon the unreported test development research performed at the Educational Testing Service between 1976 and 1978.

Developmental validity usually means test scores exponentially increase with either age or grade. But from grades 4 through 8, the NJTRS's means do not exponentially increase; instead, they remain relatively flat, a test plateau. To explain this, the publishers hypothesize that students develop elementary reasoning skills at about grade 4. However, the interaction between a child's age and item format (O'Brien & Shapiro, 1968; Roberge, 1970) might partially explain the test's ostensible plateau.

Concurrent validity comes from two studies that correlated the NJTRS with measures of college achievement. The first study, with over 600 college freshmen, found moderate correlations with the New Jersey College Basic Skills Placement Test, an exam consisting of five academic achievement subtests in the areas of reading, math, and writing. The second study, with 150 college students, reported moderate correlations between the NJTRS and the Scholastic Aptitude Test math and verbal subtests, and small but significant correlations to college grade-point average. Both studies support the interrelationship between the NJTRS and achievement with college-level students, but not with middle-school students, the intended test takers.

A major shortcoming of the NJTRS is the absence of a comprehensive test manual. A manual minimally must include such missing technical information as: (*a*) definitions and examples for the taxonomy of logical reasoning; (*b*) which items correspond to particular skills in the taxonomy, a test plan; (*c*) what research served as the basis for construct validity; (*d*) which test statistics were derived with the 55-item evaluation instrument and which came from the 50-item test; and (*e*) item difficulties and point-biserial correlations for each item.

Another limit of the NJTRS is its lack of subtests. Although the test is intended to evaluate a complex curriculum project, there is only one global test score. This score, a composite of the 22 elementary reasoning skills, will not inform a teacher or program evaluator which skills a pupil has learned. It should be noted, however, that constructing a test with reliable subtests for this many skills would require a much longer test and evidence that the subtest constructs exist.

In sum, the NJTRS provides an internally consistent composite measure of a unique taxonomy of elementary reasoning skills using a clever item format. However, the publishers could make a better case for test use by providing a thorough and comprehensive report of test information.

REVIEWER'S REFERENCES
O'Brien, T. C., & Shapiro, B. J. (1968). The development of logical thinking in children. *American Educational Research Journal, 5*, 531-542.
Roberge, J. J. (1970). A study of children's abilities to reason with basic principles of deductive reasoning. *American Educational Research Journal, 7*, 583-596.

Review of the New Jersey Test of Reasoning Skills—Form B by ROSEMARY E. SUTTON, Associate Professor of Education, Cleveland State University, Cleveland, OH:

The New Jersey Test of Reasoning Skills was developed in the early 1980s to evaluate the Philosophy for Children Program (PCP). The purpose of the PCP program, developed by Dr. Matthew Lipman at Montclair State College, is to improve students' reasoning skills through classroom discussion that emphasizes generating ideas, discovering resemblances and differences, and finding reasons. Although the Philosophy for Children Program is intended for kindergarten through high school students, the New Jersey Test of Reasoning Skills was developed for use with students in the fifth through seventh grades.

The 50-item multiple-choice test represents 22 skill areas of inductive and deductive reasoning. The language is very simple and the test can be used for as low as fourth grade level. Because so many skill areas are covered, and no information is given about which questions cover which skill areas, this test can be used only to provide information about general critical thinking ability. Thus, this test may be used to evaluate a program such as the PCP, but cannot be used to diagnose specific strengths and weaknesses.

RELIABILITY. The technical information supplied was not in the form of a technical manual, but as part of a final report on the experimental Philosophy for Children Program intervention. Details about reliability indices are given only for an earlier 55-item version of this test. Cronbach's alpha for fifth grade classes ranged from .84 to .87, for sixth grade classes the range was .86 to .89, and for seventh grade classes the range was .91 to .94. The published version of the test has only 50 items. I assume five items with low point-biserial correlations (item to total test score) discussed in the technical information were eliminated, but there is no way to determine which items were eliminated or the new reliability coefficients. These reliability coefficients are high and are unlikely to be altered significantly with the elimination of five items, but the correct figures should have been supplied.

VALIDITY. Content validity was established by producing a taxonomy of the skills needed to perform the operations in the discipline of logic used in childhood and by developing questions from this taxonomy. No information is provided about why some logical skills were selected for inclusion in the test and others were not. Correlations between this test and measures of academic performance are also provided to support validity. These correlations were high and statistically significant for the majority of the measures (e.g., SAT Math, .59; SAT Verbal, .57; Reading Comprehension subtest of the New Jersey College Basic Skills Placement Test, .82). However, all of these data were gathered from samples of college students, even though this test was developed and pilot tested on middle-school children.

NORMS. Norms for 1986 were provided for fourth through eighth grade students. These norms are based on large samples, but no demographic information was provided. Earlier norms were based on 10 diverse subsamples including suburban, rural, and inner-city children. The recent norms show little change in the average number of right answers from fourth grade to eighth grade (31.1 for fourth grade and 34.1 for eighth grade, with standard deviation for both groups approximately 10).

Evaluating critical thinking and reasoning is a very difficult task and there are very few tests appropriate for this age group. While this test appears to be of some value for its original purpose of evaluating the Philosophy for Children Program, I do not recommend it for other purposes. The technical information provided is too limited. If the publishers develop an appropriate technical manual with accurate reliability indices, details about normative samples, and more information about validity, this test may be worth consideration.

[54]
North American Depression Inventories for Children and Adults.

Purpose: "Measure symptoms of depression in children and adults."
Population: Grades 2–9, Ages 15 and over.
Publication Date: 1988.
Acronym: NADI.
Scores: Total score only.

Administration: Group.
Editions, 2: Children, Adult.
Price Data, 1988: $57.50 per complete battery including examiner's manual (56 pages) and 50 of each of the two test forms (Form A, Form C); $15 per 50 test forms (specify form); $5 per scoring stencil; $7.50 per audio cassette tape; $15 per examiner's manual; $17.50 per specimen set including examiner's manual and one copy each of the two test forms.
Time: (10–20) minutes.
Comments: Self-administered; may be orally administered by audio cassette tape; originally entitled Battle's Depression Inventories for Children and Adults and is a derivative of the Culture-Free Self-Esteem Inventories.
Author: James Battle.
Publisher: Special Child Publications.

TEST REFERENCES
1. Battle, J. (1987). Test-retest reliability of Battle's Depression Inventory for Children. *Psychological Reports, 61*, 71-74.

Review of the North American Depression Inventories for Children and Adults by PATRI-CIA A. BACHELOR, Associate Professor of Psychology, California State University, Long Beach, CA:

The North American Depression Inventories (NADI) for Children (Form C) and Adults (Form A) are self-report scales that purport to measure symptoms or characteristics of depression. The NADI may be administered as an individual or group test in 10 to 20 minutes. An audiocassette enables oral administration to nonreaders. Form C consists of 25 items to which children (grades 2 through 9) respond either "yes" or "no." Form A requires that adults (ages 15 to 60 years) respond to 40 items using a 5-point scale (*Always, Usually, Sometimes, Seldom,* or *Never*). Scores are sums of responses indicating depression, hence, higher scores indicate more intense symptoms of depression. Depression scores are classified on a 5-point continuum ranging from "very high" to "very low." Battle suggested that the information gathered from client's responses may guide the discussion and effectively focus therapeutic sessions as well as provide quantitative evaluation of intervention strategy efforts.

The manual includes numerous tables of descriptive statistics, results of validity and reliability studies, and standard score conversions (percentile ranks and T scores). Administration and scoring, as facilitated by an acetate template, are simple and quick. Four case studies briefly detailing the use of the NADI in assessing the progress of therapy are also presented. However, the rationale for the development of the test was limited with respect to a theoretical or conceptual framework. Guidelines for interpretation were sparse. Most troublesome to this reviewer was the shocking lack of descriptive detail of the standardization sample. The only demographic information provided are grade level in general terms (i.e., elementary, junior high, or adult) and number of males and females who were from a "large midwestern city." Meaningful comparisons based on these data are not possible nor is an assessment of the representativeness of the norm group.

RELIABILITY ESTIMATES. Test-retest reliability coefficients for 764 elementary, 325 junior high, and 277 adult subjects over a 2-week period were presented. Pearson correlation coefficients were .79, .79, and .93, respectively, hence the stability of the scores is acceptable. It is unfortunate, however, that no estimates of internal consistency were reported.

VALIDITY ESTIMATES. The evidence presented to support the claim of construct validity of the NADI "was built-in by our identifying and incorporating items that measure depression." This is not a method of construct validation that is accepted or endorsed by the *Standards for Educational and Psychological Testing* (AERA, APA, & NCME, 1985). Hence, the claim of construct validity is currently unwarranted.

Concurrent validity was claimed by several correlational studies. Scores on both forms of the NADI were correlated with the age-level appropriate Beck's Depression Inventory. Correlations were .56, .73, and .66 for elementary, junior high, and adults, respectively. NADI scores correlated with the Culture-Free Self-Esteem Inventory (CFSEI) -.73 at the elementary level; -.72 at the junior high level; and -.74 at the adult level. The test user is reminded that the NADI is a derivative of the CFSEI, hence the reported correlations should be interpreted judiciously. The correlations presented in support of concurrent validity were minimally adequate; however, there was no information about the validation sample's socioeconomic status, ethnicity, psychological characteristics, or other demographic makeup. This omission is problematic to external validity interpretation as well as to the establishment of concurrent validity. Perhaps, other research studies using direct observation and/or interview data to measure the intensity of symptoms of depression, rather than another self-report inventory of depression or an extension of a self-esteem instrument would prove fruitful in demonstrating concurrent validity. Discriminant validity studies would also be welcomed.

SUMMARY. The NADI for Children and Adults may serve as a promising instrument to influence and focus therapeutic intervention; however, its psychometric qualities have not, to date, been sufficiently verified. Construct and concurrent validity have not been substantiated nor has internal consistency. Stability reliability was acceptable but the normative samples were not adequately described, hence, meaningful interpretations of scores are not possible. The weakness of the norming calls into question the applicability and sample comparability of the NADI. An enthusiastic endorsement for the widespread use of the NADI in schools and clinical settings awaits further research that establishes its psychometric properties.

REVIEWER'S REFERENCE

American Educational Research Association, American Psychological Association, & National Council on Measurement in Education. (1985). *Standards for educational and psychological testing.* Washington, DC: American Psychological Association, Inc.

Review of the North American Depression Inventories for Children and Adults by MICHAEL G. KAVAN, Director of Behavioral Sciences and Assistant Professor of Family Practice, Creighton University School of Medicine, Omaha, NE:

The North American Depression Inventories (NADI) for Children (Form C) and Adults (Form A) are self-report instruments designed to measure symptoms of depression in the general population and in clinical settings. Form C is comprised of 25 items, whereas Form A contains 40 items. All items were selected on their ability to measure characteristics of depression. They also represent symptoms typical of those reported by individuals experiencing depression. The author claims that such information is not only useful for classification purposes, but items may also be used to facilitate discussion concerning the direction of therapeutic sessions.

ADMINISTRATION AND SCORING. The NADI Form C and Form A may be administered to individuals or groups. Group administration of Form C is not recommended for children below grade 2. Instead, these children should respond individually to the stimulus items while the clinician records the responses in the appropriate answer box. Older children (grade 3 and above) should be able to read and follow independently the directions provided on the answer sheet. An optional audiocassette tape is available for oral administration of both Forms C and A.

Directions for Form C request the respondent to make a check mark in a "yes" or "no" box to questions that describe "how you usually feel." A total score is obtained by adding the number of items selected that represent depression. Thus, total scores may range from 0 to 25. Administration and scoring time is estimated to be 10 to 15 minutes. For Form A, the respondent is asked to describe "how you feel" by selecting one of five options: *always*, *usually*, *sometimes*, *seldom*, and *never*. Responses are converted to scores ranging from 1 to 5 and are then totaled. Total scores may range from 40 to 200. Administration and scoring time is estimated to be 15 to 20 minutes. Acetate templates are available to facilitate the scoring of both forms.

RELIABILITY. Limited reliability data are provided in the test manual. The author provides 2-week test-retest information on two samples for Form C and one sample for Form A. For Form C, correlations were .79 for 764 boys and girls in grades 2 through 6 in a large metropolitan school district, and .79 for 325 adolescents in grades 7 through 9. For Form A, the correlation for 277 adults (ages 15 through 60) in a large midwestern city was .93.

VALIDITY. The author claims that construct validity for both Forms is "built-in" by the identification and incorporation of items that measure depression. Although the manual does not specifically address content validity, it may be demonstrated by NADI item coverage of major depressive syndrome as defined by the recently revised *Diagnostic and Statistical Manual of Mental Disorders—Third Edition* (DSM-III-R) (American Psychiatric Association, 1987). Recent viewpoints suggest the essential features of depression in children and adolescents are similar to those in adults (with some recognition of age-specific effects). In terms of the NADI, Form C items cover only five of the nine symptom categories, whereas Form A

more adequately covers eight of the nine symptom groups. Both forms place heavy emphasis on the depressed mood and worthlessness/guilt symptoms of depression. No evidence exists that factor analytic studies were performed on this instrument.

Concurrent validity was determined by correlating Form C and Form A with other instruments designed to measure both depression and constructs associated with depression. Comparisons of scores obtained by elementary school children (grades 2 through 6) on Form C with scores obtained on a "modified version of Beck's Depression Inventory adapted for children" yielded correlations of .56. Form C scores were also found to be significantly correlated with scores obtained on the Culture-Free Self-Esteem Inventory for Children, Form A (-.73). Similar correlations were obtained when 248 junior high school students (grades 7 through 9) took Form C and the "adapted" Beck Depression Inventory (.73), and when a sample of 302 children in seventh through ninth grade took the Culture-Free Self-Esteem Inventory for Children, Form A (-.72).

Scores from 277 adults taking Form A correlated .66 with the Beck Depression Inventory and -.74 with the Culture-Free Self-Esteem Inventory for Adults, Form AD. NADI Form A scores have also been compared with those earned on the depression subscale of the "mini-mult version of the Minnesota Multiphasic Personality." Correlations between these two scales were .51, .24, and .64 for both sexes, males, and females, respectively. The manual fails to provide data concerning the relationship between NADI scores and independent ratings of psychiatric diagnosis. In addition, despite claims by the author that the NADI are "sensitive to change" and "have been used effectively to identify patients or clients experiencing depression, and to determine the amount of progress that has occurred as a result of psychotherapeutic treatment," no evidence (other than case reports) is provided in the manual for such contentions.

NORMS. Normative data provided in the manual are quite adequate for general samples, but are nonexistent for other important groups. Means, standard deviations, percentile ranks, and *T*-scores are provided for elementary school age, junior high school age, and adult samples. Unfortunately, no data are provided for psychiatric diagnostic samples nor are they available on minority populations. Because race-related differences have been noted on depression instruments (Politano, Nelson, Evans, Sorenson, & Zeman, 1986) it would behoove the author to provide such information in the test manual. With normative data being limited to only general groups of children, adolescents, and adults, it is quite difficult to use the information in the manual to differentiate "normals" from psychiatrically depressed groups or from individuals with other types of disorders not in the depressive domain. As a result, interpretation of NADI scores is difficult.

SUMMARY. The NADI Form C and Form A are easily administered self-report instruments designed to assess symptoms of depression in children and adults. Although more extensive reliability studies must be performed on these instruments, their validity appears to be adequate. Normative data are limited, and thus, are a weakness of this instrument. More extensive normative data would allow for the NADI to be used more confidently to identify individuals with depression in clinical settings. At the present time, use of the NADI should be limited to research settings. In this context, the NADI provides a useful and comprehensive assessment of the depressed mood and self-esteem components of depression. Those interested in an instrument that quantifies a wider range of depressive symptoms may want to examine better-researched scales such as the Beck Depression Inventory (Beck, Ward, Mendelson, Mock, & Erbaugh, 1961) and the Zung Self-Rating Depression Scale (Zung, 1965) for adults, or the Children's Depression Inventory (13; Kovacs, 1983) for younger groups.

REVIEWER'S REFERENCES

Beck, A. T., Ward, C. H., Mendelson, M., Mock, J., & Erbaugh, J. (1961). An inventory for measuring depression. *Archives of General Psychiatry, 4,* 561-571.

Zung, W. W. K. (1965). A self-rating depression scale. *Archives of General Psychiatry, 12,* 63-70.

Kovacs, M. (1983). *The Children's Depression Inventory: A self-report depression scale for school-aged youngsters.* Unpublished manuscript, University of Pittsburgh School of Medicine, Pittsburgh.

Politano, P. M., Nelson, W. M., Evans, H. E., Sorenson, S. B., & Zeman, D. J. (1986). Factor analytic evaluation of differences between Black and Caucasian emotionally disturbed children on the Children's Depression Inventory. *Journal of Psychopathology and Behavioral Assessment, 8,* 1-7.

American Psychiatric Association. (1987). *Diagnostic and statistical manual of mental disorders* (3rd ed. rev.). Washington, DC: Author.

[55]
Oliver Organization Description Questionnaire.

Purpose: Describes occupational organizations along four dimensions.
Population: Adults.
Publication Date: 1981.
Acronym: OODQ.
Scores, 4: H (Hierarchy), P (Professional), T (Task), G (Group).
Administration: Group.
Price Data, 1989: $17.50 per 50 tests; $3.50 per scoring guide ('81, 13 pages).
Time: (15–20) minutes.
Author: John E. Oliver, Jr.
Publisher: Organizational Measurement Systems Press.

Review of the Oliver Organization Description Questionnaire by PETER VILLANOVA, Assistant Professor of Psychology, Northern Illinois University, DeKalb, IL, and H. JOHN BERNARDIN, University Professor of Research, Florida Atlantic University, Boca Raton, FL:

The Oliver Organization Description Questionnaire (OODQ) is an application of Miner's (1980) four limited domain theories of organizations. Each of Miner's four theories describes a role that must be performed by individuals within an organization or subunit in order to direct and sustain effort toward organizational goal attainment. The questionnaire provides four scores, each corresponding to a specific inducement system within Miner's taxonomy. The four inducement systems are: Hierarchic, Professional, Task, and Group. The OODQ purports to measure the extent to which organizations, organizational subunits, or positions possess characteristics representative of each inducement system.

Potential uses of the scale scores derived from the test include: (*a*) identification of boundary variables that affect the applicability of various management styles and conflict resolution strategies; (*b*) assessment of the amount of change resulting from interventions such as training, organizational development, job enrichment, management by objectives, and socio-technical designs; and (*c*) a more complete report of the organizational domain in which research on organizational behavior is conducted.

Each of Miner's theories refers to a specific form of organizational inducement system operating within a prescribed domain. For example, Miner's Hierarchic (H) inducement system operates in large bureaucratic organizations where members' energy is direct by individuals who occupy traditional management positions. Management obtains its energy from a variety of "intrinsic motivational constellations," such as, for example, a desire to compete and a desire to exercise power over others (Miner, 1980, pp. 274–275).

In contrast, the Professional (P) inducement system is said to operate among individuals or organizations whose role requirements and norms are largely a function of professional standards. Intrinsic motivational constellations for the roles germane to Professional inducement systems include, for example, a desire to learn and acquire knowledge, and an identification with the values of the profession to which one belongs. Individuals may be members of professional organizations, self-employed, or serve in some professional capacity. College professors, lawyers, and chaplains are occupations that fall within this form of inducement system.

According to the scoring guide of the OODQ, the Task (T) inducement system is characteristic of organizations or positions "that receive their energy from rewards and punishments that are built into the job or task." In this form of inducement system, individuals establish specific duties and goals, their own decisions based on the situation at hand, and alone bear the responsibility for failure or success. There is little cooperation with others and success is largely determined by the individual's ability and motivation. Entrepreneurs and commissioned sales personnel are examples of positions that feature some of these characteristics.

Group inducement systems possess democratic decision-making features. The group regulates individual behavior by the application of positive or negative sanctions. Group loyalty is considered important for group maintenance and growth, and independence is discouraged. Group inducement systems are present in work situations that require close coordination among work group members who share relatively equal status. Organizations that subscribe to the socio-technical philosophy of work design tend to have more of these features.

The questionnaire consists of 43 forced-choice items with a tetradic response format and is administered without a time limit. Oliver (1982) reports that respondents required approximately one-half hour to complete the test, though some individuals completed it within 15 minutes and others required nearly 50 minutes. Each item of the three-page questionnaire begins with the words "In my work" and is followed by statements that pertain to specific job characteristics, such as "Work rules and regulations are established by" and "My training is generally." Respondents are instructed to complete each statement by selecting the one answer that best describes their work situation. For example, the former statement is followed by the following choices: (a) me–in order to insure goal accomplishment, (b) management, (c) the work group, and (d) my profession or occupation.

Psychometric data on the instrument are sparse at this time. Those data that were reported indicate adequate psychometric properties for its use as a research device. Psychometric characteristics of the test are based on a study conducted by Oliver (1980) with a sample of 438 respondents drawn from a variety of occupations representative of each of the four domains. Occupations were classified a priori as corresponding to the various inducement strategies. For example, U.S. Army officers, NCOs, and enlisted men were hypothesized to score higher on the Hierarchic inducement scale relative to the P, T, and G scales. Likewise, lawyers and dentists were hypothesized to score higher on the P scale than the H, T, and G scales.

Results of this study indicated that 72% of the initial validation sample were classified correctly. Cross-validation with a holdout sample indicated that 71% of these respondents were classified correctly. Also, 90% of the organizational units were correctly classified. Coefficient alphas for each of the four scales ranged from .82 to .88. Test-retest coefficients based on 32 members of the original sample ranged from .77 to .87. Cutting scores for classification purposes were empirically derived and are characterized by relatively small standard errors of measurement. Thus, the scales of this questionnaire possess adequate evidence for criterion-related validity, internal consistency, temporal stability, and acceptable precision for classification purposes. However, these results were generated with relatively small derivation and cross-validation samples of approximately

50–60 respondents for each scale. Caution is required by users when interpreting the findings. Moreover, extra caution may be required if a user plans to study a sample of occupations or organizations not represented in the initial sample.

Overall, the OODQ reflects a careful approach to scale development and attention to detail. The instrument possesses characteristics that make it a promising instrument for organizational diagnosis and classification in the context of Miner's taxonomy. Considerable research is still needed on the psychometric characteristics of the instrument. In its present form, however, the OODQ could be useful to consultants and organizational scholars who share a concern about the boundary conditions of various work place interventions and who accept Miner's taxonomy.

REVIEWER'S REFERENCES

Miner, J. B. (1980). Limited domain theories of organizational energy. In C. C. Pinder & L. F. Moore (Eds.), *Middle range theory and the study of organizations*. The Hague, Netherlands: Martinus Nijhoff.

Oliver, J. E. (1980). *The development of an instrument for describing organizational energy domains.* Unpublished doctoral dissertation, Georgia State University, Atlanta, GA.

Oliver, J. E. (1982). An instrument for classifying organizations. *Academy of Management Journal, 25,* 855-866.

[56]
Pediatric Extended Examination at Three.

Purpose: "To aid in the early detection and clarification of problems with learning, attention, and behavior in three- to four-year-old children."
Population: Ages 3–4.
Publication Date: 1986.
Acronym: PEET.
Scores, 20: Developmental Attainment (Gross Motor, Language, Visual-Fine Motor, Memory, Intersensory Integration), Assessment of Behavior Rating Scale (Initial Adaptation, Reactions during Assessment), Global Language Rating Scale, Physical Findings (General Physical Examination, Neurological Examination, Auditory and Vision Testing), Task Analysis (Reception, Discrimination, Sequencing, Memory, Fine Motor Output, Gross Motor Output, Expressive Language, Instructional Output, Experiential Application).
Administration: Individual.
Price Data, 1987: $54.50 per complete kit including 24 record booklets, PEET kit (ball, target, key, wooden blocks, plastic sticks, car, crayon, doll, buttoning strip, checkers, and objects for stereognosis task), stimulus booklet (35 pages), and examiner's manual (63 pages).
Time: Administration time not reported.

Authors: James A. Blackman, Melvin D. Levine, and Martha Markowitz.
Publisher: Educators Publishing Service, Inc.

Review of the Pediatric Extended Examination at Three by WILLIAM B. MICHAEL, Professor of Education and Psychology, University of Southern California, Los Angeles, CA:

The Pediatric Extended Examination at Three (PEET) was prepared by two pediatricians and a psychologist with a strong medical orientation. This instrument was designed to assess a wide range of characteristics in neurological development, in cognitive and affective behaviors, and in physical and mental health of the 3-year-old child, with applicability to the child of 4 or 5 years of age. The authors have emphasized in the manual the lack of adequate standardized diagnostic evaluation and screening procedures for the 3-year-old. The PEET is actually one of three separate parent and school questionnaires within what is known as the Aggregate Neurobehavioral Student Health and Educational Review (ANSER) System that has been prepared to evaluate developmental factors of three age groups (ages 3 to 5 for preschool and kindergarten children, ages 6 to 11 corresponding to elementary school children, and ages 12 or more relative to secondary students).

Central to the PEET are 29 developmental tasks covering five broad functional areas: Gross Motor, Language, Visual-Fine Motor, Memory, and Intersensory Integration skills, for which there are 7, 8, 6, 5, and 3 tasks, respectively. Relative to each task, detailed and quite explicit instructions are given in the manual both for administration and for scoring and interpreting the responses.

The scoring instructions described in the manual are integrated within an 8-page fold-out record form, which itself needs to be studied to afford a comprehensive grasp of the organizational structure of the PEET. In this record form, space is provided for a tabulation of detailed results of a medical examination as well as for evaluative responses in rating scales covering (*a*) eight language skills and (*b*) 25 categories of behaviors. Although the multidimensional nature of the instrument prevents use of an interpretable total score, the record form does include one summary page to highlight information of developmental attainment, behaviors manifested during assessment, general language competency, medical status, and performance in nine global task areas.

Credit must be given to the authors for the caution they have exercised in numerous places within the manual concerning accurate interpretation of scores generated—especially the caveat not to overgeneralize the results or to draw extravagant inferences. They have encouraged the use of other indicators to supplement the outcomes of the assessment furnished by the PEET.

This refreshing position may be, in part, a function of the fact that the amount of data regarding the reliability and validity of the PEET is quite limited. In fact, the only available psychometric information is presented in a 1983 article from *Developmental Behavioral Pediatrics* (Blackman, Levine, Markowitz, & Aufseeser, 1983). The first three of the four authors of this article are the same individuals as those who prepared the Examiner's Manual.

The Blackman et al. (1983) article provides background information as well as reliability and validity data for an earlier form of the PEET that was administered to a more or less "normal" community sample of 201 children and to a clinic sample of 59 subjects. These two samples of children represented participants in the Brookline Early Education Project (BEEP), a diagnostic and educational program aimed toward ascertaining the effects of providing school-based services to community families with young children.

In the two samples studied, a classification system of identifying children as manifesting behaviors of either "possible concern" or "no concern" was established. For 62 subjects, the percentage of agreement between examiners and observers on groups of items from the PEET ranged from 93.5 to 100 with corresponding kappa coefficients falling between .77 and 1.00, although caution needs to be exercised in interpreting these data in the light of the great imbalance in the proportions of individuals falling in the two categories of concern. Promising validity data were obtained in terms of significant differences in responses to key items between members of the community sample and those of the clinic sample. Correlations between the number of possible concerns within categories of the PEET and corresponding conceptually similar portions of the McCarthy Index Scales varied between .26

and .63 for the community sample of 201 subjects—all correlations being significant beyond the .001 level. Empirically derived normative data appeared to be missing from the manual except to the extent that means and standard deviations provide limited information.

In summary, the PEET as a clinical procedure has considerable merit in that it can furnish useful information for diagnosis and possibly prescription. Far more data are needed, however, to establish both the reliability and validity of the many scales. The consumer must use great care, as the authors have recommended, in the interpretation and use of the scores derived from the scales. It is to be hoped that many additional investigations will be completed in the near future so that the results obtained can be incorporated within a revised manual that will permit both a reliable and valid assessment of the whole child.

REVIEWER'S REFERENCE

Blackman, J. A., Levine, M. D., Markowitz, M. T., & Aufseeser, C. L. (1983). The Pediatric Extended Examination at Three: A system for diagnostic clarification of problematic three-year-olds. *Developmental Behavioral Pediatrics, 4*, 143.

Review of the Pediatric Extended Examination at Three by HOI K. SUEN, Associate Professor of Educational Psychology, Pennsylvania State University, State College, PA:

The Pediatric Extended Examination at Three (PEET) is a relatively comprehensive assessment tool for the detection and clarification of problems with learning, attention, and behavior in children 3 to 4 years of age. As a result of the large variability in development and behavior of children at this age, results from PEET can best be regarded as descriptive and tentative. The authors quite correctly caution potential users that PEET should be used in conjunction with other evaluative input and vision and hearing tests, as well as data from repeated observations.

PEET is an individually administered evaluation procedure in which a child is asked to perform a series of 28 tasks. Some tasks contain several similar subitems (e.g., asking a child to repeat a series of words one at a time). The reported administration time along with physical examinations and visual screening ranges between 30 and 45 minutes. Because PEET requires a lengthy one-to-one evaluation, it is not suited for large-scaled screening purposes.

It is suitable, however, for follow-up isolation of potential areas of concern after an initial screening test or referral.

The samples used for the norming, reliability estimation, and validity analyses of PEET consisted of a small (201 subjects) self-selected community sample from the Boston area and a clinic sample of 59 subjects from a hospital in Boston. Of the mothers of the community sample, 55% has a bachelor's degree or more. While 48% of the subjects were males, the ethnic composition of the community sample was not reported. Among the subjects in the clinic sample, 80% were males. It is clear that the sizes and characteristics of the samples employed in the development of PEET have severely limited the generalizability of the norms as well as evidence of reliability and validity. The use of PEET for subjects outside of the Boston area and/or with characteristics different from the norming sample will necessitate the establishment of local norms and the reassessment of reliability and validity.

The authors reported good interrater agreement indices (proportion agreements average .96, kappa coefficients range from .77 to 1.00) in classifying subjects as "possible concern" versus "no concern" in the five areas of developmental attainment assessment. In PEET, various information is also combined to yield scores in three "channels" of communication. The authors reported marginal Cronbach Alpha estimates, ranging from .695 to .731 for the three channel scores. No Cronbach Alpha was reported for the scores on the five areas of developmental attainment. Because some of these areas contain very few items (e.g., 3 items for memory and 4 items for language), had Cronbach Alphas been assessed, they could be expected to be low.

Interrater reliability estimates are generalizable only to raters with similar background and training as those used in an interrater reliability assessment study. As such, it is important to define the characteristics of the raters so that appropriate raters can be used in the future to ensure that the same level of interrater reliability can be expected. In this regard, the authors provided clear information. Specifically, interrater reliabilities were established based on data from the use of pediatricians as raters. However, the authors have gone beyond their data somewhat by suggesting that PEET may be administered by health care personnel in general or a team of physicians, nurses, and special educators. Although raters other than pediatricians may prove to be excellent ones, evidence of their interrater reliabilities has yet to be established.

It is important to note that PEET does not produce an overall score. Rather, a number of scores corresponding to various areas of development and communication are derived. Evidence of concurrent validity was reported for the communication channel scores using the McCarthy Scales of Children's Abilities and known clinical identification as criteria in separate analyses. The strength of these pieces of statistical evidence is generally adequate to suggest that PEET channel scores can be used to differentiate between children with no concerns versus those with concerns in specific channel areas.

No data on predictive validity or construct validity were gathered; nor are they necessary given the relatively modest goal of the instrument. It should be emphasized that, because of this lack of evidence of predictive and/or construct validity, PEET should not be used alone as a diagnostic tool.

Scores on PEET are used to develop profiles. The authors suggest that an area in which a child's score is at least one standard deviation below the mean should be tentatively considered an area of "potential concern." The choice of one standard deviation appears to be arbitrary and implies that about 15% of the children can be expected to be of "potential concern" in each area. Evidence from the concurrent validity studies provided partial support for the appropriateness of the one-standard-deviation cutoff score.

Overall, PEET is a psychometrically sound evaluation tool for the specific purpose of *clarifying* potential developmental areas of concern, given both raters and subjects are similar in characteristics to those used in the Boston studies. It is inappropriate for screening or clinical diagnosis. It can be used, however, as one supplemental source of information in a comprehensive diagnostic system that includes multiple alternative sources of information. The major limitation of PEET is the lack of representativeness of the normative, reliability, and validity samples. Local norms as well as local evidence of reliability and validity are needed. Unless there are sufficient subjects for the establishment of local norms, applications of PEET may not be practical.

[57]

Perceptions of Parental Role Scales.
Purpose: "To measure perceived parental role responsibilities."
Population: Parents.
Publication Date: 1982.
Acronym: PPRS.
Scores: 13 areas in 3 domains: Teaching the Child (Cognitive Development, Social Skills, Handling of Emotions, Physical Health, Norms and Social Values, Personal Hygiene, Survival Skills), Meeting the Child's Basic Needs (Health Care, Food/Clothing/Shelter, Child's Emotional Needs, Child Care), Family as an Interface With Society (Social Institutions, the Family Unit Itself).
Administration: Group.
Price Data, 1988: $20 per 50 scales; $25 per kit including manual (41 pages) and 25 scales.
Time: (15) minutes.
Comments: Self-administered.
Authors: Lucia A. Gilbert and Gary R. Hanson.
Publisher: Marathon Consulting and Press.

Review of the Perceptions of Parental Role Scales by CINDY I. CARLSON, Associate Professor of Educational Psychology, University of Texas at Austin, Austin, TX:

The Perceptions of Parental Role Scales (PPRS) represents a departure from the numerous self-report tests developed to measure parenting style and rather provides a measure of parental role behaviors or responsibilities. The items of the PPRS are reponded to on a 5-point Likert scale ranging from "not at all important as a parental responsibility" to "very important as a parental responsibility." Thus the PPRS actually provides a measure of parental attitudes and beliefs regarding the importance of particular parental roles. The PPRS was developed as a research tool, primarily for dual-worker families. However, it has demonstrated utility in educational and counseling settings.

The PPRS directions for administration and scoring are clear and easy to follow. A manual for the measure is available and adequate. No response set problems in the items are observed. However, because questionnaires regarding parenting can be susceptible to social desirability, evaluation of this response bias is encouraged for researchers using the PPRS. Limitations of the PPRS include the requirement of an eighth grade reading level and English reading knowledge to complete the measure.

Regarding the psychometric quality of the PPRS, reliability studies have demonstrated both high internal consistency, with alpha coefficients in the .81 to .91 range, and high 1-month test-retest reliability, with coefficients ranging from .69 to .90 across subscales. Thus, the reliability of the PPRS is very good.

The high internal consistency reliability coefficients demonstrate that for each of the scales, the items reflect the same behavioral domain. The criterion-related validity of the PPRS has barely been examined. In the only available study of criterion validity, females were found to score significantly higher than males on a majority of the parenting responsibilities consistent with predictions based on previous research of marital roles. Regarding construct validity, the PPRS is clearly embedded within the theoretical frameworks of role theory and socialization theory. The 13 scales of the PPRS, however, are moderately to highly intercorrelated, suggesting that the scales are measuring aspects of the same construct rather than distinct constructs. Furthermore, an examination of the intercorrelations of the scales by domain suggests that scales are not more highly correlated within than across domains. Therefore, it would appear inappropriate for researchers to derive domain scores from the PPRS.

High intercorrelation of scales is generally considered an undesirable psychometric characteristic. The authors of the PPRS argue that the intercorrelation of scales is appropriate given the content of the measure. The high intercorrelation of scales does indicate that parental role is not a differentiated construct as measured by the PPRS. Moreover, the use of the highly correlated mean individual scale scores will be problematic for certain types of statistical analyses commonly used in research. The PPRS authors acknowledge that a factor analysis might produce a smaller number of scales that would account for the variance of the measure but argue against the desirability of this goal given the rational/intuitive development of the scales of the measure. Given the lack of empirical support for the existing scale differentiation researchers using the PPRS may consider factor scores as one possible solution to the scale intercorrelation dilemma.

To summarize the validity status of the PPRS, the rational derivation of scales has provided internally consistent scales, which all reflect to a greater or lesser extent the construct of parental role, but that do not empirically support a further differentiation of the parental role construct. The lack of criterion-related validity data currently limits possible evaluation of the usefulness and meaning of the scales of the PPRS.

As is common with measures developed for research purposes, the PPRS needs more normative data. Furthermore, descriptive data on the PPRS are extremely limited. The measure was developed with a white, middle-class, university-employed sample and was subsequently administered to a Midwestern rural and urban sample. Additional characteristics of these samples are not provided in the manual. The lack of adequate sample descriptions seriously limits the ability of users to meaningfully interpret scores on the PPRS or to evaluate the generalizability of the measure.

An additional concern regarding the PPRS is the lack of attention, both in development and psychometric evaluation, to child development. It has been established that parenting practices shift with the development of their children. Although the PPRS authors acknowledge in their directions to respondents that some of the questionnaire items are more appropriate for a younger child and others for an older child, there has been no systematic investigation of the impact of a respondent's varying experiences with children of different developmental stages. For example, do childless couples, parents with preschoolers, and parents with adolescents all respond similarly to this measure? The failure of the authors to either examine this question or to provide data regarding the ages and number of children of parents in their test development sample is another serious limitation of this measure.

In summary, the PPRS provides a reliable measure of the perceived importance of a variety of parenting activities. Given the dearth of measures with this particular focus, the PPRS provides a valuable contribution to the measurement of parental attitudes for research and educational use. The usefulness of the PPRS, however, is currently limited by a lack of descriptive and criterion-related validity studies. Parent perceptions of role responsibili-

ties can be expected to vary by numerous mediating variables including ethnicity, socioeconomic status, family structure, and child-rearing experience, which have not yet been examined in validation studies of the PPRS. In addition, the possibility of a social desirability response bias must be ruled out in the PPRS. Thus the PPRS demonstrates research and educational potential that can be ascertained only with additional empirical investigation.

Review of the Perceptions of Parental Role Scales by MARK W. ROBERTS, Professor of Clinical Psychology, Idaho State University, Pocatello, ID:

The Perceptions of Parental Role Scales (PPRS) was designed to measure adult perceptions of a comprehensive set of parenting responsibilities. Each of the 13 scales consists of 5 to 7 items, with 78 items in all. The response format is a 5-point rating (1 = not at all; 3 = moderately important; 5 = very important) of "how important you believe each item is as a parental responsibility during the various stages of rearing a child under normal circumstances." Testing time is reported at 15 minutes. Respondents require at least an eighth grade reading level.

The PPRS is designed for use by social scientists investigating group perceptions of parental roles and the many variables that might influence those perceptions (Gilbert & Hanson, 1983). An initial pool of 200 items was constructed following a literature review. Item analyses were performed to select items that most adults agreed were "major responsibilities" of parents for both male and female children; gender differences were further minimized by eliminating items that statistically covaried with adult gender. Items were also selected to maximize the internal consistency of each scale and to minimize item correlations with other scales. Consequently, normative data reflect strong endorsements of all scales, low scale variance, and relatively homogeneous item content within scales. Although the manual suggests clinical uses of the PPRS (e.g., comparing spouse perceptions during marital counseling), no published studies are available to support its clinical utility. Furthermore, test construction minimizes potential clinical usefulness by attenuating individual differences.

The internal consistency of the 13 scales appears to be strong. Coefficient alphas range from .81 to .91 (median .86). An unpublished report by Dail (1984) detected alpha coefficients all above .90. Using an earlier version of the PPRS Scales, Gilbert, Hanson, and Davis (1982) reported alpha levels between .80 and .87 for 7 of the eventual 13 scales. Farnill (1985) found alpha levels ranging from .51 to .81 (median = .76) for an abbreviated version of the PPRS. Since items were selected for scale homogeneity, it was not surprising to find high coefficient alphas across four different samples of subjects and three different versions of the PPRS. Test-retest reliability coefficients range across the 13 scales from .69 to .90 (median .82). Standard errors of measurement are not available. For its intended use (group research), however, temporal reliability and internal consistency seem adequate.

Two samples of normative data are presented in the manual. Mean scale scores, scale standard deviations, and mean item scores for each scale are reported. The first sample ($n = 202$) (Gilbert & Hanson, 1983) is more heterogeneous, consisting of randomly selected fulltime university staff. Sex, age, marital status, parenthood, and employment orientation varied. Norms are presented across three nominal dimensions: gender, employment orientation (job vs. career), and married males' spouse employment status. A second more homogeneous sample ($n = 249$) (Dail, 1984) provides norms for married adults under 30 with at least one child. Data are reported by gender and residential categories. Farnill (1985), reporting norms for an Australian sample ($n = 279$) using an abbreviated PPRS Scale, found that Australian adults rank-ordered the PPRS scales quite similarly to Americans (rho = .92 for males and .79 for females). Finally, Gilbert et al. (1982) provided normative data for an earlier version of the PPRS using percent endorsement data. The published norms seem quite adequate for evaluating different subjects from different populations.

Validation of the PPRS is currently insufficient, but shows promise. Content validity is supported by the careful and comprehensive selection of items. Items appear representative of the domain of possible areas of parental responsibility. The need for 13 different scales, however, can be questioned. The median interscale correlation is reported at .56, indicating substantial shared variance. The authors reject the idea of producing more scale independence (e.g., using factor analysis) in order to protect the content validity of the PPRS. Criterion validity of the PPRS can be found in two published and three unpublished data sets. The overwhelming finding across all these sources is that parental gender is associated with a variety of PPRS scale scores. In contrast, most demographic variables (age, ethnicity, employment patterns, marital status, and ages and numbers of children) generally do not correlate with PPRS responding. Both Gilbert and Hanson (1983) and Dail (1984) found females endorsing higher levels of parental responsibility than males. Dail conceptualized different PPRS scales as representing traditional male roles ("instrumental scales") or female roles ("expressive scales"). Women, however, scored higher than men on both composite scores.

The response format of the PPRS items can be changed from rating parental responsibility to rating the preferred agent (self, spouse, or other) for discharging responsibilities or to rating parental satisfaction with current performance. Gilbert (1983), Gilbert, Gram, and Hanson (1983), and Farnill (1985) all reported that both spouses perceive that women assume more responsibility than men for discharging parental duties. Unfortunately, the later two projects reduced the number of PPRS items, rendering the data's association with the original test obscure. Gilbert et al. (1983) examined parental satisfaction with perceived role enactment and found that both sexes tended to rate the female spouse as more functional. Further, women who preferred low spouse and low other involvement with parenting were more satisfied with their own parenting than women who wanted higher levels of husband or other involvement. Intriguingly, neither spouse expected nonfamilial agents to assume much more than 10% to 20% of the responsibility for any parental role, with the exceptions of school-relevant cognitive and physical development.

Finally, the item format of the PPRS can be changed. Gilbert et al. (1982) created a male child and a female child version of the test. Parents generally agreed that most parental responsibilities were applicable regardless of child gender. When parents disagreed, it usually involved the fathers' belief that male children required more parental responsibility than female children.

The clear limitation of the PPRS is the possibility that it simply measures the cultural stereotype of parenting roles and the respondents' tendency to endorse socially desirable items. Low scale variance and gender effects are consistent with this interpretation. Criterion validation of each scale against independent measures of parenting behavior would add greatly to the current meaning of PPRS scores. Currently, an individual can be empirically identified as statistically deviant on a given scale. Such deviance, however, could reflect different beliefs, different parenting behaviors, and/or a different inclination to endorse socially desirable items. Therefore, the PPRS cannot be currently recommended as a test of valid individual differences. In contrast, the PPRS provides good normative data and serves as a good item pool for researchers interested in measuring adult perceptions of parenting responsibilities.

REVIEWER'S REFERENCES

Gilbert, L. A., Hanson, G. R., & Davis, B. (1982). Perceptions of parental role responsibilities: Differences between mothers and fathers. *Family Relations, 31*, 261-269.
Gilbert, L. A. (1983). *Working fathers: Parenting in contemporary society.* Paper presented at the annual meeting of the American Psychological Association, Anaheim, CA.
Gilbert, L. A., Gram, A., & Hanson, G. (1983). *Preferred parenting: Comparisons of working women and men.* Paper presented at the annual meeting of the American Psychological Association, Anaheim, CA.
Gilbert, L. A., & Hanson, G. R. (1983). Perceptions of parental role responsibilities among working people: Development of a comprehensive measure. *Journal of Marriage and the Family, 45*, 203-212.
Dail, P. W. (1984). Possible television influence on parental socialization: Implications for parent education (Doctoral dissertation, University of Wisconsin-Madison, 1983). *Dissertation Abstracts International, 44A*, 1712A.
Farnill, D. (1985). *Perceptions of parental responsibilities for children's career development: A neglected area.* Unpublished manuscript, Victoria College, Australia.

[58]
Personal Style Assessment.
Purpose: To assess an individual's personal style of communication.
Population: Adults.
Publication Dates: 1980–87.
Scores, 4: Thinker, Intuitor, Sensor, Feeler.
Administration: Group.
Manual: No manual.
Price Data, 1988: $40 per set of 20 including tests and answer sheets, information ('87, 4 pages), and instructor guidelines ('80, 2 pages).
Time: (15–25) minutes.
Comments: Self-administered, self-scored.

Author: Training House, Inc.
Publisher: Training House, Inc.

Review of the Personal Style Assessment by CATHY W. HALL, Assistant Professor of Psychology, East Carolina University, Greenville, NC:

The Personal Style Assessment is a measure of an individual's communication style and is designed to be used with adults. It is based on Carl Jung's theory of four psychological functions: thinking, feeling, intuiting, and sensing. Although a person is capable of using each of these functions, Jung's premise is that one function typically will dominate (superior function) and the second strongest function will usually be an auxiliary function to the first. The weaker functions may be repressed and not recognized at the conscious level. The preferable balance would be for all four functions to be equally developed. However, this is thought to occur only when the self has become actualized, and this is never fully achieved (Jung, 1971; Hall & Lindzey, 1978).

The purpose of the Personal Style Assessment is to provide a measure of each of these four functions. Four scores are computed: Thinker, Intuitor, Sensor, and Feeler. The scores are obtained by having the person respond to 10 groups of four words each. A 4 is assigned to the word that best characterizes the individual, 3 for the next best, then 2, and finally a 1 for the word that is least descriptive. The words have been assigned to one of the four scales, and a score for each scale is computed based on the person's ratings of these descriptors. The form is self-administered and self-scored.

No information was presented concerning how the descriptors were chosen or assigned to the four categories; nor were any data reported concerning the scores obtained through the self-administration. Standardization, reliability, and validity information is notably absent. Once an individual has obtained the four scores, no process is offered to judge whether significant differences exist among the scores. In fact, no treatment of the auxiliary functions and their purposes is delineated.

In addition to the above-mentioned problems in regard to standards for test development, several questions arise concerning the theoretical assumptions made by the Personal Style Assessment. Supposedly, the score is able to give the individual an understanding of his/her personal style of communicating. The authors state: "Our success in relating to others depends on the degree to which our communication style is 'in sync' with the other person's. By knowing the cues and clues that indicate a person's communication style, we are able to modify our own style to narrow the gap." Although the Personal Style Assessment *might* give an understanding to an individual about his/her own superior function, it is not at all clear how one would readily recognize another's style—let alone be able to quickly change one's style to "fit" the situation. This problem in adapting communication styles seems particularly acute because the theoretical presumption is the weaker functions may be repressed and unconscious. Is this assessment to be used by only those who have come close to being fully actualized? Jung postulated this was a prerequisite to acquiring a balance among all four functions. The authors do provide a brief four-page overview of "Your Four Communication Styles." Strengths and weaknesses of each primary style are presented as well as "typical telephone behavior," "typical office decor," and "typical style of dress." Is this how another's style is determined?

Jung's typology has been applied to various settings, and O'Brien (1985) provides a brief overview of some of the assessment devices that purport to measure typology. Other measures such as the Myers-Briggs Type Indicator (Myers & McCaulley, 1985; 10:206) provide far better validated instruments than the Personal Style Assessment. The Personal Style Assessment raises more questions than it answers and appears to be a hastily developed and superficial assessment device without any thought to proper standards for psychological test development or theoretical postulates. Jung's theory is highly complex. An individual does not gain a meaningful understanding of these theoretical assumptions by using a brief self-administered, self-scored form.

REVIEWER'S REFERENCES

Jung, C. (1971). A psychological theory of types. In *Psychological types: The collected works of C. G. Jung* (Vol. 6). Princeton, NJ: Princeton University Press.

Hall, C., & Lindzey, G. (1978). *Theories of Personality* (3rd ed.). New York: John Wiley & Sons.

Myers, I., & McCaulley, M. *Manual: A guide to the development and use of the Myers-Briggs Type Indicator.* Palo Alto, CA: Consulting Psychologists Press.

O'Brien, R. (1985). Using Jung more (and etching him in stone less). *Training, 22* (5), 53-66.

Review of the Personal Style Assessment by GERALD L. STONE, *Professor of Counseling Psychology and Director, University Counseling Service, The University of Iowa, Iowa City, IA:*

The Personal Style Assessment (PSA) is a paper-and-pencil self-assessment exercise. The instrument is designed to identify characteristics associated with four styles of communication—Intuitor, Thinker, Feeler, and Sensor. The PSA is linked to Jung's type theory as interpreted by John Bledsoe in an article in a 1976 issue of *Training,* a magazine concerned with human resources.

In the Self-Assessment exercise, participants are presented with two sheets. The first sheet contains the instructions, examples, and 10 groups of four words. Within each group of words, participants are asked to assign a 4 to the word that best characterizes them, a 3 to the next best, a 2 to the next best, and a 1 to the word that is least descriptive. The record sheet, a noncarbon reproducing scoring sheet with scoring directions, enables each participant to sum his or her scores for each of the four communication styles.

Although the two-page Self-Assessment exercise is reported to take 5 minutes to complete, the guidelines for the PSA embed the exercise in a training workshop situation. The guidelines recommend completion of the Self-Assessment followed by explanations based on Jung's work and a reprint of a four-page article titled "Your Four Communicating Styles." After hearing the explanations and reading the article, discussion questions and dyadic exercises (e.g., "guess the style of another") are recommended to the participants. Cautions are briefly mentioned about stereotyping and value-laden tendencies ("Which is the best type?"). It is suggested that each person makes use of all four styles, although the mixture differs from person to person.

There is no manual. The instrument, as well as the workshop format, are presented uncontaminated by evaluation and/or psychometric data. There is no attempt to link the instrument to other related instruments (e.g., Myers-Briggs Type Indicator, MBTI; 10:206), nor is there any evidence of behavioral validations for these communication styles.

In summary, the PSA can be categorized only as a "parlor game" until validity evidence for the instrument is presented. Although the MBTI is not without problems (e.g., type versus continuous dimensions), validation data have been presented, thus suggesting those interested in communication analyses from a Jungian perspective may be better served by the MBTI.

REVIEWER'S REFERENCE

Bledsoe, J. L. (1976). Why, when, and how to use each of your four communicating styles. *Training, 13*, 18-21.

[59]
The Pictorial Scale of Perceived Competence and Social Acceptance for Young Children.

Purpose: Measures "perceived competence and perceived social acceptance" in young children.
Population: Preschool through second grade.
Publication Dates: 1980–83.
Scores, 4: Cognitive Competence, Peer Acceptance, Physical Competence, Maternal Acceptance.
Administration: Individual.
Forms, 2: Preschool/Kindergarten, First/Second Grade.
Price Data, 1989: $15 per booklet of pictures (preschool/kindergarten for girls ['80, 54 pages], preschool/kindergarten for boys ['80, 54 pages], first/second grade for girls ['81, 54 pages], first/second grade for boys ['81, 54 pages]); $7 per manual ('83, 21 pages).
Time: Administration time not reported.
Comments: Downward extension of the Perceived Competence Scale for Children.
Authors: Susan Harter and Robin Pike in collaboration with Carole Efron, Christine Chao, and Beth Ann Bierer.
Publisher: Susan Harter.

TEST REFERENCES

1. Anderson, P. L., & Adams, P. J. (1985). The relationship of five-year-olds' academic readiness and perceptions of competence and acceptance. *The Journal of Educational Research, 79*, 114-118.
2. Simmons, C. H., & Zumpf, C. (1986). The gifted child: Perceived competence, prosocial moral reasoning, and charitable donations. *The Journal of Genetic Psychology, 147*, 97-105.
3. Lobato, D., Barbour, L., Hall, L. J., & Miller, C. T. (1987). Psychosocial characteristics of preschool siblings of handicapped and nonhandicapped children. *Journal of Abnormal Child Psychology, 15*, 329-338.

Review of The Pictorial Scale of Perceived Competence and Social Acceptance for Young Children by WILLIAM B. MICHAEL, Professor of Education and Psychology, University of Southern California, Los Angeles, CA:

In both the Preschool-Kindergarten and the First and Second Grade versions of The Pictori-al Scale of Perceived Competence and Social Acceptance for Young Children, each of the four scales—Cognitive Competence, Physical Competence, Peer Acceptance, and Maternal Acceptance—consists of six items comprising two pictures placed side by side. Each pair of pictures portrays an activity having contrasting levels of perceived competence or social acceptance. The 12 items in the first two of the four scales represent what the authors have termed Perceived Competence; the other 12 items in the third and fourth scales, Social Acceptance. Each of the two versions of the instrument geared to different age levels has two forms with parallel items, one for boys and the other for girls, with the only appreciable difference being the placement of the individual of central interest (usually intended to be the examinee in a learning or social situation) in the picture having the same gender as the subject.

Within each of the two 6-item scales pertaining to perceived competence, for three of the items the picture in the left-hand position represents high competence, and for the remaining three items, the picture in the left-hand position reflects low competence. A comparable statement can be made for the placement of pictures in the two 6-item scales portraying social acceptance.

In this individually administered scale, the examiner shows the subject simultaneously the two pictures in an item and tells the subject what is taking place in the situation portrayed. Then the examinee is asked to pick the child in the picture most like him or her and to indicate by pointing to one of four appropriate circles (two circles below each picture) whether that child is "a lot like him or her (the big circle)" or "just a little like him or her (the smaller circle)." The examinee who points to the larger circle associated with the picture revealing the presence of perceived competence or of social acceptance receives 3 points; the child who points to the smaller circle corresponding to the picture reflecting perceived competence or social acceptance earns 3 points. If the picture revealing low perceived competence or social acceptance is chosen as being like the respondent, 2 points are assigned to the small circle and 1 point to the large circle. Thus for each of the four scales, the total number of points may range from 6 to 24. The use of four alternatives receiving differential weights probably serves to reduce the presence of response sets associated with social desirability or acquiescence, as well as possible random selection of alternatives (guessing).

In the procedural manual that accompanies the test booklets, the authors have constructed what they term the "Teacher's Rating Scale of Child's Actual Competence and Social Acceptance." Its items parallel the intended content of each of the six items in the first three of the four 6-item scales administered to the children. The scale pertaining to maternal acceptance was not duplicated because the authors thought, quite appropriately, that the teacher would not be in a position in most instances to formulate accurate judgments. Also parallel to the items in the first three scales to which the children responded are four alternatives for each item description that the teacher selects, with the statements of "really true," "pretty true," "sort of true," or "not very true" carrying 4, 3, 2, or 1 points in the scoring procedure respectively. The rating scales completed by the teachers provide a basis for establishing the degree of congruence between the perceptions of teachers and those of the children in their classes. Obviously, substantial discrepancies point to the need for the teacher to increase her or his level of communication with the child and to try to determine the basis for the discrepancies noted.

Unfortunately, the publication of the very attractively prepared test forms was probably premature, as a technical manual affording information regarding validity, reliability, and normative data is not available. At the time of the preparation of this review, it was necessary for the potential consumer interested in psychometric data to consult a 1984 article, written by the two authors of the test, that appeared in *Child Development*. In this well-done article, the authors have employed subsamples of 90 preschool, 56 kindergarten, 65 first-grade, and 44 second-grade children primarily from middle-class families of Anglo ethnicity in the Denver, Colorado area to obtain means, standard deviations, internal-consistency estimates of reliability, and intercorrelations of subscales. In addition, oblique factor analyses were done of the intercorrelations among the items for two subsamples of preschool and kindergarten children and of first- and second-grade pupils to provide evidence of the factorial validity of the instrument.

For the Cognitive, Physical, Peer, and Maternal scales, reliability coefficients relative to various subgroups fell between .52 and .79, .50 and .66, .74 and .83, and .72 and .85, respectively. The two combined scales of 12 items in the competence and acceptance domains yielded corresponding reliability coefficients ranging between .66 and .80, and between .84 and .89, respectively. Both factor analyses revealed two correlated dimensions that were clearly identified as Perceived Competence and Social Acceptance. The 12 items in the Cognitive Competence and Physical Competence scales and the 12 items in the Peer Acceptance and Maternal Acceptance scales, respectively, defined the two dimensions of competence and acceptance. Intercorrelations among subscales tended to range, for the most part, between .30 and .60, with the exception of the two acceptance scales that exhibited correlations between .62 and .80.

In summary, this instrument can be anticipated to provide important information to teachers and parents concerning the self-confidence children express in their perceived competencies and perceived levels of acceptance. The relative ease of administration and the seemingly intrinsic interest of the items in sustaining the motivation of the examinees are positive features. Very much needed are normative data and additional reliability and validity studies with numerous samples of children from families of diverse cultural backgrounds and socioeconomic levels, so that more adequate interpretations can be made of the scores obtained. At the moment, the use of these scales for research purposes is to be encouraged. Other indicators of perceived cognitive capabilities and of perceived relationships in interpersonal relations are needed to supplement any data obtained from the four scales. It is hoped the authors will continue to carry out the necessary additional research and developmental work to establish this instrument as one that can provide valid assessment of early childhood behaviors hypothesized within its structure.

Review of The Pictorial Scale of Perceived Competence and Social Acceptance for Young Children by SUSAN M. SHERIDAN, Assistant Professor of Educational Psychology, University of Utah, Salt Lake City, UT:

The Pictorial Scale of Perceived Competence and Social Acceptance for Young Children (PSPCSA) is a self-report instrument designed to assess perceptions of young children in four domains (i.e., Cognitive Competence, Physical Competence, Peer Acceptance, Maternal Acceptance). The test uses a unique item format ("structured response format"), which is sensitive to the developmental capacities of young children. This format is assumed to allow children to identify more readily to test items, and to make meaningful differentiations between possible responses. The PSPCSA has some characteristics that make it a potential addition to social-emotional assessment batteries. However, several conceptual and methodological limitations reduce its overall usefulness.

MANUAL. The manual accompanying the PSPCSA provides good administration guidelines and scoring criteria. Verbal and procedural instructions are clear and concise, and they assist in making the test easy to administer. Likewise, individual scoring and profile sheets (included in an appendix) allow for simple calculation and plotting of scores.

Although the PSPCSA is "user-friendly" in terms of administration and scoring, the manual is extremely incomplete and fails to meet the *Standards for Educational and Psychological Testing* (AERA, APA, & NCME; 1985). The authors refer test users to a related publication (Harter & Pike, 1984) that describes the underlying theory, rationale, scale construction efforts, and psychometric properties of the instrument. Given that these critical issues are not presented in the manual, there is great potential for general misuse and/or misinterpretation of test data.

STANDARDIZATION. A limited normative group was used in the standardization of the PSPCSA. Although 255 preschool through second grade subjects were included, preschoolers appeared to be overrepresented ($n = 90$), and second graders appeared to be underrepresented ($n = 44$). All subjects were from middle-class neighborhoods, and 96% were Caucasian. Thus, caution must be exercised when using the test with children from other socioeconomic, cultural, and educational groups.

RELIABILITY/VALIDITY. Psychometric support for the PSPCSA is equivocal. Alpha correlation coefficients for the total test are adequate (.88 for the preschool/kindergarten sample and .87 for the first/second-grade sample). Internal consistencies for the Acceptance factor is also good (alpha = .87 for the preschool/kindergarten sample and .86 for the first/second-grade sample); however, they are lower for the Competence factor (alpha = .76 and .77 for the preschool/kindergarten and first/second-grade samples, respectively). As expected, individual subscale reliabilities are the lowest, with an alpha range of .53 to .83 across samples.

According to the authors, factor analysis with the PSPCSA revealed a two-factor solution, with the competence subscales defining one factor and the acceptance subscales defining the second. However, even with the very liberal procedure that was used (oblique promax rotation), very low correlations were obtained, especially for the preschool/kindergarten sample (with individual item loadings ranging from .19 to .58 on Factor 1 and from .23 to .70 on Factor 2). Thus, the degree to which we can interpret separate factors as reflective of the constructs they are purported to measure is questioned.

Harter and Pike (1984) provide evidence of convergent, discriminant, and predictive validity for the PSPCSA. However, because only limited data are presented, the studies reported may be inadequate in estimating the accuracy of the test with larger and more diverse groups of children.

TEST CONSTRUCTION/ITEM SELECTION. The construction of the PSPCSA is not described by the authors. However, it appears items were selected based on subjective, rather than empirical (i.e., item analysis), methods. Some of the pictures used to depict various skills and behaviors appear inconsistent with their corresponding verbal descriptions, and may be misrepresentative of the intended content or purpose of the item. Relatedly, several of the stimulus pictures fail to differentiate adequately between the intended behavioral poles, and may be confusing to young children who rely on pictorial cues when making judgments. Thus, child responses may be dependent upon an individual's interpretation of test items, rather than the test stimuli.

Additional problems with test items are apparent. For example, some items appear developmentally and conceptually inconsistent, such as "Stays overnight at friends' house" and "Eats dinner at friends' house." These items appear on the Peer Acceptance subscale at the preschool/kindergarten level; however, the degree to which children at this age normatively engage in these activities is questioned. These same items appear on the Maternal Acceptance subscale at the first/second-grade level, yet they seem to be more dependent on peer-mediated characteristics than on maternal relationship factors. The conceptual ambiguity this presents is apparent.

INTERPRETATION. Related to problems with discrete items, the interpretive framework for this test is extremely vague. A high degree of intercorrelation between subscales exists. This presents confusion regarding what the "separate" subscales actually measure, and may increase interpretive errors for users who incorrectly perceive each as an independent domain. This, coupled with the fact that factor analysis does not support the maintenance of four separate subscales, suggests emphasis should be placed on factor scores rather than individual subtest scores. However, the authors explicitly encourage the use of separate subscale scores in interpreting individual profiles. Low, medium, and high ratings for each subtest are suggested; however, these appear to be based on arbitrary cutoff scores rather than empirical support.

SUPPLEMENTAL MATERIALS. In addition to the standard test materials, a Teacher Rating Scale is supplied which corresponds by item to the child self-report. As an additional index of external validity, correlations between child and teacher ratings were calculated by the authors. Although significant correlations were obtained for the competence ratings, they were negligible for peer acceptance. However, items on the Teacher Rating Scale are poorly defined and subjective, and no psychometric evidence is available to support its use. Thus, the use of the TRS is discouraged, awaiting empirical documentation.

SUMMARY. In sum, The Pictorial Scale of Perceived Competence and Social Acceptance for Young Children has some characteristics (i.e., appealing test format, ease in implementation and scoring, acceptable reliability) that increase its potential in social-emotional assessments. However, several limitations of the scale are evident, including its inadequate test manu-al, limited standardization sample, questionable factorial validity, insufficient data on test construction, and lack of an interpretive framework. The authors fail to provide sufficient guidelines to enhance the clinical utility of the test, and the potential for misinterpretation is great. Additional research is needed to support its use in research and practice.

REVIEWER'S REFERENCES

Harter, S., & Pike, R. (1984). The pictorial scale of perceived competence and social acceptance for young children. *Child Development, 55*, 1969-1982.

American Educational Research Association, American Psychological Association, & National Council on Measurement in Education. (1985). *Standards for educational and psychological testing.* Washington, DC: American Pscyhological Association, Inc.

[60]
Pollack-Branden Inventory.

Purpose: "To identify students who are in need of remediation, that is not readily diagnosed by standardized tests, and may be manifested in certain language weaknesses symptomatic of dyslexia."
Population: Grades 1–12.
Publication Date: 1986.
Acronym: P.B.I.
Scores: Item scores only.
Administration: Individual in part.
Price Data: Available from publisher.
Authors: Cecelia Pollack and Ann Branden.
Publisher: Book-Lab.
  a) SPELLING INVENTORY.
  Time: (8–10) minutes.
  b) DICTATED SENTENCES AND HANDWRITING.
  Levels, 2: Grades 3–5, 6–12.
  Time: (9–12) minutes.
  c) SOUND/SYMBOL INVENTORY.
  Administration: Individual.
  Time: (6–8) minutes.
  d) INVENTORY OF ORAL READING SKILLS.
  Administration: Individual.
  Time: (7–10) minutes.
  e) MATHEMATICS INVENTORY.
  Time: (15–20) minutes.
  f) WRITTEN COMPOSITION.
  Population: Grades 3 and over.
  Time: Administration time not reported.

Review of the Pollack-Branden Inventory by ANNE ANASTASI, Professor Emeritus of Psychology, Fordham University, Bronx, NY:

Although the authors do not specify the type of user for whom this inventory was designed, it is apparent from statements in the User's Guide that it is intended for teachers. Its object is twofold: first, as an informal screening instrument for identifying potential dyslexics, who will then be more fully assessed by psychologists or learning disability specialists (p. 28); second, as a guide for the teacher in correcting deficiencies through an Individualized Educational Plan (IEP) prepared for each student (p. 20).

COVERAGE. Four of the six parts of the Pollack-Branden Inventory (P.B.I.) are directed primarily to problems in the use of written symbols, considered to be symptomatic of dyslexia. These include phonics, spelling, dictation, handwriting, decoding, and the handling of written grammar, syntax, and punctuation. It should be noted that on the Sound/Symbol Inventory, an adult or child who has not been taught reading by the phonics method would need considerable preliminary explanation and pretest practice to produce the sound of visually presented letters and letter combinations, such as c, x, scr, and nk, occurring outside of normal word contexts.

Although the P.B.I. was designed principally to detect errors in the structural aspects of symbolic language, it also touches on difficulties in conceptualization, in both oral reading and written expression. The latter is assessed in the optional Written Composition. A short Mathematics Inventory is also included, consisting of 28 simple computational problems, which are worked out in the Student Booklet, so that the teacher can identify the nature of the errors.

ADMINISTRATION AND SCORING. Any one of the inventories may be used singly or in combination with one or more of the others. Results from the different inventories are not aggregated into an overall measure. All instructions for administering the P.B.I. are given in the User's Guide. For the four group-administered inventories, students record all responses in the single Student Booklet. Items are arranged in increasing order of difficulty; broad guidelines are provided for entry and exit cutoffs for different grade levels, from Grade 2 (or 3) to Grade 6 (or 7) and up. For the two individually administered inventories, the student reads the items aloud from the Student Booklet and the teacher records the responses on "Error Recording Copies" and "Comprehension Questions" copies (for the Inventory of Oral Reading Skills), for which ditto masters are included in the Appendix to the User's Guide.

The Appendix also provides Error Analysis Sheets for each of the six inventories, on which the errors are classified and the number of errors in each category is recorded. On the basis of the information on these Error Analysis Sheets, the teacher rates the student's performance on each inventory by checking one of three levels: mastered, partially mastered, or not yet mastered. No guidelines are provided for this threefold evaluation; presumably the teacher judges mastery level in terms of his/her expectation for the appropriate grade level. On some inventories, several aspects of performance are evaluated. For example, in Dictated Sentences and Handwriting, there is a summary evaluation for errors (covering punctuation, capitalization, and spelling) and another for handwriting deficiencies. For the Inventory of Oral Reading Skills, there are separate mastery evaluations for rate, accuracy, fluency, and comprehension.

The User's Guide includes a case study, which is actually a demonstration of the recording and scoring procedures, rather than a case study in the usual, clinical sense. There is also an Individual Record Form and a Class Record Form for summarizing mastery levels on each inventory in the whole battery.

The organization and format of the User's Guide could be substantially improved. It is now necessary to keep turning pages back and forth from text to Appendix in order to locate the relevant forms. Moreover, the headings introducing each separate inventory are inconspicuous in type and position on the page. It would have been helpful for the user to have the ditto masters of different record sheets (now in the Appendix) as a separate packet. It would have been still better to have all the necessary record sheets available for use in the required quantities.

INDIVIDUALIZED EDUCATIONAL PLAN (IEP). Insofar as can be determined from the User's Guide, the IEP for each student (p. 20, pp. 27–28) is essentially a translation of the entries on the Error Analysis Sheets for the six inventories into a set of educational objectives. These objectives call for teaching the specific items where errors occurred, such as particular misspelled words.

CONSTRUCTION OF THE P.B.I. The User's Guide contains one paragraph explaining the basis for selecting both the variables to be assessed in the six parts of the inventory and the specific items within each. Essentially, the instrument was developed through the authors' personal clinical experience. The short section labeled "Test Development" opens and closes as follows: "The authors have had the experience of diagnosing and remediating dyslexic students over a period of sixteen years with over 1,000 subjects of all ages ranging from first grade through adulthood . . . . The present P.B.I. represents a distillation of their experience" (p. 4). No data (quantitative or qualitative) are reported regarding norms, reliability, or validity, nor are any other published sources cited.

OVERVIEW. The P.B.I. is not a test in the usual psychometric sense. In its present form, it consists of a set of carefully chosen materials that can be used by experienced teachers who have some knowledge of dyslexia and of the phonics method of teaching reading. The authors do not call the P.B.I. a test, but use the term "inventory," both for the entire battery and for the separate parts. Nevertheless, even when all qualifications and limitations are taken into account, it would be desirable to make available some empirical data, in whatever form, about such questions as how well teachers are able to use the materials, what difficulties they encounter in administering and scoring the inventories, how children screened by the P.B.I. as potential dyslexics fare when examined comprehensively by professional specialists and when judged by classroom performance, what level of achievement actually corresponds to mastery at different grade levels, how effective the Individualized Educational Plan is, and to what extent it leads to improvement beyond the specific items covered by the P.B.I.

Review of the Pollack-Branden Inventory by VERNA HART, Professor, Program in Special Education, School of Education, University of Pittsburgh, Pittsburgh, PA:

The Pollack-Branden Inventory (P.B.I.) is a criterion-referenced test designed to generate a profile of characteristics of students with dyslexia as well as generate a plan for remediation of their difficulties. Its title states it is "For Identification of Learning Disabilities, Dyslexia and Classroom Dysfunction."

The P.B.I. is based on the authors' experience diagnosing and remediating students with dyslexia and presents what they call a "dyslexic pattern." With the current professional interest in differentiating students with learning disabilities, dyslexia, and reading disabilities, the title of the test makes it seem particularly relevant. However, careful examination of the contents of the inventory results in questioning its ability to diagnose the targeted audiences. The main problems center on the lack of information regarding the test construction, its reliability, and its validity. The User's Guide offers little information regarding any of these.

Because a criterion-referenced test is to generalize from a few items to the broader domain from which those items were sampled, a well-defined domain seems necessary. This appears to be missing in the inventory. Although some broad considerations for identifying dyslexia are noted, they are undocumented and lack specificity. There is a heavy emphasis on phonics and a statement that a knowledge of specific phonic rules must be the basis for reteaching. Auditory and cognitive processing abilities are not assessed. Knowledge of spelling, writing, and computation rules receive great emphasis in the items and error analysis, but there is no documentation that a lack of such knowledge can be used to identify those with dyslexia or learning disabilities.

Further weaknesses are the lack of rationale for the types of items included, documentation of the representativeness of the test items, and the extent to which they measure the traits of learning disabilities, dyslexia, and classroom dysfunction. Information is not provided that would show that the dyslexic or the person with learning disability can be described by using the test scores.

In addition, there are too few items to cover the content tested. For example, 36 spelling words, the total administered to those in grade 6 and up, are analyzed for 26 different types of errors. Although a few of the errors can be found in more than one word, most of the errors examined can be found in only one. With words like *obsequious* and the commonly misspelled *accommodate* among them, one questions whether the score obtained is representative of a person with learning disabilities or dyslexia, or even whether the score represents an individual's ability to use specific spelling rules.

This lack of sufficient numbers of items, as well as lack of item statistics, is seen throughout all of the subinventories. The error analysis to be used for each inventory has a larger number of analyses than the item pool would warrant. There are also cutoff points and timed responses in several of the inventories, but no rationale for them. They are offered as absolutes in one of the subinventories and as "broad guidelines" in another. There are no data regarding the consistency of responses of the students, nor of the scoring, particularly of the Written Composition which has subjective components.

Although the authors state that error analysis rather than numerical scores will identify dyslexia and provide for remediation, scores of all the subinventories are converted to numbers; 1 = mastered, 2 = partially mastered, and 3 = not yet mastered, again with no rationale. These numbers are then transferred to an Individual Record Form. Thus, when looking at the Individual Record Form, it is impossible to determine where the individual difficulties exist for any particular child.

Nearly a third of the text of the brief User's Guide is devoted to writing the Individualized Educational Plan (IEP) and completing the Class Record Form from the results of the inventory. Although the idea is a very good one, the sequence is confusing. After the IEP is written, the guide states "there is a probable indication of dyslexia which should be affirmed by more complete assessment procedures." If the IEP is that mandated by P.L. 94–142, the child would have to be assessed by using more than one appropriately normed instrument and determined to have a learning disability *before* the writing of the IEP, which by law must have certain components and participants. Equally confusing is the Class Record Form with the names of several students and level of mastery noted for each of the subinventories. Instructions are given for the teacher to determine which skills have Level 3s and to teach them to the entire class because all students lack mastery. Does this mean that all of the students in the class have been assessed with the instrument? No additional information is provided, but even assuming such a fact, the Class Record Form could not be used as recommended, for there is no information offered as to the areas within the inventories where the children are experiencing difficulties.

Given the three levels of achievement, criterion-oriented validity is also missing. There is no evidence provided that relates to the question of whether assignment for particular intervention on the basis of scores will result in greater achievement than random assignment, regardless of test scores, to various treatments.

In addition to the problems with test construction, reliability, and validity, the test has several typing, spelling, and other errors. Two of these could affect the test scores: poor sentence structure in the Inventory of Oral Reading Skills, and a dollar-sign ($) requirement for a correct answer in one of the mathematics answers when none is shown in the problem in the student booklet.

Although the idea of a very short, easy-to-administer test to identify learning disabilities, dyslexia, and classroom dysfunction is a good one, this instrument was not constructed with the rigorousness needed to accomplish this goal. Until much more work is completed on the inventory, it should not be used for the purpose designated.

[61]

Pre-School Behaviour Checklist.

Purpose: "To help identify children with emotional and behavioural problems by providing a tool for the systematic and objective description of behaviour."
Population: Ages 2–5.
Publication Date: 1988.
Acronym: PBCL.
Scores: Total score only.
Administration: Group.
Price Data, 1989: £17.20 per administration kit; £5.75 per checklist; £5.70 per manual; £3.40 per scoring overlay.
Time: (8–10) minutes.
Comments: Behavior checklist.
Authors: Jacqueline McGuire and Naomi Richman.
Publisher: NFER-Nelson Publishing Co., Ltd. [England].

Review of the Pre-School Behaviour Checklist by ROGER D. CARLSON, Visiting Associate Professor of Psychology, Whitman College, Walla Walla, WA:

The potential user of the Pre-School Behaviour Checklist (PBCL) must consider the use of this checklist with respect to two issues of paramount importance: the specific content of the items that are included and the criterion used for referring a child for further professional attention.

The authors' choice of the Checklist's items make the PBCL inherently value-laden. The choice must be carefully examined in light of the values of the user and the uses to be made of the checklist. Checklist items seem representative of ones that would be valued by preschool workers. The items are based partly on interviews with preschool workers as to their observations concerning what behaviors are considered problematic in this age group of children.

The potential user must understand that both the purposes of the Checklist's development, as well as the items and results of its use, are developed for the furtherance of institutional or group goals rather than those that are necessarily best for the individual child. The authors are to be commended on their recognition that the results of the Checklist can lead to administrative reform. However, in commenting on potential administrative uses of the scale, the authors fail to suggest questions that keep the focus of attention upon the best interests of the child. Examples are given that imply the thrust of administrative reform is not so much in the direction of criticizing institutional structure and practices as causative of a child's disruptive behavior (reform of institutional structure, aims, goals, and priorities), as it is to make changes that can result in the more effective control of children (staffing shortages, training deficits, comparisons to other institutions). Furthering the best interests of the institution may not always further the best interests of the child.

With institutional goals and values in mind, however, the items seem to be good ones when held up against the validation procedures that were undertaken by the authors. Validity studies included agreements between psychiatric judgments and PBCL scores of 122 children, as well as staff member judgments and PBCL scores of 113 children. In the latter, overall agreement was 81 percent. The PBCL did well in identifying 23 children with behavior problems in a therapeutic day center compared with 123 children in nursery school classes and 67 in local authority day nurseries. The finding that the scores of day nursery children tended to be higher than those of nursery school children coincides with the fact that day nurseries tend to take children with families under stress—

thus giving support for the validity of the PBCL.

A problem endemic to the use of checklists and psychometrics generally is the use of nominally scaled items answered in a binary fashion and then summated into a ratio-scaled score. In the case of the PBCL, the authors created a criterion point for referring children for further counsel. Fortunately, because of careful external validation procedures, the criterion seems to be a well-founded value. Children who had scores exceeding the criterion were those who by and large were judged to be either in need of referral or who were in treatment programs of various kinds.

Although no individual item analyses are reported by the authors, factor and cluster analyses were reported that reveal three groupings of items: conduct/restless (too active, not liked, poor concentration, difficult to manage, etc.), isolated/immature (unclear speech, reluctant to talk, withdrawn from peers, wanders), and emotional (miserable, demands attention, whines, sensitive). Seventy-three scores on the PBCL were correlated with those of a similar instrument, the Preschool Behaviour Questionnaire (Behar & Stringfield, 1974) for the same children, and yielded a Pearson product moment correlation coefficient of .89 ($p < .001$).

Interrater reliability studies revealed 83 percent agreement between raters of the same child (Pearson $r = .68$, $n = 108$, $p < .001$). Agreement between raters in terms of the criterion point selected for referral occurred only 38 percent of the time. The authors suggest that disagreement between raters is due to differences in familiarity with the child, as well as to the authors' deliberate selection of a criterion that would maximize the PBCL's sensitivity. Therefore, the authors report their selection of a criterion point for referral has a tendency to identify false positives rather than to reject false negatives. No statistically significant differences were found between professionals using the checklist with different levels of training (teachers or nursery nurses). Test-retest reliability was found to be respectably high over a 2-week period ($r = .88$, $p < .001$). Measures of internal consistency also were high (Cronbach's alpha = .83, and Spearman-Brown split-half method, $r = .83$).

Overall, for an instrument of its type that attempts to ascertain how well a child fits into a social context and meets social expectations, the PBCL appears to be a very well-researched and documented one. Although the items have been developed on the basis of professionals' judgments of face value, and perhaps are overly arbitrary given the goals, situations, and concerns of the authors, it is not a carelessly conceived checklist. Likewise, although over-reliance on quantification often can lead to overlooking the tangible goals, aims, and concerns of the developer and user of such a checklist, the authors are explicit in stating caveats in the PBCL's development and use, so as to dissuade the user from the inadvertent use of a "number magic."

REVIEWER'S REFERENCE

Behar, L., & Stringfield, S. (1974). A behavior rating scale for the pre-school child. *Developmental Psychology, 10*, 601-610.

Review of the Pre-School Behaviour Checklist by GARY STONER, *Assistant Professor, School Psychology Program, College of Education, University of Oregon, Eugene, OR:*

The Pre-School Behaviour Checklist (PBCL) manual contains the following statement: "The PBCL is designed to help identify children with emotional and behavioural problems by providing a tool for the systematic and objective description of behaviour. It is intended for use with 2- to 5-year-olds and, unlike most checklists, allows staff to look at the severity as well as the incidence of a particular behaviour." Whether the PBCL actually lives up to this description is questionable. In fact, all behavior rating scales provide subjective, indirect measures of behavior, with endorsed items or ratings reflecting a rater's impressions that are influenced by her or his environment, expectations, professional training, and other variables.

The PBCL consists of 22 items, each comprised of three or four alternative descriptions of the behavior or characteristics of young children. Raters are asked to choose the alternative that best describes the child's current behavior. Item selection was based on a combination of the authors' research and experience with preschool children, as well as discussions with staff working in nurseries and preschools in and around London, England.

Apparently as a function of face validity, the authors consider items to be members of five different categories: (*a*) emotional difficulties (5 items); (*b*) conduct problems (5 items); (*c*) capacity to concentrate and play constructively

(3 items); (*d*) social relations (3 items); and (*e*) a catch-all category (5 items) focusing on speech and language, habits, wetting, and soiling. A few items are unclear as to whether the descriptions are of the target child, or of other children and caregivers (e.g., "Seems to be liked by other children" and "Easy to manage and control"). Additionally, several items are composed of alternatives that are potentially confusing to raters in that more than one behavior, adjective, or adverb is used in the description (e.g., the choices for one item are "Rarely demands a great deal of attention," "Sometimes asks for a lot of attention, but can work or play independently," "Frequently demands attention"). An alternative, and perhaps more clear approach, would have items consist of a description (e.g., demands attention) and numerically coded choices indicating frequency (e.g., $0 = rarely$, $1 = sometimes$, and $2 = often$).

Clearly stated administration directions are printed at the beginning of each PBCL; however, the rater is referred to the manual for further details on completing the checklist. The one-paragraph explanation to raters in the manual could be integrated readily with those directions on the checklist to eliminate the need for two sources of directions.

Each item rating is scored either 0, 1, or 2, and these scores are summed to yield a total score. A cutoff score of 12 is suggested for use to screen for children who have "definite problems" and thus are in need of follow-up services.

Empirical support for this cutoff score is minimal. For example, test-retest reliability estimates based on ratings 2 weeks apart by the same raters yielded a .88 correlation, and 91% agreement regarding a child's falling above or below the cutoff score of 12. Another report suggested, however, that with ratings of 108 children by one observer resulting in 29 children above the cutoff score, an independent rating identified 11 of those 29 children (or 38%) in the same category.

In discussing score interpretation, the authors discuss the clinical usefulness of high scores, low scores, and scores above the cutoff point, thus accurately indicating that any given score could be cause for concern for any given child. If any score is important, however, it follows that what is crucial is *how* a child obtains a score, and not the score itself. Also, if *any* score yielded by the instrument is potentially educationally or clinically significant, then these scores may add nothing meaningful about child behaviors beyond information gathered via staff observations and anecdotal reports.

Another criticism of the PBCL is that normative data are not even mentioned in the PBCL Handbook. Within the 2–5-year-old age range one should expect a great deal of variability in behaviors such as social initiation, toileting skills, interfering with others, crying, ability to concentrate, and required amount of attention from staff. In addition, staff expectations for these children would be expected to vary widely, and thus influence their ratings of items such as "too active," "some reluctance to play with other children," and "rarely fearful, mild fears only." Differing expectations also will influence one's interpretation about whether a particular item endorsement is indicative of a problem.

The authors of the PBCL manual suggest the instrument is useful for making a variety of important decisions about children. These are:

1. Screening for children in need of further services, based on a nonempirically derived cutoff score of 12. This is the only use of the instrument supported by any data.

2. Intervention planning, based on a "pattern of scores" that "can readily be used . . . as a basis for discussion and to encourage development of ideas on intervention" (p. 4). It would be premature either to conclude that an intervention is warranted based on a PBCL score, or to plan an intervention based on a pattern of scores. For example, an intervention may be unwarranted, given circumstances such as unrealistic expectations on the part of a rater or the developmental appropriateness of the behavior of interest.

3. Program evaluation or "how successful programmes of intervention are proving" (p. 4). Unfortunately, no evidence is presented to suggest the PBCL is sensitive to changes in children's behavior in preschool settings due to intervention or education.

4. Program planning, which suggests administration with respect to all children in a given setting to contribute to decisions regarding, for example, inservice training and resource development and allocation. Here again, data are

needed to validate the usefulness of the PBCL in making these types of decisions.

In summary, the content of the PBCL appears to be reasonably thorough and complete for a brief rating scale intended to screen for problems in need of attention with target preschool children. Unfortunately, the manner in which some items assess a content area may contribute to a lack of clarity as to what is being measured. Finally, despite the authors' broader claims, only minimal empirical support for the PBCL as a screening tool is provided. For this purpose, practitioners also should consider alternative, well-developed instruments such as the Social Skills Rating System (Gresham & Elliott, 1990).

REVIEWER'S REFERENCE

Gresham, F. M., & Elliott, S. N. (1990). Social Skills Rating System. Circle Pines, MN: American Guidance Service.

[62]
Preliminary Diagnostic Questionnaire.

Purpose: To assess the functional capacities of persons with disabilities in relation to employability. **Population:** Persons involved with vocational rehabilitation agencies or facilities and workers' compensation claimants. **Publication Date:** 1981. **Acronym:** PDQ. **Scores:** 8 subscales: Work Information, Preliminary Estimate of Learning, Psychomotor Skills, Reading Retention, Work Importance, Personal Independence, Internality, Emotional Functioning. **Administration:** Individual. **Restricted Distribution:** Restricted to persons who have completed the publisher's training course and are certified; group training by arrangement. **Price Data, 1990:** $100 per person per complete self-paced training kit; $50 per 100 client booklets. **Time:** (60) minutes. **Comments:** Orally administered. **Authors:** Joseph B. Moriarty. **Publisher:** West Virginia Research and Training Center.

Review of the Preliminary Diagnostic Questionnaire by STEVE GRAHAM, Associate Professor, and DEBRA NEUBERT, Assistant Professor of Special Education, University of Maryland, College Park, MD:

The Preliminary Diagnostic Questionnaire (PDQ) is a screening instrument designed to provide vocational rehabilitation counselors with a quick assessment of clients' cognitive, physical, and emotional functioning as well as their disposition to work. The instrument is described as a casework tool, or an assistive device for gathering information on a client's functional assets and limitations, developing tentative hypotheses concerning employability, formulating additional questions and client assessment needs, and determining eligibility for rehabilitation services. The authors of the PDQ indicate that an additional advantage of the instrument is that it helps to structure the diagnostic process by providing counselors with a framework for gathering, analyzing, synthesizing, and sharing information with their clients.

The PDQ is given individually and reportedly takes only 1 hour to administer. Much of the information collected from the client is obtained through a structured interview format. The developers of the instrument claim that adequate administration requires the diagnostic interviewing skills of a trained and experienced vocational rehabilitation counselor. As a result, the instrument is available only to persons who have received training and certification through the West Virginia Research and Training Center (WVRC), the developer of the PDQ. In order to obtain certification, counselors must complete seven training modules, administer the PDQ to five clients, and submit their work to the WVRC for evaluation and feedback.

The instrument includes nine sections: demographic data and eight scales. Demographic data include questions concerning the client's employment history, social environment, medication, and so forth. Six of the demographic items (sex, marital status, work status, disability, education, and age) are used to calculate a client's probability of competitive employment. The utility of this estimate is questionable, because important factors such as severity of disability, motivation to work, physical capabilities, and so forth are not considered. Furthermore, it is not clear how this scale was devised or if clients' scores on this measure are adequate predictors of their employability.

The first four scales of the PDQ are performance-based. The Work Information subtest includes questions designed to tap the client's knowledge of the world of work. The questions are generally oriented to knowledge of blue collar jobs and unions. The relevance of some of the items (for example, "What is George Meany famous for?") is questionable. The

Preliminary Estimate of Learning (PEL) subtest reportedly measures intellectual functioning. The PEL consists primarily of general information questions. Although the authors of the PDQ indicated correlations between the PEL and the Wechsler Adult Intelligence Scale ranged from .70 to .78, they also found that the word recognition (reading) subtest from the Wide Range Achievement Test had a similar association (.79) with the PEL, thus raising questions as to what the subtest actually measures. The Psychomotor Skills subtest involves copying geometric figures from the Beery Developmental Test of Visual-Motor Integration and filling and addressing an envelope. Although such measures are economical, they tap a very limited range of the variety of motor behaviors necessary across a wide range of occupations. The Reading subtest involves reading a passage with paragraphs ranging from 4th to 11th grade level. In addition to this rather unusual format, the accompanying comprehension questions deal almost exclusively with retention; inference and other reading skills that may be important to job success are not emphasized.

The last four scales of the PDQ employ a self-report format. Work Importance is measured by having clients note their degree of agreement/disagreement with statements regarding attitudes, perceptions, and values concerning employment. The Estimate of Personal Independence assesses the client's physical limitations in terms of self-care, mobility, and range of motion. The subtest Internality measures the client's locus of control with regard to work-related situations. It must be noted that concurrent validity for this scale has not been adequately established, as the authors of the PDQ have not examined the association between this measure and more traditional measures of locus of control. Finally, Emotional Functioning is assessed by asking clients to indicate how often they exhibit behavior representative of anxiety, depression, aggression, withdrawal, and bizarreness.

One significant drawback to the PDQ is that the authors do not provide a technical manual. Information concerning normative data, reliability, and validity are included in several published and unpublished reports. This arrangement makes it difficult for users to judge the technical adequacy of the instrument.

Moreover, these reports do not contain important information such as a detailed description of how the scales were constructed.

The PDQ was standardized on a sample of 2,972 vocational rehabilitation clients from 30 states. Unfortunately, data on the normative sample are incompletely reported. Procedures for selecting persons for inclusion in the normative sample are vague; it does not appear that a systematic plan was used to select a representative sample. Although the normative sample was reasonably similar in terms of sex, race, age, education, marital status, work status, and area of disability to a randomly selected sample of all clients served in Vocational Rehabilitation agencies nationwide, additional information detailing the specific characteristics of the standardization sample, such as severity of disability or more detailed information on ethnicity (more than White, Black, or Other), are needed.

In the available published and unpublished reports, the authors of the PDQ review a variety of studies they claim provide support for the reliability and validity of the instrument. Until both further and independent investigations are undertaken, the results from these studies must be interpreted cautiously. A particular concern relates to the reliability of specific subtests, especially because the PDQ is used to make decisions about individual clients. Test-retest reliability coefficients were unavailable for two scales and were less than .80 on four others. Similarly, on a measure of internal consistency, the reliability coefficients for three scales were less than .80. It also does not appear that the majority of the scales are predictive of employment, as measured by presence or absence of earnings or earnings above or below the minimum wage. Moreover, it is not clear if the instrument or the individual scales discriminate between the disabled who have difficulty obtaining employment and nondisabled groups.

The authors of the PDQ should be commended for providing appropriate cautions for the administration and interpretation of the instrument. For instance, the PDQ is not recommended for persons with severe visual, hearing, or communicative handicapping conditions. Furthermore, the instrument, in our estimation, is not appropriate for clients with severe handicapping conditions.

In summary, the PDQ appears to be best suited for experimental work. Additional evidence on the normative sample, reliability, and validity is needed before the PDQ can be recommended as an instrument for making individual assessments on vocational rehabilitation clients.

Review of the Preliminary Diagnostic Questionnaire by THOMAS G. HARING, Associate Professor in Special Education, University of California, Santa Barbara, CA:

The expressed purpose of the Preliminary Diagnostic Questionnaire (PDQ) is to provide an initial assessment of the functional capabilities of vocational rehabilitation clients through a combination of structured interview questions and test items that assess specific abilities presumed to predict employability. This instrument allows a quick screening (approximately 1 hour) of vocational abilities, attitudes, and degree of physical independence through the use of eight subscales relevant to vocational rehabilitation: Work Information, Preliminary Estimate of Learning, Psychomotor Skills, Reading Ability and Comprehension, Work Importance, Estimate of Personal Independence, Internality, and Emotional Functioning. Results are recorded on a convenient profile that allows analysis across the eight sections in stanines. The PDQ was developed to be more than an initial diagnostic assessment. It attempts to provide a structure for organizing casework, conducting counseling sessions, and treating motivational and emotional barriers to successful vocational placement and planning rehabilitation goals. The PDQ is available only in conjunction with training from the West Virginia Research and Training Center. In order to use the PDQ, a counselor must be certified.

REVIEW OF TRAINING MODULES. The training for certification is composed of seven modules: introduction to the PDQ; philosophic basis of functional assessment; administration of the PDQ; interpretation of case studies; techniques of diagnostic interviews; interpretation of locus of control; and casework implications of the PDQ including guidelines for conducting therapeutic interviews.

An analysis of the written materials in the training package suggested the content of the training modules goes beyond the information needed to use the PDQ. The modules provide fairly detailed descriptions of counseling methods that can be used to probe beyond the test items themselves to determine motivational, emotional, and family factors that might impede or facilitate the vocational rehabilitation process. The training modules do a nice job of giving guidelines for interpreting the profiles of scores across the eight subscales. Patterns of scores are identified that might suggest a need for further exploration through interviews with the client or more comprehensive testing in specific areas. The strengths of the training modules are: (*a*) The manuals are written in a style easily understandable to counselors who may not be formally trained in assessment, (*b*) the modules include a broad range of suggestions for interpretation and problem solving with clients, and (*c*) the information provided is more than adequate to use the PDQ effectively.

There are, in my view, some shortcomings with the training modules as well: (*a*) The focus of the training and interpretation examples are generally with clients who are fairly verbal and capable of responding to more traditional question-and-answer formats. The PDQ training modules are not set up to allow training and interpretation of clients with more moderate and severe developmental disabilities, a population the field of vocational rehabilitation is coming under increasing congressional pressure to serve. (*b*) In several places the manuals (e.g., the manuals on motivation, interviewing, and management implications) go beyond data collection and interpretation of interview results into therapeutic procedures. This may pose a potential problem if the theoretical orientation of the user does not correspond to that promoted within the modules. This material, which is basically extraneous to use of the PDQ, makes the amount of training seem unnecessarily great. (*c*) The training and interpretation guidelines given relate to a concept of vocational rehabilitation that is rooted in the assessment of underlying traits and abilities (e.g., general intelligence and internal vs. external locus of control) that deals with vocational development as a predictive process and an interpersonal counseling process, rather than as a job of matching the specific service needs of a client with the specific demands of a range of work environments. Curiously, the training manuals discuss the characteristics of jobs and work environments in relation to subscale scores and client characteristics quite infrequently. Thus, the PDQ may be of somewhat limited use in guiding directly the selection of jobs or in direct planning of vocational options.

Content Analysis of the PDQ.

DEMOGRAPHIC DATA. In addition to the eight subscales, the PDQ includes a form for the collection of routine demographic information. This form may be useful to vocational rehabilitation counselors in organizing data from external sources relevant to case management and planning. Using the demographic section, the user can estimate the probability of future competitive employment based on six variables: sex, marital status, current work status, type of disability, education level, and age. To do this analysis, the data from the cover sheet are categorized by using a simple numerical code. The coded number is then transferred to a table that gives the likelihood of competitive employment for a person with that specific set of demographic variables. While most of the decisions needed to use this probability table and formulate the code are relatively straightforward, there are two areas of ambiguity. First, in classifying the primary disability of a client, six choices are offered: Visual, Hearing, Orthopedic, Amputation, Mental, and Other. The descriptions in the manual are not clear as to what types of disabilities should be classified as "Mental." For example, would this include adventitious brain injury and all levels of mental retardation, as well as psychiatric disorders? In addition, it is unclear what disabilities were lumped together to create the "other" category. The breadth of the types and severities of disabilities that are lumped together makes the use of these tables a rough estimate at best, and at worst, misleading as to the employment potential of an individual.

Whether or not a person is currently employed is by far the strongest predictor of future employment. For example, a woman who is married, currently employed, orthopedically disabled, has 15 years of education, and is 41 to 60 years old, has a probability of successful employment of .97. If she were not currently employed, this probability would drop to .26. It is impossible to estimate the effects of factors, such as just being laid off, on these probabilities. The authors point out these data should be used only as a rough estimation of future employability. The use of these data in the allocation of services, however, is another issue that requires closer ethical scrutiny and stronger discussion in the manual. In my view, these data are far too cursory for such use.

WORK INFORMATION. The authors state the purpose of the Work Information subscale is to determine if "the individual has assimilated enough work information to function effectively on the job." An analysis of the items on this subscale raises questions at the face-validity level as to the scale's ability to perform this task. Seventeen items on the scale are scored as right or wrong. The items range from being able to define the difference between being laid off and being fired, knowing what a part-time job is, and knowing what a time clock is, to knowing who George Meany is and defining the acronyms AFL-CIO and OSHA. Five of the 17 items on the scale relate to knowledge of unions; thus, workers with experience in non-union settings may have a more difficult time with this test. The authors acknowledge the test is similar to a verbal section on an ability test in content and construction. Given the brevity of the test and the fact the test apparently was not constructed based on a content analysis by experts in analysis of characteristics of work settings (as would be a typical procedure from which to claim content validity in tests of this type), the claim that this test assesses work information needed to function on the job is not well justified.

There is a high likelihood this section of the PDQ taps heavily into a more general ability factor than it does the specific skills needed to function effectively in a workplace. The correlation between the Work Information subscale and the WAIS Information subtest ($n = 43$) was .63. In addition, in a factor analytic study the Work Information section loaded significantly on Factor 1, which was interpreted as indicating general intellectual ability.

The internal consistency coefficient (KR-20) on a sample of 151 clients from West Virginia was .85. In addition, the internal consistency of the Work Information section was assessed by correlating the individual items from the subscale with the total score on a sample of 292 clients from 16 states achieving correlations "at the level of .38 or higher" (p. 41). Mean correlations and the entire range of correlations

are not reported. A test-retest correlation of .81 ($n = 28$) was reported. As with other technical descriptions within the manual, much information that would be important in making informed decisions about the use of the PDQ is missing or poorly stated. The samples used in the validity and reliability studies are too small, unsystematic, and inadequately described.

PRELIMINARY ESTIMATE OF LEARNING (PEL). The PEL was designed to give a quick estimate of intelligence. It contains 30 items scored as correct or incorrect that reflect general knowledge rather than reasoning or problem solving. The items range from knowing in what month Christmas is celebrated, how many days are in a week, and who is the president, to who wrote *Paradise Lost*, what is a definition of entomology, and who wrote "Night on Bald Mountain." In analyzing the content of this subscale, the items measure knowledge most likely acquired through participation in education and strongly favor the recall of learned facts. As such, persons who have limited participation in formal academic instruction would have a more difficult time with this subscale. For example, such fact-based instruction is rarely employed in special education. The PEL was validated on a sample of 151 clients from the West Virginia Rehabilitation Institute. The population is not adequately described. The manual states the sample contains "a higher percentage of mentally retarded than would the average field caseload." With this sample, the internal consistency (KR-20) of .97 indicates high internal consistency. Using a national sample of 292 clients from 16 states (again with only cursory descriptions of the sampling of disabilities), item-to-total correlation ranged from .26 to .66, indicating a moderate level of internal consistency. Using the West Virginia sample, the PEL correlated .79 with the WAIS Information score ($n = 43$), .71 with the WAIS full scale score ($n = 100$), .74 with the Peabody General Information score ($n = 50$), and .78 with the Peabody Reading Comprehension Score ($n = 15$). These moderate correlations are typical for a short form test such as this.

A study comparing PEL scores of mentally retarded and nonretarded clients indicated scores in the mentally retarded group were significantly lower. To assess test-retest reliability, 28 clients from the West Virginia sample were retested after 30 days. The test-retest coefficient was .97.

The sample sizes employed in the reliability and validation studies for the PEL are much smaller than generally acceptable in more comprehensive tests of general intelligence. In addition, the samples are poorly described in terms of degrees and types of disabilities and other relevant characteristics of the populations used in the studies. The national sample was predominantly white; the only minority group represented was black (12%). The logic for selection of the 16 states in the national sample and the method of sampling clients within those states are not given.

PSYCHOMOTOR SKILLS. The section on psychomotor skills consists of two tasks. The first task is to fold a piece of paper for insertion into an envelope and address the envelope. Four criteria are given to score the correctness of the paper-folding task. The second task consists of a reprint of five items from the Developmental Test of Visual-Motor Integration (VMI) by Beery and Buktenica (1967). The VMI consists of copying figures (e.g., circles and three-dimensional stars) from samples. The scoring protocol for these five items is taken directly from the VMI and calls for judgments concerning the accuracy of copying the figures. Referring to the VMI manual, the five items selected correspond to developmental norms of 5 years, 6 months; 7 years, 11 months; 11 years, 2 months; 12 years, 8 months; and 13 years, 8 months.

The use of the VMI reflects the PDQ's underlying approach to measurement based on the assessment of underlying abilities in contrast to a more direct assessment of vocationally relevant skills. While the paper-folding task does show face validity for vocational placement, the VMI does not.

The method of determining the norms for this subsection is bewildering. A sample of 58 students from West Virginia University were administered five drawing items *not* on the VMI. The mean from this test was 3.1 correct drawings. The authors then assume these college students would have obtained a perfect score on the 4 envelope tasks from the VMI. Thus, an estimated score of 7.1 was derived. This was compared to the mean score on the Psychomotor Section (that is, drawings plus paper folding) of 6.82 from the national sample

of 292 vocational rehabilitation clients. Apparently, these data were used to determine that a score of 7 ought to determine the middle score for norming purposes. However, the relevance of the study with college students using a different series of test items is difficult to determine. An item-to-total correlation was "above .37." The mean and range are not given. An ANOVA was conducted that compared the performance of clients diagnosed as mentally retarded to other clients. The report claims the group with mental retardation was significantly lower; however, the p value is not given.

Overall, the Psychomotor section is not well validated. It does not include measures with the necessary predictive relationship to vocational placement.

READING. The Reading section appears to be useful in that the ability to read and comprehend written material and to recall written facts may have important implications in planning a program of vocational rehabilitation. The PDQ offers a quick assessment of reading skills. The Reading section is administered orally and consists of reading a story that is approximately one page in length. Errors of refusal, omission, reversal, insertion, and mispronunciation are scored. In addition, the client is given an 18-item reading comprehension test after reading the passage twice, once orally and once silently.

One hundred thirteen vocational rehabilitation clients from West Virginia were administered this section to determine the norms. This sample produced a mean of 10.6. The national sample of 292 clients achieved a mean of 11.39. The mean from the norm table is given at 12 to 14. The reason for this discrepancy is not given. A group of 26 West Virginia clients was retested after 1 month. The test-retest coefficient was .78. The internal consistency of the reading section was tested with 113 West Virginia clients and yielded a coefficient (KR-20) of .85, indicating a reasonably high level of internal consistency.

WORK IMPORTANCE. The Work Importance section consists of a 10-item, 4-point, Likert scale. This section is designed to assess the client's attitude toward work. Clients are asked to indicate the extent of their agreement with statements such as "I am satisfied with most aspects of my life" and "My chances of getting a job are excellent." A good feature of this subscale is the inclusion of items that assess the degree of support the client feels from friends and family in obtaining employment. It also provides an assessment of the client's own perspective of the importance of employment in his or her own life. This information could be critical in developing a vocational rehabilitation plan.

The norms for this section were developed with a sample of students from West Virginia University and the 292 clients from the national sample. In the college sample, the coefficient alpha was .85, indicating a high degree of internal consistency. In addition, the range of item-to-total correlations was from .44 to .61, which is an acceptable level for Likert-type scales.

PERSONAL INDEPENDENCE. This section is designed to assess a client's physical abilities. The personal independence section consists of 29 items. On 20 items, the client verbally indicates if he or she can do a response without assistance, with an assistive device, with the assistance of another person, or cannot do the response. The responses include eating, drinking, dressing, and walking up and down steps. The remaining nine items are of a demonstration type in which the client is asked to raise his or her right arm above the head, stand on his or her left foot, and kneel on the floor. The information from this section may be very important in matching a client's current physical capabilities to the demands of various jobs and employment settings. The scale was designed so a perfect score (indicating no functional physical limitations) would yield a score in the middle stanine. A comparison of scores from orthopedically disabled clients with nonorthopedically disabled clients indicated this scale can discriminate physically disabled clients from nondisabled clients.

INTERNALITY. This section is composed of a 15-item, 4-point, Likert-type scale that assesses a client's degree of internal versus external locus of control. The scale has good face validity for use in vocational rehabilitation settings because generally the items reflect attitudes toward supervisors, and reasons for work-related events such as getting fired or getting promoted.

The production of the norms for this subscale is described inadequately in the manual. Scores of 0 (strongly external) through 60 (strongly internal) were possible. The sample of West Virginia clients had a mean of 29.17. A sample of 58 college students had a mean of 35.41, and the national sample of clients had a mean of 32.31. However, the authors designated 41 to 42 as the midpoint of the scale. In interpreting these data, it is typical that a college population will have mean scores that are somewhat strongly indicative of internal locus of control, yet the midpoint of this scale is set *above* the mean for the college sample. Many users will look at the profile and expect that scores above the midpoint indicate an internal locus of control and scores below that point indicate an external locus of control. In fact, the presentation of data in stanine scores means the fifth stanine correponds to the mean. The manual states, "Scores below the fifth stanine on the PDQ Internality section suggest persons who feel unable to control the events that shape their lives." An external locus of control is presumably a negative predictor of vocational success. Based on the PDQ profile, to score at the mean or into the internal range, a vocational rehabilitation client would have to score well above the mean from the validation study and above the mean of a college sample. Based on a standard deviation of 5.44 for the national sample, the midpoint of the profile is set almost 2 standard deviations above the mean. The discrepancy between the field test data and the construction of the norms is not explained or justified. Without further explanation and justification, I would not recommend the use of the profile in assessing the locus of control of vocational rehabilitation clients. Problems of this type call into question the adequacy of the construction of the PDQ.

EMOTIONAL FUNCTIONING. This section is designed to provide a preliminary assessment of the emotional functioning and psychological well-being of a client. The section consists of 20 items such as "I get nervous" and "I get mad." The client indicates the frequency of that characteristic on a 4-point scale: *never, sometimes, often, always.* The inclusion of this section is a valuable addition to the PDQ because it has been well accepted for some time that social emotional factors are powerful predictors of future successful employment (Goldstein, 1964).

On this subscale the mean for the national sample was used to set the midpoint of the scale. The test-retest reliability was assessed after 30 days with 28 clients yielding a coefficient of .89. An internal consistency coefficient of .87 indicates strong internal consistency. A statistical comparison comparing the scores of clients classified as having a mental illness with those not classified suggested significant differences between the groups. However, the mean for the mentally ill group (61.18) was less than 1 standard deviation (8.21) from the midpoint of the scale (64), indicating that although the scale will pick up significant differences in group averages, there is considerable overlap in the distribution of scores between individuals with mental illness and those not classified.

SUMMARY EVALUATION. The PDQ was designed to fill a substantial need in the diagnosis, planning, and management of vocational rehabilitation casework. An adequately developed scale that allowed the rapid collection of data across the areas sampled by the PDQ would be of great use if viewed, as the authors advocate, as a screening instrument to determine which more comprehensive tests and assessments are needed to get a clear picture of the vocational rehabilitation of a client. The Reading section, Work Importance section, and Personal Independence section show the highest degrees of usefulness and technical adequacy. Unfortunately, the overall development of the PDQ contains numerous psychometric shortcomings that should preclude its use until further and more rigorous scaling, reliability studies, and validity studies are undertaken.

REVIEWER'S REFERENCE

Goldstein, H. (1964). Social and occupational adjustment. In H. A. Stevens & R. Heber (Eds.), *Mental retardation: A review of research* (pp. 214-258). Chicago: University of Chicago Press.

[63]
Prescriptive Teaching Series.

Purpose: "To give the educator a concrete tool with which to work and to enable him to more effectively plan educational experiences."
Population: Grades 1–8.
Publication Date: 1971.
Acronym: PTS.
Scores: 6 skill areas: Math Skills, Reading and Language Skills, Auditory Skills, Motor Skills, Visual-Motor Skills, Visual Skills.
Administration: Individual.
Price Data, 1987: $15 per 20 Visual Skills booklets; $15 per 20 Visual-Motor Skills booklets; $20 per 25 Motor Skills booklets; $20 per 25

Auditory Skills booklets; $20 per 25 Reading and Language Skills booklets; $35 per 25 Math Skills booklets; $5 per manual (8 pages); $63 per specimen set including 1 copy of all booklets and manual.
Time: (10–20) minutes per test.
Comments: Skills checklist; can accumulate data for 4 rating periods; booklets available as separates.
Author: Sue Martin.
Publisher: Psychologists and Educators, Inc.

Review of the Prescriptive Teaching Series by RANDY W. KAMPHAUS, Associate Professor of Educational Psychology, The University of Georgia, Athens, GA:

According to the author the Prescriptive Teaching Series (PTS) is intended to aid the individualization of instruction by identifying appropriate instructional goals for pupils at the elementary school level. The scales of the PTS include Visual, Visual-Motor, Motor, Auditory, Reading and Language, and Math. These, however, are not scales that are directly administered to students. The rating scales are used by teachers to rate the skill level of individual students. Each skill is rated on a 4-point scale where "0 = *not introduced; no opportunity,* 1 = *introduced, but not achieved,* 2 = *partially achieved,* 3 = *satisfactorily achieved.*" The number of items in each curricular domain is large. Even shorter scales such as the Auditory Skills scale includes 31 items. These 31 items also have items with "sub-items" that require rating.

One of the more interesting comments made in the manual is that the PTS scales are not tests. Consequently, the author eschews the need for evidence of concurrent or predictive validity studies or reliability investigations. There are no psychometric data whatsoever included in the manual. Less than half a page is devoted to the topics of reliability and validity.

The individual scales are presented on 8½ x 11 inch sheets and are color coded. The layout of the scales seems reasonable and readily understandable by classroom teachers. The typesetting of the scales is rather crude. In fact, it looks as if some of the graphics were done by hand with a pencil and ruler. From a practical standpoint some of the domains seem so lengthy that I suspect that teachers may be resistant to using them. The Math Skills scale, for example, includes 315 items for the teacher to rate, but this does not include ratings of "sub-items" that can be rather lengthy in and of themselves. For example, on Item 62 having to do with multiplication, the teacher has to rate the child's overall competence in multiplication as well as knowledge of the multiplication tables for every number combination from 1 through 9.

In terms of psychometric evidence, the author makes a case for the quality of the item pool selected. The author maintains that the item pool was selected after considerable review of the elementary school curriculum and related research. It would be helpful if the manual were to give more detail as to the specific sources used for item development and whether or not the opinions of other content experts besides the author were used in the process of item selection. The author concludes that the item pools possess "high face validity" and, as such, the demands of content validity are satisfied. Face validity, of course, is something of a controversial topic in psychometric circles. It should, however, never be considered as a substitute for establishing the content validity of a scale as was apparently done in the case of the PTS.

With regard to conducting statistical investigations of the psychometric properties of the various checklists the author concludes, "No subscale scores or total scores are obtained in the booklets. With such a format comparative statistics are difficult at the very least. Since the series is not a test, it does not lend itself to the traditional parametric statistical analyses common to tests per se." I do not agree with the author's argument that the validity and reliability of the PTS checklist should not be investigated. This can be done without the computation of total scores. This lack of psychometric information results in the PTS being an unknown entity. It would be difficult to make the case to educators that the PTS checklists assess all or some degree of the core skills necessary for elementary school achievement. It also should not be argued that the PTS is "an instrument to indicate pupil progress and achievement," without having some evidence of the reliability with which pupil progress and achievement is assessed by these scales.

My conclusion regarding the PTS is that this is an informal group of checklists for the assessment of academic skills that has a paltry amount of evidence to support its use for the purposes given in the manual. Based on the

data currently available on the PTS, it should be considered as an experimental measure that will require local norming, reliability, and validation studies if it is going to be used for making important curricular decisions.

Review of the Prescriptive Teaching Series by DEBORAH KING KUNDERT, *Assistant Professor of Educational Psychology and Statistics, University at Albany, State University of New York, Albany, NY:*

The Prescriptive Teaching Series (PTS) is a criterion-referenced checklist of learning concepts and skills to use in diagnosing students' strengths and weaknesses and plotting students' progress. Six booklets included in the series are intended to serve as a tangible list of teaching goals in the areas of Visual Skills, Visual-Motor Skills, Motor Skills, Auditory Skills, Reading and Language Skills, and Math Skills. An eight-page manual is included with the series, though the author states that it is "not the purpose of this *manual* to become a *test* manual by indicating exactly how each item should be observed or tested." The age range for which the PTS is appropriate is not indicated, but a review of the skills would seem to indicate that it might address skills taught in elementary school.

According to the manual, items were selected based on research of elementary curricula. Furthermore, it is stated that items were sequenced on the checklists based on "repeated research." In examining the checklists, this reviewer questioned the sequential and developmental order of some of the items. For example, in the reading and language booklet under the word knowledges skill, "understands the meaning of proverbs" is rated as the first item and "has an adequate sight vocabulary" is rated as the seventh item. Logically and developmentally, this does not appear to be correct. In addition to inappropriate item orderings, this reviewer also questioned the classification of some of the skills on the checklists (e.g., syllabication was listed as an alphabetizing skill). Finally, some of the items on the PTS were vague, and therefore it would seem that they would be difficult to rate (e.g., "does not demonstrate significant difficulties in oral reading").

Educators using the PTS rate a student based on their knowledge of student performance or based on planned observations. The rating scale used across all of the booklets is as follows: 0 = *not introduced/no opportunity*; 1 = *introduced, but not achieved*; 2 = *partially achieved*; 3 = *satisfactorily (functionally) achieved*. The manual does not include any directions or criteria on which to distinguish between the different levels (e.g., how would one differentiate between partial and satisfactory achievement?).

Evidence of the psychometric properties of the PTS is lacking and/or inappropriate. According to the manual, the reliability of the scale is inherent and "lies in its item validity." Raters are cautioned that consistency is important, though no estimates of interrater reliability are reported. The PTS is based on "established developmental skills and learned concepts." As such, it is stated that the checklist has high face validity which incorporates content validity. It is unclear to this reviewer what this statement means. The author goes on to state that "concurrent or predictive validity studies would provide little more information" because the PTS is not a test. This is a serious omission; what inferences can be drawn from the ratings, and how might the ratings be used in instructional planning?

The author of the PTS claims that the checklist is not a test. It seems to this reviewer that this scale is a criterion-referenced measure, or it might be classified as an informal measure. Criterion-referenced and informal measures may serve a purpose in the assessment process, but certain, specific information is necessary for examiners to use the instrument appropriately. Specific criteria have been outlined by Popham (1978) for developing and selecting criterion-referenced measures (e.g., adequate number of items, focus, validity).

In summary, the PTS was designed to identify areas of dysfunction among children and adolescents. The absence of specific item selection procedures, detailed administration and scoring guidelines, interpretation details, as well as the lack of important reliability and validity data, preclude the use of the PTS at this time. It is unclear how the use of this checklist would aid in determining student strengths and weaknesses and in planning educational remediation programs.

REVIEWER'S REFERENCE

Popham, W. J. (1978). *Criterion-referenced measurement*. Englewood Cliffs, NJ: Prentice-Hall, Inc.

[64]

Productivity Environmental Preference Survey.

Purpose: "An inventory for the identification of adult preferences of conditions in a working and/or learning environment."
Population: Adults.
Publication Dates: 1979–82.
Acronym: PEPS.
Scores, 20: Sound, Light, Warmth, Formal Design, Motivated/Unmotivated, Persistent, Responsible, Structure, Learning Alone/Peer-Oriented Learner, Authority-Oriented Learner, Several Ways, Auditory Preferences, Visual Preferences, Tactile Preferences, Kinesthetic Preferences, Requires Intake, Evening/Morning, Late Morning, Afternoon, Needs Mobility.
Administration: Group.
Price Data, 1988: $6 per 60 answer sheets with questions; $4 or less per individual profile (produced when sent in for computer scoring); $.40 per individual interpretative booklet; $9 per manual ('82, 61 pages); $11 per specimen set including answer sheet, interpretative booklet, and manual.
Time: (20–30) minutes.
Comments: Computer scored.
Authors: Gary E. Price, Rita Dunn, and Kenneth Dunn.
Publisher: Price Systems, Inc.

Review of the Productivity Environmental Preference Survey by CRAIG N. MILLS, Executive Director, GRE Testing and Services, Educational Testing Service, Princeton, NJ:

The Productivity Environmental Preference Survey (PEPS) is a 100-item survey designed to diagnose adults' productivity and learning styles. According to the manual, the results can be used to structure the workplace to maximize output and the instrument can also be used for recruiting, screening, selecting, and promoting individuals. Unfortunately, evidence to support these claims is not provided.

CONTENT AND INSTRUMENT DEVELOPMENT. The PEPS instrument was developed by "identifying the research variables that appeared to describe the ways individuals prefer to learn or work." The manual does not contain a reference list of the research, nor does it specifically identify the variables identified in the research. Thus, it is not possible for the prospective user to evaluate the appropriateness of the content of the items. The instrument was refined through two pilot administrations. The first administration sample is not described.

The second sample is described as "non-random" and consisted of 589 adults.

In a factor analysis, 31 factors with eigenvalues greater than 1.00 were identified. This resulted in 21 scores. Exactly how 21 scores resulted from 31 factors is unclear.

No information is reported to indicate that data related to observed productivity or work/learning environment were collected during instrument development. There is also no explanation provided of how the lists of suggested environmental modifications were developed.

The technical information provided is difficult to interpret. For example, the following are reported for one measure: Standard Deviation = 1.85; Reliability = .83; Standard Error of Measurement = .68. Calculating the standard error of measurement by multiplying the standard deviation by the square root of 1.0 minus reliability does not yield the same result.

Average scores are also difficult to interpret. For example, in one area there are three items and the mean is reported as 2.95. It appears that means were developed for items in a true/false format. If so, it seems unlikely that this scale is meaningful. An alternative explanation is that this mean is based on administration of the items in a Likert format (the current format of the measure). However, other areas in the same table have means of less than 1.0, an unlikely occurrence.

SCORES AND INTERPRETATION. Scores are reported as standard scores with a mean of 50 and a standard deviation of 10. For each of the 21 scores, desirable features of the work or learning environment are suggested for individuals with scores of 60 and above or 40 and below. Given the low reliabilities of the scales and the size of the standard error of measurement, there appears to be a limited psychometric basis for making the distinctions between individuals with scaled scores that are 10 points from the mean. No justification is provided for the use of these scores as cutoff points, nor is there evidence that the suggested actions are supported empirically.

RELIABILITY. "Hoyt" reliabilities are reported, but information related specifically to the manner in which they were calculated is not provided. The reliabilities are low. None exceed .90 and five are under .50. This is not surprising, given the limited number of questions that can be related to a given score. Nonetheless, the reliabilities suggest that the results are not likely to be particularly useful for decision-making purposes.

It appears the reliabilities were obtained through administration of the survey in a True-False format. The manual states the format of the survey has been changed to a Likert scale, partly to address the reliability issue. Data from the survey in its revised form are not provided.

VALIDITY. The lack of validity evidence is particularly troubling, given the drawbacks pointed out previously with regard to instrument development, score interpretation, and reliability. Several research studies are reported in the manual, but they suffer, in general, from small sample sizes. More importantly, they do not address the construct or predictive validity of the instrument; they only provide descriptive information.

To determine the construct validity of the instrument, data would need to be gathered not only on people's environmental preferences, but also on their current environment and their current productivity. Without data on current environment, the user has data only on preferences and no data on how important the preferences might be. With respect to predictive validity, information would need to be available demonstrating that changing a work or learning environment to more or less closely match the respondent's stated preferences increases or decreases productivity in the expected direction. No such data are provided.

The manual indicates the survey can be useful in structuring environments to increase productivity in learning or working situations. However, none of the studies summarized in the manual are related to a work environment. To the extent the samples are described, the research appears to have been conducted exclusively with undergraduate and graduate students.

SUMMARY. The Productivity Environmental Preference Survey collects information about individuals' preferences related to 21 environmental factors. It provides recommendations for structuring an environment to maximize productivity. Technical information is sparse, but indicates that the instrument is not likely to be sufficiently reliable for decision making. The research summarized in support of the measure does not adequately address the construct validity of the measure, its predictive power, or the recommendations for environmental changes made on the basis of the scores.

Review of the Productivity Environmental Preference Survey by BERTRAM C. SIPPOLA, Associate Professor of Psychology, University of New Orleans, New Orleans, LA:

The Productivity Environmental Preference Survey (PEPS) is the adult version of the Learning Style Inventory (LSI; 37), which exists in versions for students in grades 3 and 4 and in grades 5–12. Both tests are authored by Rita and Kenneth Dunn and Gary E. Price. The PEPS consists of 100 items (5-point Likert scale) that yield scores on 20 factors. It is designed for easy administration, with all of the items and instructions appearing on an Opscan answer sheet. Scoring may be done by the publisher or the test may be taken and scored on a microcomputer.

The LSI is one of many somewhat similar instruments (some with almost identical names) (e.g., Canfield, 1976–80, 9:609; Renzulli & Smith, 1978, 9:608). These test instruments assume that students differ in terms of their preferred "style" in the learning process and that matching the educational environment to preferred style will maximize learning. The LSI shares with those tests noted above an apparent insularity from other measures, with each test reflecting its own authors' beliefs.

Some learning-style scales are based on theoretical work, such as that of Murray (1938, 1951) ("environmental press": the phenomenological experience of one's interaction with the environment) or Weber (1946) (the common-denominator characteristics of organizational settings). Murray's work provides the basis for at least two well-known sets of measures, the Stern Environment Indexes (Stern, Walker, Pace, Winters, Archer, Meyer, & Steinhoff, 1957–72) and the Social Climate Scales (Moos & Associates, 1974–87). Each of these, as well as the PEPS, includes forms that deal with adult preferences in "work" or other settings (Organizational Climate Index and Work Environment Scale, respectively).

The authors of the LSI (and others) argue that such theoretical bases are inappropriate. They emphasize the importance of the empirical development of their instruments using content and item analysis and factor analytic

studies. They note that such continuing studies (G. E. Price, personal communication, to Buros Institute of Mental Measurements, July 19, 1988) have led to the recent reduction of PEPS factors from 21 to 20. The authors stress that the "scale does not measure underlying psychological motivation . . . Rather, it yields information concerned with . . . patterns through which the highest levels of productivity tend to occur. . . . *how* an employee prefers to produce or learn best, not why" (1982, p. 2). Thus, the major interpretive portion of their manual is devoted to "suggestions" for adapting the working or learning environment, based on an individual's or a group's scores on the profile (raw scores are reported and standard scores are listed and graphed as plus or minus one standard deviation). There is little justification presented for all of these prescriptions, and very few other data are presented to indicate criterial validity. Thus, there is no evidence that carrying out the prescriptions would have a demonstrable effect on improved productivity, or even on job performance in general.

Currently, the PEPS Manual is undergoing revision; a revised version was not available at the time of review. Most of the data presented in the 1982 Manual deal with the PEPS' reliability and internal structure. These data illustrate the continuing process of clarifying factor structure and revising the instrument. As a result, the current PEPS factor structure represents a mixed bag of constructs: physical environmental variables, personality or motivational characteristics of the individual, social preferences, and even task-structuring behaviors. The physical variables have face validity; temperature, noise/sound levels, lighting levels, and amount of formal structure (possibly even time of day) are all standard variables discussed in the environment and behavior literature. However, it must be noted that instruments such as the PEPS do not assess an environment, or even a perceived environment, but simply ask raters to indicate what they believe they prefer (cf. James Richards' review of the Moos Social Climate Scales in the *Eighth Mental Measurements Yearbook*, 1978). The environmental literature is rife with examples of environmental effects of which the subject was not aware. Reported are some studies correlating productivity style and GPA (undergraduate and graduate) that suggest one direction for further validation studies, but they do not extend the PEPS outside of "learning environments."

The reliabilities reported seem to be in the acceptable ranges. However, it is worth noting that they report only 68% of the reliabilities are equal to or greater than .60; seven factors have reliabilities greater than .80, but none reaches .90. The standardization sample is rather ill-defined (589 adults "from several states and from various academic and industrial settings"). In general, insufficient data are presented to allow the reader to assess independently the applicability of the PEPS to different groups of workers in regard to "real" environments. Data are reported for right-versus left-handers, and for field-dependent versus field-independent.

Would I use this survey? It is, as claimed, easy to use; sample raters finished in 12 to 28 minutes. These raters felt it was a "simplistic" test; its apparent superficiality may stem from the lack of theoretical basis, which means individual items are tied directly to the factors or scales. We would not use it for individual personnel decisions, in that it seems to lack the validity to withstand employee challenges. The authors seem to suggest that its best use is as a "counseling measure," by a supervisor or a placement advisor. The PEPS provides quickly and systematically the kind of information that could be developed in an interview. It could thus be used as a preliminary stage to the "interview." It could also be an interesting component of a research program that included both environmental assessment and performance/productivity measures as outcome criteria.

REVIEWER'S REFERENCES

Murray, H. A. (1938). *Explorations in personality*. New York: Oxford University Press.
Weber, M. (1946). *Essay in sociology* (H. H. Garth & C. W. Mills, Trans.). New York: Oxford University Press.
Murray, H. A. (1951). Toward a classification of interaction. In T. Parsons & E. A. Shils (Eds.), *Toward a general theory of action* (pp. 434-464). Cambridge, MA: Harvard University Press.
Stern, G. G., Walker, W. J., Pace, C. R., Winters, C. L., Jr., Archer, N. S., Meyer, D. L., & Steinhoff, C. R. (1957-72). Stern Environment Indexes. Syracuse, NY: Evaluation Research Associates.
Moos, R. H., & Associates. (1974-87). The Social Climate Scales. Palo Alto, CA: Consulting Psychologists Press.
Canfield, A. A. (1976-80). Learning Styles Inventory. Rochester, MI: Humanics Media.
Renzulli, J. S., & Smith, L. H. (1978). Learning Styles Inventory. Mansfield Center, CT: Creative Learning Press.
Richards, J. M., Jr. (1978). [Review of The Social Climate Scales]. In O. K. Buros (Ed.), *The eighth mental measurements*

yearbook (Vol. I, pp. 1085-1087). Highland Park, NJ: The Gryphon Press.

[65]

Progressive Achievement Tests in Reading: Reading Comprehension and Reading Vocabulary Tests.

Purpose: "To assist teachers in determining the level of development attained by their students in the basic skills of reading comprehension and word knowledge."

Population: Years 3–9 in Australian school system.

Publication Dates: 1973–86.

Acronym: PAT.

Scores, 2: Reading Comprehension, Reading Vocabulary.

Administration: Group.

Levels: 2 parallel forms for both Comprehension and Vocabulary: A, B; 6 parts: Part 2 (Year 3), Part 3 (Year 4), Part 4 (Year 5), Part 5 (Year 6), Part 6 (Year 7), Part 7 (Year 8), Part 8 (Year 9).

Price Data: Available from publisher.

Time: 40(50) minutes Reading Comprehension, 30(40) minutes Reading Vocabulary.

Author: Australian Council for Educational Research Ltd.

Publisher: Australian Council for Educational Research Ltd. [Australia].

Cross References: For information on an earlier edition, see T3:1912 (4 references); for a review of an earlier edition by Douglas A. Pidgeon, see 8:738 (1 reference); see also T2:1579 (1 reference); for excerpted reviews by Milton L. Clark and J. Elkins, see 7:699.

TEST REFERENCES

1. Share, D. L., & Silva, P. A. (1986). The stability and classification of specific reading retardation: A longitudinal study from age 7 to 11. *British Journal of Educational Psychology, 56*, 32-39.
2. Williams, S., McGee, R., Anderson, J., & Silva, P. A. (1989). The structure and correlates of self-reported symptoms in 11-year-old children. *Journal of Abnormal Child Psychology, 17*, 55-71.

Review of the Progressive Achievement Tests in Reading: Reading Comprehension and Reading Vocabulary Tests by PAUL C. BURNETT, Lecturer in Psychology, Queensland University of Technology—Kelvin Grove Campus, Brisbane, Australia:

This is the second edition of the Progressive Achievement Tests in Reading (PATR). The first edition produced in 1973 (see 8:735) was an Australian adaption of the New Zealand Council of Educational Research's 1969 edition (see 7:699). The PATR is a group-administered test of Reading Comprehension and Reading Vocabulary for students in years (i.e., grades) 3–9 (ages 8–14). Two alternative forms of the tests are available in reusable booklets. The Reading Comprehension tests each have 97 items while the Reading Vocabulary tests have 125. The starting points for the year level are staggered with examinees completing an average of 44 Reading Comprehension items (range 40–47) and an average of 57 Reading Vocabulary items (range 45–65). This overlapping format is effective, in that it allows for the assessment of seven year levels with the minimum amount of questions and materials.

The PATR materials are well developed and produced with all resources clearly labelled for easy identification. The 54-page manual is excellent in terms of format and thoroughness. It includes a description of the tests, an outline of the uses of the test, a section that delineates the administration and scoring directions, information regarding the interpretation and use of the test scores, and a description of the tests' technical information. The following are specifically addressed in the latter section: test construction, standardization, test and item statistics, reliability, validity, and norming.

The Reading Comprehension tests measure factual and inferential comprehension of prose material while the Reading Vocabulary tests assess word knowledge. The rationale for assessing these skills centers on Bloom's conceptualization of comprehension and knowledge. The purpose of the test is presented as being to assist teachers in determining the level of skill development attained by their students in reading comprehension and vocabulary. A major use of the tests is as screening devices to identify children who are in need of special assistance in the remedial or extension areas. However, further diagnostic assessment would be needed to devise remedial programs for students whose results indicated developmental delays in reading skills or reading difficulties.

The administration instructions are comprehensive and easy to follow. Specific instructions are highlighted and easy to read to students. The tests' answer sheets can be hand or machine scored. Raw scores are translated into percentile ranks, percentile ranges at the 68% confidence interval, and stanine scores. Norms for each year level are presented but no age norms are given.

An extensive renorming of the PATR was completed in November 1984. The norming samples were large, ranging from 726 to 986 for each year level, and were selected using a complex sampling design. Government, Catholic, and Independent schools were represented. The reliability for each scale was evaluated using the KR-20 formula. Consistently high reliability coefficients are reported (range .84 to .94). These figures are similar to those obtained with the previous Australian and New Zealand samples. A weakness of the current norming was the failure to collect new validity data. A small amount of outdated validity data collected during previous standardization are reported. It would have been useful to present meaningful, updated concurrent validity data.

In summary, the second edition of the PATR is the renorming of a well-developed and well-constructed test. The updated manual is extensive and thorough with the exception of the validity section. Some of the criticisms forwarded by previous reviewers have been rectified. For example, the previous manual had separate norms for each of the states and the Australian Capital Territory whereas the new manual presents Australia-wide norms. Additionally, the many meaningless concurrent validity correlations reported in the previous manual are not in the updated manual.

REVIEWER'S REFERENCE

Bloom, B. S. (1956). *Taxonomy of educational objectives: The classification of educational goals, handbook I: Cognitive domain.* New York: McKay.

Review of the Progressive Achievement Tests in Reading: Reading Comprehension and Reading Vocabulary Tests by RICHARD LEHRER, Associate Professor of Educational Psychology, University of Wisconsin-Madison, Madison, WI:

The Progressive Achievement Tests in Reading consist of multiple-choice measures of Reading Comprehension and Vocabulary. The Reading Comprehension test includes a commendable variety of genres (narrative, descriptive, and expository), cultural themes, and content areas. Comprehension questions tap both explicit and inferential knowledge of the test passages. The Reading Vocabulary test presents a word in the context of a sentence and requires students to select the best synonym from a list of five alternatives.

Both tests appear easy to administer and score. The directions provided in the accompanying teacher's handbook are well written. Indeed the entire manual is exemplary, providing information about the intentions and theoretical predilections of the test constructors, clear directions, and substantial guidance in the interpretation of students' scores. Other strengths of the measures include high reliability (KR-20) and two alternate forms for both Reading Comprehension and Vocabulary Knowledge.

The standardization sample is Australian. The standardization sample was extensive, and the manual reports a stratified random sampling procedure based upon school enrollments and geographical location. It appears that one could use the associated norms with confidence. Unfortunately, there is no international standardization sample reported. Hence, these measures could not be used as intended in other English-speaking countries.

The only other caveat is that the validation of the measures is not reported nearly as well as other aspects of these tests. For example, the manual reports high correlations of the comprehension tests with two other measures of "reading" without specifying clearly the nature of these other measures. It is not clear if the correlations between the vocabulary and comprehension tests are higher than those between each test and other measures of vocabulary and reading comprehension. Thus the extent to which the Vocabulary and Reading Comprehension tests measure separate but related abilities is unknown. Nevertheless, the tests should provide teachers with useful, normative information about their students' reading abilities.

In summary, the Progressive Achievement Tests in Reading Comprehension and Vocabulary are easy to administer and score, and appear valid for the purposes for which they were designed. The Reading Comprehension test in particular samples a commendable number of genres, cultural themes, and content areas. The accompanying teachers' manual is clearly written and provides useful information about the interpretation of students' scores. When used with Australian students, these tests should help teachers make informed decisions about suitable instructional materials for their students.

[66]

PSB-Reading Comprehension Examination.

Purpose: "To reveal the student's comprehension or understanding of what he or she reads."
Population: Secondary and postsecondary students applying or enrolled in terminal vocational or occupational programs.
Publication Dates: 1978–87.
Scores: Total score only.
Administration: Group.
Price Data, 1988: $5 per test booklet; $3 per student for answer sheet and scoring and reporting service; $10 per technical manual ('80, 50 pages); $8 per specimen set including test booklet, answer sheet, and administrator's manual ('78, 5 pages).
Time: 30(40) minutes.
Author: Psychological Services Bureau, Inc.
Publisher: Psychological Services Bureau, Inc.

Review of the PSB-Reading Comprehension Examination by JOSEPH C. CIECHALSKI, Assistant Professor of Counselor Education, East Carolina University, Greenville, NC:

The PSB-Reading Comprehension Examination is a Level A test (i.e., a test that can be administered and interpreted with the materials provided by the publisher) designed to measure understanding of what is read. It was constructed for students interested in enrolling in an occupational or paraprofessional career program.

The test consists of four reading passages of between 325 and 450 words. Each reading passage is followed by either 10 or 15 multiple-choice items (with four options) for a total of 50 items. In examining the items, this reviewer found that 90% of them appeared to be dependent on the reading passages. Therefore, the test appears to measure reading comprehension rather than general knowledge.

ADMINISTRATION AND SCORING. Directions for administering the test are presented in the Administrator's Manual and test booklet. The directions in the Administrator's Manual are detailed, yet easy to follow.

The time limit of 30 minutes was designed to allow most of the students time to complete. Examinees are informed in the general directions of the test booklet that they are not expected to answer all of the items.

The examinees use a separate answer sheet to record their responses. These answer sheets are scored by the publisher, and the results are returned using a "Class Record and Report Sheet" and the "Student Test Record and Profile Chart."

STANDARDIZATION AND NORMS. The general standardization population contained 3,654 students. In terms of grade level, the norming population represented persons who attained between 8th and 16th grade levels. Population ages ranged from 16 to 60 years. In addition, 52.6% of the population were males and 47.7% were females.

Special norms were provided for practical/vocational nursing programs. These norms were based on a sample of 3,213 individuals drawn from nine regions in the United States. Out of 1,316 schools contacted, 265 were represented. These included adult schools, colleges, community and junior colleges, vocational-technical schools, hospitals, and public and private schools.

According to the Technical Manual, minority groups comprised 16% of the general norms and 13% of the special norms. The authors state that, before actual publication, the test "was reviewed by members of different ethnic groups for possible offensive, stereotyped, culturally restricted, or racialist material."

Local norms may be prepared by the publisher. However, the publisher believes the general national norms give more useful information than local norms.

RELIABILITY. Test-retest reliability was reported for 324 cases as .95 over a 15-to-30-day time interval. A standard error of measurement of 3.5 was also reported in this category.

Split-half reliability was not reported. The authors address this issue by claiming that split-half reliability results in an "overestimate of reliability." The authors explain their reasoning further in the Technical Manual. Additional evidence of reliability is needed.

VALIDITY. Evidence of concurrent validity was demonstrated by correlating the test with the Preliminary Scholastic Aptitude Test ($n = 203$) which resulted in a coefficient of .89. A coefficient of .93 was reported using both the PSB-Aptitude for Practical Nursing Examination ($n = 78$) and the School and College Ability Test ($n = 213$). Using the Reading Comprehension subtest of the Nelson-Denny Reading Test ($n = 123$), a coefficient of .73 was reported. A coefficient of .71 was reported using the Otis Quick Scoring Mental Ability Test ($n = 152$).

Predictive validity was established using data provided by a vocational technical school.

Using overall GPA and State Board scores as the criteria, the correlations of .87 and .85 were reported respectively ($n = 124$). For three cosmetology programs, a correlation coefficient of .91 was reported using the scores obtained from a state licensing examination ($n = 127$).

Construct validity was not specifically reported. The authors view construct validity as a "generalized concept" that is included in other types of validity. They also state this examination has "some" content validity.

INTERPRETATION AND SCORING. The scores are reported as raw scores and percentiles using the "Class Record and Report Sheet" and the "Student Test Record and Profile Chart." These forms are very easy to use and understand. For example, using the "Student Test Record and Profile Chart," examinees who scored below the 25th percentile or above the 75th percentile can be readily identified. In addition, the Technical Manual adequately describes the use of percentiles.

Stanines can be found for individuals in terminal vocational and practical nursing programs using the tables provided in the Technical Manual.

SUMMARY. Test items depend upon the information obtained from the passages, thus the test appears to be a valid measure of reading comprehension. However, additional research regarding the reliability of this instrument is needed. An alternate form would have been useful in establishing reliability. Therefore, until additional reliability data are provided, I would recommend this test be used for its intended purpose but with some caution.

Review of the PSB-Reading Comprehension Examination by BRANDON DAVIS, Research Fellow, Ball State Neuropsychology Laboratory, and JOHN A. GLOVER, Director of Research, Teachers College, Ball State University, Muncie, IN:

The PSB-Reading Comprehension Examination is suggested by its authors to be a Level A assessment device. It is designed specifically for students who are enrolled, or who have intentions of being enrolled, in terminal occupational postsecondary education programs (e.g., landscape technologists, legal secretaries, dental laboratory technicians, etc.). As such, this test has the very singular purpose of assessing levels of reading comprehension with such students and, as stated in the manual, users of the test are advised against using the test with other population groups for other assessment purposes. The test has a 30-minute time limit and consists of four passages with 50 accompanying questions. One assessment score is obtained that is translatable into accompanying percentiles. Computer scoring also is available from the publisher.

The publishers present a modest, yet well-defined, rationale of their intentions for this measure. They suggest the measure will be useful in the selection process of students interested in vocationally oriented courses. The measure also is offered as a potential screening device for possible interventions with those students who score below the 40th percentile. However, the measure was not designed as a diagnostic reading test. The publisher has indicated that the test measures the examinee's ability: (a) to understand direct statements; (b) to interpret passages; (c) to see the intent of those writing passages; (d) to observe the organization of ideas; and (e) to extract information from passages with respect to ideas and purposes. While the test does have a 30-minute time limit and technically may be referred to as a "speed test," the publishers intend the measure to be used as a "power test." Previous administrations have determined 90% of the norm-group examinees completed the test in the allowed time.

The strength of any norm-referenced measure is its technical sophistication. In this regard, the material presented in the PSB-Reading Comprehension Examination manual provides a more than adequate basis for psychometric review. The test is based on 3 years of study and research, having been subjected to a series of tryouts, analyses, and revisions. The end result is a test that has a 4-passage/50-question format. The passages range from 325 to 450 words in length and were, according to the manual, based on textbooks used by students in vocational programs. Unfortunately, the manual does not provide a referenced list of examined textbooks, nor some indication of the "readability" (if in fact this was determined) of the textbooks upon which the passages were based. Further, the manual reveals that all passage material was reviewed by "authorities" in the field of reading; however, there are no accompanying citations, nor an indication of the criticisms and suggestions made by these authorities.

Actual standardization procedures were undertaken with a fairly large group of examinees for whom the test was intended. Sampling was carried out in nine broadly defined areas of the United States with four distinct community population sizes: Rural, Suburban, Urban I, and Urban II (i.e., more than 100,000). Also taken into consideration were varieties of schools, programs, ages, types of course instruction, and socioeconomic status. Students' grade levels ranged from Grade 8 to Grade 16, with approximately 83% of the students having 11 to 13 years of education. Ages in the sample ranged from 16 to 60 years, with approximately 60% of the sample in the 16–20-year bracket. Of the total sample, 52.6% were males and 47.4% were females. Minority representation was not specifically included in the sample; however, a post-hoc analysis by the publishers suggested approximately 16% of the sample were minorities. The manual also provides a section on norms for special populations and mentions the publisher's offer to assist those interested in developing local norms.

Test-retest reliability ($N = 324$), the only reliability function quoted in the manual, was .95 with a mean raw score of 26.95, a *SD* of 15.65, and a *SEM* of 3.50. Formal selection procedures were not undertaken to establish content validity. The publishers justify this anomaly because the materials are representative of textbooks judged to be appropriate by a group of "experts."

Concurrent validity, however, was given a more appropriate evaluation by the authors. The PSB-Reading Comprehension Examination was compared to the verbal subtests of the Preliminary Scholastic Aptitude Test (PSAT) and the PSB-Aptitude for Practical Nursing Examination, and with the comprehension subtest of the Nelson-Denny Reading Test. Pearson product-moment correlations were .89 and .73 respectively for first and last mentioned comparisons.

Based on the previous and other samples, predictive validities are offered, which range between .91 and .85, between the measure and both grade-point averages and state examinations. Unfortunately, these latter mentioned tests are poorly referenced.

In sum, this test is a viable assessment device for those persons involved in selection procedures at vocational schools. The norming procedures, while not necessarily complete, offer good evidence of the measure's reliability and validity. From a technical standpoint the book is poorly referenced. However, the publishers of the PSB-Reading Comprehension Examination have succeeded in developing a test for a very select population, and quite appropriately portray its limitations for populations other than those for whom it is intended. Taken in this vein, the test represents an appropriate choice for reviewing the reading comprehension abilities of students applying for vocational programs.

REVIEWER'S REFERENCES

Educational Testing Service. (1970). Preliminary Scholastic Aptitude Test. Princeton, NJ: Educational Testing Service.
Evans, A. S., Yanuzzi, J. R., & Stouffer, G. A. (1972). Aptitude Test for Practical Nursing Examination. St. Thomas, PA: Psychological Services Bureau.
Educational Testing Service. (1973). School and College Ability Test. Princeton, NJ: Educational Testing Service.
Brown, J. I., Nelson, M. J., & Denny, E. C. (1976). Nelson-Denny Reading Test. Boston, MA: Houghton Mifflin.

[67]
The Psychap Inventory.

Purpose: Measures how happy an individual is as a person in order to help one understand how to "get more happiness and satisfaction from life."
Population: Adolescents and adults.
Publication Dates: 1971–85.
Acronym: PHI.
Scores, 5: Achieved Happiness, Happy Personality, Happy Attitudes and Values, Happiness Life-Style, Total.
Administration: Group.
Forms: 2 sets of equivalent forms: Set 1 (Forms A and B), Set 2 (Forms C and D).
Price Data, 1988: Available from publisher for 4 color-coded testing booklets, answer sheets, scoring stencils, general interpretation sheet, administration and scoring directions sheets, copy of the article "Psychap Inventory" which serves as a manual, and complete computer program including diskette and information for administration, scoring, and interpretive reporting.
Time: (10–15) minutes per form.
Comments: IBM or compatible with 64K and 1 single-sided drive required for administration of microdiskette version.
Author: Michael W. Fordyce.
Publisher: Cypress Lake Media.

Review of The Psychap Inventory by GEORGE ENGELHARD, JR., Assistant Professor of Educational Studies, Emory University, Atlanta, GA:

The Psychap Inventory (PHI) is a self-report instrument developed by Michael W. Fordyce to measure personal happiness. There are two sets of alternate forms available; Set 1 (Forms A and B) is the original and most researched set, and Set 2 (Forms C and D) was added later in order to produce a wider range of response by including more extreme response alternatives.

There are 80 items in each form, and items consist of two paired statements that describe a characteristic believed to distinguish between a happy and unhappy person; for example, "I am content" is paired with "I am not content." In addition to a total score on the PHI, scores from four subscales are also provided: Achieved Personal Happiness Scale (16 items), Happy Personality Scale (24 items), Happiness Attitudes and Values Scale (19 items), and Happiness Life-Style Scale (21 items).

The PHI was previously called the Self Description Inventory. A technical manual is not available; however, an article by Fordyce (1985) and a Supplement (Fordyce, 1987) with numerous summary tables are provided. The items in the PHI were developed on the basis of earlier reviews of the literature that led to the identification of the characteristics of "happy individuals." Responses to a pool of items were correlated with a two-item measure of happiness (Fordyce, 1977) and the Depression Adjective Checklist (Lubin, 1967) in order to select the final set of items. According to the author, the PHI is designed for use in research, counseling, and clinical assessment. The author also recommends its use as a diagnostic instrument to identify "strengths and weaknesses" related to happiness which are directly associated with Fordyce's "fourteen fundamentals to increase personal happiness" program (Fordyce, 1981).

The PHI has been used primarily with community college students in Florida. The normative data, as well as most of the technical evidence for the PHI, are based almost exclusively on this population. This is not necessarily a major weakness, but does need to be kept in mind by the potential user. The potential user also needs to be warned about problems with the Supplement; a great deal of data are presented (over 400 pages of tables) and the tables are poorly organized. For example, the correlations over time between Forms A and B are reported in the chronological order in which the studies were conducted, rather than by length of time between testings. A major improvement would be to add summaries to the tables which might include the median correlations and ranges over the data reported. A technical manual that summarizes the relevant information and integrates the validity studies would be even more helpful to the user. The Supplement, as currently presented, tends to be more of a hindrance than a help in evaluating the PHI.

Preliminary norms are based on samples of 1,437 community college students for Forms A and B, and 527 students for Forms C and D. Means and standard deviations are also presented in the Supplement for other selected populations, such as married individuals, retired businessmen, lesbians in professional careers, and college professors. Although most of the examinees are from Florida, Fordyce (1985) indicates that he has presented a "somewhat representative cross-section of adult Americans" (p. 24). This claim for national representativeness is not adequately documented.

No estimates of the internal consistency of the PHI are presented. The test-retest correlations for each form and subscales are also not reported. These are serious weaknesses making it impossible to judge the reliability of the PHI and the appropriate standard errors to use with the scores. It is somewhat surprising this evidence is not provided, given the extensive data which are presented for the correlations between forms. Short-term and long-term equivalent forms reliabilities are fairly high. Short-term equivalent forms correlations average around .92 (same testing session to a week interval); the correlations between forms over longer time periods are typical for instruments of this type with average correlations of about .86 (2- to 3-week interval) and .74 (3-month interval).

Fordyce (1985, 1987) reports on an extensive set of validity studies. In terms of convergent validity, the PHI correlates positively with other measures of happiness and negatively with a variety of indices of depression. The concurrent validity also appears to be adequate, with the PHI correlating with other personality characteristics that the literature on subjective well-being (Diener, 1984) suggests as being associated with happiness. Overall, the evidence for the validity of the PHI is fairly strong in terms of its correlations with other self-report inventories of various personality characteristics, such as the Minnesota Multiphasic Personality Inventory (Hathaway & McKinley, 1951), Edwards Personal Preference Schedule (Edwards, 1959), and the Myers-Briggs Type Indicator (Myers, 1962).

An important question that is not addressed is whether or not the classification of the items into subscales of the PHI makes any sense. Either a content validity study or an item factor analysis (Bock, Gibbons, & Muraki, 1988) would contribute to our knowledge regarding the internal structure of the PHI. Without this type of information, it is not clear that the classification of the items into subscales is based on anything other than the whim of the author.

In the section on the comparability of forms, Fordyce (1985) claims that the forms can be considered as being "identical," and he later suggests the forms be used in "tandem (since no two are identical), especially in time series and repeated measures designs" (p. 9), and in the "monitoring or follow-up assessment of programs" (p. 26). Given the differences in the means and standard deviations between the forms, they are clearly *not* comparable. If different forms were used in a time series study, it would not be possible to separate form effects from individual changes in happiness over time. Further, an unscrupulous evaluator could use Form D ($M = 45.39$ for the normative sample) for the pretest where scores tend to be lower on the average, and then use Form A ($M = 55.16$ for the normative sample) for the posttest on which the examinees are likely to have higher scores regardless of any program effects. This can be resolved by using standard scores and equating the four forms onto an equal interval scale.

In summary, much of the early work on subjective well-being arose from survey research conducted with various indicators of the quality of life. Some of the earlier measures of "happiness" were single items included in larger surveys (Diener, 1984). The PHI represents significant progress over this work and represents a step towards the development of an instrument to measure important aspects of individual happiness. Although the PHI appears to offer a promising measure of self-reported levels of well-being, the lack of evidence regarding reliability (internal consistency estimates and test-retest correlations) is a serious weakness. The validity coefficients are comparable to those found for similar self-report inventories of personality characteristics. In spite of the strong buy-this-instrument and enroll-in-my-program tone that permeates the material, the PHI should be considered by researchers interested in the assessment of subjective well-being. The evidence presented does not support the usefulness of the PHI for counseling or clinical assessment.

REVIEWER'S REFERENCES

Hathaway, S. R., & McKinley, J. C. (1951). Minnesota Multiphasic Personality Inventory. San Antonio, TX: The Psychological Corporation.

Edwards, A. L. (1959). Edwards Personal Preference Schedule. San Antonio, TX: The Psychological Corporation.

Myers, I. (1962). Myers-Briggs Type Indicator. Palo Alto, CA: Consulting Psychologists Press, Inc.

Lubin, B. (1967). Depression Adjective Check List. San Diego, CA: EdITS/Educational and Industrial Testing Service.

Fordyce, M. W. (1977). Development of a program to increase personal happiness. Journal of Counseling Psychology, 24, 511-521.

Fordyce, M. W. (1981). The psychology of happiness: A brief version of the fourteen fundamentals. Fort Myers, FL: Cypress Lake Media.

Diener, E. (1984). Subjective well-being. Psychological Bulletin, 95, 542-575.

Fordyce, M. W. (1985). The Psychap Inventory: A multiscale test to measure happiness and its concomitants. Social Indicators Research, 18, 1-33.

Fordyce, M. W. (1987). Research and tabular supplement for the Psychap Inventory. Fort Myers, FL: Cypress Lake Media.

Bock, R. D., Gibbons, R., & Muraki, E. (1988). Full-information item factor analysis. Applied Psychological Measurement, 12, 261-280.

Review of The Psychap Inventory by ALFRED L. SMITH, JR., Personnel Psychologist, Federal Aviation Administration, U.S. Department of Transportation, Washington, DC:

The Psychap Inventory purports to be a multidimensional measure of the full range of happiness characteristics and its major concomitants. At first glance, a measure of "happiness" seems overly simplistic and lacking sufficient merit to warrant much attention. This idea was reinforced by the test materials which have spelling, typographical, and grammatical errors, and seemingly naive or obvious comments on the profiles and reports that are to be given to the test taker. For example, test takers are told how their scores compare to those who "score happily," and that those who get a high score are "probably a pretty happy person because of" their similarity to the "happiest people." It is likely that people who might be given this inventory can as easily tell their therapist about their happiness or unhappiness as they can complete the inventory. Voluntary clients are likely to be fairly willing to do so and involuntary clients probably can fake the answers either way.

On second glance and careful review of Fordyce (1985), the journal article which serves as the only manual for the instrument, there does appear to be considerable value to using The Psychap in some circumstances. Most notable of these is for the situation for which it was developed—as a diagnostic tool for use in conjunction with a prescriptive program for increased happiness. The author, of course, hopes users of the inventory will also use his program for building happiness. Inventory items were designed to mesh with this program, and so to identify specific areas where a person can take steps to become more satisfied (e.g., developing relationships with people, self-knowledge and self-acceptance, or a more optimistic outlook).

It is likely that this inventory can be more helpful than interview techniques in helping people to pinpoint strengths and weaknesses contributing to their own sense of happiness, well-being, or self-satisfaction, and to set goals and objectives for positive change. Development of The Psychap is based on a firm empirical base. Clearly, considerable time and effort have gone into the identification of what constitutes and is concomitant to happiness and how to measure it. The instrument contains conceptually developed subscales covering four aspects: Achieved Personal Happiness, Happy Personality, Happiness Attitudes and Values, and Happiness Life-Style.

Extensive research reported in the journal article/manual provides information about the instrument's reliability and validity. Two sets of alternate forms exist (A–B and C–D). Within each set, alternate forms reliability (called test-retest by the author) is high. No attempt has been made to identify the two sets as equivalent, because C and D were specifically designed to eliminate response bias by creating more extreme items. Means obtained on C and D are consistently lower across studies. Review of the items clearly shows that some are so extreme that almost no one could pick the "happy" alternative. Perhaps a better approach to understanding response bias would be to examine results obtained under instructions to "fake happy" or "fake unhappy."

The author has gone to considerable length to examine the construct validity of the inventory by looking at convergent and divergent validity using concurrent administration of a lengthy number of personality instruments. Evidence is provided of positive relationships between scores on The Psychap and such things as extroversion, emotional stability, and vitality. There are strong negative relationships between happiness scores and negative emotions such as hostility, depression, and anxiety. Reliability and validity data reported in Fordyce (1985) are easily comprehended, but the cumbersome and unwieldy tables provided with the test materials are of little help to instrument evaluation for clinical use (although one might appreciate them for research use). Although norms are available, both Fordyce and this reviewer agree more work on norms is needed.

Fordyce has concluded, based on the research with The Psychap and other research, that happiness is so basic a personality factor that attempts to measure it by almost any means will be successful (even, as suggested early in this review, just by asking people). This is probably true. One could probably use almost any of the personality instruments against which The Psychap was evaluated. The latter has the advantage, however, of being less threatening as the issue is "happiness," not "self-concept" or "personality" or negative-toned concepts such as "depression," and wording and content of the items reflect this. As stated earlier, it also has the advantage of items and subscales of items geared toward specific focuses for change.

In summary, The Psychap Inventory has been well researched and considerable effort has been expended to ensure it covers the full domain of that which goes along with and/or characterizes happiness. Thus, it appears to have acceptable psychometric properties. It provides a fairly nonthreatening way to identify such things as values, attitudes, characteristics, and behaviors that directly contribute to a person's happiness and/or satisfaction (or lack thereof), and is likely to be of use in counseling normal populations. Test materials need to be brought up to professional standards, however, including a concise manual to replace the lengthy journal article currently serving as a manual.

REVIEWER'S REFERENCE

Fordyce, M. W. (1985). The Psychap Inventory: A multi-scale test to measure happiness and its concomitants. *Social Indicators Research, 18*, 1-33.

[68]
Psychoeducational Profile.

Purpose: "To identify uneven and idiosyncratic learning patterns."
Population: Autistic, psychotic, and developmentally disabled children functioning at preschool age levels.
Publication Date: 1979.
Acronym: PEP.
Scores, 13: Pathology (Affect, Relating, Use of Materials, Sensory Modes, Language), Developmental Functions (Imitation, Perception, Fine Motor, Gross Motor, Eye-Hand Integration, Cognitive Performance, Cognitive Verbal, Developmental Score).
Administration: Individual.
Parts, 2: Pathology, Developmental Functions.
Price Data, 1989: $29 per manual (234 pages); $12 per pad of profile sheets.
Time: (45–75) minutes.
Comments: Volume 1 in the Individualized Assessment and Treatment for Autistic and Developmentally Disabled Children series; other test materials (e.g., jar of bubbles, tactile blocks) must be supplied by examiner.
Authors: Eric Schopler and Robert Jay Reichler.
Publisher: PRO-ED, Inc.

Review of the Psychoeducational Profile by GERALD S. HANNA, *Professor of Educational Psychology and Measurement, Kansas State University, Manhattan, KS:*

The Psychoeducational Profile (PEP) was developed to enable direct translation of assessment results into individualized teaching programs and to pinpoint each examinee's emerging skills (Volume I, p. xi). This diagnosis theme recurs repeatedly throughout the manual. Moreover, a profile enables graphic comparison of relative strengths and weaknesses by means of estimated age equivalents, and a companion volume "explains how the diagnostic information from the PEP is translated into individualized teaching programs" (Volume I, p. 3).

Clearly, profile analysis is used in interpreting PEP results. Therefore, issues of central importance to the informed professional use of the instrument concern reliability and validity of differences among scores in the profile.

RELIABILITY. The manual provides no data regarding the reliability of the (a) total scores, (*b*) subscores, or (*c*) differences among the subscores that are used for programming.

VALIDITY. Although validity is argued on several bases, the only case this reviewer found at all persuasive was the case made for content validity. However, as the authors recognized, the key validity question is, "'Can the PEP be used for effective educational and home programming?' There are no formal data, but there is empirical clinical evidence, because the PEP has been used successfully as the main programming instrument for 10 years in our program and within a statewide program in North Carolina. These programs have received considerable recognition for their effectiveness by both professionals and parents" (Volume I, pp. 91–92). Overall, then, users are provided with no meaningful validity research, only with authorial testimony that the instrument has been considered effective by those who have used it.

NORMATIVE DATA. A sample of 276 normal children between ages 1 and 7 were chosen from the Chapel Hill-Carrboro area, apparently mainly on the basis of availability. The demographic data provided leave the impression that (*a*) the sample did not closely parallel the population of the country; and (*b*) the subsamples were not well matched from age to age.

The only kind of derived score provided is estimated age equivalents. Yet age-equivalent scores are well-known to be unsuitable for profile analysis, owing to (*a*) the likelihood of unequal variability among the subscales and (*b*) unequal units of measure. This inadequacy alone would compromise the suitability of the PEP for pinpointing examinee weaknesses.

SUMMARY. Interpretation of PEP scores is seriously handicapped by the inadequacy of the sample and the inappropriateness of the kind of derived score provided. The absence of meaningful validity studies for the recommended purpose of the instrument is also a concern. Perhaps most damaging is the total lack of evidence that scores and profiles are reliable enough to warrant use in educational programming. Collectively, these limitations lead this reviewer to view the release of the PEP as quite premature and to be unable to recommend it for applied use.

Review of the Psychoeducational Profile by MARTIN J. WIESE, School Psychologist, Wilkes County Schools, Wilkesboro, NC:

The Psychoeducational Profile (PEP) is designed to offer a developmental approach to the assessment of autistic and psychotic children. It is an inventory of behaviors and skills used to identify idiosyncratic learning patterns. The PEP provides information on developmental functioning in seven areas: Imitation, Perception, Fine Motor, Gross Motor, Eye-Hand Integration, Cognitive Performance, and Cognitive Verbal Skills. In addition to the seven developmental areas, the PEP also provides a Pathology Scale that indicates the severity of the child's behaviors. The Pathology Scale is divided into five subunits: Affect, Relating/ Cooperating/Human Interest, Play/Interest, Sensory Modes, and Language. In total, the test scores yield a profile depicting relative strengths and weaknesses in several different areas.

The PEP consists of a set of toys and play activities presented to the child by an examiner who also observes, evaluates, and records the child's responses. The test materials for the PEP can be constructed according to the instructions found in the Appendices or an assembled kit may be purchased directly. The test items are developmentally arrayed from ages 1 to 7 and minimize the amount of language needed to understand the directions. Standardized verbal directions have been avoided and nonverbal gestures and demonstrations are acceptable administration techniques.

The child is scored on each developmental item as passing, failing, or emerging according to criteria established in the manual. All developmental items are scored during administration and the pathology items are scored immediately following the testing situation. Scoring criteria for the pathology items are based on clinical judgment (e.g., appropriate, age-appropriate, or within normal limits). After the examiner has scored all items, the scores are transferred to the Test Profile. The profile provides a graphical representation of the test scores for easier interpretation.

Interpretation of the PEP scores and the profile provides information on the nature of the child's difficulties. The profile is used to determine the best approximation of the educational expectations for the subject. Uneven profiles are thought to be characteristic of psychotic or retarded children. Planning for the child includes working on the individual child's strengths and weaknesses. It is recommended that a written summary or report complement the subject's scores, and a sample outline for the report is provided in the manual.

It is important to note the PEP is not a test in the traditional framework of a norm-referenced test, nor is it a criterion-referenced test. As a result, normative data on the PEP are limited. A normal comparison group was used, not as a standardization group, but to assist in the construction of the scales. A sample of 276 normal children, all from North Carolina, were tested with the PEP to arrange the items developmentally and to construct the scales. One limitation is that the majority of the children in the initial sample were white and from high socioeconomic groups. Again, the normal comparison sample was not intended to be used as a standardization group because the PEP is not designed to yield an overall standard score. The main purpose of the test is to provide information on the child's idiosyncratic learning patterns.

There are a number of other limitations and difficulties with the PEP. First, there are no reliability or validity studies reported in the manual. The authors defend the lack of measurement data by stating the test should not be used to construct a standard score that allows comparisons with other children. Therefore, each administration is individualized to the child and reliability should not be an issue.

Similarly, no validity studies are reported. Even so, the authors suggest the PEP has good content validity and construct validity but do not cite any empirical evidence. No established procedure was used to identify the seven developmental function areas, even though the manual states the activities were empirically established as suitable for the target population. It is not clear how the content domains were specified, and it appears the items and procedures evolved through a series of trial and error modifications.

Finally, even though it was designed to guide programming and planning for autistic children, there has been no formal evaluation of the PEP's effectiveness for this purpose. The authors close, stating the PEP has been used many years and has received considerable

recognition for its effectiveness by other professionals.

Overall, the PEP does provide a method of gaining information about children considered untestable by standard means. Unfortunately, its lack of reported validity and reliability undermines its effectiveness as an assessment instrument. At a minimum, the authors should determine test-retest reliability if the PEP is to be used to measure educational progress with autistic and communication-disordered children.

[69]
Racial Attitude Test.

Purpose: Measures attitudes toward an examiner-selected group of people using a generic semantic differential method.
Population: Adults.
Publication Date: 1989.
Scores, 8: Physical, Ego Strength (Dominance, Control, Anxiety, Ethics, General Social, On the Job), You Would Object.
Administration: Group.
Manual: No manual.
Price Data, 1989: $19.95 per test booklet which may be photocopied for local use.
Time: Administration time not reported.
Comments: No reliability or validity; no norms.
Author: Thomas J. Rundquist.
Publisher: Nova Media, Inc.

Review of the Racial Attitude Test by RICH-ARD I. LANYON, Professor of Psychology, Arizona State University, Tempe, AZ:

There is no stretch of the imagination by which the Racial Attitude Test could be considered a test in the accepted sense of the term for psychology. The entirety of the material available from the publisher and the author consists of four sheets of thick paper, stapled in the corner, for which a price of $9.95 is stated on the front page. Also given on the front page is the address of the publisher and ISBN number. The second and third sheets list 46 bipolar items preceded by the following instructions: "The selected group to what degree have these traits 1 to 5. Circle your choice of 1, 2, 3, 4, or 5. For example, for the trait Dirty to Clean, one would pick a number from 1 to 5 to show what degree from Dirty to Clean he felt the selected group had." The 46 items are grouped into eight categories, the names of which are given below. The number of items in each category ranges from 2 through

13. Following the 46 items is the statement, "When you complete the survey, please bring the test up to the administrators."

The fourth sheet gives instructions for interpretation. I quote it in full. (Heading) "Evaluating Results." (Paragraph) "If testing more than one person, Xeroxing of the question sheet is allowed. This is figured in your initial price. We allow you to Xerox up to 25 copies. After that a new test booklet should be purchased. Generally, a high score for each question or each section (Physical, Ego Strength, Control, Anxiety, Ethics, General Social, On the Job, You Would Object) means a more positive attitude by the test taker toward the group. However, the reality of the general population's attitude for a selected group as shown in each question would need to be based on extensive testing. For some of the traits there may be a difference of opinion as to whether it is positive or negative."

A telephone call to the author revealed that nothing further was available, but that data were currently being collected "from a couple of colleges." No mention was made of test development procedures, item analyses, reliability, validity, norms, or a manual.

Clearly the Racial Attitude Test is not usable as an assessment instrument in its present form, and it should be withdrawn from the market until further development work is done. Guidelines for such test development can be found in the 1985 *Standards for Educational and Psychological Testing* published jointly by the American Psychological Association and other organizations.

A general comment on the study and assessment of racism is in order. Two aspects are usually addressed: (*a*) the *content* of stereotypes, as to what attitudes are salient in judging different races; and (*b*) *social distance*, as to how willing people are to engage with the race in a variety of activities of differing social distance. The two sections of the Racial Attitude Test do conform to this structure, suggesting that there might be a foundation for the ultimate development of a useful instrument. Readers wishing to advance their own knowledge of this area are referred to Brewer and Kramer (1985) and McConahay, Hardee, and Batts (1981).

REVIEWER'S REFERENCES

McConahay, J. B., Hardee, B. B., & Batts, V. (1981). Has racism declined in America? *Journal of Conflict Resolution, 25,* 563-579.

American Educational Research Association, American Psychological Association, & National Council on Measurement in Education. (1985). *Standards for educational and psychological testing.* Washington, DC: American Psychological Association, Inc.

Brewer, M. B., & Kramer, R. M. (1985). The psychology of intergroup attitudes and behavior. *Annual Review of Psychology, 36,* 219-243.

Review of the Racial Attitude Test by STEVEN G. LoBELLO, Assistant Professor of Psychology, Auburn University at Montgomery, Montgomery, AL:

The Racial Attitude Test is a 46-item scale which may be administered individually or in groups. The test is designed to measure attitudes toward any ethnic, religious, or racial group specified by the examiner. The test has three scales that are ambiguously entitled You Would Object/Accept, Physical, and Ego Strength (Dominance, Control, Anxiety, Ethics, General Social, and On the Job are subscales). The You Would Object/Accept scale asks the test taker to rate level of acceptance of the specified group in various social situations. The format is a bipolar Likert-type scale with adjectival opposites to which the test taker responds by circling a number 1 (negative) through 5 (positive). High scores on each scale or item are presumed to reflect more positive attitudes toward the specified group.

The only test instructions provided are three very awkwardly worded lines at the top of the first page of the test. There is no test manual and, consequently, there are no norms, reliability, or validity data. There is no information provided about internal consistency of the individual scales, some of which consist of fewer than four items. There is a brief, one-paragraph information sheet attached to the back of the test which provides no information about test construction, for whom the test was designed, or how the scores should be used. The purpose of the test is patently transparent with no provision for measuring social desirability, or overrater or underrater response sets.

In summary, the Racial Attitude Test reflects a naive and irresponsible approach to test construction with no attention given to even the minimum psychometric standards as outlined in the *Standards for Educational and Psychological Testing* (1985, AERA, APA, & NCME). Anyone choosing to use this test could not have the slightest confidence that it is actually measuring racial attitudes toward a specified group. The Racial Attitude Test is actually a nontest and it should not be used until the author provides adequate supporting data.

REVIEWER'S REFERENCE

American Educational Research Association, American Psychological Association, & National Council on Measurement in Education. (1985). *Standards for educational and psychological testing*. Washington, DC: American Psychological Association, Inc.

[70]

Reading Comprehension Inventory.

Purpose: To assess a student's strengths and weaknesses in reading and to determine a student's capacity to extract meaningful information from narrative passages.
Population: Grades K–6.
Publication Date: 1988.
Acronym: RCI.
Scores: 3 sets of structural features: Narrative Elements, Response Level, Information Sequencing.
Administration: Group.
Price Data, 1988: $24.95 per starter set including 20 workbooks with student profiles and manual (33 pages); $18 per 20 workbooks with student profiles; $8.50 per manual; $13 per specimen set.
Time: Administration time not reported.
Author: Gerard Giordano.
Publisher: Scholastic Testing Service, Inc.

Review of the Reading Comprehension Inventory by ALICE J. CORKILL, Assistant Professor of Psychology, University of Western Ontario, London, Ontario, Canada:

The Reading Comprehension Inventory attempts to assess the functional and operational skills of elementary school age readers. The test consists of six narrative passages beginning with a simple five-sentence story and progressing to a more complex four-paragraph story. Each passage is followed by five questions which are designed to assess the following five Narrative elements of the passage: character(s), location(s), time(s), plot, and rationale. Each question also provides information concerning the Response Level: factual, critical, or extrapolative and Information Sequencing: presituational, situational, or postsituational.

The first passage, "Snake," is the least complex on all features requiring only simple, factual, situational responses to the five questions. The passages gradually become more complex with the last passage, "Fire," requiring complex information in all areas.

The passages may be read orally or silently during administration. Test administrators are encouraged to have the examinee continue with the test until comprehension falls below 60 percent. How this is to be determined, however, is not discussed. These procedures suggest the inventory is individually administered, although this is not clearly stated in the administrator's manual.

An "Analysis of Questions" is provided for each of the six passages. The analysis provides answers to each question, a point value for each correct response, and a description of the Narrative Element, the Response Level, and the Information Sequencing as assessed by each question. Each of the five questions that accompany a passage is differentially weighted. Simple, factual information may receive a small number of points while more complex, interpretive questions garner a larger number of points. The weights were devised by a group of "20 experienced teachers" (no other information about the teachers or their experience is provided) who read each passage and distributed a total of 100 points to five questions that they created which assessed each of the five narrative elements. As a result, the point values assigned to each narrative element vary from passage to passage.

In four of the six passages the answers provided for the question assessing the location narrative element are incomplete or incorrect. For example, in the passage titled "Creature" the examinee is questioned about the location of a trap set to capture the creature. The answer provided is "backyard," however, the passage states, "They decided to set a trap in their yard." As a result, "yard" or "outside" might be better answers and although "backyard" could be considered appropriate, it is not necessarily the best or most correct response. In the other passages the responses seem somewhat incomplete. The examinee has access to the passage while responding to the questions. As a consequence, detailed or specific answers are readily available and could be expected. Other passages with problems with this narrative element include "Alone," "Crash," and "Fire."

For two passages, "Cave" and "Creature," additional correct responses could be provided for the question assessing rationale (often more than one correct response is provided). For the passage "Crash" the character question may be asking for too much to be inferred from the passage. If administrators of the test are inclined to employ a literal use of the responses provided in the test manual, the results of the test may incorrectly identify an examinees' strengths and/or weaknesses.

In each instance an examinee receives all the points assigned to a question or none of the points. A brief perusal of the responses provided in the administrator's manual, however, clearly shows that some responses are more complete or precise. Since more than one correct response is provided, in many instances, a possibility worth considering would be to assign more correct responses, in terms of detail or specificity, with higher point values and less correct or complete responses with lower point values.

Each test booklet includes the six test passages and a strength and weakness worksheet. This worksheet is to be used by the administrator in an effort to identify an examinee's pattern of strengths and weaknesses. The administrator is instructed to assign and total an examinee's points. These point totals are not used for anything, at least not according to the manual. Careful examination of the sample strength and weakness worksheet, however, suggests that the point total indicates percentage of comprehension. Further use of the strength and weakness worksheet is in identifying areas in which an examinee excels or fails. Insufficient information is provided for this use of the strength and weakness worksheet. A more complete example or more than one example of using the worksheet would be beneficial.

Half of the administrator's manual is devoted to 23 instructional activities designed to address the identified deficiencies of an examinee. This is a potentially valuable portion of the manual; however, use of these activities may be restricted by the nature of the problems associated with use of the strength and weakness worksheet.

No reliability or validity information is provided in the administrator's manual. The lack of information in this area is a critical deficiency in the Reading Comprehension Inventory. Some attempt should be made to determine the reliability of the instrument, perhaps via test-retest if no other option seems suitable. The validity of the inventory also needs to be established, if only the content validity. The value of this instrument cannot be completely determined without evidence of reliability and validity.

If the problems associated with scoring procedures are rectified, the Reading Comprehension Inventory could be a valuable instrument for use by classroom teachers. Its value lies in ease of administration, teacher scoring, and suggested instructional activities developed to assist in strengthening identified deficiencies. Its shortcomings center on incomplete or incorrect responses, lack of directions for completing the strength and weakness worksheet, and undocumented reliability and validity information.

Review of the Reading Comprehension Inventory by BRANDON DAVIS, Research Fellow, Ball State Neuropsychology Laboratory, and JOHN A. GLOVER, Director of Research, Teachers College, Ball State University, Muncie, IN:

The Reading Comprehension Inventory (RCI) was designed to evaluate reading comprehension in school-aged children from a criterion-referenced standpoint; age ranges are not included in the manual. The test consists of six reading passages, each accompanied by five differentially weighted questions. This weighting process is intended to correspond both to different items within each passage and also across the six passages; with the first passage being the simplest with respect to comprehension issues and the sixth passage being the most complicated. Accordingly, item values are given weights ranging from 5 to 60 points. There is no total score, but rather individual scores for each story with the diagnostician circling weaknesses in each story based on the three possible categories of assessment for each question and the three to five subcategories for each category. The manual includes a series of exercises that purport to offer guidance in the remediation of the identified comprehension deficits.

In a poorly delineated introduction, the author suggests that the test "is an actual test of reading comprehension rather than a test of skills that correlate with reading." One is left with the impression that the author has presumed comprehension is easily bifurcated from the myriad of other cognitive skills in reading. Indeed, this perception appears confirmed as the author has offered nothing in the way of approximate readability levels for any of the six passages. Further, the manual suggests that students can be assessed in either an oral or silent diagnostic mode; and while the author suggests the test is intended as a classroom evaluation tool, the manual does not specify whether such assessment is to be carried out in an individual or group fashion.

The author offers a gratuitous figure (Figure 1, p. 1) in the introduction of the manual enjoining the reader in an appreciation of the fact that the processes of reading bring to bear on the reader a variety of physical, linguistic, cognitive, academic, social, and emotional factors. Apparently, the RCI is designed to respond to this blending of intellective factors in the six passages making up the test.

The six passages are arranged in order of increasing complexity based on the matrix of three sets of features (i.e., Narrative Elements, Response Level issues, and Information Sequencing concerns) with corresponding levels of structure within each set (i.e., character, location, time, plot, and rationale for the Narrative Elements; factual, critical, and extrapolative issues for the Response Level set; and, presituational, situational, and postsituational concerns for the Sequencing of Information set). The last story respresents the most complex interaction of these variables, while the first story represents the simplest interaction.

Such an assessment outline would seem to suggest a sophisticated attempt directed toward the assessment of the comprehension processes in the student. Unfortunately, the technical information in the manual does little to substantiate this impression. In fact, it is not apparent that any criteria, as delineated in *Standards for Educational and Psychological Testing* (AERA, APA, & NCME, 1985), have been applied in the test's construction. There is no information available as to the test's reliability or validity. The author does not make mention of the differential issues of criterion-referencing versus norm-referencing. However, it appears from its construction that it would best fit into the norm-referenced category. Even allowing for the fact that this test is criterion-referenced, one might expect some reference to minimal issues of psychometric test construction (Carver, 1974; Salvia & Ysseldyke, 1981; Womer, 1974). One singular reference to test construction suggests the process of assigning values to each of the five questions in the six stories was carried out with the collaboration of 20 experienced teachers.

Also notable by its absence is support for those concepts on which the construction of the test is based. Indeed, there is no theoretical or empirical support offered lending credence to the author's perspective on issues of reading comprehension. In the introduction of the manual the author suggests that his test attempts to measure the reading process (i.e., comprehension) in tandem with all the other mechanical skills of reading (i.e., syllabification, phonics, spelling, word derivation, etc.) rather than separate from them. However, appropriate test construction would have better dealt with this issue. In fact, without the necessary psychometric concerns that would control for the age and grade levels of words chosen in his passage, it would be impossible to assume that the test (*a*) is assessing comprehension, or (*b*) is appropriate for a given segment of the school population. In fact, such inappropriate test construction would allow word recognition to confound issues of comprehension to the degree that word recognition, not comprehension, is actually being assessed.

In sum, the RCI attempts to represent a defined theoretical perspective on the assessment of reading comprehension. Unfortunately, the author has neglected to support this perspective by applying basic test construction principles to his measure and has offered only a minimum of technical data. For instance, even criterion-referenced measures should include the targeted school population. Essentially, the RCI represents an extremely arbitrary and subjective attempt at test construction. There are significant problems with every aspect of this measure.

REVIEWER'S REFERENCES

Carver, R. P. (1974). Two dimensions of tests: Psychometric and edumetric. *American Psychologist, 29* (7), 512-518.

Womer, F. B. (1974). What is criterion-referenced measurement? In W. E. Blanton, R. Farr, & J. J. Tuinman (Eds.), *Measuring reading performance* (pp. 34-43). Newark, DE: International Reading Association.

Salvia, J., & Ysseldyke, J. E. (1981). *Assessment in special and remedial education.* Boston: Houghton-Mifflin.

American Educational Research Association, American Psychological Association, & National Council on Measurement in Education. (1985). *Standards for educational and psychological testing.* Washington, DC: American Psychological Association, Inc.

[71]

Reading Evaluation Adult Diagnosis (Revised).

Purpose: Assess existing reading competencies.
Population: Illiterate adult students.
Publication Dates: 1972–82.
Acronym: READ.

Scores: 4 parts, 26 scores: Sight Words (List A, List B, List C, List D), Word Analysis Skills (Letter Sounds Not Identified, Letter Names Not Identified, Reversal Problems, Consonant-Vowel-Consonant Not Known, CV-CC, Initial Blends Not Known, Final Blends Not Known, Initial Digraphs Not Known, Final Digraphs Not Known, Variant Vowel Problems (R-Controlled, L-Controlled, W-Controlled, Y-Controlled, Vowel Digraphs, and Vowel Plus E), Suffixes Not Known, Soft C and G Problems, Silent Letter Problems, Multi-Syllabic Word Problems), Reading/Listening Inventory (Word Recognition, Reading Comprehension, Listening Comprehension), Group Screening Test.
Administration: Individual in part; student responds orally in part.
Price Data, 1989: $7.25 per test booklet/manual('82, 55 pages); $1.50 per tester's recording pad; $20 per test trainer's kit including trainer's guide and cassette tape.
Time: Administration time not reported.
Comments: Examiner must be trained to administer test.
Authors: Ruth J. Colvin and Jane H. Root.
Publisher: Literacy Volunteers of America, Inc.

TEST REFERENCES

1. Fox, B. J., & Fingeret, A. (1984). Test review: Reading Evaluation Adult Diagnosis (revised). *Journal of Reading, 28,* 258-261.

Review of the Reading Evaluation Adult Diagnosis (Revised) by MARY E. HUBA, Professor of Research and Evaluation, Iowa State University, Ames, IA:

The Reading Evaluation Adult Diagnosis (Revised) is an evaluation instrument to be used as part of an instructional program designed for adults and teens by the Literacy Volunteers of America, Inc. The intended administrators of the test are instructors (tutors) in adult basic reading, and references are continually made in the test manual to *Tutor*, the basic text designed by the same authors for training tutors to teach. The tutors (and thus testers) are assumed to be those who have had no experience in teaching.

The primary evaluation instrument is an individually administered diagnostic test to assist tutors in assessing both student reading needs and student reading progress. The test is organized into three parts that are standard elements in many reading tests (Sight Words, Word Analysis Skills, Reading/Listening Inventory). The manual is well organized and the paragraphs to be used in the Reading/Listening portion of the test are appropriate in content for an adult audience. Testers are trained in an 18-hour workshop in which instructions are provided from an audio-cassette tape and a leader is present to facilitate understanding. In addition to training in the administration and scoring of right/wrong items, instruction in evaluating oral reading ability (i.e., recording omissions, substitutions, self-corrections, etc.) is also included.

The authors recommend that the test be given both before and after the tutoring experience, although according to the manual, the test can be readministered at any time to assess student status. The approach appears to be criterion-referenced in the Sight Word and Word Analysis sections. In the former, words are sampled from successive quarters of "the list of the 300 words most commonly used in print." No citation for this reference is provided. This list apparently forms the corpus of sight words taught in the instructional program. In the latter, skills commonly included in reading inventories and presumed to be essential for mastering the reading task are presented. In contrast, in the Reading/Listening section, the authors purport that paragraphs evaluated with a readability formula correspond in difficulty to those typically found in elementary textbooks from grades 1 to 5.5.

Another evaluation instrument described in the manual is a Group Screening Test for use with a large number of students in order to "help determine which students should be tested further." The test is a word-matching exercise assessing speed and accuracy of visual perception. Twenty-five target words (primarily two- and three-syllable words) are presented vertically on a page. Next to each are four alternatives, one of which is the target word. The student must underline the word that is the same as the target word. Responses are not scored for accuracy; rather, the only score consists of the number of seconds to complete the test. According to the authors, "experience has shown that students who require more than seventy-five seconds to complete this test will probably have many reading problems," and "further diagnosis is advised."

The chief concern with these instruments is that absolutely no information whatsoever is provided in the manual regarding their psychometric properties. According to the publisher, two in-house studies have been conducted, but summaries were not available at the time of this review. The purpose of the tests is to make inferences regarding reading skill in an instructional setting in which learning is presumed to take place. However, no evidence that scores can effectively address this purpose (validity) is presented. Further, without data supporting reliability, confidence in the consistency of scores is not possible. The limitation this creates is particularly evident for the Group Screening Test in which neither the content nor the score is directly related to the reading task. Empirical evidence that scores are related to those from a more detailed test or assessment process is needed.

The need for psychometric information is also critical with regard to several of the authors' recommendations for use of the diagnostic test. First, minimal information about scoring procedures for the subtests is provided by the authors. For most subtests, the guideline is simply that three or more errors signal a need for instruction in the area. No data are presented to verify the usefulness of this cutoff, and further, no norms are presented. For subtests that must be mastered in order to read (like letter sounds) and in which the items represent the entire universe of items in the domain, a purely criterion-referenced approach may not be inappropriate. However, for these sections, as well as for other areas of the test in which items are samples from a universe, normative data for various groups of adults would be instructive. Since several critical aspects of the testing situation are rather atypical (i.e., type of instructor—volunteers usually having no formal training in reading education, learners—illiterate or low-achieving adults, and instructional setting—informally arranged meetings either individually or in groups), data on the ability of the instrument to detect learning effects under these conditions are needed.

Second, on the Sight Word and Reading/Listening portions of the diagnostic test, the paragraphs to be read either by the student or by the tutor change from pretest to posttest. Evidence of their equivalence is needed. Third, for the Word Analysis portions of the diagnostic test, the items do not change from pretest to posttest. There appears to be no recognition on the authors' part that, for some subtests (such as decoding CVCs, CVCCs, digraphs, and blends), administering the tests as often as desired

during instruction may weaken the ability to infer that posttest scores are the result of increased reading ability.

In sum, the use of this test, either in the specific setting for which it is intended or in other settings, is not recommended until information supporting the reliability and validity of test scores is available. Also needed is information supporting the effectiveness of the training program in producing reliable test administrators. The issue of using volunteers without formal academic training in the assessment and remediation of reading difficulties is also relevant; however, it is considered to be outside the scope of this review.

Review of the Reading Evaluation Adult Diagnosis (Revised) by DIANE J. SAWYER, Director, Consultation Center for Reading, Syracuse University, Syracuse, NY:

Reading Evaluation Adult Diagnosis (Revised) (READ) is a carefully constructed tool that permits a systematic approach to describing the word- and passage-reading skills of an adult who reads below a fifth grade level (approximately). It was designed to provide diagnostic information in word recognition and analysis with the hope that specific weaknesses might be addressed through tutoring. Further, READ provides an estimate of the difficulty level of text material that might be used in tutoring or offered for independent reading between tutoring sessions. Comprehension questions following passages require primarily literal recall, although some questions do encourage linkages between text and personal experience.

READ is an informal reading inventory. Normative data for interpreting test performance are not available. Instead, analysis of reader behavior is dependent upon examiner skill. Because this test is intended for use by volunteer tutors from various walks of life, the quality of the test booklet/manual and possible instructional interpretations is critical. In addition, the volunteer examiner/tutor is referred to *TUTOR*, a separate handbook also published by Literacy Volunteers of America, Inc. (LVA). Preparation or training to administer READ is offered through LVA chapter offices or a test trainers kit (a trainer's guide and audio cassette) offered for purchase through LVA. In this reviewer's opinion, it would be very difficult for anyone lacking previous background in teaching reading to learn to administer and interpret the test without guidance beyond that which is provided in the test trainers kit.

No specific information is offered regarding the reliability or validity of READ. However, both construct and content validity are apparent and consistent with the purposes for which this test was designed. Within the "discrete skills" view of reading, proficiency in reading is presumed dependent upon mastery of a hierarchy of specific content such as that contained in the word lists and word analysis subtests of READ. Meaning is presumed to be in the text and the reader's task is to accurately decode words so that the author's meaning may become apparent. Difficulties in decoding words must, therefore, be addressed through direct instruction in specific phonic elements or in the use of context clues to aid recognition. Clearly the "discrete skills" approach is the view of reading upon which development of READ is predicated. The tasks, as well as interpretations of failure on the tasks, are consistent with this approach and with the typical content and sequence of instruction that would be provided to someone after completion of READ.

The absence of information regarding reliability is a more serious concern. Tutors are urged to administer READ as soon after the first "get acquainted" meeting as possible. Most adults who are poor readers are embarrassed by their reading performance. It may be that adults would do worse than usual if required to read aloud before a virtual stranger who is carefully writing down all errors. This would seem to pose a serious threat to the accuracy of the profile of skill needs obtained. Test-retest reliability data appear essential to support the stability of scores before recommendations based on these scores are to be carried out by tutors.

Another problem is related to the manner in which reading materials are selected for instruction and recreation based on the reading level score obtained using READ. Though many cautions are provided in the manual concerning the selection of material that is appropriate for adults both in terms of difficulty and content, no specific sources or examples are offered. The passages used to estimate reading level are taken from adult experience stories and thus reflect adult experiences, vocabulary, and syntax. Although a readability formula was used to

rank a given passage at beginning second grade, for example, it will be inherently more adult than a trade book written for beginning second graders to read. Further, adults reading that trade book are likely to make more errors because of the constrained vocabulary and syntax which seems unnatural to them. It would seem critical that more specific suggestions be offered to tutors regarding selection of reading materials if READ is to serve adequately the objective of identifying the appropriate level of material through which instruction should be offered.

Overall, READ is a well-constructed informal reading inventory (IRI) with good potential to serve the identification of specific instructional needs within the traditional discrete skills approach to reading acquisition. However, as with most IRIs, the potential usefulness of READ is commensurate with the training and experience of its user.

[72]
Reading Style Inventory.
Purpose: "To identify the individual reading style preferences and strengths of youngsters when they read."
Population: Grades 1–12.
Publication Dates: 1980–87.
Acronym: RSI.
Scores: 30 elements: Environmental Stimuli (Sound-Quiet, Sound-Music/Talking, Light, Temperature, Design-Formal/Informal, Design-Organization), Emotional Profile (Peer-Motivated, Adult-Motivated, Self-Motivated, Persistence, Responsibility, Structure-Choices, Structure-Directions, Structure-Work Checked When, Structure-Work Checked by Whom), Sociological Preferences (Prefers Reading to a Teacher, With Peers, Alone, With Peers and the Teacher, With One Peer, Intake, Prefers Reading in the Morning, Prefers Reading in Early Afternoon, Prefers Reading in Late Afternoon, Prefers Reading in the Evening, Mobility), Perceptual Strengths/Preferences (Auditory Strengths, Visual Strengths, Tactual Preferences, Kinesthetic Preferences).
Administration: Group; individual for first grade.
Price Data, 1990: $10 per 25 test booklets; $8 per 30 answer sheets; $12 per manual ('84, 76 pages); $20 per specimen set including test booklet, sample profiles, Research Supplement ('83, 39 pages), manual, and free processing of 1 RSI.
Foreign Language Edition: Spanish edition available.
Time: (20–40) minutes.

Comments: Based upon learning style model; scoring service offered by publisher.
Author: Marie Carbo.
Publisher: National Reading Styles Institute, Inc.

TEST REFERENCES

1. Carbo, M. (1984). Research in learning style and reading: Implications for instruction. *Theory Into Practice*, 23 (1), 72-76.

Review of the Reading Style Inventory by JERI BENSON, Associate Professor of Measurement, Statistics and Evaluation, University of Maryland, College Park, MD:

The Reading Style Inventory (RSI) consists of 52 items to which a student responds using either a three-choice or two-choice format to indicate their reading preferences. The scale is thought to measure 30 elements of reading style grouped into four stimuli: Environmental, Emotional, Sociological, and Physical. The items were developed based upon student comments and observations of students while reading. However, the author provides no information as to how many initial items were generated nor whether item analyses were used to produce the final set of 52 items.

From a rough categorization of items, there appear to be 28 items covering the three areas of Environmental, Emotional, and Sociological stimuli with the remaining 24 items representing Physical stimuli. Given the purpose of the RSI is primarily diagnostic, there appears to be an overrepresentation of items in the Physical area and too few in the remaining three areas. It would be helpful if the author would provide a table of specifications indicating which item measures which stimulus and the rationale for the breakdown. In addition, a rationale should be given as to why 14 of the items have a 3-point response scale and 38 items have a 2-point response scale. Finally, a Spanish version of the RSI is available, but no psychometric data are provided nor information as to the quality of the item translation or equivalence to the English version.

The author is to be commended for the emphasis she places on setting a good testing environment for the student (especially younger students). Carefully worded warm-up exercises are provided so the students understand what is meant by indicating a "preference." Another strength of the RSI is that no special administrator training is necessary other than familiarization with the items and item format.

Many helpful illustrations to aid the classroom teacher in developing and providing appropriate reading instruction and supporting material are given in the printouts and Chapters VI and VII of the manual. However, some rationale as to how the suggestions were developed would be useful. Are the recommendations based upon the research in the field of reading? If so, the authors should cite the research.

A glaring omission in the technical manual is the scoring protocol for the RSI. The answer sheets must be sent to the author for scoring. This procedure represents an additional expense. Although very detailed diagnostics per student and for the class as a whole are provided, it would be helpful psychometrically to know what combination of items went into developing the diagnostic profile. Additionally, no normative data are provided in terms of score profiles for different grades (ages), gender, reading ability, or other relevant background factors.

The only reliability data presented are from a study involving students in grades 2, 4, 6, and 8. There were approximately 70 students per grade for the total sample of 293 drawn from inner-city and suburban areas of New York. Test-retest reliabilities of .63 to .77 were reported, over a 1-month interval. Although these data are acceptable, evidence for the stability of the RSI across all grades in more than one geographical area is needed.

With regard to the reported content validation of the scale, the author indicates that practitioners stated the RSI items "accurately measured the elements of reading style." A more precise description of the practitioners is required for content validation; in fact, the persons chosen for the content validation are often described as *experts* in the field. Thus, while the items "appear" to reflect reading style, a more controlled study describing the procedures used to obtain the item evaluations by acknowledged experts in the field of reading/learning is warranted.

The author should provide the concurrent validity correlations between the RSI and the other "instruments that measure similar variables" in the technical manual itself and not just refer to the studies (p. 12). Furthermore, the two comments on pages 12–13 of the Research Supplement that (*a*) the RSI was selected in a nationwide survey as "one of fourteen learning style instruments that qualified for inclusion in the *Learning Styles Network's Instruments Assessment Analysis*," and (*b*) the respondents to the nationwide survey indicated that the "RSI printouts were accurate" are not validity data and should be removed from the validity section of the manual.

In terms of establishing the construct validity of the RSI, the known-group procedure of reporting mean level differences from the samples used in the reliability study cited above are presented. The data are impressive, but a few statistical questions remain. Given that data were available on grade, gender, and reading ability, why were one-way ANOVA results presented instead of factorial ANOVA results? Table 8 is titled two-way ANOVAS, yet only one variable (reading level) is described for the results. With so many subtests (elements), was the probability of a type I error controlled either by a multivariate analysis or a Bonferonni adjustment for the ANOVAs reported? Generally, the communication of information in the Research Supplement and Research Update could be improved by having a psychometrician edit these documents.

In sum, the RSI appears to be a promising diagnostic tool to enable teachers to provide specific reading instruction and materials for their students. If the author can provide additional data on the consistency of the RSI over all grades, specific content and concurrent validity data, information as to how the RSI is scored, and data for the Spanish version, I could recommend the RSI for general use. Given the present data, however, I can recommend the RSI only for use in research settings.

Review of the Reading Style Inventory by ALICE J. CORKILL, Assistant Professor of Psychology, University of Western Ontario, London, Ontario, Canada:

The Reading Style Inventory (RSI) is designed to identify individual differences in reading preferences and strengths as differentiated by a set of 52 questions that assess 30 separate elements. The 30 elements are based on learning styles (see elements listed in test entry). The Inventory is not a reading skills test and should not be considered as such. Rather it is designed to provide information about how a student learns best. The purpose in using the Inventory is not only to discover an individual's reading preferences, but to provide information that will assist in designing reading instruction with the best fit to an individual's personal reading style.

Students who cannot read at a beginning fourth grade reading level must have the Inventory read to them. As a result, students in the lower elementary grades will need considerable assistance when taking the Inventory. In addition, a computer scan sheet is used as the answer sheet. Some students may not be able to use the sheet. In these instances it is suggested the students be allowed to mark in the test booklet, then requiring the teacher to mark the answer sheet at a later time.

The Inventory is scored by the publisher with no other option available. Each student who takes the Inventory is provided with an "Individual Reading Style Profile" which includes a diagnosis in perceptual strengths and preferences, the preferred reading environment, an emotional profile, the sociological preferences, and the physical preferences of each child. It also includes recommended strategies for teaching reading based on that child's preferences with references to suggestions listed in the RSI manual.

In addition each profile includes recommendations of reading methods and reading materials. The reading methods listed include the phonic method, the linguistic method, the Orton-Gillingham Method, the whole-word method, individualized methods, the Carbo recorded-book method, the language-experience method, and the Fernald word-tracing method (for more complete descriptions see the administrator's manual). The reading materials listed include Basal reader programs, language-experience programs, individualized programs, and supplementary reading materials (which include games, activity cards, reading kits, skill development books and duplicating masters, and audio-visual materials). Each method or type of material is listed as either highly recommended, recommended, acceptable, or not recommended for an individual based on his/her responses to the Inventory.

A "Reading Style Group Profile" is also available. The group profile compiles the information from individual profiles to reveal group patterns. Two different methods of reporting group profiles are currently in use (only one is listed in the manual). The two group profiles differ in the format of data presentation. In the method described in the manual, the data are presented in the following format: name of examinee on the left margin and preferences or reading method recommendations across the top of the page. In the second method, the data are presented such that individuals are grouped by response strength on preferences and by the degree of recommendation (highly recommended, recommended, acceptable, or not recommended) on the reading method recommendations. The group profiles provide the same information as the individual profiles. This component of the RSI may be particularly useful for classroom teachers who may choose to use the profile information when selecting activities, reading materials, or reading methods for an entire class.

The questions in the Inventory are simple and easy to understand. For example, students are asked to choose between statements similar to the following: "A) I read best where it's quiet with no music playing, B) I read best where there is music playing, C) I read about the same where it's quiet or where there is music playing." Suggestions for preparing younger students to take the Inventory are included in the RSI manual.

As with any self-report inventory, it is possible students will not provide accurate information. This may be especially true when considering older students. Students beyond grades 7 or 8 may find the statements too simplistic. The questions are obviously geared toward younger students. Most students beyond elementary school who read regularly already know what their preferences are in terms of reading style. In addition, the recommended reading methods and materials are geared toward younger readers. As a result, the information provided by the Inventory may be of little value with regard to older students.

The reliability of the instrument was established via a test-retest method using 293 second-, fourth-, sixth-, and eighth-grade students. The sample was taken from inner-city and suburban schools in New York City and Nassau County, New York, and considered the reading ability (high, average, or below average) of the student as a critical variable. The test-retest reliability coefficients range from .55 to .81, with most coefficients falling between .67 and .72. Because of the nature of this self-report inventory, the reported reliability is acceptable. Assessing other types of reliability (i.e., coefficient alpha) might provide information that would assist in improving the Inventory. In addition, a more representative sample, including older students (the Inventory is listed for use with grades 1 through 12) and/or other geographic locations, might enhance the usefulness of the Inventory.

The validity of the instrument has been addressed in several ways. The content validity was assessed by 87 educators representing 23 states, 93% of whom stated that the RSI measured the elements of reading style in an accurate, appropriate, and representative fashion. In addition, the Inventory has been submitted to experts in the field for review and was selected by the National Center for the Study of Learning/Teaching Styles for inclusion in the *Learning Styles Network's Instruments Assessment Analysis*, one of only 14 instruments that qualified.

The RSI manual devotes considerable attention to suggestions for matching reading styles with reading programs. Several studies (reported in a research update booklet provided with the Inventory) have suggested that educators, specifically elementary teachers, who match students' reading preferences with appropriate reading materials and methods, observed considerable improvement in reading skill. This is especially evident for students with learning disabilities. As a consequence, if the results of this inventory are viewed in a prescriptive fashion a considerable increase in reading skill may be the final product.

The incremental value of the Reading Style Inventory is unclear. It may provide assistance to teachers of beginning reading or special education by suggesting the best method and materials for teaching reading on an individual or small group basis. The results of the Inventory match closely with teacher observations of students, so much so that teacher observation may provide ample information for making reading method and material decisions, thus rendering the information from an inventory like the RSI redundant. In contrast, the reported research suggests significant gains in reading skill by matching reading style with teaching methods. If the RSI is the only method for acquiring this information, it may be well worth the time required to administer and score it.

[73]
Reynolds Adolescent Depression Scale.
Purpose: "To assess depressive symptomatology in adolescents."
Population: Ages 13–18.
Publication Dates: 1986–87.
Acronym: RADS.
Scores: Total score only.
Forms, 3: HS, I, G.
Comments: Self-report measure.
Author: William M. Reynolds.
Publisher: Psychological Assessment Resources, Inc.
a) FORM HS.
Administration: Individual and small group.
Price Data, 1988: $25 per complete kit including scoring key, HS answer sheets, and manual ('87, 47 pages).
Time: [5–10] minutes.
Comments: Hand-scored.
b) FORM I.
Administration: Individual in part.
Price Data, 1988: $47.50 or less per 10 prepaid answer sheets including scoring and reporting by publisher; $12 per manual.
Time: [5–10] minutes.
Comments: Machine-scored.
c) FORM G.
Administration: For large groups.
Price Data, 1988: $100 or less per 50 prepaid answer sheets including scoring and reporting by publisher; $12 per manual.
Time: [5–10] minutes.
Comments: Machine-scored; for screening programs and research projects.

TEST REFERENCES
1. Reynolds, W. M., & Coats, K. I. (1986). A comparison of cognitive-behavioral therapy and relaxation training for the treatment of depression in adolescents. *Journal of Consulting and Clinical Psychology, 54,* 653-660.
2. Nieminen, G. S., & Matson, J. L. (1989). Depressive problems in conduct-disordered adolescents. *Journal of School Psychology, 27,* 175-188.

Review of the Reynolds Adolescent Depression Scale by BARBARA J. KAPLAN, Associate Professor of Psychology, State University of New York College at Fredonia, Fredonia, NY:

The Reynolds Adolescent Depression Scale (RADS) is described by its authors as being a measure of depressive symptomatology rather than being a diagnostic measure of depression. As such, it appears that the RADS may be most effectively used for research purposes and not as a clinical screening measure or an aid to diagnosis. This type of quickly administered self-rating scale should not be considered as a substitute for more extensive diagnostic interviewing, a point the authors of the RADS make in several places.

The standardization sample for the RADS consisted of 2,460 adolescents drawn from grades 7 through 12 at two junior high schools and one high school in a midwestern community. Information regarding heterogeneity of the sample is reported and suggests that racial mix and the range of socioeconomic status are reflected in the norming of the test. Though the standardization sample was drawn from only one geographic location, the authors report that subsequent data do not indicate that additional locations would change the norms. In the process of its construction and revision, the test was administered to over 10,000 adolescents.

Multiple measures of the internal consistency of the RADS demonstrate high internal consistency. A brief discussion of the difficulties of evaluating test-retest reliability in assessing mood accompanies and clarifies data presented for retests of different samples at intervals of 6 weeks, 3 months, and 1 year. Concurrent validity for the RADS is demonstrated through joint administration of the RADS and the Hamilton Rating Scale (Hamilton, 1960).

The data and analyses demonstrating the RADS's psychometric qualities are impressive, and the authors have taken pains to compare their test results with other measures of depression and to provide some evaluation of the clinical significance of high and low scores. A useful feature of the RADS is the opportunity to convert raw scores to percentile ranks for sex, grade, and sex x grade. Analyses are available by age, race, and sex. Test means reflect the higher scores for females that are reported in numerous studies of depression.

The question still remains, does the RADS add anything to already existing measures of depression? I believe the answer is no. There is neither a theory of adolescence nor of adolescent depression that illuminates or justifies the construction of the test. The items on the RADS are significantly and highly correlated with other measures of depression, even though those measures were not specifically designed for adolescents. In addition, other individual characteristics such as anxiety and general self-esteem are highly correlated with the RADS.

These correlations have absolute values ranging from .65 to .80. Although a number of studies of depression show low self-esteem and high anxiety as elements in the clinical picture of depression, the RADS offers little in the way of increased discriminability of these several factors.

Although weak on theory, the RADS appears to be equal to many of the other, more commonly used self-report measures of depression. In assessing the outcome of various therapeutic or educational interventions or in research where some measure of adolescent depressive symptoms might be needed, the RADS would be a reasonable choice. However, if comparisons with other studies of depression are indicated, one of the more popular measures of depression such as the Beck Depression Inventory (BDI; Beck, Ward, Mendelson, Mock, & Erbaugh, 1969), the Hamilton (1960), or the Zung (1965) rating scales would be a better choice.

REVIEWER'S REFERENCES

Hamilton, M. (1960). A rating scale for depression. *Journal of Neurology, Neurosurgery, and Psychiatry, 23,* 56-62.

Beck, A. T., Ward, C., Mendelson, M., Mock, J., & Erbaugh, J. (1961). An inventory for measuring depression. *Archives of General Psychiatry, 4,* 561-571.

Zung, W. W. K. (1965). A self-rating depression scale. *Archives of General Psychiatry, 12,* 63-70.

Review of the Reynolds Adolescent Depression Scale by DEBORAH KING KUNDERT, Assistant Professor of Educational Psychology and Statistics, University at Albany, State University of New York, Albany, NY:

The Reynolds Adolescent Depression Scale (RADS) is a questionnaire designed to assess the severity of depression in adolescents. Examinees respond to 30 sentences that describe feelings using a 4-point Likert-type format indicating how they usually feel (*almost never, hardly ever, sometimes,* or *most of the time*). The scale may be used for adolescents 13–18 years-of-age, it is appropriate for group or individual administration, and it may be machine or hand scored. Three different forms are available, depending on scoring and administration preference.

The primary use of the RADS is to assess symptoms associated with depression. The author indicates that this questionnaire was not designed to provide a diagnosis of specific depressive disorder; specific diagnosis would require a more extensive evaluation. As out-

lined in the manual, the RADS may be used as part of a screening procedure for identifying the extent of depressive symptomatology among adolescents (e.g., in schools or institutions). The author provides a multiple-stage screening method for assessment of depression in schools in the manual. Another application of the RADS is in the evaluation of prevention and treatment programs for depression.

Responses on the RADS are based on frequency of occurrence and are weighted from 1 to 4 points, with a total score range of 30 to 120. The author uses a cutoff score approach (at or above 77) to identify those who need further evaluation. According to the author, this cutoff score indicates a "level of symptom endorsement associated with clinical depression."

Standardization of the RADS is based on a sample of 2,460 students from a suburban/rural midwestern high school. Since completion of the initial field testing, additional data from a variety of sources have been collected (over 10,000 subjects). These data have not been found to differ significantly from the original sample. Significant differences were found for sex and grade, but not for race. As a result, separate norm tables for converting raw scores to percentile ranks are provided for sex and grade. Limited information (one study) is provided on using this questionnaire with special populations.

To estimate the reliability of the RADS, internal consistency and test-retest procedures were used. Coefficient alphas ranged from .90 to .94 and the split-half estimate was .91. Test-retest evaluations were conducted at 6 weeks (.80), 3 months (.79), and 1 year (.63).

Several types of validity data are presented for the RADS. The content validity of the scale was assessed by examining the congruence of questionnaire items with clinically specified symptomatology and item-total scale correlations. The RADS items were developed to reflect descriptive components of depression; items were not developed based on a specific theory of depression. Following this orientation, items on the RADS reflect the symptomatology outlined in *DSM-III* for major depression and dysthymic disorder, as well as symptoms of depression specified by the Research Diagnostic Criteria (RDC). Items assess cognitive, somatic, psychomotor, and interpersonal areas. The author indicates that not all symptoms associated with depression are assessed by the RADS. The item-total correlations are presented as additional evidence of the content validity of the questionnaire. The majority of these correlations ranged from the .50s to the .60s, with a median correlation of .53.

Criterion-related validity of the RADS was examined using the Hamilton Rating Scale clinical interview. These measures were administered to a sample of 111 adolescents. The correlation between the RADS and the rating scale was .83.

Evidence offered for construct validity is in the form of significant correlations of the RADS with other self-report measures of depression (e.g., Beck Depression Inventory, Children's Depression Inventory). In addition, significant correlations between the RADS and related constructs (e.g., self-esteem, anxiety, loneliness) are reported to support the construct validity of the scale. Lower correlations between the RADS and variables unrelated to depression (e.g., social desirability, academic achievement) suggest minimal relationship between these variables and RADS scores. Results of factor analytic studies are presented as descriptive information, and not as validity investigations, since the scale was developed based on symptomatology and not on a theory.

The clinical validity of the RADS was evaluated by examining treatment sensitivity and diagnostic efficacy. Results from two studies indicate a high level of classificatory agreement between RADS scores and clinical severity ratings (using the Hamilton Rating Scale; 89% agreement) and between the RADS and clinical interviews (using the Schedule for Affective Disorders and Schizophrenia-SADS; 82% agreement). Further evidence for the clinical utility of the RADS was obtained from the results of a study comparing treatment approaches for depression (cognitive-behavioral vs. relaxation training vs. waiting list controls).

A technical analysis of the RADS indicates that it is a moderately well-developed instrument that clinicians should find useful as a screening measure of depressive symptoms in adolescents. The manual is clearly and concisely written, which meets the author's expectation that it should serve as both a technical guide and a clinical guide for evaluating depression in adolescents. The ease of administration and scoring are additional assets. As indicated by the author, only initial investigations supporting the psychometric properties of the RADS are presented; further research will contribute to a better understanding of the relationship between the RADS and depression in adolescents.

[74]
Screening Children for Related Early Educational Needs.
Purpose: "To focus on early academic related behaviors in the areas of oral language, reading, writing, and mathematics."
Population: Ages 3–7.
Publication Dates: 1981–88.
Acronym: SCREEN.
Scores, 5: Achievement Quotient, Language, Reading, Writing, Math.
Administration: Individual.
Price Data, 1988: $69 per complete kit including 25 Profile/Record forms, 25 student workbooks, Picture Book, and examiner's manual ('88, 100 pages).
Time: (25–50) minutes.
Authors: Wayne P. Hresko, D. Kim Reid, Donald D. Hammill, Herbert P. Ginsburg, and Arthur J. Baroody.
Publisher: PRO-ED, Inc.

Review of Screening Children for Related Early Educational Needs by DAVID W. BARNETT, Professor, School Psychology and Counseling, University of Cincinnati, Cincinnati, OH:

Screening Children for Related Early Educational Needs (SCREEN) is considered by the authors to be an achievement measure, or alternatively, a measure of academically related behaviors pertinent to identifying children with mild to moderate learning difficulties. The stated purposes of SCREEN are identifying young children with possible delays in "early academic areas" (p. 6), determining strengths and weaknesses, and monitoring progress of children in intervention programs through retesting. The administration time is reported to be between 15 to 40 minutes, depending on the child's age and ability.

SCREEN comprises the following components: Oral Language, Reading, Writing, and Mathematics. However, as examples, early "writing" tasks include pointing to pictures of a stamp or pencil, while an early "reading" item involves identifying the top of a book. In addition, a global SCREEN Early Achievement Quotient (SEAQ) is provided, based on the child's performance on the four components. Items for inclusion were selected from other measures available from the same publisher: The Test of Early Language Development (TELD; 9:1250) (Hresko, Reid, & Hammill, 1981); The Test of Early Reading Ability (TERA; 9:1253) (Reid, Hresko, & Hammill, 1981); Test of Early Written Language (TEWL) (Hresko, 1988); and Test of Early Mathematics Ability (TEMA; 9:1252) (Ginsburg & Baroody, 1983).

The administration and scoring of SCREEN are relatively straightforward. Some common materials must be supplied by the examiner (i.e., blocks, coins, chips, or other items for counting). The provided test materials include a Picture Book, a Student Workbook, and a Profile/Record Form. Scoring is unambiguous for the most part. Correct items are given 1 point and incorrect responses receive 0 points. Suggested entry items based on chronological age are used to reduce testing time by indicating places to begin. In addition, basal and ceiling levels are used for the SEAQ. Testing is continued from the entry level until six consecutive items are missed. If the child is unsuccessful on the first item, the examiner proceeds backwards until six consecutive items are passed. After the basal is established, the examiner proceeds from the original starting point and discontinues testing following six consecutive failed items. Computer scoring is available.

To aid in test interpretation, standard scores, percentiles, and descriptive phrases are included (i.e., *very superior* and *superior* at one extreme, to *poor* and *very poor* at the other). The standard scores, including the SCREEN Early Achievement Quotient and the four component quotients, have a mean of 100 and standard deviation of 15.

The technical characteristics of SCREEN include a reasonably large standardization sample ($N = 1,355$ children in 20 states). However, no information is given concerning SES. Children of poverty are typically underrepresented in standardization efforts but are disproportionately referred. The number of cases at half-year age levels from age 3 to age 7-11 ranged from 105 to 174. The older children in the sample (from age 6 upward) are better represented than younger children.

Reliability was analyzed through the use of coefficient alpha, Rasch, and test-retest procedures. By half-year age intervals, overall alphas were .95 or higher for all intervals except children from 3.6 to 3.11 (alpha = .85). Coefficient alphas for individual subtests were typically lower; only 17.5% were above .90. Thus, the components should be interpreted with caution. The test-retest results (2-week interval, no sample size given, ages 6 to 7.3) were quite high, ranging from .87 to .98 with a median of .93 for components.

Validity evidence is presented in several overlapping ways. Content validity was closely related to test construction as mentioned. Construct validity was supported by significant correlations between SCREEN performance, chronological age, school experience, other developmental measures, and discrimination of identified groups of children with or without learning problems. Criterion-related validity was supported by the correlations between the original measures from which the items were selected and a range of various criterion measures. The correlations ranged from .40 to .75 with a median of .55. Criterion-related validity is also suggested by the correlations between SCREEN and several alternative criterion measures. The resulting validity coefficients range from .46 to .68 with a median of .54. The SCREEN Overall Score was moderately related to various measures of intelligence (i.e., ranged from .44 to .66, with a median of .57).

Several cautions to potential users should be mentioned. First, one of the stated purposes of the SCREEN is to enable practitioners to develop profiles of specific strengths and weaknesses. In fact, the authors encourage the use of profile interpretations of the SCREEN. Given the high degree of intercorrelations found between SCREEN subtests, actual profiles may be quite tenuous, if not impossible, to interpret. For example, the correlation between Language and Reading was .95, and the correlation between Reading and Math was .96. The intercorrelations frequently exceed scale reliabilities at various age levels. Thus, it is quite likely that a general factor underlies the scale. Furthermore, given the many examples of moderate relationships with alternative screening measures, the reliability of *decisions* (e.g., whether or not a child is "at risk") is likely to be quite low.

Second, because the SCREEN is purported to be a screening measure, the test user should be cognizant of important issues related to screening (Adelman, 1982; Barnes, 1982). If used for wide-scale screening efforts, such measures can be error-prone and are not likely to be cost-effective, especially in situations in which the base rates of children with educational needs are either very high or low. Because many preschool programs include well-developed curriculum and opportunities for ongoing teacher/parent observation and consultation, curriculum-based alternatives to screening merit primary consideration.

Third, the SCREEN has an inadequate floor and ceiling for the ages that encompass the intended use of the scale. As examples of the former problem, children who receive a raw score of 1 at ages 3.0 to 3.5 receive a scaled score of 86 on the SCREEN LQ. At the same age level, a raw score of 1 is equivalent to a scaled score of 100 on the SCREEN MQ. At the other extreme, children at age level 7.6 to 7.11 with raw scores of 17 (out of a possible 18) receive standard scores of 100 on three out of four subtests.

Fourth, the item gradients are quite uneven throughout the test, which may result in interpretive difficulties. As an example, a child between the ages of 5.6 to 5.11 who achieves a raw score of 9 on the SCREEN WQ (writing component) receives a scaled score of 100. A child of the same age who receives credit for one more correct item (a raw score of 10) receives a scaled score of 113. At the other extreme, a child aged 3.6 with a raw score of 21 receives a SCREEN SEAQ equal to 119, whereas a child receiving a raw score of 31 has a SCREEN SEAQ of 123.

In sum, despite the fact that overall reliabilities and evidence for validity are similar to many other screening devices, the goal of developing "academic profiles" for young children cannot be met by this device. Although the only potential use of this scale would be to help identify young children based on downward extensions of PL 94-142 to meet state regulations that are developing with respect to PL 99-457, based on the technical properties of the scales, such decisions are likely to be associated with high error rates. Numerous screening alternatives are available, founded on practices related to organizational/systems approaches to screening, parent and teacher consultation, and curriculum-based methods.

REVIEWER'S REFERENCES

Hresko, W. P., Reid, D. K., & Hammill, D. D. (1981). The Test of Early Language Development. Austin, TX: PRO-ED, Inc.

Reid, D. K., Hresko, W. P., & Hammill, D. D. (1981). The Test of Early Reading Ability. Austin, TX: PRO-ED, Inc.

Adelman, H. S. (1982). Identifying learning problems at an early age: A critical appraisal. *Journal of Clinical Child Psychology*, *11*, 255-261.

Barnes, K. E. (1982). *Preschool screening: The measurement and prediction of children at-risk.* Springfield, IL: Thomas.

Ginsburg, H. P., & Baroody, A. J. (1983). Test of Early Mathematics Ability. Austin, TX: PRO-ED, Inc.

Hresko, W. P. (1988). Test of Early Written Language. Austin, TX: PRO-ED, Inc.

Review of Screening Children for Related Early Educational Needs by LIZANNE DeSTEFANO, Assistant Professor of Educational Psychology, University of Illinois at Urbana-Champaign, Champaign, IL:

Screening Children for Related Early Educational Needs (SCREEN) measures the early development of academic abilities in children 3 through 7 years of age. Item analysis was used to identify for inclusion on the SCREEN the most discriminating items on four well-known tests of early development: The Test of Early Language Development (TELD; 9:1250); (Hresko, Reid, & Hammill, 1981)—18 items; The Test of Early Reading Ability (TERA; 9:1253) (Reid, Hresko, & Hammill, 1981)—18 items; the Test of Early Written Language (TOWL) (Hresko, 1988)—16 items; and the Test of Early Mathematics Ability (TEMA; 9:1252) (Ginsburg & Baroody, 1983)—18 items.

In an excellent historical review of research and practice, the authors describe the test as a direct assessment of academic achievement for young children, clearly differentiating it from traditional indirect or predictive measures, such as developmental inventories or readiness measures. The stated purposes of the test include: to identify students who are below their peers in certain academic areas and who may be candidates for early intervention; to identify strengths and weaknesses in individual students; to document students' progress as a consequence of early intervention programs; and to serve as a measure of early academic achievement in research. The authors stress the use of the test as a screening device, offering suggestions for further assessment if weaknesses are noted in the SCREEN. Given the recent growth in early intervention programs as a result of the implementation of PL 99-457, the appearance of this test is timely.

The SCREEN is divided into four components: Oral Language, Reading, Writing, and Mathematics. The SCREEN Early Achievement Quotient (SEAQ) is based on the child's total score on all components, representing a global measure of early academic achievement. Similar quotients, with means equal to 100 and standard deviations of 15, are available for each of the four components. Percentile scores are also available. No grade or age equivalents are used, which may be seen as a disadvantage by teachers and others who are used to using these metrics, but because of problems with interpretation and the quality of these scores, the authors should be commended for not promoting their use.

Because of the variety in the types of skills measured, the test demands a broad repertoire of responses from the child. He/she must read, copy, write, manipulate small objects, analyze small black and white line drawings presented in a Picture Book, respond verbally with words and sentences, and attend to rather long oral instructions. Although all of these responses are among those most often called upon in school learning, the wide response demand may confound the content being measured for some items, and may place students with certain disabilities at a disadvantage. For example, a mathematics item asks the child to count out 19 pennies (or other small item) from a larger group. If a child has problems with a pincer grasp or other fine motor skills, failure on this task may not reflect lack of the number concept 19, but rather inability to perform the motor demands of the task. To offset this problem, alternative explanations for weakness on a particular item or subset of items should be considered in the manual.

The manual is well written, providing detailed instructions for administration of the SCREEN along with some general guidelines for testing young children and suggestions for modifying the test to make it more valid for certain geographic locations and types of children. A script is provided for the examiner. Examples of correct responses are provided as an aid to scoring. Unfortunately, the script and the scoring examples are in the Examiner's Manual and not the Picture Book, making it rather cumbersome for the examiner to juggle

the manual, Picture Book, and other materials. An adaptive testing format uses the child's age to determine the starting point for the test. Basal and ceiling rules are used to minimize the number of items administered and the resulting testing time. A computerized scoring package is available (Hresko & Schlieve, 1988).

The manual provides a clear description of the procedures for scoring and using the test, including suggestions and cautions for interpreting each type of score, guidelines for sharing results, extraneous influences on test performance to consider in test interpretation, and a discussion of the distinction among legal, statistical, and clinical discrepancies between scores. The authors should be commended for the cautious approach they have taken in the interpretation and use of test scores, as well as their effort made to educate users of the test with regard to basic test theory.

The standardization sample consisted of 1,355 children ages 3 years to 7 years 11 months, in 20 states. Over 100 children are included in each 6-month age cohort. Characteristics of the sample relative to sex, place of residence, race, geographic region, ethnicity, and age are presented and compare favorably with national figures for the *Statistical Abstract of the United States* (1985). Information on the procedure for obtaining subjects, ability levels, and the socioeconomic information for the sample is not reported, making it difficult to judge the overall quality of the sample. Users of the test should be encouraged to develop local norms in order to better understand the performance of children in their school in relation to the standardization sample.

Internal consistency of the test was measured using both coefficient alpha and Rasch analysis. Both techniques provided evidence that the SCREEN has sufficient internal consistency to be used to make educational decisions about children. As is the case for reliable tests, the standard error of measurement for each component and for the overall test was small. Test-retest reliability studies, conducted with two groups of unreported size and age, produced stability coefficients from .87 to .98. Given the instability of some constructs such as intelligence at lower age levels, it seems further analysis of the stability of SCREEN scores over short intervals of time by age is warranted.

Evidence of construct, criterion, and content validity is presented in the manual. Content validity is attributed to the validity of the parent instruments and the process used to select items for the SCREEN. As evidence of criterion validity, component scores were correlated with each of the tests from which they were taken. These correlations exceeded .90. In addition, a table showing the correlation of SCREEN scores with scores on several selected criterion tests was presented. Although significant, these correlations were moderate, indicating the SCREEN measures something different from traditional tests for this age.

As evidence of construct validity, students' mean scores on the SCREEN were shown to increase as they became older and as they progressed from grade to grade. Correlations of SCREEN scores with a variety of intelligence measures were moderate to moderately high (.44 for the Math Quotient to .66 for SEAQ), indicating the abilities measured on the SCREEN and those measured on intelligence tests are highly related. The component scores in each content area (Reading, Oral Language, Writing, and Mathematics) were highly intercorrelated (.84 to .98), supporting the premise that they all contribute to the measurement of a unitary construct, early academic achievement, but calling into question whether each component measures a unique set of skills. Although one of the stated purposes of the test was to identify strengths and weaknesses by comparing performance across components, the high intercorrelation indicates this comparison may not be a valid one. It may be that interpretation should be limited to only the SEAQ. In a test of the SCREEN's ability to distinguish between children with normal learning capacity and children who are learning disabled, the test was administered to 22 six-year-old children. Differences between the handicapped and nonhandicapped groups averaged between 21 and 28 points in favor of the nonhandicapped group. Unfortunately, as for many of the reliability and validity studies, the sample was not well described, limiting the use of this information.

In summary, the SCREEN is a well-constructed direct assessment of early academic skills. It is probably best used as a measure of global academic achievement, to identify students for more intensive evaluation and perhaps remediation, thus meeting a great need in the growing field of early intervention. Unfortunately, many of the reliability and validity studies for the SCREEN used small or poorly described samples. Additional work in this area is warranted, along with research examining the relationship of performance on the SCREEN to school performance in later years.

REVIEWER'S REFERENCES

Hresko, W. P., Reid, D. K., & Hammill, D. D. (1981). The Test of Early Language Development. Austin, TX: PRO-ED, Inc.
Reid, D. K., Hresko, W. P., & Hammill, D. D. (1981). The Test of Early Reading Ability. Austin, TX: PRO-ED, Inc.
Ginsburg, H. P., & Baroody, A. J. (1983). Test of Early Mathematics Ability. Austin, TX: PRO-ED, Inc.
Statistical abstract of the United States. (1985). Washington, DC: U.S. Bureau of the Census.
Hresko, W. P. (1988). Test of Early Written Language. Austin, TX: PRO-ED, Inc.
Hresko, W. P., & Schlieve, P. L. (1988). PRO-SCORE System for the SCREEN (Apple and IBM versions). Austin, TX: PRO-ED, Inc.

[75]

Self-Perception Profile for College Students.

Purpose: To measure college students' self-concept.
Population: College students.
Publication Date: 1986.
Scores: 13 domains: Creativity, Intellectual Ability, Scholastic Competence, Job Competence, Athletic Competence, Appearance, Romantic Relationships, Social Acceptance, Close Friendships, Parent Relationships, Finding Humor in One's Life, Morality, Global Self-Worth.
Administration: Group.
Price Data, 1989: $9 per manual (84 pages).
Time: 30(40) minutes.
Authors: Jennifer Neemann and Susan Harter.
Publisher: University of Denver.

Review of the Self-Perception Profile for College Students by ROBERT D. BROWN, Carl A. Happold Distinguished Professor of Educational Psychology, University of Nebraska-Lincoln, Lincoln, NE:

Three inventories are included in this package of self-perception instruments: "What Am I Like," "Importance Ratings," and a "Social Support" scale. The instruments can be used separately or as part of a package. The "What Am I Like" inventory is designed to assess college students' self-rating of their global self-worth and in 12 specific domains: Creativity, Intellectual Ability, Scholastic Competence, Job Competence, Athletic Competence, Appearance, Romantic Relationships, Social Acceptance, Close Friendships, Parent Relationships, Humor, Morality, and a Global Self-Worth rating. Each of the content domain subscales has four items and the Global Self-Worth subscale has six items. Estimated completion time is 30 minutes. The "Importance Ratings" inventory parallels the Self-Worth inventory with two items for each of the 12 content domain scales. Finally, the "Social Support" scale has four items each for subscales labelled: Close Friends, Mother, Father, People in Campus Organizations, and Instructors.

The scales and scoring information are provided in the manual and the authors inform readers that they should feel free to copy the instruments directly from the manual.

The "What I Am Like" inventory items ask students to select which one of two self-descriptions (e.g., "Some students are not satisfied with their social skill," and "Other students think their social skills are just fine") are *Really true for me* or *Sort of true for me*. The self-descriptions are on the same lines with the word "But" between them. There is no middle response of "undecided" or "neither." Responses are recorded either on the left margin or on the right margin, depending upon which statement the student believes describes them. Items are scored on a 1 to 4 scale where 4 represents the most competent or adequate self-judgment. Half the items have the high competency phrasing on the left and the other half have the high competency phrasing on the right. Response formats for the "Importance Ratings" and "Social Support" scales are similar and the items are also similar in general content.

The "What I Am Like" inventory parallels similar instruments designed by Harter and associates for use with children, adolescents, and adults. The college student form was developed to fill the developmental gap between the adolescent and adult populations.

The current form of the instruments was developed using data obtained from 300 students, mostly single and Caucasian. Internal consistency assessed by coefficient alphas for the "What I Am Like" inventory were reasonably high for the Self-Worth scales with only one scale below .80. Factor analysis with an oblique rotation and using a scree test resulted in 12 scales perfectly matching the designed scales. (The Global Self-Worth scale was not included.) Intercorrelations among the scales range

from low (e.g., Athletic to Scholastic Competence, $r = .02$), to modest (Social Acceptance to Morality, $r = .24$), to moderate (Intellectual Ability to Scholastic Competence, $r = .65$). Reliabilities were less strong for the "Importance Ratings" scales ranging from .53 to .84 but reasonably high for the "Social Support" scale with the range from .76 to .90.

A variety of preliminary validity data are reported which provide interesting as well as supportive information. Gender differences are noted with males having higher self-worth ratings on Appearance and Athletic Competence, but lower importance ratings on Intellectual Ability, Scholastic Competence, and Close Friendships. Unexpectedly, the authors found no gender differences on the social support scales. Overall, Appearance, Social Acceptance, Job Competence, Scholastic Competence, and Intellectual Ability correlated most strongly with the Global Self-Worth scale on the "What I Am Like" inventory and the same general pattern held for the "Importance Ratings."

The authors suggest ways the instruments can be used for research purposes such as examining the relationship of resilience to stress and self-esteem and for individual therapy. In the latter use, they provide examples of how profiles of the self-worth and importance ratings can provide useful insights as well as how to use discrepancy scores. Such information can be useful for helping students determine what aspects of their self they wish to develop.

Personality measures designed specifically for use with a college population are too rare. Too many instruments were developed using clinical populations or focus extensively on problems. One of the most prominent instruments available for use with a normal college population for developmental purposes is the Student Developmental Task and Lifestyle Inventory (83) which has proven useful for research purposes and for working with individual students. Researchers, counselors, and trained mentors will find it appropriate to consider use of these self-perception scales as well. Indeed, a worthwhile research topic would be to explore the relationship among the scales on these instruments and how receptive they are to intervention strategies.

If the self-perception inventories are deficient, beyond the fact that only preliminary validity data are available, it is because of what is omitted rather than what is present. It is unfortunate that the designers did not go further beyond the domains they already had covered in the adolescent and adult version than they did. Several domains immediately come to mind such as leisure-recreational skills, self-management (e.g., stress management) skills, aesthetic/artistic competency, multicultural awareness, and basic living skills (e.g., budgeting, car maintenance). Two important domains are also missing from the social support domains: other students and religious/church affiliation. As I read the Campus Organization subscale items I suspect that most students will respond by thinking about their peers in general rather than solely campus organizations, but it would have been cleaner to have such a peer scale titled as such.

As noted earlier, the authors tell readers to feel free to copy the scales. This fact, plus the fine preliminary work performed on these scales, should make them useful to researchers and others interested in trying to understand and assist college students during their college years.

Review of the Self-Perception Profile for College Students by STEPHEN F. DAVIS, Professor of Psychology, Emporia State University, Emporia, KS:

Although self-concept scales have been developed for children, adolescents, and adults, such an instrument has been lacking for the college-age population. The rather extensive and thorough manual for the Self-Perception Profile for College Students indicates that while some scales/domains from the adolescent and adult instruments developed previously by one of the authors are appropriate for college students, others are not. Therefore, several of the domains tested by this new instrument were contributed by each of these previous tests. A total of 13 domains, including Global Self-Worth, comprises the present test.

The full scale consists of 54 items—four items each for Domains 1–12 and six items for the Global Self-Worth domain. Each question asks the examinee "to indicate which of two types of students they are most like." This is accomplished by checking one of two boxes (*Really True, Sort of True*) for one of the two student types described by each item. One description is positive while the second is negative. Within each domain the items are balanced with regard to the number of positive and negative statements that appear first. As the pairs of answer boxes are located at opposite ends of each item, there may well be a tendency to check one box in each pair. While such an admonition is built into the instructions to the examiner, it will need to be emphasized to the students and the first few answers monitored to avoid more than one response per item. The full scale may be individually or group administered within approximately 30 minutes. A set of clear instructions to be read to the students is included.

The response to each item is assigned a score of 1, 2, 3, or 4 depending upon the degree of competence or self-judgement reflected by the answer. These scores are then summed on a domain-by-domain basis to yield a separate score for each subscale.

It is noteworthy that the students ($N = 300$; 70 males, 230 females) employed for the development of this instrument were predominantly freshmen (47.33%) from the University of Denver and Colorado State University. Very few juniors (13.66%) and seniors (7.66%) were represented in the sample. Additionally, a majority (84%) were commuters. The mean age of this predominantly Caucasian (93%), predominantly single (94%) sample was 19.8 years. Such demographics suggest potential areas of concern for the representativeness of the sample. As "the target population of this measure is the traditional full-time college student, ages 17–23," the potential usefulness of the instrument may be limited somewhat.

The reliabilities of the four-item subscales, as measured by coefficient alpha, ranged from .76 to .92 with only one domain (Job Competence) falling below .80. Suggesting the absence of ceiling and floor effects, subscale means clustered around 3.00 (sd = approximately .80). Three reliable gender effects were reported. Females scored higher on Close Friendship, while males scored higher on Athletic Competence and Appearance. The results of Cattell's scree test "indicated that twelve factors should be extracted, and these corresponded perfectly to the intended twelve subscales." A subsequent principle components factor analysis yielded high factor loadings (average = .78, range = .52–.92) with no cross-loadings.

In an attempt to place this scale within the theoretical model of William James who proposed that global self-esteem resulted from an "evaluation of the ratio of one's *successes* to one's *pretensions*," an Importance Scale also was developed. By determining the discrepancy between the competence score for a domain and the importance score of that domain, the authors suggest that they have operationalized James' theory. The Importance Scale consists of 24 questions (2 from each domain).

The items for the Importance Rating Scale are balanced and scored in the same manner as are those for the Self-Perception Profile. The internal reliabilities (coefficient alpha) range from .53 to .84 with only three subscales falling below .72. For two-item subscales such figures are quite acceptable. Other descriptive measures show that the importance means are rather high (range = 2.68–3.75) with one-half of the measures falling above 3.50. The standard deviations fall within an acceptable range of .45 to .83.

The most sensitive use of the importance scores appears to be in conjunction with the global measure of self-worth. When importance *and* competency scores are plotted for each domain for high, medium, and low self-worth subjects it is clear that while the importance ratings did not vary, the competence scores decreased dramatically from high to low self-worth. Although this is an excellent and informative use of these scores, the rationale behind the formation of the three self-worth categories is not explained or substantiated. They were formed "For demonstration purposes only." Hence, other configurations and results are possible.

Finally, recognizing that self-worth may be related to the process of socialization, the authors have included a Social Support Scale evaluating the importance of Close Friends, Mother, Campus Organizations, Father, and Instructors. This scale, which has a total of 20 items (4 per subscale), is administered and scored in the same manner as the Self-Perception Profile. The subscale reliabilities (coefficient alpha) range from .76 to .90. Although the subscale means are rather high (3.10–3.64) there is sufficient variability (*sd* range = .53–.70).

Reflecting some lack of organization in preparing the manual, it is not until page 45 that one finds information concerning validity and the target population for the Self-Perception Profile. (Such information is not given for the Importance Ratings and Social Support scales.) As these sections are rather short, they should have been incorporated directly into an earlier section. As validity information is presented for only three subscales (Social Acceptance, Close Friendships, and Parent Relationships), it is clear that additional work is needed in this area. The fact, however, that all three reported measures are quite reliable ($p = .001$) is encouraging. Similarly, the authors occasionally refer to appendices that may have been planned but which are not to be found in the completed manual.

The descriptive portion of the manual concludes with a section on applications. The authors suggest the Self-Perception Profile can be used in research, as a predictor of the resilience to stress, and as a therapeutic adjunct. The remainder of the manual is devoted to complete versions of each of the three scales, scoring keys, and an Individual Profile Form.

As the user is given permission to reproduce the scales and the profile form, all of the necessary elements for administering, scoring, and interpreting this scale are contained in this manual. Based upon the information provided here, the Self-Perception Profile and its two related scales should prove to be quite informative and helpful to those interested in evaluation of the self-concept of college-age subjects.

[76]

Sentence Comprehension Test, Revised Edition.

Purpose: "To assess children's comprehension of English and/or Panjabi."
Population: Ages 3–5.
Publication Dates: 1979–87.
Acronym: SCT.
Scores: 10 subtests: Simple Intransitive, Simple Transitive, Intransitive with Adjective, Plural, Past, Future, Negative, Prepositions, Embedded Phrase, Passive.
Administration: Individual.
Price Data, 1988: £30.55 per complete set including 25 record forms (English version), 25 record forms (Panjabi bilingual version), picture book ('87, 45 pages), and manual ('87, 43 pages); £5.20 per 25 record forms (English version); £6.90 per 25 record forms (Panjabi bilingual version); £16.70 per picture book; £12.65 per manual.

Foreign Language Edition: Panjabi bilingual version available.
Time: (10–20) minutes.
Authors: Kevin Wheldall, Peter Mittler, Angela Hobsbaum, Dorothy Gibbs (Panjabi bilingual version), Deirdre Duncan (Panjabi bilingual version), and Surinder Saund (Panjabi bilingual version).
Publisher: NFER-Nelson Publishing Co., Ltd. [England].
Cross References: For reviews by Francis X. Archambault and Mavis Donahue of the experimental edition, see 9:1107.

TEST REFERENCES

1. Gregory, H. M., & Beveridge, M. C. (1984). The social and educational adjustment of abused children. *Child Abuse & Neglect, 8*, 525-531.

Review of the Sentence Comprehension Test, Revised Edition by GABRIEL DELLA-PIANA, Professor of Educational Psychology, University of Utah, Salt Lake City, UT:

The Sentence Comprehension Test (SCT), Revised Edition, has the same purpose and structure as the earlier experimental edition. The test is designed "to measure a child's ability to comprehend sentences of varying length and grammatical complexity by requiring him to select appropriately from sets [of four] pictures" the one representing an orally presented stimulus sentence. The major changes introduced in the revised version are reduced testing time (due to fewer subtests) and redrawing of all pictures (for clarity, elimination of sex stereotyping, and including multicultural representation of persons illustrated). In addition, new studies of reliability and validity and some normative data support the revised edition.

The intended use of this measure of comprehension of orally presented sentences is primarily diagnostic, "[to] help . . . pinpoint the sentence constructions" that are causing the child some difficulty and to "lead to more systematic and specific approaches to remediation." It is also intended as a "quick screening device" to identify children whose performance deviates markedly from other children. Thus, the key questions to be addressed are: adequacy of reliability, validity, and norms for these purposes; ease of administration and scoring by testers; and usefulness of the manual to support the intended interpretations and uses of test results.

The administration procedure is simple and the record form is easy to use. An example illustrates the procedure. The tester presents a set of four black and white drawings (e.g., a black ladder, a white ladder, a black chair, and a white chair). The tester then asks the child to look at the pictures and says, "Show me the black chair." While feedback and help are given on practice items, during the actual test only noncontingent social reinforcement is given. A record form has a matrix of four squares corresponding to the four drawings coded as T (for target or correct response) or for type of error (e.g., S for subject error, V for verb error, etc.). The procedure allows the tester to attend to the child rather than to written instructions. Scoring is also simple, allowing a quick tally.

There are no statements concerning the qualifications needed to properly administer, score, or interpret the test, and there is little help in the manual to support interpretations and uses recommended. For example, the manual advises that "although one can say that the child scored 30/40 on the Test, it is more useful to examine the profile of subtests." But no examples of profiles are given, nor is there any information about how one might interpret and use a profile. The fact that "failure on specific test items or on the Test as a whole may result from . . . boredom . . . failure to scan pictures, listen to the message or relate what is heard to what is seen; or being too interested in the picture" suggests the need for training and for examples or guides to such analyses. However, none are to be found.

The test-retest reliability of .79 for total score and .77 for number of subtests passed on an N of 50 is only fair. The Spearman-Brown coefficient was .77 on the first test and .83 on the second testing. Because the age range tested sampled 3-, $3^1/_2$-, 4-, $4^1/_2$-, and 5-year-olds, one might expect higher reliabilities. Yet, at lower age levels, high reliabilities are often difficult to obtain. At any rate, it would be worth exploring what contributes to the only moderately high reliabilities obtained. Reliability data are not reported for separate age levels, even though normative data were gathered on a sample of 30 3-year-olds and 50 each of $3^1/_2$-, 4-, $4^1/_2$-, and 5-year-olds.

Data are presented showing approximate ages by which 50 percent and 75 percent of children tested have passed each subtest. Also, graphs show the mean total score and subtest pass rates for each age level. These data are appropriate to "screening" decisions, as suggested earlier in the manual. However, one would also want to recommend local testing for normative data because the normative sample in the study is small, and one might expect local variations in spite of the sample being selected to represent the general population in the "Registrar General's categories."

Validity is supported by SCT mean scores developing linearly over ages for the test as a whole but not for all subtests. Also, for the test as a whole, subtests passed and mean vocabulary age of the sample increase linearly for age groups along with SCT scores. However, because the manual suggests that it is more useful to examine the profile of subtests than the total score, validity relevant to interpreting the profiles would be very helpful.

Finally, this reviewer is not an expert on bilingual assessment and did not refer to the Panjabi bilingual version of the test in the above review. A quick overview suggests that the test has promise. However, this reviewer will have to leave it to others to assess whether or not the test has possibilities for assessing whether language problems of this population are problems with English or with language in general.

In summary, the SCT does appear to sample oral sentence comprehension in a way that identifies specific grammatical structures that require further diagnosis or remedial attention. Many of the earlier difficulties in the test have been corrected in the current version. However, the diagnostic possibilities of the test continue to warrant further development. In the hands of an experienced clinical educational diagnostician, the test has its most immediate current use.

[77]

Short Category Test, Booklet Format.

Purpose: A sensitive indicator of brain damage measuring an individual's ability to solve problems requiring careful observation, development of organizing principles, and responsiveness to feedback.
Population: Ages 15 and over.
Publication Dates: 1986–87.
Acronym: SCT.
Scores: Total score only.
Subtests, 5: 1, 2, 3, 4, 5.

Administration: Individual.
Price Data, 1989: $105 per complete kit; $79.50 per set of stimulus cards, 5 booklets ('86, 20 cards per booklet); $13.50 per 100 answer sheets ('87); $17.50 per manual ('87, 40 pages).
Time: (15–30) minutes.
Comments: Revision of the Halstead-Reitan Category Test (9:463).
Authors: Linda Wetzel and Thomas J. Boll.
Publisher: Western Psychological Services.

Review of the Short Category Test, Booklet Format by SCOTT W. BROWN, Associate Professor of Educational Psychology, University of Connecticut, Storrs, CT:

The Short Category Test (SCT) is designed to assess an individual's ability to solve problems requiring abstract concept formation, based on the presentation of geometric shapes and configurations. The SCT does this without the equipment requirements and in less time than the longer Category Test. It transforms Halstead's nine subtests containing 360 items, presented using a semiautomated slide format with a rear projection screen, into five subtests of 20 items each, presented using a booklet format. The purpose of the SCT is to serve as a screening tool for individuals between the ages of 15 years through adulthood in a variety of medical and educational settings. The scores obtained from this instrument are purported to assess an individual's use of abstract principles, adaptive skills, and cognitive flexibility.

During administration of the SCT, the individual views figures or designs and responds with a number between 1 and 4, based on what rule the picture suggests to him or her. The response format may be either manual (pointing) or oral. The examiner provides feedback to each response by stating "right" or "wrong." All 100 items are administered to all subjects.

The SCT retains many of the original principles of the Category Test, with each SCT subtest containing various geometric shapes, lines, colors, and/or figures focusing on one of the following organizing principles: (*a*) the number of figures in a linear array; (*b*) the ordinal position of the atypical figure in a linear display; (*c*) the identification of the atypical quadrant; and (*d*) the number of quadrants joined by solid lines. The individual being assessed must view the cards, generate a hypothesis about the rule for the correct response, and check that rule against the feedback provided by the examiner.

The manual reports reliability and validity data for both the SCT and the Category Test. A reliability coefficient of .81 was obtained for the SCT using the split-half procedure with a Spearman-Brown correction formula. However, as the manual notes, the reliability coefficient must be interpreted with some caution because the items are linked together within subtests (because of feedback), resulting in some artifacts.

Test-retest reliability coefficients were not reported for the SCT, failing to provide an indication of the potential practice effects resulting from multiple testings. This is an extremely important unfortunate deficit because the manual states the SCT may be used to assess changes that could result from various treatments.

Criterion-related and discriminative validity procedures are reported in the manual. The results of a study correlating the scores obtained by a group of 50 undergraduates on the Category Test and the SCT indicates that the two tests are highly related (.93 and .80, depending on the order of administration), suggesting the two tests are measuring similar abilities. Further analyses revealed a statistically significant practice effect when the Category Test was administered first, but not when the SCT was administered first. Unfortunately, the authors misinterpret this as evidence indicating a lack of a practice effect for the SCT.

Discriminative validity was assessed using a group of individuals with psychiatric and neurological diagnoses and a group of volunteers with no neurological damage. Analyses between the error scores of the "brain-damaged" and "non-brain-damaged" subjects indicated a high degree of predictability for group membership after controlling for age and education level ($p < .001$). When cutoff scores were used based on the creation of two age groups, those 45 years and younger and those 46 years and older, 83% of the total group were correctly classified. Additional analyses examining the correlation coefficients of a group of neurological patients for the SCT and the Category Test with several other neuropsychological measures yielded similar correlation coefficients. The validity data reported in the manual suggest that the SCT may be an effective screening tool for detecting neurological impairments affecting problem-solving abilities and that the results will be similar to those obtained on the Category Test.

The normative sample consisted of 120 volunteers and an independent clinical sample of 70 psychiatric and neurological patients. The manual reports the breakdown of the normal sample for sex, age, education, occupational level, and race with all stratifying variables within the appropriate range, except for age. No individuals in the normal sample were under the age of 20, yet the SCT manual reports that the test can be used for individuals 15 years of age and older. Without the age group of 15 to 19 included as part of the normative sample, the use of the SCT with this age group is inappropriate.

Analyses of the scores of the 190 subjects in the normative group controlled for the age and educational level of the individual. Subsequent analyses yielded two different cutoff scores, a cutoff score of 41 errors for subjects 45 and under and a cutoff score of 46 for subjects 46 and over, correctly classifying 83% of the total group as either brain-damaged or non-brain-damaged. Normative tables are provided for both age groups indicating percentiles and T-scores.

The SCT manual is well written and organized containing the pertinent psychometric and administration information. The inclusion of case studies using the SCT enables the examiner to interpret the scores and response patterns of different types of patients.

In summary, the SCT provides an alternative to the Category Test to assess impairments in the problem-solving abilities of individuals suspected of psychiatric or neurological dysfunctions. Two problems that need to be addressed when considering the use of the SCT are the age of the individual and practice effects. Using the SCT with individuals under the age of 20 should be done with extreme caution because there are no normative data available for this age group. Further, without test-retest reliability estimates, the practice effects from multiple administrations of the SCT are unknown. The SCT should provide, however, very similar results to the Category Test in a shorter amount of time and with less equipment.

Review of the Short Category Test, Booklet Format by HOPE J. HARTMAN, *Associate Professor of Social & Psychological Foundations, School of Education, The City College, City University of New York, New York, NY:*

The Halstead-Reitan Category Test (HRCT; 9:463) was revised because this sensitive screening device indicating brain damage had several limitations resulting in its frequent exclusion from clinical assessments. Administration was very time consuming, the equipment was expensive and broke down frequently, and it was difficult to use at bedside. Additionally, research has demonstrated that it is subject to practice effects, making improved retesting results difficult to interpret.

Several prior attempts to shorten the HRCT and simplify its administration included slides, cards, and booklet formats. These efforts were of limited value due to item sequencing problems and lack of, or unsuccessful, cross-validation results. Additional weaknesses were in reliability data, norms, and other psychometric information.

The Short Category Test, Booklet Format (SCT) was developed to: cut administration time by at least half, simplify the equipment needed, ensure the test's comparability to the original test in relation to standard neurological batteries, and discriminate between brain-damaged and non-brain-damaged individuals.

A spiral-bound booklet contains the 20 items (cards) which result in 5 subtests. In each subtest, items selected in sequence from the HRCT are organized according to a single principle, either number of objects, ordinal position of figures on the card, number of quadrants, or missing quadrant. The task is to formulate an organizing concept for each card sequence. The subject responds to each card by orally answering "one," "two," "three," or "four," or by pointing to the answer on the card shown. The test administrator marks the response and says "right" or "wrong." Item selection had an empirical base, but because no gender or race data were provided for the sample, generalizability of item appropriateness is unclear.

One source of confusion in the manual is an inconsistency between the narrative description of the test and Table 1. The narrative implies the second subtest has the organizing principle of "ordinal position," while Table 1 identifies the organizing principle of Subtest 2 as "original position." Some careful editing of the manual is in order.

Administration and scoring procedures appear relatively simple. In fact, the manual states administration and scoring can be done by a trained paraprofessional.

The rationale underlying the scoring procedure seems questionable. Instructions provide the subject with more cues for obtaining the correct answer on Subtest 2 than on Subtest 1, yet weigh these subtest errors the same. Although the manual mentions that Subtest 1 often is considered a warm-up exercise, all nine figures illustrating the answer sheet and scoring show the "Total Raw Error Scores" as the sum of *all* subtests. The Appendix contains a table providing Normalized *T*-Scores and Percentile Rank Equivalents corresponding to the Total Raw Error Score. The table provides separate data for Older and Younger Adults; age 45 is the cutoff.

The Percentile Rank Equivalents provided in the manual are potentially confusing. Why are they used instead of percentile ranks? The manual states that a person with a percentile rank equivalent score of 58 had *more errors* than approximately 58% of the normative sample in the appropriate age group. Therefore, the higher the "percentile rank equivalent score," the *worse* the level of performance. Conventionally, a "percentile rank" score means the higher the percentile rank, the *better* the level of performance. Representation of percentile rank equivalent data on the table in the Appendix by "%," the *percentage* symbol, could engender misinterpretation. Use of "%ileE" or "PRE" would be clearer.

The manual provides some reliability and validity data. Estimation procedures produced corrected split-half reliability coefficients of .81 for the SCT and .89 for the HRCT. The manual states both are probably artificially high because of item interdependence. There were no significant differences between the HRCT and SCT for even-odd item means. Test-retest reliability data were provided for the HRCT, but not for the SCT. No standard error of measurement data were reported.

In demonstrating equivalence between the two versions, the authors controlled for practice effects between the SCT and the HRCT by counterbalancing order of presentation and correlated percent of error scores. Subjects were primarily women undergraduates (only 14 males); race was unspecified. Pearson product-moment correlations were .93 for HRCT-SCT and .80 for SCT-HRCT. With HRCT-SCT presentation order, reliability was .84; with SCT-HRCT order, reliability was .42 (Summers & Boll, 1987), suggesting a significant lack of practice effects for the SCT. This implies better SCT scores upon retesting are more likely to reflect improved mental functioning than improvement on the HRCT. SCT items and the test overall were demonstrated to correlate with other neuropsychological measures. Correlation patterns were similar to comparisons of those tests to the HRCT.

The manual reports discriminative validity of the SCT for distinguishing brain-damaged from non-brain-damaged individuals. After controlling for age and education, ANCOVA results showed highly significant discriminability for these groups. Using age-corrected cutoff scores ("41" ≤ age 45; "46" ≥ age 46), 83% of normative and impaired subjects combined were classified correctly. This is an impressive hit rate for a single test and comparable to the classification rate of the HRCT. The manual states interpretations should be made by professionals with advanced clinical training and experience, and within the context of other measures. It also notes the test taker must have adequate motivation, vision, and attention span.

Standardization data appear to be primarily from white, middle-class males. The clinical sample was fairly homogeneous: primarily middle class, with high school education; the ratio of males to females was approximately 3:1 (15 females). Race was unspecified. The nonimpaired sample was somewhat more heterogeneous: a wider range of socioeconomic status and educational levels, and relatively balanced for gender. However, most individuals had at least a high school education and 87.5% were white. Research showed both age and educational level to affect significantly SCT performance. When comparing clinical and normal samples, the developers controlled for age and education. Norms are provided for different age groups but not different educational levels. The manual notes interpretations should take this into account. Race and gender were *not considered*. Research on nonverbal material demonstrates males and females, as well as Blacks and

Whites, may differ significantly in their performance.

Overall, the SCT is appealing in format, short, and easy to use. Its apparent lack of practice effects is noteworthy. It may contribute to clinical diagnostic practice and treatment by serving as an improved alternative to the HRCT. However, before an unqualified recommendation can be given, several improvements are necessary. First, components of the manual and scoring statistics should be improved. Second, additional research is needed to test its reliability further, and to generate norms based on educational level. Finally, research is needed to determine whether the SCT's validity and norms can be generalized across race and gender.

REVIEWER'S REFERENCE

Summers, M., & Boll, T. (1987). Comparability of a short booklet version and the traditional form of the Category Test. *International Journal of Clinical Neuropsychology, 9* (4), 158-161.

[78]

Social Reticence Scale.

Purpose: To assess an individual's shyness.
Population: High school and college and adults.
Publication Date: 1986.
Acronym: SRS.
Scores: Total score only.
Administration: Individual or group.
Price Data, 1987: $4 per 25 test booklets; $1.50 per scoring key; $10 per manual (30 pages); $11 per specimen set including test booklet, scoring key, and manual.
Time: (5–10) minutes.
Author: Warren H. Jones.
Publisher: Consulting Psychologists Press, Inc.

TEST REFERENCES

1. Briggs, S. R. (1988). Shyness: Introversion or neuroticism? *Journal of Research in Personality, 22*, 290-307.

Review of the Social Reticence Scale by OWEN SCOTT, III, Clinical Psychologist, The Psychology Clinic, Baton Rouge, LA:

The Social Reticence Scale (SRS) is a brief (20-item), self-administered instrument designed to measure shyness. The authors conceptualize shyness as a form of social anxiety that inhibits effective performance in social situations. The word shyness does not appear in the title or items in order to avoid communicating the exact construct being measured to respondents. Each of the items is rated on a 5-point, Likert-type scale with half of the items scored in the reverse direction. Information on the reading level of the test is not provided;

similarly, no recommendations are given as to the age range for whom the test is intended. Inspection of the items suggests that it is probably appropriate for persons of high school age and educational level and above. The potential range of scores is 20 to 100. The test can be quickly and easily administered and scored using the scoring key provided with the test. The test score may be computed by hand or with the aid of a calculator.

The stated purpose of the test is to provide an index of shyness for basic research on personality variables and for applied uses, which include assessing the relative degree of individuals' shyness, providing feedback to persons on their shyness, and assessing treatment effects in interventions aimed at reducing shyness. The authors recommend against using the SRS at the present time for diagnostic purposes, such as determining whether an individual needs treatment for shyness or other problems, due to the lack of empirical data on these issues.

The manual provides a very satisfactory summary of the rationale, development, and validation of the SRS in a clear and succinct style. Substantial evidence is presented for the reliability and validity of the instrument. Internal consistency and test-retest reliability of the SRS, as determined in a sample of 252 college students and replicated in a heterogeneous sample of over 1,100 high school and college students and adults, are impressive. For example, test-retest correlations for a sample of 101 college students over an 8-week interval were .81, .89, and .87 for men, women, and the combined sample, respectively. Similarly, a great deal of data are presented to show the SRS is a valid measure of shyness as intended by the authors. Typical of the construct validity findings are correlations between the SRS and the first order factors of the Sixteen Personality Factor Questionnaire (16PF). As expected, the SRS correlated significantly with all components of the second-order factor Introversion-Extraversion in the expected directions, with the greatest correlation (-.82) occurring for Factor H (shy, threat-sensitive vs. bold, adventurous). Smaller, but significant, correlations were also found with two anxiety factors, guilt-proneness (Factor 0), and ergic tension (Factor Q4). In addition to showing good convergent and discriminant validity, a particularly impressive finding was the correlation between SRS

scores and judges' ratings of brief, videotaped self-descriptions by the 30 respondents ($r = .50$ for ratings of shyness, $p < .002$). The SRS has also been found in several studies to predict self-reported indices of social activity and support. Other evidence is presented to show the SRS does measure shyness rather than related constructs (e.g., sociability and fear of negative evaluation) and that it does not appear excessively influenced by social desirability.

Replicated factor analyses of the SRS revealed that it has two correlated factors, isolation from others and ease of social communication. The authors provide directions for computing subscale scores, should the test user wish to do so.

For the applied user, tables presenting means and standard deviations for several normative groups, most notably college students, high school students, and nonclinical adults, are provided. Data on the distribution of SRS scores in terms of percentages of 2,645 respondents scoring within 9-point ranges (e.g., 20–28, 29–37, etc.) are presented in an Appendix.

The manual of the SRS concludes with recommendations for future research on shyness as related to the use of the test.

The authors are to be commended for providing a conservative and incisive analysis of promising directions for research that illuminates the present and potential utility of the SRS. In general, the SRS is a reliable, valid, and solidly constructed instrument for the measurement of shyness. It is short and easy to administer, yet it possesses very satisfactory psychometric properties. Researchers in the area of shyness would be advised to consider this instrument strongly when selecting a self-report measure of the construct. The SRS also has much promise for clinical applications, although, as the authors point out, additional research is needed to determine the full extent of clinical implications of shyness and to identify cutoff scores for classifying subjects in relation to criteria of interest (e.g., impaired ability to form important relationships). For the applied user, the systematic collection of normative data on various populations of interest (e.g., persons of different ages, ethnic groups, and geographic regions) would add to the utility of the test. Overall, the SRS compares very favorably to other specific self-report measures of shyness and warrants the consideration of researchers and clinicians interested in this variable.

Review of the Social Reticence Scale by WIL-LIAM K. WILKINSON, Assistant Professor of Counseling and Educational Psychology, New Mexico State University, Las Cruces, NM:

The Social Reticence Scale (SRS) is a 20-item, self-report instrument designed to measure shyness. Respondents rate SRS items on a 5-point Likert-type scale (1 = *not at all characteristic*, 5 = *extremely characteristic*) yielding a total score used to evaluate interpersonal reticence. The normative sample consists primarily of college students ($N = 2,250$), but also includes separate samples of high school students, adults, convicted felons, hospital workers, and parents of adolescents in counseling.

One of the strongest features of the SRS is its evidence of reliability and validity. Regarding reliability, the stability of self-reported ratings across an 8-week administration period is reported as .87 for a sample of 101 college students. This stability coefficient meets appropriate standards as an estimate of reliability.

Further, evidence regarding the three major components of validity are all discussed in the test manual. In terms of content validity, the test manual clearly distinguishes the steps in the derivation of SRS items. For instance, items were derived from Zimbardo's (1981) analysis of shyness as defining seven interpersonal areas (e.g., problems in meeting strangers, excessive self-consciousness, etc.), with three items then written for each of the seven domains. Subsequently, items were statistically analyzed, and only those items demonstrating appropriate statistical standards were retained. Thus, the SRS appears content valid with respect to the shyness construct.

Evidence of validity is presented in three forms. Concurrent validity was investigated by correlating the SRS with four other measures of shyness. The correlations varied from .72 to .81, revealing that SRS scores are highly related to scores on other measures of the shyness construct. In addition, SRS scores obtained for 128 freshmen during the first week of college were related to the number of new friends, social network and its density, and social supports established 2 months later, thus testing predictive validity. The correlations were signif-icantly negative, thus revealing that low scores on the SRS (low shyness) predicted the presence of more new friends, denser social network, and more social support than those with high SRS scores. As further evidence of predictive validity, SRS scores predicted judges' ratings of shyness for 30 college students observed individually during a 2-minute period of self-disclosure.

The SRS also appears construct valid. That the instrument predicts scores on other measures of shyness lends support to this statement. In addition, the SRS does not appear to measure constructs antithetical to shyness. For example, SRS scores are negatively related to the Sixteen Personality Factor Questionnaire (16PF; 9:1136) scales pertaining to social boldness ($r = .-61$) and outgoing ($r = -.82$), and also are inversely correlated with extraversion ($r = -.73$) and assertiveness ($r = -.63$).

In sum, although there is little doubt the SRS provides sufficient evidence of reliability and validity, there are troublesome aspects to the SRS. Of particular concern is the interpretation of individual scores. Interpretation is problematic for the following reasons.

First, determining a respondent's degree of shyness relative to the normative group is limited, because the only normative data presented are means, standard deviations, and percentages within raw score intervals (20–28, 29–37, etc.). Using just this descriptive information, the test interpreter is limited to comparing a respondent's score with the mean score of the normative sample. Interpretation of the SRS would be significantly improved if each raw score in the normative sample was converted to a derived score, such as percentiles or T-scores. Derived scores would help determine the magnitude of a respondent's shyness relative to the normative sample, and enable more precise statements to be made regarding what raw score constitutes a "significant" degree of shyness.

Even if derived scores were included for the SRS, a more pervasive issue is the fact that the distribution of raw scores for the normative sample looks positively skewed. Positive skewness may exist in that about 88 percent of the scores fall below the raw score point of 64, although the theoretical median value of the raw scores should be 60 (multiplying the midpoint value of three for each item by the number of items). In other words, a rough interpolation suggests that around 80 percent of the normative sample averaged an endorsement of three or less per item. Yet, is it safe to conclude that a respondent with a raw score of 60 (the theoretical median) is "significantly" shy? Probably not, although this raw score would surpass approximately 80 percent of the normative sample. Thus, test interpreters need to guard against the possibility of interpreting SRS scores as indicative of shyness when, in fact, they are not.

Because SRS interpretation is severely limited, the instrument is clearly not appropriate for diagnostic purposes. To the test developer's credit, the test manual warns potential test consumers not to use the SRS for diagnostic reasons. This does not mean the SRS cannot be used in applied settings. Rather, its applied use is restricted to individual feedback in cases where shyness is clearly an interpersonal weakness.

The exact degree of a respondent's shyness (e.g., relative magnitude) will have to be determined by the test interpreter through conversion of the raw score to a derived score. Further, what constitutes a "significant" degree of shyness must be carefully considered in light of the potentially skewed distribution of raw scores observed for the normative sample. To guard against the possibility of overinterpreting SRS results, it may be advisable to adopt a relatively high raw score value (e.g., 80 or above) as suggestive of "significant" shyness.

The SRS might be useful in research efforts. Before adopting the SRS, however, as an investigative tool, its relative strengths and weaknesses should be compared to other instruments of shyness, such as the measures developed by Morris (1984), and Cheek and Buss (1981), as well as other well-known instruments that seem to measure constructs similar to shyness (e.g., 16PF).

REVIEWER'S REFERENCES

Cheek, J. M., & Buss, A. N. (1981). Shyness and sociability. *Journal of Personality, 41*, 330-339.
Zimbardo, P. G., & Radl, S. L. (1981). *The shy child.* New York: McGraw-Hill.
Morris, T. L. (1984). *A longitudinal study of personality influences on social support.* Unpublished master's thesis, University of Tulsa, Tulsa, OK.

[79]

Social Skills Inventory, Research Edition.

Purpose: "To assess basic social communication skills."
Population: Ages 14 and over reading at or above the eighth grade level.
Publication Date: 1989.
Acronym: SSI.
Scores, 7: Emotional Expressivity, Emotional Sensitivity, Emotional Control, Social Expressivity, Social Sensitivity, Social Control, Total.
Administration: Group and individual.
Price Data, 1990: $20 per 25 test booklets; $3 per scoring key; $25 per 50 answer sheets; $14 per manual (24 pages); $17 per specimen set (includes manual, test booklet, scoring key); scoring service offered by publisher.
Time: (30–45) minutes.
Comments: Test booklet title is Self-Description Inventory; self-administered.
Authors: Ronald E. Riggio.
Publisher: Consulting Psychologists Press, Inc.

TEST REFERENCES

1. Riggio, R. E., Tucker, J., & Throckmorton, B. (1987). Social skills and deception ability. *Personality and Social Psychology Bulletin, 13*, 568-577.

Review of the Social Skills Inventory, Research Edition by JUDITH C. CONGER, Director of Clinical Training, Purdue University, West Lafayette, IN:

RATIONALE. The Social Skills Inventory (SSI) is a 90-item self-report inventory designed to measure social communication skills. The six scales tap three major areas—Expressivity, Sensitivity, and Control. These are each measured on two levels, Emotional and Social, thus yielding six domains. The author indicates the total SSI score reflects "a global level of social skill development indicative of overall social competence or social intelligence" (p. 2). Although most researchers would agree the social competence construct is multidimensional in nature, they might not agree that social communication skills, social skills, social competence, and social intelligence are equivalent or interchangeable terms owing to the fact their meanings are tied to the social, behavioral, or individual difference traditions that spawned them. Further, although the author discusses "social intelligence" in terms of general intelligence in an effort to discriminate between them, the "apparent" similarity stops there. That is, it should be noted that traditional intellectual measures are based on performance or samples of behavior: this measure is not. It is designed to measure the *self-report* of social behavior and not the behavior itself.

The development of the SSI is tied to previous work in nonverbal communication (e.g., Rosenthal, 1979; Friedman, 1979) and is reported to be an extension of the Affective Communication Test (ACT; Friedman, Prince, Riggio, & DiMatteo, 1980). The ACT is a measure of nonverbal expressiveness. The measure was developed originally for social psychological research. The exact nature of the item pool from which the measure is derived or the construction of the items in the SSI is not reported in detail, although the author reports several years of pretesting and refinement in the selection of the items. Further, the measure is embedded in a theoretical context and is part of an active, ongoing research program by the author.

RELIABILITY. Internal consistency estimates for the individual scales and the total scale are reported. Most appear to be adequate, although the internal consistency of the Emotional Expressivity and Emotional Sensitivity scales for males is only .62 and .67, respectively (total range = .62–.87). Although two samples of both men and women were tested, complete descriptive data are reported only on Sample 1.

Test-retest reliability is based on a 2-week interval ($N = 40$) and ranges from .81 to .96 for the individual scales, with the reliability of the total SSI being .94. These are strong test-retest estimates; however, evidence for the stability of the SSI over longer time intervals is needed.

VALIDITY CONSIDERATIONS. Evidence for the validity of the SSI is derived from several sources. With regard to the internal structure, the author states the relationship among the component social skills should be positive, given that the possession of one skill should predispose one to possess other skills. The intercorrelations among the scales, although indicating a preponderance of positive relationships, also indicate some variability. That is, roughly one third of the correlations are negative and some scales show no relationship or a weak relationship to other scales. Most notably, Social Sensitivity shows no meaningful relationship to Emotional Expressivity in the total sample matrix or in the matrices for each sex. Further, although most of the scales correlate positively with the total SSI score, social sensitivity correlates extremely weakly or not at all ($rs = .06, -.03,$ or $.00$).

Inspection of the intercorrelations among the scales does not suggest six different factors; however, the author reports a factor analysis using a confirmatory factor analytic approach that indicates the presence of six different factors. This approach allows the investigator to specify a model, a priori, that is then tested. Although this particular model was not rejected, it is also possible that a simpler model using fewer factors would not be rejected either. This approach requires the testing of different models against one another, which if done, was not reported. Thus, the argument for six factors based just on this analysis is not compelling and needs replication.

The SSI shows a range of correlations with other measures, most strongly with the ACT and more weakly with the Profile of Nonverbal Sensitivity (PONS). The correlational results suggest the SSI is tapping some of the same constructs measured by these other inventories (16 Personality Factor Questionnaire [16PF], Personality Research Form [PRF], Eysenck Personality Inventory [EPI], etc.). However, some of these correlations raise questions about the nature of what is being measured in terms of the subscales. For example, the Social Sensitivity scale (SS) correlates most highly with Public Self-Consciousness (.58) and Social Anxiety (.37), while relationships with the ACT and PONS were minimal. The SS scale also had virtually no relationship to the total SSI score. This scale may be measuring something other than that which was intended and probably needs further examination. One of the strongest scales in the SSI is Social Expressivity (SE). The test-retest reliability (.96) is as good as that of the total SSI (.94). Often its relationship to other measures is similar in patterning to the total SSI and the strength of those relationships was often as good, if not better, than the total SSI. Future researchers may want to examine how well this scale performs in comparison to the total SSI, as it may do just as well in some situations.

Other validity work appears to be ongoing in terms of relating the SSI to performance measure of social competence, as well as indirect measures such as social networks. Although the manual indicates this research is favorable, specific data are not always reported. All studies are, however, referenced. Further, there appears to be an ongoing research program by Riggio and his colleagues which is a credit to the author and should shed additional light on the SSI.

Although the test is designed for use with adults at an eighth-grade reading level, the primary population used in the development and investigation of the SSI was made up of college students at the undergraduate and graduate levels. To the author's and publisher's credit, this is clearly spelled out in the manual.

In summary, the SSI appears to be a serious attempt to design a self-report measure of social competence. This is a worthy goal. The SSI definitely has some strengths and some weaknesses. More specifically, clearer evidence regarding validity is needed. Further research guided by additional clarification of the theory should shed light on these issues.

Review of the Social Skills Inventory, Research Edition by SUSAN M. SHERIDAN, Assistant Professor of Educational Psychology, University of Utah, Salt Lake City, UT:

The Social Skills Inventory (SSI) is a self-report measure for adults based on an information-processing model of social skills. It consists of six scales that measure social communication skills on two levels: Emotional and Social. Expressivity, Sensitivity, and Control are evaluated in each. The SSI appears to be theoretically and psychometrically sound, and has several positive characteristics that contribute to its utility. When used in conjunction with behavioral measures of social skills, the SSI may be a helpful instrument in research and applied settings.

MANUAL. The manual for the SSI is clear and complete. Sections on theory and background, procedural details, psychometric qualities, and research applications are included. The procedures for administration, scoring, and interpretation are well documented, and appear to be especially helpful to test users.

ADMINISTRATION AND SCORING. The SSI is very user-friendly in terms of its administration and scoring procedures. The instrument is self-administered, and is appropriate for individuals with an eighth-grade reading level. Items are written clearly, and the SSI could be adapted easily to group administrations.

Scoring of the SSI is clear and simple. Items are scored on a 5-point Likert scale, with scores on the six scales ranging from 15–75. A total

score is provided that is described as a global level of social skill or competence. Scoring is aided by the use of a scoring template. Descriptive data and cutoff scores for each scale and for the Total SSI are reported, with separate norms for males and females.

One potential scoring problem with the SSI is the way it handles unanswered items. The author, Riggio, notes that a protocol containing more than 15 unanswered items is invalid; however, the necessary number of completed items within each scale is not reported. He further recommends that unanswered items be given a score of 3 (the midway point on the 5-point scale), implying that this will not greatly effect a protocol that contains few unanswered items across scales. However, if a test contains several unanswered items within the same scale, and the respondent rated the majority of items within that scale consistently high or low, it may significantly alter the scale score and test profile for that individual. It may be more appropriate to compute the mean for completed items, and impose this mean rating onto unanswered items. This procedure appears to be more sensitive to individual responses in the profile analysis.

STANDARDIZATION. A limited normative group was used in the standardization of the SSI. Descriptive statistics and cutoff scores from two undergraduate college samples are reported ($n = 453$ and 199, respectively). Although the author recommends cautious interpretation when using the scale with other populations, he discusses other applications of the instrument in detail (e.g., counseling, couples research, and leadership training). Further research in these areas is needed before the instrument can be put to widespread use.

TEST DEVELOPMENT. Riggio (1989) reports that early pretesting of the SSI was done on hundreds of items. Two versions of the test were constructed, tested, and refined; however, specific procedures of item development and evaluation are not provided. A 105-item scale was used in the validity studies; however, one social skill scale (Social Manipulation) was subsequently eliminated with no rationale, yielding the final version with 90 items.

RELIABILITY/VALIDITY. The SSI has good psychometric properties. Test-retest reliabilities of the separate scales range from .81 to .96 (2-week interval), and alpha coefficients range from .62 to .87. Across male and female samples, the three emotional scales revealed the lowest alpha coefficients, suggesting lower consistency within these subtests.

Riggio reported the results of several validity studies using a variety of instruments (including the Affective Communication Test, Bem Sex-Role Inventory, 16 Personality Factor Questionnaire, Personality Research Form, and Eysenck Personality Inventory). A great deal of data are provided that generally support the convergent and discriminant validity of the scale. Although several predicted relationships emerged, some unexpected relationships were also found. Unfortunately, many of the instruments used in the studies may be unfamiliar to test users, and the overwhelming presentation of the data makes this information difficult to interpret. It should also be noted that college student samples were used in all of the validity studies, limiting the scale's use pending future research.

Evidence of factorial validity is also provided for the SSI. Factor analysis was conducted by grouping items for each of the scales into sets of five items each, resulting in 18 total item sets. The purpose for this grouping procedure is unclear; however, the author reported it was due to the large number of items on the test. A six-factor solution with varimax rotation was used, and all six of the predicted factors emerged with strong factor loadings. One possible exception is with a subset of items purported to load on the Social Expressivity scale. A relatively low factor loading (.28), along with a high intercorrelation with the Social Control scale (.66) suggests that interpretation of this factor may be difficult.

INTERPRETATION. Factor analysis of the SSI generally allows test users to interpret subscales as reflective of the underlying constructs they are purported to measure. Descriptive statistics, cutoff scores by sex, and sample profiles are provided to aid in the interpretation of individual profiles.

Riggio argues the basic social skill components are assumed to be additive (i.e., contributing to a total score), but also recognizes appropriately that the relation between any single skill area and "social effectiveness" is not always linear. According to the author, "It is not only the extent to which individuals have developed particular social skills . . . that is important, but it is the balance among them that is related to overall social competence" (p. 7). Thus, he recommends the use of an "imbalance score" using the standard deviation of the six social skill scales for each individual. A formula to compute standard deviation is provided, but is very cumbersome and impractical for clinicians in its current form.

One fundamental assumption of the test is that individuals can, in fact, be accurate raters of their own social skills; however, this assumption has no empirical support. Test users must recognize that the SSI is primarily a self-*perception* instrument, and this distinction should be clarified when interpreting individual profiles.

SUMMARY. The SSI has several characteristics that make it an appealing instrument, including its ease in administration and scoring, and its sound psychometric qualities. It shows potential as a meaningful component in the assessment of social skills. However, continued research with broader samples is needed before the scale can be used clinically with confidence.

[80]

Spellmaster.
Purpose: "A method of analyzing spelling errors for sequential prescriptive instruction."
Population: Elementary and junior high school students.
Publication Dates: 1974–87.
Scores: Total score only on each test.
Administration: Group.
Levels: 8 overlapping levels.
Price Data, 1987: $59 per complete kit; $9 per 50 student answer sheets; $5 per 25 scoring forms (specify level 1–8); $24 per examiner's manual ('87, 107 pages).
Time: Administration time not reported.
Comments: "Criterion-referenced"; 27 tests.
Author: Claire R. Greenbaum.
Publisher: PRO-ED, Inc.
Cross References: For reviews by C. Dale Carpenter and Steve Graham of an earlier edition, see 9:1162.

Review of the Spellmaster by PATTI L. HARRISON, Associate Professor of Behavioral Studies, College of Education, The University of Alabama, Tuscaloosa, AL:

Spellmaster is designed to yield prescriptive, criterion-referenced information for planning spelling instruction. Its use is limited, however, due to absence of technical data. The system consists of several levels and types of spelling tests, as well as supplementary word lists, guidelines for teaching spelling, and examples of spelling activities. The manual does not describe any similarities or differences between the current and 1974 editions.

Spellmaster, which may be group or individually administered, includes three entry level tests and eight levels each of comprehensive regular word, irregular word, and homophone tests. Each entry test requires about 10 minutes for administration and each comprehensive test requires about 20 minutes. Examiners administer items by saying the words and using them in sentences; students write the words on an answer sheet.

Administration begins with an entry test (regular word, irregular word, or homophones). Each entry test has eight levels which correspond to levels on the comprehensive tests. Entry tests provide quick estimates of students' mastery, instructional, and frustration spelling levels. Students' instructional level on an entry test indicates the level of the comprehensive test to be administered.

Regular word tests are emphasized for diagnostic testing and error analyses. Regular word tests contain phonetically regular words that can be spelled according to dependable generalizations. The tests measure phonetic and structural *elements* such as consonants, beginning blends, endings, and open and closed syllables. An average grade range is indicated for each level. Levels 1 and 2 measure auditory elements; levels 3 through 6, auditory and visual elements; and levels 6 through 8, conceptual elements.

Irregular word tests measure spelling of words that violate phonic rules. Homophone tests measure spelling of words that have the same pronunciations as other words, but different meanings. Error analyses are not provided and use of these tests is not clearly described. The author indicates only that the tests are usually administered after regular phonic patterns are learned and may be used with students designated as top spellers on the regular word tests.

For the level of regular word, irregular word, and homophone tests administered to the student, the number of correctly spelled words is calculated. Error analyses for regular word levels are accomplished on scoring forms that list parts of words and their corresponding

elements. Only a few elements are measured at each level; scorers may indicate that students made errors corresponding to an element not measured, but lower levels must be administered to conduct error analyses for these elements. Therefore, administration of any level provides only a partial analysis of spelling errors. In addition, many elements occur infrequently, with the majority of elements occurring only 2 or 3 times, resulting in a limited sampling for elements.

Guidelines for interpretation focus on the total number of correctly spelled words. The manual indicates the number of correct words that identify top, middle, and bottom spellers. Top spellers may be given the next highest regular word level or the irregular words or homophones tests, or may be excused from systematic spelling instruction. Middle spellers may be given instruction at their level and bottom spellers may be retested at a lower level. No guidelines are given for interpreting the error analyses of regular words, a notable omission given the purpose of the system.

With the exception of a brief statement concerning field testing, *no information about test development or psychometric properties is reported in the Spellmaster manual*. Many types of technical data are required for appropriate use of Spellmaster and absence of technical data greatly limits the confidence that can be placed in test results. The fact that Spellmaster is criterion-referenced, and not norm-referenced, does not excuse the author from supplying evidence of appropriate developmental procedures, reliability, and validity.

There is no evidence that any part of Spellmaster represents spelling skills necessary in today's schools. The author simply states that words on Spellmaster are likely to be seen in classroom materials and the regular word elements are frequently applied. Detailed information concerning selection of words and elements for the tests is necessary to judge the relationship between test content and school curriculum at each grade level.

Data must support the author's assumptions that regular word levels measure cumulative elements, that item difficulty corresponds to the grade ranges specified for levels, and that homophone items are sequenced according to difficulty. Entry level tests should be equated to their corresponding comprehensive tests.

Criteria for identifying top, middle, and bottom spellers should be based on accepted standards for mastery and take into account normative data for students at different grade levels. Without information about the relationship between test content and school curriculum, item data, and data supporting criteria for mastery, school personnel have no way of determining the relationship between Spellmaster results and expected performance on actual classroom materials at each grade level.

Standard data are needed to support reliability of decisions using total scores and error analyses. Correlations between Spellmaster and other measures, analysis of Spellmaster scores for previously identified good and poor spellers, and data concerning effectiveness of remediating weaknesses identified by Spellmaster represent just three of many investigations needed to support construct and criterion-related validity.

In conclusion, the organization of Spellmaster is attractive and supplementary spelling lists and teaching activities may be useful in some classrooms. However, the tests are not recommended for use. Content validity is of primary importance for criterion-referenced tests, yet the Spellmaster manual provides no evidence that the tests represent an adequate sample of spelling skills needed in schools. There are no item, normative, reliability, and construct and criterion-related validity data to support decisions resulting from scores. Without this necessary technical information, teachers should not identify poor spellers or plan instruction using Spellmaster tests.

Review of the Spellmaster by MARGARET ROGERS WIESE, Assistant Professor of School Psychology, Appalachian State University, Boone, NC:

The Spellmaster Assessment and Teaching System (Spellmaster), revised in 1987 after initial publication in 1974, is a criterion-referenced test and instructional system designed to measure and teach spelling skills. The test is group or individually administered and purports to identify spelling strengths and weaknesses of children in primary grades and junior high. Teaching techniques and multimodal activities are provided to help remediate skill weaknesses.

The major changes in Spellmaster since the initial publication seem to be in test packaging and introduction of the entry level tests. Currently, the assessment system comprises four categories of tests including entry level, regular word, irregular word, and homophone. Each of the four categories of tests is broken down into eight test levels. Although no empirical evidence is provided, the author suggests these eight test levels contain spelling skills typically learned between grades K–10.

Between grades K–10? The manual initially states the tests and teaching materials are appropriate for primary grade children and junior high youngsters, then goes on to suggest that high schoolers, adults, and children who speak English as a second language would benefit as well. This is confusing information. The manual needs to specifically state for which age ranges the materials were developed. In addition, if the materials were designed for a broader population, then appropriate forms should be provided.

The second problem with test administration concerns the regular word entry level tests that serve as the beginning point in the assessment sequence. Cutoff scores are provided for these tests and they yield information concerning the mastery, frustration, and instructional levels of test takers. The problem is that no explanation is provided for how cutoff scores were determined. Also, do these cutoffs have any relation to an outside standard? This is important information that is missing from the manual.

The third administrative problem concerns the discontinue rule during group administration. The manual recommends that examiners discontinue group testing when it is clear that students have met their respective frustration levels (i.e., when four items in one level have been missed). However, in a classroom of 25 students, how is the examiner supposed to simultaneously review everyone's response sheet to insure that premature termination does not occur? It is unrealistic to require the examiner to perform this feat.

Once the regular word entry level test has been administered, the examiner proceeds with further testing using the other entry level tests and the regular word test, irregular word test, and homophone test. These latter tests provide information concerning knowledge of phonic and structural spelling elements, knowledge of irregular spelling rules, and ability to spell homophones. The tests are all administered via dictation whereby words are dictated in isolation, then within a sentence, then repeated in isolation. Students are provided with separate answer sheets to record responses.

Scoring the irregular word and homophone tests is easily achieved by matching the response to the stimulus word and calculating raw scores based on the total number of correct responses. Scoring the regular word tests requires additional procedures because each response is scored several times. First, the whole word is scored for overall accuracy and second, the word is scored for the accuracy of the phonic and structural elements that make it up. Omissions, additions, and sequencing errors are also noted. Special scoring forms are provided for scoring each of the eight levels of the regular word test.

The manual supplies cutoff scores that allow for instructional groupings into "top spellers," "middle spellers," and "bottom spellers" but again, does not specify how these cutoffs were determined. The groupings are intended to help teachers identify students who need additional instruction or further testing.

All testing and teaching materials, with the exception of the student answer sheets and scoring forms, are provided in an attractive soft-cover ring binder. Two methods for organizing test results are available in the binder and can be duplicated: class data sheets and individual progress records. Both general and specific test administration directions are given in the front of the binder with actual test items contained in the appendices. This results in the examiner having to flip back and forth in the manual during test administration. Supplementary regular word tests are also provided in the back of the binder along with an array of instructional activities for helping to remediate spelling difficulties. However, these instructional activities do not specify the objective of the task or what demonstrates mastery of a skill.

Although reviews of the previous edition of the Spellmaster clearly highlighted weaknesses in reliability and validity as well as test development, no substantive improvements within these areas over the last 13 years seem to have occurred. In this reviewer's opinion, the most important limitation of the Spellmaster continues to be the lack of test development, reliability, and validity data. A test manual typically contains technical psychometric information. The Spellmaster manual does not. A review of the test manual yields no specific information concerning test item development and selection. The authors suggest that classroom teachers and specialists provided input in helping to shape the materials but do not specify the nature of this input.

A field test in New England using over 2,500 children is described but no information regarding when field testing occurred, or the age ranges, socio-economic levels, and racial and ethnic composition of the participants is provided. This is crucial data which needs to be documented adequately.

In summary, the absence of reliability and validity data and test development information significantly limits the applicability of these materials. In order to make this program more meaningful, test-retest reliability data, standard errors of measurement, content validity data, and criterion validity data must be collected and documented. Also, the manual should contain information concerning examiner qualifications. Although the Spellmaster is attractively designed and packaged and contains a variety of interesting teaching strategies, psychometric weaknesses must be addressed before the system can be recommended for use.

[81]
State-Trait Anger Expression Inventory, Research Edition.

Purpose: To provide "concise measures of the experience and expression of anger."
Population: Ages 13 and over.
Publication Dates: 1979–88.
Acronym: STAXI.
Scores, 8: State Anger, Trait Anger, Angry Temperament, Angry Reaction, Anger-in, Anger-out, Anger Control, Anger Expression.
Administration: Group.
Forms, 2: HS, G.
Price Data, 1989: $39 per complete kit (includes manual ['88, 27 pages], 50 test booklets, and 50 rating forms); $18 per 50 test booklets; $14 per 50 rating forms; $9 per manual; scoring service offered by publisher.
Time: (15–17) minutes.
Comments: Test booklet title is Self-Rating Questionnaire.
Author: Charles D. Spielberger.
Publisher: Psychological Assessment Resources, Inc.

TEST REFERENCES

1. Stoner, S. B., & Spencer, W. B. (1987). Age and gender differences with the Anger Expression Scale. *Educational and Psychological Measurement*, 47 (2), 487-492.

Review of the State-Trait Anger Expression Inventory, Research Edition by BRUCE H. BISKIN, Senior Psychometrician, American Institute of Certified Public Accountants, New York, NY:

The State-Trait Anger Expression Inventory (STAXI) is the product of several decades of research by Charles D. Spielberger and his associates. As noted in the manual, the STAXI was developed as part of long-term study of anxiety, anger, and curiosity. This research program also spawned the often-used State-Trait Anxiety Inventory (STAI; 9:1186).

The STAXI attempts to measure several facets of anger. The Inventory comprises 44 items, which may be conceptualized as representing two domains: anger experience and anger expression. Anger experience is represented by two 10-item scales: State Anger (S-Anger) and Trait Anger (T-Anger). T-Anger includes two four-item subscales: Angry Temperament and Angry Reaction. Anger expression is represented by three eight-item scales: Anger-in (AX/In), Anger-out (AX/Out), and Anger Control (AX/Con). A total Anger Expression (AX/EX) score may be computed from the latter three scales, though the manual notes, "The psychometric properties of the AX/EX scale have not been thoroughly investigated" (p. 11).

The test booklet for the self-scoring version (Form HS) is printed clearly in a larger-than-average typeface and is accompanied by a self-scoring answer form. The computer-scorable form (Form G) is printed in a smaller, but bolder, typeface. This version contains the items directly on the answer form.

The STAXI items are grouped into three parts: Part I comprises the S-Anger items; Part II comprises the T-Anger items; and Part III comprises AX/In, AX/Out, and AX/Con. The instructions for each part are clear and seem appropriate for the constructs they measure. The self-scoring form booklet contains a profile chart that can be completed by the administrator. This chart requires the administrator to enter percentile scores instead of raw scores, which some may find confusing at first.

The STAXI manual is impressive. I found it to be well written and complete. It reports six sets of norms: adolescents, college students, and adults, each reported for men and women separately. The norms are reported as both percentiles and T-scores in Appendix A. The manual also reports several special interest norms in Appendix B. As Spielberger appropriately points out, STAXI users should apply these norms with care and, where feasible, develop local norms whenever those reported in the manual are inappropriate for the user's purpose.

There are some apparent inconsistencies in the normative data, however. Tables 1 and 2 of the manual (p. 4) report means, standard deviations, and sample size for each of the six norm groups. The sample sizes do not correspond to those reported in the text on page 3. Also, the tabled means do not correspond to T-scores of 50 as reported in Appendix A. These apparent discrepancies should be clarified in future editions of the manual. In addition, I suggest including sample sizes in the norm tables in Appendix A for clarity.

I appreciated the amount of detail included in the chapter on "Conceptual Issues and Scale Development." Though this chapter may be too technical for some users, it conveys clearly the major issues that Spielberger and his associates confronted in developing the STAXI. It also describes how their concept of anger expression changed to include Anger/Control. Psychometric information is extensive, if not complete (see below). Median reliability (coefficients alpha) reported in the manual for all the STAXI scales is about .82. The scales measuring angry feelings (S-Anger and T-Anger) are somewhat more internally consistent (median = .85) than those for anger expression (AX/In, AX/Out, and AX/Con; median = .78).

The manual also reports item-remainder correlations within and across scales. These provide evidence for both convergent and discriminant validity of the STAXI items. For example, each item on the T-Anger scale correlates more highly with its own scale than it does with the T-Anxiety or T-Curiosity scales. Spielberger also reports the results of factor analyses of the various scales, which support further the STAXI's construct-related validity. These analyses seem to have been carefully carried out. Curiously, none of the correlations among the STAXI scales are reported. These should be included in the next revision of the manual. This would provide further evidence regarding the STAXI's construct-related validity.

Test-retest correlations are not included in the manual. Besides providing additional reliability estimates, such correlations could serve as further validity indicators. For example, presumably T-Anger should have larger test-retest correlations than S-Anger does, even for short time intervals between administrations.

In contrast with the high quality of the inventory forms, the manual's layout is less than optimal. The typeface is small, and there is little space between words and lines. As a result, I found it somewhat difficult to read. I expect many readers with even minor visual impairments would find it even more difficult to read than I did. With so much care put into the content of the STAXI manual and the formats of the Inventory forms, I was surprised and disappointed by the manual's presentation. Perhaps when PAR reprints the manual, it could improve the layout.

SUMMARY. The STAXI is a welcome addition to those few instruments now available to measure various aspects of anger. It has an excellent conceptual foundation and very good measurement characteristics. However, until the STAXI's research and clinical bases grow, its scores should be interpreted cautiously by users.

Review of the State-Trait Anger Expression Inventory, Research Edition by PAUL RETZLAFF, Assistant Professor of Psychology, University of Northern Colorado, Greeley, CO:

The State-Trait Anger Expression Inventory (STAXI) assesses two major types of anger, State Anger and Trait Anger. Trait Anger is additionally subdivided into Angry Temperament and Angry Reaction. The STAXI additionally measures three primary modes of anger expression: Anger-in, Anger-out, and Anger Control. Finally, an overall Anger Expression score is derived from the three primary anger expression scales.

There are two forms of the test for administration. The first is a hand-scored form. The questions are on a two-page booklet and a separate answer sheet is used for endorsement. The separate answer sheet is a multipart form that allows for immediate scoring by examining the carbon copy. The scoring is a little difficult, as only item numbers are listed for keying and no arrows or color coding are on the sheet for visual aid. The second form of the test is a single computer form that can be given to subjects for research and then mailed to the publisher for group scoring. Computer-scoring access may assist future research efforts with the STAXI.

The test has a total of 44 items endorsed on a 4-point scale. State and Trait Anger have 10 items each. The two Trait subscales of Temperament and Reaction have only four items apiece. This small number of items appears minimal for a scale. Each of the three primary anger expression scales has eight items, with Anger Expression a composite of the three primary scores.

Different test development approaches were used in the construction of the STAXI. The State and Trait scales were developed via a domain construction technique. The Anger Expression scales were developed by factor analytic methods. As such, item level statistics, item inclusion/exclusion, and potential overlap were not well managed across the test as a whole.

Internal consistencies are generally good for the main scales: State Anger (.93), Trait Anger (.87), Anger-in (.82), Anger-out (.74), and Anger Control (.84). The 4-item Temperament subscale holds up well with around .86, but the other 4-item Reaction scale suffers with .70s. The composite Anger Expression scale would have a reliability that is a function of the underlying 24 items, but this coefficent is not reported in the manual. Information of test validity is, perhaps, the most problematic aspect of the test. Due to its recent release, there are relatively few validity estimates presented in the manual. There is no reported evidence that the State Anger scale is sensitive to experimental manipulations. Although anger manipulation would be difficult, some study of frustrating driver's license applicant procedures or questionable football replay videos may be indicated. Trait Anger is correlated with hostility scales, but in the introduction to the test, the author points out the need to separate the domains of anger, hostility, and aggression. Convergent and divergent validity for the anger expression scales involve intercorrelation with state-trait anxiety and curiosity. Why these variables were chosen is not explained and perhaps others (e.g., hostility, depression) would be more appropriate. Finally, perhaps too much of the research is in the form of unpublished theses and dissertations.

Additionally, a complete intercorrelation matrix of all the STAXI scales is not made available. With the parallel construction of the scales, it is particularly important to prove scale specificity. The correlations reported are high between Anger-out and Anger Control, as well as between Anger-out and Trait Anger.

In summary, the STAXI is designed to tap an important domain, is easy to administer and score, and will probably be as popular as the State-Trait Anxiety Inventory (9:1186). Its face validity is good. Although suggesting a piecemeal construction, its scales are rigorously developed. Reliabilities are generally good, but additional validity estimates are necessary.

[82]
Stress Response Scale.
Purpose: A measure of children's emotional status "designed for children referred for possible emotional adjustment problems."
Population: Grades 1–8.
Publication Dates: 1979–86.
Acronym: SRS.
Scores, 6: Impulsive (Acting Out), Passive-Aggressive, Impulsive (Overactive), Repressed, Dependent, Total.
Administration: Group.
Price Data, 1988: $8 per 25 rating scales; $8 per 25 profile sheets (specify male or female); $18.50 per sample set including manual ('86, 26 pages).
Special Edition: *The Stress Response Scale for Children: A Profile Analysis Program.* 1985; "a program for the interactive entry of SRS data"; 2 modes: clinical applications, research applications; Apple II/II+/IIe/IIc (64K RAM) or IBM-PC/XT/AT (or 100% compatibles) required; printer is recommended, but not required; $79 per program and manual; Mark D. Shermis and Louis A. Chandler; Mark D. Shermis.
Time: Administration time not reported.
Comments: Ratings by parents or teachers; manual title is *The Stress Response Scale for Children, 1986 Revision.*
Author: Louis A. Chandler.
Publisher: Louis A. Chandler.

Review of the Stress Response Scale by MARY LOU KELLEY, Associate Professor of Psychology, Louisiana State University, Baton Rouge, LA:

The Stress Response Scale is a 40-item rating scale designed to measure children's emotional status. Items are short descriptors of children's behavioral or emotional responses rated on a 6-point scale (0 = *never* to 5 = *always*). The scale is intended to be completed either by parents or teachers, depending on who is making the referral for evaluation.

Scale content is based heavily upon the author's theoretical beliefs. The scale was developed on the assumption that children's reactions to stress represent behavioral responses to specific stimuli characterized as stressors. Maladaptive behaviors are considered extreme examples of normal coping responses. Based upon the author's "stress response" model, which utilizes two dimensions of personality (introversion-extraversion and passive-active), four patterns of behavior emerge. The items of the Stress Response Scale are grouped according to the four symptom patterns labelled: Dependent, Impulsive, Passive-Aggressive, and Repressed.

Factor analytic studies generally supported the item groupings. Factor analysis yielded five factors that accounted for 64% of the variance. The symptom clusters noted remained consistent with the conceptual underpinnings of the test. However, the "Impulsive" symptom grouping was represented by two factors. Illustrative items included in each factor are: (*a*) *Impulsive-Acting Out*: demanding, selfish, impulsive; (*b*) *Impulsive-Overactive*: easily excited, not quiet or withdrawn, talkative; (*c*) *Dependent*: lack of participation, lacks self-confidence, lacks independence; (*d*) *Passive-Aggressive*: daydreams, underachiever, doesn't care about schoolwork; and (*e*) *Repressed*: worries, sensitive, easily upset, afraid of new situations.

The author provides a well-written, well-organized, and informative manual. The manual describes the intended uses of the test, the conceptual basis behind the test, and the target population with whom the test is used. The procedures for administering and scoring the test are unambiguous and simple. The manual details the reliability and validity of the test in a very clear, user-friendly manner.

The test has been standardized with a relatively large sample, and norms are available for boys and girls at varying ages. Thus, the test takes into account developmental and gender differences often seen in children. Standard scores and percentile rankings are easily derived from tables provided in the manual. Profile charts are available for both males and females at different ages, making the test easy to score by trained personnel. It is unclear, however, whether the standardization data are based on parent or teacher ratings.

The reliability of the test is well documented, based on information detailed in the manual and other publications. The test has been shown to be internally consistent and to possess good test-retest reliability, both in terms of total scores and factor scores. However, it appears the author has not examined interrater reliability, which could potentially be quite low, given the lack of behavioral specificity of the items. For example, agreement between mothers and fathers or teachers and parents apparently has not been evaluated.

The author is to be commended for the extent of measurement validation that has been conducted on the SRS. The author and others have examined the construct, content, factorial, discriminant, and criterion-related validity of the instrument. For example, factor-analytic studies suggested that 64% of the variance was accounted for with the five-factor solution described earlier. This factor analysis included 34 of the 40 items contained in the test. With regard to criterion-related validity, Chandler, Shermis, and March (1985) evaluated the ability of the scale to predict psychiatric group membership. The authors compared the SRS subscale scores with psychiatric diagnoses given to the children by clinicians. This study and other work by Chandler indicated that scores obtained from the measure predicted group membership.

It should be clear the SRS appears to have a number of positive features and the instrument may be a useful screening measure in clinical settings. The test is very brief and probably takes only a few minutes to complete because many of the items are just one or two words. A clear, succinct manual describing the test and scoring criteria makes the measure easy to use.

In spite of the positive features of the test, I have some reservations about the reliability of the test. The items generally are very global descriptors of children's emotions and behavior, and therefore are particularly subject to rater bias.

Although the author purports that the SRS measures responses to stress and that this construct is supported in the literature, it is not clear how this test differs from other available instruments not based on the same conceptual underpinnings. For example, other instruments measure children's maladaptive behavioral and emotional responses. Whereas the author's conceptualization of stress may or may not be accurate, I fail to understand how the conceptualization is reflected in the SRS in ways that make the test unique.

Thus, in spite of the positive features of the SRS, it is not clear how this instrument is better than other more behaviorally anchored instruments such as the Child Behavior Checklist (CBCL; 12). The CBCL, for example, contains more items and several additional factors (Achenbach & Edelbrock, 1979). The CBCL also has more comprehensive reliability and validity data supporting the instrument. However, should the reader be interested in a brief instrument that assesses global characteristics in children as perceived by an adult caretaker, the SRS is one test to consider.

REVIEWER'S REFERENCES

Achenbach, T., & Edelbrock, C. (1979). The Child Behavior Profile: II. Boys aged 12–16 and girls aged 6–11 and 12–16. *Journal of Consulting and Clinical Psychology, 47*, 223-233.

Chandler, L. A., Shermis, M. D., & Marsh, J. (1985). The use of the Stress Response Scale in diagnostic assessment. *Journal of Psychoeducational Assessment, 3*, 16-29.

Review of the Stress Response Scale by WILLIAM K. WILKINSON, Assistant Professor, Department of Counseling and Educational Psychology, New Mexico State University, Las Cruces, NM:

The Stress Response Scale (SRS) is a rating scale appropriate for use with children aged 5 to 14. The 40-item instrument is completed by an adult familiar with the target child's behavior, with each statement rated from 0 (*never*) to 5 (*always*). The scale is constructed to yield one global score, and six separate profile types—Acting Out, Passive-Aggressive, Overactive, Dependent, Repressed, and Mixed—which purportedly reflect a child's "emotional status." The global SRS raw score is convertible to both *T*-scores and percentile ranks. The normative sample for the SRS consists of 947 schoolchildren in western Pennsylvania who were rated by their respective teachers.

The SRS test materials include a technical manual that provides information concerning the intended use and application of the scale, a conceptual model on which the test was based, reliability, validity, normative information, and guidelines for scoring and interpretation. The 40 statements comprising the SRS are contained on one response sheet. A particularly nice feature of the instrument is the inclusion of computer software designed to aid in scoring and interpretation. This material is presented in a binder containing clear, step-by-step instructions for computer use. Finally, separate profile sheets are included for those test users opting to hand score and interpret SRS data. Overall, the SRS is professionally marketed, with test materials nicely organized and clearly identifiable.

In reviewing the SRS technical manual and several published articles concerning the scale, several concerns are noteworthy. Perhaps the most pervasive difficulty involves the nature of the stress construct and its measurement.

For example, the construct of stress is not directly measured by the SRS, but rather, is an explanatory variable that may account for maladaptive levels of those personality characteristics purportedly measured by the instrument. The SRS is not designed to measure stress response per se; rather, it provides data in the form of adult ratings of children on traits such as shy, defiant, and cooperative. An interpretation regarding why an adult rates a child at any particular level of a measured trait, whether stress response or some other reason, goes beyond the scope of the SRS and would require careful analysis and interpretation across a wide array of assessment procedures. Unfortunately, because the instrument was named the Stress Response Scale, it may mislead test users to purchase the scale as a direct measure of stress response, or to interpret a child's score as a result of stress. Clearly, caution is needed in these respects.

Given the SRS is not a measure of stress response, then what does it measure? Although the technical manual contains terms such as "emotional status," "emotional adjustment," "coping strategies," "personality," "stress response," "behavior," and "response style," the items and factor descriptions appear consistent with other trait measures (e.g., Eysenck, Cattell, Conners, Achenbach). In fact, the technical manual notes the similarities between SRS factors and other personality descriptions, although no empirical data regarding these relationships are presented. The lack of these data undermines a test user's confidence in the instrument's construct validity.

There is evidence of factorial validity—the profile factors are stable in unique samples

(nonreferred vs. clinic referred), but these data do not address the issue of similarities or differences between the SRS factors and those measured by other scales. Further, establishing the stability of the factors across different samples does not entirely support the statement in the manual that "emotional adjustment reactions may be seen as extreme patterns of normal coping behavior." This statement could be verified through the inclusion of the separate profile scores (means and standard deviations) for the nonreferred versus clinic-referred groups. Ideally, both the total score and each profile factor score should be significantly greater for the clinic-referred children than their nonreferred peers. However, the only information in the technical manual is that clinic-referred children receive higher total score ratings than the nonreferred children.

Regarding separate profile scores, instead of presenting descriptive statistics concerning group differences across the five profile factors, data regarding the frequencies of SRS profile types for the entire normative sample ($N = 857$) and a group of clinic-referred children ($N = 84$) are given. The evidence presented hardly supports the SRS as a diagnostic tool, because only one (Acting Out) of the five SRS factors (excluding the mixed profile) reached acceptable levels of statistical significance in differentiating the proportions of each sample within diagnostic categories.

Further, although two studies are cited as support for the scale's ability to predict diagnostic group membership, these data are either difficult to evaluate or inherently limited. For instance, the statement that the SRS reduces error in predicting psychiatric group membership is hard to interpret without further explanation (e.g., what type of error, what was the procedure for initial classification, what were the diagnostic categories, was the reduction statistically significant, how tested, etc.). Also, that SRS scores predict a diagnostic criterion with two outcomes—special education or a specific type of special education—is troublesome because the criterion suffers from such a restricted range. Thus, further support of predictive validity is clearly needed if the instrument is to gain a reputation as being diagnostically useful.

As for reliability data, this information is presented in terms of stability of ratings across a test-retest period of one month. The correlations for separate scale scores range from .72 to .90, demonstrating the SRS meets technically adequate levels of stability reliability. However, it should be noted that these reliability correlations were obtained with teachers only, so that the reliability of ratings for different groups (parents) is presently unknown.

In general, it seems the conclusions reached in the SRS manual are far overstated, given the instrument's format and technical qualities. Test users should know the limitations of rating formats in general (e.g., items emphasize problem behavior, bias in rater perception) and keep these weaknesses in mind when judging the appropriateness of the SRS for assessment and treatment planning.

Further, the conclusion that the SRS provides data about the impact of stress on a child's behavioral adjustment clearly goes beyond the scope of the instrument. If a measure of stress response was desired, stress, and response to it, would be operationally defined, directly measured, and ultimately validated. None of these steps is found in the SRS, emphasizing the point that the instrument is not intended to measure either stress response or the effects of stress on personality.

Rather, the only legitimate conclusion is the instrument appears to measure selected personality traits. Thus, the SRS may be appropriate as a measure of certain personality dimensions, pending the collection of necessary validation data regarding the traits it purportedly measures. Until then, the use of this scale is not recommended.

[83]
Student Developmental Task and Lifestyle Inventory.

Purpose: "Assisting students in understanding their own development and establishing goals and plans to shape their own futures."
Population: College students ages 17–24.
Publication Date: 1987.
Acronym: SDTLI.
Scores, 12: Establishing and Clarifying Purpose Task (Educational Involvement Subtask, Career Planning Subtask, Life Management Subtask, Lifestyle Planning Subtask, Cultural Participation Subtask), Developing Mature Interpersonal Relationships Task (Peer Relationships Subtask, Tolerance Subtask, Emotional Autonomy Subtask), Academic Autonomy Task, Salubrious Lifestyle Scale, Intimacy Scale, Response Bias Scale.

Administration: Group.
Price Data, 1987: $45 per 50 reusable test booklets; $20 per 50 answer sheets; $12.50 per 50 Understanding and Using the SDTLI: A Guide for Students (6 pages); $9 per manual (50 pages).
Time: (30–40) minutes.
Comments: Revision of the Student Developmental Task Inventory, Revised, Second Edition.
Authors: Roger B. Winston, Jr., Theodore K. Miller, and Judith S. Prince.
Publisher: Student Development Associates, Inc.
Cross References: For reviews by Fred H. Borgen and Steven D. Brown of the Second Edition, see 9:1199 (5 references).

TEST REFERENCES
1. Furr, J. D., Staik, I. M., & Bagby, S. A. (1984). The assessment of developmental tasks in college women. *College Student Journal, 18,* 253-256.
2. Blann, F. W. (1985). Intercollegiate athletic competition and students' educational and career plans. *Journal of College Student Personnel, 26,* 115-118.
3. Williams, M., & Winston, R. B., Jr. (1985). Participation in organized student activities and work: Differences in developmental task achievement of traditional aged college students. *NASPA Journal, 22* (3), 52-59.
4. Itzkowitz, S. G., & Petrie, R. D. (1986). The Student Developmental Task Inventory: Scores of northern versus southern students. *Journal of College Student Personnel, 27,* 406-413.
5. Stonewater, J., Daniels, M. H., & Heischmidt, K. (1986). The reliability and validity of the Student Developmental Task Inventory-2: Pilot studies. *Journal of College Student Personnel, 27,* 70-74.
6. Straub, C. A., & Rodgers, R. F. (1986). An exploration of Chickering's theory and women's development. *Journal of College Student Personnel, 27,* 216-224.
7. Winston, R. B., Jr., & Polkosnik, M. C. (1986). Student Developmental Task Inventory (2nd Edition): Summary of selected findings. *Journal of College Student Personnel, 27,* 548-559.

Review of the Student Developmental Task and Lifestyle Inventory by MARY HENNING-STOUT, Assistant Professor of Counseling Psychology, Lewis and Clark College, Portland, OR:

The purpose of the Student Developmental Task and Lifestyle Inventory (SDTLI) is to gauge the social-emotional development of college students. The SDTLI and its earlier versions have been most commonly applied in the articulation of developmental tasks that face individual students. The authors suggest that the successful completion of these tasks is necessary for continued progress both in the prevailing culture and within one's historical cohort. According to the authors who ground their inventory in the theory of Chickering (1969), these tasks lead to development and clarification of life purpose, mature interpersonal relationships, academic autonomy, mature intimacy, and healthy lifestyles.

This version of the SDTLI, published in 1987, represents a second revision of the Student Developmental Task Inventory first published in 1974 (Prince, Miller, & Winston, 1974). The current version differs from the others in its response to psychometric questions of scale structure, to consumer objections to the exclusive focus on heterosexual relationships, and to the need for addressing lifestyle issues such as cultural activity and health maintenance. In addition, a response bias scale is built into the most recent version of this inventory.

ADMINISTRATION. The SDTLI may be administered individually or to groups provided the groups complete the inventory under supervision. Accompanying the test materials is a guide for students that provides step-by-step instructions to examinees for completing, scoring, and interpreting the instrument. Given the complexity of the notion of developmental tasks and the likelihood of students being unfamiliar with it, facilitation of response interpretation by a qualified examiner seems advisable.

Students respond to 140 questions by indicating whether the stem is representative (true) or not representative (false) of their current experience. Their responses are made on a form with a carbon and scoring guide attached.

Scores are obtained for three "developmental tasks" (Establishing and Clarifying Purpose, Developing Mature Interpersonal Relationships, and Academic Autonomy) and three scales (Salubrious Lifestyle, Intimacy, and Response Bias). Based on factor analytic findings reported in the manual, these seem to be six distinct constructs. The first two tasks break into subtasks which are also scored.

Once recorded, the raw scores can be converted to T scores using the tables provided in the manual. The authors suggest that normative interpretation of inventory results be confined to use in program evaluation and research studies. When the scale is used with an individual for counseling or advising, ideopathic interpretation of scale scores and individual items is advised. This interpretation can then be applied in consultation with the individual to plan for personal change.

PSYCHOMETRIC PROPERTIES. The descriptions of research presented in the manual indicate that the reliability and validity of this instrument are well established. Reliability was gauged using test-retest and internal consistency

procedures. In both instances, reliability was sufficient to warrant acceptance of the consistency of this inventory's results. Validity was also measured in two ways. Construct validity was given initial support with reports of the factor analyses conducted to develop the test (and reported in the test development section of the manual). Additional research on the constructs of this measure were not reported. The potential user of the SDTLI is encouraged to seek information on more recent construct validation as it may be presented in the professional literature. The presentation of evidence of the scale's concurrent validity is more thorough. The SDTLI shows appropriate correlation with the Mines-Jensen Interpersonal Relationship Inventory, the Iowa Developing Autonomy Inventory Scales, and selected scales from the Omnibus Personality Inventory.

One potential weakness of the scale is evident in the standardization sample ($n = 1,200$). The authors admit the middle-class bias of the items in the scale suggesting that, "The primary reason for this is that colleges in North America are basically middle-class social institutions." Information on the socioeconomic status of the standardization sample is not provided and is, therefore, assumed consistent with the above statement. In general, the information provided on the standardization process is minimal. There is no indication of how selection was made and whether the distributions reported are stratified categories. Most of the subjects are from the Southeastern United States ($n = 394$) and the fewest are from the Western United States ($n = 62$).

Descriptive statistics on the standardization sample reveal that women's and men's score were significantly different on the Intimacy and Salubrious Lifestyle Scales. Standardized scores for these two scales are provided by gender. Additional reported statistical data indicate other discrepancies that are not accounted for in standardized scoring. For example, Blacks scored significantly lower on the Intimacy Scale and Southeasterners scored significantly lower than Westerners and Northeasterners on the three developmental tasks. No explanation or caution accompanies these statistics.

PRACTICAL AND RESEARCH UTILITY. Along with the problems mentioned above regarding the potential bias in standardization and item content of the SDTLI, there is an additional bias that emerges as a result of the fact that this instrument is based on Chickering's (1969) work. That work and his subsequent research efforts with Havighurst (Chickering & Havighurst, 1981) focused primarily on the experiences of men in the typical college age group. The designation and selection of scales based on this research and theory may preclude consideration of some of the developmental tasks faced by minority and women college students. It is likely that both men and women experience the developmental challenges represented in this inventory, a likelihood partially supported by the factor analytic data emerging from the standardization sample in which women outnumbered men by approximately 7:4. The question of what may be overlooked given a theoretical perspective emerging from research focusing on the experience of white men remains an important one for the authors of this instrument. Research in this area by the authors is encouraged.

The suggestions for application of this measure offered in the manual are useful and clear. The primary consumers of this scale would be counselors, advisors, and student life staff for undergraduate programs. The individualized use of the scale seems most appropriate as an ideopathically interpreted vehicle for therapeutic interchange between a student and service provider.

The suggestions made by the authors for application of this instrument as a program evaluation or research tool are excellent. As a part of needs assessment for program development and subsequent evaluation, the SDTLI seems well suited. The suggestions for use with advising and training students in peer support also seem appropriate for this measure. For the purposes of research, the authors provide useful cautions and direction, especially regarding the vulnerability of this instrument to social desirability response sets and the importance of examiner-examinee rapport.

In summary, the SDTLI is a psychometrically sound inventory that can prove useful in program development and has potential research applications. Its utility for individual assessment seems best if the results are interpreted ideopathically and used to enhance the psychotherapeutic communication process. The possible limitations of this scale as described

above stem from its basis in theory which has emerged from research focused primarily on white men. This focus does not render the scale irrelevant for women and minorities, but does perhaps overlook developmental tasks that are important for the excluded groups.

REVIEWER'S REFERENCES

Chickering, A. W. (1969). *Education and identity*. San Francisco: Jossey-Bass.
Chickering, A. W., & Havighurst, R. J. (1981). The life cycle. In A. W. Chickering (Ed.), *The modern American college: Responding to the new realities of diverse students and a changing society*. San Francisco: Jossey-Bass.

Review of the Student Developmental Task and Lifestyle Inventory by WILLIAM D. PORTERFIELD, Academic Coordinator and Adjunct Assistant Professor of Educational Administration, Commission on Interprofessional Education and Practice, The Ohio State University, Columbus, OH:

The Student Developmental Task and Lifestyle Inventory (SDTLI) is a revision of the Student Developmental Task Inventory—2 published by Winston, Miller, and Prince in 1979. The SDTLI (1987) is intended for use with traditional college age students (17–24 years old) to provide a snapshot of their developmental accomplishments in areas of Establishing and Clarifying Purpose, Developing Mature Interpersonal Relationships, and Developing Academic Autonomy. Scores are also obtained for a Salubrious Lifestyle Scale, a Response Bias Scale, and an experimental Intimacy Scale. The authors note a number of uses for the instrument in the college setting including individual counseling, student development research, and programming.

The theoretical base for the SDTLI is derived from A. W. Chickering's study of college students (1969) and Chickering and Havighurst's (1981) revision of the earlier research. Chickering outlines seven vectors of student development. The vectors of development consist of patterns of attitudes and behaviors that seem to be consistent among college students. The SDTLI, thus, has a solid and identifiable theoretical base, and represents a major accomplishment in translating some of Chickering's (1969) ideas into educational practice.

The authors note that the instrument is contextually based in middle class values, and attempt to note the basic values that are inherent in the instrument. This, in the reviewer's opinion, is a valuable statement of limitations of the instrument, as well as an excellent statement for researchers and educators considering using the instrument with various populations and campuses.

The instrument consists of 140 items to which respondents mark whether the item is true or false within the context of their personal experiences. The instrument is self-scoring through use of a carbon sheet between the answer sheet and the score sheet. The instrument takes approximately 25 to 30 minutes to complete. Thus, in terms of administration and scoring, the instrument should receive high marks for efficiency and cost effectiveness to the user.

The package of materials includes an extensive manual with descriptions of the developmental tasks and scales. Additionally, the manual includes extensive normative data for use in interpreting scores. Current normative data are based on respondents from 20 colleges and universities in the United States and Canada. An extensive treatment of reliability and validity estimates is also included in the manual. The manual is professionally presented, and achieves a balance in content between the interests of the potential researcher and the practitioner. The manual is easily read and interpreted.

The manual also discusses the significance of data on racial ethnic backgrounds, age, and gender. This is a strength of the research on the SDTLI as well as the manual. Clearly, continued research on the differences in student development across these groups is needed, and the SDTLI authors are sensitive to this need in their own research, and in the presentation of their results. Appropriate cautions about the generalizability of test results are noted throughout the manual.

The package of materials on the SDTLI also includes a Guide for Students. This six-page worksheet assists students in understanding their tests, the results of their tests, and offers concrete suggestions for facilitating their own growth. This makes the instrument and the packet of materials very attractive for programmers and counselors in higher education.

In summary, the SDTLI represents a solid research effort geared toward college students aged 17–24. Additionally, the research effort has a definitive theoretical base. The instrument is effective and efficient in terms of administra-

tion and scoring. The manual is detailed in terms of interpretation of results, and as a general guide for higher education practitioners. Limitations and potential uses of the instrument are stated with clarity. A reviewer of the instrument manual could, based on the data presented, make judgments about the relative utility of the materials in research and programming. The instruments and materials are reasonably priced.

The SDTLI is a useful and efficient instrument for higher education practitioners involved in working with traditional college-aged students. It is also a useful tool for further research with college students. This instrument could be valuable to graduate programs as a teaching tool, and to graduate students as one of the more valid and reliable measures of Chickering's vectors of college student development.

REVIEWER'S REFERENCES
Chickering, A. W. (1969). *Education and identity*. San Francisco: Jossey-Bass.
Chickering, A. W., & Havighurst, R. J. (1981). The life cycle. In A. W. Chickering and Associates (Eds.), *The modern American college: Responding to the new realities of diverse students and a changing society*. San Francisco: Jossey-Bass.

[84]

Study Habits Evaluation and Instruction Kit.

Purpose: "To identify the areas of weakness in study habits that individual students have, and to provide students with a means of improving their study habits."

Population: New Zealand secondary school students (Forms 4–6).

Publication Date: 1979.

Acronym: SHEIK.

Scores, 7: The Place of Study, Study Times, Organization for Study, Textbook Reading Skills, Taking Notes, Studying for Examinations, Examination Technique.

Administration: Group.

Price Data: Available from publisher.

Time: (30–40) minutes.

Comments: Self-administered; self-scored.

Authors: Peter F. Jackson, Neil A. Reid, and A. Cedric Croft.

Publisher: New Zealand Council for Educational Research [New Zealand].

Review of the Study Habits Evaluation and Instruction Kit by SANDRA L. CHRISTEN-SON, Assistant Professor of Educational Psychology, University of Minnesota, Minneapolis, MN:

The Study Habits Evaluation and Instruction Kit (SHEIK) is self-administered and self-scored by secondary school students for the purposes of identifying areas of weakness in study habits and suggesting ways to improve study habits. SHEIK is comprised of the Inventory of Study Habits and seven instructional lessons. The kit is an inventory, not a test; therefore, it is commendable that information is provided related to construction, standardization, norming procedures, reliability, and validity. However, limited information is provided on specific characteristics of the standardization sample, resulting in questions about the usefulness of the norms. Normative data are restricted to New Zealand secondary school students.

The seven areas examined by the inventory, Place of Study, Study Times, Organization for Study, Textbook Reading Skills, Taking Notes, Studying for Examinations, and Examination Techniques, have good face validity. In addition, internal consistency estimates of reliability for each scale are adequate, and obtained intercorrelations for the seven scales of the inventory suggest the scales are sufficiently independent dimensions. Reported criterion validity data indicate that the relationship between achievement and the behaviors sampled by the Inventory of Study Habits is explained by more than mental ability.

The reliability and validity of the inventory are adequate. Although group use of SHEIK is possible, users should note that the inventory is designed to be self-administered and interpreted by the student. Student motivation and well-developed reading skills may be prerequisites for successful student use of the inventory. For many students, direction from and interaction with teachers may be essential in order to accurately complete and interpret the inventory. The inventory may not be informative or helpful for students who are most in need of study skills instruction.

A global strength of the kit is its focus on an assessment-intervention link. Seven instructional units, corresponding to each area examined, are provided in the kit. Students are provided with information to improve study habits in each of seven areas by reading a three- to four-page lesson, completing a review exercise that highlights salient points, and engaging in a class discussion. Users should be aware that the information provided in each instructional unit is very general. The empirical basis for the content of the instructional unit is not provided. In addition, there is no application of the skills to course content materials nor a discussion of metacognitive approaches to study skills. The instructional material, if not supplemented by teachers, may at most inform students of what areas are important in developing good study skills. Without supplemental materials, it is unclear whether students would apply the information to completion of school assignments.

SHEIK is adequate for introducing students to the basics of study skills; however, it is very limited as a study skills instructional program. The Study Habits Evaluation and Instruction Kit was published one decade ago, which may explain its lack of inclusion of more recent research on approaches to study skills, application of skills to existing course content, and use of learning strategies.

Review of the Study Habits Evaluation and Instruction Kit by KENNETH A. KIEWRA, Associate Professor of Educational Psychology, University of Nebraska-Lincoln, Lincoln, NE:

Study skill training is being implemented in increasing numbers of secondary schools. A problem is that few secondary school personnel are trained in evaluating students' current skills or in developing and implementing a program to increase study skill proficiency. Fortunately, there are several evaluation and instruction programs marketed for these purposes. This review describes and critiques one such secondary school program called the Study Habits Evaluation and Instruction Kit (SHEIK).

SHEIK has two objectives—the identification of weaknesses in study habits and improvement in study habits. The kit includes an Inventory of Study Habits to meet the first objective, and Instructional Units to meet the second objective. The materials are intended for group or individual use. I will discuss the Inventory and Instructional Units, in turn, before making concluding comments.

INVENTORY OF STUDY HABITS. The Inventory consists of a reusable Item Booklet and a consumable booklet that combines a Response Sheet, Marking Key, and Profile Sheet. The Item Booklet contains seven, 25-item, self-report scales, each assessing a different aspect of studying. The seven scales are as follows:

1. The Place of Study: The physical conditions under which studying is done.

2. Study Times: The time of day and amount of time associated with studying.

3. Organization of Study: The efficient organization of study time.

4. Textbook Reading Skills: The use of skills involved in effective reading.

5. Taking Notes: The practice of taking notes from text or lectures.

6. Studying for Examinations: The methods used and time spent studying for exams.

7. Examination Technique: The techniques used during examinations.

Students mark their responses on the Response Sheet. The response mode for all items consists of five choices ranging from "never or almost never" to "always or almost always." As students mark the Response Sheet, their responses show through onto the Marking Key on the opposite side of the page indicating a score of 0, 1, or 2 for each item. Students are instructed to total these numbers within each scale and arrive at a raw score ranging from 0–50. Students then enter the seven raw scores onto the Profile Sheet. This enables them to compare their performance with the performance of other students at that grade level by using percentile ranks. The norms used in these comparisons are based on results from a total of about 1,500 randomly selected students in grades 10, 11, and 12 from 30 secondary schools in New Zealand. The schools were selected to represent schools differing with respect to location, size, and type. Students can also use provided *t*-scores from the Profile Sheet to compare their relative performance on the various scales. This helps them to see their area(s) of greatest need. The authors state that students can self-administer the Inventory within a 40-minute period. It is unclear, however, whether that time estimate includes the activities of marking answers and interpreting results.

RELIABILITY AND VALIDITY OF THE INVENTORY. The internal consistency of the Inventory was calculated using both split-half and Kuder-Richardson Formula 8 (KR-8) estimates. Both estimates showed that the Inventory was reliable with coefficients ranging from .75 to .88 for the split-half estimates, and from .77 to .90 for the KR-8 estimates.

The authors did not calculate test-retest reliability. Therefore, nothing is known about the stability of scores. Without this information, it would be unwise to administer the Inventory prior to and following instruction, and to then assume that performance changes on the Inventory were the result of instruction.

The validity of each scale of the Inventory was calculated against a composite score of four subtests on the School Certificate exam for 11th and 12th grade students. All correlations between the scales and the criteria were significant at the .01 level. When both Inventory scale scores and a standardized measure of intelligence were used to predict performance on the composite subtests of the School Certificate Exam, results indicated that the Inventory scale scores measured behaviors related to the composite score beyond that measured by general intelligence.

Subscale correlations were also calculated to determine the degree of interdependence among the subscales. Ideally, test constructors want specific scales to measure relatively independent behaviors. Results, however, indicated that scores from each scale correlated significantly ($p < .01$) with each of the other scale scores. Intercorrelations between individual scale scores and total score were not reported. These data suggest that individual scales might not measure the particular study habit(s) they purport to measure.

DEVELOPMENT OF THE INVENTORY. The original Inventory was modeled after and adapted from existing inventories. How it is different is not addressed. It was field tested using approximately 1,500 secondary students throughout New Zealand. At each administration, the students' teachers provided information on the overall academic achievement of each student. This information was used to select items that discriminated between high and low achievers. The final items were then reviewed by guidance counselors or counseling trainers and final revisions (that are unspecified) were made.

There are several problems associated with development. First, initial item construction was not apparently tied to any theoretically- or empirically-based model of studying. For example, the Inventory does not tap whether students process information at a surface level or more generative level (Wittrock, 1974), whether students make internal and external connections while studying (Mayer, 1984), or whether they are motivated (Nolan & Haladyna, in press) or behave metacognitively (Flavell, 1981).

A second problem concerns the faulty logic used to select items. Items that discriminated between high and low achievers were retained. However, it was never established to what degree high achievers were successful because of their study habits. It is possible that high achievement occurred not because of effective study habits, but in spite of them. High achievement was perhaps more the result of high intelligence, knowledge, or motivation. Some studies, in fact, show that high achievers are not at all strategic (Thomas & Rowher, 1986).

A third problem is that Inventory items were reviewed solely by people affiliated with guidance counseling. My hunch is that training for these people in learning theory, in general, and study skills, in particular, is quite limited. The Inventory should also be validated by experts in Psychology and Educational Psychology who are focused on learning and cognition as they apply to studying.

INSTRUCTIONAL UNITS. The Instructional Units, which can also be used in groups or individually, consist of seven reusable booklets with the same names as the comparable scales of the Inventory. Each is three or four pages long and provides topical advice, in a didactic manner, under a series of convenient headings and subheadings. The booklets seem well written, age appropriate, organized, and interesting. Often, they contain illustrations and graphics that facilitate learning.

Accompanying each instructional booklet is a one-page (front and back) Review Section intended to summarize the lesson and to help the students to evaluate their learning. Part I of each Review Section contains a paragraph about the topic containing approximately 25 blank spaces for the student to complete. One limitation of this exercise is that many of the blanks can be completed without ever having studied the material. For example, "Homework and revision *should* be done when you are alert." Therefore, this exercise is more for the purpose of review than self-testing.

Part II presents a problem for students to solve such as "Develop a personal study time plan for a normal school week." Suggested responses for both Parts I and II are provided on the back of each Review Sheet.

My general impression of the instructional materials is that they are superficially presented and the content is outdated. With respect to the breadth of the materials, techniques and strategies are presented in almost a laundry list fashion. Students are given little conditional knowledge for understanding how and why the strategies are effective, nor about potential applications. Research has shown that conditional knowledge is an important component of strategy instruction (e.g., Paris & Jacobs, 1984).

Several important and contemporary ideas are absent from the instructional materials. Students using these materials would not be trained to do the following: orchestrate strategies such as note taking and review; identify knowledge patterns and text structures; represent information in spatial forms such as hierarchies, sequences, and matrices; relate new information to prior knowledge; study differentially for various types of learning tasks (i.e., declarative knowledge, procedural knowledge); increase self-motivation; self-monitor performance; conduct error analysis.

CONCLUSION. The materials are sleek, easy to use, and might even be somewhat helpful to those who can pick up a helpful study hint or two in a short time with little effort. For the most part though, they are hollow. They offer minimal knowledge about the learning system, few effective strategies, and virtually no opportunity to practice skills. Procedural skills such as reading, note taking, and reviewing require considerable practice. Furthermore, SHEIK is neither empirically founded nor empirically tested. There is no evidence demonstrating that students achieve higher in school because of this program.

REVIEWER'S REFERENCES

Wittrock, M. C. (1974). Learning as a generative process. *Educational Psychologist, 11,* 87-95.

Flavell, J. H. (1981). Cognitive monitoring. In W. P. Dickson (Ed.), *Children's oral communication skills.* New York: Academic Press.

Mayer, R. E. (1984). Aids to text comprehension. *Educational Psychologist, 19,* 30-42.

Paris, S. G., & Jacobs, J. E. (1984). The benefits of informed instruction for children's reading awareness and comprehension skills. *Child Development, 55,* 2083-2093.

Thomas, J. W., & Rohwer, W. D. (1986). Academic studying: The role of learning strategies. *Educational Psychologist, 21,* 19-41.

Nolan, S. B., & Haladyna, T. M. (in press). Motivation and studying in high school science. *Journal of Research in Science Teaching.*

[85]
Study Process Questionnaire.

Purpose: "To assess the extent to which a tertiary student at college or university endorses different approaches to learning and the more important motives and strategies comprising those approaches."
Population: College students.
Publication Dates: 1985–87.
Acronym: SPQ.
Scores, 10: Surface Motive, Surface Strategy, Deep Motive, Deep Strategy, Achieving Motive, Achieving Strategy, Surface Approach, Deep Approach, Achieving Approach, Deep-Achieving Approach.
Administration: Individual or group.
Price Data, 1989: A$4.85 per 10 questionnaires, $2.50 per 10 answer sheets; $3 per score key; $29.95 per monograph entitled Student Approaches to Learning and Studying ('87, 151 pages); $13.20 per manual ('87, 44 pages).
Time: 20(40) minutes.
Comments: Secondary counterpart of the Learning Process Questionnaire (36).
Author: John Biggs.
Publisher: Australian Council for Educational Research Ltd. [Australia].
Cross References: For a review by Robert D. Brown of both the Learning Process Questionnaire and the Study Process Questionnaire and a review by Cathy W. Hall of the Learning Process Questionnaire, see 36.

TEST REFERENCES
1. Watkins, D., Hattie, J., & Astilla, E. (1986). Approaches to studying by Filipino students: A longitudinal investigation. *British Journal of Educational Psychology, 56,* 357-362.

Review of the Study Process Questionnaire by CATHY W. HALL, Assistant Professor of Psychology, East Carolina University, Greenville, NC:

The Study Process Questionnaire (SPQ) is a 42-item, self-report questionnaire that measures process factors involved in learning strategies and learning motives with tertiary students. (There is an accompanying questionnaire, Learning Process Questionnaire [LPQ], for use with secondary students.) Biggs (1987) points out that the three motives and strategies are likely to lead to different levels of learning. The surface approach is likely to lead to the accurate but unintegrated recall of information for a brief period of time in order to meet minimal requirements. The deep approach leads to the greatest structural complexity and is motivated by need to pursue personal interests in a particular area. Finally, the achieving approach is seen when a student is motivated to do well and employs a strategy that is likely to lead to whatever goals are necessary to achieve high grades. Problems may arise when there is a discrepancy between a student's motive and strategy regarding a particular subject, or when a student's approach is not in line with the requirements of a course of study. The SPQ provides a way of assessing these areas in order to make an instructional decision and/or a decision to refer the student for academic counseling.

Three primary learning approaches are measured (surface, deep, and achieving) with each factor having two subscales consisting of motives and strategies. Nine scores are possible given the three motives, three strategies, and three approaches. In addition to these nine scores, an additional score is possible for a Deep-Achieving Approach which combines the salient aspects of the deep *and* achieving processes. Biggs (1987) also discusses a Surface-Achieving Approach, but norming data are not provided for this approach. The range of scores is 7 to 35 for each of the motive and strategy subscales. Scoring for the SPQ may be done by hand, machine, computer, or by sending the protocols to the Australian Council for Educational Research.

The SPQ was standardized on an Australian population of 2,402 subjects at five universities and ten colleges (Centers for Advanced Education—CAEs). Subjects were not chosen on a random basis, as with the LPQ, and the author notes this limitation. Norm tables are provided in the manual for males and females scores, universities and CAEs, and further broken down into Arts, Education, and Science disciplines. Subject representation in each of these groups is limited and variable and represents a significant problem of this assessment device.

Reliability and validity data are presented for the SPQ. Test-retest information was not available due to the sampling restrictions. Internal consistency data demonstrated satisfactory results as reported in the manual with a range of .51 to .85. Construct validity specific to the SPQ was assessed by utilizing students' self-rated performance, satisfaction with performance, and future education goals. Correlations with actual performance (grade-point average—GPA) were obtained in a study conducted by Watkins and Hattie (1981) and were supportive of the SPQ.

The manual does not provide information on minority representation, subject age, demographic variables, or socioeconomic variables. However, a detailed account of these variables can be found in *Student Approaches to Learning and Studying* (Biggs, 1987). In addition to the above, Biggs' text offers detailed information concerning theoretical development, relevant research, and implications of the SPQ.

Use of the SPQ outside Australia should be done with the understanding that the norms are limited and more information is needed on the utilization of these learning approaches in an educational setting. Research has indicated that other factors, such as ability to understand and use language effectively, may also need to be taken into consideration when interpreting the SPQ (Wilson, 1987).

The SPQ provides a promising research tool for the assessment of learning approaches and studying the development of metacognition. If administered outside Australia, additional factor analyses and normative data would be helpful and informative. The author addresses the limitations and the need for future research with this instrument in his text. The manual is far from comprehensive, however, and it is strongly recommended that anyone choosing to adopt the SPQ also acquire the text—*Student Approaches to Learning and Studying* (Biggs, 1987).

REVIEWER'S REFERENCES

Watkins, D., & Hattie, J. (1981). The learning processes of Australian university students: Investigations of contextual and personological factors. *British Journal of Educational Psychology*, 51, 384-393.
Biggs, J. (1987). *Student Approaches to Learning and Studying*. Melbourne: Australian Council for Educational Research.
Wilson, A. (1987). Approaches to learning among third world tertiary science students: Papua New Guinea. *Research in Science & Technological Education*, 5 (1), 59-67.

[86]
Style of Learning and Thinking.
Purpose: To indicate a student's learning strategy and brain hemisphere preference in problem solving.
Population: Grades K–5, 6–12.
Publication Date: 1988.
Acronym: SOLAT.
Scores, 3: Whole Brain, Left Brain, Right Brain.
Administration: Group.
Forms, 2: Elementary, Youth.
Price Data, 1988: $28 per 35 tests (specify Elementary or Youth Form); $10 per Administrator's manual (46 pages); $15 per specimen set including manual and 1 each Elementary and Youth Form questionnaires.
Time: [30–40] minutes.
Comments: Self-scored.
Author: E. Paul Torrance.
Publisher: Scholastic Testing Service, Inc.

TEST REFERENCES
1. Torrance, E. P. (1987). Some evidence regarding development of cerebral lateralization. *Perceptual and Motor Skills, 64* (1), 261-262.

Review of the Style of Learning and Thinking by KENNETH A. KIEWRA, *Associate Professor of Educational Psychology, University of Nebraska-Lincoln, Lincoln, NE, and* DAMIAN McSHANE, *Associate Professor of Psychology, Utah State University, Logan, UT:*

The Style of Learning and Thinking (SOLAT) is an inventory for determining a student's brain hemisphere preference (left, right, or integrative) and associated learning style in problem solving. Its purpose, although not stated, is probably to help educators assist students in identifying their brain hemisphere/learning style profile and in planning solutions for strengthening their profile. Below, the materials are briefly described and three basic assumptions are presented that must be met in order to support the use of SOLAT.

DESCRIPTION OF MATERIALS. There are two SOLAT forms: the Elementary Form intended for first through fifth grade students, and the Youth Form intended for students in grades 6 through 12. Both forms can be administered in classroom-size groups, although it is suggested that first graders be tested in smaller groups. The Elementary Form contains 25 items and the Youth Form contains 28 items. In both forms, items present a pair of statements and the student is directed to place a check mark next to one of them, both of them, or neither of them based on how the statements "fit" the responder. For each item, one statement purportedly describes a behavior representative of left-brain dominance (e.g., "I like to get to work and not be silly," or "I think well when I sit straight up"), whereas the other statement supposedly describes a behavior representative of right-brain dominance (e.g., "I like to be silly and play around" or "I think well lying down on my back"). The student who marks both statements from a pair is said to be integrative and functioning from a whole-brain perspective. People who are left-brain dominant purportedly display learning styles associated with conformity, organization, logic, detail, and verbal processing. People who are right-brain dominant are supposedly more nonconforming, explorative, intuitive, global, and spatially oriented.

As students mark the test sheet their responses are recorded onto an answer key through carbon paper. The answer key has designated each statement as indicative of left- (L) or right-brain (R) dominance. A student simply totals the number of Ls, the number of Rs, and the number where both statements were checked—whole-brained (W). (The number of items for which neither statement was checked is not totalled.) These three scores are entered respectively onto three raw score scales. A vertical line is then drawn through each point so that it crosses a standard score scale above these scales and a percentile scale below. Students then estimate their standard and percentile scores. Finally, the raw, standard, and percentile scores for left, right, and whole are entered onto a chart to aid interpretation.

BASIC ASSUMPTIONS GOVERNING THE USE OF SOLAT. We think that there are three assumptions that govern the use of SOLAT. These are that (*a*) the left and right hemispheres of the brain are uniformly responsible for different thoughts and behaviors; (*b*) SOLAT is a reliable and valid instrument; and (*c*) learning styles instruction should be developed to support, compensate for, or facilitate individual learning styles.

The assumption that the left and right hemispheres of the brain are uniformly responsible for certain types of thoughts and behaviors is not well supported (e.g., Bradshaw & Nettlton, 1983). Most neuroscientists dismiss the popularized idea of simple left- and right-brain lateralization, and favor a view suggesting a more complex functional model that includes neural networks spanning multiple regions of the brain. PET scan studies, for example, show major involvement by multiple regions of the brain, spanning the left and right regions, in both simple and complex tasks. Furthermore, even if one attempted to categorize thoughts and behaviors by regions of the brain in a gross fashion, then a left-right distinction is still too simplistic. The posterior and anterior regions of the brain are generally associated with certain thoughts and behaviors such as initial processing of visual stimuli and complex thinking, respectively.

The second assumption deals with the reliability and validity of the SOLAT. *Reliability* data are surprisingly limited (or unreported). The manual reports a single estimate of reliability for the Elementary Form based on 129 sets of responses (Cronbach Alpha was .77 for the Left Scale, and .73 for the Right Scale) and a single estimate for the Youth Form based on the responses of 441 eighth graders (Cronbach Alpha was .77 for the Left Scale, and .74 for the Right Scale). Also limited are data on test-retest reliability. Data on the Elementary Form are based on 41 elementary students, (grade level(s) unspecified), whereas the Youth Form is based on the scores from 106 high school students (grade level(s) unspecified). Product-moment reliability coefficients were .74 (L), .61 (R), and .67 (W) for the elementary students, and .73 (L), .57 (R), and .47 (W) for the high school students. All reliability data are unpublished. Overall, these data generally support SOLAT's reliability. Additional tests by grade level, however, are warranted particularly at the elementary school level.

With respect to *content validity* there is very little clinical or research support (Bradshaw & Nettlton, 1983; Bryden, 1982; Geschwind & Galaburda, 1987) for the proposition that SOLAT items are related to and/or differentiate particular hemisphere-specific, lateralized functions. In addition, a multiple-choice, self-report, paper-and-pencil format cannot control for "attentional," pre-existing "set," and "activation" variables that affect hemisphere lateralized response tendencies.

With respect to *construct validity*, the author reports roughly 40 studies showing that performance on the SOLAT is related to certain characteristics such as visual and verbal learning styles, and to group affiliation such as artists, musicians, and the gifted. One limitation of these studies is that the bulk of them are in relation to the right subscale only. Groups as varying as the gifted, psychologists, coaches, underachievers, elementary students, and students with behavior problems all scored high on the right subscale. It is difficult to integrate findings showing that measurement students scored high on the left subscale, whereas educational psychology students (who are very similar) scored high on the right subscale; or why public administrators scored high on the right subscale, whereas business students scored high on the left subscale; or why both gifted/honors students and underachievers scored high on the right subscale.

Serious questions arise concerning the *concurrent validity* of the SOLAT when the few studies using widely accepted techniques and measures are examined. The only study using dichotic listening found no significant relationships with SOLAT scores. Another study using conjugate lateral eye movements (CLEM) found no significant relationships, and a second study using CLEM found no relationship to right or whole-brain subscales and only a small correlation with the left subscale.

Much more troubling are results of the study with the Differential Aptitude Test (DAT) which showed Verbal Reasoning, Abstract Reasoning, and Spelling subtest scores significantly correlated with the right subscale and not the left as would be expected given the nature of these subtests. Conversely, Numerical and Mechanical Reasoning subtest scores correlated with the left subscale, not the right. Similar confusion results from the finding that the Armed Services Vocational Aptitude Clerical Composite score is negatively correlated with the left subscale, contrary to expectations based on the constructs involved.

The author does not try to resolve the contradiction inherent in the finding that while three visual-spatial tests were found to correlate positively with the right subscale, the Bender-Gestalt was negatively correlated with the right subscale. Finally, whereas right-hemisphere-specific contributions to reading and math performance have been widely published, the SOLAT right subscale is negatively correlated with Stanford Achievement Tests in reading and math.

In summary, while the author emphasizes the left-brain orientation of educational systems, the most robust findings are that an incredibly diverse set of populations score higher on the right subscale, and that most of the relationships with subtest scores on other instruments and measures are in relation to the right subscale. In fact, some of the language-based, left-hemisphere-oriented subscales on other measures are correlated positively with the right subscale, raising serious questions about content

and construct validity, regardless of SOLAT's internal consistency.

Even had the SOLAT met the previous two assumptions we doubt that it has much of a place in school learning. We agree with the author that students should use a range of thinking in solving academic problems as well as personal and social ones. However, it is suggested that the link between these thinking styles and brain hemisphere preference is weak, misleading, and unnecessary.

Given that the ultimate objective of the SOLAT is to facilitate a range of thinking, it is on this ground that the materials are most inadequate. Surprisingly, little is said in the Administrator's Manual about interpretation or implications. With respect to interpretation, readers are told that "a standard score of 120 [the 84th percentile] may be regarded as identifying a dominant pattern," and that "some children may not have any dominant pattern." The manual suggests that teachers should help students to clarify fuzzy profiles by "wondering" along with them. The implications of the survey are not clear. Teachers are encouraged to help students to "select . . . the greatest weakness" from their profile, and have "time set aside for discussing improvement." How profiles can be improved is not addressed in the manual other than to say that students should "capitalize on their strengths, and to work towards a whole-brained kind of functioning."

For those still interested in using some instrument to measure brain hemisphere preference, we recommend Gordon's (1983) Cognitive Laterality Battery (CLB). It is a group-administered test that takes about an hour to administer. Although the use of a self-report instrument is still problematic, Horner and Freider (1989) found a significant relationship between the CLB and *extreme* responses on a cognitive style questionnaire.

REVIEWER'S REFERENCES

Bryden, M. P. (1982). *Laterality: Functional asymmetry in the intact brain.* New York: Academic Press.

Bradshaw, J. L., & Nettlton, N. C. (1983). *Human cerebral asymmetry.* Englewood Cliffs, NJ: Prentice Hall.

Gordon, H. W. (1983). Cognitive Laterality Battery. Pittsburgh, PA: University of Pittsburgh Western Psychiatric Institute and Clinic.

Geschwind, N., & Galaburda, A. M. (1987). *Cerebral lateralization.* Cambridge, MA: M.I.T. Press.

Horner, M. D., & Freider, D. (1989, February). The relationship between cognitive style and cognitive competency.

Paper presented at the Seventeenth Annual Conference of the International Neuropsychological Society, Vancouver, BC.

Review of the Style of Learning and Thinking by DONALD U. ROBERTSON, *Professor of Psychology, and* VIRGINIA L. BROWN, *Director, Institute for Research and Community Service, Indiana University of Pennsylvania, Indiana, PA:*

According to the author, E. Paul Torrance, the Style of Learning and Thinking (SOLAT) was developed in response to the need to assist educators to utilize the rapidly expanding knowledge and new information related to specialized functioning of brain hemispheres. Specifically, Torrance asserts that recent research indicates the left and right cerebral hemispheres each have the following independent and specialized functions: The left hemisphere "seems to be the locus of logical, analytical, propositional thought" and is the center of most language, information ordering, and time sense; "the right hemisphere seems to be the locus of visuospatial and appositional thought and imagination," is nonverbal, and "makes itself known through dreams and fantasy." With respect to information processing, the left hemisphere is considered to be linear and sequential whereas the right hemisphere is nonlinear and capable of relating and associating information simultaneously. Early versions of the SOLAT were designed to tap these two cerebral functions in adults.

Unspecified "item analyses" of the adult SOLAT produced a 25-item Elementary form for children in grades K to 5 (norms are provided for grades 1 to 5) and a 28-item Youth form for grades 6 to 12. The adult version is now called the Human Information Processing Survey (10:144), and the SOLAT refers to the two versions for children and youth. Test items consist of a pair of statements; one statement is considered to reflect right cerebral hemispheric functioning, the other left hemisphere. Children are instructed to check the statement that is true of them and are permitted to check both or neither statement of each pair. Raw scores for the Right Brain scale are computed by adding the number of items for which only the right hemisphere statement was checked, the Left Brain score by summing the left only statements, and the Whole Brain score by summing the items for which both statements were checked. Although the test giver is cautioned to note the number of items for which no statements were checked, test scores are not affected by it. Because of this feature, the test in effect has a variable length. However, the transformation of raw scores to standard scores and percentiles does not take this into account. A child who completed only the first five items on the test and left the remainder blank could receive the same score on two of the three scales as a child who omitted no items. Test-retest reliability (stability) coefficients and coefficient alpha are reported for both forms. Test-retest coefficients (10-week delay) for the Left, Right, and Whole Brain scales were .71, .61, and .67 for the Elementary form and .73, .57, and .47 for the Youth form (12-week delay). The test authors assert that "the reliabilities are satisfactory for this type of test." Although they may be satisfactory for the test, they are not satisfactory for use of the test with individual children in an attempt to identify learning style. Coefficient alphas were also relatively low: .77 and .73 for the Left and Right scales on the Elementary form and .77 and .74 for the Youth form.

Norms for the test are based on a large sample (4,315) of students in grades 1 through 12. The composition of the sample is not, however, well described. We are told the states from which the students came and the overall racial composition of the sample, but the distribution of these variables across grades is not given. No information about the gender composition of the sample, socioeconomic status, characteristics of the schools (e.g., urban or rural, large or small), or inclusion/exclusion criteria (were learning disabled children included?) was given. There are no norms for kindergarten children; the sample size of the first graders is small; and separate norms for males and females are not provided.

The test manual contains nearly seven pages of validity information, all of which was based on previous forms of the test and much of which is with adults. Four types of validity evidence were presented: content, construct, concurrent, and predictive. Torrance argues that these studies are relevant because the Youth and Elementary form items came from the same item pool. In other words, the contention is that if we can demonstrate valid measurement of a construct in an adult population, then it is possible to use similar measurement procedures to assess the construct in children. Despite the assertion of a kind of validity generalization that probably should be demonstrated, the argument hinges on the construct validity of the original measures.

Although there are many ways of providing evidence that bears on the construct validity of a measurement, at a minimum one must clearly identify properties of the construct and rudimentary elements of the empirical relationships into which the construct should and should not enter. The construct validity evidence that is provided in the test manual consists of brief descriptions of about 30 studies that either compare groups such as gifted adolescents with norms or correlate the previous forms of the SOLAT with other paper-and-pencil tests (such as the What Kind of Person are You? test). This sort of cataloging of studies, while it may seem impressive to some, is not evidence of construct validity. Critical issues such as response sets, method variance, and discriminant validity are not mentioned.

The basic issue is what construct(s) is being measured and what are the empirical relationships entailed. Is this a measure of hemispheric dominance, hemispheric preference (and if so, what is that?), learning style, or personality traits? At times the author seems to suggest all of the above, creating the illusion that because there is some basic research which indicates hemispheric specialization that the SOLAT is measuring (a) a biologically based construct, that (b) results in individual differences in information processing, that (c) are related to the way children best learn, and (d) is reflected in behavioral preferences for activities such as lying on one's back or sitting up straight. The rather lengthy chain of hypotheses is not supported by data that consist of correlations between paper-and-pencil tests and group differences. Finally, as Messick (1981) and others have pointed out, without some evidence of construct validity one cannot determine what a test score means.

Direct evidence for validity of the Youth and Elementary forms of the SOLAT is almost nonexistent. One study with the Youth form was discussed in much detail, but was based on a sample of six second-graders. Three unpublished studies were cited as initial evidence for the Youth form; two were conducted by eighth grade students and one by a high school

sophomore. There is no way to evaluate the adequacy of these studies.

In summary, the reliability of the SOLAT is relatively poor and does not qualify it for individual use. The direct validity information about the Youth and Elementary forms is inadequate. The major shortcoming of this test is the conceptual looseness associated with the nature of the construct being measured and the direction of validation research.

REVIEWER'S REFERENCE

Messick, S. (1981). Constructs and their vicissitudes in educational and psychological measurement. *Psychological Bulletin, 89,* 575-588.

[87]
Suffolk Reading Scale.

Purpose: "To provide a standardized measure of reading attainment and to monitor the progress of individuals and groups."
Population: Ages 6–12.
Publication Dates: 1986–87.
Scores: Total score only.
Administration: Group.
Levels: 3 overlapping levels: Level 1 (ages 6–7), Level 2 (ages 8–10), Level 3 (ages 10–12); 2 parallel forms: A, B.
Price Data, 1987: £5.20 per set of 10 Level 1A booklets or Level 1B booklets or Level 2A booklets or Level 2B booklets; £6.35 per set of 10 Level 3A booklets or Level 3B booklets; £5.75 per set of 25 Level 3 answer sheets; £6.90 per Teacher's Guide ('87, 48 pages); scoring service for Level 3 offered by publisher.
Time: (35–45) minutes.
Author: Fred Hagley.
Publisher: NFER-Nelson Publishing Co., Ltd. [England].

Review of the Suffolk Reading Scale by ROBERT B. COOTER, JR., Associate Professor of Elementary Education, Brigham Young University, Provo, UT:

DESCRIPTION. The Suffolk Reading Scale is a group-administered norm-referenced test of reading ability intended for children from 6 to 12 + years of age. Three levels of the Suffolk Reading Scales are available (1, 2, 3) with two alternate forms (Forms A and B).

Each level of the test presents the child with sentences arranged in increasing difficulty with a single word missing (e.g., *The milkman drove down the _____*). The task is to supply the missing word from multiple choices shown below the sentence (e.g., *robe road door milk read*). Children simply circle the word in the test booklet for Levels 1 and 2. They may do likewise on Level 3 or use a machine-scored answer sheet. This modified cloze format provides the sole basis for reading assessment with the Suffolk.

TEST DEVELOPMENT AND TECHNICAL FEATURES. The genesis of the Suffolk Reading Scale is very interesting and admirable. Educators in Suffolk County, England saw a need "to update and improve upon the tests currently being used . . . and to avoid disjointed results from the use of different tests with different age groups." Thus, educators in the County of Suffolk set out to create a new test matching their curricular standards and to establish local norms for the new test.

Teachers in 42 schools in Suffolk were selected to work on the project with teachers selected from all levels and across a variety of subject specializations. They were asked to suggest material relating to the reading experiences in their classes. This process yielded some 500 potential items. Finally, a panel of "Advisory Teachers" and "Educational Psychologists" edited the items using preestablished criteria.

Two provisional forms of the test were constructed for further development within Suffolk. During the Autumn term of 1982, the Suffolk Reading Scale was administered to some 300 children in the county at each age level (6+, 8+, 10+, and 12+). These results were then subjected to item analysis by the National Foundation for Educational Research (NFER) using both classical item analysis and Rasch scaling methods.

Following the initial construction and field use of the Suffolk Reading Scale, it was decided to establish national norms prior to publication. The NFER assisted in this effort and developed a standardization sample of children across the 6+ to 13+ age range attending schools in England, Wales, and Northern Ireland. Socioeconomic considerations were taken into account in the development of the sample. Some 38,625 students participated in the standardization process conducted in March of 1986.

Scores on the Suffolk Reading Scale may be interpreted in several ways from the norm tables. A student's raw score may be converted into a Standard Score (SS), Percentile Rank (PR), and/or a Grade Equivalent (GE). Section III of the manual provides useful directions for interpretation and use of derived scores.

Reliability estimates for the Suffolk are satisfactory. Several estimates of the test's reliability were made including checks for internal consistency and test-retest reliability. Test-retest results indicate reliability coefficient scores ranging from a low of .89 for Level 3, Form B to a high of .96 for Level 1, Form B. Internal consistency estimates (KR-20) range from .92 (Level 3, Form A) to .95 (Level 1). The author points out that these data are based on a "first occasion of testing only"; that is, the children had never taken either form of the test before. Thus, one might expect scores to be slightly higher on subsequent testings.

Validity was primarily determined by comparing students' test performance with teachers' estimates of their reading ability. In addition, readability levels of children's current school reading books were considered. Correlations were computed using the Rasch Ability Score, which forms the basis of age equivalent scores for the Suffolk Reading Scale. When comparing teacher estimates of pupils' reading ability with performance on the Scale, correlation coefficients ranged from .76 to .83. Readability level of pupils' current reading books compared to reading ability estimates derived from the Suffolk Reading Scale yielded correlations ranging from .61 to .74. These figures indicate that the Suffolk Reading Scale is associated with both teacher estimates of reading level and with the readability level of their school reading books.

Finally, the Suffolk Reading Scale has at least a degree of curricular validity by virtue of the method of test construction used. As mentioned above, teachers from all grade levels and content specialities were involved in the construction of the test items. Although this would not seem to represent a rigorous application of curricular validity standards, some recognition of the process seems warranted.

EVALUATION AND CONCLUSIONS. The Suffolk Reading Scale represents a significant contribution to the reading assessment field, not so much because of its content, but for the process it represents. Many reading assessment theorists recognize that standardized tests are significant indicators of educational progress when used as part of an overall evaluation

(Calfee, 1987). This being the case, then one may likely conclude that a test of reading ability constructed by local professionals and normed using local populations would be preferable to other commercial tests. If a similar process were adopted by all school systems then validity of measurement would be greatly improved. However, as a commercial test of reading ability for general application, the Suffolk Reading Scale has a number of serious problems.

One major difficulty with the Scale is that it does not reflect recent advances in our understanding of the reading process (Valencia & Pearson, 1987). Important factors such as affect, concepts about print, reading/study skills, and even basic word identification/recognition strategies are not addressed. In essence the Scale is a series of modified cloze sentences of progressive difficulty, a task generally considered to measure inferential comprehension and context clues. Thus, one can in no way consider this test to be a comprehensive test of reading skill.

A second related problem is the failure of the Scale's author either to articulate or adhere to any known construct or understanding of the reading process. Nowhere in the Teacher's Guide is a rationale offered indicating reasoning behind the format of the test, or exclusion of important aspects of the reading process. Our only insight into test construction is the knowledge that teachers were asked to generate items for inclusion in the scales. Failure to explain the philosophical underpinnings of any assessment instrument creates a great deal of suspicion regarding overall validity.

It is difficult to determine how the Suffolk Reading Scale has any great benefit to classroom instruction beyond determining gross reading levels. Because no specific reading abilities have been identified or correlated to test scores it would appear that the Scales could only be used for school or district reporting. Possibly the Scale could be used for initial screenings of reading ability for children in Great Britain.

Finally, the test makers should consider inclusion of a section in the Teacher's Guide explaining how these test results may be used as part of an overall assessment package. Limitations of the test should be pointed out and suggestions for building a complete assessment program offered. The 1990s are likely to call not only for the integration of more holistic teaching methods in the classroom, but also for the inclusion of process-oriented measures of reading ability.

REVIEWER'S REFERENCES

Calfee, R. C. (1987). The school as a context for assessment of literacy. *The Reading Teacher, 40*, 738-743.
Valencia, S., & Pearson, P. D. (1987). Reading assessment: Time for change. *The Reading Teacher, 40*, 726-732.

Review of the Suffolk Reading Scale by RICHARD LEHRER, Associate Professor of Educational Psychology, University of Wisconsin-Madison, Madison, WI:

The Suffolk Reading Scale consists of multiple-choice, sentence-completion items that may be administered either individually or to a group. The items sample a commendable range of content areas. Other strengths include easy administration, simple scoring, and high reliability. The national standardization sample also appears adequate, so the accompanying standard scores are meaningful.

Despite these strengths, the Scale suffers from an essentially theory-free approach toward the assessment of reading. It seems as if the Scale measures vocabulary and neglects other aspects of reading, such as comprehension. The validation of the Scale offers little assistance in resolving this dilemma. The only validity data presented in the manual consist of correlations between teachers' estimates of students' reading ability and the scores obtained from administration of the Scale. It is not clear how teachers' estimates were scaled, nor is it clear if the teachers who provided the estimates were also those who were involved in the original test construction. Moreover, because many test items were created from materials the children were reading, it is not surprising that teachers' estimates of children's reading ability and children's performance on the Scale were associated highly.

No other forms of concurrent validity are provided nor is any attempt made at discriminating between the Scale and other forms of mental assessment, including other measures of reading skill. Hence, very little can be concluded at this time about the validity of the Suffolk Reading Scale.

An additional problem is that the Scale may not be valid across cultures, due to the inclusion of terms such as "petrol" and "lorry" that are apt to be unfamiliar to children in the United

States. The directions for administration are also vague, leaving it to individual teachers to translate into practice phrases such as, "Explain that they have to choose one word which best fits into the sentence."

In summary, the Suffolk Reading Scale provides an easy and quick assessment of some aspects of children's reading skills, perhaps primarily vocabulary. Although the Scales are reliable, they suffer from a vaguely defined theory of reading and an inadequate attempt at validation. At the present time, more established measures of reading skills may be a better choice for the assessment of children's reading.

[88]
Survey of Functional Adaptive Behaviors.

Purpose: To assess an individual's skill level of adaptive behavior.
Population: Ages 16 and over.
Publication Date: 1986.
Acronym: SFAB.
Scores, 5: Residential Living Skills, Daily Living Skills, Academic Skills, Vocational Skills, SFAB Total Score.
Administration: Individual.
Manual: No manual.
Price Data, 1988: $24.50 per 25 surveys.
Authors: Jack G. Dial, Carolyn Mezger, Theresa Massey, Steve Carter, and Lawrence T. McCarron.
Publisher: McCarron-Dial Systems.

Review of the Survey of Functional Adaptive Behaviors by STEVEN W. LEE, Assistant Professor of Educational Psychology and Research, University of Kansas, Lawrence, KS:

The Survey of Functional Adaptive Behaviors (SFAB) was designed as a comprehensive rating of adaptive behavior for individuals 16 years of age or older. A 12-page protocol is provided to those administering the test. Data on the standardization sample, including reliability and validity of the instrument, are provided in a 4-page handout.

The SFAB is an untimed test that can be completed by (*a*) case history information, (*b*) interview, or (*c*) behavioral observation. No empirical data are provided indicating these three rating methods provide equivalent adaptive behavior ratings. Regardless of the method used to obtain the information, a rating of 2 (Task performed independently), 1 (Task performed inadequately or requires assistance, prompting, or cueing), or 0 (Task not per-

formed) is used by the evaluator to rate each of 135 behavioral items.

These items are divided into four skill areas. The four skill areas include: Residential Living, Daily Living, Academic, and Vocational Skills areas. Standard scores for each skill area can be obtained as well as a Total Adaptive Behavior score. A secondary rating system is mentioned that seems to be designed to identify the training needs (i.e., none, remedial, or adaptive devices needed) for the client being evaluated for each of the 135 behavioral items. The scoring and uses for this secondary system are, however, not elucidated.

No manual is provided for the SFAB. The psychological reasoning or theory underlying the test is not provided, nor is any description of item selection, item analysis, or other research leading to the development of the test. Furthermore, no information regarding how the test should be interpreted is included, nor are there any warnings against possible misuses of the instrument. The educational qualifications for the test users are not mentioned. Specific instructions related to each of the three methods of administration of the SFAB are not provided, so the user cannot determine how to use case histories, behavioral observations, or interviews to complete the SFAB in a manner consistent with that of the normative sample. For example, in using the interview method, who should be the respondent? Are the behavioral observations to be structured or unstructured, and over what period of time should the behavioral observations be done? Scoring of the SFAB protocol is done in a clear and straightforward manner; however, converting the raw scores into standard scores is more difficult. No continuous norm tables are provided with the SFAB. As a result, interpolation or rounding will often be necessary to obtain standardized *T*-scores for SFAB raw scores. Neither the SFAB protocol nor the associated handout provides a method for obtaining standard scores not listed in the table. This problem introduces additional and unnecessary error into estimates of adaptive behavior skills.

The normative sample of the SFAB included 567 adults with ages ranging from 15 to 62. These adults had a mean IQ of 85 ($SD = 17$). The sample was appropriately stratified for both race and sex according to the U.S. population; however, the sampling procedure was not clearly specified and did not appear to be randomized. Forty percent of the sample ($n = 245$) had neurological damage, while 57 percent ($n = 322$) were intellectually in the average range and competitively employed. However, of this latter group, 195 were visually impaired, 92 were nondisabled, and information on the remaining 35 was not provided. The U.S. region of residence of the sample was noted only for the neurologically impaired group. No measures of central tendency or variability are provided for the normative sample. This is particularly unfortunate, given the unique nature of the sample (i.e., visually and neurologically impaired), as psychological and educational measures with large normative samples are difficult to obtain for these specialized groups. Given the unique characteristics of large groups within the sample, accurate estimates of adaptive behavior from the obtained scores would be quite difficult to make.

The reliability of the SFAB was reportedly assessed by interrater and test-retest methods. Test-retest reliability over a 7-to-14-day period, using 100 neurologically and visually disabled persons, was quite good and ranged in the high .80s to low .90s for the skill areas, and was $r = .92$ for the Total Adaptive Behavior score. No true interrater reliability was reported as no simultaneous ratings of behaviors were made. The rating method (i.e., case history, interview, or behavioral observation) used in the above mentioned study was not specified; therefore, the consumer would not know which method yielded the above mentioned results. No other data on the reliability of the SFAB were provided.

The validity of the SFAB was assessed through a comparison with other McCarron-Dial measures of adaptive behavior (Behavior Rating Scale [BRS] and Street Survival Skills Questionnaire [SSSQ]). These criterion measures were not described except through abbreviations, so the consumer could not evaluate their adequacy as criterion instruments. A concurrent validity study was reported with 52 mentally retarded adults. In this study, the SFAB correlated at $r = .90$ with Part I and $r = .65$ with Part II of the AAMD Adaptive Behavior Scale. Although these results are encouraging, the AAMD-ABS is viewed as having questionable psychometric viability (Sattler, 1988).

Finally, the authors report a "concurrent validity" study comparing SFAB scores for 372 sighted adults in eight different levels on the vocational continuum from daycare to professional competitive employment. The correlations of the SFAB with these vocational levels would potentially provide criterion-related validity. For this comparison, however, the Pearson Product Moment correlation coefficient was inappropriately used. The correct correlational statistic for comparing interval (SFAB) with nominal data (vocational level) is Eta.

In summary, the SFAB is deficient as a normative measure of adaptive behavior. The instrument has no clearly designated manual. No descriptive statistics of the normative sample are provided. Information on the development of the test, qualifications of users, administration methods, and scoring procedure are either unclear, confusing, or nonexistent. As noted above, the psychometric properties of the tool are weak. The main value of the SFAB may be as an informal tool used to evaluate adaptive behavior of adults without making comparisons to the normative sample.

REVIEWER'S REFERENCE

Sattler, J. M. (1988). *Assessment of children* (3rd ed.). San Diego: Jerome M. Sattler.

Review of the Survey of Functional Adaptive Behaviors by STEVEN I. PFEIFFER, *Director, Institute of Clinical Training and Research, The Devereux Foundation, Devon, PA:*

The Survey of Functional Adaptive Behaviors (SFAB) is described as a comprehensive rating scale of adaptive behavior. The scale consists of 135 items clustered within four skill areas. "Residential Living Skills" consists of self-care and home management (30 items). "Daily Living Skills" is made up of money management; community, social, and recreational resources; and travel (40 items). "Academic Skills" includes numerical reasoning, functional language, and literacy and writing (20 items). "Vocational Skills" incorporates physical ability and vocational attributes (45 items).

The scale is one of a set of tests developed and published by the McCarron-Dial Systems, with the support of the Texas Commission for the Blind.

The scale is appropriate for clients 16 years of age and older, and the authors state the instrument may be rated from case history information, interview, and/or behavioral observation. Clients are rated on a 3-point scale of skill level: Task performed independently (accommodations permitted); Task performed inadequately or requires assistance, prompting, or cueing; and Task not performed. When a client obtains a skill-level rating on any item indicating either inadequate performance or task not performed, a secondary rating is provided that allows the examiner to record whether intervention or adaptive accommodation may be needed.

Test results are expressed on the record form in standard scores, based on a normative sample of 567 adults (aged 15–62). Reliability and validity studies were based on this same normative group. Reliability indices appear adequate—test/retest scores of .92 for the SFAB Total Score and .85 to .94 for the four factor scores. However, validity data are rather meager; the authors report only one concurrent validity study, with the SFAB correlating .80 with the AAMD Adaptive Behavior Scale (*n* = 52). A second validity study indicated that the SFAB correlated .88 with one of eight assigned vocational program levels of independence (*n* = 372).

The scale is a promising instrument, with a great majority of the 135 items tapping relevant adaptive behaviors and critical normative developmental skills. The SFAB does not omit any significant domains and is quite easy to rate and score. However, the scale has its weaknesses, some rather critical. First and foremost, there is no technical manual. Information on technical adequacy was provided in a four-page letter summarizing the research sent by the publisher, McCarron-Dial Systems. No information was available on the underlying theoretical model, rationale for the four scales, or how the items were selected and evaluated. It is unclear how ratings based on review of a case history, clinical interview, or behavioral observation can yield sufficiently similar and valid scores.

Instructions are sketchy and consist of only one paragraph on the record form. Although the secondary rating procedure is a unique and valuable feature, the record form provides no information on how to determine whether remediative intervention for the particular skill is indicated. Many of the academic skill items are too difficult for developmentally disabled individuals, which raises the question of the specific proposed use for the scale. The normative sample was primarily drawn from the southwestern United States, and 42% of the subjects were visually impaired (legally or totally blind).

The SFAB seems to cover adequately the domain of skills and competencies considered important in programming for developmentally disabled adults. However, the scale does not meet minimal technical standards and will need restandardization and more extensive norms, rigorous reliability and validity studies, and a technical manual before it can be endorsed as anything but a research tool.

[89]
The TARC Assessment System.

Purpose: "Provides a short-form behavioral assessment of the capabilities of retarded or otherwise severely handicapped children on a number of skills related to education."
Population: Ages 3–16.
Publication Date: 1975.
Acronym: TARC.
Scores, 17: Self-Help Skills (Toileting, Washing, Eating, Clothing Management, Total), Motor Skills (Small Muscle Coordination, Large Muscle Coordination, Pre-Academic Skills, Total), Communication Skills (Receptive, Expressive, Pre-Academic, Total), Social Skills (Observed Behavior, Pre-Academic Skills, Total), Total.
Administration: Individual.
Price Data, 1989: $16 per complete kit including 10 assessment sheets and manual (7 pages); $13 per 10 assessment sheets; $5 per manual.
Time: Administration time not reported.
Comments: Behavior checklist.
Authors: Wayne Sailor and Bonnie Jean Mix.
Publisher: PRO-ED, Inc.

Review of the TARC Assessment System by STEVEN W. LEE, Assistant Professor of Educational Psychology and Research, University of Kansas, Lawrence, KS:

The TARC (Topeka [Kansas] Association for Retarded Citizens) Assessment System was developed as a "quick assessment" which provides a "snapshot" of the current functioning level of mentally retarded and severely handicapped children. The TARC "kit" provides a seven-page manual, with 10 eight-page assessment sheets. The manual provides some psychometric information as well as instructions on scoring and interpreting the TARC. The assessment sheet is well laid out and easy to use. Instructions for scoring are also provided on the assessment sheet, including a page for charting the examinee's profile. The assessment is untimed and should be done by an examiner after at least 3 weeks of observation of the child. No other special qualifications of the examiner are mentioned. If a skill to be rated has not been observed, it is recommended that the examiner "test" these directly, although the procedure for doing this is not elucidated.

The TARC was developed using a "narrow sampling" of behaviors in representative skill areas presumably to provide an estimate of the examinee's current skills in various domains. Items on the TARC are grouped into subsections (e.g., Toileting, Washing, Eating, Clothing Management, etc.) that are subsumed under the Self-Help, Motor, Communication, and Social Skill areas. The sum of section scores provides a Total Score. There are two types of items on the TARC, scaled and categorical items. On the scaled items, the rater circles a numbered statement from a graduated, behaviorally anchored list of skills that have been observed by the examiner in a specific skill area (e.g., eating or dressing). The categorical items are a nongraduated list of behaviors within a skill area. The examiner must endorse all the behaviors within the skill area that can be successfully completed by the examinee. For example, in the Large Muscle Coordination area some skills are: walks, runs, hops on one foot, skips, climbs, swings, etc.

The manual reports that standardization was completed on 283 "severely handicapped" children between the ages of 3 and 16. Severely handicapped is defined as those children who were moderately mentally retarded or below (AAMD classification), as well as autistic, cerebral palsied, perceptually handicapped, or learning disabled. The rationale or method for selecting the sample was not provided, nor were the norms subdivided by age, sex, handicap, or IQ. Also omitted is the geographic location from which the sample was drawn, although presumably it was drawn from the Kansas area. The omission of the sample characteristics limits accurate interpretation of the TARC results. For example, might we expect a 3-year-old diagnosed as TMR to have fewer basic skills than TMR children who are 10 years older? Yet, if the 3-year-old is lower in skills with reference to the 3- to 16-year-old normative sample, his or her TARC scores may be interpreted as low, even though the child may have average skills when compared with other TMR preschool children. This is a serious deficit if the test is to be used in a normative way.

Subsection, section, and the total raw scores are plotted on a profile sheet (located on page 2 of the assessment sheet). In this way, raw scores can be converted to standard scores with a mean of 50 and a standard deviation of 20. The average range may then be construed as 30 to 70. Given the large age range and varying handicapping conditions in the standardization sample, a high degree of variability or error exists within the ratings which serves to limit the discriminative power of the test. In addition, the TARC has a limited ceiling in the Toileting, Washing, Eating, Clothing Management, Receptive, and Expressive Language subskill areas, further reducing the ability of the test to discriminate among functionally retarded children in these areas.

No psychometric information is provided on how the test was developed. Reliability data are provided in the form of an interrater reliability study using 66 severely handicapped children (50 of whom were institutionalized and 16 who were in day care). Interrater correlations were poor for the Self-Help ($r = .59$) and Motor ($r = .63$) scales, average for the Communication ($r = .77$) and Social ($r = .78$) scales, and good for the Total ($r = .85$) scale. A test-retest reliability study is mentioned, with reliability coefficients for the above mentioned scales exceeding the .80s over a 6-month time span. Unfortunately, no sample, examiners, or setting characteristics are provided for this study. No standard errors of measurement or validity data are provided in the TARC manual.

Instructions for interpreting the TARC are included in the manual. These instructions seem to confuse the differences between normative and relative strengths and weaknesses. According to the TARC authors, relative strengths or weaknesses are defined as scores that fall above or below a standard score of 50, respectively. Two problems are noted here. First from a normative perspective, scores falling within ± 1 standard deviation of the mean would be considered average range scores and therefore could not be considered strengths or weaknesses. Second, *relative* strengths or weaknesses can be defined as those skill areas that are significantly higher or lower than the other skill areas in a specific child's profile. For example, a child with standard scores of around 20 in the Self-Help, Motor, and Communication skill areas may have a *relative* strength in Social Skills with a standard score of 40 (but still below the mean). Due to these problems, the instructions for interpretation of the TARC are quite problematic.

In sum, the TARC is quite limited as a normative measure of adaptive behavior. Accurate interpretation of TARC scores would be quite difficult given the lack of norms divided by age, sex, or handicapping condition. In addition, the limited ceiling in a number of the subskill areas, and the misleading instructions for interpretation serve to minimize the normative usefulness of the instrument. Add to these problems the equivocal reliability data and no published validity information, and the TARC cannot be considered a psychometrically viable, normative measure of adaptive behavior. However, as is mentioned in the manual, the TARC may be valuable as an informal assessment or screening tool leading to a more comprehensive assessment of adaptive behavior. The TARC may also be helpful in the development of instructional objectives for severely handicapped children.

Review of The TARC Assessment System by PAT MIRENDA, Assistant Professor of Special Education and Communication Disorders, University of Nebraska-Lincoln, Lincoln, NE:
The TARC Assessment System, so named because it was developed with the cooperation of the Topeka (Kansas) Association for Retarded Citizens, is intended to be used as an alternative to more complex omnibus assessment inventories used with children with mental retardation or other severe handicaps. It is not intended to replace comprehensive assessment instruments, but rather to provide a general picture of a child's functioning in a number of areas. In order to do so the TARC provides an inventory to be completed by someone who "knows" the target child— "knowing" being defined as having spent a minimum of 3 weeks observing the child in a group or class setting. The inventory is completed by circling the option under each subsection that most closely describes the child's ability. These responses are then totaled to

arrive at a raw score and plotted on a profile sheet that allows a comparison with standard scores (mean = 50, standard deviation = 20). Thus, the final scores are not stated in terms of either developmental or mental age and are not necessarily related to IQ or other common indices of this type.

The manual provides standardization information based on a population of 283 male and female children labelled moderately, severely, or profoundly handicapped and ranging in age from 3–16. No socioeconomic or racial/ethnic information about the subjects is provided, nor are the male/female ratio, the mean age of subjects, or information about the age range distribution made available. Information about the subjects' residence is not stated although at least subgroups of the sample are identified as living in an institution and a day-care situation. According to the manual, the sample included children with mental retardation, autism, cerebral palsy, perceptual handicaps, and learning disabilities; however, neither the proportions nor mean IQs of these subgroups are stated in the manual. Salvia and Ysseldyke (1988) recommend that the minimum number of subjects for which a full range of percentiles can be computed is 100; and that, therefore, a norm sample should contain at least 100 subjects per age. Based on this criterion, a sample that spans 13 years (ages 3–16) should have at least 1,300 subjects. Using this standard, the sample of 283 subjects for the TARC is inadequate. Furthermore, the lack of information about the sample group along the parameters mentioned previously seriously detracts from the utility of the instrument, as the specific population for whom its use would be appropriate is not at all clear.

The manual provides an intercorrelation matrix in which each subsection is correlated with each other subsection based on this sample. The matrix indicates that all correlations are significant at the $p < .05$ level (range = .54–.98) and that the Motor Skills section is the most predictive of the total inventory score. Interrater reliability was calculated on a subsample of 66 severely handicapped children, 50 of whom lived in an institution. The raters were two staff or teachers who were familiar with the children. The resulting "coefficients of correlation" (the exact procedure used is not named) on the subsections were found to be between .59 (Self-Help) and .78 (Social), with an overall correlation of .85; all were significant at $p < .01$. Test-retest reliabilities were conducted with the same subsample 6 months after the first administration and are reported as all being .80 or greater. Neither concurrent or construct validity information is provided, nor are any references available that indicate the source or sources of the items appearing on the inventory. Thus, within the limits of the standardization sample size, the TARC appears to be at least moderately reliable both across raters and over time, and is internally consistent in most areas. However, the sample size used for standardization is seriously deficient, the sample is inadequately described, and there is no information provided about the validity of the test items or their derivation.

The manual provides no guidelines concerning the use of the TARC assessment information to plan educational programs, aside from general statements that "the low points on the profile can be used to formulate educational goals and instructional objectives for the child" and that "many individual categorical items can also be translated into instructional objectives," with an example provided of how this might occur. Further, the test is quite out of date in terms of the type of educational program currently considered to be state-of-the-art for students with severe handicaps. Indeed, it is an irony that the first author of this now-outdated 1975 test is today one of the leading innovators in the area of integration and functional curricula for persons with severe handicaps. While the TARC measures functional skill ability more than many other assessments of its kind, it fails to provide a wide range of functional, chronological-age-appropriate items intended to measure educational needs in both school and community settings. Alternative assessment instruments that do provide such information include: the *Teaching Research Curriculum for Handicapped Adolescents and Adults: Assessment Procedures* (Peterson, Trecker, Egan, Fredericks, & Bunse, 1983); and the *Individual Student Community Life Skill Profile System for Severely Handicapped Students* (Freagon, Wheeler, McDaniel, Brankin, & Costello, 1983).

Overall, the TARC is an example of the type of assessment that was developed in the mid-1970s as an alternative to the standard, developmentally-normed instruments often used with children who experience severe handicaps.

It is seriously deficient in the size and description of the standardization sample used but otherwise appears to be moderately reliable. The validity of the TARC as an assessment instrument is questionable, and it should not be used (nor was it intended to be used) as a substitute for a comprehensive educational assessment in a variety of functional, relevant life skill domains. It may be used to pinpoint general areas of educational concern when used along with other measures.

REVIEWER'S REFERENCES

Freagon, S., Wheeler, J., McDaniel, K., Brankin, G., & Costello, D. (1983). *Individual student community life skill profile system for severely handicapped students*. DeKalb, IL: DeKalb County Special Education Association.
Peterson, J., Trecker, N., Egan, I., Fredericks, B., & Bunse, C. (1983). *Teaching research curriculum for handicapped adolescents and adults: Assessment procedures*. Monmouth, OR: Teaching Research.
Salvia, J., & Ysseldyke, J. E. (1988). *Assessment in special and remedial education* (4th ed.). Boston: Houghton Mifflin.

[90]

Test of Economic Knowledge.

Purpose: Measures knowledge of economic concepts.
Population: Grades 8–9.
Publication Date: 1987.
Acronym: TEK.
Scores: Total score only.
Administration: Group.
Forms, 2: A, B.
Price Data: Available from publisher.
Time: (40–45) minutes.
Comments: "Designed to replace the Junior High School Test of Economics."
Authors: William B. Walstad and John C. Soper.
Publisher: Joint Council on Economic Education.

Review of the Test of Economic Knowledge by WILLIAM A. MEHRENS, *Professor of Educational Measurement, Michigan State University, East Lansing, MI:*

The Test of Economic Knowledge and the accompanying Examiner's Manual are described as a "standardized nationally-normed test and discussion guide for the junior high school level." The test replaces the Junior High School Test of Economics (a review by Ehman [1978] of that test appeared in the *8th MMY*). Each of the two forms of the test contain 39 items, of which 20 are common items to each form.

The test developers apparently took very seriously the criticisms made by Ehman of the previous test. He was critical of item development as well as the poor content validity and lack of construct validity of the Junior High School Test of Economics. The current test is a vast improvement over its predecessor.

The content of the test is based on the 1984 publication of the Joint Council on Economic Education: *A Framework for Teaching the Basic Concepts*. The test was developed by "a national committee of test experts, economists, and classroom teachers." These individuals, and their affiliations, are listed in the Examiner's Manual. This committee developed the test specifications, selected and revised old items that fit the specifications, and wrote new items. Two 50-item versions were tried out in an initial field test, the data were used for revisions, the revised drafts (each with 44 items) were tried out, there were more revisions, and finally two 40-item versions were developed. One item from each form was dropped based on data from the national norm group. Thus, the final versions each have 39 items with, as mentioned, 20 items in common.

The Examiner's Manual presents a two-way table of specifications for the content: concepts by cognitive levels. There are four broad content categories: fundamental economic concepts (25.6%), microeconomic concepts (33.3%), macroeconomic concepts (28.2%), and international economic concepts (12.8%). Each broad category is divided into several subcategories. The cognitive levels are knowledge (33.3%), comprehension (30.8%), and application (35.9%). Each item in each form is keyed to the table of specifications, although the authors admit the classifications may be somewhat arbitrary. This reviewer thought the classifications were about on target. At any rate, the table of specifications and the item classifications are explicit and are published as part of the available materials. Individuals considering the use of this test can determine whether the content validity of the test is adequate for their particular purposes. The authors state they followed "guidelines suggested by the National Advisory Committee regarding the economic content that *ought* to be tested."

The items appear to be well written. The manual presents a rationale for each item, the percentage of the norm group that got the item correct (for two samples—those with and without economic training), and the corrected item-total correlation. In addition, tables showing the percentage of all students responding to each of the four options and the percentage of omitted responses are presented. For all but two items, the percentage correct was greater for the group that had economic training. For one of the two exceptions, the percentages were equal and for the other item, the percentage was actually greater for the group that had not had economic training. This was a supply-demand model item. One of the foils was too attractive—perhaps correct (46% marked one foil and only 26% marked the keyed answer).

The norms were obtained from a nationwide sample of 6,887 students (3,230 for Form A and 3,657 for Form B). Separate norms tables are given for each form, and a conversion table is given equating Form A scores to Form B scores. The equating was accomplished through the equipercentile approach, but the manual also presents the linear converting equation for those who would prefer to use it. The forms are comparable. The norms sample comes from 91 different schools (listed in the appendix of the manual), and is diverse with respect to geographical regions, type of area (urban, etc.), and school size. While "no claim is made that the group tested is exactly representative of the student population enrolled in the 8th and 9th grades nationwide . . . A case can be made that the norm sample contains a representative distribution of students by general ability, socio-economic status, ethnic-racial mix, and other characteristics." This quoted statement from the manual seems exactly right to me. A table in the manual presents the means and standard deviations for various subgroups that have and have not been exposed to economics instruction. The groups are by sex, grade level, scholastic aptitude (3 levels), race/origin, type of community, region, course type, and income level.

Cronbach's alpha is .82 on Form A and .85 on Form B. Standard errors are about 2.8. These are adequate for the "low stakes" uses suggested for the test. Content validity evidence is presented *via* the table of specifications, as mentioned earlier, and users can draw their own conclusions about the appropriateness of the content for the domain to which they wish to infer. Construct validity evidence is meager, but students with economics instruction do perform about 3.3 points higher on the tests than those without instruction.

The manual suggests that the test(s) can be used as a pretest, a posttest, or midway into the course (for formative evaluations). Generally the suggested uses of the test are appropriate.

In summary, the Test of Economic Knowledge is a carefully developed test with fairly complete evidence concerning the technical qualities of the items and the test as a whole. Educators interested in obtaining evidence on the knowledge seventh and eighth grade students have of the economic content covered should give serious consideration to this test. It is certainly far better constructed than the average teacher-constructed test would be over this content.

REVIEWER'S REFERENCE

Ehman, L. H. (1978). [Review of Junior High School Test of Economics.] In O. K. Buros (Ed.), *The eighth mental measurements yearbook* (pp. 1429-1430). Highland Park, NJ: The Gryphon Press.

Review of the Test of Economic Knowledge by ANTHONY J. NITKO, *Professor, School of Education, University of Pittsburgh, Pittsburgh, PA:*

This test measures knowledge in four areas: fundamental economic ideas, microeconomics, macroeconomics, and international economics. There are two forms, each containing 39 four-option, multiple-choice items. The authors suggest the forms be used as pretest and posttest.

The test samples the domain of economic concepts defined by the Joint Council on Economic Education's (JCEE) revised Master Curriculum Guide in Economics. The test's development relied heavily on a committee composed of three economists, two social studies teachers, and a foundation vice president. The final version was reviewed by a panel of five economists.

The authors correctly caution teachers who disagree with the learning objectives implied by the test to use it judiciously or not at all. As Ochoa (1985) stated when reviewing the high school version of this test, most American students are taught economics in social studies courses with broad, integrative objectives, and therefore, an economist's definition of economic education may be too narrow "to determine what is taught or tested in the context of preparing citizens who need to be able to understand, analyze, and decide whether economic practices are desirable or not" (p. 1567).

According to the manual, the primary value of the test is "to assess understanding of the basic economic concepts (sic) that students should know to fulfill present and future roles as consumers, workers, and voters" (p. 2). The test's narrow domain and limited item designs attenuate the attainment of this broad interpretation of the test scores, however. For example, the stem of item 5 reads, "Specialization allows more goods and services to be produced with a given quantity of resources because it results in . . ." Items written in such abstract academic language, instead of in concrete common language, do not seem capable of testing a student's deeper understanding of economic explanations of everyday events. The great majority of items are of the incomplete sentence variety, which further increases their complexity for average eighth and ninth grade readers. More sophisticated item types (e.g., those involving tabular material, scenarios, and interpretive materials) are not used, so the full range of "understanding" performances are not represented in the test.

Factors other than understanding basic economic concepts appear to influence the test scores inordinately. A student's general vocabulary and reading abilities play a heavier than necessary role. This view is supported by the (*a*) correlation (.54 and .56) of the test scores with a vocabulary test (Quick Word Test), (*b*) relatively low mean scores of the norm groups, (*c*) relatively small differences (mean of 3 to 4 points) between students trained and untrained in economics, and (*d*) mean test score differences favoring white students over blacks and students from high-income families over those from low-income families.

Coefficient alphas are .82 for Form A and .85 for Form B, and the standard error of measurement for each form is approximately 2.8. The latter seems rather large. The manual does not report test-retest or alternate forms reliabilities. These are especially important to someone planning to use the test to measure gain from instruction. Although the two forms of the test have 20 items in common, it should not be assumed that the form's raw scores are interchangeable. Form B is slightly easier and slightly more variable than Form A. A table for equating scores is provided, however. Teachers and program evaluators should use the equated scores, rather than the raw scores, when both forms are being administered.

The manual encourages interpreting a class's results at the item level. A unique and especially useful feature is that a "rationale" for why the keyed answer is considered the best choice is printed in the manual beside the text of the item. Also reported for each item are the percent of the norm group choosing each alternative and the percent of the economics-instructed and noninstructed groups choosing the correct alternative. The rationales and percentages are helpful when a teacher "goes over the test" with students who took it.

Percentile ranks norms are provided for various eighth and ninth grade subgroups and aggregations of subgroups, some as small as 210 students. More important than norm group size, however, is that the schools selected for the standardization sample do not seem to be representative of their states.

The manual suggests using any variety of answer sheet that permits students to mark 39 items with four options each. This suggestion is too cavalier because sometimes the use of different answer-sheet formats will alter a test's norms. This point should be subjected to further research.

Because of the test's narrow focus, it cannot be used as a valid basis for grading students. The manual provides insufficient data to estimate the reliability of individual students' pretest-to-posttest gain scores, but it is likely this reliability is low. Caution should be exercised, too, when measuring group growth. The average difference between students with and without exposure to economics training is only about 3 or 4 points, and Form B is about 1 point easier than Form A. One wonders whether a difference of a few points after a term or two of economics represents a practical gain in students' understanding of economic principles, especially because such a gain can be obtained by memorizing the basic terminology.

SUMMARY. The Test of Economic Knowledge is a useful tool for assessing a rather narrow view of what should constitute a junior high school student's understanding of economic concepts and principles. The test does not seem to sample a wide range of economic applications, nor does it test an ability to explain phenomena typically experienced by eighth and ninth grade students as they go about their daily routine. Even if one adopts the narrow definition of economics education implied by the test items, one should exercise caution when interpreting students' test scores. The scores appear to be influenced unduly by a student's general vocabulary reserve and reading ability.

REVIEWER'S REFERENCE

Ochoa, A. S. (1985). [Review of Test of Economic Literacy.] In J. V. Mitchell, Jr. (Ed.), *The ninth mental measurements yearbook* (pp. 1567-1568). Lincoln, NE: Buros Institute of Mental Measurements.

[91]
Test of English Proficiency Level.

Purpose: "To determine a student's instructional level for placement in an English as a Second Language Program."
Population: Limited-English-proficient students in secondary and adult programs.
Publication Date: 1985.
Acronym: TEPL.
Scores: 4 skill area scores: Oral, Structure, Reading, Writing.
Administration: Individual in part.
Price Data, 1987: $49.95 per complete set including test booklet blackline masters, student answer sheet blackline masters, Scantron scoring key, hand-scored scoring key, and manual (89 pages); $7.50 per 50 Scantron answer forms.
Time: Oral Section, (5–20) minutes; Written Section, 60(70) minutes.
Author: George Rathmell.
Publisher: The Alemany Press.

Review of the Test of English Proficiency Level by ALAN GARFINKEL, Associate Professor of Spanish and Foreign Language Education, Purdue University, West Lafayette, IN:

The Test of English Proficiency Level (TEPL) offers the prospective purchaser a clearly defined purpose, along with convincing evidence of success in fulfilling that purpose. For these reasons, it can be recommended as a useful classroom tool despite its lack of complete quantitative data on reliability and validity.

One of the problems facing some tests is an overly ambitious statement of purpose that can be interpreted as an attempt to make a test look useful for all purposes. Because a test is more likely to successfully fulfill a specific purpose than a broad range of purposes, the author and publisher of this test are to be congratulated for staking out the arena of placement for their work in measurement without being excessively ambitious in setting goals.

Placement, as defined in the TEPL manual, involves more than a simple decision on whether or not a given student needs English as a Second Language instruction. Placement measures must be able to assist in selecting an appropriate point for each student on a range from zero proficiency to native proficiency, keeping in mind that an English as a Second Language student can achieve "peer-appropriate second language conversational skills" in about 2 years, while needing 5 to 7 years to achieve parity with peers in second language academic skills. Because these chronological estimates cannot be applied to all students in all English as a Second Language classes, the TEPL authors wisely state its results in levels named with letters rather than numbers. This avoids confusion with chronologically determined levels of instruction.

Further, the TEPL does measure knowledge "about the language," and the measured concept of placement also includes a "dynamic continuum of different but interacting skills." This careful thinking about purpose makes an important contribution to the usefulness of the TEPL.

Content validity of the instrument is self-evident to the experienced instructor. That determination is supported by the use of well-known measures of readability in preparing the TEPL and by comparisons with other tests. Similarly, additional confidence in the TEPL is provided by association with well-known English as a Second Language practitioners and by publication by a firm known for excellence in the ESL field.

The TEPL is not norm referenced. It is intended to estimate placement level for one student, not to measure the achievement of large groups. However, the test's structure and reading sections have been used in an attempt to estimate reliability. Further efforts to establish validity are now under way. Their results would certainly be valuable additions to future editions of the manual. It would also be well to determine interscorer reliability on a reasonably large sample of scorers and students. Showing such reliability could be demonstrated would further enhance the confidence of prospective users.

The manual is made all the more complete by including recommendations of a range of useful teaching materials and resources. It is not useful to compare this test to others, because none of the other well-known tests for English as a Second Language specifically measure placement level as defined by the TEPL manual.

The TEPL was published in 1985 after years of experimentation. This reviewer applauds the ongoing efforts to provide new information on reliability and validity while recommending the test for widespread use in making English as a Second Language placement decisions.

Review of the Test of English Proficiency Level by MAURICE TATSUOKA, Professor Emeritus of Psychology, University of Illinois at Urbana-Champaign, Champaign, IL:

This test purports to measure what the author characterizes as a full range of language skills, consisting of oral proficiency, the ability to identify correct structures in sentences, reading comprehension, and the ability to communicate in written English. The oral part, which must be administered on a one-on-one basis, is said to take between 5 and 20 minutes (depending on how far the examinee can progress), while the three written subtests, which may be administered to a group, take 60 minutes. The test is intended for limited-English-proficient students in secondary and adult programs designed to teach English as a second language. Its results are given not in numerical scores but by classifying examinees in one of seven instructional levels in each of the four skill areas, for the purpose of placing each student in what is judged to be the appropriate level in the program.

The oral section consists of five sets of six questions each, arranged in increasing order of difficulty. Nineteen of the questions refer to a series of pictures labeled A through S, and the remaining 11 are general ones, such as "Do you like to go to the movies?" and "Is it raining today?". In order to earn credit for their answers, examinees must answer in complete sentences that contain certain key clauses specified in the manual.

The written section contains five open-ended questions that require writing sentences or paragraphs about specified topics, interspersed among 88 multiple-choice questions embedded in 11 passages that alternately test for structure-identification and reading comprehension. (Actually, the passages in which the questions dealing with structure-identification occur are not single-theme narratives but sets of six sentences each.)

Besides the tests, the manual includes a list of "suggested materials for each of the four skills and at each of the seven levels," and a separate list of teacher resources intended to help teachers both in testing and instruction in English as a Second Language programs at the secondary or adult level.

At the end of the manual there is a set of answer and scoring sheets, including ruled boxes for the examinee to write answers to four of the five open-ended writing questions. (The fifth and last writing question is, for some reason, to be answered on a separate sheet.) The answer sheets for all but the oral and written questions include both hand-scorable and machine-scorable types.

For overall clarity of instructions, completeness, and "face validity" of the questions, this reviewer gives the Test of English Proficiency Level (TEPL) fairly high scores. As for "completeness," the manual even has a two-page section entitled "Questions and Answers About T.E.P.L.," presumably to allay some doubts a potential user of the test might entertain about it. However, some of the answers given are themselves questionable, as I shall indicate below. But first, to dwell a little longer on the positive aspects of the test: I believe, for one thing, that the gradation in difficulty of the questions—from easy to hard—is done quite effectively and smoothly. Also, even the easiest questions do not seem to insult the intelligence of the adolescent/adult examinees. The pictures for 19 of the oral questions are drawn quite expertly and attractively. In the written test, the reading-comprehension questions, in particular, are carefully constructed to be nontrivial, attention-holding, and informative of things and ways American for the immigrant examinee. Another positive—even remarkable—aspect of the test is that each page of the written test and of the answer sheets carries the statement, "Permission granted to reproduce for classroom use," alongside the copyright statement. One somehow wonders whether the publisher does not regret the overly generous stance of the author (who is the copyright holder) and the fact the manual and test booklet were not published separately—with permission "to reproduce for classroom use" granted for neither. (However, I do *not* suggest that this be done in future editions!)

Coming now to the negative aspects, by far the worst, in this reviewer's opinion, is the paucity of technical information given about the test. The $2^{1}/_{3}$ pages (pp. 30–32) devoted to this matter give the mean, median, standard deviation, standard error of measurement, and *a* reliability coefficient of the set of 88 items constituting the structure-identification and reading-comprehension parts of the written test, but *no* validity coefficient. (Even for the reliability coefficient—which, incidentally, is mis-typeset as "reliability factor"—it is not stated what *type* of coefficient it is: split-half, test-retest, KR-20, or what?) The table on page 32 giving "comparisons with [seven] other tests" is not accompanied by a description of just how these comparisons were derived. Data on means and percentile ranks are compared with TEPL classifications for three of the tests. For the other four tests (for which only the "corresponding levels" are given), one wonders whether they might not have been made by "intuitive Procrustes fitting."

In the two-page "Questions and Answers" section referred to above (pp. 34–35), it is claimed that "The structure and reading parts of T.E.P.L. have undergone a standardization process as a check on validity," but the meager data given on page 30 hardly constitute a standardization, much less a validation, of the test. It is stated several times in the manual that further data are "now being gathered" to provide more accurate statistical analyses, but it seems the 3 or 4 years that have elapsed since the test first appeared should have been sufficient to permit at least the addition of an appendix giving some validation data. Another self-serving answer is given to the question, "Is T.E.P.L. less reliable than norm-referenced tests?" (viz., "In terms of comparing scores with large-scale averages, yes; but that is not its function"). This sounds like gobbledygook to me.

A minor but nevertheless non-negligible irritation the manual caused me was that, at two places in the instructions for the oral test (pp. 50 and 52), "i.e." is used when "e.g." is clearly intended. This is a fairly common error even among sophisticated writers, but its commission in a manual of an English test sets a poor example, to say the least.

[92]
Test of Legible Handwriting.
Purpose: Assesses handwriting legibility.
Population: Ages 7.6–17.11.
Publication Date: 1989.
Acronym: TOLH.
Scores: 6 writing sample scores: Creative Essay, Biographical Sketch, Correspondence, Report, Previous Work Sample, Legibility Quotient.
Administration: Group.
Price Data, 1989: $39 per complete kit including examiner's manual (62 pages) and 50 profile/scoring forms; $21 per 50 profile/scoring forms; $20 per examiner's manual.
Time: 15(20) minutes per writing sample.
Authors: Stephen C. Larsen and Donald D. Hammill.
Publisher: PRO-ED, Inc.

Review of the Test of Legible Handwriting by GREGORY J. CIZEK, *Program Associate, American College Testing, Iowa City, IA:*

The authors of the Test of Legible Handwriting (TOLH) build a strong case for the need for handwriting assessment. They note that "of all school subjects, handwriting typically receives the least attention and generally is the most poorly taught." They also comment that "an individual's failure to learn to write legibly may adversely affect academic success and have implications for later occupational and social success."

However, despite the perceived importance of the skill, handwriting assessment apparently occurs infrequently. Further, the authors note that "at present, no norm-referenced, nationally standardized tests of handwriting are available that permit the valid and reliable assessment of a person's [handwriting] ability." It is suggested that one reason handwriting assessment and research into handwriting may be lagging is that instruments with demonstrated reliability and validity have been unavailable. The TOLH was put forth to address these critical needs in the area of handwriting assessment.

ADMINISTRATION AND SCORING. The TOLH is easily administered to students in grades 2 through 12. The authors recommend that examiners who administer the test have "formal training in assessment," a "basic understanding of testing statistics," and "specific information about educational evaluation." It is doubtful that such expertise is truly necessary to administer the TOLH, although it may be helpful. Those characteristics certainly should

be required of anyone interpreting the test results, as the authors note.

Administration of the TOLH is accomplished by obtaining a sample (or samples) of the student's handwriting. The sample can be an extant piece of writing or can be elicited through use of one of the two picture prompts provided. Clear directions are provided for use with the picture prompts. It should be noted that students are *not* informed they are being evaluated for handwriting legibility. Therefore, a "usual" handwriting sample is obtained, rather than one that reflects maximum performance. TOLH test results should be interpreted in this light.

Scoring of the TOLH is accomplished by matching the student's writing sample to one of three basic scoring protocols—one for right-slant or perpendicular cursive, one for left-slant cursive, and one for manuscript or modified manuscript handwriting. Within each of the three protocols are four graded writing guides. A raw score from 1 to 9 results from matching the student's writing sample as closely as possible to one of the guides. When matching writing samples to the guides, scorers are instructed to "rate the sample as holistically as possible" and to "disregard specific deficits such as spacing, letter formation, inconsistent slant, and so forth."

INTERPRETATION. Several scores can be obtained from the TOLH. The authors warn that "raw scores have no clinical, instructional, or diagnostic value." However, percentile ranks, standard scores, grade-equivalent scores, and a "legibility quotient" are provided, along with a list of descriptors from "very poor" to "very superior" corresponding to the range of standard scores. Appropriate guidelines for interpreting these scores are also given. Admirably, a section of the TOLH is also devoted to "Cautions in Interpreting Test Scores" and information regarding sources of measurement error is provided.

NORMS. The TOLH was normed in 1987 using 1,723 students, ages 7 to 17, from 19 states. Information regarding how the sample was obtained is provided, as are demographic characteristics of the standardization sample. Overall, the sample appears to be highly appropriate and nationally representative.

RELIABILITY. The authors report several indices to describe the reliability of scores on the

TOLH. The average index of internal consistency (coefficient Alpha) across four age ranges is reported to be .86. An average test-retest correlation of .90 is also reported. An adjusted test-retest correlation to isolate the temporal stability of the TOLH is reported as .97.

Perhaps the most important aspect of reliability is the extent to which a student's writing sample receives consistent scores across raters. To investigate this, two trained raters each scored 70 writing samples and obtained an interrater reliability coefficient of .95.

All of the reliability evidence presented regarding the TOLH appears impressive. Users of the TOLH should be cautioned, however, about being overly impressed by the high reliability indices. The manual for the TOLH errs in not providing the detailed training procedures required for a user to actually obtain the reported degree of reliability. For example, it is recommended that users of the TOLH "become thoroughly familiar with the contents of [the] test manual" and "practice scoring the sample stories." These instructions seem inadequate.

Also conspicuously absent is strong advice to the user to gather multiple writing samples and to consider having multiple raters assign scores to a writing sample. It has long been known that implementing these procedures can greatly reduce error variance associated with ratings of handwriting (Feldt, 1962). Such an omission is surprising in light of the fact that the TOLH allows for the various scores reported to be based on the combination of scores from as many as five writing samples.

VALIDITY. The manual for the TOLH includes a somewhat weak attempt to define the construct of "legible handwriting." However, the rather circular definition provided may be about as good as construct definition gets in the area of handwriting; it has often been noted by researchers in the area that "the term [legibility] resists precise definition" (Graham, 1986, p. 64).

Several kinds of validity evidence are provided for the TOLH. The authors' claims regarding the content validity of the TOLH are moderately supported. It is noted that factors affecting legibility were incorporated into the scoring guides. However, the use of nonstructured responses to picture prompts means that critical elements of legibility (e.g., letter formation) may not be sampled.

Some evidence for construct validity is also reported. It is reported that mean scores on the TOLH across grade levels differed significantly, supporting the notion that handwriting skill generally increases with age. Comparison of TOLH scores with scores on the Test of Written Language—2 (TOWL-2) by Hammill and Larsen (1988) showed small correlations with other written language skills such as spelling and style. Finally, a group of 30 students with poor handwriting as judged by their teachers were administered the TOLH. Their mean score on the TOLH was significantly below average. Similar analyses for samples with average and superior handwriting are not reported.

Moderate evidence is offered to substantiate a claim of high criterion-related validity. The coefficient of .92 was obtained by correlating the ratings (1 to 5) of experienced teachers for 30 student handwriting samples with TOLH scores (1 to 9) for the same samples. It is somewhat unsurprising that the two similar measures correlated highly. Perhaps, for subsequent versions of the TOLH, expanded research into its criterion-related validity will be reported.

OTHER FEATURES. The TOLH contains several very helpful features. As previously mentioned, an Appendix to the TOLH manual contains several writing samples for test administrators' practice use. Another excellent characteristic is an entire chapter of the manual devoted to assessing and remediating handwriting problems. The authors are to be commended for recognizing the important link between assessment and instruction.

Finally, although the TOLH is touted as "an ecological approach to holistic [handwriting] assessment," the authors recognize the importance of identifying specific handwriting deficiencies. A diagnostic scoring form is provided for use with student writing samples elicited using the TOLH picture prompts. The diagnostic form allows the user to assess the formation of individual letters, alignment, spacing, slant, letter size, rate, and other characteristics. Results from this checklist can be translated into specific remediation strategies.

SUMMARY. The TOLH is used to obtain and evaluate student handwriting samples for legibility. The test does not attempt to provide criterion-referenced information, that is, the level of handwriting considered to be perfect, worst, or acceptable. Instead, the TOLH provides norm-referenced information about a student's handwriting legibility. The instrument is extremely easy to administer, the scoring guides are straightforward, and the tables used to obtain derived scores are reasonably easy to use with some practice.

Norms for the TOLH appear to have been recently and rigorously developed. The reliability data provided indicate that the instrument is quite reliable, although the user should be cautioned that such high reliability indices will probably not be realized in less controlled situations. The manual for the TOLH fails to provide users with detailed training procedures necessary to obtain reliable scores.

The TOLH manual presents evidence for several aspects of validity. Although the validity evidence and research presented are only weak to moderate, the authors commendably inform the user about proper interpretations and uses of TOLH scores.

The TOLH should fill the need for a reliable, standardized, norm-referenced assessment of handwriting legibility. In addition to filling this need, it also provides a means of identifying specific handwriting deficiencies and, admirably, provides users with guidance for remediation.

REVIEWER'S REFERENCES

Feldt, L. S. (1962). The reliability of measures of handwriting quality. *Journal of Educational Psychology, 53,* 288-292.

Graham, S. (1986). A review of handwriting scales and factors that contribute to variability in handwriting scores. *Journal of School Psychology, 24,* 63-71.

Hammill, D. D., & Larsen, S. C. (1988). Test of Written Language—2. Austin, TX: PRO-ED, Inc.

Review of the Test of Legible Handwriting by STEVE GRAHAM, *Associate Professor of Special Education, University of Maryland, College Park, MD:*

The Test of Legible Handwriting (TOLH) was developed to measure the readability of children's and adolescents' handwriting, grades 2 through 12. According to the authors, this norm-referenced test can be used to identify students who have handwriting problems, to pinpoint students' specific strengths and weaknesses in penmanship, and to document students' progress in developing handwriting skills. The authors of the test also indicate that

it is a suitable tool for use in research involving penmanship.

The TOLH is administered individually by collecting between one and five handwriting samples from the target student. One sample is collected by asking the student to write a story in response to a picture (either a prehistoric or a futuristic space picture) contained in the accompanying test protocol. The other samples include a previous specimen of the student's handwriting taken from actual schoolwork, as well as a biographical sketch, a correspondence (e.g., personal or business letter), and a report taken under more controlled conditions.

Each of the obtained handwriting samples is scored by matching the student's specimen as closely as possible to a set of graded samples with scores ranging from 1 to 9. Three different sets of graded samples are available: one for manuscript writing, another for cursive writing that is either perpendicular or slanted to the right, and a final scale for cursive writing that slants left. Although the test developers do not provide a rationale for devising two separate scales for cursive writing, there is some evidence to suggest that reliability in handwriting assessment can be increased when the slant of students' handwriting is taken into consideration (Herrick & Erlebacher, 1963).

The raw scores obtained for each of the handwriting specimens are converted to standard scores and percentile ranks. If more than one handwriting specimen is collected, a legibility quotient ($M = 100$, $SD = 15$) is also computed. The authors should be commended for not including tables for grade- or age-equivalent scores as part of the test. They do, however, provide examiners with a formula for computing grade-equivalent scores, but they appropriately caution against their use.

In addition to the general measure of legibility obtained for the student's handwriting sample(s), the test protocol includes a section for completing an informal analysis of handwriting errors. Two checklists are provided, one for manuscript and one for cursive. Both checklists contain three sections: errors in the formation of individual letters, difficulties in spatial relationships (e.g., alignment, uniformity of slant, spacing, and so forth), and rate of writing. The inclusion of the "rate of writing" section is questionable, because the method used to collect student specimens is influenced not only by handwriting speed but by factors involved in planning the written product. A more appropriate assessment would involve measuring the speed at which a familiar selection is copied.

The TOLH was standardized on 1,723 students ranging in age from 7 to 17 years of age. Although the sample is similar to national norms on a number of variables such as sex, race, ethnicity, and residence, data on the normative sample are incompletely reported. For example, no information on the SES or handedness of the students in the normative sample is provided. The description of procedures for selecting students is also vague. One means of selecting students, for instance, involved asking previous purchasers of PRO-ED tests (PRO-ED, Inc. publishes the TOLH) to administer the TOLH to 20 or 30 children in their area.

The developers of the TOLH do not present a strong or convincing case regarding the reliability and validity of the instrument. Interscorer reliability of the test was established by having two members of the "PRO-ED research department" independently score the same 70 handwriting specimens. The obtained reliability coefficient was high (.95), but it is unlikely that normal users of the scale would obtain an equivalent level of reliability (see Graham, 1986; and Graham, Boyer-Schick, & Tippets, 1989 for evidence regarding this point). Similarly, the data the authors present to support the validity of the instrument are quite meager; only a few studies were reported and they typically involved small numbers of subjects or handwriting samples. The data that are presented provide little insight into what the test actually measures; for example, does it measure general legibility or does a single element such as letter formation or neatness primarily account for the variability in students' scores on the test?

It should also be noted the TOLH does not include samples of the least able and best possible handwriting. Moreover, a scale that measures only nine gross levels is probably not sufficiently precise to monitor gradual improvement; it is probably best used as a general gauge of handwriting competence. The authors, however, do provide valuable suggestions in the test manual concerning additional handwriting assessment and instruction. They further include

eight practice samples for examiners to score. Surprisingly, a suggested legibility score for each individual sample is not provided.

In summary, two noteworthy aspects of the TOLH include the inclusion of separate scoring scales for different types of writing and the emphasis on the collection of multiple samples of students' penmanship. Nonetheless, the TOLH appears to be best suited as a screening device for identifying students in need of instructional assistance. Even this recommendation must be tempered, though, because the reliability and validity of the instrument have yet to be adequately established.

REVIEWER'S REFERENCES

Herrick, V., & Erlebacher, A. (1963). The evaluation of legibility in handwriting. In V. Herrick (Ed.), *New horizons for research in handwriting* (pp. 207-236). Madison: University of Wisconsin Press.

Graham, S. (1986). A review of handwriting scales and factors that contribute to variability in handwriting scores. *Journal of School Psychology, 24,* 63-71.

Graham, S., Boyer-Shick, K., & Tippets, E. (1989). The validity of the handwriting scale from the Test of Written Language. *Journal of Educational Research, 82,* 166-171.

[93]

Test of Relational Concepts.

Purpose: "To identify deficits in the comprehension of relational concepts."

Population: Ages 3-0 to 7-11.

Publication Date: 1988.

Acronym: TRC.

Scores, 1: Concept Score.

Administration: Individual.

Price Data, 1989: $64 per complete kit including examiner's manual (31 pages), picture book (118 pages), and 50 record forms; $37 per picture book; $9 per 50 record forms; $21 per examiner's manual.

Time: (10–15) minutes.

Comments: Orally administered; examiner must have previous training in the administration and interpretation of individual measures.

Authors: Nellie K. Edmonston and Nancy Litchfield Thane.

Publisher: PRO-ED, Inc.

Review of the Test of Relational Concepts by ROGER D. CARLSON, Independent Consultant, Springfield, OR:

The Test of Relational Concepts (TRC) is based upon an unusually carefully developed research and theoretical base. The authors have documented the cognitive, developmental, and psycholinguistic bases for their decisions to include the domains tested by the items. An extensive bibliography of substantive research is included in the manual. The artistic work in the test book is quite well done, and characterizations are without ambiguity.

One thousand children from 3 to almost 8 years of age were used in the norming. Considerable effort was made to assure that the sample was demographically representative of various aspects of the U.S. population, namely regional, urban versus rural, occupational, racial, and sexual representativeness. The sample used for norming appears to represent quite closely those demographic characteristics of the U.S. In the norming study, the test was administered by volunteer professionals or supervised student clinicians. The examiner qualifications for the test call for any professional trained in the administration and interpretation of individual evaluation instruments. Given the quite specific nature of administration and the clearly discrete and unambiguous response choices available, it appears that restricting administration to only persons who have such training may be overly stringent.

Measures of test-retest reliability and internal consistency yielded quite respectable correlation coefficients. Breakdowns by ages also yield satisfactorily high coefficients with the lowest occurring at the higher age levels.

Empirical validity measures were used by relating results of the TRC to those obtained by the Peabody Picture Vocabulary Test—Revised, the Boehm Test of Basic Concepts (Form B), and teachers' ratings. Correlations of TRC results with each of those measures were .619, .866, and .450 respectively. (All correlations were significant at the .0001 level.) It is interesting that the authors note significant correlations with teacher judgments. One wonders whether more economical results might be gotten by teacher judgments; the test may be of most value where such judgments are not available or where the test is used in a corroborative fashion.

Perhaps the weakest aspect of the TRC is that it uses only one item to sample each domain of interest. Although a case could be made that if the child "has" the relational concept, then he/she would get all items of its type correct all of the time. Thus a single sampling from a domain represents the child's knowledge of the concept. Such argumentation does not take into account contextual and cultural familiarity and developmental progression of a given concept. A child may only gradually come to acquire a thoroughgoing knowledge of a given concept. Further, children may know the difference between their right and left hands, but not which of two objects placed before them is on their left. Likewise, a child may know that a hat is *on* one's head, but not that the book is *on* the table. By using only a sampling of one item from each domain, the authors seem to imply that cognition is an all-or-nothing logical phenomenon that takes place in a cultural vacuum. For these reasons, it would be of interest to see whether a longer form may have yielded different results in the pilot testing of the TRC.

Overall, the TRC has been developed in a way consistent with the highest standards of test development. Unusually painstaking work was undertaken in the theoretical and research literature reviews, and the results of that work were used in developing the test. A norming sample was used that would assure representativeness of the major demographic characteristics of the U.S. The only reservation about the TRC is item selection, which was not thoroughly discussed. Research comparing results of the TRC with more, and with more varied items measuring the specific relational concepts, is recommended.

Review of the Test of Relational Concepts by LENA R. GADDIS, Assistant Professor of Psychology, University of Southern Mississippi, Hattiesburg, MS:

The Test of Relational Concepts (TRC) is intended for use as a screening measure of the comprehension of concepts whose mastery is often considered imperative to the academic success of young children. It consists of 56 items, all of which are administered to every child. The stimulus book presents simple line drawings from which the child must select the alternative (via a pointing response) that matches the statement made by the examiner. Also contained in the stimulus book are the examiner's verbal directions, which make administration of the TRC quite simple. Likewise, scoring is accomplished easily.

NORMS. The standardization sample consisted of 1,000 children, 100 at each of 10 six-month age groups between the ages of 3-0 and 7-11. The sample closely resembles the U.S. population in the 1980 census report with regard to gender, geographic region, urban/rural residence, occupational categories, and ethnicity.

SCORES. The test yields both percentile ranks and standard scores ($m = 50$, $sd = 10$), which are not interchangeable because they were derived separately from the raw scores. The authors recommend that users consider a standard score of 40 or below be used to identify children in need of special assistance.

As is the case with many tests of a developmental nature, the TRC does not have adequate floor and ceiling at the extreme age levels (i.e., it is not possible to obtain scores 3 standard deviations above and below the mean, which would accommodate in excess of 99% of the population). For example, at the age level of 7.6–7.11, the range of possible standard scores is 1 to 62, meaning that an obtained *perfect* raw score would correspond to a standard score only slightly more than 1 standard deviation above the mean. This is not necessarily a weakness of the test in that it would be expected that many children over the age of 6 years may have indeed mastered the "basic" concepts covered by the test, but it is certainly worthy of discussion in the manual in order to guard against any possible misuse of the test. Frequently users will adopt the use of any test designated as a "screening" instrument to identify children for further assessment for possible services of either gifted programs or services appropriate for "at risk" children. The TRC would not be appropriate for either of these purposes, in that it would certainly fail to identify either young low-functioning or older high-functioning youngsters.

RELIABILITY. Test-retest reliability (1- to 4 4-week interval; $n = 196$) across the 10 age levels is good ($r = .95$). Adequate test-retest reliability was noted for each of the age levels of 3-0 to 6-11 (range = .80 to .96). However, the reliability coefficients for the two upper age levels are inadequate (range = .48 to .70). Internal consistency reliability estimates were adequate, with a reported KR-20 coefficient of .97 for the entire sample and coefficients ranging from .79 to .93 for the individual age levels.

VALIDITY. The authors went to great lengths to ensure the construction and design of the TRC were based on a thorough review of the relevant literature, which speaks to its content validity. Also, care was taken to control for extraneous factors (e.g., visual-perception, test and response format) so that the user can have confidence the TRC measures what it claims. Evidence provided to support the criterion validity of the TRC included significant correlations with the Peabody Picture Vocabulary Test—Revised ($n = 203$, $r = .62$) and the Boehm Test of Basic Concepts ($n = 144$, $r = .87$). Additionally, it was found to relate significantly with teachers' ratings of subjects' ($n = 489$) knowledge of the concepts encompassed by the TRC ($r = .45$). As acquisition of language comprehension, and hence concepts, is theorized to be developmental in nature, the finding that the mean scores get progressively higher with each successive age level is offered as support for construct validity of the TRC.

Although there is considerable evidence for validity of the TRC, many validation domains have not been sufficiently tapped or have gone untapped. For example, no studies regarding the predictive validity of the TRC are reported. This is of particular concern, considering the test is intended as a screening instrument. Related questions that remain unanswered include: (*a*) How adequately does it identify children who are truly deficient in the comprehension of concepts?; and (*b*) to what extent does it overidentify or underidentify such children? Also, once a child is identified as deficient by the test, where does the user proceed—should the examiner conduct a more extensive evaluation or are we to assume the items that comprise the scale can then be used to prepare an instructional plan for each individual child or to aid a teacher in planning his/her instruction for the entire class?

SUMMARY. The TRC is a screening measure of the comprehension of concepts. It possesses fair to good psychometric qualities. It has good content validity, an excellent standardization sample, and adequate reliability at all but the two upper age levels. There is evidence to support the concurrent validity of the TRC, but there is no evidence provided for predictive validity. The test is easily administered and scored and the manual is quite readable. Limitations of the manual include failure on the part of the authors to caution the consumer more strongly regarding the questionable reliability evident for the upper age groups and failure to discuss the inherent ceiling and floor effects, and possible related misuses of the TRC.

With the recent emphasis on early identification and intervention, it is not surprising there has been a deluge of preschool instrumentation emerging, a number of which tap the construct of basic concepts. Among all other similar measures, is the TRC the instrument of choice? Although the authors note the TRC includes items representative of a number of concepts (e.g., temporal, quantitative, dimensional, spatial), there is no evidence that these domains are sufficiently tapped and the TRC yields only a single score. In contrast, the Bracken Basic Concept Scale (BBCS; Bracken, 1984; 10:33) yields scores for seven categories in addition to the total score. Thus, the BBCS allows the user to better determine the pattern of individual strengths and weaknesses. Additionally, Bracken (1984) provides the user with guidelines for criterion-referenced interpretation, remediation, and developing Individualized Educational Plans. In conclusion, many consumers will find the BBCS more useful in planning remediation and performing program evaluation. However, with additional documentation of the predictive validity of the TRC, it should serve the user well (at the lower age ranges) as a screening device.

REVIEWER'S REFERENCE

Bracken, B. A. (1984). Bracken Basic Concept Scale. The Psychological Corporation: San Antonio, TX.

[94]
Tests of Adult Basic Education, Forms 5 and 6, and Survey Form.

Purpose: "Designed to measure achievement in reading, mathematics, language, and spelling."
Population: Adults in basic education programs.
Publication Dates: 1957–87.
Acronym: TABE.
Administration: Group.
Levels: 4 overlapping levels: E (Easy) (grades 2.6–4.9), M (Medium) (grades 4.6–6.9), D (Difficult) (grades 6.6–8.9), A (Advanced) (grades 8.6–12.9).
Forms, 3: Survey Form, Complete Battery (Form 5), Complete Battery (Form 6).
Price Data, 1988: $18.75 per 25 Practice Exercise and Locator Test test books; $9.35 per 25 Practice Exercise and Locator Test SCOREZE answer sheets; $9.50 per 50 Practice Exercise and Locator Test hand-scorable answer sheets; $9.50 per 50 Practice Exercise and Locator Test answer sheets for SCANTRON stand-alone scanner; $9.50 per 50

Practice Exercise and Locator Test answer sheets for SCANTRON computer-linked scanner; $7.75 per Practice Exercise and Locator Test hand-scoring stencil; $6 per Norms Book ('87, 146 pages); $8.50 per Test Coordinator's Handbook ('87, 59 pages); $8.50 per Technical Report ('87, 60 pages); $12 per Multi-Level Test Review Kit (specimen set) including Test Reviewer's Guide, descriptive brochure, Examination Materials booklet, Practice Exercise and Locator Test, Practice Exercise and Locator Test answer sheets, 1 test book of the Survey Form and for each level of the Complete Battery (Form 5), Complete Battery Examiner's Manual with answer key (for all levels), Survey Form Examiner's Manual with answer key (for all levels), Complete Battery hand-scorable answer sheet, SCANTRON answer sheets, Norms Book, and Group Record Sheet.
Time: 20(25) minutes for the Practice Exercise and Locator Test.
Comments: Locator tests included to determine appropriate level of either test form to be administered; optional practice test also included; Apple and IBM software available to aid scoring.
Author: CTB/McGraw-Hill.
Publisher: CTB/McGraw-Hill.

a) SURVEY FORM.
Purpose: Shortened version of Form 5 to be used for screening purposes.
Publication Date: 1987.
Scores, 3: Total Reading, Total Mathematics, Total Language.
Price Data: $34 per 25 test books including Examiner's Manual with answer key (specify Level E, M, D, or A); $12 per 25 SCOREZE answer sheets (specify level); $9.50 per 50 hand-scorable answer sheets; $9.50 per 50 SCANTRON answer sheets (for computer-linked scanners); $9.50 per 50 SCANTRON answer sheets (for stand-alone scanners) (specify Reading and Mathematics or Language); $9.50 per 50 NCS answer sheets; $7.75 per hand-scoring stencil for use with hand-scorable answer sheet (specify level); $6 per Examiner's Manual with answer key (for use with Practice Exercise and Locator Test).
Time: 108(128) minutes.

b) COMPLETE BATTERY, FORMS 5 AND 6.
Publication Dates: 1957–87.
Scores, 11: Reading (Vocabulary, Comprehension, Total), Mathematics (Computation, Concepts and Applications, Total), Language (Mechanics, Expression, Total), Total Battery, Spelling.
Forms, 2: 5, 6 (parallel forms).
Price Data: $34 per 25 test books including Examiner's Manual with answer key (specify Level E, M, D, or A and Form 5 or 6); $12 per

25 SCOREZE answer sheets (specify Reading, Mathematics, or Language and Spelling and Level E, M, D, or A); $18 per 50 hand-scorable answer sheets; $9.50 per 50 SCANTRON answer sheets for use with computer-linked scanners (specify Reading, Mathematics, or Language and Spelling); $9.50 per 50 SCANTRON answer sheets for use with stand-alone scanners (specify Reading, Mathematics, or Language and Spelling); $9.50 per 50 NCS answer sheets (specify Reading, Mathematics, or Language and Spelling); $23.25 per 3 hand-scoring stencils (specify Level E, M, D, or A); $5.30 per 25 Individual Diagnostic Profile/Analysis of Learning Difficulties (specify Level E, M, D, or A); $.80 per Complete Battery Group Record Sheet; $6 per Examiner's Manual with answer key; $9.50 per Large-Print Edition Locator Test test book; $20 per Large-Print Edition test book (specify Level E, M, D, or A); $5.60 per 10 Large-Print Edition hand-scorable answer sheets; $5.60 per 10 Large-Print Edition Locator Test answer sheets.

Special Edition: Large-Print Edition available for Form 5.

Time: 203(223) minutes.

Cross References: For reviews by Thomas F. Donlon and Norman E. Gronlund of an earlier edition, see 8:33 (1 reference); for a review by A. N. Hieronymus and an excerpted review by S. Alan Cohen of an earlier edition, see 7:32.

TEST REFERENCES

1. Stewart, W. W., Davis, P. D., Wilson, R. C., & Porter, T. (1981). Expressed versus tested vocational interests of incarcerated and non-incarcerated adolescents. *Journal of Applied Rehabilitation Counseling, 12,* 126-129.
2. Kender, J. P., Greenwood, S., & Conard, E. (1985). WAIS-R performance patterns of 565 incarcerated adults characterized as underachieving readers and adequate readers. *Journal of Learning Disabilities, 18,* 379-383.

Review of the Tests of Adult Basic Education, Forms 5 and 6, and Survey Form by ROBERT W. LISSITZ, Professor of Education and Psychology and Chairperson, Department of Measurement, Statistics, and Evaluation, University of Maryland, College Park, MD:

The Tests of Adult Basic Education (TABE) examination is designed to assess achievement in Reading, Mathematics, Language, and Spelling. Equivalent Forms 5 and 6 are intended to provide norm-referenced scores as well as criterion-referenced scores for basic skills. The test is organized in four separate levels—Easy, Medium, Difficult, and Advanced. The level of the test to be administered is determined by a Locator Test consisting of 25 mathematics items and 25 vocabulary items. There is also a

Survey Form that is a shortened version of the TABE 5 and has items from all areas except Spelling. Its purpose is to provide, with less time investment, benchmark scores for Reading, Mathematics, and Language. It also uses the Locator Test, which takes 37 minutes. Combined with Reading (22 minutes), Mathematics (28 minutes), and Language (21 minutes), the Survey Form still takes 1 hour and 48 minutes, plus time for whatever practice exercises or orientation is allocated to the assessment. If a school is looking for a quick test to use for students to get a general evaluation, this is probably not going to be satisfactory.

There are numerous booklets available, including one for norms, a technical manual, a coordinator's manual, an examiner's manual for the Survey Form, and another for Forms 5 and 6. Along with sample copies of the tests, there are inches of material to read. Fortunately, the material is well written and attractively presented. The test and supporting documents were professionally done and clearly will be a competitive product in the marketplace.

The test was developed by examining current curriculum guides, textbooks, and instructional programs obtained from adult education programs throughout the country (Technical Manual, p. 5). The material was used to identify a common set of basic skills, and items were written by professionals, many of whom were experienced teachers. A "Tryout Edition" was reviewed for content, instructions, and time limits. The process for development also included extensive review for potential bias against Blacks, Hispanics, and Asians. No information is given about the Hispanic and Asian samples.

The development process is the sole basis for validity of the tests. Content validity is the only type of validity justification. Because the user is encouraged to test for diagnostic purposes and the test is likely to be used for admissions and classification decisions as well, some criterion-validity evidence should supplement the curriculum analysis as supporting evidence. The test also emphasizes its potential usage with a wide variety of educational environments (adult offenders, juvenile offenders, and vocational/technical school enrollees), but no justification, even content validity, is included for these.

The TABE subtests were correlated with the subtests of the Tests of General Educational

Development (GED) and the set of coefficients is interesting to examine. They provide a multimethod, multitrait matrix, but unfortunately no discussion of differential validity is provided. Further, the GED is either passed or not passed, and the predictability of this overall decision, using the TABE, would be a nice addition to the manual.

All test analyses utilized the 3-parameter IRT model and LOGIST-5 computer program (from Educational Testing Service). The information function is calculated and the conditional Standard Error of Measurement (SEM) is presented as a function of the scale score. This is quite important, particularly because the SEM curves are presented for each of the four levels of test difficulty. In many of the cases the Advanced and Difficult forms do not differ in their SEM curves as much as we might expect or might hope. In these cases, they are interchangeable test forms, as far as accuracy of estimation is considered. Another concern with the reliability of the test is that only internal consistency is estimated (using KR20). Additional evidence, such as test-retest and parallel form reliabilities, would be helpful to users of the test. In fact, no discussion of the equivalence of Forms 5 and 6 was found in the material submitted for review.

There is some useful information from an equating study of Form 5 and Form 3 (from 1976). Scale score to scale score conversion tables are available, according to the technical manual. The California Achievement Tests (CAT E) provided a set of anchor items for use in the equating study, and these permit an additional conversion table for the TABE 5 and 6 to the CAT E and F. These test conversion tables, and the work relating the TABE to the GED, are potentially very helpful. For a technical manual, however, there is not much detail on any of these additions.

One of the more interesting tables in the Technical Manual (p. 35, also in the section on equating and norming) shows that 49% of the norming sample were in the 15-to-24-year age group and an additional 31% were in the 25-to-34-year age range. This is a very young adult group and it is not clear to the reviewer why there were any persons under age 18 in the norms sample at all, given the name of the test (Tests of *Adult* Basic Education). It was also surprising that almost 71% of the norming

sample were males (5,731 out of 8,125). One of the nice features of the test is the availability of norms for adult offenders, juvenile offenders, and vocational/technical school enrollees.

Another strong feature of the TABE is the use of the Locator Test, although it would be more defensible if additional information was provided. For example, this reviewer would like to see a description of the process used in deciding to have only mathematics and vocabulary items in the Locator, and to see how the cutoffs are justified for referral to each of the four levels. Evidence of the effect of the referral test upon the efficiency of the testing process would also be useful. Additional validation work is needed to justify the Locator process as well.

The material on test reports for the teacher and/or student is also not as convincing as I would have liked. For example, the design of the reports would be more user friendly with pictorial representations of the SEM as a band on the latent ability rather than a numerical presentation.

In summary, the TABE, Forms 5 and 6, and the Survey Form are well-done instruments with considerable justification for their use. The supporting material is nicely done, although the technical manual would benefit from considerable expansion, particularly with additional work on reliability and validity.

Review of the Tests of Adult Basic Education, Forms 5 and 6, and Survey Form by STEVEN J. OSTERLIND, Associate Professor and Director, Center for Educational Assessment, University of Missouri-Columbia, Columbia, MO:

The Tests of Adult Basic Education (TABE) examination, Forms 5 and 6, is a completely rewritten version of the popularly used earlier TABE forms. Virtually every aspect of test construction was done anew for the TABE, Forms 5 and 6: The content was reorganized after a thorough review of relevant curricular materials, all of the test's items were freshly prepared, an entirely new standardization process was undertaken, a Locator test was added, the test's reports were redesigned, and most of the ancillary materials were rewritten. Also, a microcomputer software package for scoring answer sheets, looking up norms, and calculating objectives mastery information is available for the first time.

The publisher's claims for the information yielded by this new assessment instrument are manifold. According to CTB/McGraw-Hill, the TABE, Forms 5 and 6, can (a) predict the probability of passing the Tests of General Educational Development (GED); (b) provide objective-referenced curriculum scores; (c) produce norm-referenced scores (to four specific adult populations); and (d) can be equated to earlier TABE Forms 3 and 4. Further, throughout the promotional brochures and administration materials, the publisher boasts of technical rigor, citing claims of "reliability" again and again. We shall examine the merit of these claims later in this review.

Several features are added to the TABE, Forms 5 and 6, that make it attractive to users. In particular, the Practice Exercise, the various scoring options, the microcomputer-based system for interpreting results, and the reports are all appealing features of this instrument. The Practice Exercise is a brief and useful activity intended to acquaint examinees with the format for test items they will confront on the test. The score reports—of which there are two, an individual report (that may be obtained with or without objectives performance) and a summary report—are pleasing and will likely prove easily read by test users. The scoring options are especially alluring. Either a convenient SCO-REZE answer sheet or a scannable form may be used. The administrator must then access the TABE Norms System through a microcomputer, or the same information can be gotten through a series of lookup tables. The Locator Test will probably be useful to test administrators, despite the shortcoming of having only vocabulary and mathematics items included.

Two ancillary publications, the Test Coordinator's Handbook and the Examiner's Manual, are especially helpful. CTB/McGraw-Hill's success in using parallel materials in other achievement tests has proven to the TABE's benefit. They are easily read, attractively formatted, and very informative to workaday practitioners.

All of these features are clear pluses for a testing system that is obviously trying to be "user friendly."

When one looks beyond these superficial aspects of the test, however, and into the merits for valid interpretations of the numbers yielded by this instrument, serious concerns arise. For example, little technical information is offered about such important aspects of test construction as scaling, norming, score comparability, and equating. Yet, claims to each of these aspects are made in the promotional literature. For example, the Technical Report provides scant data about the validity of the score interpretations recommended. This is too serious an omission to call it an oversight. Weak Pearson correlation coefficients to GED scores are about all that is presented for external-related validity evidence. Nothing at all is mentioned about data gathered for supporting diagnostic uses of the test.

Only cursory information about the norming sample is provided, but this is obviously one of the areas of greatest interest to test users. A table cites their numbers but no information is provided about the relevant characteristics of this sample. The same criticism is true for the equating study cited. The reader is left to wonder what happened. The materials say a study was conducted, but it is not described and the results are not presented for inspection.

As another example, information about standard errors of the various subtests is not provided in any meaningful way. Beyond printing in the Technical Report IRT standard error curves (without accompanying explanation and without mentioning their relevance to score interpretation for test users), one is left uninformed about this important aspect of mental measurements.

The issue of test bias is important, both in fact and in perception about a test. Here, the test's developers seem to have invested more energy in explaining the procedures used than in some other equally important areas.

In summary, while there are appealing aspects of the ease of use of the TABE, Forms 5 and 6, it appears CTB/McGraw-Hill did not follow the precepts put forth in the Standards for Educational and Psychological Testing (AERA, APA, & NCME, 1985) to a disturbing degree, especially as it concerns that most-important-of-all-test-development concerns: valid interpretations of the scores. This leads one to recommend that if the TABE, Forms 5 and 6, is adopted for use, it should be done so by users who are aware that much about the psychometric underpinnings of this test is unexplained.

REVIEWER'S REFERENCE
American Educational Research Association, American Psychological Association, & National Council on Measurement in Education. (1985). *Standards for educational and psychological testing*. Washington, DC: American Psychological Association, Inc.

[95]
Tests of Reading Comprehension.
Purpose: "They aim at assessing the extent to which readers are able to obtain meaning from text."
Population: Grades 3–7, 6–10.
Publication Date: 1987.
Acronym: TORCH.
Scores, 14: Grasshoppers; The Bear Who Liked Hugging People; Lizards Love Eggs; Getting Better; Feeding Puff; Shocking Things; Earthquakes!; The Swamp-creature; The Cats; A Horse of Her Own; Iceberg Towing; The Accident; The Killer Smog of London; I Want to be Andy; The Red Ace of Spades.
Administration: Individual or group.
Levels: 2 overlapping test booklets: A, B.
Price Data, 1988: A$50 per complete kit including test booklet A, test booklet B, 16 answer sheets, set of photocopy master sheets, and manual (84 pages).
Time: Untimed.
Comments: "Content-referenced" and/or "norm-referenced."
Authors: Leila Mossenson, Peter Hill, and Geoffrey Masters.
Publisher: Australian Council for Educational Research, Ltd. [Australia].

Review of the Tests of Reading Comprehension by ROBERT B. COOTER, JR., Associate Professor of Elementary Education, Brigham Young University, Provo, UT:

The Tests of Reading Comprehension (TORCH) are a set of 14 group-administered reading tests for use with students in Years (grades) 3 to 10. The TORCH is untimed and provides both norm-referenced and "content-referenced" information for classroom use. Each testing package contains an Examiner's Manual, Test Booklets A and B, consumable TORCH Answer Sheets, and a very helpful set of Photocopy Masters of the TORCH Answer Sheets.

The TORCH passages were selected from published materials and reflect a wide variety of fiction and nonfiction literature. Test Booklet A is intended for Years (grades) 3 to 7, and Test Booklet B is for Years 6 to 10. Students are instructed to read each passage of text, then complete a retelling of the passage. The retelling is very much like a cloze passage with key words or ideas missing. Students fill in the gaps with one or more of their own words. The TORCH authors feel that this process allows readers to produce their own reconstruction of the author's intended meaning, and acts as a probe causing them to consider particular details in the text.

Scoring on the TORCH is done much more holistically than with most reading assessment instruments. Score keys are presented in the examiner's manual that suggest several appropriate responses for each blank in the retelling, as well as responses judged to be unacceptable. If the student offers a response not included in the key, examiners are instructed to judge the semantic similarity of the student's answer to responses on the list. Although this scoring process may take considerably longer, the results should be much more valid and offer useful classroom implications.

Another appealing aspect of the TORCH is the availability of what the authors refer to as "content-referenced" interpretations. By analyzing the 302 items from all 14 subtests the authors were able to identify 11 distinct kinds of comprehension tasks (e.g., Provide subject of story, Infer emotion, Reconstruct the writer's general message). By applying student responses to a "TORCH Scale" included at the bottom of each answer sheet the examiner is able to easily deduce which comprehension tasks need attention.

The examiner's manual is very well written and offers many useful suggestions for administering and scoring the TORCH. Particularly helpful are the numerous figures and tables detailing such information as comparisons between student ability levels and test difficulty, sources for reading passages, case study examples illustrating how to use the scoring keys, and reading comprehension tasks rated according to a scale of increasing difficulty. Examiners should find it relatively easy to familiarize themselves with the materials and procedures after a careful reading of the Manual.

TECHNICAL CONSIDERATIONS. The TORCH was developed in 1982 by staff of the Western Australian Education Department. As mentioned above, all passages were selected from published materials. The authors especially wanted to avoid what they termed "stilted prose," that which has limited content and carefully controlled vocabulary. A balance was maintained between questions of a literal and inferential nature.

Standardization of the TORCH was carried out in 1982 and 1984 in Western Australian Government schools. The TORCH performance scale, which runs from near zero to about 100, was developed through a calibration and equation process using Rasch measurement methods. This allows for the direct comparison of ability estimates of children who have taken different tests and allows for the selection of tests that are appropriate to the reading levels of individual children. Full details of the calibration and equating of the TORCH tests in Western Australia are offered in the Manual.

Reliability estimates for the TORCH, indicating the extent to which the test offers consistent results, seem to be quite satisfactory. The Kuder-Richardson (KR-20) procedure was employed and provides some indication of the internal consistency of the test items. Reliability coefficients range from .90 to .93 for the various passages. Generally a subtest reliability coefficient of .75 is considered acceptable, so the TORCH figures are very adequate.

Validity is generally considered to be an estimate of how well a test measures the skill or ability it is intended to measure. Two types of validity often considered by test makers are content (or curricular) validity and construct validity. The TORCH authors have failed to provide any direct evidence of either. However, they have not left the issue entirely unattended. Care has been taken in the construction of the TORCH to identify 11 specific comprehension abilities assessed on the 14 passages through a kind of factor analysis procedure. Thus, educators can review the list and compare these abilities to the school curriculum. To the extent that the test has identified abilities of interest to local personnel, it may be considered either valid or invalid. No evidence concerning construct validity is provided in the TORCH manual. In summary, one must conclude that very little evidence of validity has been offered by the authors.

Finally, the authors have included a very thorough appendix that provides other technical benefits. Perhaps the most notable is a listing of the 11 comprehension tasks identified through factor analysis and a key that matches each ability to test item examples. The difficulty level for each ability has been computed along with text and exercise sample items. This allows examiners not only to review a definition of the ability, but also to see a concrete example of each. Correlation of comprehension skills on the test to the school curriculum is made much easier with this very functional appendix.

SUMMARY AND CONCLUSIONS. The Tests of Reading Comprehension (TORCH) represent a step forward in the literacy assessment field. It appears that the primary advantages of the TORCH have to do with reliability, holistic scoring, and classroom applicability. First, there is little question that the TORCH is a reliable instrument when used with students in Western Australia. The normative work was completed with a reasonable degree of rigor and should provide data of some use to school administrators. In addition, the manual indicates that educators in other school systems may develop their own local norms by following a procedure described by Chew and others (1984). Development of local norms is an important step in the overall improvement of literacy assessment. Second, and probably the most important aspect of the TORCH, is its use of more holistic scoring procedures. Allowing examiners to evaluate each response qualitatively moves comprehension assessment closer to the source, namely students' thought processes. Understanding what they do and do not understand has direct implications for classroom intervention. Third, performance on the TORCH may be applied to classroom instruction in at least two ways: (a) through the qualitative analysis of test item responses (as mentioned above), and (b) through the correlation of test performance to specific reading comprehension tasks using the TORCH Scale. This second procedure permits the identification of specific strengths and deficits in reading comprehension that may be most helpful in curricular decision making.

As with all assessment instruments, the TORCH has several limitations. One concern has to do with the identification of the 11 comprehension tasks assessed by the TORCH. It seems that the test was developed first and that identification of the comprehension abilities assessed followed. This would appear to be backwards. For an assessment instrument to be truly valid one should first identify the belief system or philosophy of reading subscribed to by the school system, generate a list of competencies to be measured that are consistent with that belief system, and finally, develop test items keyed to each competency. In that way the test is driven by the curriculum and not the other way around. The TORCH is not driven by a well-defined belief system, but seems to be driven by itself. A common classroom result in this scenario is teachers teaching to the test rather than having the test serve as an independent measure of student growth.

Another problem with the TORCH is that the format of the test (modified cloze) assumes that the child is capable of working independently, is capable of writing well enough to be understood, and possesses sufficient inferential comprehension skills to guess missing words in mutilated sentences. Certainly the cloze format works well with many students, but not with all. Thus, if a student fails to perform well on the TORCH, one should not conclude that s/he has poor comprehension ability without further investigation using other assessment techniques.

The Tests of Reading Comprehension (TORCH) are an interesting new addition to the arsenal of commercial reading measures presently available. Perhaps as school systems, reading specialists, and researchers experiment with potential uses of the TORCH we will learn of its true significance as part of a comprehensive assessment program. At present it appears that its greatest contribution is the insight it offers into more qualitative forms of cognitive-process assessment.

REVIEWER'S REFERENCE

Chew, A. L., Kesler, E. B., & Sudduth, D. H. (1984). A practical example of how to establish local norms. *The Reading Teacher, 38*, 160-163.

Review of the Tests of Reading Comprehension by DIANE J. SAWYER, Director, Consultation Center for Reading, Syracuse University, Syracuse, NY:

The Tests of Reading Comprehension (TORCH) was developed to assess comprehension competence by engaging students in completing a printed retelling of a passage read. Students fill in blanks (similar to the Cloze procedure). Eleven different kinds of tasks tap comprehension processes. Blanks associated with each of these tasks are presented for each passage. These tasks include: provide story subject given multiple references, verbatim recall of parts of sentences, completion of simple rewordings of text, completion of paraphrases, connecting pronouns with referent, connecting ideas separated in text, giving details in the presence of distracting ideas, giving details in the presence of competing answers, giving evidence of understanding motive underlying actions, reconstructing the writer's general message from specific statements, inferring emotion from scattered clues, and writer's tone.

A student is asked to read just one passage and to complete the retelling of that passage in one untimed sitting. Passages in each booklet are ordered according to difficulty and range in length from 200 to 900 words. Each is an excerpt from a longer passage but can stand alone as a short story or descriptive article in its own right. For each student, the teacher/administrator is to select a passage whose difficulty is closely aligned with the student's reading competence. All children in a given class or at a given grade level need not read the same passage. Analysis of the items missed on the retelling allows the teacher to identify the kinds of comprehension tasks the student can accomplish and provides direction for focusing instruction on those tasks next in need of development. Adequate guidance for interpreting responses into a list of instructional needs is provided in the manual.

In addition to diagnostic information, some normative data are also available. The norming population was drawn from schools in Western Australia. Eight passages were used with the norming sample (over 6,000 students in grades 3–10). Norms for the remaining six passages appear to have been estimated based upon scores obtained from an earlier administration in Western Australia. National Australian norms were derived statistically through a procedure (Rasch calibration and common item-linking procedures) that linked student scores on a TORCH passage to the same student's score on the Progressive Achievement Tests in Reading. Raw scores on any passage are converted to a standard score (TORCH score) that may be compared to the normal curve. For example, a TORCH score of 45 is associated with the 85th percentile rank among third graders, the 47th percentile for fifth graders, and the 15th percentile for seventh graders. The authors do caution users that differences in the student population served, as well as in the time of the year when testing takes place, makes it advisable for schools to establish their own norms. This reviewer would add the caution that differences in the reading curricula between Australia and the United States/Canada is an equally strong reason for developing local norms to assist in interpreting TORCH performance, if comparisons are deemed important.

Reliability of the TORCH is reported in terms of Kuder-Richardson reliability coefficients calculated for only the eight passage retellings used in the norming study. These range between .90 and .93 and suggest a strong degree of internal consistency for those passages. No comment regarding reliability for the remaining six passages is offered. These reliability coefficients were also used to compute the standard error of measurement (*SEM*) for each of the 14 retellings. These range from 3 raw-score points at the mid-range of scores to 7 raw-score points at the two extremes. The authors caution that very high or very low scores are probably not valid indicators of a child's reading competence. In cases of extreme scores teachers are urged to discuss the retelling with the child and to consider another administration of an easier or harder passage.

The authors state that since content validity must be established largely on the basis of subjective examination of the test's content in relation to accepted curricula, "the best approach is for the teacher to work systematically through the items of each test, to evaluate the appropriateness of the content for a class, and to test the extent to which the test and the objectives match the teacher's set of objectives."

TORCH appears to be an excellent attempt to shift the focus of comprehension assessment from product to process; from a concern for discrete skills to a concern for strategies engaged. However, in its current form TORCH is best thought of as an informal assessment, dependent upon significant levels of teacher expertise to select an appropriate passage for a given child and to interpret performance. For example, in a figure comparing student ability with test difficulty (Figure 1, p. 3, TORCH manual) it appears that a given third grader might be assigned any one of the first four passages in Booklet A since item difficulty for each ranges well below third grade level. However, some passage 1 items appear to be challenging for most fourth graders, but difficult passage 2 items might not be sufficiently challenging for very able third graders. Further, passage 3 appears to have many more easy items than either of the first two passages, yet some items would be challenging for most fifth graders. It seems reasonable to expect that teachers might have to use these passages several times in order to gain sufficient insight into their unique demands before efficient assignment of students to passages might be achieved.

Further, reliability appears to be only partially specified for the test passages and the question of validity has been left to the judgement of the user. Under these circumstances, potential users are cautioned to consider TORCH an instrument still in the process of becoming a useful tool. How useful it may one day be is essentially dependent upon the skills and energies of the user.

Finally, the normative data reflect only the performance of the children of Western Australia on Australian reading curricula. It would seem imprudent to compare the TORCH performance of children in the United States or Canada to that of the norming group.

[96]
Time Perception Inventory.

Purpose: Measures perceptions of time use including degree of personal concern about time usage and frame of reference (past, present, future) used.

Population: Students in time management courses.

Publication Dates: 1976–87.

Scores, 4: Time Effectiveness, Orientation (Past, Present, Future).

Administration: Group.

Price Data, 1989: $25 per complete kit; $17.50 per 10 inventories including profile; $8.25 per manual ('87, 8 pages).

Time: Administration time not reported.

Comments: Manual has been revised; self-administered.

Author: Albert A. Canfield.

Publisher: Western Psychological Services.

Review of the Time Perception Inventory by DOUGLAS J. McRAE, Senior Evaluation Consultant, CTB, Ann Arbor, MI:

PURPOSE. The Time Perception Inventory (TPI) is designed to provide data on (*a*) the way in which individuals view their use of time and (*b*) the general time frame of reference (past, present, future) individuals use in thinking about the world.

DESCRIPTION. The TPI consists of two parts. Part 1 (Time Effectiveness) consists of 10 "How often do you . . ." questions, to which the examinee responds on a 4-point scale (*Rarely, Occasionally, Frequently, A Great Deal*). Each response for each question is weighted, and a total score is obtained by adding the weights assigned for each of the 10 responses. This total score may then be converted to a percentile score for interpretation. Part 2 (Orientation) consists of eight items designed to elicit an individual's tendency to think in the past, the present, or the future. Again, each response is weighted, and separate total scores are obtained for Past, Present, and Future scales by adding the weights assigned to each of the eight responses. The total scores may then be converted to percentiles for interpretation. The TPI is self-administered without time limits. It typically takes 10 minutes or less to complete.

RATIONALE. The TPI is most typically used in courses on time management. Scores on the Time Effectiveness component (Part 1) are designed to determine whether a person feels he/she has a problem managing time. Low scores on the Time Effectiveness component may be used to identify people who are susceptible to effective learning of time management skills. Scores on the Orientation component (Part 2) may be used as a self-analysis that may be related back to specific job assignments. The suggestion is made that a balanced orientation profile (roughly equal emphasis on Past, Present, and Future) may be the most productive profile for business people.

TECHNICAL INFORMATION. The revised manual available to the reviewer contained a minimum of technical information. The manual indicated the percentile scores for all four scales were based on a sample of more than 2,000 primarily white, male, middle-class, middle-aged, middle-management students taking classes at a midwestern university's business school or attending time use seminars conducted by the author. No information was provided on the derivation of weights used to produce scores for the four scales, nor was reliability or validity information provided.

EVALUATION. The Time Perception Inventory is potentially useful as an instrument to elicit a self-examination about effective use of time and one's orientation regarding time. It may be used as a discussion starter in courses or seminars on effective time management. It does not have a thorough enough rationale or a sufficiently strong technical base to support inferences of potential effectiveness in job assignments or inferences for diverse populations of individuals. Therefore, its appeal as a guidance instrument is extremely limited. However, as a lead-in for discussion of time management, it may be an effective instrument.

[97]
Transit Operator Selection Inventory.
Purpose: "To identify those applicants who . . . have a high probability of success as bus drivers."
Population: Applicants for municipal and urban transit bus operators.
Publication Dates: 1979–84.
Acronym: TOSI.
Scores, 1: Probability of Successful Performance.
Administration: Group.
Price Data, 1988: $11 or less per booklet (minimum order 25) for mail-in scoring method (price includes booklets, scoring, and reports); $12 or less per booklet (minimum order 25) for telephone-scoring method (price includes booklets, scoring, and reports); $6.50 or less per booklet (minimum order 250) for PC-based scoring systems (available with or without data collection for analysis, price includes booklets and software diskettes for IBM-PCs and compatibles); $7.50 per booklet (1,000 minimum) for PC-based scoring system including booklets, software diskettes, and leased IBM-compatible PC.
Time: (60) minutes.
Comments: All first-time users must submit a job analysis questionnaire entitled Skills and Attributes Inventory (SAI) to demonstrate their bus operator job is similar to those for which the test battery was validated.
Author: Melany E. Baehr.
Publisher: London House, Inc.

Review of the Transit Operator Selection Inventory by LAWRENCE M. RUDNER, Director of the Educational Resources Information Center Clearinghouse on Tests, Measurement and Evaluation (ERIC/TME), American Institutes for Research, Washington, DC and Director of Research, LMP Associates, Chevy Chase, MD:

Virtually every urban area is faced with the problem of selecting transit operators. Poor selection can result in hiring individuals prone to having accidents, using sick leave, being absent, abusing drugs, and receiving traffic violations. This, in turn, can lead to a poor public image, increased liability, increased administrative problems, and increased costs. A test that can improve hiring and thus reduce the problems associated with poor selection decisions should be welcomed by any transit authority.

Developing a test that can be used with multiple population groups and that can withstand the test of time, however, is not an easy task. Based on extensive federally funded research, the Transit Operator Selection Inventory (TOSI) comes close to meeting this standard. But, the TOSI is not without its problems. Three areas warranting careful consideration are local validity, the age of the test, and its reliance on self-report data.

The TOSI consists of three subtests that quantify the applicant's background, skills, and emotional health. The Background subtest uses 35 biodata items and emphasizes job history. The Skills subtest is a self-report instrument in which applicants rate themselves on 96 skills related to bus driving. In the Emotional Health subtest, applicants are asked to rate themselves on 108 psychological characteristics related to working with the public. Several scale scores are available in addition to a composite "Probability of Successful Performance" (PSP) index. Consistent with good practice, the publisher advocates that this PSP score be used with other selection procedures, such as interviews, driving record checks, and driving tests.

The TOSI was developed over a 9-year period with funding from the U.S. Department of Transportation. An extensive job analysis was conducted, a test instrument was piloted, and the final instrument was validated using a variety of concurrent and predictive validation procedures. Special attention was paid to racial and gender differences. The original validation study, conducted in 1975, included over 1,000 bus drivers.

A more recent validation study (circa 1985) involving 210 bus drivers showed an adjusted multiple correlation of .45 between PSP scores, on one hand, and long-term quarterly rates of chargeable accidents, sick days, traffic citations, absenteeism, and supervisory suspensions. Mean PSP scores for Blacks, Whites, and Hispanics were extremely close (all approximately equal to .54) and the different groups had similar validity coefficients. These results were quite similar to the original validation studies.

Despite its impressive history, the TOSI is not necessarily appropriate for all transit authorities. Three possible threats are the congruence between the skills measured on the TOSI and those needed by a particular transit authority, aging of the test, and dependence on self-report data. The publisher has long recognized the first threat and requires a local job analysis. An instrument is available to assist with that task.

Aging of the TOSI is of concern. As the job of bus driver changes with new technology and new demands, the validity of the TOSI can be expected to decline. Relying on demographic characteristics, the predictive validity of biodata questions are particularly time-bound. For example, an annual income of $10,000 may have been highly associated with success as a bus driver in 1975. Such a response would probably detract from predictive validity in 1991. The biodata portion of the TOSI contains numerous items that appear to be time-sensitive.

Another concern is dependence on self-report data. This format allows the test to cover a wide range of skills and attributes related to success as a bus driver. Rather than asking a person to answer 10 questions on depth perception, for example, the TOSI asks one question—How good is your depth perception? The trade-off is that there is no information regarding the accuracy of the individual's response. Because the answer is easy to fake and there is an incentive for applicants to exaggerate their situation or ability, an individual's scores will not necessarily reflect his or her history, skills, or attributes. This trade-off underscores the need stated by the publisher to go beyond the TOSI in evaluating bus driver applicants.

[98]
Wolfe Microcomputer User Aptitude Test.

Purpose: To evaluate the practical and analytical skills required for the effective use of microcomputers.
Population: Applicants for positions involving the use of microcomputers.
Publication Dates: 1986–88.
Scores: Item scores and total score only.
Administration: Group.

Price Data, 1989: $55 per test (scored by publisher) including test manual ('86, 5 pages); additional $35 per candidate for 2-hour scoring service available from publisher by phone.
Foreign Language Edition: French edition available.
Time: 75(80) minutes.
Author: Richard Label.
Publisher: Wolfe Personnel Testing & Training Systems, Inc.

Review of the Wolfe Microcomputer User Aptitude Test by ROBERT FITZPATRICK, Consulting Industrial Psychologist, Pittsburgh, PA:

This is intended to be a test of aptitude for those who will use microcomputers in their work. It is not aimed at selecting computer programmers.

The test consists of four problems, each of which was designed to evaluate an ability thought to be important in typical work with microcomputers. Problem 1 simulates the operation of a spreadsheet. Problem 2 is a complex clerical checking task. Problem 3 includes three reasoning items, using some concepts found in computer programming. Problem 4 requires the examinee to follow complex instructions in another context similar to a computer program.

The problems seem ingeniously designed and are fun to work. However, there is no rationale given for their design, and there seems no reason to suppose these problems would do a better job in selecting computer users than would conventional tests of comprehension, following instructions, and reasoning. No evidence is provided that these are the most important abilities for computer users.

The Manual is skimpy and vague. It is not clear whether the test is to be timed. A time is stated for each problem, but apparently this is done merely to help the examinee stay within a total time of "approximately" 75 minutes. The examiner is not explicitly instructed to enforce a time limit. The Manual says the test may be administered with "only clerical supervision," and that "Once begun, it is self-instructive." However, the instructions are somewhat complex and not entirely clear. Some substantial reading comprehension is needed to deal with the instructions.

No reliability data are presented. It seems likely that the reliability is low, because the number of separate items is small and some of these are interdependent. For example, in Problem 1, there are only five items; to get the correct answer to item 2 (except by accident), one must have answered item 1 correctly; and the same relationship holds between items 3 and 2.

No scoring procedures or norms are provided in the Manual. The publisher offers a scoring service, which includes recommendations for hiring or training. However, the user is in the dark as to the bases for these recommendations. There is no apparent reason for the scoring to be complex or esoteric. The publisher owes the potential user either (*a*) instructions for scoring and norms or (*b*) an explanation of the reason for scoring secrecy.

The publisher has provided a report of one criterion-related validity study. Only part of the study is relevant to the intended application of the test. That part is based on a sample of only 35 college students, and the resulting correlation is low. The publisher's summary of the overall study is misleading and, in part, inaccurate.

The Wolfe Microcomputer User Aptitude Test could possibly be used in some specialized research. However, in view of the lack of evidence for validity or reliability, the secrecy of scoring, and the lack of normative information, it is decidedly not recommended for use in personnel selection.

CONTRIBUTING TEST REVIEWERS

ANNE ANASTASI, Professor Emeritus of Psychology, Fordham University, Bronx, NY

FRANCES X. ARCHAMBAULT, JR., Professor of Educational Psychology and Department Head, The University of Connecticut, Storrs, CT

JAMES T. AUSTIN, Assistant Professor of Psychology, New York University, New York, NY

PATRICIA A. BACHELOR, Associate Professor of Psychology, California State University, Long Beach, CA

LYLE F. BACHMAN, Professor of Applied Linguistics, University of California at Los Angeles, Los Angeles, CA

DAVID W. BARNETT, Professor of School Psychology and Counseling, University of Cincinnati, Cincinnati, OH

CAMILLA PERSSON BENBOW, Professor of Psychology, Iowa State University, Ames, IA

JERI BENSON, Associate Professor of Measurement, Statistics and Evaluation, University of Maryland, College Park, MD

H. JOHN BERNARDIN, University Professor of Research, Florida Atlantic University, Boca Raton, FL

BRUCE H. BISKIN, Senior Psychometrician, American Institute of Certified Public Accountants, New York, NY

CAROL A. BOLIEK, Assistant Research Scientist, Speech and Hearing Sciences, University of Arizona, Tucson, AZ

R. A. BORNSTEIN, Associate Professor of Psychiatry, Neurosurgery and Neurology, The Ohio State University, Columbus, OH

ROBERT D. BROWN, Carl A. Happold Distinguished Professor of Educational Psychology, University of Nebraska-Lincoln, Lincoln, NE

SCOTT W. BROWN, Associate Professor of Educational Psychology, University of Connecticut, Storrs, CT

VIRGINIA L. BROWN, Director, Institute for Research and Community Service, Indiana University of Pennsylvania, Indiana, PA

PAUL C. BURNETT, Lecturer in Psychology, Queensland University of Technology—Kelvin Grove Campus, Brisbane, Australia

R. T. BUSSE, Graduate Student, Department of Educational Psychology, University of Wisconsin-Madison, Madison, WI

CAMERON J. CAMP, Associate Professor of Psychology, University of New Orleans, New Orleans, LA

CINDY I. CARLSON, Associate Professor of Educational Psychology, University of Texas at Austin, Austin, TX

ROGER D. CARLSON, Visiting Associate Professor of Psychology, Whitman College, Walla Walla, WA

SANDRA L. CHRISTENSON, Assistant Professor of Educational Psychology, University of Minnesota, Minneapolis, MN

JOSEPH C. CIECHALSKI, Assistant Professor of Counselor Education, East Carolina University, Greenville, NC

GREGORY J. CIZEK, Program Associate, American College Testing, Iowa City, IA

JUDITH C. CONGER, Director of Clinical Training, Purdue University, West Lafayette, IN

ROBERT B. COOTER, JR., Associate Professor of Elementary Education, Brigham Young University, Provo, UT

ALICE J. CORKILL, Assistant Professor of Psychology, University of Western Ontario, London, Ontario, Canada

MERITH COSDEN, Assistant Professor of Education, University of California, Santa Barbara, CA

WILLIAM L. CURLETTE, Professor of Educational Foundations, Georgia State University, Atlanta, GA

BRANDON DAVIS, Research Fellow, Ball State Neuropsychology Laboratory, Ball State University, Muncie, IN

STEPHEN F. DAVIS, Professor of Psychology, Emporia State University, Emporia, KS

GABRIEL DELLA-PIANA, Professor of Educational Psychology, University of Utah, Salt Lake City, UT

LIZANNE DESTEFANO, Assistant Professor of Educational Psychology, University of Illinois at Urbana-Champaign, Champaign, IL

ESTHER E. DIAMOND, Educational and Psychological Consultant, Evanston, IL

DAVID N. DIXON, Professor and Department Chair, Department of Counseling Psychology and Guidance Services, Ball State University, Muncie, IN

RON EDWARDS, Professor of Psychology and Director of School Psychology Training, University of Southern Mississippi, Hattiesburg, MS

ARTHUR S. ELLEN, Assistant Professor of Psychology, Pace University, New York, NY

STEPHEN N. ELLIOTT, Professor of Educational Psychology, University of Wisconsin-Madison, Madison, WI

GEORGE ENGELHARD, JR., Assistant Professor of Educational Studies, Emory University, Atlanta, GA

JOHN M. ENGER, Professor of Education, Arkansas State University, State University, AR

JOAN ERSHLER, Postdoctoral Student, School Psychology Program, University of Wisconsin, Madison, WI

JULIAN FABRY, Counseling Psychologist, Myers Rehabilitation Institute, Omaha, NE

R. W. FAUNCE, Consulting Psychologist, Minneapolis, MN

ANNE R. FITZPATRICK, Manager of Applied Research, CTB/McGraw-Hill, Monterey, CA

ROBERT FITZPATRICK, Consulting Industrial Psychologist, Pittsburgh, PA

STEPHEN G. FLANAGAN, Clinical Associate Professor, Department of Psychology, The University of North Carolina at Chapel Hill, Chapel Hill, NC

ROBERT K. GABLE, Professor of Educational Psychology, and Associate Director, Bureau of Educational Research and Service, University of Connecticut, Storrs, CT

LENA R. GADDIS, Assistant Professor of Psychology, University of Southern Mississippi, Hattiesburg, MS

GLORIA A. GALVIN, Assistant Professor of Psychology, Ohio University, Athens, OH

ALAN GARFINKEL, Associate Professor of Spanish and Foreign Language Education, Purdue University, West Lafayette, IN

JOHN A. GLOVER, Director of Research, Teachers College, Ball State University, Muncie, IN

BERT A. GOLDMAN, Professor of Education, University of North Carolina, Greensboro, NC

ROLAND H. GOOD, III, Assistant Professor of Counseling and Educational Psychology, College of Education, University of Oregon, Eugene, OR

HARRISON G. GOUGH, Professor of Psychology, Emeritus, University of California, Berkeley, CA

STEVE GRAHAM, Associate Professor of Special Education, University of Maryland, College Park, MD

CATHY W. HALL, Assistant Professor of Psychology, East Carolina University, Greenville, NC

GERALD S. HANNA, Professor of Educational Psychology and Measurement, Kansas State University, Manhattan, KS

THOMAS G. HARING, Associate Professor of Special Education, University of California, Santa Barbara, CA

PATTI L. HARRISON, Associate Professor of Behavioral Studies, College of Education, The University of Alabama, Tuscaloosa, AL

VERNA HART, Professor, Program in Special Education, School of Education, University of Pittsburgh, Pittsburgh, PA

HOPE J. HARTMAN, Associate Professor of Social and Psychological Foundations, School of Education, The City College, City University of New York, New York, NY

MARY HENNING-STOUT, Assistant Professor of Counseling Psychology, Lewis and Clark College, Portland, OR

JOHN R. HESTER, Associate Professor of Psychology, Francis Marion College, Florence, SC

MARY E. HUBA, Professor of Research and Evaluation, Iowa State University, Ames, IA

JAN N. HUGHES, Associate Professor of Educational Psychology, Texas A&M University, College Station, TX

PATSY ARNETT JAYNES, Second Language Program Evaluation Specialist, Jefferson County Public Schools, Golden, CO

JEFFREY JENKINS, Attorney, Keleher & McLeod, P.A., Albuquerque, NM

RANDY W. KAMPHAUS, Associate Professor of Educational Psychology, The University of Georgia, Athens, GA

BARBARA J. KAPLAN, Associate Professor of Psychology, State University of New York College at Fredonia, Fredonia, NY

WALTER KATKOVSKY, Professor of Psychology, Northern Illinois University, DeKalb, IL

MICHAEL G. KAVAN, Director of Behavioral Sciences and Assistant Professor of Family Practice, Creighton University School of Medicine, Omaha, NE

JERARD F. KEHOE, District Manager, Selection and Testing, American Telephone & Telegraph Co., Morristown, NJ

MARY LOU KELLEY, Associate Professor of Psychology, Louisiana State University, Baton Rouge, LA

KENNETH A. KIEWRA, Associate Professor of Educational Psychology, University of Nebraska-Lincoln, Lincoln, NE

HOWARD M. KNOFF, Associate Professor of School Psychology and Director of the School Psychology Program, University of South Florida, Tampa, FL

ERNEST J. KOZMA, Professor of Education, Clemson University, Clemson, SC

DEBORAH KING KUNDERT, Assistant Professor of Educational Psychology and Statistics, University at Albany, State University of New York, Albany, NY

RICHARD I. LANYON, Professor of Psychology, Arizona State University, Tempe, AZ

STEVEN W. LEE, Assistant Professor of Educational Psychology and Research, University of Kansas, Lawrence, KS

RICHARD LEHRER, Associate Professor of Educational Psychology, University of Wisconsin-Madison, Madison, WI

S. ALVIN LEUNG, Assistant Professor of Educational Psychology, University of Nebraska-Lincoln, Lincoln, NE

MARY A. LEWIS, Director, Organizational and Employment Technology, PPG Industries, Inc., Pittsburgh, PA

ROBERT W. LISSITZ, Professor of Education and Psychology and Chairperson, Department of Measurement, Statistics, and Evaluation, University of Maryland, College Park, MD

STEVEN G. LOBELLO, Assistant Professor of Psychology, Auburn University at Montgomery, Montgomery, AL

DOUGLAS J. MCRAE, Senior Evaluation Consultant, CTB, Ann Arbor, MI

DAMIAN MCSHANE, Associate Professor of Psychology, Utah State University, Logan, UT

DAVID J. MEALOR, Chair of Educational Services Department, College of Education, University of Central Florida, Orlando, FL

WILLIAM A. MEHRENS, Professor of Educational Measurement, Michigan State University, East Lansing, MI

KEVIN MENEFEE, Certified School Psychologist, Omaha Public Schools, Omaha, NE

WILLIAM B. MICHAEL, Professor of Education and Psychology, University of Southern California, Los Angeles, CA

CRAIG N. MILLS, Executive Director, GRE Testing and Services, Educational Testing Service, Princeton, NJ

PAT MIRENDA, Assistant Professor of Special Education and Communication Disorders, University of Nebraska-Lincoln, Lincoln, NE

DEBRA NEUBERT, Assistant Professor of Special Education, University of Maryland, College Park, MD

ANTHONY J. NITKO, Professor, School of Education, University of Pittsburgh, Pittsburgh, PA

JANET NORRIS, Assistant Professor of Communication Disorders, Louisiana State University, Baton Rouge, LA

JOHN E. OBRZUT, Professor of Educational Psychology, University of Arizona, Tucson, AZ

STEVEN J. OSTERLIND, Associate Professor and Director, Center for Educational Assessment, University of Missouri-Columbia, Columbia, MO

STEVEN V. OWEN, Professor of Educational Psychology, University of Connecticut, Storrs, CT

CHARLES K. PARSONS, Professor of Management, Georgia Institute of Technology, Atlanta, GA

STEVEN I. PFEIFFER, Director, Institute of Clinical Training and Research, The Devereux Foundation, Devon, PA

JOSEPH G. PONTEROTTO, Associate Professor of Education, Division of Psychological and Educational Services, Fordham University, New York, NY

WILLIAM D. PORTERFIELD, Academic Coordinator and Adjunct Assistant Professor of Educational Administration, Commission on Interprofessional Education and Practice, The Ohio State University, Columbus, OH

G. MICHAEL POTEAT, Assistant Professor of Psychology, East Carolina University, Greenville, NC

PAUL RETZLAFF, Assistant Professor of Psychology, University of Northern Colorado, Greeley, CO

MARK W. ROBERTS, Professor of Clinical Psychology, Idaho State University, Pocatello, ID

DONALD U. ROBERTSON, Professor of Psychology, Indiana University of Pennsylvania, Indiana, PA

DONALD L. RUBIN, Associate Professor of Language Education, The University of Georgia, Athens, GA

LAWRENCE M. RUDNER, Director of the Educational Resources Information Center Clearinghouse on Tests, Measurement and Evaluation (ERIC/TME), American Institutes for Research, Washington, DC and Director of Research, LMP Associates, Chevy Chase, MD

DARRELL SABERS, Professor of Educational Psychology, University of Arizona, Tucson, AZ

DIANE J. SAWYER, Director, Consultation Center for Reading, Syracuse University, Syracuse, NY

OWEN SCOTT, III, Clinical Psychologist, The Psychology Clinic, Baton Rouge, LA

SUSAN M. SHERIDAN, Assistant Professor of Educational Psychology, University of Utah, Salt Lake City, UT

BERTRAM C. SIPPOLA, Associate Professor of Psychology, University of New Orleans, New Orleans, LA

ALFRED L. SMITH, JR., Personnel Psychologist, Federal Aviation Administration, U.S. Department of Transportation, Washington, DC

RONALD K. SOMMERS, Professor of Speech Pathology and Audiology, Kent State University, Kent, OH

JACLYN B. SPITZER, Chief, Audiology and Speech Pathology, Veterans Administration Medical Center, West Haven, CT, and Associate Clinical Professor, Department of Surgery (Otolaryngology), Yale University School of Medicine, New Haven, CT

GARY J. STAINBACK, Senior Psychologist, Department of Pediatrics, East Carolina University, School of Medicine, Greenville, NC

STEPHANIE STEIN, Assistant Professor of Psychology, Central Washington University, Ellensburg, WA

WILLIAM A. STOCK, Professor of Exercise Science, Arizona State University, Tempe, AZ

GERALD L. STONE, Professor of Counseling Psychology and Director, University Counseling Service, The University of Iowa, Iowa City, IA

GARY STONER, Assistant Professor, School Psychology Program, College of Education, University of Oregon, Eugene, OR

MICHAEL J. SUBKOVIAK, Professor and Chair of Educational Psychology, University of Wisconsin-Madison, Madison, WI

HOI K. SUEN, Associate Professor of Educational Psychology, Pennsylvania State University, State College, PA

GAIL M. SULLIVAN, Chief, Geriatric Medicine, and Associate Chief of Staff for Education, Veterans Administration Medical Center, Newington, CT, and Assistant Professor of Medicine, University of Connecticut, Farmington, CT

ROSEMARY E. SUTTON, Associate Professor of Education, Cleveland State University, Cleveland, OH

MAURICE TATSUOKA, Professor Emeritus of Psychology, University of Illinois at Urbana-Champaign, Champaign, IL

CAROLYN TRIAY, Department of Psychology, University of New Orleans, New Orleans, LA

NICHOLAS A. VACC, Professor and Chairperson, Department of Counselor Education, University of North Carolina, Greensboro, NC

PETER VILLANOVA, Assistant Professor of Psychology, Northern Illinois University, DeKalb, IL

ALEX VOOGEL, Assistant Professor, TE-

SOL/MATFL Program, Monterey Institute of International Studies, Monterey, CA

JOHN F. WAKEFIELD, Associate Professor of Education, University of North Alabama, Florence, AL

ALIDA S. WESTMAN, Professor of Psychology, Eastern Michigan University, Ypsilanti, MI

MARGARET ROGERS WIESE, Assistant Professor of School Psychology, Appalachian State University, Boone, NC

MARTIN J. WIESE, School Psychologist, Wilkes County Schools, Wilkesboro, NC

WILLIAM K. WILKINSON, Assistant Professor of Counseling and Educational Psychology, New Mexico State University, Las Cruces, NM

ROBERT T. WILLIAMS, Professor, School of Occupational and Educational Studies, Colorado State University, Fort Collins, CO

W. GRANT WILLIS, Associate Professor of Psychology, University of Rhode Island, Kingston, RI

HILDA WING, Personnel Psychologist, Federal Aviation Administration, Washington, DC

CLAUDIA R. WRIGHT, Assistant Professor of Educational Psychology, California State University, Long Beach, CA

DAN WRIGHT, School Psychologist, Ralston Public Schools, Ralston, NE

THOMAS A. WROBEL, Assistant Professor of Psychology, University of Michigan-Flint, Flint, MI

JAMES E. YSSELDYKE, Professor of Educational Psychology, University of Minnesota, Minneapolis, MN

INDEX OF TITLES

This title index lists all the tests included in The Supplement to the Tenth Mental Measurements Yearbook. *Citations are to test entry numbers, not to pages—e.g., 54 refers to test 54 and not page 54. (Test numbers along with test titles are indicated in the running heads at the top of each page, while page numbers, used only in the Table of Contents but not in the indexes, appear at the bottom of each page.) Superseded titles are listed with cross references to current titles, and alternative titles are also cross referenced. An (N) appearing immediately after a test number indicates that the test is a new, recently published test, and/or that it has not appeared before in a Buros Institute publication. An (R) indicates that the test has been revised or supplemented since last reviewed in a Mental Measurements Yearbook.*

INDEX OF ACRONYMS

This Index of Acronyms refers the reader to the appropriate test in The Supplement to the Tenth Mental Measurements Yearbook. In some cases tests are better known by their acronyms than by their full titles, and this index can be of substantial help to the person who knows the former but not the latter. Acronyms are only listed if the author or publisher has made substantial use of the acronym in referring to the test, or if the test is widely known by the acronym. A few acronyms are also registered trademarks (e.g., SAT); where this is known to us, only the test with the registered trademark is referenced. There is some danger in the overuse of acronyms, but this index, like all other indexes in this work, is provided to make the task of identifying a test as easy as possible. All numbers refer to test numbers, not page numbers.

CLASSIFIED SUBJECT INDEX

The Classified Subject Index classifies all tests included in The Supplement to the Tenth Mental Measurements Yearbook *into 14 major categories: Achievement, Behavior Assessment, Developmental, Education, English, Intelligence and Scholastic Aptitude, Mathematics, Miscellaneous, Neuropsychological, Personality, Reading, Social Studies, Speech and Hearing, and Vocations. Each category appears in alphabetical order and tests are ordered alphabetically within each category. Each test entry includes test title (first letter capitalized), population for which the test is intended (lower case), and the test entry number in* The Supplement to the Tenth Mental Measurements Yearbook. *All numbers refer to test entry numbers, not to page numbers. Brief suggestions for the use of this index are presented in the introduction.*

ACHIEVEMENT

Adult Basic Learning Examination, Second Edition, adults with less than 12 years of formal schooling, see 1

Guidance Centre Classroom Achievement Tests, grades 3–8, 9–12, see 29

National Educational Development Tests, grades 9–10, see 52

BEHAVIOR ASSESSMENT

Child Behavior Checklist, ages 2–18, see 12

Survey of Functional Adaptive Behaviors, ages 16 and over, see 88

DEVELOPMENTAL

Battelle Developmental Inventory Screening Test, birth to age 8, see 9

Dallas Pre-School Screening Test, ages 3–6, see 18

Missouri Kindergarten Inventory of Developmental Skills, Alternate Form, ages 48–72 months, see 48

Pediatric Extended Examination at Three, ages 3–4, see 56

The Pictorial Scale of Perceived Competence and Social

Acceptance for Young Children, preschool through second grade, see 59

Pre-School Behaviour Checklist, ages 2–5, see 61

Psychoeducational Profile, autistic, psychotic, and developmentally disabled children functioning at preschool age levels, see 68

The TARC Assessment System, ages 3–16, see 89

EDUCATION

Classroom Communication Screening Procedure for Early Adolescents: A Handbook for Assessment and Intervention, grades 5–10, see 14

Educational Leadership Practices Inventory, teachers and administrators, see 23

Learning Styles and Strategies, teachers, see 38

Prescriptive Teaching Series, grades 1–8, see 63

Screening Children for Related Early Educational Needs, ages 3–7, see 74

Tests of Adult Basic Education, Forms 5 and 6, and Survey Form, adults in basic education programs, see 94

ENGLISH

Basic English Skills Test, limited-English-speaking adults, see 8

Descriptive Tests of Language Skills, beginning students in two- and four-year institutions, see 20

English Language Skills Assessment in a Reading Context, beginning, intermediate, and advanced students of English as a second language from upper elementary to college and adult students, see 25

Informal Writing Inventory, grades 3–12, see 33

Sentence Comprehension Test, Revised Edition, ages 3–5, see 76

Spellmaster, elementary and junior high school students, see 80

Test of English Proficiency Level, limited-English-proficient students in secondary and adult programs, see 91

INTELLIGENCE AND SCHOLASTIC APTITUDE

New Jersey Test of Reasoning Skills—Form B, reading level grade 5 and over, see 53

Test of Relational Concepts, ages 3-0 to 7-11, see 93

MATHEMATICS

American High School Mathematics Examination, high school students competing for individual and school awards, see 5

American Invitational Mathematics Examination, American and Canadian high school students, see 6

American Junior High School Mathematics Examination, American and Canadian students in grade 8 or below, see 7

Early Mathematics Diagnostic Kit, ages 4–8, see 22

Mathematics 7, ages 6-10 to 7-9, see 45

MISCELLANEOUS

Adult Growth Examination, ages 19–71, see 2

The Marriage and Family Attitude Survey, adolescents and adults, see 44

Perceptions of Parental Role Scales, parents, see 57

Pollack-Branden Inventory, grades 1–12, see 60

Study Habits Evaluation and Instruction Kit, New Zealand secondary school students (Forms 4–6), see 84

Test of Legible Handwriting, ages 7.6–17.11, see 92

NEUROPSYCHOLOGICAL

Cognitive Behavior Rating Scales, patients with possible neurological impairment, see 15

Dementia Rating Scale, individuals suffering from brain dysfunction, see 19

Mini Inventory of Right Brain Injury, ages 18 and over, see 47

Short Category Test, Booklet Format, ages 15 and over, see 77

PERSONALITY

READING

SOCIAL STUDIES

SPEECH AND HEARING

VOCATIONS

PUBLISHERS DIRECTORY AND INDEX

This directory and index give the addresses and test entry numbers of all publishers represented in The Supplement to the Tenth Mental Measurements Yearbook. *Please note that all numbers in this index refer to test entry numbers, not page numbers. Publishers are an important source of information about catalogs, specimen sets, price changes, test revisions, and many other matters.*

International Training Consultants, Inc., P.O. Box 35613, Richmond, VA 23235-0613: 39

Joint Council on Economic Education, 432 Park Avenue, South, New York, NY 10016: 90

Literacy Volunteers of America, Inc., Widewaters One Office Building, 5795 Widewaters Parkway, Syracuse, NY 13214-1846: 71
London House, Inc., 1550 Northwest Highway, Suite 302, Park Ridge, IL 60068: 97

Management Research Associates, R.R. 25, Box 26, Terre Haute, IN 47802: 23
Marathon Consulting and Press, P.O. Box 09189, Columbus, OH 43209-0189: 57
Mathematical Association of America; American Mathematical Society, Walter E. Mientka, Ph.D., Executive Director, University of Nebraska-Lincoln, Dept. of Mathematics & Statistics, 917 Oldfather Hall, Lincoln, NE 68588-0322: 5, 6, 7
McCarron-Dial Systems, P.O. Box 45628, Dallas, TX 75245: 24, 88
Robert F. Morgan, Ph.D., Pacific Graduate School of Psychology, 935 E. Meadow Drive, Palo Alto, CA 94303-4233: 2

National Computer Systems, Inc., Professional Assessment Services Division, P.O. Box 1416, Minneapolis, MN 55440: 11
National Reading Styles Institute, Inc., P.O. Box 39—Dept. W, Roslyn Heights, NY 11577: 72
New Zealand Council for Educational Research, Education House West, 178-182 Willis St., Box 3237, Wellington, New Zealand: 84
Newbury House Publishers, Inc., 10 East 53rd Street, New York, NY 10022: 25
NFER-Nelson Publishing Co., Ltd., Darville House, 2 Oxford Road East, Windsor, Berkshire SL4 1DF, England: 22, 27, 34, 45, 61, 76, 87
Nova Media, Inc., 1724 No. State, Big Rapids, MI 49307: 69

Organizational Measurement Systems Press, P.O. Box 1656, Buffalo, NY 14221: 55

Price Systems, Inc., Box 1818, Lawrence, KS 66044: 37, 64
PRO-ED, Inc., 8700 Shoal Creek Blvd., Austin, TX 78758-6897: 47, 68, 74, 80, 89, 92, 93
Psychological Assessment Resources, Inc., P.O. Box 998, Odessa, FL 33556-0998: 15, 19, 49, 73, 81
The Psychological Corporation, 555 Academic Court, San Antonio, TX 78204-0952: 1, 10, 21, 40
Psychological Services Bureau, Inc., P.O. Box 4, St. Thomas, PA 17252: 66
Psychologists and Educators, Inc., Sales Division, P.O. Box 513, Chesterfield, MO 63006: 44, 63

Saville & Holdsworth Ltd., The Old Post House, 81 High Street, Esher, Surrey KT10 9QA, England: 41
Scholastic Testing Service, Inc., 480 Meyer Road, P.O. Box 1056, Bensenville, IL 60106-8056: 33, 70, 86
Science Research Associates, Inc., 155 N. Wacker Drive, Chicago, IL 60606-1780: 52
Mark D. Shermis, Ph.D., EDB 504, The University of Texas at Austin, Austin, TX 78712-1296: 82
SOARES Associates, 111 Teeter Rock Road, Trumbull, CT 06611: 3
Special Child Publications, P.O. Box 33548, Seattle, WA 98133: 54
Student Development Associates, Inc., 110 Crestwood Drive, Athens, GA 30605: 83

Training House, Inc., P.O. Box 3090, Princeton, NJ 08543: 42, 43, 58

University Associates, Inc., 8517 Production Avenue, San Diego, CA 92121-2280: 17

West Virginia Research and Training Center, One Dunbar Plaza, Suite E, Dunbar, WV 25064: 62
Western Psychiatric Institute and Clinic, 3811 O'Hara Street, Pittsburgh, PA 15213-2593: 13
Western Psychological Services, 12031 Wilshire Blvd., Los Angeles, CA 90025: 4, 50, 77, 96
Wolfe Personnel Testing & Training Systems, Inc., Box 319, Oradell, NJ 07649: 98

INDEX OF NAMES

This analytical index indicates whether a citation refers to authorship of a test, a test review, or a reference for a specific test. Numbers refer to test entries, not to pages. The abbreviations and numbers following the names may be interpreted as follows: "test, 73" indicates authorship of test 73; "rev, 86" indicates authorship of a review of test 86; "ref, 45(30)" indicates authorship of reference number 30 in the "Test References" section for test 45; "ref, 13r" indicates a reference (unnumbered) in one of the "Reviewer's References" sections for test 13. Names mentioned in cross references are also indexed.

Marlowe, D. A.: ref, 4r
Marsh, J.: ref, 13(29), 82r
Martin, D.: ref, 44r
Martin, D. V.: test, 44
Martin, E.: ref, 36(1)
Martin, M.: test, 44; ref, 44r
Martin, S.: test, 63
Massey, T.: test, 24, 88
Massman, P. J.: ref, 12(99)
Masters, G.: test, 95
Mathematical Association of America: test, 5
Matson, J. L.: ref, 12(12), 13(27)r, 73(2)
Mattis, S.: test, 19
Mattison, R. E.: ref, 12(112)
Mayer, R. E.: ref, 84r
Mayes, S. D.: ref, 34(9)
McArdle, J.: ref, 12(112)
McCarron, L. T.: test, 24, 88
McCauley, E.: ref, 12(75,82)
McCaulley, M.: ref, 58r
McCaulley, M. H.: ref, 38r
McCombs, A.: ref, 13(17)
McConahay, J. B.: ref, 69r
McConaughy, S. H.: ref, 12(34,58,59,100)
McCormick, K.: ref, 9r
McDaniel, K.: ref, 89r
McGee, R.: ref, 65(2)
McGiboney, G. W.: ref, 34(4)
McGuire, J.: test, 61
McIntosh, J.: ref, 13(3)
McIntyre, A.: ref, 12(60)
McKay, V.: ref, 12(49)
McKinley, J. C.: ref, 67r
McLean, M.: ref, 9r
McLinden, S. E.: ref, 9r
McMahon, R. J.: ref, 12(3)
McNulty, G.: ref, 19r
McRae, D. J.: rev, 51, 96
McShane, D.: rev, 86
Mealor, D. J.: rev, 15
Medler, B.: ref, 44r
Mehrens, W. A.: rev, 90
Melchior, L. A.: test, 4
Mendelson, M.: ref, 54r, 73r
Menefee, K.: rev, 45
Messick, S.: ref, 86r
Meyer, D. L.: ref, 64r
Meyer, E. C.: ref, 12(32)
Meyer, N. E.: ref, 13(26)
Mezger, C.: test, 24, 88
Michael, W. B.: rev, 56, 59
Miller, C. T.: ref, 12(81), 59(3)
Miller, J. H.: ref, 9r
Miller, T. K.: test, 83
Mills, C. N.: rev, 64
Miner, J. B.: ref, 55r
Miner, M. E.: ref, 12(115)
Mintzberg, H.: ref, 41r
Mirenda, P.: rev, 89
Missouri Department of Elementary and Secondary Education: test, 48
Mittler, P.: test, 76
Mix, B. J.: test, 89
Mock, J.: ref, 54r, 73r
Mooney, K. C.: ref, 12(83)

Moos, R. H.: ref, 64r
Morgan, R. F.: test, 2
Mori, C.: ref, 25(2)
Moriarty, J. B.: test, 62
Morris, T. L.: ref, 78r
Morton, N. W.: rev, 10
Mossenson, L.: test, 95
Mott, S. E.: ref, 9r
Mouton, J. S.: ref, 42r
Mu Alpha Theta: test, 5
Munn, D.: ref, 9r
Munson, R. F.: ref, 34(5,6)
Muraki, E.: ref, 67r
Murphy, H. A.: test, 51
Murphy, S.: ref, 33r
Murray, H. A.: ref, 64r
Murray, J. B.: ref, 37(3)
Myers, I.: ref, 58r, 67r
Myers, I. B.: ref, 38r

Naeser, M.: ref, 19r
Naglieri, J. A.: test, 21
Nastasi, B. K.: ref, 12(48)
Nation, J. E.: ref, 12(2)
National Association of Secondary School Principals: ref, 37r
National Council of Teachers of Mathematics: test, 5
National Council on Measurement in Education: ref, 4r, 7r, 8r, 18r, 22r, 26r, 28r, 34r, 35r, 59r, 69r, 70r, 94r
Neeman, J.: test, 75
Nelson, C. W.: test, 23
Nelson, J. M.: ref, 12(83)
Nelson, M. J.: ref, 66r
Nelson, R. O.: ref, 12(101), 13(15)
Nelson, W. M.: ref, 13r, 54r
Nettlton, N. C.: ref, 86r
Neubert, D.: rev, 62
Newborg, J.: test, 9; ref, 9r
Newby, H. A.: ref, 2r
Newby, R. F.: ref, 12(95)
Nieminen, G. S.: ref, 13(27), 73(2)
Nilsson, A.: ref, 12(45)
Nitko, A. J.: rev, 90
Nolan, B.: ref, 13(9)
Nolan, S. B.: ref, 84r
Norris, J.: rev, 40
Nottelmann, E. D.: ref, 12(91)
Novak, D. M.: ref, 34(12)
Nussbaum, N. L.: ref, 12(61,62,99)

O'Brien, E. J.: test, 49; ref, 49r
O'Brien, R.: ref, 58r
O'Brien, T. C.: ref, 53r
O'Brien Towle, P.: ref, 12(84)
O'Leary, K. D.: ref, 12(5), 13(4)
Obrosky, D. S.: ref, 13(29)
Obrzut, J. E.: rev, 47
Ochoa, A. S.: ref, 90r
Okun, M. A.: ref, 30r
Oliver, J. E.: ref, 55r
Oliver, J. E., Jr.: test, 55
Ollendick, T. H.: ref, 13(30)
Oller, J. W.: ref, 25r
Osterlind, S. J.: rev, 94
Owen, S. V.: rev, 34

SCORE INDEX

This Score Index lists all the scores, in alphabetical order, for all the tests included in The Supplement to the Tenth Mental Measurements Yearbook. Because test scores can be regarded as operational definitions of the variable measured, sometimes the scores provide better leads to what a test actually measures than the test title or other available information. The Score Index is very detailed, and the reader should keep in mind that a given variable (or concept) of interest may be defined in several different ways. Thus the reader should look up these several possible alternative definitions before drawing final conclusions about whether tests measuring a particular variable of interest can be located in the 10MMY-S. If the kind of score sought is located in a particular test or tests, the reader should then read the test descriptive information carefully to determine whether the test(s) in which the score is found is (are) consistent with reader purpose. Used wisely, the Score Index can be another useful resource in locating the right score in the right test. As usual, all numbers in the index are test numbers, not page numbers.